Eighth Edition

THE COMPACT READER

SHORT ESSAYS BY METHOD AND THEME

Jane E. Aaron

Assisted by Ellen Kuhl

BEDFORD/ST. MARTIN'S

Boston ◆ New York

For Bedford/St. Martin's

Developmental Editor: Anne Leung
Editorial Assistant: Marisa Feinstein
Senior Production Supervisor: Nancy J. Myers
Marketing Manager: Karita dos Santos
Project Management: Books By Design, Inc.
Cover Design: Donna Lee Dennison
Cover Art: Painting from *After Image* 2001 series by Kelly Spalding.
Composition: Achorn International, Inc.
Printing and Binding: RR Donnelley & Sons Company

President: Joan E. Feinberg
Editorial Director: Denise B. Wydra
Editor in Chief: Karen S. Henry
Director of Marketing: Karen Melton Soeltz
Director of Editing, Design, and Production: Marcia Cohen
Manager, Publishing Services: Emily Berleth

Library of Congress Control Number: 2007929236

Manufactured in the United States of America.

2   1   0   9   8   7
f   e   d   c   b   a

ISBN-10: 0-312-43347-6
ISBN-13: 978-0-312-43347-5

Acknowledgments

Barbara Lazear Ascher. "The Box Man." From *Playing After Dark* by Barbara Lazear Ascher. Copyright © 1982, 1983, 1984, 1986 by Barbara Lazear Ascher. Used by permission of Doubleday, a division of Random House, Inc.
Dave Barry. "Humvee Satisfies a Man's Lust for Winches." From *Boogers Are My Beat* by Dave Barry. Copyright © 2003 by Dave Barry. Used by permission of Crown, a division of Random House, Inc.
Judy Brady. "I Want a Wife." Originally published in *Ms.*, Vol. 1, and No. 1 December 31, 1971. Reprinted by permission of the author.
Thomas de Zengotita. "*American Idol* Worship." Originally published in *The Christian Science Monitor*, February 17, 2006. Reprinted by permission of Thomas de Zengotita, author of *Mediated: How the Media Shapes Your World and the Way You Live in It.*

Acknowledgments and copyrights continue at the back of the book on page 411, which constitutes an extension of the copyright page.

PREFACE

The eighth edition of *The Compact Reader,* like its predecessors, combines three texts in one brief volume: a short-essay reader, a rhetorical reader, and a thematic reader. Remarkably thorough given its size, the book complements nearly three dozen professional and student essays with all the editorial apparatus of a larger book — at a lower price. Three introductory chapters guide students through the process of critical reading, writing, and revising. Then ten chapters focus on the rhetorical methods of development, with each chapter's brief selections both illustrating a method and centering on a common theme. This edition features a new appendix on research and documentation, nineteen new essays, and heightened emphases on critical reading and thesis statements, making *The Compact Reader* even more stimulating and helpful for both students and instructors.

THREE READERS IN ONE

The core of *The Compact Reader* remains its selections. Thirty-five short essays and twenty paragraphs provide interesting reading that will enliven class discussion and spark good writing. The selections represent both emerging writers — including a student in every chapter — and established writers such as Joan Didion, Langston Hughes, Dave Barry, and Anna Quindlen. Fourteen professional essays, five student essays, and nine paragraphs are new to this edition.

The Compact Reader's unique structure suits courses that call for brief essays with either a rhetorical or a thematic approach:

- The essays in *The Compact Reader* average just two to four pages apiece so that students can read them quickly, analyze them thoroughly, and emulate them successfully. A few longer essays, such as Jessica Mitford's "Embalming Mr. Jones," help students make the transition to more challenging material.
- Above all, the essays offer clear models for writing, but they also show the rhetorical methods — narration, example, comparison,

and so on—at work in varied styles for varied purposes. In Chapters 4–12, three essays and two annotated paragraphs illustrate each method. Chapter 13, on argument, expands on this format with a more detailed introduction to the method and, new to this edition, two additional essays for further study.

- Each rhetorical chapter also has an overlapping thematic focus that shows the method developing the same general subject and provides diverse perspectives to stimulate students' critical thinking, discussion, and writing. Six themes are new to this edition.

4. Description	Sensing the natural world
5. Narration	Recalling childhood
6. Example	Using language
7. Division or analysis	Looking at popular culture
8. Classification	Sorting group identities (new)
9. Process analysis	Examining the human body (new)
10. Comparison and contrast	Evaluating stereotypes (new)
11. Definition	Clarifying family relationships (new)
12. Cause-and-effect analysis	Understanding markets and consumers (new)
13. Argument and persuasion	Debating law and order (new)

The new themes are designed to appeal to a broad range of students, including those whose interests lie outside the humanities. In addition, the thematic connections in the newly expanded Chapter 13 (argumentation) have been tightened, all of the selections now tackle related issues of criminal justice, and, for the first time, two final essays take opposing positions on a controversial debate.

AN INTRODUCTION TO READING AND WRITING

A thorough introduction to critical reading and the writing process appears in the first three chapters:

- Chapter 1 demonstrates the reading process, showing a student's annotations on a sample passage and providing detailed analysis of a professional essay, Barbara Lazear Ascher's "The Box Man." A new boxed checklist on critical reading summarizes the chapter's most important guidelines for easy reference.
- Chapter 2 covers the initial stages of composing, from assessing the writing situation through drafting, following the student's response to Ascher's essay and first draft. Because students often have diffi-

culty focusing their writing, this chapter now offers an expanded discussion of forming and expressing a thesis.

- Chapter 3 discusses revising and editing, from rethinking the thesis through reshaping paragraphs, reworking sentences, and changing words. The chapter includes boxed checklists for revision and editing, as well as revised and final drafts by the student responding to Ascher's essay.

The Compact Reader's emphasis on the union of reading and writing carries through the entire book:

- A detailed, practical introduction to each of the ten rhetorical methods opens with a discussion of the basic concepts to look for when reading, analyzes two sample paragraphs that illustrate the method, and suggests specific strategies for developing an essay using the method, from choosing a subject through editing the final draft. The introductions draw connections among purpose, subject, and method, helping students analyze and respond to any writing situation. A final "Note on Thematic Connections" explains how the chapter's paragraphs and essays relate to one another.
- A new appendix, "Working with Sources," outlines the basics of using readings and conducting research to support writing. Emphasizing the essential skills of summarizing, paraphrasing, quoting, avoiding plagiarism, and using MLA documentation, this new section shows students how to synthesize information and ideas from their reading to develop and support their own ideas. The appendix concludes with a sample student essay that illustrates the elements of source-based writing.
- To help students find what they need in the book, a guide to the elements of writing appears inside the back cover. This index covers Chapters 2 and 3, all the rhetorical introductions, and the new appendix.

UNIQUE EDITORIAL APPARATUS

In addition to the features already mentioned, *The Compact Reader* offers numerous aids for students and teachers:

- Complementing the expanded section on thesis statements in Chapter 2, the introduction to each rhetorical method now breaks out the discussion of forming a thesis, highlighting the importance of writing with a thesis and making the advice easy to locate.

- The introduction to each rhetorical method also features a "Focus" box that covers an element of writing especially relevant to that method, such as verbs in narration, paragraph coherence in comparison and contrast, and tone in argument and persuasion. Each box appears with a revising and editing checklist that extends Chapter 3's more general checklists to the particular method.

- Quotations and a journal prompt precede every essay. These pre-reading materials get students thinking and writing about the essay's topic, helping them to form and express their own ideas before they read the essay itself.

- Headnotes about the author and the essay place every selection in a context that helps focus students' reading.

- Detailed questions after each essay guide students' analysis of meaning, purpose and audience, method and structure, and language. A question labeled "Other Methods" highlights the author's use of combined methods.

- At least four writing topics after each selection give students specific direction for their own work. Among these, a "Journal to Essay" topic helps students build their journal writing into a finished essay; a "Cultural Considerations" topic leads students to consider similarities and differences among cultures; and a "Connections" topic encourages students to make thematic or rhetorical links to other selections in the book.

- Additional writing topics appear at the ends of each chapter. "Writing with the Method" lists ideas for applying the chapter's method of development, and "Writing about the Theme" suggests ways to draw on the chapter's resources to explore its topic.

- A glossary at the end of the book defines and illustrates more than a hundred terms, with specific cross-references to longer discussions in the text.

HELPFUL INSTRUCTOR'S MANUAL AND WEB SITE

Resources for Teaching THE COMPACT READER, bound into the instructor's edition of the book, aims to help teachers integrate the text into their courses and use it in class. It includes an overview of the book's organization and chapters, ideas for combining the reader with other course materials, and varied resources for each selection: teaching tips, a content quiz, a vocabulary quiz, and detailed answers to all of the critical reading questions. The manual also reprints one essay from each rhetorical chapter with annotations that identify the author's thesis and use of mixed methods.

Students have access to a range of helpful resources on *The Compact Reader*'s companion Web site (*http://bedfordstmartins.com/compactreader*). Annotated links for each of the book's themes and writers direct students to further reading. And *Re:Writing* provides free, open, and easy-to-use resources in *The Bedford Research Room*, *The St. Martin's Tutorial on Avoiding Plagiarism*, and *Exercise Central*: checklists and tutorials on working with sources, model documents, style and grammar exercises, visual analysis activities, research guides, bibliography tools, and much more.

ACKNOWLEDGMENTS

Many instructors helped to shape this edition of *The Compact Reader*, offering insights from their experience and suggestions for improvement. Many thanks to Nancy Allen, Angelo State University; Joseph Brogunier, University of Maine; Candyce Carter, McQueen High School; Jill Collen, Northwest Iowa Community College; Judith Dearlove, Meredith College; Deborah A. Dessaso, University of the District of Columbia; Joy Dworkin, Missouri Southern State University; Edward Glenn, Miami-Dade College North; Susan Guzman-Trevino, Temple College; Judy Grigg Hansen, College of Southern Idaho; Marie Iglesias-Cardinale, Genesee Community College; Jean Knight, Klamath Community College; Pamela Kraft, Ohio University—Chillicothe; Terry Mathias, Southeastern Illinois College; Eric Mein, Northwest Iowa Community College; Rebecca Mooney, Bakersfield College; Virginia Polanski, Stonehill College; Patricia Portanova, Bridgewater State College; Linda Riddell, Victor Valley College; Robert Roehm, Palmdale High School; Su Senapati, Abraham Baldwin Agricultural College; Hoang-Anh Tran, University of North Carolina at Wilmington; Matthew Usner, Harold Washington College; Allen Williams, Cincinnati State College; Cynthia Wiseman, Borough of Manhattan Community College and Hunter College; Lucette Wood, Linn-Benton Community College; and Angus Woodward, Our Lady of the Lake College. Special thanks as well to Kim Sanabria, Eugenio María de Hostos Community College, whose contributions to the seventh edition continue to influence the book's content and features.

Ellen Kuhl was an invaluable collaborator on this edition of *The Compact Reader*. She drew on her editorial experience with past editions of the book—and dozens of other college textbooks—to propose ideas for new features, suggest specific revisions, and provide extensive help with new selections and new apparatus.

The people at Bedford/St. Martin's once again contributed greatly to this project. Joan Feinberg, Karen Henry, and Steve Scipione provided encouraging and supportive leadership. Anne Leung and Kaitlin Hannon, assisted by Marisa Feinstein, helped to conceive the book's features and select new readings, coordinated efforts with the students whose essays appear throughout, and managed myriad details. And Emily Berleth and Nancy Benjamin deftly shepherded the manuscript through production. Deep and happy thanks to all.

CONTENTS

---

3   **WRITING**   **31**
                   REVISING AND EDITING

---

4   **DESCRIPTION**   **55**
                   Sensing the Natural World

| **5** | **NARRATION**
Recalling Childhood | **81** |

6	EXAMPLE Using Language	**111**

7	DIVISION OR ANALYSIS Looking at Popular Culture	**140**

8 CLASSIFICATION
Sorting Group Identities 168

---

9   PROCESS ANALYSIS
            Examining the Human Body   **195**

| **13** | ARGUMENT AND PERSUASION | **320** |
| | Debating Law and Order | |

APPENDIX
WORKING WITH SOURCES   373

Chapter 1

READING

This collection of essays has one purpose: to help you become a more proficient reader and writer. It combines examples of good writing with explanations of the writers' methods, questions to guide your reading, and ideas for your own writing. In doing so, it shows how you can adapt the processes and techniques of others as you learn to communicate clearly and effectively on paper.

Writing well is not an inborn skill but an acquired one: you will become proficient only by writing and rewriting, experimenting with different strategies, listening to the responses of readers. How, then, can it help to read the work of other writers?

- Reading others' ideas can introduce you to new information and give you new perspectives on your own experience. Many of the essays collected here demonstrate that personal experience is a rich and powerful source of material for writing. But the knowledge gained from reading can help pinpoint just what is remarkable in your experience. And by introducing varieties of behavior and ways of thinking that would otherwise remain unknown to you, reading can also help you understand where you fit in the scheme of things. Such insight not only reveals subjects for writing but also improves your ability to communicate with others whose experiences naturally differ from your own.

- Reading exposes you to a broad range of strategies and styles. Just seeing that these vary as much as the writers themselves should assure you that there is no fixed standard of writing, while it should also encourage you to find your own strategies and style. At the same time, you will see that writers do make choices to suit their subjects, their purposes, and especially their readers. Writing is rarely easy, even for the pros; but the more options you have to choose from, the more likely you are to succeed at it.

- Reading makes you sensitive to the role of audience in writing. As you become adept at reading the work of other writers critically, discovering intentions and analyzing choices, you will see how a writer's decisions affect you as audience. Training yourself to read attentively and critically is a first step to becoming a more objective reader of your own writing.

READING ATTENTIVELY

This chapter offers strategies for making the most of your reading in this book and elsewhere. These strategies are reinforced in Chapters 4–13, each of which offers opportunities for careful reading with two paragraphs, one student essay, and two professional essays. Each chapter also introduces a method of developing a piece of writing:

description	process analysis
narration	comparison and contrast
example	definition
division or analysis	cause-and-effect analysis
classification	argument and persuasion

These methods correspond to basic and familiar patterns of thought and expression, common in our daily musings and conversations as well as in writing for all sorts of purposes and audiences: college term papers, lab reports, and examinations; business memos and reports; letters to the editors of newspapers; articles in popular magazines.

As writers we draw on the methods, sometimes unconsciously, to give order to our ideas and even to find ideas. For instance, a writer narrates, or tells, a story of her experiences to understand and convey the feeling of living her life. As readers, in turn, we have expectations for these familiar methods. When we read a narrative of someone's experiences, for instance, we expect enough details to understand what happened, we anticipate that events will be told primarily in the order they occurred, and we want the story to have a point — a reason for its being told and for our bothering to read it.

Making such expectations conscious can sharpen your skills as a critical reader and as a writer. A full chapter on each method explains how it works, shows it at work in paragraphs, and gives advice for using it to develop your own essays. The essays in each chapter provide clear examples that you can analyze and learn from (with the help of specific questions) and can refer to while writing (with the help of specific writing suggestions).

To make your reading more interesting and also to stimulate your writing, the sample paragraphs and essays in Chapters 4–13 all focus on a common subject, such as childhood, popular culture, or stereotypes. You'll see how flexible the methods are when they help five writers produce five unique pieces on the same theme. You'll also have a springboard for producing your own unique pieces, whether you take up some of the book's writing suggestions or take off with your own topics.

READING CRITICALLY

When we look for something to watch on television or listen to on the radio, we often tune in one station after another, pausing just long enough each time to catch the program or music being broadcast before settling on one choice. Much of the reading we do is similar: we skim a newspaper, magazine, or online document, noting headings and scanning paragraphs to get the gist of the content. But such skimming is not really reading, for it neither involves us deeply in the subject nor engages us in interaction with the writer.

To get the most out of reading, we must invest something of ourselves in the process, applying our own ideas and emotions and attending not just to the substance but to the writer's interpretation of it. This kind of reading is **critical** because it looks beneath the surface of a piece of writing. (The common meaning of *critical* as "negative" doesn't apply here: critical reading may result in positive, negative, or even neutral reactions.)

Critical reading can be enormously rewarding, but of course it takes care and time. A good method for developing your own skill in critical reading is to prepare yourself beforehand and then read the work at least twice to uncover what it has to offer.

Preparing

Preparing to read need involve no more than a few minutes as you form some ideas about the author, the work, and your likely response to the work:

- What is the author's background, what qualifications does he or she bring to the subject, and what approach is he or she likely to take? The biographical information provided before each essay in this book should help answer these questions; many periodicals and books include similar information on their authors.
- What does the title convey about the subject and the author's attitude toward it? Note, for instance, the quite different attitudes conveyed by these three titles on the same subject: "Safe Hunting," "In Touch with Ancient Spirits," and "Killing Animals for Fun and Profit."
- What can you predict about your own response to the work? What might you already know about the author's subject? Based on the title and other clues, are you likely to agree or disagree with the author's views? *The Compact Reader* helps ready you for reading by providing two features before each selection. First, quotations from varied writers comment on the selection's core theme to give you a range of views. And second, a prompt labeled "Journal Response" encourages you to write about your existing views on or experiences with the author's subject before you see what the author has to say. By giving you a head start in considering the author's ideas and approach, writing *before* reading encourages you to read more actively and critically.

Reading Actively

After developing some expectations about the piece of writing, read it through carefully to acquaint yourself with the subject, the author's reason for writing about it, and the way the author presents it. (Each essay in this book is short enough to be read in one sitting.) Try not to read passively, letting the words wash over you, but instead interact directly with the work to discover its meaning, the author's intentions, and your own responses.

One of the best aids to active reading is to make notes on separate sheets of paper or, preferably (if you own the book), on the pages themselves. As you practice making notes, you will probably develop a personal code meaningful only to you. As a start, however, try this system:

- Underline or bracket passages that you find particularly effective or that seem especially important to the author's purpose.
- Circle words you don't understand so that you can look them up when you finish.
- Put question marks in the margins next to unclear passages.
- Jot down associations that occur to you, such as examples from your own experience, disagreements with the author's assumptions, or links to other works you've read.

When you have finished such an active reading, your annotations might look like those below. (The paragraph is from the end of the essay reprinted on pp. 7–11.)

The first half of our lives is spent stubbornly denying it. As children we acquire language to make ourselves understood and soon learn from the blank stares in response to our babblings that even these, our saviors, our parents, are strangers. In adolescence when we replay earlier dramas with peers in the place of parents, we begin the quest for the best friend, that person who will receive all thoughts as if they were her own. Later we assert that true love will find the way. True love finds many ways, but no escape from exile. The shores are littered with us, Annas and Ophelias, Emmas and Juliets, all outcasts from the dream of perfect understanding. We might as well draw the night around us and find solace there and a friend in our own voice.

true?

What about his own? Audience = women?

Ophelia + Juliet from Shakespeare. Others also?

In other words, just give up?

To answer questions like those in the annotations, count on rereading the essay at least once. Multiple readings increase your mastery of the material; more important, once you have a basic understanding of a writer's subject, a second and third reading will reveal details and raise questions that you might not have noticed on the first pass. Reading an essay several times also helps you to uncover how the many parts of the work—for instance, the sequencing of information, the tone, the evidence—contribute to the author's purpose.

Using a Reading Checklist

When rereading an essay, start by writing a one- or two-sentence summary of each paragraph—in your own words—to increase your mastery of the material (see p. 378). Then let the essay rest in your mind for at least an hour or two before approaching it again. On subsequent readings, dig beneath the essay's surface by asking questions such as those in the following checklist. Note that the questions provided after each essay in this book offer more targeted versions of the ones below. Combining the questions in the checklist with the questions for individual readings will ensure a thorough analysis of what you read.

CHECKLIST FOR CRITICAL READING

- Why did the author write about this subject?
- Who is the author's intended audience? What impression did the author wish to make on readers?
- What is the author's point? Can you find a direct statement of the main idea of the essay, or is the author's thesis implied?
- What details does the author provide to support the main idea of the essay? Is the supporting evidence reliable? complete? convincing?
- How does the author organize his or her ideas? What effect does the sequencing of information have on the overall impact of the essay?
- What do the language and tone used in the essay reveal about the author's meaning, purpose, and attitude?
- How successful is the essay as a whole, and why?

ANALYZING A SAMPLE ESSAY

A procedure for a critical reading—and the insights to be gained from it—can best be illustrated by examining an actual essay. The paragraph on page 5 comes from "The Box Man" by Barbara Lazear Ascher. The entire essay is reprinted here in the same format as other selections in this book, with quotations from other writers to get you thinking about the essay's subject, a suggestion for exploring your attitudes further in your journal, a note on the author, and a note on the essay.

You are where you live.
　　　　　　　　　　　　　　　　　　　　　　—Anna Quindlen

People who are homeless are not social inadequates. They are people without homes.
　　　　　　　　　　　　　　　　　　　　　　—Sheila McKechnie

How does it feel / To be without a home / Like a complete unknown / Like a rolling stone?
　　　　　　　　　　　　　　　　　　　　　　—Bob Dylan

Journal Response　In your journal write briefly about how you typically feel when you encounter a person who appears to be homeless. Are you sympathetic? disgusted? something in between?

Barbara Lazear Ascher

Born in 1946, American writer Barbara Lazear Ascher is known for her insightful, inspiring essays. She obtained a BA from Bennington College in 1968 and a JD from Cardozo School of Law in 1979. After practicing law for two years, Ascher turned to writing full-time. Her essays have appeared in a diverse assortment of periodicals, including the New York Times, Vogue, *the* Yale Review, Redbook, National Geographic Traveler, *and* AARP: The Magazine. *Ascher has also published a memoir of her brother, who died of AIDS,* Landscape without Gravity: A Memoir of Grief *(1993), and several collections of essays:* Playing after Dark *(1986),* The Habit of Loving *(1989), and* Dancing in the Dark: Romance, Yearning, and the Search for the Sublime *(1999). She is editorial director of Delphinium Books and teaches writing workshops at Bennington College.*

THE BOX MAN

In this essay from Playing after Dark, *the evening ritual of a homeless man prompts Ascher's reflection on the nature of solitude. By describing the Box Man alongside two other solitary people, Ascher distinguishes between chosen and unchosen loneliness.*

The Box Man was at it again. It was his lucky night.　　　　　　　　1

　　The first stroke of good fortune occurred as darkness fell and the　2
night watchman at 220 East Forty-fifth Street neglected to close the
door as he slipped out for a cup of coffee. I saw them before the Box

Man did. Just inside the entrance, cardboard cartons, clean and with their top flaps intact. With the silent fervor of a mute at a horse race, I willed him toward them.

3   It was slow going. His collar was pulled so high that he appeared headless as he shuffled across the street like a man who must feel Earth with his toes to know that he walks there.

4   Standing unselfconsciously in the white glare of an overhead light, he began to sort through the boxes, picking them up, one by one, inspecting tops, insides, flaps. Three were tossed aside. They looked perfectly good to me, but then, who knows what the Box Man knows? When he found the one that suited his purpose, he dragged it up the block and dropped it in a doorway.

5   Then, as if dogged by luck, he set out again and discovered, behind the sign at the parking garage, a plastic Dellwood box, strong and clean, once used to deliver milk. Back in the doorway the grand design was revealed as he pushed the Dellwood box against the door and set its cardboard cousin two feet in front — the usual distance between coffee table and couch. Six full shopping bags were distributed evenly on either side.

6   He eased himself with slow care onto the stronger box, reached into one of the bags, pulled out a *Daily News,* and snapped it open against his cardboard table. All done with the ease of IRT Express passengers whose white-tipped, fair-haired fingers reach into attaché cases as if radar-directed to the *Wall Street Journal.* They know how to fold it. They know how to stare at the print, not at the girl who stares at them.

7   That's just what the Box Man did, except that he touched his tongue to his fingers before turning each page, something grandmothers do.

8   One could live like this. Gathering boxes to organize a life. Wandering through the night collecting comforts to fill a doorway.

9   When I was a child, my favorite book was *The Boxcar Children.* If I remember correctly, the young protagonists were orphaned, and rather than live with cruel relatives, they ran away to the woods to live life on their own terms. An abandoned boxcar was turned into a home, a bubbling brook became an icebox. Wild berries provided abundant desserts and days were spent in the happy, adultless pursuit of joy. The children never worried where the next meal would come from or what February's chill might bring. They had unquestioning faith that berries would ripen and streams run cold and clear.

And unlike Thoreau,[1] whose deliberate living was self-conscious and purposeful, theirs had the ease of children at play.

Even now, when life seems complicated and reason slips, I long to live like a Boxcar Child, to have enough open space and freedom of movement to arrange my surroundings according to what I find. To turn streams into iceboxes. To be ingenious with simple things. To let the imagination hold sway.   *10*

Who is to say that the Box Man does not feel as Thoreau did in his doorway, not "crowded or confined in the least," with "pasture enough for . . . imagination." Who is to say that his dawns don't bring back heroic ages? That he doesn't imagine a goddess trailing her garments across his blistered legs?   *11*

His is a life of the mind, such as it is, and voices only he can hear. Although it would appear to be a life of misery, judging from the bandages and chill of night, it is of his choosing. He will ignore you if you offer an alternative. Last winter, Mayor Koch[2] tried, coaxing him with promises and the persuasive tones reserved for rabid dogs. The Box Man backed away, keeping a car and paranoia between them.   *12*

He is not to be confused with the lonely ones. You'll find them everywhere. The lady who comes into our local coffee shop each evening at five-thirty, orders a bowl of soup and extra Saltines. She drags it out as long as possible, breaking the crackers into smaller and smaller pieces, first in halves and then halves of halves and so on until the last pieces burst into salty splinters and fall from dry fingers onto the soup's shimmering surface. By 6 p.m., it's all over. What will she do with the rest of the night?   *13*

You can tell by the vacancy of expression that no memories linger there. She does not wear a gold charm bracelet with silhouettes of boys and girls bearing grandchildren's birthdates and a chip of the appropriate birthstone. When she opens her black purse to pay, there is only a crumpled Kleenex and a wallet inside, no photographs spill onto her lap. Her children, if there are any, live far away and prefer not to visit. If she worked as a secretary for forty years in a downtown office, she was given a retirement party, a cake, a reproduction of an antique perfume atomizer and sent on her way. Old colleagues — those who   *14*

[1] Henry David Thoreau (1817–62) was an American essayist and poet who for two years lived a solitary and simple life in the woods. He wrote of his experiences in *Walden* (1854). [Editor's note.]

[2] Edward Koch was the mayor of New York City from 1978 through 1989. [Editor's note.]

traded knitting patterns and brownie recipes over the water cooler, who discussed the weather, health, and office scandal while applying lipstick and blush before the ladies' room mirror — they are lost to time and the new young employees who take their places in the typing pool.

Each year she gets a Christmas card from her ex-boss. The envelope   *15* is canceled in the office mailroom and addressed by memory typewriter. Within is a family in black and white against a wooded Connecticut landscape. The boss, his wife, who wears her hair in a gray page boy, the three blond daughters, two with tall husbands and an occasional additional grandchild. All assembled before a worn stone wall.

Does she watch game shows? Talk to a parakeet, feed him cuttle-   *16* bone, and call him Pete? When she rides the buses on her Senior Citizen pass, does she go anywhere or wait for something to happen? Does she have a niece like the one in Cynthia Ozick's story "Rosa," who sends enough money to keep her aunt at a distance?

There's a lady across the way whose lights and television stay on   *17* all night. A crystal chandelier in the dining room and matching Chinese lamps on Regency end tables in the living room. She has six cats, some Siamese, others Angora and Abyssinian. She pets them and waters her plethora of plants — African violets, a ficus tree, a palm, and geraniums in season. Not necessarily a lonely life except that 3 a.m. lights and television seem to proclaim it so.

The Box Man welcomes the night, opens to it like a lover. He   *18* moves in darkness and prefers it that way. He's not waiting for the phone to ring or an engraved invitation to arrive in the mail. Not for him a P.O. number. Not for him the overcrowded jollity of office parties, the hot anticipation of a singles' bar. Not even for him a holiday handout. People have tried and he shuffled away.

The Box Man knows that loneliness chosen loses its sting and   *19* claims no victims. He declares what we all know in the secret passages of our own nights, that although we long for perfect harmony, communion, and blending with another soul, this is a solo voyage.

The first half of our lives is spent stubbornly denying it. As children   *20* we acquire language to make ourselves understood and soon learn from the blank stares in response to our babblings that even these, our saviors, our parents, are strangers. In adolescence when we replay earlier dramas with peers in the place of parents, we begin the quest for the best friend, that person who will receive all thoughts as if they were her own. Later we assert that true love will find the way. True love finds many ways, but no escape from exile. The shores are littered with us,

Annas and Ophelias, Emmas and Juliets,[3] all outcasts from the dream of perfect understanding. We might as well draw the night around us and find solace there and a friend in our own voice.

One could do worse than be a collector of boxes.

21

Even read quickly, Ascher's essay would not be difficult to comprehend: the author draws on examples of three people to make a point at the end about solitude. In fact, a quick reading might give the impression that Ascher produced the essay effortlessly, artlessly. But close, critical reading reveals a carefully conceived work whose parts work independently and together to achieve the author's purpose.

One way to uncover underlying intentions and relations like those in Ascher's essay is to work through a series of questions about the work. The following questions proceed from the general to the specific—from overall meaning through purpose and method to word choices—and they parallel the more specific questions after the essays in this book. Here the questions come with possible answers for Ascher's essay. (The paragraph numbers can help you locate the appropriate passages in Ascher's essay as you follow the analysis.)

Meaning

What is the main idea of the essay—the chief point the writer makes about the subject, to which all other ideas and details relate? What are the subordinate ideas that contribute to the main idea?

Ascher states her main idea (or thesis) near the end of her essay: in choosing solitude, the Box Man confirms the essential aloneness of human beings (paragraph 19) but also demonstrates that we can "find solace" within ourselves (20). (Writers sometimes postpone stating their main idea, as Ascher does here. Perhaps more often, they state it near the beginning of the essay. See pp. 22–25.) Ascher leads up to and supports her idea with three examples—the Box Man (paragraphs 1–7, 11–12) and, in contrast, two women whose loneliness seems unchosen (13–16, 17). These examples are developed with specific details

---

[3] These are all doomed heroines of literature. Anna is the title character of Leo Tolstoy's novel *Anna Karenina* (1876). Emma is the title character of Gustave Flaubert's novel *Madame Bovary* (1856). Ophelia and Juliet are in Shakespeare's plays—the lovers, respectively, of Hamlet and Romeo. [Editor's note.]

from Ascher's observations (such as the nearly empty purse, 14) and from the imagined lives these observations suggest (such as the remote, perhaps nonexistent children, 14).

Occasionally, you may need to puzzle over some of the author's words before you can fully understand his or her meaning. Try to guess the word's meaning from its context first, and then check your guess in a dictionary. (To help master the word so that you know it next time and can draw on it yourself, use it in a sentence or more of your own.)

Purpose and Audience

Why did the author write the essay? What did the author hope readers would gain from it? What did the author assume about the knowledge and interests of readers, and how are these assumptions reflected in the essay?

Ascher seems to have written her essay for two interlocking reasons: to show and thus explain that solitude need not always be lonely and to argue gently for defeating loneliness by becoming one's own friend. In choosing the Box Man as her main example, she reveals perhaps a third purpose as well—to convince readers that a homeless person can have dignity and may achieve a measure of self-satisfaction lacking in some people who do have homes.

Ascher seems to assume that her readers, like her, are people with homes, people to whom the Box Man and his life might seem completely foreign: she comments on the Box Man's slow shuffle (paragraph 3), his mysterious discrimination among boxes (4), his "blistered legs" (11), how miserable his life looks (12), his bandages (12), the cold night he inhabits (12), the fearful or condescending approaches of strangers (12, 18). Building from this assumption that her readers will find the Box Man strange, Ascher takes pains to show the dignity of the Box Man—his "grand design" for furniture (5), his resemblance to commuters (6), his grandmotherly finger licking (7), his refusal of handouts (18).

Several other apparent assumptions about her audience also influence Ascher's selection of details, if less significantly. First, she assumes some familiarity with literature—at least with the writings of Thoreau (9, 11) and the characters named in paragraph 20. Second, Ascher seems to address women: in paragraph 20 she speaks of each person confiding in "her" friend, and she chooses only female figures from literature to illustrate "us, . . . all outcasts from the dream of perfect understanding." Finally, Ascher seems to address people who are familiar with, if not actually residents of, New York City: she refers to a New York street address (2); alludes to a New York newspaper, the *Daily News*, and a New York subway line, the IRT Express (6); and mentions the city's mayor (12). However, readers who do not know the literature Ascher cites, who are not women, and who do not know New York City are still likely to understand and appreciate Ascher's main point.

Method and Structure

What method or methods does the author use to develop the main idea, and how do the methods serve the author's subject and purpose? How does the organization serve the author's subject and purpose?

Ascher's primary support for her idea consists of three examples (Chapter 6) — specific instances of solitary people. The method of example especially suits Ascher's subject and purpose because it allows her to show contrasting responses to solitude: one person who seems to choose it and two people who don't.

As writers often do, Ascher relies on more than a single method, more than just example. She develops her examples with description (Chapter 4), vividly portraying the Box Man and the two women, as in paragraphs 6–7, so that we see them clearly. Paragraphs 1–7 in the portrayal of the Box Man involve retelling, or narrating (Chapter 5), his activities. Ascher uses division or analysis (Chapter 7) to tease apart the elements of her three characters' lives. And she relies on comparison and contrast (Chapter 10) to show the differences between the Box Man and the other two in paragraphs 13 and 17–18.

While using many methods to develop her idea, Ascher keeps her organization fairly simple. She does not begin with a formal introduction or a statement of her idea but instead starts right off with her main example, the inspiration for her idea. In the first seven paragraphs she narrates and describes the Box Man's activities. Then, in paragraphs 8–12, she explains what appeals to her about circumstances like the Box Man's and she applies those thoughts to what she imagines are his thoughts. Still delaying a statement of her main idea, Ascher contrasts the Box Man and two other solitary people, whose lives she sees as different from his (13–17). Finally, she returns to the Box Man (18–19) and zeroes in on her main idea (19–20). Though she has withheld this idea until the end, we see that everything in the essay has been controlled by it and directed toward it.

Language

How are the author's main idea and purpose revealed at the level of sentences and words? How does the author use language to convey his or her attitudes toward the subject and to make meaning clear and vivid?

One reason Ascher's essay works is that she uses specific language to portray her three examples—she *shows* them to us—and to let us know what she thinks about them. For instance, the language changes markedly from the depiction of the Box Man to the next-to-last paragraph on solitude. The Box Man comes to life in warm terms: Ascher watches him with "silent fervor" (paragraph 2); he seems "dogged by luck" (5); he sits with "slow care" and opens the newspaper with "ease" (6); his page turning reminds Ascher of "grandmothers" (7); it is conceivable that, in Thoreau's word, the Box Man's imagination has "pasture" to roam, that he dreams of "heroic ages" and a "goddess trailing her garments" (11). In contrast, isolation comes across as a desperate state in paragraph 20, where Ascher uses words such as "blank stares," "strangers," "exile," "littered," and "outcasts." The contrast in language helps to emphasize Ascher's point about the individual's ability to find comfort in solitude.

In describing the two other solitary people—those who evidently have not found comfort in aloneness—Ascher uses words that emphasize the heaviness of time and the sterility of existence. The first woman "drags" her meal out and crumbles crackers between "dry fingers" (13), a "vacancy of expression" on her face (14). She lacks even the trinkets of attachment—a "gold charm bracelet" with "silhouettes" of grandchildren (14). A vividly imagined photograph of her exboss and his family (15)—the wife with "her hair in a gray page boy," "the three blond daughters"—emphasizes the probable absence of such scenes in the woman's own life.

Ascher occasionally uses incomplete sentences (or sentence fragments) to stress the accumulation of details or the quickness of her impressions. For example, in paragraph 10 the incomplete sentences beginning "To" sketch Ascher's dream. And in paragraph 18 the incomplete sentences beginning "Not" emphasize the Box Man's withdrawal. Both of these sets of incomplete sentences gain emphasis from **parallelism**, the use of similar grammatical form for ideas of equal importance (see p. 47). The parallelism begins in the complete sentence preceding each set of incomplete sentences—for example, ". . . I long to live like a Boxcar Child, to have enough open space and freedom of movement. . . . To turn streams into iceboxes. To be ingenious with simple things. To let the imagination hold sway." Although incomplete sentences can be unclear, these and the others in Ascher's essay are clear: she uses them deliberately and carefully, for a purpose. (Inexperienced writers often find it safer to avoid any incomplete sentences until they have mastered the complete sentence.)

These notes on Ascher's essay show how one can arrive at a deeper, more personal understanding of a piece of writing by attentive, thoughtful analysis. Guided by the questions at the end of each essay and by your own sense of what works and why, you'll find similar lessons and pleasures in all of this book's readings.

Chapter 2

WRITING

GETTING STARTED
THROUGH DRAFTING

Analyzing a text in the way shown in the preceding chapter is valuable in itself: it can be fun, and the process helps you better understand and appreciate whatever you read. But it can make you a better writer, too, by showing you how to read your own work critically, broadening the range of strategies available to you, and suggesting subjects for you to write about.

The essays collected in this book are accompanied by a range of material designed to help you use your reading to write effectively. Every reading is followed by several detailed questions that will help you read it critically and examine the writing strategies that make it successful. Accompanying the questions are writing topics—ideas for you to adapt and develop into essays of your own. Some of these call for your analysis of the essay; others lead you to examine your own experiences or outside sources in light of the essay's ideas. Chapters 4–13 each conclude with two additional sets of writing topics: one group provides a range of subjects for using the chapter's method of development; the other encourages you to focus on thematic connections in the chapter.

To help you develop your writing, *The Compact Reader* also offers several tools that guide you through the process of composing effective essays. This chapter and the next, on writing, offer specific ways to strengthen and clarify your work as you follow the stages of the **writing process**: getting started, forming a thesis, organizing, drafting, revising, and editing. (You may want to refer back to these chapters as your writing skills develop. See the inside back cover for a guide to the topics covered.) Complementing this overview are the more specific introductions to the methods of development in Chapters 4–13 — narration, comparison and contrast, definition, and so on. These method introductions follow the pattern set here by also proceeding from beginning to end of the writing process, but they take up particular concerns of the method, such as organizing a narrative or clarifying a definition.

A word of caution: for the sake of clarity, this book guides you through the writing process in stages, shifting the focus from inventing to shaping to revising and editing. But as you'll discover, these stages are actually somewhat arbitrary. Writers rarely move in straight lines through fixed steps, like locomotives over tracks. Instead, just as they do when thinking, writers continually circle back over covered territory, each time picking up more information or seeing new relationships, until their meaning is clear to themselves and can be made clear to readers. No two writers proceed in exactly the same way, either, so your writing process may differ considerably from your classmates'. A successful writing process is the one that works best for you.

GETTING STARTED

Every writing situation involves several elements: you communicate a *thesis* (idea) about a subject to an *audience* of readers for a particular *purpose*. At first you may not be sure of your idea or your purpose. You may not know how you want to approach your readers, even when you know who they are. Your job in getting started, then, is to explore options and make choices.

Considering Your Subject and Purpose

A subject for writing may arise from any source, including your own experience or reading, a suggestion in this book, or an assignment from your instructor. In the previous chapter, Barbara Lazear Ascher's essay on a homeless man demonstrates how an excellent subject can be found from observing one's surroundings. Whatever its source, the subject should be something you care enough about to probe deeply and to stamp with your own perspective.

This personal stamp comes from your **purpose**, your reason for writing. The purpose may be one of the following:

- To explain the subject so that readers understand it or see it in a new light.
- To persuade readers to accept or reject an opinion or to take a certain action.
- To entertain readers with a humorous or exciting story.
- To express the thoughts and emotions triggered by a revealing or instructive experience.

A single essay may sometimes have more than one purpose: for instance, a writer might both explain what it's like to be disabled and try to persuade readers to respect special parking zones for the disabled. Your reasons for writing may be clear to you early on, arising out of the subject and its significance for you. But you may need to explore your subject for a while—even to the point of writing a draft—before you know what you want to do with it.

Considering Your Audience

Either very early, when you first begin exploring your subject, or later, as a check on what you have generated, you may want to make a few notes on your anticipated audience. The notes are optional, but thinking about audience definitely is not. Your topic and purpose, as well as your thesis, supporting ideas, details and examples, organization, style, tone, and language—all should reflect your answers to the following questions:

- What impression do you want to make on readers?
- What do readers already know about your subject? What do they need to know?
- What are readers' likely expectations and assumptions about your subject?
- How can you build on readers' previous knowledge, expectations, and assumptions to bring them around to your view?

These considerations are obviously crucial to achieve the fundamental purpose of all public writing: communication. Accordingly, they come up again and again in the chapter introductions and the questions after each essay.

Discovering Ideas

Ideas for your writing — whether your subject itself or the many smaller ideas and details that comprise what you have to say about it — may come to you in a rush, or you may need to search for them. Writers use a variety of searching techniques, from jotting down thoughts while they pursue other activities to writing concentratedly for a set period. Here are a few techniques you might try.

Journal Writing

Many writers keep a **journal**, a record of thoughts and observations. Whether in a notebook or in a computer file, journal entries give you an opportunity to explore ideas just for yourself, free of concerns about readers who will judge what you say or how you say it. Regular journal entries can also make you more comfortable with the act of writing and build your confidence. Indeed, writing teachers often require their students to keep journals for these reasons.

In a journal you can write about whatever interests, puzzles, or disturbs you. Here are just a few possible uses:

- Record your responses to your reading in this book and other sources.
- Prepare for a class by summarizing the week's reading or the previous class's discussion.
- Analyze a relationship that's causing you problems.
- Imitate a writer you admire, such as a poet or songwriter.
- Explore your reactions to a movie or a television program.
- Confide your dreams and fears.

Any of this material could provide a seed for a writing assignment, but you can also use a journal deliberately to develop ideas for assignments. One approach is built into this book: before every essay you will find several quotations and a suggestion for journal writing — all centering on the topic of the essay. In responding to the quotations and journal prompt preceding Barbara Lazear Ascher's "The Box Man" (p. 7), you might explore your feelings about homeless people or recount a particular encounter with a homeless person. One student, Grace Patterson, wrote this journal entry in response to the material preceding Ascher's essay:

> It seems that nothing works to solve the problem of
> homeless people. My first reaction is fear--especially
> if the person is really dirty or rambling on about some-
> thing, I just walk away as fast as I can. Can't say I'm
> proud of myself though--there's always guilt--I should
> be helping. But how? I like what Bob Dylan says--a home
> is important, so how must it feel to be without one?

Writing for herself, Patterson felt free to explore what was on her mind, without worrying about correctness and without trying to make it clear to external readers what she meant by words such as *fear* and *guilt*. By articulating her mixed reactions to homelessness, Patterson established a personal context in which to read Ascher's essay, and that context made her a more engaged, more critical reader.

Patterson used journal writing for another purpose as well: to respond to Ascher's essay *after* she read it.

> Ascher gives an odd view of homelessness--hadn't really
> occurred to me that the homeless man on the street
> might want to be there. Always assumed that no one
> would want to live in filthy clothes, without a roof.
> What is a home anyway--shelter? decor? a clothes
> closet? Can your body and few "possessions" = home?

As this entry's final question makes clear, Patterson didn't come to any conclusions about homelessness or about Ascher's essay. She did, however, begin to work out ideas that would serve as the foundation for a more considered critical response later on. (Further stages of Patterson's writing process appear throughout the rest of this chapter.)

Freewriting

To discover ideas for a particular assignment, you may find it useful to try **freewriting**, or writing without stopping for a set amount of time, usually ten to fifteen minutes. In freewriting you push yourself to keep writing, following ideas wherever they lead, paying no attention to completeness or correctness or even sense. When she began composing an essay response to Barbara Lazear Ascher's "The Box Man," Grace Patterson produced this freewriting:

> Something in Ascher's essay keeps nagging at me. Almost ticks me off. What she says about the Box Man is based on certain assumptions. Like she knows what he's been through, how he feels. Can he be as content as she says? What bothers me is, how much choice does the guy really have? Just cuz he manages to put a little dignity into his life on the street and refuses handouts-- does that mean he chooses homelessness? Life in a shelter might be worse than life on the street.

Notice that this freewriting is rough: the tone is very informal, as if Patterson were speaking to herself; some thoughts are left dangling; some sentences are shapeless or incomplete; a word is misspelled (*cuz* for *because*). But none of this matters because the freewriting is just exploratory. Writing fluently, without halting to rethink or edit, actually pulled insights out of Patterson. She moved from being vaguely uneasy with Ascher's essay to conceiving an argument against it. Then, with a more definite focus, she could begin drafting in earnest.

If you have difficulty writing without correcting and you compose on a word processor, you might try **invisible writing**: turn the computer's monitor off while you freewrite, so that you can't see what you're producing. When your time is up, turn the monitor back on to work with the material.

Brainstorming

Another discovery technique that helps to pull ideas from you is **brainstorming**, listing ideas without stopping to censor or change them. As in freewriting, write without stopping for ten or fifteen minutes, jotting down everything that seems even remotely related to your subject. Don't stop to reread and rethink what you have written; just keep pulling and recording ideas, no matter how silly or dull or irrelevant they seem. When your time is up, look over the list to find the promising ideas and discard the rest. Depending on *how* promising the remaining ideas are, you can resume brainstorming, try freewriting about them, or begin a draft.

Using the Methods of Development

The ten methods of development discussed in Chapters 4–13 can also help you expand your thinking. Try asking the following questions to open up ideas about your subject:

- *Description* (Chapter 4): How does the subject look, sound, smell, taste, and feel?
- *Narration* (Chapter 5): What is the story in the subject? How did it happen?
- *Example* (Chapter 6): How can the subject be illustrated? What are instances of it?
- *Division or Analysis* (Chapter 7): What are the subject's parts, and what is their relationship or significance?
- *Classification* (Chapter 8): What groups or categories can the subject be sorted into?
- *Process Analysis* (Chapter 9): How does the subject work, or how does one do it?
- *Comparison and Contrast* (Chapter 10): How is the subject similar to or different from something else?
- *Definition* (Chapter 11): What are the subject's characteristics and boundaries?
- *Cause-and-Effect Analysis* (Chapter 12): Why did the subject happen? What were or may be its consequences?
- *Argument and Persuasion* (Chapter 13): Why do I believe as I do about the subject? Why do others have different opinions? How can I convince others to accept my opinion or believe as I do?

FORMING A THESIS

How many times have you read a work of nonfiction and wondered, "What's the point?" Whether consciously or not, we expect a writer to *have* a point, a central idea that he or she wants readers to take away from the work. We expect that idea to determine the content of the work — so that everything relates to it — and we expect the content in turn to demonstrate or prove the idea.

Arriving at a main idea, or **thesis**, is thus an essential part of the writing process. Sometimes your thesis will occur to you at the moment you hit on your subject — for instance, if you think of writing about the new grading policy because you want to make a point about its unfairness. More often, you will need to explore your subject for a while — even to the point of writing a draft or more — before you pin down just what you have to say. Even if your thesis will evolve, however, it's a good idea to draft it early because it can help keep you focused as you generate more ideas, seek information, organize your thoughts, and so on.

Identifying Your Main Point

A thesis is distinct from the subject of an essay. The subject is what an essay is about; the thesis captures a writer's unique understanding of that subject. In the case of "The Box Man," for example, the subject is homelessness, but Ascher's thesis — that one homeless man's quiet dignity should serve as a model for how the rest of us go about our lives — makes a strong point that readers may not have contemplated on their own. Student writer Grace Patterson writes about the same subject — homelessness — but she makes a completely different point: that a homeless person's "choice" to live on the streets is not a choice at all.

The distinction between a subject and a thesis is evident throughout this book. Each chapter of readings focuses on a single subject — such as childhood, popular culture, or the human body — yet the individual essays demonstrate the writers' unique perspectives on particular aspects of those general topics. The readings in Chapter 4, for instance, all center on the subject of nature, but no two take the same approach. David Mura writes to describe the discomfort caused by typhoon season in Tokyo; Diane Ackerman strives to capture the breathtaking beauty of icebergs; Marta K. Taylor uses a car ride in the desert to explain the protections offered by family; Dagoberto Gilb writes about his yard to make a point about cultural conflict; and Joan Didion considers the ways in which California's weather affects the mental health of the state's inhabitants.

To move from a general subject to a workable thesis for your own writing, keep narrowing your focus until you have something to say about the subject. For example, if you wanted to write about family, you'd quickly discover that the topic — which fills whole books — is too broad to work with in a brief essay. You could then narrow the subject to adoptive families, but even that covers too much territory. By consistently tightening your focus, you might eventually realize that what interests you is adopted children who want to contact their birth parents and that you want to explain how it is possible, if difficult, to locate the necessary information. In a few steps, you've turned a broad subject into a main point worth making. The process isn't always simple, but it is a necessary first step in finding a thesis.

Drafting and Revising a Thesis Sentence

Once you've narrowed your subject and have something to say about it, the best way to focus on your thesis is to write it out in a **thesis sentence** (or sentences): an assertion that makes your point about the subject. In these two sentences from the end of "The Box Man" (p. 7), Barbara Lazear Ascher asserts the main idea of her essay:

> [We are] all outcasts from the dream of perfect understanding. We might as well draw the night around us and find solace there and a friend in our own voice.

Ascher's thesis statement, while poetic, nonetheless ties together all of the other ideas and details in her essay; it also reflects her purpose in writing the essay and focuses her readers on a single point. All effective thesis sentences do this: they go beyond generalities or mere statements of fact to express the writer's opinion about the subject. Notice the differences in the following sentences Grace Patterson considered for her response to "The Box Man":

GENERAL STATEMENT   Homelessness is a serious problem in America.

STATEMENT OF FACT   Some homeless people avoid staying in temporary shelters.

EFFECTIVE THESIS SENTENCE   For the homeless people in America today, there are no good choices.

The first sentence offers an opinion, but because it's a very broad assertion that few would dispute, it fails to capture readers' interest or make a significant point. The second sentence merely expresses a fact, not a main idea worth developing in an essay. The final sentence, however, makes a strong assertion about a narrow subject and gives readers an idea of what to expect from the rest of the essay.

Because the main point of an essay may change over the course of the writing process, your own thesis sentence may also change, sometimes considerably. The following examples show how one writer shifted his opinion and moved from an explanatory to a persuasive purpose between the early stages of the writing process and the final draft.

EARLY THESIS SENTENCE   With persistence, adopted children can often locate information about their birth parents.

FINAL THESIS SENTENCE   Adopted children are unfairly hampered in seeking information about their birth parents.

The final sentence makes a definite assertion ("Adopted children are unfairly hampered") and clearly conveys the persuasive purpose of the essay to come. Thus the sentence lets readers know what to expect: an argument that adopted children should be treated more fairly when they seek information about their birth parents. Readers will also expect some discussion of what hampers an adoptee's search, what is "unfair" and "fair" in this situation, and what changes the author proposes.

Most commonly, the thesis sentence comes near the beginning of an essay, sometimes in the first paragraph, where it serves as a promise to examine a particular subject from a particular perspective. But as Ascher demonstrates by stating her thesis at the end, the thesis sentence may come elsewhere as long as it controls the whole essay. The thesis may even go unstated, as other essays in this book illustrate, but it still must govern every element of the work as if it were announced.

ORGANIZING

Writers vary in the extent to which they arrange their material before they begin drafting, but most do establish some plan. A good time to do so is after you've explored your subject and developed a good stock of ideas about it. Before you begin drafting, you can look over what you've got and consider the best ways to organize it.

Creating a Plan

A writing plan may consist of a list of key points, a fuller list including specifics as well, or even a detailed formal outline — whatever gives order to your ideas and provides some direction for your writing.

As you'll see in later chapters, many of the methods of development suggest specific structures, most notably description, narration, classification, process analysis, and comparison and contrast. But even when the organization is almost built into the method, you'll find that some subjects demand more thoughtful plans than others. You may be able to draft a straightforward narrative of a personal experience with very little advance planning. But a nonpersonal narrative, or even a personal one involving complex events and time shifts, may require more thought about arrangement.

Though some sort of plan is almost always useful when drafting, resist any temptation at this stage to pin down every detail in its proper place. A huge investment in planning can hamper you during drafting, making it difficult to respond to new ideas and even new directions that may prove fruitful.

Thinking in Paragraphs

Most essays consist of three parts: an introduction and a conclusion (discussed in the next section) and the **body**, the most substantial and longest part, which develops the main idea or thesis.

As you explore your subject, you will discover both ideas that directly support your thesis and more specific examples, details, and other evidence that support these ideas. In the following outline of Grace Patterson's "A Rock and a Hard Place" (pp. 52–54), you can see how each supporting idea, or subpoint, helps to build the thesis sentence:

THESIS SENTENCE   For the homeless people in America today, there are no good choices.

SUBPOINT   A "good choice" is one made from a variety of options determined and narrowed down by the chooser.

SUBPOINT   Homeless people do not necessarily choose to live on the streets.

SUBPOINT   The streets are the only alternative to shelters, which are dangerous and dehumanizing.

Patterson uses specific evidence to develop each subpoint in a paragraph. In essence, the paragraphs are like mini-essays with their own main ideas and support. (See pp. 33–34 for more on paragraph structure.)

When you seek a plan in your ideas, look first for your subpoints, the main supports for your thesis. Use these as your starting points to work out your essay one chunk (or paragraph) at a time. You can sketch the supporting details and examples into your organizational plan, or you can wait until you begin drafting to get into the specifics.

Considering the Introduction and Conclusion

You'll probably have to be drafting or revising before you'll know for sure how you want to begin and end your essay. Still, it can be helpful to consider the introduction and conclusion earlier, so you have a sense of how you might approach readers and what you might leave them with.

The basic opening and closing serve readers by demonstrating your interest in their needs and expectations:

- The **introduction** draws readers into the essay and focuses their attention on the main idea and purpose, often stated in a thesis sentence.
- The **conclusion** ties together the elements of the essay and provides a final impression for readers to take away with them.

These basic forms allow considerable room for variation. Especially as you are developing your writing skills, you will find it helpful to state your thesis sentence near the beginning of the essay; but sometimes you can place it effectively at the end, or you can let it direct what you say in the essay but never state it at all. One essay may need two paragraphs of introduction but only a one-sentence conclusion, whereas another essay may require no formal introduction but a lengthy conclusion. How you begin and end depends on your subject and purpose, the kind of essay you are writing, and the likely responses of your readers. Specific ideas for opening and closing essays are included in each chapter introduction and in the Glossary under *introductions* and *conclusions*.

DRAFTING

However detailed your organizational plan is, you should not view it as a rigid taskmaster while you are drafting your essay. Drafting is the chance for you to give expression to your ideas, filling them out, finding relationships, drawing conclusions. If you are like most writers, you will discover much of what you have to say while drafting. In fact, if your subject is complex or difficult for you to write about, you may need several drafts just to work out your ideas and their relationships.

Writing, Not Revising

Some writers draft rapidly, rarely looking up from the paper or keyboard. Others draft more in fits and starts, gazing out the window or doodling as much as writing. Any method that works is fine, but one method rarely works: collapsing drafting and revising into one stage, trying to do everything at once.

Write first; then revise. Concentrate on *what* you are saying, not on *how* you are saying it. You pressure yourself needlessly if you try to produce a well-developed, coherent, interesting, and grammatically correct paper all at once. You may have trouble getting words on paper because you're afraid to make mistakes, or you may be distracted by mistakes from exploring your ideas fully. Awkwardness, repetition, wrong words, grammatical errors, spelling mistakes — these and other more superficial concerns can be attended to in a later draft. The same goes for considering your readers' needs: like many writers, you may find that attention to readers during the first draft inhibits the flow of ideas.

If you experience writer's block or just don't know how to begin your draft, start writing the part you're most comfortable with. Writing in paragraph chunks, as described on page 26, will also make drafting more manageable. You can start with your thesis sentence — or at least keep it in view while you draft — as a reminder of your purpose and main idea. But if you find yourself pulled away from the thesis by a new idea, you may want to let go and follow, at least for a while. If your purpose and main idea change as a result of such exploration, you can always revise your thesis accordingly.

Grace Patterson's First Draft

Some exploratory work by the student Grace Patterson appears on pages 20 and 21. What follows is the first draft she subsequently wrote on homelessness. The draft is very rough, with frequent repetitions, wandering paragraphs, and many other flaws. But such weaknesses are not important at this early stage. The draft gave Patterson the opportunity to discover what she had to say, explore her ideas, and link them in rough sequence.

```
                          Title?
        In the essay, "The Box Man," Barbara Lazear
   Ascher says that a homeless man who has chosen solitude
   can show the rest of us how to "find . . . a friend in
   our own voice." Maybe. But her case depends on the Box
   Man's choice, her assumption that he had one.
        Discussions of the homeless often use the word
   choice. Many people with enough money can accept the
```

condition of the homeless in America when they tell themselves that many of the homeless chose their lives. That the streets are in fact what they want. But it's not fair to use the word choice here: the homeless don't get to choose their lives the way most of the rest of us do. For the homeless people in America today, there are no good choices.

What do I mean by a "good choice"? One made from a variety of options determined and narrowed down by the chooser. There is plenty of room for the chooser to make a decision that he will be satisfied with. When I choose a career, I expect to make a good choice. There is plenty of interesting fields worth investigating, and there is lots of rewarding work to be done. It's a choice that opens the world up and showcases its possibilities. If it came time for me to choose a career, and the mayor of my town came around and told me that I had to choose between a life of cleaning public toilets and operating a jackhammer on a busy street corner, I would object. That's a lousy choice, and I wouldn't let anyone force me to make it.

When the mayor of New York tried to take the homeless off the streets, some of them didn't want to go. People assumed that the homeless people who did not want to get in the mayor's car for a ride to a city shelter chose to live on the street. But just because some homeless people chose the street over the generosity of the mayor does not necessarily mean that life on the streets is their ideal. We allow ourselves as many options as we can imagine, but we allow the homeless only two: go to a shelter, or stay where you are. Who narrowed down the options for the homeless? Who benefits if they go to a shelter? Who suffers if they don't?

Homeless people are not always better off in shelters. I had a conversation with a man who had lived on

the streets for a long time. The man said that he had
spent some time in those shelters for the homeless, and
he told me what they were like. The shelters are
crowded and dirty and people have to wait in long lines
for everything. People are constantly being herded
around and bossed around. It's dangerous--drug dealers,
beatings, theft. Dehumanizing. It matches my picture of
hell. From the sound of it, I couldn't spend two hours
in a shelter, never mind a whole night. I value my
peace of mind and my sleep too much, not to mention my
freedom and autonomy.

When homeless people sleep in the street, though,
that makes the public uncomfortable. People with enough
money wish the homeless would just disappear. They
don't care where they go. Just out of sight. I've felt
this way too but I'm as uneasy with that reaction as I
am at the sight of a person sleeping on the sidewalk.
And I tell myself that this is more than a question of
my comfort. By and large I'm comfortable enough.

The homeless are in a difficult enough situation
without having to take the blame for making the rest of
us feel uncomfortable with our wealth. If we cannot offer the homeless a good set of choices, the opportunity
to choose lives that they will be truly satisfied with
then the least we can do is stop dumping on them (?).
They're caught between a rock and a hard place: there
are not many places for them to go, and the places
where they can go afford nothing but suffering.

Chapter 3

WRITING

REVISING AND EDITING

The previous chapter took you through the first-draft stage of the writing process, when you have a chance to work out your meaning without regard for what others may think. This chapter describes the crucial next stages, when you actively consider your readers: revising to focus and shape the work and editing to clarify and polish.

Revision and editing are different tasks. In revising, you make fundamental changes in content and structure: you work below the surface of the draft. Then in editing, you make changes in the revised draft's sentences and words: you work on the surface, attending to style, grammar, punctuation, and the like. The separation of these two stages is important because attention to little changes distracts from a view of the whole. If you try to edit while you revise, you'll be more likely to miss the big picture. You may also waste effort perfecting sentences you'll later decide to cut.

REVISING

Revision means "re-seeing," looking at your draft as a reader sees it: mere words on a page that are only as clear, interesting, and significant as the writer has made them.

31

Reading Your Own Work Critically

Perhaps the most difficult challenge in revising is reading your own work objectively, as a reader would. To gain something like a reader's critical distance from your draft, try one or more of the following techniques:

- Put your first draft aside for at least a few hours—and preferably overnight—before attempting to revise it. You may have further thoughts in the interval, and you will be able to see your work more objectively when you return to it.
- Ask another person to read and comment on your draft. Your teacher may ask you and your classmates to exchange drafts so that you can help each other revise. But even without such a procedure, you can benefit from others' responses. Keep an open mind to readers' comments, and ask questions when you need more information.
- Make an outline of your draft by listing what you cover in each paragraph. Such an outline can show gaps, overlaps, and problems in organization. (See also p. 26.)
- Read the draft aloud or into a recorder. Speaking the words and hearing them can help to create distance from them.
- Imagine you are someone else—a friend, perhaps, or a particular person in your intended audience—and read the draft through that person's eyes, as if for the first time.
- If you write on a word processor, print a double-spaced copy of your draft. It's much easier to read text on paper than on a computer screen, and you can spread out printed pages to see the whole paper at once. Once you've finished revising, making the changes on the computer requires little effort.

Looking at the Whole Draft

Revision involves seeing your draft as a whole, focusing mainly on your purpose and thesis, the support for your thesis, and the movement among ideas. You want to determine what will work and what won't for readers—where the draft strays from your purpose, leaves a hole in the development of your thesis, does not flow logically or smoothly, digresses, or needs more details. (See the revision checklist on p. 40.) Besides rewriting, you may need to cut entire paragraphs, condense paragraphs into sentences, add passages of explanation, or rearrange sections.

Purpose and Thesis

In the press of drafting, you may lose sight of why you are writing or what your main idea is. Both your purpose and your thesis may change as you work out your meaning, so that you start in one place and end somewhere else or even lose track of where you are.

Your first goal in revising, then, is to see that your essay is well focused. Readers should grasp a clear purpose right away, and they should find that you have achieved it at the end. They should see your main idea, your thesis, very early, usually by the end of the introduction, and they should think that you have proved or demonstrated the thesis when they reach the last paragraph.

Like many writers, you may sometimes start with one thesis and finish with another, in effect writing into your idea as you draft. In many cases you'll need to rewrite your thesis statement to reflect what you actually wrote in your draft. Or you may need to upend your essay, plucking your thesis out of the conclusion and starting over with it, providing the subpoints and details to develop it. You'll probably find the second draft much easier to write because you know better what you want to say, and the next round of revision will probably be much cleaner.

Unity

When a piece of writing has **unity**, all its parts are related: the sentences build the central idea of their paragraph, and the paragraphs build the central idea of the whole essay. Readers do not have to wonder what the essay is about or what a particular paragraph has to do with the rest of the piece.

UNITY IN PARAGRAPHS Earlier we saw how the body paragraphs of an essay are almost like mini-essays themselves, each developing an idea, or subpoint, that supports the thesis. (See p. 26.) In fact, a body paragraph should have its own thesis, called its **topic**, usually expressed in a **topic sentence** or sentences. The rest of the paragraph develops the topic with specifics.

In the following paragraph from the final draft of Grace Patterson's "A Rock and a Hard Place" (pp. 52–54), the topic sentence is italicized:

> *The fact is that homeless people are not always better off in shelters.* I recently had a conversation with a man named Alan Doran who had lived on the streets for a long time. He said that he had spent some time

in shelters for the homeless, and he told me what they are like. They're dangerous and dehumanizing. Drug dealing, beatings, and theft are common. The shelters are dirty and crowded, so that residents have to wait in long lines for everything and are constantly being bossed around. No wonder some homeless people, including Alan, prefer the street: it affords some space to breathe, some autonomy, some peace for sleeping.

Notice that every sentence of this paragraph relates to the topic sentence. Patterson achieved this unity in revision (see pp. 42–43). In her first draft the last sentences of this paragraph focused on herself rather than the conditions of homeless shelters:

> It matches my picture of hell. From the sound of it, I couldn't spend two hours in a shelter, never mind a whole night. I value my peace of mind and my sleep too much, not to mention my freedom and autonomy.

If you look back at the full paragraph above, you'll see that Patterson deleted these sentences and substituted a final one that focuses on the paragraph's topic, the conditions of the shelters for the homeless themselves.

Your topic sentences will not always fall at the very beginning of your paragraphs. Sometimes you'll need to create a transition from the preceding paragraph before stating the new paragraph's topic, or you'll build the paragraph to a topic sentence at the end, or you'll divide the statement between the beginning and the end. (Patterson's second paragraph, on p. 53, works this way, defining a good choice at the beginning and a bad choice at the end.) Sometimes, too, you'll write a paragraph with a topic but without a topic sentence. In all these cases, you'll need to have an idea for the paragraph and to unify the paragraph around that idea, so that all the specifics support and develop it.

UNITY IN ESSAYS Just as sentences must center on a paragraph's main idea, so paragraphs must center on an essay's main idea, or thesis. Readers who have to ask "What is the point?" or "Why am I reading this?" generally won't appreciate or accept the point.

Look at the outline of Grace Patterson's essay on pages 24–25. Her thesis sentences states, "For the homeless people in America today, there are no good choices," and each paragraph clearly develops this idea: what is a good choice, whether the homeless choose to live on the streets, and why shelters are not good alternatives to the streets.

This unity is true of Patterson's final draft but not of her first draft, where she drifted into considering how the homeless make other people uncomfortable. The topic could be interesting, but it blurred Patterson's focus on the homeless and their choices. Recognizing as much, Patterson deleted her entire second-to-last paragraph when she revised (see p. 43). Deleting this distracting passage also helped Patterson clarify her conclusion.

Like Patterson, you may be pulled in more than one direction by drafting, so that you digress from your thesis or pursue more than one thesis. Drafting and then revising are your chances to find and then sharpen your focus. Revising for unity strengthens your thesis.

Coherence

Writing is **coherent** when readers can follow it easily and can see how the parts relate to each other. The ideas develop in a clear sequence, the sentences and paragraphs connect logically, and the connections are clear and smooth. The writing flows.

COHERENCE IN PARAGRAPHS Coherence starts as sentences build paragraphs. The example on the next page (also reprinted in Chapter 4 on description) shows several devices for achieving coherence in paragraphs:

- Repetition or restatement of key words (underlined twice in the example).
- Pronouns such as *it* and *they* that substitute for nouns such as *ice* and *birds* (circled in the example).
- Parallelism, the use of similar grammatical structures for related ideas of the same importance (underlined once in the example). See also page 47.
- Transitions that clearly link the parts of sentences and whole sentences (boxed in the example). See the Glossary, page 402, for a list of transitions.

Check all your paragraphs to be sure that each sentence connects with the one preceding and that readers will see the connection without having to stop and reread. You may not need all the coherence devices Ackerman uses, or as many as she uses, but every paragraph you write will require some devices to stitch the sentences into a seamless cloth.

COHERENCE IN ESSAYS Reading a coherent essay, the audience does not have to ask "What does this have to do with the preceding paragraph?"

Pastel icebergs roamed around us, some tens of thousands of years old. Great pressure can push the air bubbles out of the ice and compact it. Free of air bubbles, it reflects light differently, as blue. The waters shivered with the gooseflesh of small ice shards. Some icebergs glowed like dull peppermint in the sun—impurities trapped in the ice (phytoplankton and algae) tinted them green. Ethereal snow petrels flew around the peaks of the icebergs, while the sun shone through their translucent wings. White, silent, the birds seemed to be pieces of ice flying with purpose and grace. As they passed in front of an ice floe, they became invisible. Glare transformed the landscape with such force that it seemed like a pure color. When we went out in the inflatable motorized rafts called Zodiacs to tour the iceberg orchards, I grabbed a piece of glacial ice and held it to my ear, listening to the bubbles cracking and popping as the air trapped inside escaped. And that night, though exhausted from the day's spectacles and doings, I lay in my narrow bunk, awake with my eyes closed, while sunstruck icebergs drifted across the insides of my lids, and the Antarctic peninsula revealed itself slowly, mile by mile, in the small theater of my closed eyes.

—Diane Ackerman, from
A Natural History of the Senses

or "Where is the writer going here?" The connections are apparent, and the organization is clear and logical.

Transitions work between paragraphs as well as within them to link ideas. When the ideas in two paragraphs are closely related, a simple word or phrase at the start of the second one may be all that's needed to show the relation. In each example below, the italicized transition opens the topic sentence of the paragraph:

> *Moreover*, the rising costs of health care have long outstripped inflation.

> *However*, some kinds of health-care plans have proved much more expensive than others.

When a paragraph is beginning a new part of the essay or otherwise changing direction, a sentence or more at the beginning will help explain the shift. In the next example, the first sentence summarizes the preceding paragraph, the second introduces the topic of the new paragraph, and the third gives the paragraph's topic sentence:

Traditional health-care plans have *thus* become an unaffordable luxury for most individuals and businesses. The majority of those with health insurance *now* find themselves in so-called managed plans. Though they do vary, managed plans share at least two features: they pay full benefits only when the insured person consults an approved doctor, and they require prior approval for certain procedures.

Notice that italicized transitions provide further cues about the relationship of ideas.

Organization

Though transitions can provide signposts to alert readers to movement from one idea to another, they can't achieve coherence by themselves. Just as important is an overall organization that develops ideas in a clear sequence and directs readers in a familiar pattern:

- A **spatial organization** arranges information to parallel the way we scan people, objects, or places: top to bottom, left to right, front to back, near to far, or vice versa. This scheme is especially useful for description (Chapter 4).
- A **chronological organization** arranges events or steps as they occurred in time, first to last. Such an arrangement usually organizes a narrative (Chapter 5) or a process analysis (Chapter 9) and may also help with cause-and-effect analysis (Chapter 12).
- A **climactic organization** proceeds in order of climax, usually from least to most important, building to the most interesting example, the most telling point of comparison, the most significant argument. A climactic organization is most useful for example (Chapter 6), division or analysis (Chapter 7), classification (Chapter 8), comparison and contrast (Chapter 10), definition (Chapter 11), and argument and persuasion (Chapter 13), and it may also work for cause-and-effect analysis (Chapter 12).

The introduction to each method of development in Chapters 4–13 gives detailed advice on organizing with these arrangements and variations on them.

When revising your draft for organization, try outlining it by jotting down the topic sentence of each paragraph and the key support for each topic. The exercise will give you some distance from your ideas and words, allowing you to see the structure like a skeleton. Will your readers grasp the logic of your arrangement? Will they see why you move from each idea to the next one? After checking the overall structure, be sure you've built in enough transitions between sentences and paragraphs to guide readers through your ideas.

Development

When you **develop** an idea, you provide concrete and specific details, examples, facts, opinions, and other evidence to make the idea vivid and true in readers' minds. Readers will know only as much as you tell them about your thesis and its support. Gaps, vague statements, and unsupported conclusions will undermine your efforts to win their interest and agreement.

Development begins in sentences, when you use the most concrete and specific words you can muster to explain your meaning. (See pp. 49–50.) At the level of the paragraph, these sentences develop the paragraph's topic. Then, at the level of the whole essay, these paragraphs develop the governing thesis.

The key to adequate development is a good sense of your readers' needs for information and reasons. The list of questions on page 18 can help you estimate these needs as you start to write; reconsidering the questions when you revise can help you see where your draft may fail to address, say, readers' unfamiliarity with your subject or possible resistance to your thesis.

The introduction to each method of development in Chapters 4–13 includes specific advice for meeting readers' needs when using the method to develop paragraphs and essays. When you sense that a paragraph or section of your essay is thin but you don't know how to improve it, you can also try the discovery techniques given on pages 19–21 or ask the questions for all the methods of development on page 22.

Tone

The **tone** of writing is like the tone of voice in speech: it expresses the writer's attitude toward his or her subject and audience. In writing we express tone with word choice and sentence structure. Notice the marked differences in these two passages discussing the same information on the same subject:

> Voice mail can be convenient, sure, but for callers it's usually more trouble than it's worth. We waste time "listening to the following menu choices," when we just want the live person at the end. All too often, there isn't even such a person!

For callers the occasional convenience of voice mail generally does not compensate for its inconveniences. Most callers would prefer to speak to a live operator but must wait through a series of choices to reach that person. Increasingly, companies with voice-mail systems do not offer live operators at all.

The first passage is informal, expresses clear annoyance, and with *we* includes the reader in that attitude. The second passage is more formal and more objective, reporting the situation without involving readers directly.

Tone can range from casual to urgent, humorous to serious, sad to elated, pleased to angry, personal to distant. The particular tone you choose for a piece of writing depends on your purpose and your audience. For most academic and business writing, you will be trying to explain or argue a point to your equals or superiors. Your readers will be interested more in the substance of your writing than in a startling tone, and indeed an approach that is too familiar or unserious or hostile could put them off. In other kinds of writing, you have more latitude. A warm and lighthearted tone may be just right for a personal narrative, and a touch of anger may help to grab the reader's attention in a letter to a magazine editor.

Tone is something you want to evaluate in revision, along with whether you've achieved your purpose and whether you've developed your thesis adequately for your audience. But adjusting tone is largely a matter of replacing words and restructuring sentences, work that could distract you from an overall view of your essay. If you think your tone is off base, you may want to devote a separate phase of revision to it, after addressing unity, coherence, and the other matters discussed in this section on revision.

For advice on sentence structures and word choices, see the section on editing, beginning on page 44.

Using a Revision Checklist

The following checklist summarizes the advice on revision given here. Use the checklist to remind yourself what to look for in your first draft. But don't try to answer all the questions in a single reading of the draft. Instead, take the questions one by one, rereading the whole draft for each. That way you'll be able to concentrate on each element with minimal distraction from the others.

CHECKLIST FOR REVISION

- What is your purpose in writing? Will it be clear to readers? Do you achieve it?

- What is your thesis? Where is it made clear to readers?

- How unified is your essay? How does each body paragraph support your thesis? (Look especially at your topic sentences.) How does each sentence in the body paragraphs support the topic sentence of the paragraph?

- How coherent is your essay? Do repetition and restatement, pronouns, parallelism, and transitions link the sentences in paragraphs?

- Does the overall organization clarify the flow of ideas? How does your introduction work to draw readers in and orient them to your purpose and thesis? How does your conclusion work to pull the essay together and give readers a sense of completion?

- How well developed is your essay? Where might readers need more evidence to understand your ideas and find them convincing?

- What is the tone of your essay? How is it appropriate for your purpose and your audience?

Note that the introductions to the methods of development in Chapters 4–13 also have their own revision checklists. Combining this list with the one for the method you're using will produce a more targeted set of questions. (The guide inside the back cover will direct you to the discussion you want.)

Grace Patterson's Revised Draft

Considering questions like those in the revision checklist led the student Grace Patterson to revise the rough draft we saw on pages 28–30. Patterson's revision follows. Notice that she made substantial cuts, especially of digressions near the end of the draft. She also revamped the introduction, tightened many passages, improved the coherence of paragraphs, and wrote a wholly new conclusion to sharpen her point. She did not try to improve her style or fix errors at this stage, leaving these activities for later editing.

~~Title?~~ *A Rock and a Hard Place*

In the essay / "The Box Man /" Barbara Lazear Ascher

says that a homeless man who has chosen solitude can show

the rest of us how to "find . . . a friend in our own

voice." Maybe. But ~~her~~ *Ascher's* case depends on the Box Man's

choice, her assumption that he <u>had</u> one.

Discussions of the homeless often use the word

choice. Many ~~people with enough money can accept the~~ *of us with homes would like to think*

~~condition of the homeless in America when they tell~~

~~themselves~~ that many of the homeless chose their lives.

~~That the streets are in fact what they want. But it's not~~

~~fair to use the word~~ <u>~~choice~~</u> ~~here: the homeless don't get~~

~~to choose their lives the way most of the rest of us~~

~~do.~~ *But* ₍ₐ₎ /or the homeless people in America today, there are no

good choices.

What do I mean by a "good choice"? ~~One~~ *A good choice is* made from a

variety of options determined and narrowed down by the

chooser. There is plenty of room for the chooser to make a

decision that he will be satisfied with. When I choose a

career, I expect to make a good choice. There is plenty of

interesting fields worth investigating, and there is lots

of rewarding work to be done. ~~It's a choice that opens the~~

~~world up and showcases its possibilities.~~ ₍ₐ₎ *However,* /f ~~it came time~~

~~for me to choose a career, and~~ the mayor of my town came

around and told me that I had to choose between a life of

cleaning public toilets and operating a jackhammer on a

busy street corner, I would object. That's a lousy choice,

and I wouldn't let anyone force me to make it.

When the mayor of New York tried to take ~~the~~ homeless∧ *people*
he likewise offered them a bad choice.
off the streets, ∧~~some of them didn't want to go. People~~
They could
~~assumed that the homeless people who did not want to~~∧ get
or they could stay
in the mayor's car for a ride to a city shelter∧~~chose to~~
People assumed that the homeless people who
~~live~~ on the street. ~~But just because some homeless people~~
refused a ride to the shelter wanted to live on the street. But that
~~chose the street over the generosity of the mayor does not~~
assumption is not necessarily true.
~~necessarily mean that life on the streets is their ideal.~~

We allow ourselves as many options as we can imagine, but
both unpleasant.
we allow the homeless only two/, ~~go to a shelter, or stay~~

~~where you are. Who narrowed down the options for the~~

~~homeless? Who benefits if they go to a shelter? Who~~

~~suffers if they don't?~~

Homeless people are not always better off in
Last Sunday,
shelters.∧I had a conversation with a man who had lived
He
on the streets for a long time. ~~The man~~ said that he had

spent some time in those shelters for the homeless, and
They're dangerous and
he told me what they were like. ~~The shelters are crowded~~
dehumanizing. Drug dealing, beatings, and theft are common.
~~and dirty and people have to wait in long lines for~~
The shelters are dirty and crowded, so that residents have to wait in
~~everything. People are constantly being herded around and~~
long lines for everything and are constantly
∧*bossed around.* ~~It's dangerous--drug dealers, beatings,~~

~~theft. Dehumanizing. It matches my picture of hell. From~~
No wonder some homeless people prefer the street: some space to
~~the sound of it, I couldn't spend two hours in a shelter,~~

breathe, some autonomy, some peace for sleeping.
~~never mind a whole night. I value my peace of mind and my~~
~~sleep too much, not to mention my freedom and autonomy.~~

~~When homeless people sleep in the street, though,~~
that makes the public uncomfortable. People with enough
money wish the homeless would just disappear. They don't
care where they go. Just out of sight. I've felt this way
too but I'm as uneasy with that reaction as I am at the
sight of a person sleeping on the sidewalk. ~~And I tell~~
~~myself that this is more than a question of my comfort.~~
~~By and large I'm comfortable enough.~~

The homeless are in a difficult enough situation
without having to take the blame for making the rest of us
feel uncomfortable with our wealth. If we cannot offer the
homeless a good set of choices, the opportunity to choose
lives that they will be truly satisfied with then the
least we can do is stop dumping on them (?). They're
caught between a rock and a hard place: there are not
many places for them to go, and the places where they
can go afford nothing but suffering.

Focusing on the supposed choices the homeless have may make us
feel better, but it distracts attention from the kinds of choices that are
really being denied the homeless. The options we take for granted—a
job with decent pay, an affordable home—do not belong to the home-
less. They're caught between no shelter at all and shelter that
dehumanizes, between a rock and a hard place.

EDITING

In **editing** you turn from global issues of purpose, thesis, unity, coherence, organization, development, and tone to more particular issues of sentences and words. In a sense revision occurs beneath the lines, in the deeper meaning and structure of the essay. Editing occurs more between the lines, on the surface of the essay.

Like revision, editing requires that you gain some distance from your work so that you can see it objectively. Try these techniques:

- Work on a clean copy of your revised draft. If you write on a computer, edit on a printout rather than on the computer: it's more difficult to spot errors on a screen.
- Read your revised draft aloud or into a recorder so you can hear the words. But be sure to read what you have actually written, not what you may have intended to write but didn't.
- To catch errors, try reading your draft backward sentence by sentence. You'll be less likely to get caught up in the flow of your ideas.
- Profit from your past writing experiences by keeping a personal checklist of problems that others have pointed out to you. Add this personal checklist to the one on page 40.

Making Sentences Clear and Effective

Clear and effective sentences convey your meaning concisely and precisely. In editing you want to ensure that readers will understand you easily, follow your ideas without difficulty, and stay interested in what you have to say.

Conciseness

In drafting, we often circle around our ideas, making various attempts to express them. As a result, sentences may use more words than necessary to make their points. To edit for conciseness, focus on the following changes:

- *Put the main meaning of the sentence in its subject and verb.* Generally, the subject should name the agent of your idea, and the verb should describe what the agent did or was. Notice the difference in these two sentences (the subjects and verbs are italicized):

  WORDY   According to some experts, the *use* of calculators by students *is* sometimes a reason why they fail to develop computational skills.

CONCISE   According to some experts, *students* who use calculators sometimes *fail* to develop computational skills.

By focusing on the key elements of the idea, the students and their occasional failure, the edited sentence saves seven words and is easier to follow.

- *Use the active voice.* In the active voice, a verb describes the action *by* the subject (*We grilled vegetables*), whereas in the passive voice, a verb describes the action done *to* the subject (*Vegetables were grilled*, or, adding who did the action, *Vegetables were grilled by us*). The active voice usually conveys more information in fewer words than the passive. The active is also clearer, more direct, and more forceful because it always names the actor.

    WORDY PASSIVE   Calculators *were withheld* from some classrooms by school administrators, and the math performance of students with and without the machines *was compared*.

    CONCISE ACTIVE   School administrators *withheld* calculators from some classrooms and *compared* the math performance of students with and without the machines.

- *Delete repetition and padding.* Words that don't contribute to your meaning will interfere with readers' understanding and interest. Watch out for unneeded repetition or restatement, such as that italicized in the following sentence:

    WORDY   Students *in the schools* should have ample practice in computational skills, *skills* such as long division and using fractions.

    CONCISE   Students should have ample practice in computational skills, such as long division and using fractions.

Padding occurs most often with empty phrases that add no meaning:

    WORDY   *In this particular regard, the nature* of calculators *is such that they* remove the drudgery from computation but can also *for all intents and purposes* interfere with the development of important cognitive skills.

    CONCISE   Calculators remove the drudgery from computation but can also interfere with the development of important cognitive skills.

Emphasis

Once your sentences are as concise as you can make them, you'll want to see that they give the appropriate emphasis to your ideas. Readers will look for the idea of a sentence in its subject and its verb, and they will expect words and word groups to clarify or add texture to the idea by modifying it. You can emphasize important ideas in various ways by altering the structure of sentences. Following is a summary of the most common techniques.

- *Use subordination to de-emphasize what's less important.* **Subordination** places minor information in words or word groups that modify the sentence's subject and verb:

  UNEMPHATIC *Computers can manipulate* film and photographs, and *we cannot trust* these media to represent reality. [The sentence has two subject-verb structures (both in italics), and they seem equally important.]

  EMPHATIC *Because* computers can manipulate film and photographs, we cannot trust these media to represent reality. [*Because* makes the first subject-verb group into a modifier, de-emphasizing the cause of the change and emphasizing the effect.]

- *Use coordination to balance equally important ideas.* **Coordination** uses *and*, *but*, *or*, or *nor* to join two or more ideas and emphasize their equality. It can link the ideas of separate sentences in one sentence:

  UNEMPHATIC Two people may be complete strangers. A photograph can show them embracing.

  EMPHATIC Two people may be complete strangers, *but* a photograph can show them embracing.

- *Use the ends and beginnings of sentences to highlight ideas.* The end of a sentence is its most emphatic position, and the beginning is next most emphatic. Placing the sentence's subject and verb in one of these positions draws readers' attention to them. In these sentences the core idea is in italics:

  UNEMPHATIC With computerized images, *filmmakers can entertain us*, placing historical figures alongside today's actors.

  EMPHATIC With computerized images that place historical figures alongside today's actors, *filmmakers can entertain us*.

  EMPHATIC *Filmmakers can entertain us* with computerized images that place historical figures alongside today's actors.

- *Use short sentences to underscore points.* A very short sentence amid longer sentences will focus readers' attention on a key point:

UNEMPHATIC   Such images of historical figures and fictional characters have a disadvantage, however, in that they blur the boundaries of reality.

EMPHATIC   Such images of historical figures and fictional characters have a disadvantage, however. They blur the boundaries of reality.

Parallelism

Parallelism is the use of similar grammatical structures for elements of similar importance, either within or among sentences.

PARALLELISM WITHIN A SENTENCE   Smoking can *worsen heart disease* and *cause lung cancer.*

PARALLELISM AMONG SENTENCES   Smoking has less well-known effects, too. *It can cause* gum disease. *It can impair* circulation of blood and other fluids. And *it can reduce* the body's supply of vitamins and minerals.

Parallelism can help relate sequential sentences, improving paragraph coherence (see pp. 35–37). It also clarifies when sentences or elements within them are equivalent, so that readers see the relationship automatically. Without the signal of parallelism in the first sentence below, the reader must stop to work out that both italicized elements are nonmedical consequences:

NONPARALLEL   Smoking has nonmedical consequences as well, including *loss of productivity* for smokers at work and *insurance expenses are high* for smokers.

PARALLEL   Smoking has nonmedical consequences as well, including smokers' *lower productivity* at work and *higher expenses for insurance.*

Variety

Variety in the structure and length of sentences helps keep readers alert and interested, but it also does more. By emphasizing important points and de-emphasizing less important points, varied sentences make your writing clearer and easier to follow. The first passage below is adapted from "How Boys Become Men," an essay by Jon Katz. The second is the passage Katz actually wrote.

UNVARIED   I was walking my dog last month past the playground near my house. I saw three boys encircling a fourth. They were laughing and pushing him. He was skinny and rumpled, and he looked frightened. One boy knelt behind him. Another pushed him from the front. The trick was familiar to any former boy. The victim fell backward.

VARIED   Last month, walking my dog past the playground near my house, I saw three boys encircling a fourth, laughing and pushing him. He was skinny and rumpled, and he looked frightened. One boy knelt behind him while another pushed him from the front, a trick familiar to any former boy. He fell backward.

Katz's actual sentences work much better to hold and direct our attention because he uses several techniques to achieve variety:

- *Vary the lengths of sentences.* The eight sentences in the unvaried adaptation range from four to thirteen words. Katz's four sentences range from three to twenty-two words, with the long first sentence setting the scene and the short final sentence creating a climax.
- *Vary the beginnings of sentences.* Every sentence in the adaptation begins with its subject (*I, I, They, He, One boy, Another, The trick, The victim*). Katz, in contrast, begins one sentence with a transition and a modifier (*Last month, walking my dog past the playground near my house . . .*).
- *Vary the structure of sentences.* The sentences in the adaptation are all similar in structure, marching like soldiers down the page and making it difficult to pick out the important events of the story. Katz's version emphasizes the important events by making them the subjects and verbs of the sentences, turning the other information into modifiers that either precede or follow.

Choosing Clear and Effective Words

The words you use can have a dramatic effect on how readers understand your meaning, perceive your attitude, and respond to your thesis.

Denotations and Connotations

The **denotation** of a word is its dictionary meaning, the literal sense without emotional overtones. A **connotation** is an emotional association the word produces in readers. Using an incorrect or inappropriate word will confuse readers momentarily; several such confusions can undermine readers' patience.

Using a word with the wrong denotation muddies meaning. Be especially careful to distinguish between words with similar sounds but different meanings, such as *sites* and *cites* or *whether* and *weather*, and between words with related but distinct meanings, such as *reward* and *award* or *famous* and *infamous*. Keeping a list of the new words you acquire will help you build your vocabulary.

Using words with strong connotations can shape readers' responses to your ideas. For example, consider the distinctions among *feeling, enthusiasm, passion,* and *mania*. Describing a group's *enthusiasm* for its cause is quite different from describing its *mania*: the latter connotes much more intensity, even irrationality. If your aim is to imply that the group's enthusiasm is excessive, and you think your readers will respond well to that characterization, then *mania* may be the appropriate word. But words can backfire if they set off inappropriate associations in readers.

Consult a dictionary whenever you are unsure of a word's meanings. For connotations, you'll find a wide range of choices in a thesaurus, which lists words with similar meanings. A thesaurus doesn't provide definitions, however, so you'll need to check unfamiliar words in a dictionary.

Concrete and Specific Words

Clear, exact writing balances abstract and general words, which provide outlines of ideas and things, with concrete and specific words, which limit and sharpen.

- **Abstract words** name ideas, qualities, attitudes, or states that we cannot perceive with our senses of sight, hearing, touch, smell, and taste: *liberty, hate, anxious, brave, idealistic.* **Concrete words**, in contrast, name objects, persons, places, or states that we can perceive with our senses: *newspaper, police officer, Mississippi River, red-faced, tangled, screeching.*
- **General words** name groups: *building, color, clothes.* **Specific words** name particular members of a group: *courthouse, red, boot-cut jeans.*

You need abstract and general words for broad statements that set the course for your writing, conveying concepts or referring to entire groups. But you also need concrete and specific words to make meaning precise and vivid by appealing to readers' senses and experiences. The following examples show how much clearer and more interesting a sentence becomes when its abstractions and generalities are brought down to concrete and specific details:

VAGUE   The pollution was apparent in the odor and color of the small stream.

EXACT   The narrow stream, just four feet wide, smelled like rotten eggs and ran the greenish color of coffee with nonfat milk.

The first sentence leaves it to readers to imagine the size, odor, and color of the stream. A few readers may guess at details, but most won't bother: they'll just pass on without getting the picture. In contrast, the second sentence *shows* the stream just as the writer experienced it, in disturbing detail.

Concrete and specific language may seem essential only in descriptions like that of the polluted stream, but it is equally crucial in any other kind of writing. Readers can't be expected to understand or agree with general statements unless they know what evidence the statements are based on. The evidence is in the details, and the details are in concrete and specific words.

Figures of Speech

You can make your writing concrete and specific, even lively and forceful, with **figures of speech**, expressions that imply meanings beyond or different from their literal meanings. Here are some of the most common figures:

- A **simile** compares two unlike things with the use of *like* or *as*: *The car spun around like a top. Coins as bright as sunshine lay glinting in the chest.*
- A **metaphor** also compares two unlike things, but more subtly, equating them without *like* or *as*: *The words shattered my fragile self-esteem. The laboratory was a prison, the beakers and test tubes her guards.*
- **Personification** is a simile or metaphor that attributes human qualities or powers to things or abstractions: *The breeze sighed and whispered in the grasses. The city squeezed me tightly at first but then relaxed its grip.*
- **Hyperbole** is a deliberate overstatement or exaggeration: *The dentist filled the tooth with a bracelet's worth of silver. The children's noise shook the walls and rafters.*

By briefly translating experiences and qualities into vividly concrete images, figures of speech can be economical and powerful. But be careful not to combine figures and thus create confusing or absurd images in readers' minds. This mixed metaphor conjures up conflicting images of bees and dogs: *The troops swarmed the field like pit bulls ready for a fight.*

Fresh Language

In trying for concrete and specific words, we sometimes resort to **clichés**, worn phrases that have lost their descriptive power: *tried and true, ripe old age, hour of need*. Many clichés are exhausted figures of speech, such as *heavy as lead, thin as a rail*, or *goes on forever*.

If you have trouble recognizing clichés in your writing, be suspicious of any expression you have heard or read before. When you do find a cliché, cure it by substituting plain language (for instance, *reliable* for *tried and true*) or by substituting a fresh figure of speech (*thin as a sapling* for *thin as a rail*).

Using an Editing Checklist

The following checklist summarizes the editing advice given in this section and adds a few other technical concerns as well. Some of the items will be more relevant for your writing than others: you may have little difficulty with variety in sentences but may worry that your language is too general. Concentrate your editing efforts where they're needed most, and then survey your draft to check for other problems.

CHECKLIST FOR EDITING

- How clear and concise is each sentence? Have you put the main meaning in the subject and verb? Have you relied on the active voice of verbs? Is there repetition and padding to delete?

- How well do sentences emphasize their main ideas with subordination, coordination, ends and beginnings, or length?

- Where is parallelism needed within or between sentences to increase clarity and coherence?

- Where should groups of sentences be more varied in length and structure to improve clarity and readability?

- Which words should be changed either because they have the wrong denotations or because their connotations are inappropriate for your meaning or your audience?

- Where should you make your meaning less abstract and general with concrete and specific words or with figures of speech? Where do clichés need editing?

- If you have referred to the work of another writer or conducted research to develop any of your points, are quotations marked and your sources identified? (See the Appendix for a full discussion of working with sources.)

- Where do sentences need editing for grammar or punctuation—so that, for instance, pronouns such as *he* and *him* are used correctly, subjects and verbs agree, sentences are complete, and apostrophes fall in the right places? Concentrate on finding errors that readers have pointed out in your work before, and refer to a grammar handbook as necessary.

- Where might spelling be a problem? Look up any word you're not ab-solutely sure of. (You'll still have to proofread a spell-checked paper; the programs don't catch everything.)

Grace Patterson's Editing and Final Draft

The following paragraph comes from the edited draft of Grace Patter-son's "A Rock and a Hard Place." Then Patterson's full final draft ap-pears with notes in the margins highlighting its thesis, structure, and uses of the methods of development. If you compare the final version with the first draft on pages 28–30, you'll see clearly how Patterson's revising and editing transformed the essay from a rough exploration of ideas to a refined, and convincing, essay.

EDITED PARAGRAPH

~~What do I mean by~~ A "good choice"? A good choice is one
made from a variety of options determined and narrowed
down by the chooser. ~~There is plenty of room for the
chooser to make a decision that he will be satisfied with.~~
When I choose a career, I expect to make a good choice.
There are many ~~is plenty of~~ interesting fields to ~~worth~~ investigate, e,
and there is much ~~lots of~~ rewarding work to do. ~~be done.~~ If the
mayor of my town suddenly ~~came around and~~ told me that I would have ~~had~~ to
choose between a career ~~life~~ of cleaning public toilets and
one of ~~operating a jackhammer on a busy street corner, I would
object. That's a bad ~~lousy~~ choice. ~~and I wouldn't let anyone
force me to make it.~~

FINAL DRAFT

A Rock and a Hard Place

In the essay "The Box Man" Barbara Lazear
Ascher says that a homeless man who has chosen
solitude can show the rest of us how to "find
. . . a friend in our own voice"(11). Maybe he
can. But Ascher's case depends on the Box Man's
choice, her assumption that he <u>had</u> one.
Discussions of the homeless often involve the
word <u>choice</u>. Many of us with homes would like to
think that many of the homeless chose their
lives. But for the homeless people in America
today, there are no good choices.

A "good choice" is one made from a variety
of options determined and narrowed down by the
chooser. When I choose a career, I expect to make
a good choice. There are many interesting fields
to investigate, and there is much rewarding work
to do. If the mayor of my town suddenly told me
that I would have to choose between a career of
cleaning public toilets and one of operating a
jackhammer on a busy street corner, I would
object. That's a <u>bad</u> choice.

When the mayor of New York tried to remove
the homeless people from the streets, he offered
them a similarly bad choice. They could get in
the mayor's car for a ride to a city shelter, or
they could stay on the street. People assumed
that the homeless people who refused a ride to
the shelter <u>wanted</u> to live on the street. But the
assumption is not necessarily true. We allow
ourselves as many options as we can imagine, but
we allow the homeless only two, both unpleasant.

The fact is that homeless people are not
always better off in shelters. I recently had a

Right margin annotations:

Introduction:
establishes point
of contention with
Ascher's essay

Thesis sentence
(see pp. 24–25)

Definition and
comparison of
good choices and
bad choices

Examples

Application of
definition to home-
less; analysis of
choice offered

Cause-and-effect
analysis: why home-
less avoid shelters

conversation with a man named Alan Doran who had
lived on the streets for a long time. He said
that he had spent some time in shelters for the
homeless, and he told me what they are like.
They're dangerous and dehumanizing. Drug dealing,
beatings, and theft are common. The shelters are
dirty and crowded, so that residents have to wait
in long lines for everything and are constantly
being bossed around. No wonder some homeless
people, including Alan, prefer the street: it
affords some space to breathe, some autonomy,
some peace for sleeping.

Description of shelter

Comparison of shelter and street

Focusing on the supposed choices the homeless have may make us feel better. But it distracts our attention from something more important
than our comfort: the options we take for granted
--a job with decent pay, an affordable home--are
denied the homeless. These people are caught between no shelter at all and shelter that dehumanizes, between a rock and a hard place.

Conclusion: returns to good vs. bad choices; sums up with a familiar image

Works Cited

Ascher, Barbara Lazear. "The Box Man." The
    Compact Reader. 8th ed. Ed. Jane E. Aaron.
    Boston: Bedford/St. Martin's, 2008. 7-11.
Doran, Alan. Personal interview. 27 Sept. 2007.

Chapter 4

DESCRIPTION

Sensing the Natural World

Whenever you use words to depict or re-create a scene, an object, a person, or a feeling, you use **description**. A mainstay of conversation between people, description is likely to figure in almost any writing situation: an e-mail home may describe a new roommate's spiky yellow hair; a laboratory report may describe the colors and odors of chemicals; a business memo may examine the tastes and textures of competitors' low-fat potato chips; an insurance claim may explain the condition of an apartment after a kitchen fire. Because the method builds detail and brings immediacy to a subject for readers, description is an important part of most essay writing as well.

READING DESCRIPTION

Description draws on perceptions of the five senses—sight, hearing, smell, taste, and touch—to understand and communicate a particular experience of the world. A writer's purpose in writing and his or her involvement with the subject will largely determine how objective or subjective a description is.

- **Objective description** strives for precision and objectivity, trying to convey the subject impersonally, without emotion. This is the kind of description required in scientific writing—for instance, a medical diagnosis or a report on an experiment in psychology—where cold facts and absence of feeling are essential for readers to judge the accuracy of procedures and results. It is also the method of news reports and of reference works such as encyclopedias.
- **Subjective description**, in contrast, draws explicitly on emotions, giving an impression of the subject filtered through firsthand experience. Instead of withdrawing to the background, the writer invests feelings in the subject and lets those feelings determine which details he or she will describe and how he or she will describe them. State of mind—perhaps loneliness, anger, or joy—can be re-created by reference to sensory details such as numbness, heat, or sweetness.

In general, writers favor objective description when their purpose is explanation and subjective description when their purpose is self-expression or entertainment. But the categories are not exclusive, and most descriptive writing mixes the two. A news report on a tropical storm, for instance, might objectively describe bent and broken trees, fallen wires, and lashing rain, but the reporter's selection of details gives a subjective impression of the storm's fearsomeness.

Whether objective or subjective or a mixture of the two, effective description requires a **dominant impression**—a central theme or idea about the subject to which readers can relate all the details. The dominant impression may be something a writer sees in the subject, such as the apparent purposefulness of city pedestrians or the expressiveness of an actor. Or it may derive from an emotional response to the subject, perhaps pleasure (or depression) at all the purposefulness, perhaps admiration (or disdain) for the actor's technique. Whatever its source, the dominant impression serves as a unifying principle that guides both the writer's selection of details and the reader's understanding of the subject.

One aid in creating a dominant impression is a consistent **point of view**, the position from which a writer approaches a subject. Point of view in description has two main elements:

- A real or imagined *physical* relation to the subject: a writer could view a mountain, for instance, from the bottom looking up, from fifteen miles away across a valley, or from an airplane passing overhead. The first two points of view are fixed because the writer remains in one position and scans the scene from there; the third is moving because the writer changes position.

- A *psychological* relation to the subject, a relation partly conveyed by pronouns. In subjective description, where feelings are part of the message, writers might use *I* and *you* freely to narrow the distance between themselves and the subject and between themselves and the reader. But in the most objective, impersonal description, writers will use *one* ("One can see the summit") or avoid self-reference altogether in order to appear distant from and unbiased toward the subject.

Once a physical and psychological point of view has been established, readers come to depend on it. Thus a sudden and inexplicable shift from one view to another—zooming in from fifteen miles away to the foot of a mountain, abandoning *I* for the more removed *one*—can disorient readers and distract them from the dominant impression.

ANALYZING DESCRIPTION IN PARAGRAPHS

David Mura (born 1952) is a poet, essayist, and critic. This paragraph comes from his book *Turning Japanese* (1991), a memoir of his time in Japan as a *sansei*, or a third-generation Japanese American. Mura describes Tokyo during the rainy season.

And then the rains of June came, the typhoon season. Every day endless streaks of gray drilled down from the sky. A note held, passing from monotone into a deeper, more permanent dirge. The air itself seemed to liquefy, like the insides of a giant invisible jellyfish. In the streets the patter grew into pools, then rushes and torrents. Umbrellas floated, black bobbing circles, close as the wings of bats in underground caves. In the empty lot across the street, the grass turned a deep, tropical green; then the earth itself seemed to bubble up in patches, foaming. In the country, square after square of rice field filled to the brim and overflowed. In the city, the city of labyrinths, the rain became another labyrinth, increased the density of inhabitants; everything seemed thicker, moving underwater.

Specific, concrete details (underlined once)

Figures of speech (underlined twice)

Point of view: moving; psychologically somewhat distant

Dominant impression: overwhelming, intense wetness

Diane Ackerman (born 1948) is a poet and essayist who writes extensively on the natural world. The following paragraph comes from *A Natural History of the Senses* (1991), a prose exploration of sight, hearing, touch, taste, and smell.

Pastel icebergs <u>roamed</u> around us, some tens of thousands of years old. Great pressure can push the air bubbles out of the ice and compact it. Free of air bubbles, it reflects light differently, as blue. The <u>waters shivered</u> <u>with the gooseflesh of small ice shards.</u> Some icebergs <u>glowed like dull peppermint</u> in the sun—impurities trapped in the ice (phytoplankton and algae) tinted them green. Ethereal snow petrels flew around the peaks of the icebergs, while the <u>sun shone through their translu-</u><u>cent wings.</u> <u>White, silent,</u> the <u>birds seemed to be pieces</u> <u>of ice flying with purpose and grace.</u> As they passed in front of an ice floe, they became invisible. Glare transformed the landscape with such force that it seemed like a pure color. When we went out in the inflatable motorized rafts called Zodiacs to tour <u>the iceberg orchards,</u> I grabbed a piece of glacial ice and held it to my ear, listening to the <u>bubbles cracking and popping</u> as the air trapped inside escaped. And that night, though <u>ex-</u><u>hausted</u> from the day's spectacles and doings, I lay in my <u>narrow bunk,</u> awake with my eyes closed, while <u>sun-</u><u>struck icebergs drifted across the insides of my lids,</u> and the Antarctic peninsula revealed itself slowly, mile by mile, in the <u>small theater of my closed eyes.</u>

> Specific, concrete details (underlined once)
>
> Figures of speech (underlined twice)
>
> Point of view: fixed, then moving; psychologically close
>
> Dominant impression: awesome, chilly brightness

DEVELOPING A DESCRIPTIVE ESSAY
Getting Started

The subject for a descriptive essay may be any object, place, person, or state of mind that you have observed closely enough or experienced sharply enough to invest with special significance. A chair, a tree, a room, a shopping mall, a movie actor, a passerby on the street, a feeling of fear, a sense of achievement—anything you have a strong impression of can prompt effective description.

Observe your subject directly, if possible, or recall it as completely as you can. Jot down the details that seem to contribute most to the impression you're trying to convey. You needn't write the description of the details yet—that can wait for drafting—but you do want to capture the possibilities in your subject.

You should start to consider the needs and expectations of your readers early on. If the subject is something readers have never seen or felt before, you will need enough objective details to create a complete picture in their minds. A description of a friend, for example, might focus on his distinctive voice and laugh, but readers will also want to know something about his appearance. If the subject is essentially abstract, like an emotion, you will need details to make it concrete for readers. And if the subject is familiar to readers, as a shopping mall or an old spruce tree on campus probably would be, you will want to skip obvious objective information in favor of fresh observations that will make readers see the subject anew.

Forming a Thesis

When you have your subject, specify in a sentence the dominant impression that you want to create for readers. The sentence will help keep you on track while you search for the sensory details that will make your description concrete and vivid. It should evoke a quality or an atmosphere or an effect, as these examples do:

> His fierce anger at the world shows in every word and gesture.

> The mall is a thoroughly unnatural place, like a space station in a science-fiction movie.

Such a sentence can serve as the thesis of your essay. You don't necessarily need to state it outright in your draft; sometimes you may prefer to let the details build to a conclusion. But the thesis should hover over the essay nonetheless, governing the selection of every detail and making itself as clear to readers as if it were stated.

Organizing

Though the details of a subject may not occur to you in any particular order, you should arrange them so that readers are not confused by shifts among features. You can give readers a sense of the whole subject in the introduction to the essay: objective details of location or size or shape, the incident leading to a state of mind, or the reasons for describing a familiar object. In the introduction, also, you may want to state your thesis — the dominant impression you will create.

The organization of the body of the essay depends partly on point of view and partly on dominant impression. If you take a moving point of view — say, strolling down a city street — the details will probably arrange themselves naturally. But a fixed point of view, scanning a subject from one position, requires your intervention. When the subject is a landscape, a person, or an object, you'll probably want to use a spatial organization: near to far, top to bottom, left to right, or vice versa. (See also p. 37.) Other subjects, such as a shopping mall, might be better treated in groups of features: shoppers, main concourses, insides of stores. Or a description of an emotional state might follow the chronological sequence of the event that aroused it (thus overlapping description and narration, the subject of the next chapter). The order itself is not important, as long as there is an order that channels readers' attention.

Drafting

The challenge of drafting your description will be bringing the subject to life. Whether it is in front of you or in your mind, you may find it helpful to consider the subject one sense at a time—what you can see, hear, smell, touch, taste. Of course, not all senses will be applicable to all subjects; a chair, for instance, may not have a noticeable odor, and you're unlikely to know its taste. But proceeding sense by sense can help you uncover details, such as the smell of a tree or the sound of a person's voice, that you may have overlooked.

Examining one sense at a time is also one of the best ways to conceive of concrete words and figures of speech to represent sensations and feelings. For instance, does *acid* describe the taste of fear? Does an actor's appearance suggest the smell of soap? Does a shopping mall smell like new dollar bills? In creating distinct physical sensations for readers, such representations make meaning inescapably clear. (See pp. 48–50 and the box opposite for more on specific, concrete language and figures of speech.)

Revising and Editing

When you are ready to revise and edit, use the following questions and box as a guide.

- *Have you in fact created the dominant impression you intended to create?* Check that you have plenty of specific details and that each one helps to pin down one crucial feature of your subject. Cut irrelevant details that may have crept in. What counts is not the number of details but their quality and the strength of the impression they make.
- *Are your point of view and organization clear and consistent?* Watch for confusing shifts from one vantage point or organizational scheme to another. Watch also for confusing and unnecessary shifts in pronouns, such as from *I* to *one* or vice versa. Any

FOCUS ON CONCRETE AND SPECIFIC LANGUAGE

For readers to imagine your subject, you'll need to use concrete, specific language that appeals to their experiences and senses. (See pp. 49–50 for the meanings of *concrete* and *specific*.) The first sentence below shows a writer's first-draft attempt to describe something she saw. After editing, the second sentence is much more vivid.

VAGUE   Beautiful, scented wildflowers were in the field.

CONCRETE AND SPECIFIC   Backlighted by the sun and smelling faintly sweet, an acre of tiny lavender flowers spread away from me.

The writer might also have used figures of speech (see p. 50) to show what she saw: for instance, describing the field as "a giant's bed covered in a quilt of lavender dots" (a metaphor) or describing the backlighted flowers as "glowing like tiny lavender lamps" (a simile).

When editing your description, keep a sharp eye out for vague words such as *delicious, handsome, loud,* and *short* that force readers to create their own impressions or, worse, leave them with no impression at all. Using details that call on readers' sensory experiences, say why delicious or why handsome, how loud or how short. When stuck for a word, conjure up your subject and see it, hear it, touch it, smell it, taste it.

Note that *concrete* and *specific* do not mean "fancy": good description does not demand five-dollar words when nickel equivalents are just as informative. The writer who uses *rubiginous* instead of *rusty red* actually says less because fewer readers will understand the less common word and all readers will sense a writer showing off.

shifts in point of view or organization should be clearly essential for your purpose and for the impression you want to create.

A NOTE ON THEMATIC CONNECTIONS

The writers represented in this chapter all set out to explore something in nature. They probably didn't decide consciously to write a description, but turned to the method intuitively as they chose to record the perceptions of their senses. In a paragraph, David Mura captures the dense unpleasantness of a seemingly endless downpour (p. 57). In another paragraph, Diane Ackerman describes the sharp, lasting images of a sea of icebergs (p. 58). Marta K. Taylor's essay on a nighttime car ride climaxes in a lightning storm (p. 62). Dagoberto Gilb's essay on a desert lawn examines the cultural tensions in a border town (p. 66). And Joan Didion's essay on a wind coming from the mountains above Los Angeles shows how an air current can transform a city (p. 72).

Memory is the diary that we all carry about with us.   — Oscar Wilde

A childhood is what anyone wants to remember of it.   — Carol Shields

*I might have seen more of America when I was a child if I hadn't had to
spend so much of my time protecting my half of the back seat from
incursions by my sister.*   — Calvin Trillin

Journal Response   Recall a childhood event such as a family outing, a long
car ride, a visit to an unfamiliar place, or an incident in your neighborhood.
Imagine yourself back in that earlier time and write down details of what
you experienced and how you felt.

--------------------- Marta K. Taylor ---------------------

*Marta K. Taylor was born in 1970 and raised in Los Angeles. She attended a
"huge" public high school there before being accepted into Harvard University.
She graduated from Harvard in 1992 with a degree in chemistry and from
Harvard Medical School in 1998. She is now a physician in Philadelphia, where
she specializes in ear, nose, and throat surgery.*

DESERT DANCE

(STUDENT ESSAY)

*Taylor wrote this description of a nighttime ride when she was a freshman in college
taking the required writing course. The essay was published in the 1988–89
edition of* Exposé, *a collection of student writing published by Harvard.*

We didn't know there was a rodeo in Flagstaff. All the hotels were   *1*
filled, except the really expensive ones, so we decided to push on to
Winslow that night. Dad must have thought we were all asleep, and
so we should have been, too, as it was after one A.M. and we had been
driving all day through the wicked California and Arizona desert on
the first day of our August Family Trip. The back seat of our old station
wagon was down, allowing two eleven-year-old kids to lie almost
fully extended and still leaving room for the rusty green Coleman ice-
chest which held the packages of pressed turkey breast, the white bread,

and the pudding snack-pacs that Mom had cleverly packed to save on lunch expenses and quiet the inevitable "Are we there yet?" and "How much farther?"

Jon was sprawled out on his back, one arm up and one arm down, reminding me of Gumby or an outline chalked on the sidewalk in a murder mystery. His mouth was wide open and his regular breath rattled deeply in the back of his throat somewhere between his mouth and his nose. Beside the vibration of the wheels and the steady hum of the engine, no other sound disturbed the sacred silence of the desert night. 2

From where I lay, behind the driver's seat, next to my twin brother on the old green patchwork quilt that smelled like beaches and picnics — salty and a little mildewed — I could see my mother's curly brown head slumped against the side window, her neck bent awkwardly against the seat belt, which seemed the only thing holding her in her seat. Dad, of course, drove — a motionless, soundless, protective paragon of security and strength, making me feel totally safe. The back of his head had never seemed more perfectly framed than by the reflection of the dashboard lights on the windshield; the short, raven-colored wiry hairs that I loved so much caught and played with, like tinsel would, the greenish glow with red and orange accents. The desert sky was starless, clouded. 3

Every couple of minutes, a big rig would pass us going west. The lights would illuminate my mother's profile for a moment and then the roar of the truck would come and the sudden, the violent sucking rush of air and we would be plunged into darkness again. Time passed so slowly, unnoticeably, as if the whole concept of time were meaningless. 4

I was careful to make no sound, content to watch the rising and falling of my twin's chest in the dim light and to feel on my cheek the gentle heat of the engine rising up through the floorboards. I lay motionless for a long time before the low rumbling, a larger sound than any eighteen-wheeler, rolled across the open plain. I lifted my head, excited to catch a glimpse of the rain that I, as a child from Los Angeles, seldom saw. A few seconds later, the lightning sliced the night sky all the way across the northern horizon. Like a rapidly growing twig, at least three or four branches, it illuminated the twisted forms of Joshua trees and low-growing cacti. All in silhouette — and only for a flash, though the image stayed many moments before my mind's eye in the following black. 5

The lightning came again, this time only a formless flash, as if God were taking a photograph of the magnificent desert, and the long, 6 straight road before us—empty and lonely—shone like a dagger. The trees looked like old men to me now, made motionless by the natural strobe, perhaps to resume their feeble hobble across the sands once the shield of night returned. The light show continued on the horizon though the expected rain never came. The fleeting, gnarled fingers grasped out and were gone; the fireworks flashed and frolicked and faded over and over—danced and jumped, acting out a drama in the quick, jerky movements of a marionette. Still in silence, still in darkness.

   I watched the violent, gaudy display over the uninhabited, endless ex-   7
panse, knowing I was in a state of grace and not knowing if I was dreaming but pretty sure I was awake because of the cramp in my neck and the pain in my elbow from placing too much weight on it for too long.

Meaning

1. What does Taylor mean by "state of grace" in paragraph 7? What associations does this phrase have? To what extent does it capture the dominant impression of this essay?
2. If you do not know the meaning of any of the words below, try to guess it from its context in Taylor's essay. Test your guesses in a dictionary, and then try to use each word in a sentence or two of your own.

paragon (3)	gnarled (6)	marionette (6)
silhouette (5)	frolicked (6)	gaudy (7)
strobe (6)		

Purpose and Audience

1. Why does Taylor open with the sentence "We didn't know there was a rodeo in Flagstaff"? What purposes does the sentence serve?
2. Even readers familiar with the desert may not have had Taylor's experience of it in a nighttime lightning storm. Where does she seem especially careful about describing what she saw? What details surprised you?

Method and Structure

1. What impression or mood is Taylor trying to capture in this essay? How does the precise detail of the description help to convey that mood?
2. Taylor begins her description inside the car (paragraphs 1–5) and then moves out into the landscape (5–7), bringing us back into the car in her final thought. Why does she use such a sequence? Why do you think she devotes about equal space to each area?

3. Taylor's description is mainly subjective, invested with her emotions. Point to elements of the description that reveal emotion.
4. **Other Methods**   Taylor's description relies in part on narration (see Chapter 5). How does narrative strengthen the essay's dominant impression?

Language

1. How does Taylor's tone help convey the "state of grace" she feels inside the car? Point out three or four examples of language that establish that mood.
2. Why do you think Taylor titles her essay "Desert Dance"?
3. Notice the words Taylor uses to describe Joshua trees (paragraphs 5–6). If you're already familiar with the tree, how accurate do you find Taylor's description? If you've never seen a Joshua tree, what do you think it looks like, based on Taylor's description? (Next time you're in the library, look the tree up in an encyclopedia to test your impression.)
4. Taylor uses similes to make her description vivid and immediate. Find several examples, and comment on their effectiveness. (See p. 50 for more on similes.)
5. Taylor's last paragraph is one long sentence. Does this long sentence work with or against the content and mood of the paragraph? Why and how?

Writing Topics

1. **Journal to Essay**   Using subjective description, expand your journal entry about a childhood event (p. 62) into an essay. Recalling details of sight, sound, touch, smell, even taste, build a dominant impression for readers of what the experience was like for you.
2. Taylor's essay illustrates her feelings not only about the desert but also about her father, mother, and twin brother. Think of a situation when you were intensely aware of your feelings about another person (friend or relative). Describe the situation and the person in a way that conveys those feelings.
3. **Cultural Considerations**   Though she had evidently seen the desert before, Taylor had not seen it the way she describes it in "Desert Dance." Write an essay in which you describe your first encounter with something new—for instance, a visit to the home of a friend from a different social or economic background, a visit to a big city or a farm, an unexpected view of your own backyard. Describe what you saw and your responses. How, if at all, did the experience change you?
4. **Connections**   Both Taylor and Diane Ackerman (in the paragraph on p. 58) experience awe at a natural wonder. In a brief essay, analyze how these writers convey their sense of awe so that it is concrete, not vague. Focus on their words and especially on their figures of speech. (See p. 50 for more on figures of speech.)

Be it ever so humble, there's no place like home.   —John Howard Payne

Our houses are such unwieldy property that we are often imprisoned rather than housed in them.   —Henry David Thoreau

The grass is always greener on the other side of the fence.   —Proverb

Journal Response   To keep our living spaces comfortable, we all have to perform tasks that can feel tedious or even pointless. What household chore do you dislike (or enjoy) the most? Write a journal entry that describes the chore and how you feel about doing it.

Dagoberto Gilb

A fiction writer, essayist, and journeyman carpenter, Dagoberto Gilb was born in 1950 in Los Angeles. After enrolling in junior college with some doubts about his academic ability, Gilb "just went nuts over books" and earned a BA in philosophy and an MA in religion from the University of California at Santa Barbara. He had difficulty finding work after college and for fifteen years scraped together a living with irregular construction jobs while keeping a journal on the side. The son of a Mexican mother and a German American father, Gilb celebrates mestizaje (mixed) culture and often examines the experiences and perspectives of working-class Latinos in his work. He has published three collections of short stories, Winners on the Pass Line *(1985),* The Magic of Blood *(1993), and* Woodcuts of Women *(2001); a novel,* The Last Known Residence of Mickey Acuña *(1994); and a collection of essays,* Gritos *(2003). Gilb is a regular contributor to the* New Yorker *and* Harper's Magazine *and has received many honors and prizes, including the Hemingway Foundation/PEN Award, a* New York Times *notable book designation, and a National Endowment for the Arts fellowship. He currently lives in Austin, Texas, and teaches creative writing at Texas State University–San Marcos.*

MY LANDLADY'S YARD

Dagoberto Gilb's writing can be both deceptively simple and deliberately provocative. In the following piece, first published in the Texas Observer *and later reprinted as the opening essay in* Gritos, *Gilb finds surprising meanings in the seeming futility of yard work.*

It's been a very dry season here. Not enough rain. And the sun's be- 1
ginning to feel closer. Which, of course, explains why this is called the
desert. Why the kinds of plants that do well enough in the region—creosote, mesquite, ocotillo, yucca—aren't what you'd consider lush, tropical blooms. All that's obvious, right? To you, I'm sure, it's obvious,
and to me it is, too, but not to my landlady. My landlady doesn't think
of this rock house I rent in central El Paso as being in the desert. To
her, it's the big city. She's from the country, from a ranch probably just
like the one she now calls home, a few miles up the paved highway in
Chaparral, New Mexico, where the roads are graded dirt. She must still
see the house as she did when she lived here as a young wife and
mother, as part of the city's peaceful suburbs, which it certainly was
thirty years ago. She probably planted the shrubs and evergreens that
snuggle the walls of the house now, probably seeded the back- and
front-yard grass herself. And she wants those Yankee plants and that
imported grass to continue to thrive as they would in all other American, nondesert neighborhoods, even if these West Texas suburbs moved
on to the east and west many years ago, even if the population has
quadrupled and water is more scarce, and expensive, than back then.

So I go ahead and drag around a green hose despite my percep- 2
tion that *gold*, colorless and liquid, is pouring out onto this desert, an
offering as unquenchable and ruthless as to any Aztec deity (don't
water a couple of days and watch how fast it dries away). Superstitions,
if you don't mind my calling them that, die hard, and property values
are dependent on shared impressions. I'm not ready to rent and load
another U-Haul truck.

With my thumb over the brass fitting and squeezed against the 3
water, I use the digits on my other hand to pluck up loose garbage.
You've heard, maybe, of West Texas wind. That explains why so much
of it lands here on my front yard, but also a high school is my backyard: the school's rear exit is only a dirt alley and fence away from my
garage, and teenagers pass by in the morning, during lunch, and when
school lets out. I find the latest Salsa Rio brand of Doritos, Big Gulp
Grande cups, paper (or plastic or both) bowls with the slimy remains
of what goes for cheese on nachos from the smiley-faced Good Time
Store two blocks away, used napkins, orange burger pouches, the new
glossy-clean plastic soda containers, waxy candy wrappers from
Mounds and Mars and Milky Way. Also beer cans and bottles, grocery-
store bags both plastic and paper, and fragments from everything else
(believe me) possible.

I'm betting you think I'm not too happy about accumulating such   4
evidence. You're right. But I'm not mentioning it to complain. I want
the image of all the trash, as well as the one of me spraying precious
water onto this dusty alkaline soil, to get your attention. Because both
stand for the odd way we live and think out here, a few hundred miles
(at least) from everyplace else in the United States.

My green grass in the desert, for instance. My landlady wants   5
thick, luxuriant grass because that's the way of this side of the border,
and this side is undeniably better, whatever misconception of place and
history and natural resources the desire for that image depends on. It's
not just her, and it's not just lawns. Take another example: a year ago
about this time, police cars squealed onto the asphalt handball and basketball courts on the other side of the school fence to regain control
of a hundred or so students lumped around a fight, most of them
watching, some swinging baseball bats. What happened? According to
the local newspaper, the fight broke out between a group of black students, all of them dependents of Fort Bliss military personnel (as their
jargon has it), and a group of Hispanic students. "Hispanic" is the current media term for those of descent from South of the Border. Even
around here. Which is the point: that even in this town—the other side
of the concrete river considered the official land of Spanish-language
history and culture—the latest minority-language terminology is used
to describe its historic, multigenerational majority population. With the
exception of one high school on the more affluent west side of town,
Anglos are the overwhelming minority; at the high school behind my
backyard the ratio must be ten to one. Though Mexico has been the
mother of this region, and remains so, it's the language and understanding of The North that labels the account of the school incident:
"Hispanic" students, black dependents of GIs.

If green grass is the aspiration, the realization of an American fan-   6
tasy, then the trash is from the past, the husks of a frontier mentality
that it took to be here, and stay, in the first place. Trash blowing by,
snared by limbs and curbs and fences, is a display of what was the attitude of the West. The endlessness of its range. The ultimate principle
of every man, woman, animal, and thing for itself. The meanness required to survive. The wild joy that could abandon rules. The immediacy of life. Or the stupidity of the non-Indian hunter eating one meal,
then leaving behind the carcass. Except that vultures and coyotes and
finally ants used to clean that mess up. The remains of the modernized
hunt don't balance well in nature or its hybrid shrubs, do not biodegrade. And there are a lot more hunters than before.

Trash contradicts the well-tended lawn. And in my neighborhood, not all is Saint Augustine or Bermuda.[1] Hardy weeds sprout and grow tall everywhere, gray-green century plants shoot stalks beside many homes. El Paso is still crossing cultures and times, the wind blows often, particularly this time of year, the sun will be getting bigger, but the pretty nights cool things off here on the desert. Let me admit this: I'd like it if grass grew well in my backyard. What I've got is patchy at best, and neglected, the brown dirt is a stronger color than the green. So the other day, I soaked that hard soil, dug it up, threw seed grown and packaged in Missouri, covered it with peat humus from Menard, Texas, and I'm waiting.

Meaning

1. Gilb starts his essay with the observation that grass cannot thrive in the desert and that watering is a waste of both money and natural resources. So why does he try to grow a lawn?
2. In his conclusion, Gilb writes, "What I've got is patchy at best, and neglected, the brown dirt is a stronger color than the green." What does he mean? Is he talking about the yard, or something else?
3. If you're unsure of any of the following words, try to guess what they mean from the context of Gilb's essay. Then look them up to see if you were right. Use each word in a sentence or two of your own.

lush (1)	digits (3)	husks (6)
graded (1)	alkaline (4)	snared (6)
Yankee (1)	luxuriant (5)	hardy (7)
unquenchable (2)	misconception (5)	peat humus (7)
deity (2)	aspiration (6)	

Purpose and Audience

1. Gilb writes about his yard to make a point about something else entirely: cultural tensions in a border town. How does grass in this essay function as a symbol? (If necessary, see *symbol* in the Glossary.)
2. In describing the plot of land that surrounds his home, Gilb shifts the possessive pronoun from *my landlady's* yard in the title to *my* backyard in the conclusion. What does this shift reveal about Gilb's reasons for writing about his home?

---

[1] Varieties of cultivated grass. [Editor's note.]

3. This piece was originally written for a regional magazine with a strong political bent. What, then, could Gilb assume about his audience? How are those assumptions reflected in his essay? (You might want to take a look at an issue of the *Texas Observer* or the magazine's Web site, *http://www.texasobserver.org*, for clues.)

Method and Structure

1. What dominant impression of his yard does Gilb create?
2. What point of view does Gilb take toward his subject?
3. **Other Methods** Gilb uses several methods of development in addition to description — for instance, paragraphs 2–6 use division (Chapter 7) to analyze the political and cultural meanings of green grass in the desert, and paragraph 3 gives several examples (Chapter 6) of the garbage that litters the yard. Most notably, paragraph 5 uses definition (Chapter 11) to explore the Texas media's use of the term *Hispanic*. Why is the label so important to Gilb?

Language

1. Gilb's essay includes many sentence fragments. Identify at least two examples. Is this sloppy writing, or does Gilb break the rules of sentence grammar for a purpose? What do Gilb's fragments contribute to (or take away from) his essay? Explain your answer.
2. In several places throughout his essay, Gilb uses figures of speech to add depth to his description. Locate two examples that you find especially striking and explain their effect. (If necessary, see *figures of speech* in the Glossary.)
3. How many of the five senses does Gilb appeal to in his description? Find words or phrases that seem especially precise in conveying sensory impressions.

Writing Topics

1. **Journal to Essay** Write an essay about something in or around your home that holds emotional significance for you. Your subject could be related to the chore you wrote about in your journal entry (p. 66), or it could have to do with a home-improvement project that you found especially frustrating or rewarding. Describe the object or space to reveal both its physical attributes and its significance to you.
2. In paragraph 5, Gilb characterizes his landlady's attitude as the belief that the American "side of the border . . . is undeniably better" than the Mex-

ican side. Does he agree with her? Write an essay that identifies and analyzes Gilb's position on the issue of cultural assimilation in American border towns, paying close attention to each of his examples and explaining how he reaches his conclusions.

3. **Cultural Considerations**   Our dreams for the future are often influenced by the family, community, or larger culture in which we grew up. Think of a personal goal that seems to have come at least partly from other people. In an essay describe the goal and your feelings about it, and explain the origins of your feelings as best you can.

4. **Connections**   Both Gilb and Marta K. Taylor, in "Desert Dance" (p. 62), write about the Southwest desert, Gilb from the perspective of an adult who lives and works there and Taylor from the perspective of a child who visits during a family vacation. Compare and contrast what the landscape means to them. How do their respective points of view affect their experiences and attitudes? Be sure to include examples from both essays to support your comparison.

It's an ill wind that blows nobody any good.   —Proverb

Meanings, moods, the whole scale of our inner experience, find in nature the "correspondences" through which we may know our boundless selves.
                                                          —Kathleen Raine

How we are all more or less creatures of Sun, Shadow, and Imagination, impressed or depressed by weather!   —The Gardener

Journal Response   Write a journal entry about a natural phenomenon that affected you, such as a lightning storm, a hurricane, or a blizzard. How did the event make you act and feel?

Joan Didion

One of America's leading nonfiction writers, Joan Didion consistently applies a journalist's eye for detail and a terse, understated style to the cultural dislocation pervading modern American society. She was born in 1934 in Sacramento, a fifth-generation Californian, and she has attended closely to the distinctive people and places of the American West. After graduating from the University of California at Berkeley in 1956, Didion lived for nearly a decade in New York City before returning permanently to California. She has contributed to many periodicals, and her essays have been published in Slouching towards Bethlehem *(1968),* The White Album *(1979),* Salvador *(1983),* Essays and Conversations *(1984),* Miami *(1987),* After Henry *(1992),* Political Fictions *(2001), and* Fixed Ideas: America since 9.11 *(2003). Didion has also published five novels:* Run River *(1963),* Play It as It Lays *(1970),* A Book of Common Prayer *(1977),* Democracy *(1984), and* The Last Thing He Wanted *(1996). With her late husband, the writer John Gregory Dunne, she wrote screenplays for movies, among them* Panic in Needle Park *(1971),* A Star Is Born *(1976),* True Confessions *(1981), and* Up Close and Personal *(1996). Didion's most recent book is* The Year of Magical Thinking *(2005), a personal memoir of her emotional state in the wake of her husband's sudden death.*

THE SANTA ANA

In describing the violent effects of a hot, dry wind on Los Angeles, Didion ranges typically outward from herself to the people figuring in local news reports. "The Santa Ana" first appeared in the Saturday Evening Post *in 1967*

and later appeared as part of "Los Angeles Notebook," an essay collected in
Slouching towards Bethlehem.

There is something uneasy in the Los Angeles air this afternoon, some   1
unnatural stillness, some tension. What it means is that tonight a Santa
Ana will begin to blow, a hot wind from the northeast whining down
through the Cajon and San Gorgonio Passes, blowing up sandstorms
out along Route 66, drying the hills and the nerves to the flash point.
For a few days now we will see smoke back in the canyons, and hear
sirens in the night. I have neither heard nor read that a Santa Ana is
due, but I know it, and almost everyone I have seen today knows it too.
We know it because we feel it. The baby frets. The maid sulks. I rekindle a waning argument with the telephone company, then cut my losses
and lie down, given over to whatever it is in the air. To live with the
Santa Ana is to accept, consciously or unconsciously, a deeply mechanistic view of human behavior.

I recall being told, when I first moved to Los Angeles and was liv-   2
ing on an isolated beach, that the Indians would throw themselves into
the sea when the bad wind blew. I could see why. The Pacific turned
ominously glossy during a Santa Ana period, and one woke in the night
troubled not only by the peacocks screaming in the olive trees but by
the eerie absence of surf. The heat was surreal. The sky had a yellow
cast, the kind of light sometimes called "earthquake weather." My
only neighbor would not come out of her house for days, and there
were no lights at night, and her husband roamed the place with a machete. One day he would tell me that he had heard a trespasser, the
next a rattlesnake.

"On nights like that," Raymond Chandler[1] once wrote about the   3
Santa Ana, "every booze party ends in a fight. Meek little wives feel the
edge of the carving knife and study their husbands' necks. Anything can
happen." That was the kind of wind it was. I did not know then that
there was any basis for the effect it had on all of us, but it turns out to
be another of those cases in which science bears out folk wisdom. The
Santa Ana, which is named for one of the canyons it rushes through, is
a *foehn* wind, like the *foehn* of Austria and Switzerland and the *ham-
sin* of Israel. There are a number of persistent malevolent winds, perhaps the best known of which are the mistral of France and the
Mediterranean sirocco, but a *foehn* wind has distinct characteristics: it

---

[1] Chandler (1888–1959) is best known for his detective novels featuring Philip Mar-
lowe. [Editor's note.]

occurs on the leeward slope of a mountain range and, although the air begins as a cold mass, it is warmed as it comes down the mountain and appears finally as a hot dry wind. Whenever and wherever a *foehn* blows, doctors hear about headaches and nausea and allergies, about "nervousness," about "depression." In Los Angeles some teachers do not attempt to conduct formal classes during a Santa Ana, because the children become unmanageable. In Switzerland the suicide rate goes up during the *foehn*, and in the courts of some Swiss cantons the wind is considered a mitigating circumstance for crime. Surgeons are said to watch the wind, because blood does not clot normally during a *foehn*. A few years ago an Israeli physicist discovered that not only during such winds, but for the ten or twelve hours which precede them, the air carries an unusually high ratio of positive to negative ions. No one seems to know exactly why that should be; some talk about friction and others suggest solar disturbances. In any case the positive ions are there, and what an excess of positive ions does, in the simplest terms, is make people unhappy. One cannot get much more mechanistic than that.

Easterners commonly complain that there is no "weather" at all in Southern California, that the days and the seasons slip by relentlessly, numbingly bland. That is quite misleading. In fact the climate is characterized by infrequent but violent extremes: two periods of torrential subtropical rains which continue for weeks and wash out the hills and send subdivisions sliding toward the sea; about twenty scattered days a year of the Santa Ana, which, with its incendiary dryness, invariably means fire. At the first prediction of a Santa Ana, the Forest Service flies men and equipment from northern California into the southern forests, and the Los Angeles Fire Department cancels its ordinary non-firefighting routines. The Santa Ana caused Malibu to burn the way it did in 1956, and Bel Air in 1961, and Santa Barbara in 1964. In the winter of 1966–67 eleven men were killed fighting a Santa Ana fire that spread through the San Gabriel Mountains.

Just to watch the front-page news out of Los Angeles during a Santa Ana is to get very close to what it is about the place. The longest single Santa Ana period in recent years was in 1957, and it lasted not the usual three or four days but fourteen days, from November 21 until December 4. On the first day 25,000 acres of the San Gabriel Mountains were burning, with gusts reaching 100 miles an hour. In town, the wind reached Force 12, or hurricane force, on the Beaufort Scale; oil derricks were toppled and people ordered off the downtown streets to avoid injury from flying objects. On November 22 the fire in the San Gabriels was out of control. On November 24 six people were killed in automobile accidents, and by the end of the week the Los Angeles *Times* was keeping a box score of traffic deaths. On November 26 a prominent Pasadena attorney, depressed about money, shot and killed his wife, their two sons, and himself. On November 27 a South Gate divorcée, twenty-two, was murdered and thrown from a moving car. On November 30 the San Gabriel fire was still out of control, and the wind in town was blowing eighty miles an hour. On the first day of December four people died violently, and on the third the wind began to break.

It is hard for people who have not lived in Los Angeles to realize   6
how radically the Santa Ana figures in the local imagination. The city burning is Los Angeles's deepest image of itself: Nathanael West perceived that, in *The Day of the Locust*; and at the time of the 1965 Watts riots what struck the imagination most indelibly were the fires.[2] For days one could drive the Harbor Freeway and see the city on fire, just as we had always known it would be in the end. Los Angeles weather is the weather of catastrophe, of apocalypse, and, just as the reliably long and bitter winters of New England determine the way life is lived there, so the violence and the unpredictability of the Santa Ana affect the entire quality of life in Los Angeles, accentuate its impermanence, its unreliability. The wind shows us how close to the edge we are.

Meaning

1. Does Didion describe purely for the sake of describing, or does she have a thesis she wants to convey? If so, where does she most explicitly state this thesis?

2. What is the dominant impression Didion creates of the Santa Ana wind? What effect does it have on residents of Los Angeles?

3. Explain what Didion means by a "mechanistic view of human behavior" (paragraph 1). What would the opposite of such a view of human behavior be?

4. How might Didion's last sentence have two meanings?

5. Based on their context in the essay, try to guess the meanings of any of the following words that you don't know. Test your guesses in a dictionary, and then try out your knowledge of each word by using it in sentences of your own.

[2] *The Day of the Locust* (1939), a novel about Hollywood, ends in riot and fire. The August 1965 disturbances in the Watts neighborhood of Los Angeles resulted in millions of dollars in damage from fires. [Editor's note.]

flash point (1)   malevolent (3)   derricks (5)
mechanistic (1)   leeward (3)   indelibly (6)
ominously (2)   cantons (3)   apocalypse (6)
surreal (2)   mitigating (3)   accentuate (6)
machete (2)   incendiary (4)

Purpose and Audience

1. Why do you think Didion felt compelled to write about the Santa Ana? Consider whether she might have had a dual purpose.
2. What kind of audience is Didion writing for? Primarily people from Los Angeles? How do you know? Does Didion identify herself as an Angelina?

Method and Structure

1. Didion doesn't describe the Santa Ana wind itself as much as its effects. Why does she approach her subject this way? What effects does she focus on?
2. Didion alternates between passages of mostly objective and mostly subjective description. Trace this movement throughout the essay.
3. What is the function of the quotation from Raymond Chandler at the beginning of paragraph 3? How does it serve as a transition?
4. **Other Methods**   The essay is full of examples (Chapter 6) of the wind's effects on human beings. How do these examples help Didion achieve her purpose?

Language

1. Note Didion's frequent use of the first person (*I* and *we*) and of the present tense. What does she achieve with this point of view?
2. What is the effect of the vivid imagery in paragraph 2? In what way is this imagery "surreal" (fantastic or dreamlike)?

Writing Topics

1. **Journal to Essay**   Using Didion's essay as a model, write a descriptive essay about something that annoys, frightens, or even crazes you and others. Your subject could be a natural phenomenon, such as the one you described in your journal entry (p. 72), or something else: bumper-to-bumper traffic at rush hour, long lines at the department of motor vehicles or another government agency, lengthy and complicated voice-mail menus that

end up in busy signals. You may use examples from your own experience and observation, from experiences you have read or heard about, or, like Didion, from both sources.

2. Didion tries to explain the Santa Ana phenomenon scientifically in paragraph 3 as having something to do with an excess of positive ions in the air. But she admits that nobody knows why there are more positive than negative ions or why that fact should translate into human unhappiness. To what extent do you think our moods can be explained by science? Are our emotions simply the by-products of brain chemistry, as some scientists would suggest? Write an essay, using description and narration (Chapter 5), about someone you know (or know of) whose moods are affected by forces beyond his or her control. Be sure to include enough detail to create a vivid portrait for your readers.

3. **Cultural Considerations**   Didion perceives the Santa Ana as a cultural phenomenon in Los Angeles that affects the attitudes, relationships, and activities of residents "just as the reliably long and bitter winters of New England determine the way life is lived there" (paragraph 6). Consider a place you know well and describe how some aspect of the climate or weather affects the culture, "the way life is lived," not only during a particular event or season but throughout the year.

4. **Connections**   Both Didion and Marta K. Taylor, in "Desert Dance" (p. 62), describe dramatic natural phenomena that occur in the American West. Compare the way Taylor describes a desert lightning storm in paragraphs 5 and 6 of her essay to Didion's description, in paragraph 2, of the surreal landscape of the Santa Ana. How does each writer combine striking images and original figures of speech to convey a strong sense of mood and a feeling in the reader that he or she is there? Do you think one author's description is more successful than the other's? Why?

Description

Choose one of the following topics, or any topic they suggest, for an essay developed by description. The topic you decide on should be something you care about so that description is a means of communicating an idea, not an end in itself.

PEOPLE

1. An exceptionally neat or messy person
2. A person whose appearance and mannerisms are at odds with his or her real self
3. A person you admire or respect
4. An irritating child
5. A person who intimidates you (teacher, salesperson, doctor, police officer, fellow student)

PLACES

6. A shopping mall
7. A frightening place
8. A place near water (ocean, lake, pond, river, swimming pool)
9. A place you daydream about
10. A prison cell, police station, or courtroom
11. A cellar, attic, or garage
12. Your room

ANIMALS AND THINGS

13. Birds at a bird feeder
14. A work of art
15. A pet or an animal in a zoo
16. A favorite childhood toy
17. A prized possession
18. The look and taste of a favorite or detested food

SCENES

19. The devastation caused by a natural disaster
20. A scene of environmental destruction
21. A yard sale or flea market
22. Late night or early morning
23. The scene at a concert (rock, country, folk, classical, jazz)

SENSATIONS

24. Waiting for important news
25. Being freed of some restraint
26. Sunday afternoon
27. Writing
28. Skating, running, bodysurfing, skydiving, or some other activity
29. Extreme hunger, thirst, cold, heat, or fatigue

Sensing the Natural World

1. Although we tend to think of nature as unspoiled wilderness, some of the writers in this chapter recognize that the natural world can be difficult to cope with. Joan Didion's description of the Santa Ana wind (p. 72) and David Mura's description of rain (p. 57) are most notable in this respect, but even Dagoberto Gilb's examination of the allure of a green lawn (p. 66) emphasizes the desert's hostility to plant life. Write a descriptive essay about a natural environment that is special to you, emphasizing its blemishes rather than its beauty.

2. All of the writers in this chapter demonstrate strong feelings for the place, thing, or phenomenon they describe, but the writers vary considerably in the ways they express their feelings. For example, Joan Didion's own discomfort in the Santa Ana wind colors all of her perceptions, whereas Marta K. Taylor's description of an electrical storm mixes serenity and awe (p. 62). Write an essay analyzing the tone of these and the three other selections in this chapter: David Mura's paragraph on typhoons, Diane Ackerman's paragraph on icebergs (p. 58), and Dagoberto Gilb's "My Landlady's Yard." Discuss which pieces you find most effective and why.

3. Each writer in this chapter vividly describes a specific place or thing that represents some larger, abstract concept: for example, Dagoberto Gilb's backyard represents cultural conflict, and Marta Taylor's desert lightning represents the awesomeness of nature. Think of a specific, tangible place or thing in your life that represents some larger, abstract idea and write a descriptive essay exploring this relationship.

Chapter 5

NARRATION

Recalling Childhood

You **narrate** every time you tell a story about something that happened. Narration helps us make sense of events and share our experiences with others; consequently, it is one of the longest-standing and most essential methods of communicating. (As the writer Joan Didion famously put it, "We tell stories in order to live.") You can use narration to entertain friends by retelling an amusing or scary experience, to explain the sequence of events in a chemistry experiment, to summarize a salesclerk's actions in a letter complaining about bad customer service, to explain what went wrong in a ball game, or to persuade skeptics by means of several stories that the forestry industry is sincere about restoring clear-cut forests. Storytelling is instinctive to the ways we think and speak; it's no surprise, then, that narration should figure into so much of what we read and write.

READING NARRATION

Narration relates a sequence of events that are linked in time. By arranging events in an orderly progression, a narrative illuminates the stages leading to a result. Sometimes the emphasis is on the story itself, as in fiction, biography, autobiography, some history, and much journalism. But often a narrative serves some larger point, as when a paragraph or a brief story about an innocent person's death helps to strengthen an argument for stricter handling of drunk drivers. When used as a primary means of developing an essay, such pointed narration usually relates a sequence of events that led to new knowledge or had a notable outcome. The point of the narrative — the idea the reader is to take away — then determines the selection of events, the amount of detail devoted to them, and their arrangement.

Though narration arranges events in time, narrative time is not real time. An important event may fill whole pages, even though it took only minutes to unfold; and a less important event may be dispensed with in a sentence, even though it lasted hours. Suppose, for instance, that a writer wants to narrate the experience of being mugged in order to show how courage came unexpectedly to his aid. He might provide a slow-motion account of the few minutes' encounter with the muggers, including vivid details of the setting and of the attackers' appearance, a moment-by-moment replay of his emotions, and exact dialogue. At the same time, he will compress events that merely fill in background or link main events, such as how he got to the scene of the mugging or the follow-up questioning by a police detective. And he will entirely omit many events, such as a conversation overheard at the police station, that have no significance for his point.

The point of a narrative influences not only which events are covered and how fully but also how the events are arranged. There are several possibilities:

- A straight chronological sequence is most common because it relates events in the order of their actual occurrence. It is particularly useful for short narratives, for those in which the last event is the most dramatic, or for those in which the events preceding and following the climax contribute to the point being made.
- The final event, such as a self-revelation, may come first, followed by an explanation of the events leading up to it.
- The entire story may be summarized first and then examined in detail.
- **Flashbacks** — shifts backward rather than forward in time — may recall events whose significance would not have been apparent earlier. Flashbacks are common in movies and fiction: a character in the midst of one scene mentally replays another.

In addition to providing a clear organization, writers also strive to adopt a consistent **point of view**, a position relative to the events, conveyed in two main ways:

- Pronouns indicate the storyteller's place in the story: the first-person *I* if the narrator is a direct participant; the third-person *he*, *she*, *it*, or *they* if the writer is observing or reporting.
- Verb tense indicates the writer's relation in time to the sequence of events: present (*is*, *run*) or past (*was*, *ran*).

Combining the first-person pronoun with the present tense can create great immediacy ("I feel the point of the knife in my back"). At the other extreme, combining third-person pronouns with the past tense creates more distance and objectivity ("He felt the point of the knife in his back"). In between extremes, writers can combine first person with past tense ("I felt ...") or third person with present tense ("He feels ..."). The choice depends on their actual involvement in the narrative and on their purpose.

ANALYZING NARRATION IN PARAGRAPHS

Michael Ondaatje (born 1943) is a poet, fiction writer, essayist, and filmmaker. The following paragraph is from *Running in the Family* (1982), Ondaatje's memoir of his childhood in Ceylon, now called Sri Lanka, off the southern tip of India.

After my father died, a grey cobra came into the house. My stepmother loaded the gun and fired at point blank range. The gun jammed. She stepped back and reloaded but by then the snake had slid out into the garden. For the next month this snake would often come into the house and each time the gun would misfire or jam, or my stepmother would miss at absurdly short range. The snake attacked no one and had a tendency to follow my younger sister Susan around. Other snakes entering the house were killed by the shotgun, lifted with a long stick and flicked into the bushes, but the old grey cobra led a charmed life. Finally one of the old workers at Rock Hill told my stepmother what had become obvious, that it was my father who had come to protect his family. And in fact, whether it was because the chicken farm closed down or because of my father's presence in the form of a snake, very few other snakes came into the house again.

Margin notes:

Chronological order

Past tense

Transitions (underlined)

Point of view: participant

Purpose: to relate a colorful, mysterious story

Andre Dubus (1936–99) wrote essays and fiction. This paragraph comes from his essay "Under the Lights," which was published first in the *Village Voice* and then in Dubus's collection *Broken Vessels* (1991).

In the spring of 1948, in the first softball game during the afternoon hour of physical education in the dusty schoolyard, the two captains chose teams and, as always, they chose other boys until only two of us remained. I batted last, and first came to the plate with two or three runners on base, and while my teammates urged me to try for a walk, and the players on the field called Easy out, Easy out, I watched the softball coming in waist high, and stepped and swung, and hit it over the right fielder's head for a double. My next time at bat I tripled to center. From then on I brought my glove to school, hanging from a handlebar.

Chronological order

Past tense

Transitions (underlined)

Point of view: direct participant

Purpose: to relate the author's transformation into a baseball player

DEVELOPING A NARRATIVE ESSAY
Getting Started

You'll find narration useful whenever relating a sequence of events can help you make a point, sometimes to support the thesis of a larger paper, sometimes *as* the thesis of a paper. If you're assigned a narrative essay, probe your own experiences for a situation such as an argument involving strong emotion, a humorous or embarrassing incident, a dramatic scene you witnessed, or a learning experience like a job. If you have the opportunity to do research, you might choose a topic dealing with the natural world (such as the Big Bang scenario for the origin of the universe) or an event in history or politics (such as how a local activist worked to close down an animal-research lab).

Explore your subject by listing all the events in sequence as they happened. At this stage you may find the traditional journalist's questions helpful:

- Who was involved?
- What happened?
- When did it happen?
- Where did it happen?
- Why did it happen?
- How did it happen?

These questions will lead you to examine your subject from all angles. Then you need to decide which events should be developed in great detail because they are central to your story; which merit compression because they merely contribute background or tie the main events together; and which should be omitted altogether because they are irrelevant to the story or might clutter your narrative.

While you are weighing the relative importance of events, consider also what your readers need to know in order to understand and appreciate your narrative.

- What information will help locate readers in the narrative's time and place?
- How will you expand and compress events to keep readers' attention?
- What details about people, places, and feelings will make the events vivid for readers?
- What is your attitude toward the subject—lighthearted, sarcastic, bitter, serious?—and how will you convey it to readers in your choice of events and details?
- What should your point of view be? Do you want to involve readers intimately by using the first person and the present tense? Or does that seem overdramatic, less appropriate than the more detached, objective view that would be conveyed by the past tense or the third person or both?

Forming a Thesis

Whatever your subject, you should have some point to make about it: Why was the incident or experience significant? What does it teach or illustrate? If you can, phrase this point in a sentence before you start to draft. For instance:

> I used to think small-town life was boring, but one taste of the city made me appreciate the leisurely pace of home.

> A recent small earthquake demonstrated the hazards of inadequate civil defense measures.

Sometimes you may need to draft your story before the point of it becomes clear to you, especially if the experience had a personal impact or if the event was so recent that writing a draft will allow you to gain some perspective.

Whether to state your main point outright in your essay, as a thesis sentence, depends on the effect you want to have on readers. You might use your introduction to lead to a statement of your thesis so that readers will know from the start why you are telling them your story. Then again, to intensify the drama of your story, you might decide to withhold your thesis sentence for the conclusion or omit it altogether. Remember, though, that the thesis must be evident to readers even if it isn't stated: the narrative needs a point.

Organizing

Narrative essays often begin without formal introductions, instead drawing the reader in with one of the more dramatic events in the sequence. But you may find an introduction useful to set the scene for your narrative, to summarize the events leading up to it, to establish the context for it, or to lead in to a thesis statement if you want readers to know the point of your story before they start reading it.

The arrangement of events in the body of your essay depends on the actual order in which they occurred and the point you want to make. To narrate a trip during which one thing after another went wrong, you might find a strict chronological order most effective. To narrate an earthquake that began and ended in an instant, you might sort simultaneous events into groups — say, what happened to buildings and what happened to people — or you might arrange a few people's experiences in order of increasing drama. To narrate your experience of city life, you might interweave events in the city with contrasting flashbacks to your life in a small town, or you might start by relating one especially bad experience in the city, drop back to explain how you ended up in that situation, and then go on to tell what happened afterward. Narrative time can be manipulated in any number of ways, but your scheme should have a purpose that your readers can see, and you should stick to it.

Let the ending of your essay be determined by the effect you want to leave with readers. You can end with the last event in your sequence, or the one you have saved for last, if it conveys your point and provides a strong finish. Or you can summarize the aftermath of the story if it contributes to the point. You can also end with a formal conclusion that states your point — your thesis — explicitly. Such a conclusion is especially useful if your point unfolds gradually throughout the narrative and you want to emphasize it at the finish.

Drafting

Drafting a narrative can be less of a struggle than drafting other kinds of papers, especially if you're close to the events and you use a straight chronological order. But the relative ease of storytelling can be misleading if it causes you to describe events too quickly or write without making a point. While drafting, be as specific as possible. Tell what the people in your narrative were wearing, what expressions their faces held, how they gestured, what they said. Specify the time of day, and describe the weather and the surroundings (buildings, vegetation, and the like). All these details may be familiar to you, but they won't be to your readers.

At the same time, try to remain open to what the story means to you, so that you can convey that meaning in your selection and description of events. If you know before you begin what your thesis is, let it guide you. But the first draft may turn out to be a search for your thesis, so that you'll need another draft to make it evident in the way you relate events.

In your draft you may want to experiment with dialogue — quotations of what participants said, in their words. Dialogue can add immediacy and realism as long as it advances the narrative and doesn't ramble beyond its usefulness. In reconstructing dialogue from memory, try to recall not only the actual words but also the sounds of speakers' voices and the expressions on their faces — information that will help you represent each speaker distinctly. And keep the dialogue natural sounding by using constructions typical of speech. For instance, most speakers prefer contractions such as *don't* and *shouldn't* to the longer forms *do not* and *should not*; and few speakers begin sentences with *although*, as in the formal-sounding "Although we could hear our mother's voice, we refused to answer her."

Whether you are relating events in strict chronological order or manipulating them for some effect, try to make their sequence in real time and the distance between them clear to readers. Instead of signaling sequence with the monotonous *and then ... and then ... and then* or *next ... next ... next*, use informative transitions that signal the order of events (*afterward, earlier*), the duration of events (*for an hour, in that time*), or the amount of time between events (*the next morning, a week later*). (See the Glossary under *transitions* for a list of such expressions.)

Revising and Editing

When your draft is complete, revise and edit it by answering the following questions and considering the information in the box.

- *Is the point of your narrative clear, and does every event you relate contribute to it?* Whether or not you state your thesis, it should be obvious to readers. They should be able to see why you have lingered over some events and compressed others, and they should not be distracted by insignificant events and details.

- *Is your organization clear?* Be sure that your readers will understand any shifts backward or forward in time.
- *Have you used transitions to help readers follow the sequence of events?* Transitions such as *meanwhile* or *soon afterward* serve a dual purpose: they keep the reader on track, and they link sentences and paragraphs so that they flow smoothly. (For more information, see pp. 35 and 36 and the Glossary under *transitions*.)
- *If you have used dialogue, is it purposeful and natural?* Be sure all quoted speech moves the action ahead. And read all dialogue aloud to check that it sounds like something someone would actually say.

FOCUS ON VERBS

Narration depends heavily on verbs to clarify and enliven events. Strong verbs sharpen meaning and encourage you to add other informative details:

WEAK   The wind *made* an awful noise.

STRONG   The wind *roared* around the house and *rattled* the trees.

Forms of *make* (as in the example above) and forms of *be* (as in the next example) can sap the life from narration:

WEAK   The noises *were* alarming to us.

STRONG   The noises *alarmed* us.

Verbs in the active voice (the subject does the action) usually pack more power into fewer words than verbs in the passive voice (the subject is acted upon):

WEAK PASSIVE   We *were besieged* in the basement by the wind, as the water at our feet *was swelled* by the rain.

STRONG ACTIVE   The wind *besieged* us in the basement, as the rain *swelled* the water at our feet.

(See also p. 45 on active versus passive voice.)

While strengthening verbs, also ensure that they're consistent in tense. The tense you choose for relating events, present or past, should not shift unnecessarily.

INCONSISTENT TENSES   We *held* a frantic conference to consider our options. It *takes* only a minute to decide to stay put.

CONSISTENT TENSE   We *held* a frantic conference to consider our options. It *took* only a minute to decide to stay put.

A NOTE ON THEMATIC CONNECTIONS

All the authors in this chapter saw reasons to articulate key events in their childhoods, and for that purpose narration is the obvious choice. Michael Ondaatje, in a paragraph, recalls his stepmother's inability to kill a cobra, perhaps because it embodied his dead father (p. 83). Andre Dubus, in another paragraph, records his transformation from a benchwarmer to a baseball player (p. 84). Annie Dillard's essay recounts the ecstasy of being chased by an adult for pelting his car with a snowball (p. 90), while Langston Hughes pinpoints the moment during a church revival when he lost his faith (p. 97). And Kaela Hobby-Reichstein's narrative recalls some disturbing girlhood experiences with racism (p. 102).

We wove a web in childhood, / A web of sunny air. —Charlotte Brontë

*When she was good, / She was very, very good, / But when she was bad she
was horrid.* —Henry Wadsworth Longfellow

Go directly—see what she's doing, and tell her she mustn't. —Punch

Journal Response   In a short journal entry, reflect on a time you misbehaved
as a child. Was it exciting? scary? How did the adults in your life react?

Annie Dillard

*A poet and essayist, Annie Dillard is part naturalist, part mystic. She was born
in 1945 in Pittsburgh. Growing up in that city, she was an independent child
given to exploration and reading. (As an adult, she reads nearly a hundred
books a year.) After graduating from Hollins College in the Blue Ridge Mountains of Virginia, Dillard settled in the area to investigate her natural surroundings and to write. Dillard demonstrated her intense, passionate
involvement with the world of nature and the world of the mind early in her
career with* Pilgrim at Tinker Creek *(1974), a series of related essays that
earned her national recognition and a Pulitzer Prize. Dillard's prolific output
since then has spanned several genres, including poetry in volumes such as*
Tickets for a Prayer Wheel *(1974),* Holy the Firm *(1977), and* Mornings Like
This *(1995); essays collected in* Teaching a Stone to Talk *(1982),* The Writing
Life *(1989), and* For the Time Being *(1999); literary criticism in* Living by Fiction *(1982) and* Encounters with Chinese Writers *(1984); the autobiography*
An American Childhood *(1987); and, most recently, a novel,* The Maytrees
*(2007). In 1999 she was inducted into the American Academy of Arts and Let-
ters. Dillard currently lives in North Carolina and is professor emeritus at
Wesleyan University.*

THE CHASE

In her autobiography, An American Childhood, *Dillard's enthusiasm for life
in its many forms colors her recollections of her own youth. "The Chase" (editor's title) is a self-contained chapter from the book that narrates a few minutes of glorious excitement.*

Some boys taught me to play football. This was fine sport. You thought   *1*
up a new strategy for every play and whispered it to the others. You
went out for a pass, fooling everyone. Best, you got to throw yourself
mightily at someone's running legs. Either you brought him down or
you hit the ground flat out on your chin, with your arms empty before
you. It was all or nothing. If you hesitated in fear, you would miss and
get hurt: you would take a hard fall while the kid got away, or you
would get kicked in the face while the kid got away. But if you flung
yourself wholeheartedly at the back of his knees — if you gathered and
joined body and soul and pointed them diving fearlessly — then you
likely wouldn't get hurt, and you'd stop the ball. Your fate, and your
team's score, depended on your concentration and courage. Nothing
girls did could compare with it.

Boys welcomed me at baseball, too, for I had, through enthusias-   *2*
tic practice, what was weirdly known as a boy's arm. In winter, in the
snow, there was neither baseball nor football, so the boys and I threw
snowballs at passing cars. I got in trouble throwing snowballs, and have
seldom been happier since.

On one weekday morning after Christmas, six inches of new snow had   *3*
just fallen. We were standing up to our boot tops in snow on a front
yard on trafficked Reynolds Street, waiting for cars. The cars traveled
Reynolds Street slowly and evenly; they were targets all but wrapped
in red ribbons, cream puffs. We couldn't miss.

I was seven; the boys were eight, nine, and ten. The oldest two   *4*
Fahey boys were there — Mikey and Peter — polite blond boys who lived
near me on Lloyd Street, and who already had four brothers and sisters.
My parents approved of Mikey and Peter Fahey. Chickie McBride was
there, a tough kid, and Billy Paul and Mackie Kean too, from across
Reynolds, where the boys grew up dark and furious, grew up skinny,
knowing, and skilled. We had all drifted from our houses that morning
looking for action, and had found it here on Reynolds Street.

It was cloudy but cold. The cars' tires laid behind them on the   *5*
snowy street a complex trail of beige chunks like crenellated castle
walls. I had stepped on some earlier; they squeaked. We could have
wished for more traffic. When a car came, we all popped it one. In the
intervals between cars we reverted to the natural solitude of children.

I started making an iceball — a perfect iceball, from perfectly white   *6*
snow, perfectly spherical, and squeezed perfectly translucent so no
snow remained all the way through. (The Fahey boys and I considered

it unfair actually to throw an iceball at somebody, but it had been known to happen.)

I had just embarked on the iceball project when we heard tire   7
chains come clanking from afar. A black Buick was moving toward us down the street. We all spread out, banged together some regular snow-balls, took aim, and, when the Buick drew nigh, fired.

A soft snowball hit the driver's windshield right before the driver's   8
face. It made a smashed star with a hump in the middle.

Often, of course, we hit our target, but this time, the only time   9
in all of life, the car pulled over and stopped. Its wide black door opened; a man got out of it, running. He didn't even close the car door.

He ran after us, and we ran away from him, up the snowy   10
Reynolds sidewalk. At the corner, I looked back; incredibly, he was still after us. He was in city clothes: a suit and tie, street shoes. Any nor-mal adult would have quit, having sprung us into flight and made his point. This man was gaining on us. He was a thin man, all action. All of a sudden, we were running for our lives.

Wordless, we split up. We were on our turf; we could lose ourselves   11
in the neighborhood backyards, everyone for himself. I paused and con-sidered. Everyone had vanished except Mike Fahey, who was just rounding the corner of a yellow brick house. Poor Mikey, I trailed him. The driver of the Buick sensibly picked the two of us to follow. The man apparently had all day.

He chased Mikey and me around the yellow house and up a back-   12
yard path we knew by heart: under a low tree, up a bank, through a hedge, down some snowy steps, and across the grocery store's deliv-ery driveway. We smashed through a gap in another hedge, entered a scruffy backyard and ran around its back porch and tight between houses to Edgerton Avenue; we ran across Edgerton to an alley and up our own sliding woodpile to the Halls' front yard; he kept coming. We ran up Lloyd Street and wound through mazy backyards toward the steep hilltop at Willard and Lang.

He chased us silently, block after block. He chased us silently over   13
picket fences, through thorny hedges, between houses, around garbage cans, and across streets. Every time I glanced back, choking for breath, I expected he would have quit. He must have been as breathless as we were. His jacket strained over his body. It was an immense discovery, pounding into my hot head with every sliding, joyous step, that this or-dinary adult evidently knew what I thought only children who trained at football knew: that you have to fling yourself at what you're doing, you have to point yourself, forget yourself, aim, dive.

Mikey and I had nowhere to go, in our own neighborhood or out   *14*
of it, but away from this man who was chasing us. He impelled us forward; we compelled him to follow our route. The air was cold; every
breath tore my throat. We kept running, block after block; we kept im-
provising, backyard after backyard, running a frantic course and choosing it simultaneously, failing always to find small places or hard places
to slow him down, and discovering always, exhilarated, dismayed, that
only bare speed could save us — for he would never give up, this man —
and we were losing speed.

He chased us through the backyard labyrinths of ten blocks before   *15*
he caught us by our jackets. He caught us and we all stopped.

We three stood staggering, half blinded, coughing, in an obscure   *16*
hilltop backyard: a man in his twenties, a boy, a girl. He had released
our jackets, our pursuer, our captor, our hero: he knew we weren't
going anywhere. We all played by the rules. Mikey and I unzipped our
jackets. I pulled off my sopping mittens. Our tracks multiplied in the
backyard's new snow. We had been breaking new snow all morning.
We didn't look at each other. I was cherishing my excitement. The
man's lower pants legs were wet; his cuffs were full of snow, and there
was a prow of snow beneath them on his shoes and socks. Some trees
bordered the little flat backyard, some messy winter trees. There was
no one around: a clearing in a grove, and we the only players.

It was a long time before he could speak. I had some difficulty at   *17*
first recalling why we were there. My lips felt swollen; I couldn't see
out of the sides of my eyes; I kept coughing.

"You stupid kids," he began perfunctorily.   *18*

We listened perfunctorily indeed, if we listened at all, for the chew-   *19*
ing out was redundant, a mere formality, and beside the point. The
point was that he had chased us passionately without giving up, and so
he had caught us. Now he came down to earth. I wanted the glory to
last forever.

But how could the glory have lasted forever? We could have run   *20*
through every backyard in North America until we got to Panama. But
when he trapped us at the lip of the Panama Canal, what precisely
could he have done to prolong the drama of the chase and cap its
glory? I brooded about this for the next few years. He could only have
fried Mikey Fahey and me in boiling oil, say, or dismembered us piece-
meal, or staked us to anthills. None of which I really wanted, and none
of which any adult was likely to do, even in the spirit of fun. He could
only chew us out there in the Panamanian jungle, after months or
years of exalting pursuit. He could only begin, "You stupid kids," and

continue in his ordinary Pittsburgh accent with his normal righteous anger and the usual common sense.

    If in that snowy backyard the driver of the black Buick had cut off   *21* our heads, Mikey's and mine, I would have died happy, for nothing has required so much of me since as being chased all over Pittsburgh in the middle of winter — running terrified, exhausted — by this sainted, skinny, furious red-headed man who wished to have a word with us. I don't know how he found his way back to his car.

Meaning

1. What lesson did Dillard learn from the experience of the chase? Where is her point explicitly revealed?
2. In paragraph 2 Dillard writes, "I got in trouble throwing snowballs, and have seldom been happier since." What exactly is Dillard saying about the relationship between trouble and happiness? Do you think she is recommending "getting in trouble" as a means to happiness? Why, or why not?
3. If you do not know the meanings of the following words, try to guess them from the context of Dillard's essay. Test your guesses in a dictionary, and then try to use each word in a sentence or two of your own.

crenellated (5)	compelled (14)	perfunctorily (18, 19)
translucent (6)	improvising (14)	redundant (19)
embarked (7)	labyrinths (15)	exalting (20)
impelled (14)	obscure (16)	

Purpose and Audience

1. What seems to be Dillard's purpose in "The Chase": to encourage children to get into trouble? to encourage adults to be more tolerant of children who get into trouble? to do something else?
2. In her first paragraph, Dillard deliberately shifts from the first-person point of view (using *me*) to the second (using *you*). What is the effect of this shift, and how does it contribute to Dillard's purpose?

Method and Structure

1. Why do you think Dillard chose narration to illustrate her point about the difference between children and adults? What does she gain from this method? What other methods might she have used?
2. In this straightforward narrative, Dillard expands some events and summarizes others: for instance, she provides much more detail about the

chase in paragraph 12 than in paragraphs 13 and 14. Why might she first provide and then pull back from the detail in paragraph 12?

3. How does the last sentence of paragraph 2 — "I got in trouble throwing snowballs, and have seldom been happier since" — serve to set up the story Dillard is about to tell?

4. **Other Methods**   Dillard makes extensive use of description (Chapter 4). Locate examples of this method and analyze what they contribute to the essay as a whole.

Language

1. How would you characterize Dillard's style? How does the style reflect the fact that the adult Dillard is writing from a child's point of view?

2. What does Dillard mean by calling the man who chases her "sainted" (paragraph 21)? What is her attitude toward this man? What words and passages support your answer?

3. Consider Dillard's description of cars: traveling down the street, they looked like "targets all but wrapped in red ribbons, cream puffs" (paragraph 3), and their tires in the snow left "a complex trail of beige chunks like crenellated castle walls" (5). What is the dominant impression created here?

Writing Topics

1. **Journal to Essay**   Write a narrative essay about the incident of misbehavior you explored in your journal entry (p. 90). Use the first-person, *I*, strong verbs, and plenty of descriptive details to render vividly the event and its effects on you and others.

2. Write a narrative essay about a time you discovered that an "ordinary adult" knew some truth you thought only children knew. What was that truth, and why did you believe until that moment that only children knew it? What did this adult do to change your mind?

3. Though Dillard focuses on a time when no harm was done, the consequences of throwing snowballs at moving cars could be quite serious. Rewrite the essay from the point of view of someone who would *not* glorify the children's behavior — the man driving the Buick, for instance, or one of the children's parents. How might one of these people narrate these events? On what might he or she focus?

4. **Cultural Considerations**   Childhood pranks like throwing snowballs at cars are tolerated more in some cultural groups than in others. In a narrative essay, retell an event in your childhood when you felt you were testing the rules of behavior in your culture. Make your motivations as clear as possible, and reflect on the results of your action.

5. **Connections**   Annie Dillard and Alaina Wong ("China Doll," p. 251) share an exuberant attitude toward their childhoods, at least toward the small portions they describe in their essays. But Wong focuses on a concrete, specific object, while Dillard focuses on an event. Write an essay examining the effects each essay has on you, and why. What techniques does each writer use to create these effects?

Nothing is more restful than conformity. —Elizabeth Bowen

We all try to be alike in our youth. —Alec Tweedie

This above all: to thine own self be true, / And it must follow, as the night the day, / Thou canst not then be false to any man. —William Shakespeare

Journal Response When have you experienced a powerful desire to think, look, or act like others, especially your peers? Write a journal entry about your experience.

——————— **Langston Hughes** ———————

A poet, fiction writer, playwright, critic, and humorist, Langston Hughes described his writing as "largely concerned with depicting Negro life in America." He was born in 1902 in Joplin, Missouri, and grew up in Illinois, Kansas, and Ohio. After dropping out of Columbia University in the early 1920s, Hughes worked at odd jobs while struggling to gain recognition as a writer. His first book of poems, The Weary Blues *(1925), helped seed the Harlem Renaissance, a flowering of African American music and literature centered in the Harlem district of New York City during the 1920s. The book also generated a scholarship that enabled Hughes to finish college at Lincoln University. In all of his work — including* The Negro Mother *(1931),* The Ways of White Folks *(1934),* Shakespeare in Harlem *(1942),* Montage of a Dream Deferred *(1951),* Ask Your Mama *(1961), and* The Best of Simple *(1961) — Hughes captured and projected the rhythms of jazz and the distinctive speech, subtle humor, and deep traditions of African American people. He died in New York City in 1967.*

SALVATION

A chapter in Hughes's autobiography, The Big Sea *(1940), "Salvation" is a simple yet compelling narrative about a moment of deceit and disillusionment for a boy of twelve. As you read Hughes's account, notice how the opening two sentences set up every twist of the story.*

I was saved from sin when I was going on thirteen. But not really saved.   *1*
It happened like this. There was a big revival at my Auntie Reed's
church. Every night for weeks there had been much preaching, singing,

praying, and shouting, and some very hardened sinners had been brought to Christ, and the membership of the church had grown by leaps and bounds. Then just before the revival ended, they held a special meeting for children, "to bring the young lambs to the fold." My aunt spoke of it for days ahead. That night, I was escorted to the front row and placed on the mourner's bench with all the other young sinners, who had not yet been brought to Jesus.

My aunt told me that when you were saved you saw a light, and something happened to you inside! And Jesus came into your life! And God was with you from then on! She said you could see and hear and feel Jesus in your soul. I believed her. I have heard a great many old people say the same thing and it seemed to me they ought to know. So I sat there calmly in the hot, crowded church, waiting for Jesus to come to me. 2

The preacher preached a wonderful rhythmical sermon, all moans and shouts and lonely cries and dire pictures of hell, and then he sang a song about the ninety and nine safe in the fold, but one little lamb was left out in the cold. Then he said: "Won't you come? Won't you come to Jesus? Young lambs, won't you come?" And he held out his arms to all us young sinners there on the mourner's bench. And the little girls cried. And some of them jumped up and went to Jesus right away. But most of us just sat there. 3

A great many old people came and knelt around us and prayed, old women with jet-black faces and braided hair, old men with work-gnarled hands. And the church sang a song about the lower lights are burning, some poor sinners to be saved. And the whole building rocked with prayer and song. 4

Still I kept waiting to *see* Jesus. 5

Finally all the young people had gone to the altar and were saved, but one boy and me. He was a rounder's son named Westley. Westley and I were surrounded by sisters and deacons praying. It was very hot in the church, and getting late now. Finally Westley said to me in a whisper: "God damn! I'm tired o' sitting here. Let's get up and be saved." So he got up and was saved. 6

Then I was left all alone on the mourner's bench. My aunt came and knelt at my knees and cried, while prayers and songs swirled all around me in the little church. The whole congregation prayed for me alone, in a mighty wail of moans and voices. And I kept waiting serenely for Jesus, waiting, waiting—but he didn't come. I wanted to see him, but nothing happened to me. Nothing! I wanted something to happen to me, but nothing happened. 7

I heard the songs and the minister saying: "Why don't you come?   8
My dear child, why don't you come to Jesus? Jesus is waiting for you.
He wants you. Why don't you come? Sister Reed, what is this child's
name?"

"Langston," my aunt sobbed.   9

"Langston, why don't you come? Why don't you come and be   10
saved? Oh, Lamb of God! Why don't you come?"

Now it was really getting late. I began to be ashamed of myself,   11
holding everything up so long. I began to wonder what God thought
about Westley, who certainly hadn't seen Jesus either, but who was
now sitting proudly on the platform, swinging his knickerbockered legs
and grinning down at me, surrounded by deacons and old women on
their knees praying. God had not struck Westley dead for taking his
name in vain or for lying in the temple. So I decided that maybe to save
further trouble, I'd better lie, too, and say that Jesus had come, and get
up and be saved.

So I got up.   12

Suddenly the whole room broke into a sea of shouting, as they saw   13
me rise. Waves of rejoicing swept the place. Women leaped in the air.
My aunt threw her arms around me. The minister took me by the hand
and led me to the platform.

When things quieted down, in a hushed silence, punctuated by a   14
few ecstatic "Amens," all the new young lambs were blessed in the
name of God. Then joyous singing filled the room.

That night, for the last time in my life but one — for I was a big boy   15
twelve years old — I cried. I cried, in bed alone, and couldn't stop.
I buried my head under the quilts, but my aunt heard me. She woke
up and told my uncle I was crying because the Holy Ghost had come
into my life, and because I had seen Jesus. But I was really crying because I couldn't bear to tell her that I had lied, that I had deceived everybody in the church, that I hadn't seen Jesus, and that now I didn't believe
there was a Jesus anymore, since he didn't come to help me.

Meaning

1. What is the main point of Hughes's narrative? What change occurs in him
   as a result of his experience?
2. What finally makes Hughes decide to get up and be saved? How does this
   decision affect him afterward?
3. What do you make of the title and the first two sentences? What is Hughes
   saying here about "salvation"?

4. If you are unfamiliar with any of the following words, try to guess what they mean from the context of Hughes's essay. Test your guesses in a dictionary, and then try to use each word in a sentence or two of your own.

dire (3)
rounder (6)
deacons (6)

Purpose and Audience

1. Why do you think Hughes wrote "Salvation" as part of his autobiography more than two decades after the experience? Was his purpose simply to express feelings prompted by a significant event in his life? Did he want to criticize his aunt and the other adults in the congregation? Did he want to explain something about childhood or about the distance between generations? What passages support your answer?
2. What does Hughes seem to assume about his readers' familiarity with the kind of service he describes? What details help make the procedure clear?
3. How do dialogue, lines from hymns, and details of other sounds (paragraphs 3–10) help re-create the increasing pressure Hughes feels? What other details contribute to this sense of pressure?

Method and Structure

1. Why do you think Hughes chose narration to explore the themes of this essay? Can you imagine an argumentative essay (Chapter 13) that would deal with the same themes? What might its title be?
2. Where in his narrative does Hughes insert explanations, compress time by summarizing events, or jump ahead in time by omitting events? Where does he expand time by drawing moments out? How does each of these insertions and manipulations of time relate to Hughes's main point?
3. In paragraph 1 Hughes uses several transitions to signal the sequence of events and the passage of time: "for weeks," "Then just before," "for days ahead," "That night." Where does he use similar signals in the rest of the essay?
4. **Other Methods**   Hughes's narrative also explains a process (Chapter 9): we learn how a revival meeting works. Why is this process analysis essential to the essay?

Language

1. What does Hughes's language reveal about his adult attitudes toward his experience? Does he feel anger? bitterness? sorrow? guilt? shame? amusement? What words and passages support your answer?

2. Hughes relates his experience in an almost childlike style, using many short sentences and beginning many sentences with *And*. What effect do you think he is trying to achieve with this style?

3. Hughes expects to "see" Jesus when he is saved (paragraphs 2, 5, 7), and afterward his aunt thinks that he has "seen" Jesus (15). What does each of them mean by *see*? What is the significance of the difference in Hughes's story?

Writing Topics

1. **Journal to Essay**   Continuing from your journal entry (p. 97), write a narrative essay about a time when others significantly influenced the way you thought, looked, or acted — perhaps against your own true beliefs or values. What was the appeal of the others' attitudes, appearance, or behavior? What did you gain by conforming? What did you lose? Use specific details to explain how and why the experience affected you.

2. Hughes says, "I have heard a great many old people say the same thing and it seemed to me they ought to know" (paragraph 2). Think of a piece of information or advice that you heard over and over again from adults when you were a child. Write a narrative essay about an experience in which you were helped or misled by that information or advice.

3. **Cultural Considerations**   It seems that Hughes wants to be saved largely because of the influence of his family and his community. Westley (paragraphs 6 and 11) represents another kind of influence, peer pressure, that often works against family and community. Think of an incident in your own life when you felt pressured by peers to go against your parents, religion, school, or another authority. Write a narrative essay telling what happened and making it clear why the situation was important to you. What were the results?

4. **Connections**   When Hughes doesn't see Jesus and then lies to satisfy everyone around him, he feels betrayed and pained. How does Hughes's experience differ from the one cheerfully reported by Michael Ondaatje (p. 83), in which a potentially deadly snake is said to be Ondaatje's deceased father, "come to protect his family"? Write an essay analyzing what elements these narratives have in common and any significant differences between them.

Racism and class hatred are a learned activity, and as a kid I found myself in a society that was all too ready to teach it. —Henry A. Giroux

Sometimes, I feel discriminated against, but it does not make me angry. It merely astonishes me. How can any deny themselves the pleasure of my company? —Zora Neale Hurston

I have a dream that my four little children will one day live in a nation where they will not be judged by the color of their skin but by the content of their character. —Martin Luther King Jr.

Journal Response   In a journal entry, look back on a time in your past when you were surprised by another person's opinion of one of your friends. Try to convey how your perspectives differed and why your point of view seemed more logical to you at the time. Has your perspective changed now that you're an adult?

Kaela Hobby-Reichstein

Kaela Hobby-Reichstein was born in 1981 and grew up in Philadelphia. A teacher got her interested in writing while she was a high school student at Germantown Friends School, and she immersed herself in writing projects as an undergraduate at the University of Massachusetts Amherst. Hobby-Reichstein worked to support herself as she completed her undergraduate thesis and spent some time in the African country of Ghana before graduating with a degree in African American studies in 2007. She hopes to return to Africa to do development work in microfinance with an international organization.

LEARNING RACE
(STUDENT ESSAY)

Hobby-Reichstein, who reports that she is "still fascinated by race," first wrote this essay while in high school and rewrote it for her required freshman writing course in 1999. In her narrative she recounts two episodes from her childhood to re-create the gradual discovery of an ugly truth.

A few weeks ago as we sat down for lunch, my best friend, Ryan, asked   1
me when I learned what race was. My mind searched and searched, but I couldn't pin down an answer. It was not an easy question. I have

known Ryan since I was two. We grew up in neighboring apartments where we shared a wall as well as each other's toys and families. I can't remember a time without her or the exact moment I realized I was white, she was black, and what that meant. Of course, I always knew the creamy pink color of my skin and deep brown color of her skin weren't the same, but really understanding this took me many years.

My first memory is from kindergarten, Ms. Oakleaf's class at   2
C. W. Henry Elementary School. It was a normal day. The room, like most kindergarten classrooms, was overflowing with bright colors and various animal posters. The kids sat at their respective tables scratching their heads because of the recent lice invasion in our cubbies. Ms. Oakleaf stood at the front of the class swimming in her dated plaid pants suit and announced our next project.

"Children, would you all please stand in front of your easels."   3

Our chairs made an extremely annoying metallic noise as we   4
jumped from our plastic seats and pushed each other on the way to our easels.

"I would like you to put on your smocks and paint a picture of   5
your family for me."

At my easel, I velcroed my smock behind my neck and assessed the   6
colors they had set out for us. There was the usual red, yellow, blue, green, purple, and orange as well as two new colors, skin colors, brown and peach. First, I painted a rainbow in the top left corner of my paper because back then there were rainbows in everything I painted. Second, I painted a stick figure of myself with colorful clothing, curly blue hair and peach skin. I dipped my finger into the paint to make sure it was the right color. Next to me I painted my father. I chose the brown paint for him because his skin is darker than mine. Next to my father I painted my mother with peach paint. And next to her I painted my half brother in brown paint. My color selection seemed logical to me. In Ryan's family, she and her mom were the same color, brown. Her father and her stepbrother were peach, like me. Girls in a family were one color and boys in a family were another.

Ms. Oakleaf came around when we had all finished our paintings   7
and informed me my painting was wrong. She had met my family and knew all four of us were white. At the time, she wouldn't explain why it was wrong. She told me to talk to my parents about it when I got home, which I did. When my mom's Honda pulled up in front of the school, I ran outside, with my painting in hand. I asked her if Dad was light black or dark white and told her I thought he was light black. She laughed for a long time and then told me my father was not black but

white. I painted a new picture of my family that night with all peach people and a rainbow in the corner and learned that my family and I were white and Ryan and her mom were black.

Though I was now aware that people were different colors, I didn't   8
really know what those colors meant. My mother cooked mostly bland foods: oatmeal, boiled chicken, and potatoes. Ryan's family ate grits, crabs, fried chicken, and added lots of spices to everything. My mom told me to say "Ryan and I" rather than "me and Ryan." Ryan's mom said "y'all" and "ain't." Ryan's family loved listening to loud music, and my family didn't really listen to music at all. Ryan's Barbies were black. My mom felt Barbie degraded women. Ryan's mom used a pick when she did her hair, and my mom used a brush, though we both screamed just as loud. There were no concrete things that made her black and me white, and growing up across the hall from each other, I'm sure we had picked up a number of each other's cultural attributes.

It was also with Ryan that I learned about bigotry. I think I was   9
in fourth grade, though I'm not really sure. Her father was driving us to dinner at her grandmother's house. Her grandmother lived in Fort Richmond, which could be described as a blue-collar Italian neighborhood, where the rest of her father's family lived. The streets were lined with old American cars. Along the river, factories that employed most of the neighborhood puffed out huge clouds of smoke. Everyone lived in a row house and therefore knew everyone else's business. It was the middle of the summer, and as we pulled up we saw a group of kids gathered around the fire hydrant cooling off and joking around in the powerful spray. We begged her dad to let us go play with the other kids, and he parked the car as we ran down the street toward the kids. As we got closer, they looked up. Their eyes froze on our little bodies, and their smiles turned to frowns.

"Get out of here."   10

"What do you think you are doing?"   11

"You don't belong here, monkey."   12

"Nigger lover, get that nigger out of here."   13

We stopped and stared at them, examining their faces for reasons, 14 logic, justification. They threw rocks at us and we ran. At that moment, I learned the feeling of hatred and it hurt. My head ached from sobbing, my body hurt from running so hard and fast, and my stomach turned remembering the looks on their faces and the way the words rolled off their tongues. My eyes burned with injustice as I imagined being able to fry them with a look. Shards of childlike innocence caught in my throat, making it impossible to respond or even speak. It is a feeling that I have felt many times since then and has yet to soften. I felt it when I saw Ryan's mom put a pretty peach Band-Aid on her smooth chocolate leg, trying not to notice the obvious color clash. I felt it when my next-door neighbor was called a "dirty black man" by a judge in a courtroom full of white people. I felt it when a black man on the bus called me a cracker and spit on my jacket.

So that is how I learned race, to tell the differences between me and so many, to see the bigotry and the hate differences can inspire. It is knowledge that I am glad I have. My awareness of the differences between Ryan and me have helped me understand her and myself better. We still talk every Sunday though we now live three hundred miles apart. My knowledge of hatred has helped me understand right and wrong. My experiences have made me stronger, and it is strength that allows me to speak my mind and possibly end some ignorance and hatred in the process.

Meaning

1. In paragraph 1, Hobby-Reichstein writes that "really understanding" the meaning of race "took ... many years." Where in the essay (if at all) does she share her understanding of what race means? How did Hobby-Reichstein feel about the differences between herself and her best friend as a child? How does she feel about them now?

2. Why did Hobby-Reichstein believe that "girls in a family were one color and boys in a family were another" (paragraph 6)? What does that belief reveal about her understanding of difference?

3. If you are unsure of the meanings of any of the following words, try to guess them from the context of Hobby-Reichstein's essay. Look the words up in a dictionary to test your guesses, and then use each word in a sentence or two of your own.

respective (2)   degraded (8)   justification (14)
swimming (2)   attributes (8)
grits (8)   bigotry (9)

Purpose and Audience

1. It can be very difficult to recall a painful experience in your life, yet Hobby-Reichstein chooses to do so. What do you believe is her purpose in recording these episodes from her childhood: to understand her experiences? to tell her peers about her childhood? to do something else?

2. How does dialogue help re-create the discomfort and shock Hobby-Reichstein felt as a child? Is her repetition of other people's racial slurs (such as "monkey" in paragraph 12, "nigger" in paragraph 13, and "cracker" in paragraph 14) offensive or effective? Why do you think so?

Method and Structure

1. What features of narration make it ideal for describing childhood experiences like the ones documented by Hobby-Reichstein?
2. Although Hobby-Reichstein uses chronological order to organize her experiences, the two major episodes she recounts took place four years apart and her final examples are taken from her adult life. Why do you believe she jumps between time periods? How does this manipulation of narrative time serve the overall purpose of the essay?
3. **Other Methods**   In the middle of her narration (paragraph 8), Hobby-Reichstein compares and contrasts (Chapter 10) her white family with her friend's biracial family. What differences and similarities does she highlight? Why do you think she chose these details for her comparison? What do they contribute to the purpose of her narrative?

Language

1. Hobby-Reichstein uses many figures of speech to enrich her prose, particularly when she recounts her emotional response to the taunts of the young boys: "shards of childlike innocence caught in [her] throat," her "eyes burned with injustice," and she fantasized about "being able to fry them with a look" (paragraph 14). How effective are her figures of speech in reflecting how she felt about her experiences? How do they contribute to the overall meaning of her essay?
2. Although the topic of race is very complicated, Hobby-Reichstein uses relatively simple sentence structures through most of her essay. How does the rhythm of her sentences reinforce her purpose?

Writing Topics

1. **Journal to Essay**   In "Learning Race," Hobby-Reichstein revisits two moments when she was surprised to discover that other people saw her best friend in a much different light than she did. In your journal entry (p. 102), you also recalled a moment when you were surprised by another person's opinion of one of your friends. Elaborate on that memory in a brief narrative essay. Include details of the episode that will make this memory

more vivid and real for your readers. What perspective can you bring to your experience now that you didn't have then?

2. "Learning Race" relies on narrative to recount a difficult and troubling learning experience. Using the same method, write an essay in which you recapture one of the happiest or most exciting discoveries of your childhood: for example, finding a favorite hiding place, learning a skill such as skating or playing a musical instrument, making an unexpected friend, or receiving something you deeply desired. Use straightforward chronological time if that works best, or, like Hobby-Reichstein, compress narrative time to emphasize the most significant moments.

3. **Cultural Considerations**   Many scientists and cultural critics argue that there are no significant biological differences between people of varying colors and ethnicities. Race, they say, is a *social construction*: in other words, our understandings of racial difference are the result of what we're taught by society, not a scientific truth. Hobby-Reichstein's narrative explores one instance of this kind of cultural education: as a child she saw no differences between black and white until adults pointed them out to her, and she continues to reject the labels she was given. Write an essay in which you explore your own understandings of race and try to pinpoint where they came from. When did you first learn that skin color matters in American culture? Do you believe that there are real differences between races, or do you lean toward the idea that skin color is irrelevant? Explain your answer, giving plenty of details from your own experiences.

4. **Connections**   Both Hobby-Reichstein and Marta K. Taylor, in "Desert Dance" (p. 62), write about experiences they had as children. Hobby-Reichstein recalls times of confusion and hurt; Taylor, in contrast, recaptures "a state of grace." Write an essay comparing the two writers' uses of narrative time, dramatic incidents, and language as means of showing readers their experiences.

Narration

Choose one of the following topics, or any other topic they suggest, for an essay developed by narration. The topic you decide on should be something you care about so that narration is a means of communicating an idea, not an end in itself.

FRIENDS AND RELATIONS

1. Gaining independence
2. A friend's generosity or sacrifice
3. A significant trip with your family
4. A wedding or funeral
5. An incident from family legend

THE WORLD AROUND YOU

6. An interaction you witnessed while taking public transportation
7. A storm, a flood, an earthquake, or another natural event
8. The history of your neighborhood
9. The most important minutes of a particular game in baseball, football, basketball, or some other sport
10. A school event, such as a meeting, demonstration, or celebration
11. A time when a poem, story, film, song, or other work left you feeling changed

LESSONS OF DAILY LIFE

12. Acquiring and repaying a debt, either psychological or financial
13. An especially satisfying run, tennis match, bicycle tour, one-on-one basketball game, or other sports experience
14. A time when you confronted authority
15. A time when you had to deliver bad news
16. A time when a new, eagerly anticipated possession proved disappointing
17. Your biggest social blunder

FIRSTS

18. Your first day of school, as a child or more recently
19. The first time you met someone who became important to you
20. The first performance you gave
21. A first date

ADVENTURES

22. An episode of extrasensory perception
23. An intellectual journey: discovering a new field, pursuing a subject, solving a mystery
24. A trip to an unfamiliar place

Recalling Childhood

1. While growing up inevitably involves fear, disappointment, and pain, there is usually security and joy as well. Michael Ondaatje clearly finds comfort in his dead father's reappearance as a cobra (p. 83), Andre Dubus finally earns the respect of his classmates on the softball field (p. 84), Annie Dillard relishes the thrill of being chased (p. 90), and Kaela Hobby-Reichstein believes that her childhood experiences with racism strengthened her relationship with her best friend (p. 102). Write a narrative essay about a similarly mixed experience from your childhood, making sure to describe your feelings vividly so that your readers share them with you.

2. The vulnerability of children is a recurring theme in the essays and paragraphs in this chapter. Andre Dubus, Langston Hughes (p. 97), and Kaela Hobby-Reichstein all write in some way about psychological pain. After considering each writer's situation individually, write an essay analyzing the differences among these situations. Based on these narratives, which writers seem to have the most in common? Which of their responses seem unique to children? Which are most likely to be outgrown?

3. Childhood is full of epiphanies, or sudden moments of realization, insight, or understanding. Langston Hughes and Annie Dillard both report such moments at the ends of their essays: Hughes loses faith in a Jesus who would not help him in church, and Dillard recognizes that any experience of glorious happiness must end. Write a narrative essay in which you tell of events leading to an epiphany when you were growing up. Make sure both the events themselves and the nature of the epiphany are vividly clear.

Chapter 6

EXAMPLE

Using Language

An **example** represents a general group or an abstract concept or quality. Steven Spielberg is an example of the group of movie directors. A friend's calling at 2:00 a.m. is an example of her inconsiderateness—or desperation. We habitually use examples to bring broad ideas down to specifics so that others will take an interest in them and understand them. You might use examples to entertain friends with the idea that you're accident prone, to convince family members that a sibling is showing self-destructive behavior that requires intervention, to demonstrate to voters that your local fire department deserves a budget increase, or to convince your employer that competing companies' benefits packages are more generous. Examples are so central to human communication, in fact, that you will find them in nearly everything you read and use them in nearly everything you write.

READING EXAMPLES

The chief purpose of examples is to make the general specific and the abstract concrete. Since these operations are among the most basic in writing, it is easy to see why illustration or exemplification (the use of example) is among the most common methods of writing. Examples

111

appear frequently in essays developed by other methods. In fact, as diverse as they are, all the essays in this book employ examples for clarity, support, and liveliness. If the writers had not used examples, we might have only a vague sense of their meaning or, worse, might supply mistaken meanings from our own experiences.

While nearly indispensable in any kind of writing, exemplification may also serve as the dominant method of developing an essay. When a writer's primary goal is to convince readers of the truth of a general statement—whether a personal observation or a controversial assertion—using examples is a natural choice. Any of the following generalizations, for instance, might form the central assertion of an essay developed by example:

- Generalizations about trends: "MP3 players are forcing the recording industry to rethink the way it does business."
- Generalizations about events: "Some fans at the championship game were more competitive than the players."
- Generalizations about institutions: "A mental hospital is no place for the mentally ill."
- Generalizations about behaviors: "The personalities of parents are sometimes visited on their children."
- Generalizations about rituals: "A funeral benefits the dead person's family and friends."

How many examples are necessary to support a generalization? That depends on a writer's subject, purpose, and intended audience. Two basic patterns are possible:

- A single **extended example** of several paragraphs or several pages fills in needed background and gives the reader a complete view of the subject from one angle. For instance, the purpose of a funeral might be made clear with a narrative and descriptive account of a particular funeral, the family and friends who attended it, and the benefits they derived from it.
- **Multiple examples**, from a few to dozens, illustrate the range covered by the generalization. The competitiveness of a team's fans might be captured with three or four examples. But supporting the generalization about mental hospitals might demand many examples of patients whose illnesses worsened in the hospital or (from a different angle) many examples of hospital practices that actually harm patients.

Sometimes a generalization merits support from both an extended example and several briefer examples, a combination that provides depth along with range. For instance, half the essay on mental hospitals might be devoted to one patient's experiences and the other half to brief summaries of others' experiences.

When you read essays developed by illustration and exemplification, pay attention to how writers use examples to develop a point. Rarely will a simple list do an idea justice. Effective writers, you will see, not only provide examples but also explain how those examples support their ideas.

ANALYZING EXAMPLES IN PARAGRAPHS

Deborah Tannen (born 1945), a respected scholar with a knack for popular writing, is widely known for her prolific work on how men and women communicate. The following paragraph is from the book *Talking from 9 to 5* (1994), Tannen's best-selling exploration of gender differences in workplace communication.

Women are often told they apologize too much. The reason they're told to stop doing it is that, to many men, apologizing seems synonymous with putting oneself down. <u>But there are many times when "I'm sorry" isn't self-deprecating, or even an apology; it's an automatic way of keeping both speakers on an equal footing.</u> For example, a well-known columnist once interviewed me and gave me her phone number in case I needed to call her back. I misplaced the number and had to go through the newspaper's main switchboard. When our conversation was winding down and we'd both made ending-type remarks, I added, "Oh, I almost forgot—I lost your direct number, can I get it again?" "Oh, I'm sorry," she came back instantly, even though she had done nothing wrong and *I* was the one who'd lost the number. But I understood she wasn't really apologizing; she was just automatically reassuring me she had no intention of denying me her number.

Generalization and topic sentence (underlined)

Single detailed example

William Lutz (born 1940) is an expert on doublespeak, which he defines as "language that conceals or manipulates thought. It makes the bad seem good, the negative appear positive, the unpleasant appear attractive or at least tolerable." In this paragraph from his book *Doublespeak* (1989), Lutz illustrates one use of this deceptive language.

Because it avoids or shifts responsibility, doublespeak is particularly effective in explaining or at least glossing over accidents. An air force colonel in charge of safety wrote in a letter that rocket boosters weighing more than 300,000 pounds "have an explosive force upon surface impact that is sufficient to exceed the accepted overpressure threshold of physiological damage for exposed personnel." In English: if a 300,000-pound booster rocket falls on you, you probably won't survive. In 1985 three American soldiers were killed and sixteen were injured when the first stage of a Pershing II missile they were unloading suddenly ignited. There was no explosion, said Major Michael Griffen, but rather "an unplanned rapid ignition of solid fuel."

> Generalization and topic sentence (underlined)

> Two examples

DEVELOPING AN ESSAY BY EXAMPLE
Getting Started

You need examples whenever your experiences, observations, or reading lead you to make a general statement; the examples give readers evidence for the statement so that they see its truth. An appropriate subject for an example paper is likely to be a general idea you have formed about people, things, the media, or any other feature of your life. Say, for instance, that you have noticed while watching television that many programs aimed at teenagers deal with sensitive topics such as drug abuse, domestic violence, or chronic illness. There is a promising subject: teen dramas that address controversial social issues.

After choosing a subject, you should make a list of all the pertinent examples that occur to you. This stage may take some thought and even some further reading or observation. When you're making this list, focus on identifying as many examples as you can, but keep your intended readers at the front of your mind: what do they already know about your subject, and what do they need to know in order to accept your view of it?

Forming a Thesis

Having several examples of a subject is a good starting place, but you will also need a thesis that ties the examples together and gives them a point. A clear thesis is crucial for an example paper because without it readers can only guess what your illustrations are intended to show.

To move from a general subject toward a workable thesis, try making a generalization based on what you know of individual examples, for instance:

> Some teen dramas do a surprisingly good job of dramatizing and explaining difficult social issues.

> Some teen dramas trivialize difficult social issues in their quest for higher ratings.

Either of these statements could serve as the thesis of an essay, the point you want readers to take away from your examples.

Avoid the temptation to start with a broad statement and then try to drum up a few examples to prove it. A thesis such as "Teenagers do poorly in school because they watch too much television" would require factual support gained from research, not the lone example of your brother. If your brother performs poorly in school and you attribute his performance to his television habits, then narrow your thesis so that it accurately reflects your evidence—perhaps "In the case of my brother, at least, the more time spent watching television the poorer the grades."

After arriving at your thesis, you should narrow your list of examples down to those that are most pertinent, adding new ones as necessary to persuade readers of your point. For instance, in illustrating the social value of teen dramas for readers who believe television is worthless or even harmful, you might concentrate on the programs or individual episodes that are most relevant to readers' lives, providing enough detail about each to make readers see the relevance.

Organizing

Most example essays open with an introduction that engages readers' attention and gives them some context to relate to. You might begin the paper on teen dramas, for instance, by briefly narrating the plot of one episode. The opening should lead into your thesis sentence so that readers know what to expect from the rest of the essay.

Organizing the body of the essay may not be difficult if you use a single example, for the example itself may suggest a distinct method of development (such as narration) and thus an arrangement. But an essay using multiple examples usually requires close attention to arrangement so that readers experience not a list but a pattern. Some guidelines:

- With a limited number of examples—say, four or five—use a climactic organization (p. 37), arranging examples in order of increasing importance, interest, or complexity. Then the strongest and most detailed example provides a dramatic finish.

- With very many examples—ten or more—find some likenesses among examples that will allow you to treat them in groups. For instance, instead of covering fourteen teen dramas in a shapeless list, you might group them by subject into shows dealing with family relations, those dealing with illness, and the like. (This is the method of classification discussed in Chapter 8.) Covering each group in a separate paragraph or two would avoid the awkward string of choppy paragraphs that might result from covering each example independently. And arranging the groups themselves in order of increasing interest or importance would further structure your presentation.

To conclude your essay, you may want to summarize by elaborating on the generalization of your thesis now that you have supported it. But the essay may not require a conclusion at all if you believe your final example emphasizes your point and provides a strong finish.

Drafting

While you draft your essay, remember that your examples must be plentiful and specific enough to support your generalization. If you use fifteen different examples, their range should allow you to treat each one briefly, in one or two sentences. But if you use only three examples, say, you will have to describe each one in sufficient detail to make up for their small number. And, obviously, if you use only a single example, you must be as specific as possible so that readers see clearly how it illustrates your generalization.

Revising and Editing

To be sure you've met the expectations that most readers hold for examples, revise and edit your draft by considering the following questions and the information in the box.

- *Is your generalization fully supported by your examples?* If not, you may need to narrow your thesis statement or add more evidence to prove your point.
- *Are all examples, or parts of a single example, obviously relevant to your generalization?* Be careful not to get sidetracked by interesting but unrelated information.

- *Are the examples specific?* Examples bring a generalization down to earth only if they are well detailed. For an essay on the social value of teen dramas, for instance, simply naming representative programs and their subjects would not demonstrate their social value. Each drama would need a plot or character summary that shows how the program fits and illustrates the generalization.

- *Do the examples, or the parts of a single example, cover all the territory mapped out by your generalization?* To support your generalization, you need to present a range of instances that fairly represents the whole. An essay would be misleading if it failed to acknowledge that not *all* teen dramas have social value. It would also be misleading if it presented several shows as representative examples of socially valuable teen programming when in fact they were the *only* instances of such television.

FOCUS ON SENTENCE VARIETY

While accumulating and detailing examples during drafting, you may find yourself writing strings of similar sentences:

> UNVARIED   One example of a teen drama that deals with chronic illness is *Rockingham Place*. Another example is *The Beating Heart*. Another is *Tree of Life*. These three shows treat misunderstood or little-known diseases in a way that increases the viewer's sympathy and understanding. The characters in *Rockingham Place* include a little boy who suffers from cystic fibrosis. *The Beating Heart* features a mother of four who is weakening from multiple sclerosis. *Tree of Life* deals with brothers who are both struggling with muscular dystrophy. All three dramas show complex, struggling human beings caught blamelessly in desperate circumstances.

The writer of this paragraph was clearly pushing to add examples and to expand them — both essential for a successful essay — but the resulting passage needs editing so that the writer's labor isn't so obvious and the sentences are more varied and interesting:

> VARIED   Three teen dramas dealing with chronic illness are *Rockingham Place*, *The Beating Heart*, and *Tree of Life*. In these shows people with little-known or misunderstood diseases become subjects for the viewer's sympathy and understanding. A little boy suffering from cystic fibrosis, a mother of four weakening from multiple sclerosis, a pair of brothers struggling with muscular dystrophy — these complex, struggling human beings are caught blamelessly in desperate circumstances.

For more on sentence variety, see pages 47–48.

A NOTE ON THEMATIC CONNECTIONS

The authors represented in this chapter all have something to say about language—how we use it, abuse it, or change from it. Their ideas probably came to them through examples as they read, talked, and listened, so naturally they use examples to demonstrate those ideas. In one paragraph, Deborah Tannen draws on a single example to show the layers of meaning a simple phrase can convey (p. 113). In another, William Lutz uses two examples to illustrate how evasive doublespeak can be (p. 113). Kim Kessler's essay explores the emergence of the expression *blah blah blah* to end sentences (p. 119). Kirk Johnson questions the common assumption that today's slang is contributing to a decline in the English language (p. 124). And Perri Klass's essay grapples with why doctors use peculiar and often cruel jargon and how it affects them (p. 130).

Sometimes speech is no more than a device for saying nothing.
— Simone de Beauvoir

Continual eloquence is tedious.
— Blaise Pascal

One way of looking at speech is to say it is a constant stratagem to cover nakedness.
— Harold Pinter

Journal Response   Pick a conversation filler that you have noticed, such as *you know* or *I mean*. Why do people use these fillers? Do you use them yourself? Write a journal entry reacting to these words and phrases.

Kim Kessler

Kim Kessler was born in 1975 in New York City and grew up mostly in Greenwich, Connecticut, graduating from high school there. In 1997 she graduated from Brown University and took a job at Vanity Fair *magazine.*

BLAH BLAH BLAH

(STUDENT ESSAY)

Kessler published this essay in the Brown Daily Herald *in 1996, after noticing, she says, that she and her friends "had basically stopped talking to each other in complete sentences." With ample examples and analysis, Kessler questions the uses of the title expression in place of words that the speaker, for some reason, doesn't want to utter.*

"So he says to me, 'Well it just happened. I was this and that and blah blah blah.'" 1

That's an actual quote. That was the statement one of my oh-so-articulate friends made as an explanation of a certain situation. The thing about it is that I figured I knew exactly what he meant. The more important thing about it, the thing that makes this quote notable, is that I feel as though I've been hearing it all over the place these days. It has come to my attention in the last few weeks, maybe even in the last couple of months, that it is common for peers of mine to finish their sentences with "blah blah blah." Some people have their own less common 2 versions of the phrase — e.g., "yadda yadda" or "etc., etc." — but it all amounts to the same thing. Rather than completing a thought or detailing an explanation, sentences simply fade away into a symbol of generic rhetoric.

I'm not quite sure what I think about this recently noticed phenomenon quite yet. What does it mean that I can say "blah blah blah" to you and you consider it to be an acceptable statement? 3

I guess that there are a couple of good reasons for why this is going on. First, it's a commentary on just how trite so many of those conversations we spend our time having really are. Using the phrase is a simple acknowledgment of the fact that what is about to be said has been said so many times before that it is pretty much an exercise in redundancy to say it again. Some folks "blah blah blah" me (yeah, it's a verb) when they're using the phrase as a shortcut; they are eager to get to the part of their story that *does* distinguish it from all the other stories out there. Other times people "blah blah blah" me when they think that it is not worth their time or their energy to actually recount a story for my sake. In this case I feel dismissed, rejected. You can get "blah blahed" (past tense) in an inclusive way, too. In this scenario the "blah blah" construction is used to refer to something that both you and the speaker understand. This reflects a certain intimacy between the speaker and the listener, an intimacy that transcends the need for the English language that strangers would need in order to communicate. 4

I have discovered quite a different use for the phrase. I have found that because "blah blah" is an accepted part of our everyday discourse, and because people assume that with this phrase what you are referring to is indeed the same thing that they are thinking of, it is very easy to use this construction to lie. Well, maybe "lie" isn't the best word. It's usually more of a cover-up than a lie. I'll give an example to demonstrate my meaning here. 5

I'm walking across campus at some time on some Monday. I get accosted by some acquaintance and have the gratuitous "How was your weekend?" conversation. He's asking me about my Saturday night. I reply: "It was good, you know . . . went out to dinner then to a party, blah blah blah." The acquaintance smiles and nods and then goes merrily on his way, his head filled with thoughts of me and my normal Saturday night. What he will never know (as long as he's not reading this) is that I ended that night walking many, many blocks home alone in the rain without a coat, carrying on my back, of all things, a trombone. He also does not know about the mini-breakdown and moment of personal evaluation that my lonely, wet, trombone-carrying state caused me to have under a street- 6 light in the middle of one of those many blocks. He does not know these things because he has constructed his own end to my night to fill in for my "blah blah blah." (I hope you can all handle that open display of vulnerability. It's not very often that I share like that.)

"Blah blah blah" implies the typical. I tend to use it in place of the 7 atypical, usually the atypical of the most embarrassing sort. For me, it's a cop-out. The accepted use of the phrase has allowed me a refuge, a wall of meaningless words with which to protect myself. I'm definitely abusing the term.

Maybe there are a couple of you readers who would want to in- 8 terject here and remind me that not everybody tells the *whole* truth *all* of the time. (I'd guess that there would even be a hint of sarcasm in your voice as you said this to me.) Well, I realize that. I just feel the slightest twinge of guilt because my withholding of the truth has a deceptive element to it.

But, hey, maybe I'm not the only one. Maybe everyone is manipu- 9 lating the phrase "blah blah blah." What if none of us really knows what anyone else is talking about anymore? What are the repercussions of this fill-in-the-blank type of conversation? I feel myself slipping into that very annoying and much too often frequented realm of the overly analytical, so I'm going to stop myself. To those of you who are concerned about this "blah blah" thing I am going to offer the most reasonable solution that I know of—put on your Walkman and avoid it all. The logic here is that the more time you spend with your Walkman on, the less time you spend having those aforementioned gratuitous conversations, and therefore the fewer "blah blahs" you'll have to deal with.

Meaning

1. How does Kessler's use of the phrase *blah blah blah* differ from the normal use, and why does her use bother her?
2. What is the "symbol of generic rhetoric" referred to in paragraph 2? What does Kessler mean by these words? (Consult a dictionary if you're not sure.) Does this sentence state Kessler's main idea? Why, or why not?
3. Try to guess the meanings of any of the following words you are unsure of, based on their context in Kessler's essay. Look the words up in a dictionary to test your guesses, and then use each word in a sentence of your own.

articulate (2)	transcends (4)	atypical (7)
phenomenon (3)	discourse (5)	interject (8)
trite (4)	accosted (6)	repercussions (9)
redundancy (4)	gratuitous (6)	

Purpose and Audience

1. What seems to be Kessler's purpose in this essay: to explain the various ways the phrase *blah blah blah* can be used? to argue against the overuse of the phrase? to do something else?
2. Whom did Kessler assume as her audience? (Look back at the note on the essay, p. 119, if you're not sure.) How do her subject, evidence, and tone reflect such an assumption?

Method and Structure

1. Why do you think Kessler chose to examine this linguistic phenomenon through examples? How do examples help her achieve her purpose in a way that another method might not? (Hint: What is lost when you skip from paragraph 5 to 7?)
2. What generalizations do the examples in paragraphs 4 and 6 support?
3. Which paragraphs fall into the introduction, body, and conclusion of Kessler's essay? What function does each part serve?
4. **Other Methods**   Kessler's essay attempts to define the indefinable, an expression that would seem to have no meaning. What meanings does she find for *blah blah blah*? How does this use of definition (Chapter 11) help Kessler achieve her purpose?

Language

1. How would you characterize Kessler's tone: serious? light? a mix of both? How does this tone reflect her intended audience and her attitude toward her subject?
2. Point out instances of irony in the essay. (See *irony* in the Glossary.)
3. What does Kessler achieve by addressing the reader directly throughout the essay?

Writing Topics

1. **Journal to Essay**   Reread your journal entry (p. 119), and then listen carefully for the conversation filler you've selected in the speech of your friends, the talk you observe on campus or in online chat rooms, and the dialogue in television shows and movies. Form a generalization about the way the filler functions and the purpose or purposes it serves, and then, in an essay, support that generalization with plenty of examples.
2. Write an essay expressing your opinion of Kessler's essay. For instance, how did you react to her complaint that most of her conversations with

her peers were "trite" or "gratuitous"? Do you think she is too critical of her peers? Agree or disagree with Kessler, supporting your opinion with your own examples.

3. **Cultural Considerations**   Although Kessler never explicitly says so, the phenomenon she writes about seems to apply mainly to people of her own generation. Think of an expression that you use when among a group to which you belong (family, ethnic group, others of your own gender, and so on) but feel constrained from using outside the group. Write an essay explaining and illustrating the uses of the expression in the group and the problems you experience using it elsewhere.

4. **Connections**   To what extent, if at all, does *blah blah blah* resemble the jargon of the medical profession as discussed by Perri Klass in "She's Your Basic L.O.L. in N.A.D." (p. 130)? After reading Klass's essay, list the purposes she believes medical jargon serves. Does *blah blah blah* serve similar or different purposes for Kessler and her peers? Spell your answer out in an essay, drawing on Klass's and Kessler's essays as well as your own experience for evidence.

*Slang is a language that rolls up its sleeves, spits on its hands, and goes to
work.* — Carl Sandburg

*Every age has a language of its own; and the difference in the words is often
far greater than in the thoughts.* — Augustus Hare

Correct English is the slang of prigs. — George Eliot

Journal Response Think of one or more expressions that you use when
speaking with friends or family but that you might not use in writing an
essay — private code words that you use only with your family or slang expressions such as *duh*, *like*, and *yeah, right*, the subjects of the following essay.
Write briefly about what these expressions mean to you and others who use
them.

Kirk Johnson

*Kirk Johnson was born in Salt Lake City, Utah. A Pulitzer-nominated writer
for the* New York Times *and an endurance runner, Johnson has written a book
entitled* To the Edge: A Man, Death Valley, and the Mystery of Endurance
(2001). He lives in northern New Jersey with his wife and two sons.

TODAY'S KIDS ARE, LIKE, KILLING THE ENGLISH LANGUAGE

*In "Today's Kids Are, Like, Killing the English Language," which first appeared
in the* New York Times, *Johnson takes a long look at the changes occurring
in, like, the vocabulary of younger generations. Contrary to common opinion, Johnson holds, these changes are neither superficial nor dangerous.*

As a father of two preteen boys, I have in the last year or so become a   1
huge fan of the word *duh*. This is a word much maligned by educators,
linguistic Brahmins and purists, but they are all quite wrong.

Duh *has elegance.* Duh *has shades of meaning, even sophistication.*   2
Duh *and its perfectly paired linguistic partner,* yeah, right, *are the ideal*

terms to usher in the millennium and the information age, and to highlight the differences from the stolid old twentieth century.

Even my sons might stop me at this point and quash my hyperbole 3 with a quickly dispensed, "Yeah, right, Dad." But hear me out: I have become convinced that *duh* and *yeah, right* have arisen to fill a void in the language because the world has changed. Fewer questions these days can effectively be answered with *yes* or *no*, while at the same time, a tidal surge of hype and mindless blather threatens to overwhelm old-fashioned conversation. *Duh* and *yeah, right* are the cure.

Good old *yes* and *no* were fine for their time — the archaic, black- 4 and-white era of late industrialism that I was born into in the 1950s. The *yes*-or-*no* combo was hard and fast and most of all simple: it belonged to the Manichean[1] red-or-dead mentality of the cold war, to manufacturing, to *Father Knows Best* and *It's a Wonderful Life.*

The information-age future that my eleven-year-old twins own is 5 more complicated than *yes* or *no.* It's more subtle and supple, more loaded with content and hype and media manipulation than my childhood — or any adult's, living or dead — ever was.

And *duh*, whatever else it may be, is drenched with content. Be- 6 tween them, *duh* and *yeah, right* are capable of dividing all language and thought into an exquisitely differentiated universe. Every statement and every question can be positioned on a gray scale of understatement or overstatement, stupidity or insightfulness, information saturation or yawning emptiness.

And in an era when plain speech has become endangered by the 7 pressures of political correctness, *duh* and *yeah, right* are matchless tools of savvy, winking sarcasm and skepticism: caustic without being confrontational, incisive without being quite specific.

With *duh*, you can convey a response, throw in a whole basket full 8 of auxiliary commentary about the question or the statement you're responding to, and insult the speaker all at once! As in this hypothetical exchange:

Parent: Good morning, son, it's a beautiful day.
Eleven-year-old boy: Duh.

9

And there is a kind of esthetic balance as well. *Yeah, right* is the yin to *duh*'s yang, the antithesis to *duh*'s empathetic thesis. Where

---

[1] *Manichean* means dualistic. Manicheism is the belief that the world consists of dual oppositions, such as good and evil. [Editor's note.]

duh is assertive and edgy, a perfect tool for undercutting mindless understatement or insulting repetition, *yeah, right* is laid back, a surfer's cool kind of response to anything overwrought or oversold.

New York, for example, is *duh* territory, while Los Angeles is *yeah,* 10 *right.* Television commercials can be rendered harmless and inert by simply saying, "yeah, right," upon their conclusion. Local television news reports are helped out with a sprinkling of well-placed *duh*s, at moments of stunning obviousness. And almost any politician's speech cries out for heaping helpings of both at various moments.

Adolescent terms like *like*, by contrast, scare me to death. While I 11 have become convinced through observation and personal experimentation that just about any adult of even modest intelligence can figure out how to use *duh* and *yeah, right* properly, *like* is different. *Like* is hard. *Like* is, like, dangerous.

Marcel Danesi, a professor of linguistics and semiotics at the Uni- 12 versity of Toronto who has studied the language of youth and who coined the term "pubilect" to describe the dialect of pubescence, said he believes *like* is in fact altering the structure of the English language, making it more fluid in construction, more like Italian or some other Romance language than good old hard-and-fast Anglo-Saxon. Insert *like* in the middle of a sentence, he said, and a statement can be turned into a question, a question into an exclamation, an exclamation into a quiet meditation.

Consider these hypothetical expressions: "If you're having broc- 13 coli for dinner, Mr. Johnson, I'm, like, out of here!" and "I was, like, no way!" and perhaps most startlingly, "He was, like, duh!"

In the broccoli case, *like* softens the sentence. It's less harsh and 14 confrontational than saying flatly that the serving of an unpalatable vegetable would require a fleeing of the premises.

In the second instance, *like* functions as a kind of a verbal quota- 15 tion mark, an announcement that what follows, "no way," is to be heard differently. The quote itself can then be loaded up with any variety of intonation—irony, sarcasm, even self-deprecation—all depending on the delivery.

In the third example—"He was, like, duh!"—*like* becomes a cru- 16 cial helping verb for *duh*, a verbal springboard. (Try saying the sentence without like and it becomes almost incomprehensible.)

But *like* and *duh* and *yeah, right,* aside from their purely linguistic 17 virtues, are also in many ways the perfect words to convey the sense of reflected reality that is part of the age we live in. Image manipulation, superficiality, and shallow media culture are, for better or worse, the backdrop of adolescent life.

Adults of the *yes*-or-*no* era could perhaps grow up firm in their 18 knowledge of what things "are," but in the Age of *Duh*, with images reflected back from every angle at every waking moment, kids swim in a sea of what things are "like." Distinguishing what is from what merely seems to be is a required skill of an eleven-year-old today; *like* reflects modern life, and *duh* and *yeah, right* are the tools with which such a life can be negotiated and mastered.

But there is a concealed paradox in the Age of *Duh*. The informa- 19 tion overload on which it is based is built around the computer, and the computer is, of course, built around—that's right—the good old *yes*-or-*no* binary code: billions of microcircuits all blinking on or off, black or white, current in or current out. Those computers were designed by minds schooled and steeped in the world of *yes* or *no*, and perhaps it is not too much of a stretch to imagine my sons' generation, shaped by the broader view of *duh*, finding another path: binary code with attitude. Besides, most computers I know already seem to have an attitude. Incorporating a little *duh* would at least give them a sense of humor.

Meaning

1. What is Johnson's main point? Underline the sentence that you believe best demonstrates his main idea.
2. Which slang terms does Johnson single out, and what do they contribute to the main point of his essay?
3. What is a paradox? What is the "paradox" that Johnson refers to in his last paragraph?
4. If you are uncertain of the meanings of any of the words listed below, try to guess them from the context of Johnson's essay. Then look them up to see how close your definitions were to those in the dictionary. Test out the new words by using each of them in a sentence or two.

Brahmins (1)	esthetic (9)	unpalatable (14)
hyperbole (3)	antithesis (9)	self-deprecation (15)
hype (3)	overwrought (9)	springboard (16)
blather (3)	semiotics (12)	backdrop (17)
caustic (7)	confrontational (14)	steeped (19)
incisive (7)		

Purpose and Audience

1. Do you think Johnson wants to provoke, educate, or entertain us? Or does he want to do all of these things? What evidence can you provide for your answer?

2. What clues can you find that this essay was originally published in the *New York Times*? For instance, what does Johnson seem to assume about his readers—that they're teenagers? adults? linguists? parents? Does he assume that they speak the slang he analyzes or that they approve of it? Provide examples from the essay to support your answers.

3. Johnson establishes his viewpoint in the first few paragraphs. What objections does he anticipate? How does he respond to them? How convinced are you by his response?

Method and Structure

1. Examine the quotations that Johnson offers as examples of *duh* and *yeah, right* and *like*. How well do they, along with Johnson's explanations of them, convey the meanings of the expressions? Are there places where you would like to see more examples?

2. Why do you think that Johnson does not mention *like* until halfway through the essay? Does this delay make the essay weaker or more interesting for you?

3. Weigh the evidence that Johnson gives to support his opinions. Which evidence is personal, and which is not? Are both the personal and the nonpersonal equally effective? Why, or why not?

4. **Other Methods**   Johnson's example essay is also a model of definition (Chapter 11) because he establishes the meanings of three slang terms. What are the meanings of *duh* and *yeah, right* and *like*? How is each distinct from the others?

Language

1. How would you characterize Johnson's tone in this essay—for instance, wise, argumentative, reassuring, humorous, serious, flippant, worried, irritated, confused, enthusiastic? Give examples to support your analysis. How is the tone appropriate (or not) for the audience you identified in question 2 under "Purpose and Audience"?

2. Johnson uses several pairs of contrasting words, such as "*yes-or-no*" and "red-or-dead." What similar pairs do you find? What is their significance for Johnson's thesis?

3. How does the author attempt to make his ideas accessible while also maintaining his sophistication? In your opinion, is this essay difficult to read, easy to read, or something in between? Why?

Writing Topics

1. **Journal to Essay**   Reread your journal entry and the quotations at the beginning of Johnson's essay (p. 124). Using specific examples, write an essay

about the expression or expressions you use with friends or family. What shades of meaning do the expressions have? What situations do you use them in? How do others react to them?

2. You may not agree with Johnson's opinion that certain slang expressions are ideal for our modern world and actually enrich our language. Write an essay in which you consider the opposite view: that English is actually being harmed by terms such as *duh* and *yeah, right* and *like*. You may use examples from Johnson's essay or others of your own, but be sure to support your case.

3. **Cultural Considerations**   Many English speakers use words from other languages, nonstandard forms such as *ain't* or *can't hardly*, or slang such as *duh* or *yeah, right*—and many listeners find the language richer for these additions. Yet not all ways of speaking gain equal acceptance. Write an essay in which you examine how negative stereotyping may use the language of a particular group—an accent, say, or certain slang expressions—against the members of that group. In stereotyping, what connections are drawn between the language and the perceived or imagined qualities of its speakers? What purpose might such stereotyping serve for those who do it? What effect might it have on them?

4. **Connections**   Both Johnson and William Lutz, in a paragraph from *Doublespeak* (p. 113), discuss language use among a particular group. Johnson explains how his preteen sons and their friends use certain slang expressions to reflect the reality of the world around them. Lutz, in contrast, shows how carefully chosen terminology used by the military can actually obscure meaning. Write an essay in which you examine a form of doublespeak, jargon, or slang, such as the language of teachers, journalists, or college students. Does the language used clarify or confuse reality?

*A passage is not plain English — still less is it good English — if we are
obliged to read it twice to find out what it means.* —Dorothy Sayers

I'm bilingual. I speak English and I speak educationese. —Shirley Hufstedler

You and I come by road or rail, but economists travel on infrastructure.
—Margaret Thatcher

Journal Response   What words or expressions have you encountered in
your college courses or in your college's rules and regulations that have
confused, delighted, or irritated you? Write a brief journal entry describing
the language and its effects on you.

Perri Klass

*Perri Klass is a pediatrician and a writer of both fiction and nonfiction. She was
born in 1958 in Trinidad and grew up in New York City and New Jersey. After
obtaining a BA from Harvard University in 1979, she began graduate work
in biology but then switched to medicine. Klass finished Harvard Medical School
in 1986 and practices pediatrics in Boston. Her publications are extensive: short
stories in* Mademoiselle, Antioch Review, *and other magazines; two novels,*
Recombinations *(1985) and* Other Women's Children *(1990); two collections
of essays,* A Not Entirely Benign Procedure *(1987) and* Baby Doctor: A Pediatrician's Training *(1992); and, with Eileen Costello, the parenting guide* Quirky
Kids: Understanding and Helping Your Child Who Doesn't Fit In — When to
Worry and When Not to Worry *(2003). She is the mother of two sons and one
daughter.*

SHE'S YOUR BASIC
L.O.L. IN N.A.D.

*Most of us have felt excluded, confused, or even frightened by the jargon of
the medical profession — that is, by the special terminology and abbreviations
for diseases and procedures. In this essay Klass uses examples of such language, some of it heartless, to illustrate the pluses and minuses of becoming
a doctor. The essay first appeared in 1984 as a "Hers" column in the* New York
Times.

"Mrs. Tolstoy is your basic L.O.L. in N.A.D., admitted for a soft rule-   *1*
out M.I.," the intern announces. I scribble that on my patient list. In
other words Mrs. Tolstoy is a Little Old Lady in No Apparent Distress
who is in the hospital to make sure she hasn't had a heart attack (rule
out a myocardial infarction). And we think it's unlikely that she has
had a heart attack (a *soft* rule-out).

If I learned nothing else during my first three months of working   *2*
in the hospital as a medical student, I learned endless jargon and abbreviations. I started out in a state of primeval innocence, in which I
didn't even know that "s̄ C.P., S.O.B., N/V" meant "without chest
pain, shortness of breath, or nausea and vomiting." By the end I took
the abbreviations so for granted that I would complain to my mother
the English professor, "And can you believe I had to put down *three*
NG tubes last night?"

"You'll have to tell me what an NG tube is if you want me to sym-   *3*
pathize properly," my mother said. NG, nasogastric — isn't it obvious?

I picked up not only the specific expressions but also the patterns   *4*
of speech and the grammatical conventions; for example, you never say
that a patient's blood pressure fell or that his cardiac enzymes rose.
Instead, the patient is always the subject of the verb: "He dropped his
pressure." "He bumped his enzymes." This sort of construction probably reflects that profound irritation of the intern when the nurses come
in the middle of the night to say that Mr. Dickinson has disturbingly
low blood pressure. "Oh, he's gonna hurt me bad tonight," the intern
may say, inevitably angry at Mr. Dickinson for dropping his pressure
and creating a problem.

When chemotherapy fails to cure Mrs. Bacon's cancer, what we   *5*
say is, "Mrs. Bacon failed chemotherapy."

"Well, we've already had one hit today, and we're up next, but at   *6*
least we've got mostly stable players on our team." This means that our
team (group of doctors and medical students) has already gotten one
new admission today, and it is our turn again, so we'll get whoever is
next admitted in emergency, but at least most of the patients we already
have are fairly stable, that is, unlikely to drop their pressures or in any
other way get suddenly sicker and hurt us bad. Baseball metaphor is
pervasive: a no-hitter is a night without any new admissions. A player
is always a patient — a nitrate player is a patient on nitrates, a unit
player is a patient in the intensive-care unit, and so on, until you reach
the terminal player.

It is interesting to consider what it means to be winning, or doing   *7*
well, in this perennial baseball game. When the intern hangs up the

phone and announces, "I got a hit," that is not cause for congratulations. The team is not scoring points; rather, it is getting hit, being bombarded with new patients. The object of the game from the point of view of the doctors, considering the players for whom they are already responsible, is to get as few new hits as possible.

These special languages contribute to a sense of closeness and professional spirit among people who are under a great deal of stress. As a medical student, it was exciting for me to discover that I'd finally cracked the code, that I could understand what doctors said and wrote and could use the same formulations myself. Some people seem to become enamored of the jargon for its own sake, perhaps because they are so deeply thrilled with the idea of medicine, with the idea of themselves as doctors.   8

I knew a medical student who was referred to by the interns on the team as Mr. Eponym because he was so infatuated with eponymous terminology,[1] the more obscure the better. He never said "capillary pulsation" if he could say "Quincke's pulses." He would lovingly tell over the multinamed syndromes—Wolff-Parkinson-White, Lown-Ganong-Levine, Henoch-Schonlein—until the temptation to suggest Schleswig-Holstein or Stevenson-Kefauver or Baskin-Robbins became irresistible to his less reverent colleagues.   9

And there is the jargon that you don't ever want to hear yourself using. You know that your training is changing you, but there are certain changes you think would be going a little too far.   10

The resident was describing a man with devastating terminal pancreatic cancer. "Basically he's C.T.D.," the resident concluded. I reminded myself that I had resolved not to be shy about asking when I didn't understand things. "C.T.D.?" I asked timidly.   11

The resident smirked at me. "Circling The Drain."   12

The images are vivid and terrible. "What happened to Mrs. Melville?"   13

"Oh, she boxed last night." To box is to die, of course.   14

Then there are the more pompous locutions that can make the beginning medical student nervous about the effects of medical training. A friend of mine was told by his resident, "A pregnant woman with sickle-cell represents a failure of genetic counseling."   15

Mr. Eponym, who tried hard to talk like the doctors, once explained to me, "An infant is basically a brainstem preparation." A brain-   16

---

[1] *Eponymous* means "named after"—in this case, medical terminology is named after researchers. [Editor's note.]

stem preparation, as used in neurological research, is an animal whose higher brain functions have been destroyed so that only the most primitive reflexes remain, like the sucking reflex, the startle reflex, and the rooting reflex.

The more extreme forms aside, one most important function of medical jargon is to help doctors maintain some distance from their patients. By reformulating a patient's pain and problems into a language that the patient doesn't even speak, I suppose we are in some sense taking those pains and problems under our jurisdiction and also reducing their emotional impact. This linguistic separation between doctors and patients allows conversations to go on at the bedside that are unintelligible to the patient. "Naturally, we're worried about adreno-C.A.," the intern can say to the medical student, and lung cancer need never be mentioned.   *17*

   I learned a new language this past summer. At times it thrills me to hear myself using it. It enables me to understand my colleagues, to communicate effectively in the hospital. Yet I am uncomfortably aware that I will never again notice the peculiarities and even atrocities of medical language as keenly as I did this summer. There may be specific expressions I manage to avoid, but even as I remark them, promising myself I will never use them, I find that this language is becoming my professional speech. It no longer sounds strange in my ears—or coming from my mouth. And I am afraid that as with any new language, to use it properly you must absorb not only the vocabulary but also the structure, the logic, the attitudes. At first you may notice these new alien assumptions every time you put together a sentence, but with time and increased fluency you stop being aware of them at all. And as you lose that awareness, for better or for worse, you move closer and closer to being a doctor instead of just talking like one.   *18*

Meaning

1. What point does Klass make about medical jargon in this essay? Where does she reveal her main point explicitly?
2. What useful purposes does medical jargon serve, according to Klass? Do the examples in paragraphs 9–16 serve these purposes? Why, or why not?
3. Try to guess the meanings of any of the following words on the next page that are unfamiliar. Check your guesses in a dictionary, and then use each word in a sentence or two of your own.

primeval (2)   syndromes (9)   locutions (15)
terminal (6)   reverent (9)   jurisdiction (17)
perennial (7)   pompous (15)

Purpose and Audience

1. What does Klass imply when she states that she began her work in the hospital "in a state of primeval innocence" (paragraph 2)? What does this phrase suggest about her purpose in writing the essay?
2. From what perspective does Klass write this essay: that of a medical professional? someone outside the profession? a patient? someone else? To what extent does she expect her readers to share her perspective? What evidence in the essay supports your answer?
3. Given that she is writing for a general audience, does Klass take adequate care to define medical terms? Support your answer with examples from the essay.

Method and Structure

1. Why does Klass begin the essay with an example rather than a statement of her main idea? What effect does this example produce? How does this effect support her purpose in writing the essay?
2. Although Klass uses many examples of medical jargon, she avoids the dull effect of a list by periodically stepping back to make a general statement about her experience or the jargon—for instance, "I picked up not only the specific expressions but also the patterns of speech and the grammatical conventions" (paragraph 4). Locate other places—not necessarily at the beginnings of paragraphs—where Klass breaks up her examples with more general statements.
3. **Other Methods**   Klass uses several other methods besides example, among them classification (Chapter 8), definition (Chapter 11), and cause-and-effect analysis (Chapter 12). What effects—positive and negative—does medical jargon have on Klass, other students, and doctors who use it?

Language

1. What is the tone of this essay? Is Klass trying to be humorous or tongue-in-cheek about the jargon of the profession, or is she serious? Where in the essay is the author's attitude toward her subject the most obvious?
2. Klass refers to the users of medical jargon as both *we/us/our* (paragraphs 1, 5, 6, 17) and *they/our* (7), and sometimes she shifts from *I* to *you* within

a paragraph (4, 18). Do you think these shifts are effective or distracting? Why? Do the shifts serve any function?

3. Klass obviously experienced both positive and negative feelings about mastering medical jargon. Which words and phrases in the last paragraph reflect positive feelings, and which negative?

Writing Topics

1. **Journal to Essay**   When she attended medical school, Perri Klass discovered a novel language to learn and with it some new attitudes. Working from your journal entry (p. 130), write an essay about new languages and attitudes you have encountered in college. Have you been confronted with different kinds of people (professors, other students) from the ones you knew before? Have you had difficulty understanding some words people use? Have you found yourself embracing ideas you never thought you would or speaking differently? Have others noticed a change in you that you may not have been aware of? Have you noticed changes in your precollege friends? Focus on a particular kind of obstacle or change, using specific examples to convey this experience to readers.

2. Klass likens her experience learning medical jargon to that of learning a new language (paragraph 18). If you are studying or have learned a second language, write an essay in which you explain the "new alien assumptions" you must make "every time you put together a sentence." Draw your examples not just from the new language's grammar and vocabulary but from its underlying logic and attitudes. For instance, does one speak to older people differently in the new language? make requests differently? describe love or art differently?

3. Klass's essay explores the "separation between doctors and patients" (paragraph 17). Has this separation affected you as a patient or as the relative or friend of a patient? If so, write an essay about your experiences. Did the medical professionals rely heavily on jargon? Was their language comforting, frightening, irritating? Based on your experience and on Klass's essay, do you believe that the separation between doctors and patients is desirable? Why, or why not?

4. **Cultural Considerations**   Most groups focused on a common interest have their own jargon. If you belong to such a group — for example, runners, football fans, food servers, engineering students — spend a few days listening to yourself and others use this language and thinking about the purposes it serves. Which aspects of this language seem intended to make users feel like insiders? Which seem to serve some other purpose, and what is it? In an essay, explain what this jargon reveals about the group and its common interest, using as many specific examples as you can.

5. **Connections**   Both Klass and Kirk Johnson, in "Today's Kids Are, Like, Killing the English Language" (p. 124), believe that the way we speak can signal our membership in a particular group of people: in this case, doctors or teenagers. Write an essay in which you examine the way another group of people—say, faculty members, politicians, or people from a particular region—use language to mark their group identity.

Example

Choose one of the following statements, or any other statement they suggest, and agree *or* disagree with it in an essay developed by one or more examples. The statement you decide on should concern a topic you care about so that the example or examples are a means of communicating an idea, not an end in themselves.

FAMILY

1. In happy families, talk is the main activity.
2. Grandparents relate more closely to their grandchildren than to their children.
3. Sooner or later, children take on the personalities of their parents.

BEHAVIOR AND PERSONALITY

4. Rudeness is on the rise.
5. Gestures and facial expressions often communicate what words cannot say.
6. Our natural surroundings when we are growing up contribute to our happiness or unhappiness as adults.

EDUCATION

7. The best college courses are the difficult ones.
8. Education is an easy way to get ahead in life.
9. Students at schools with enforced dress codes behave better than students at schools without such codes.

POLITICS AND SOCIAL ISSUES

10. Talk radio can influence public policy.
11. Drug or alcohol addiction does not happen just to "bad" people.
12. True-life crime mimics TV and movies.
13. Unemployment is hardest on those over fifty years old.

MEDIA AND CULTURE

14. Bumper stickers are a form of conversation among Americans.
15. The Internet divides people instead of connecting them.
16. Good art can be ugly.
17. A craze or fad reveals something about the culture it arises in.
18. The best popular musicians treat social and political issues in their songs.

19. Television news programs are beauty pageants for untalented journalists.
20. The most rewarding books are always easy to read.

RULES FOR LIVING

21. Murphy's Law: If anything can go wrong, it will go wrong, and at the worst possible moment.
22. With enough motivation, a person can accomplish anything.
23. Lying may be justified by the circumstances.
24. Friends are people you can't always trust.

WRITING ABOUT THE THEME

Using Language

1. Deborah Tannen (p. 113), William Lutz (p. 113), and Perri Klass (p. 130) discuss the power of language with a good deal of respect. Tannen refers to its social uses, Lutz to its effectiveness "in explaining ... accidents," and Klass to its support as she became a doctor. Think of a time when you were in some way profoundly affected by language, and write an essay about this experience. Provide as many examples as necessary to illustrate both the language that affected you and how it made you feel.

2. Kim Kessler (p. 119) and Kirk Johnson (p. 124) both write about forms of language that do not obey traditional grammar rules and are considered incorrect by some people. As you see it, what are the advantages and disadvantages of using nonstandard language when speaking? How effective are these forms of language as ways to communicate? Write an essay answering these questions, using examples from the essays and your own experience.

3. Perri Klass writes that medical jargon "contribute[s] to a sense of closeness and professional spirit among people who are under a great deal of stress" (paragraph 8) and that it helps "doctors maintain some distance from their patients" (17). Write an essay in which you analyze the function of "doublespeak," as presented by William Lutz. Who, if anyone, is such language designed to help? The accident victims? Survivors of these victims? Someone else? Can a positive case be made for this language?

Chapter 7

DIVISION
OR ANALYSIS

Looking at Popular Culture

Division and **analysis** are interchangeable terms for the same method. *Division* comes from a Latin word meaning "to force asunder or separate." *Analysis* comes from a Greek word meaning "to undo." Using this method, we separate a whole into its elements, examine the relations of the elements to one another and to the whole, and reassemble the elements into a new whole informed by the examination.

Analysis (as we will call it) is the foundation of **critical thinking**, the ability to see beneath the surface of things, images, events, and ideas; to uncover and test assumptions; to see the importance of context; and to draw and support independent conclusions. The method, then, is essential to college learning, whether in discussing literature, reviewing a psychology experiment, or interpreting a business case. It is also fundamental in the workplace, from choosing a career to making sense of market research. Analysis even informs and enriches life outside school or work, whether we ponder our relationships with others, decide whether a movie was worthwhile, evaluate a politician's campaign promises, or determine whether a new video game system is worth buying.

We use analysis throughout this book when looking at paragraphs and essays. And it is the basic operation in at least four other methods discussed in other chapters: classification (Chapter 8), process analysis (Chapter 9), comparison and contrast (Chapter 10), and cause-and-effect analysis (Chapter 12).

READING DIVISION OR ANALYSIS

At its most helpful, division or analysis peers inside an object, institution, work of art, policy, or any other whole. It identifies the parts, examines how the parts relate, and leads to a conclusion about the meaning, significance, or value of the whole. The subject of any analysis is usually singular—a freestanding, coherent unit, such as a bicycle or a poem, with its own unique constitution of elements. (In contrast, classification, the subject of the next chapter, usually starts with a plural subject, such as bicycles or the poems of the Civil War, and groups them according to their shared features.) A writer chooses the subject and with it a **principle of analysis**, a framework that determines how the subject will be divided and thus what elements are relevant to the discussion.

Sometimes the principle of analysis is self-evident, especially when the subject is an object, such as a bicycle or a camera, that can be "undone" in only a limited number of ways. Most of the time, however, the principle depends on the writer's view of the whole. In academic disciplines, businesses, and the professions, distinctive principles are part of what the field is about and are often the subject of debate within the field. In art, for instance, some critics see a painting primarily as a visual object and concentrate on its composition, color, line, and other formal qualities; other critics see a painting primarily as a social object and concentrate on its content and context (cultural, economic, political, and so on). Both groups use a principle of analysis that is a well-established way of looking at painting, yet each group finds different elements and thus meaning in a work.

Writers have a great deal of flexibility in choosing a principle of analysis, but the principle also must meet certain requirements: it should be appropriate for the subject and the field or discipline; it should be significant; and it should be applied thoroughly and consistently. Analysis is not done for its own sake but for a larger goal of illuminating the subject, perhaps concluding something about it, perhaps evaluating it. But even when the method culminates in evaluation—in the writer's judgment of the subject's value—the analysis should represent the subject as it actually is, in all its fullness and complexity. In analyzing a movie, for instance, a writer may emphasize one element, such as setting, and even omit some elements, such as costumes; but the characterization of the whole must still apply to *all* the elements. If it does not, readers can be counted on to notice; so the writer must single out any wayward element(s) and explain why they do not substantially undermine the framework and thus weaken the opinion.

ANALYZING DIVISION OR ANALYSIS IN PARAGRAPHS

Jon Pareles (born 1953) is the chief critic of popular music for the *New York Times*. The following paragraph comes from "Gather No Moss, Take No Prisoners, but Be Cool," a review of a concert by the rock guitarist Keith Richards.

Mr. Richards shows off by not showing off. He uses rhythm chords as a goad, not a metronome, slipping them in just ahead of a beat or skipping them entirely. The distilled twang of his tone has been imitated all over rock, but far fewer guitarists have learned his guerrilla timing, his coiled silences. When he switches to lead guitar, Mr. Richards goes not for long lines, but for serrated riffing, zinging out three or four notes again and again in various permutations, wringing from them the essence of the blues. The phrasing is poised and suspenseful, but it also carries a salutary rock attitude: that less is more, especially when delivered with utter confidence.

> Principle of analysis (topic sentence underlined): elements of Richards's "not showing off"
>
> 1. Rhythm chords as goad (or prod)
>
> 2. Timing
>
> 3. Silences
>
> 4. Riffing (or choppy playing)
>
> 5. Confident, less-is-more attitude

Luci Tapahonso (born 1953) is a poet and teacher. This paragraph is from her essay "The Way It Is," which appears in *Sign Language*, a book of photographs (by Skeet McAuley) of life on the reservation for some Navajo and Apache Indians.

It is rare and, indeed, very exciting to see an Indian person in a commercial advertisement. Word travels fast when that happens. Nunzio's Pizza in Albuquerque, New Mexico, ran commercials featuring Jose Rey Toledo of Jemez Pueblo talking about his "native land —Italy" while wearing typical Pueblo attire—jewelry, moccasins, and hair tied in a chongo. Because of the ironic humor, because Indian grandfathers specialize in playing tricks and jokes on their grandchildren, and because Jose Rey Toledo is a respected and well-known

> Principle of analysis (topic sentence underlined at end): elements of the commercial that appealed to Indians
>
> 1. Rarity of an Indian in a commercial
>
> 2. Indian dress
>
> 3. Indian humor
>
> 4. Indian tradition
>
> 5. Respected Indian spokesperson

elder in the Indian communities, word of this commercial spread fast among Indians in New Mexico. It was
the cause of recognition and celebration of sorts on the
reservations and in the pueblos. His portrayal was not   6. Realism
in the categories which the media usually associate with
Indians but as a typical sight in the Southwest. It
showed Indians as we live today — enjoying pizza as
one of our favorite foods, including humor and fun as
part of our daily lives, and recognizing the importance
of preserving traditional knowledge.

DEVELOPING AN ESSAY
BY DIVISION OR ANALYSIS
Getting Started

Analysis is one of the readiest methods of development: almost anything whole can be separated into its elements, from a lemon to a play
by Shakespeare to an economic theory. In college and at work, many
writing assignments will demand analysis with a verb such as *analyze*,
criticize, *discuss*, *evaluate*, *interpret*, or *review*. If you need to develop
your own subject for analysis, think of something whose meaning or
significance puzzles or intrigues you and whose parts you can distinguish and relate to the whole — an object such as a machine, an artwork such as a poem, a media product such as a news broadcast, an
institution such as a hospital, a relationship such as stepparenting, a
social issue such as sheltering the homeless.

Dissect your subject, looking at the actual, physical thing if possible, imagining it in your mind if necessary. Make detailed notes of all
the elements you see, their distinguishing features, and how those features work together. In analyzing someone's creation, tease out the creator's influences, assumptions, intentions, conclusions, and evidence.
You may have to go outside the work for some of this information —
researching an author's background, for instance, to uncover the political biases that may underlie his or her opinions. Even if you do not
use all this information in your final draft, it will help you see the elements and help keep your analysis true to the subject.

If you begin by seeking meaning or significance in a subject, you will
be more likely to find a workable principle of analysis and less likely to
waste time on a hollow exercise. Each question below suggests a distinct
approach to the subject's elements — a distinct principle of analysis —
that makes it easier to isolate the elements and see their connections.

To what extent is an enormously complex hospital a community in itself?

What is the function of the front-page headlines in the local tabloid newspaper?

Why did a certain movie have such a powerful effect on you and your friends?

Forming a Thesis

A clear, informative thesis sentence (or sentences) is crucial in division or analysis because readers need to know the purpose and structure of your analysis in order to follow your points. If your exploratory question proves helpful as you gather ideas, you can also use it to draft a thesis sentence: answer it in such a way that you state your opinion about your subject and reveal your principle of analysis.

QUESTION   To what extent is an enormously complex hospital a community in itself?

THESIS SENTENCE   The hospital encompasses such a wide range of personnel and services that it resembles a good-size town.

QUESTION   What is the function of the front-page headlines in the local tabloid newspaper?

THESIS SENTENCE   The newspaper's front page routinely appeals to readers' fear of crime, anger at criminals, and sympathy for victims.

QUESTION   Why did a certain movie have such a powerful effect on you and your friends?

THESIS SENTENCE   The film is a unique and important statement of the private terrors of adolescence.

Note that all three thesis statements imply an explanatory purpose—an effort to understand something and share that understanding with the reader. The third thesis sentence, however, suggests a persuasive purpose as well: the writer hopes that readers will accept her evaluation of the film.

These thesis sentences clearly convey the writers' approaches to their subjects. In contrast, the following sentence does not. With "do anything," it overstates and yet fails to specify a framework for analysis.

VAGUE   Advertisers will do anything to sell their products.

Compare this thesis sentence with the one from Shafeeq Sadiq's essay later in this chapter (p. 155). Here it is apparent that the writer will focus on the racist and sexist elements in advertising:

CLEAR   Often, these gimmicks [in advertisements] reinforce racial stereotypes and portray women in a negative light.

A well-focused thesis sentence benefits not only your readers but also you as writer, because it gives you a yardstick to judge the completeness, consistency, and supportiveness of your analysis. Don't be discouraged, though, if your thesis sentence doesn't come to you until *after* you've written a first draft and had a chance to discover your interest. Writing about your subject may be the best way for you to find its meaning and significance.

Organizing

In the introduction to your essay, let readers know why you are bothering to analyze your subject: Why is the subject significant? How might the essay relate to the experiences of readers or be useful to them? A subject unfamiliar to readers might be summarized or described, or part of it (an anecdote or quotation, say) might be used to tantalize readers. A familiar subject might be introduced with a surprising fact or an unusual perspective. An evaluative analysis might open with an opposing viewpoint.

In the body of the essay you'll need to explain your principle of analysis according to the guidelines above. The arrangement of elements and analysis should suit your subject and purpose: You can describe the elements and then offer your analysis, or you can introduce and analyze elements one by one. You can arrange the elements themselves from least to most important, least to most complex, most to least familiar, spatially, or chronologically. Devote as much space to each element as it demands: there is no requirement that all elements be given equal space and emphasis if their complexity or your framework dictates otherwise.

Most analysis essays need a conclusion that assembles the elements, returning readers to a sense of the whole subject. The conclusion can restate the thesis, summarize what the essay has contributed, consider the influence of the subject or its place in a larger picture, or (especially in an evaluation) assess the effectiveness or worth of the subject.

Drafting

If your subject or your view of it is complex, you may need at least two rough drafts of an analysis essay — one to discover what you think and one to clarify your principle, cover each element, and support your points with concrete details and vivid examples (including quotations if the subject is a written work). Plan on two drafts if you're uncertain of your thesis when you begin; you'll probably save time in the long run by attending to one goal at a time. Especially because the analysis essay says something about the subject by explaining its structure, you need to have a clear picture of the whole and relate each part to it.

As you draft, be sure to consider your readers' needs as well as the needs of your subject and your own framework:

- If the subject is unfamiliar to your readers, you'll need to carefully explain your principle of analysis, define all specialized terms, distinguish parts from one another, and provide ample illustrations.
- If the subject is familiar to readers, your principle of analysis may not require much justification (as long as it's clear), but your details and examples must be vivid and convincing.
- If readers may dispute your way of looking at your subject, be careful to justify as well as explain your principle of analysis.

Whether readers are familiar with your subject or not, always account for any evidence that may seem not to support your opinion—either by showing why, in fact, the evidence is supportive or explaining why it is unimportant. (If contrary evidence refuses to be dispensed with, you may have to rethink your approach.)

Revising and Editing

When you revise and edit your essay, use the following questions and the box on the next page to uncover any weaknesses remaining in your analysis.

- *Is your principle of analysis clear?* The significance of your analysis and your view of the subject should be apparent throughout your essay.
- *Is your analysis complete?* Have you identified all elements according to your principle of analysis and determined their relations to one another and to the whole? If you have omitted some elements from your discussion, will the reason for their omission be clear to readers?
- *Is your analysis consistent?* Is your principle of analysis applied consistently to the entire subject (including any elements you have

omitted)? Do all elements reflect the same principle, and are they clearly separate rather than overlapping? You may find it helpful to check your draft against your list of elements or your outline or to outline the draft itself.

- *Is your analysis well supported?* Is the thesis supported by clear assertions about parts of the subject, and are the assertions supported by concrete, specific evidence (sensory details, facts, quotations, and so on)? Do not rely on your readers to prove your thesis.
- *Is your analysis true to the subject?* Is your thesis unforced, your analysis fair? Is your new whole (your reassembly of the elements) faithful to the original? Be wary of leaping to a conclusion that distorts the subject.

FOCUS ON PARAGRAPH COHERENCE

With several elements that contribute to the whole of a subject, an analysis will be easy for your readers to follow only if you frequently clarify what element you are discussing and how it fits with your principle of analysis. To help readers keep your analysis straight, you can rely on the techniques of paragraph coherence discussed on pages 35–37, especially on transitions and on repetition or restatement:

- *Transitions* like those listed in the Glossary act as signposts to tell readers where you, and they, are headed. Some transitions indicate that you are shifting between subjects, either finding resemblances between them (*also, like, likewise, similarly*) or finding differences (*but, however, in contrast, instead, unlike, whereas, yet*). Other transitions indicate that you are moving on to a new point (*in addition, also, furthermore, moreover*). Consider, for example, how transitions keep readers focused in the following paragraph from "The Distorting Mirror of Reality TV," an essay by Sarah Coleman:

  Let's start with the contestants. Most producers of reality TV shows would like you to believe they've picked a group of people who span a broad spectrum of human diversity. *But* if you took the demographics of the average reality show *and* applied them to the population at large, you'd end up with a society that was 90 percent white, young, and beautiful. *In fact*, though reality TV pretends to hold up a mirror to society, its producers screen contestants *in much the same way* as the producers of television commercials and Hollywood movies screen their actors. For ethnic minorities, old people, the un-beautiful, and the disabled, the message is harsh: even in "reality" you don't exist.

- Repetition or restatement of labels for your principle of analysis or for individual elements makes clear the topic of each sentence. In the preceding passage, the repetition of *contestants* and *producers* and the substitution of *people* and *they* for each emphasize the elements under discussion. The restatement of *reality*, *TV/television*, and *diversity/demographics/population/minorities* clarifies the principle of analysis (the unreality of reality show contestants).

See the sample paragraph on page 36 for additional examples of these two techniques.

A NOTE ON THEMATIC CONNECTIONS

Because popular culture is everywhere, and everywhere taken for granted, it is a tempting and challenging target for writers. Having chosen to write critically about a disturbing, cheering, or intriguing aspect of popular culture, all the authors represented in this chapter naturally pursued the method of division or analysis. The paragraph by Jon Pareles dissects the unique playing style of the rock guitarist Keith Richards (p. 142). The other paragraph, by Luci Tapahonso, analyzes a pizza commercial that especially appealed to Native Americans (p. 142). Dave Barry's essay asks just what drivers experience when they sit behind the wheel of a Humvee (opposite). Shafeeq Sadiq's essay finds plenty of political incorrectness in advertising (p. 155). And Thomas de Zengotita's essay considers what it is about the television show *American Idol* that makes it so irresistible to viewers (p. 160).

ON CARS

The purpose of life is to produce and consume automobiles. —Jane Jacobs

It is only here, in your very own castle of rubber and steel, that you can for a short but blissful time throw off the cloak of civilizations and be the raging Hun you always wanted to be. —Adair Lara

Whither goest thou, America, in thy shiny car in the night? —Jack Kerouac

Journal Response What kind of vehicle do you drive: a hand-me-down wreck? a sporty convertible? a muscular sport-utility vehicle? a beat-up truck? an environmentally friendly hybrid? an occasional rental? Write about your first or current car, describing why you chose it, what you use it for, and the reasons you like or dislike it. If you don't have access to a car, do you hope to acquire one someday? What, when, and why—or why not?

Dave Barry

One of the most widely read contemporary writers in the United States, Dave Barry (born 1947) is known for finding laugh-out-loud humor in the most mundane elements of daily life, whether his subject is bodily functions, grammar flubs, or lawn mower races. Raised in Armonk, New York, Barry was elected class clown of his high school and earned a BA in English from Haverford College. He worked as a small-town newspaper reporter and business-writing consultant in Pennsylvania until his freelance efforts earned him a position at the Miami Herald *in 1983. Barry's weekly column, for which he won the Pulitzer Prize for commentary in 1988, was syndicated in more than five hundred newspapers across the country until he took an indefinite break in 2004. (He continues to keep a blog for the* Herald.*) Barry's columns have been collected in several anthologies, including* Dave Barry's Greatest Hits *(1988),* Dave Barry Is Not Making This Up *(2001), and* Boogers Are My Beat: More Lies, but Some Actual Journalism *(2003). He is also the author of more than two dozen best-selling humor books, including* The Taming of the Screw: Several Million Homeowner's Problems Sidestepped *(1983),* Dave Barry Slept Here: A Sort of History of the United States *(1989), and* Dave Barry's Money Secrets: Like: Why Is There a Giant Eyeball on the Dollar? *(2006). When he's not writing or traveling in search of bizarre local festivals to lampoon, Barry plays guitar with the Rock Bottom Remainders, an amateur rock band composed of himself and several fellow writers, among them Amy Tan, Stephen King, and Mitch Albom.*

HUMVEE SATISFIES A MAN'S LUST FOR WINCHES

In this column, first published on January 7, 2001, Barry launches his trade-mark wit at a favorite target: grown men's toys. Why would anybody pay in excess of $100,000 for a car? The answer, Barry suggests, is that it gives men a (false) sense of masculinity.

It is time for our popular feature "Stuff That Guys Need." Today's topic   1
is: the Humvee.

Most Americans became aware of the Humvee (military shorthand   2
for HUgely Masculine VEEhickle) during the Gulf War, when U.S.
troops, driving Humvees equipped with missile launchers, kicked Iraq's
butt and taught Saddam Hussein a lesson that he would not forget for
several weeks.[1]

After the war, a few wealthy Californians got hold of Humvees.   3
This led to some mishaps, most notably when Arnold Schwarzenegger,
attempting to open his garage door, accidentally launched a missile.
Fortunately, it landed in a noncelebrity neighborhood.

But once the "bugs" were ironed out, the Humvee became available   4
for civilian purchase. I test-drove one recently thanks to my co-worker
Terry Jackson, who is the *Miami Herald*'s automotive writer and TV
critic. That's correct: This man gets paid to drive new cars AND watch
television. If he ever dies and goes to heaven, it's going to be a big
letdown.

When I arrived at Terry's house, there was a bright-yellow Humvee   5
sitting in his driveway, covered with puddles of drool deposited by
passing guys. In terms of styling, the Humvee is as masculine as a vehicle can get without actually growing hair in its wheel wells. It's a big,
boxy thing with giant tires and many studly mechanical protuberances.
It looks like something you'd buy as part of a toy action-figure set called
"Sergeant Bart Groin and His Pain Platoon."

Terry told me this particular Humvee model cost $101,000, which   6
sounds like a lot of money until you consider its features. For example,
it has dashboard switches that enable you to inflate or deflate your tires

---

[1] In 1991, Americans led a successful United Nations effort to force Iraqis out of neigh-boring Kuwait. Saddam Hussein, the longtime dictator of Iraq, was captured during the war that began in 2003. He was tried and executed in 2006. [Editor's note.]

as you drive. Is that cool, or WHAT? In a perfect guy universe, this feature would seriously impress women.

GUY: Look! I can inflate the tires as I drive!   7

WOMAN: Pull over right now, so we can engage in wanton   8
carnality!

Unfortunately, the real world doesn't work this way. I know this   9
because when I took my wife for a ride in the Humvee, we had this
conversation:

ME: Look! I can inflate the tires as I drive!   10

MY WIFE: *Why?*   11

Another feature that my wife did not appreciate was the winch.   12
This Humvee had a SERIOUS winch in front ("It can pull down a
house," noted Terry). There's nothing like the feeling of sitting in traffic, knowing that you have a MUCH bigger winch than any of the guys
around you. Plus, a winch can be mighty handy in an emergency. Like,
suppose some jerk runs you off the road into a ditch. After a tow truck
pulls you out, you could find out where the jerk lives, then use your winch
to pull down his house.

The Humvee also boasts an engine. Terry offered to show it to me,   13
but I have a strict policy of not looking at engines, because whenever
I do, a mechanic appears and says "There's your problem right there"
and charges me $758. I can tell you this, however: The Humvee engine is LOUD. I picture dozens of sweating men under the hood, furiously shoveling coal as Leonardo DiCaprio and Kate Winslet run
gaily past.[2]

As for comfort: Despite the Humvee's ruggedness, when it's cruising on the highway, the "ride" is surprisingly similar to that of a full-size luxury sedan being dragged across a boulder field, on its roof. But   14
a truly masculine, big-winched man does not need comfort. All he
needs is the knowledge that he can take his vehicle into harsh and unforgiving terrain. And I gave the Humvee the toughest challenge you
can give a car in America. That's right: I drove it to a shopping mall
just before Christmas.

Perhaps you think I was foolhardy. Well, people said that the   15
Portuguese explorer Vasco da Gama was foolhardy, too, and do you
remember what he did? Neither do I. But if he had not done it, I
doubt that Portugal would be what it is today: a leading producer of
cork.

---

[2] DiCaprio and Winslet starred in the 1997 film *Titanic*. The doomed steamship was
powered by manually fed coal furnaces. [Editor's note.]

And thus I found myself piloting the Humvee through the mall   *16*
parking structure at roughly the speed of soybean growth, knowing
that I was competing for the one available parking space with roughly
20,000 other motorists, but also knowing that ALL of them would
have to stop their vehicles if they wanted to inflate or deflate their tires.
The pathetic wimps! I could not help but cackle in a manly way.
My wife was rolling her eyes at me, but by God I got us safely into
and out of there, and I doubt that I used more than 300 gallons of
fuel.

Meaning

1. In paragraph 5, Barry writes, "The Humvee is as masculine as a vehicle
   can get without actually growing hair in its wheel wells." How does this
   statement illustrate Barry's main idea?
2. A *winch* is a vehicle-mounted crank used for pulling items. How does
   Barry's use of the word in his title function as a pun, or a play on the similar sound of two words with very different meanings? How does the pun
   predict Barry's point about Humvees?
3. If any of the following words are new to you, try to guess their meanings
   from the context of Barry's essay. Test your guesses in a dictionary, and
   then use each new word in a sentence or two.

   protuberances (5)   carnality (8)
   wanton (8)   foolhardy (15)

Purpose and Audience

1. What is Barry's purpose in writing this essay: to persuade readers to purchase a Humvee? to explain why the vehicle is popular? to make fun of
   his coworker? to do something else?
2. Barry is relentless in his mockery of men who drive (or want to drive)
   Humvees. Find at least three examples of statements that are either obviously untrue or greatly exaggerated. What is the effect of Barry's use of
   hyperbole, and how does it contribute to his purpose? (If necessary, see
   hyperbole in the Glossary.)

Method and Structure

1. What is Barry's principle of analysis, and into what elements does he divide the Humvee? Be specific, supporting your answer with examples from
   the text.

2. How does Barry use the method of analysis for comic effect? In what ways does analysis lend itself particularly well to a humorous subject such as this one?

3. **Other Methods**   In addition to analysis, Barry employs description (Chapter 4) and example (Chapter 6) to illustrate the masculine appeal of Humvees, and he uses comparison and contrast (Chapter 10) to explore the differences in how men and women perceive several of the vehicle's features. Locate examples of each of these methods in Barry's essay. What do they add to his analysis of Humvees?

Language

1. What is Barry's tone? How seriously does he take his subject?

2. Note Barry's frequent use of informal language and colloquial phrases, such as "Is that cool, or WHAT?" (paragraph 6). What does he achieve with this attitude? (If necessary, see *colloquial language* in the Glossary.)

Writing Topics

1. **Journal to Essay**   Building on your journal entry (p. 149), write an essay in which you analyze the benefits and drawbacks of your current (or desired) means of transportation. Make a list of all the elements that constitute a particular vehicle or public conveyance (such as a bus or subway). In your essay examine each element to show what it contributes to the whole. Be sure your principle of analysis is clear to readers.

2. Barry jokes about the Humvee's poor gas mileage in the last paragraph of his essay, but his earlier reference to the Gulf War of 1991 (paragraph 2) subtly invokes many people's concern that American reliance on fossil fuels has significant environmental and political consequences. Write an argumentative essay that addresses the issue of America's use of fossil fuels seriously. To what extent should automotive manufacturers be required to meet environmental standards? Under what circumstances, if any, should personal choice be limited in the name of global responsibility? Be sure to include examples to support your opinions.

3. **Cultural Considerations**   Throughout his essay, Barry implies that the men who are drawn to Humvees are trying to compensate for something they think they lack. Most of us, however, have experienced a moment (or perhaps many moments) when we were tempted to buy something to make us feel better about ourselves—an impulse that some say is the direct result of advertising practices that create insecurities in order to exploit them. (Consider, for instance, weight loss ads suggesting that a size 10 woman is fat, the current push for tooth whitening, or cell phone campaigns showing the embarrassing consequences of a dropped call.) Choose an example

of advertising that you think appeals to a real or invented insecurity to sell a product, and analyze its message in a brief essay. Are the advertiser's techniques effective? ethical? entertaining? Be sure to identify a principle of analysis for your response and to support your argument with details from the advertisement.

4. **Connections**   Like Barry, Marta K. Taylor, in "Desert Dance" (p. 62), describes the strength and power conferred upon the male driver of a car. The two writers, however, offer very different interpretations of masculine roles and responsibilities. Whose concept of automotive masculinity strikes you as more realistic or insightful? Why? Explain your answer in an essay, using plenty of details from both readings to support your thesis.

You can tell the ideals of a nation by its advertisements. — Norman Douglas

The art of publicity is a black art. — Learned Hand

*Advertising may be described as the science of arresting the human
intelligence long enough to get money from it.* — Stephen Leacock

Journal Response Think of a TV commercial that you object to because it is
offensive or annoying in some way. Write about why it bothers you so much.

Shafeeq Sadiq

*Shafeeq Sadiq was born in 1977 in Stockton, California, where he grew up.
He graduated from high school in nearby Manteca, obtained an AA degree
from San Joaquin Delta College in Stockton, and finished his bachelor's degree
in economics at the University of California at Davis. He holds a law degree
from the University of California at Hastings and is now a practicing trial attorney in Stockton.*

RACISM AND SEXISM IN ADVERTISING

(STUDENT ESSAY)

*In this strong critique of advertising tactics, Sadiq offers detailed examples to
support his assertions. This essay was first published in the 1997* Delta Winds,
*a collection of student writing from San Joaquin Delta College. Sadiq updated
it for* The Compact Reader *in 2007.*

Political correctness is an inherent part of society today. Whether it   1
involves minorities or women, racist and sexist comments are rightfully
no longer tolerated in places such as the schoolyard and the workplace.
Why is it, then, that minorities and women are constantly being exploited in everyday advertisements? Television, print media, and billboards no longer show products, but rather show gimmicks in order to
sell the products. Often, these gimmicks reinforce racial stereotypes and
portray women in a negative light.

On every television channel, commercials sell products with the use   2
of beautiful women. These commercials range from alcoholic beverages
to Internet domain registrations. Who can forget the GoDaddy.com ad
campaign, with scantily clad Candice Michelle selling the Web site
with a series of commercials that had nothing to do with the Web site
itself? These commercials, still available for viewing on the Go Daddy
Web site, featured "window cleaner" Michelle rubbing her breasts
against an office window, "car washer" Michelle doing the same at a
car wash, and spokesperson Michelle having a "wardrobe malfunction" during a congressional hearing on censorship. The product is
mentioned only in passing. Advertisements like the Go Daddy campaign exploit women en route to their actual target: men. The series
of commercials would routinely air during sporting events such as the
NFL playoffs and Super Bowl, when the majority of the viewers are
male. They tied in quite nicely with similar commercials that are designed to sell beer.

Beer companies have been notorious for exploiting women in their   3
everyday promotions. Watching a sporting event, you can usually find
an attractive young lady being swept off her feet by a less than attractive man after he opens the beer of his choice. Or, if you are lucky, you
can witness several young women materialize on a desert island with
the male drinker after, of course, he opens his can of beer. These advertisements present women as a goal, a trophy if you will, that can
only be attained with the proper beverage. The women seldom have
anything to say besides "Yes," solidifying their portrayal as unintelligent sex objects.

Unfortunately, the exploitation does not stop with women. It touches   4
minority groups as well, especially the African American community.
In a recent issue of *Cosmopolitan* magazine, for example, an ad for
Boost Mobile features a young, African American male sitting in a hot
tub and staring into the sky. He is joined by three attractive women—
two white, one under each arm, and one African American, watching
the action farther to his left. The caption, "Pick up on a plan that pays
off," is followed by the company's tag line: "Where You At?" In promoting the product in a women's magazine, Boost unabashedly reinforces long-standing stereotypes of African American male sexuality.
Is that *really* where we are at? Are white women *really* the big "payoff" plan for today's young, African American male? Boost Mobile
would like us to think so.

African Americans are not the ony minority group exploited in ad-   5
vertising. Immigrants are regularly subjected to abuse as well. The most

recent perpetrator, Citibank, promoted its credit card rewards program in 2006 and 2007 with commercials featuring two cartoonish immigrant characters: Roman, a man with a thick European accent, mustache, and polyester suit, and his sidekick, Victor. According to Citibank's ad agency, the campaign was supposed to have "unique humor and charm" (qtd. in Petracca). Viewers disagreed. More than half the consumers polled for *USA Today*'s weekly Ad Track survey said they disliked the ads (Petracca). In the commercial, Roman states in his accented English that Citibank's cards are rewarding. "Very, very, very rewarding." The poll shows that most of us found the ads to be annoying. Very, very, very annoying.

Racism and sexism in advertising is a problem that often goes unnoticed by the consumer today. Nevertheless, it must be dealt with. The only winners in these types of ad campaigns are the advertisers themselves, who make money when we purchase their products. There needs to be a public awakening, for racism and sexism should not be used in any situation, especially not to sell products. Advertisers need to take responsibility for their own actions and end this type of exploitation. But if they do not do so willingly, we the consumers can always force them. After all, we have the dollars and the sense.

6

Works Cited

Boost Mobile. Advertisement. *Cosmopolitan* Dec. 2006: 72.

Godaddy.com. Advertisements. 3 Apr. 2007 <http:// www.godaddy.com/gdshop/media/lounge.asp>.

Petracca, Laura. "Citibank Ads Take a Risk to Go for Laughs." *USA Today* 22 Jan. 2007. 3 Apr. 2007 <http://www.usatoday.com/ money/advertising/adtrack/2007-01-22-citibank_x.htm>.

Meaning

1. What is Sadiq's thesis? Where does he state it explicitly?
2. In your own words, explain the process, described in paragraphs 2 and 3, by which advertisers use women to sell products to men. What, besides the product, are they selling?
3. What is wrong, in Sadiq's opinion, with a phone company's depicting an African American having a good time?
4. What does Sadiq mean in paragraph 4 when he says, "Boost unabashedly reinforces long-standing stereotypes of African American male sexuality"? What is he referring to?

5. If you are unfamiliar with any of the following words, try to guess their meanings from the context in which Sadiq uses them. Look the words up in a dictionary to check your guesses, and then use each one in a sentence or two of your own.

gimmicks (1)   materialize (3)   perpetrator (5)
notorious (3)   unabashedly (4)

Purpose and Audience

1. What do you think Sadiq's purpose was in writing this essay: to ask readers who think that racism and sexism have disappeared from advertising to reconsider? to convince advertisers to change their ways? to do something else?
2. What assumptions does Sadiq seem to make about his readers—their gender or age, their attitudes toward stereotypes of gender or race, their attitudes toward advertising, and so on?

Method and Structure

1. Why do you think Sadiq chose the method of analysis to talk about sexism and racism in advertising? How does the method help Sadiq achieve his purpose?
2. Each example Sadiq cites is a mini-analysis of a television commercial or magazine ad. By breaking down the commercial into its elements, he creates a new whole, a new way of looking at the commercial, that might not have been apparent before. Show how this analysis works in paragraph 4 of the essay, using the annotated paragraphs on pages 142–43 as a guide.
3. What does Sadiq accomplish in his first and last paragraphs?
4. Why do you think Sadiq cites more examples of racism than of sexism in advertising? Does he seem to think racism is more important or more widespread?
5. **Other Methods** The advertisements Sadiq analyzes are all examples (Chapter 6) used to illustrate racism or sexism in advertising, and each of these examples includes description (Chapter 4). What does this description contribute to Sadiq's thesis?

Language

1. How would you describe Sadiq's tone? How seriously does he take his subject? Is the tone appropriate, given his purpose?
2. Sadiq occasionally uses irony in analyzing advertisements, as in "Or, if you are lucky, you can witness several young women materialize on a desert

island with the male drinker after, of course, he opens his can of beer" (paragraph 3) or "Are white women *really* the big 'payoff' plan for today's young, African American male?" (4). Is the irony effective? Why, or why not? (See *irony* in the Glossary.)

Writing Topics

1. **Journal to Essay**   Expand your journal entry about a TV commercial (p. 155) into a full essay analyzing the commercial. Describe the commercial, and pinpoint why you find it annoying or offensive. Make sure your essay has a controlling thesis that draws together all the points of your analysis and asserts why the commercial has the effect it does. Alternatively, you could choose a commercial you think is unusually entertaining, amusing, or moving and explain why it works. Be sure to document your sources, as Sadiq does (see p. 157).

2. How did you react to Sadiq's essay? Do you agree with him that too many commercials remain sexist or racist in an age of supposed tolerance? Or do you find his complaints to be exaggerated, the offenses he points out rare or minor? Write an essay of your own responding to Sadiq's essay. Be sure to include examples to support your view.

3. **Cultural Considerations**   Sadiq is critical of an advertisement for Boost Mobile that he sees as depicting an African American in a negative light. However, what if the ad was created by African Americans for African Americans? Would it still seem to stereotype? And if so, do the members of a minority group have a license to employ stereotypes about themselves, either in jest or as a way of deflating the stereotypes? Write an essay in which you state your position on this issue and support it using examples.

4. **Connections**   Write a two-paragraph comparison of paragraph 4 of Sadiq's essay and the paragraph by Luci Tapahonso on page 142. Each paragraph analyzes a single advertisement, but the tones of the two paragraphs are quite different. How do the words used by each author convey his or her attitude toward the advertisement?

Television—teacher, mother, secret lover!   —Homer Simpson

Television is chewing gum for the eyes.   —Frank Lloyd Wright

The medium is the message.   —Marshall McLuhan

Journal Response   Reflect for a few moments on your favorite show on TV. Write a journal entry explaining what you like about the show, trying to get down as many details as you can.

Thomas de Zengotita

A contributing editor for Harper's Magazine, *Thomas de Zengotita (born 1943) earned a PhD in anthropology from Columbia University in 1985 and teaches at both the Dalton School (a private preparatory school in Manhattan) and New York University's Draper Graduate Program. His essays have appeared in the* Christian Science Monitor *and* Los Angeles Times; Harper's Magazine, *the* Nation, *and* Shout Magazine; *and the scholarly journal* Cultural Anthropology. *He also maintains a blog for the Huffington Post. De Zengotita's interest in the ways that mass media influence thought and behavior led him to develop the analytic concept of* mediation, *which theorizes that every aspect of our consciousness is filtered through what we see and hear in popular culture. He elaborates on this central idea of his critical work in* Mediated: How the Media Shapes Your World and the Way You Live in It *(2005), his widely acclaimed first book.*

AMERICAN IDOL WORSHIP

A major tenet of de Zengotita's theory of mediation is that the media flatter audiences by suggesting that every popular culture production is ultimately about the people who consume it. (As he explains it in his introduction to Mediated, *contemporary media offer "a place where everything is addressed to us, everything is for us, and nothing is beyond us anymore.") In this essay, written in February 2006 and published in both the* Los Angeles Times *and the* Christian Science Monitor, *de Zengotita examines how this flattery plays out in one of the most popular media productions going—the television reality show* American Idol.

When the ratings numbers came in after last week's Grammy Awards,   *1*
the news wasn't good for the professionals. A show that features amateurs had attracted a far bigger audience than had one with the likes
of Madonna, Coldplay, and U2. . . . *American Idol* drew almost twice
as many viewers as the awards show. What's going on here? Why does
this reality show consistently attract the weekly attention of close to
35 million viewers?

It's a nexus of factors shaping the "virtual revolution" unfolding   *2*
all around us, on so many fronts. Think chat rooms, MySpace.com,
blogs, life journals illustrated with photos snapped by cell phones, flash-
mobbing, marathon running, focus groups, talk radio, e-mails to news
shows, camcorders, sponsored sports teams for tots—and every garage
band in town with its own CD. What do all these platforms have in
common? They are all devoted to otherwise anonymous people who
don't want to be mere spectators. In this virtual revolution, it's not
workers against capitalists—that's so 19th century. In our mediated
world, it's spectators against celebrities, with spectators demanding a
share of the last scarce resource in the overdeveloped world—attention. The *American Idol* format combines essential elements of this
revolution.

Have you followed the ruckus over why people don't have heroes   *3*
anymore—in the old-fashioned statesman, warrior, genius, artist kind
of way? People concerned with education are especially alarmed. They
invest a lot of energy in trying to rekindle an aura of greatness around
the Founding Fathers. But it's hopeless. Ask natural-born citizens of the
mediated world who their heroes are, and their answers fall into one
of two categories: somebody in their personal lives or performers—
above all, pop music performers.

The "everyday hero" answer reflects the virtual revolution, but what   *4*
about performers? Why are they so important to their fans? Because,
in concert especially, these new kinds of heroes create an experience of
belonging that their fans would otherwise never know, living as they do
in a marketplace of lifestyles that can make one's existence feel optional.
That's why there's a religious quality to a concert when the star meets
the audience's awesome expectations and creates, in song and persona,
a moment in which each individual feels personally understood and, at
the same time, fused with other fans in a larger common identity. "Performer heroes" are, in the end, all about us. They don't summon us to
serve a cause—other than the one of being who we are. So, naturally,
they have been leaders of the virtual revolution. From their perch on
high, they make us the focus of attention.

American Idol takes the next step. It unites both aspects of the   5
relationship—in the climactic final rounds, a fan becomes an idol; the
ultimate dream of our age comes true before our eyes and in our hearts.
That's mediational magic.   6

And don't forget the power of music. *American Idol* wouldn't be   7
what it is if, say, amateur actors were auditioning. You can disagree
with someone about movie stars and TV shows and still be friends. But
you can't be friends with someone who loves the latest boy band, in a
totally unironic way, if you are into Gillian Welch. That's because
tastes in pop music go right to the core of who you are, with a depth
and immediacy no other art form can match. Music takes hold of you
on levels deeper than articulated meaning. That's why words, sustained
by music, have such power. There is nothing like a song for expressing who we are.

That brings us to the early rounds of *American Idol*, in which con-   8
testants are chosen for the final competition in Hollywood. The conventional wisdom is that they're an exercise in public humiliation, long
a staple of reality TV. That's not wrong, as far as it goes, but it isn't
just any old humiliation exercise—it is the most excruciating form of
voluntary personal humiliation the human condition allows for because
it involves the most revealing kind of performance there is, this side of
pornography. During this phase of the show, the audience, knowing
it will eventually fuse in a positive way with a finalist idol, gets to be
in the most popular clique on the planet, rendering snarky judgments
on one of the most embarrassing pools of losers ever assembled.

American Idol gives you so many ways to feel good about yourself.   9
No wonder it's a hit.   10

Meaning

1. What is de Zengotita's thesis? Where does he state it explicitly? Try to
   summarize the central meaning of de Zengotita's analysis in a sentence
   or two of your own.
2. According to de Zengotita, what elements define the "virtual revolution"
   (paragraph 2)? How does *American Idol* bring together these elements to
   create an irresistible media experience?
3. What do you think de Zengotita means when he writes, "*American Idol* . . .
   unites both aspects of the relationship—in the climactic final rounds, a fan
   becomes an idol; the ultimate dream of our age comes true before our eyes
   and in our hearts. . . . That's mediational magic" (paragraphs 5 and 6)? According to de Zengotita, how does *American Idol* transform both the contestants and the audience?

4. Try to guess the meanings of any of the following words that you are un-sure of, based on their context in de Zengotita's essay. Test your guesses in a dictionary, and then try to use each word in a sentence or two of your own.

nexus (2)	persona (4)	excruciating (8)
ruckus (3)	climactic (5)	clique (8)
rekindle (3)	unironic (7)	snarky (8)
aura (3)	articulated (7)	

Purpose and Audience

1. What do you think was de Zengotita's purpose in writing this essay? Does he want to shock, inform, persuade, or entertain his readers? Or does he have another purpose? What evidence from the text supports your view-point?

2. What assumptions does de Zengotita make about his audience? Does he assume that his readers are familiar with *American Idol*? with his theory of *mediation*? How familiar with the show (or the author's theory) would readers have to be in order to understand de Zengotita's analysis?

Method and Structure

1. De Zengotita's immediate subject of analysis is *American Idol*, but he's also using the show to examine a wider phenomenon. What is that wider phe-nomenon? How does the author's analysis of *American Idol* explain it?

2. What is de Zengotita's principle of analysis, and what elements of *Amer-ican Idol* does he analyze? How does he reassemble these elements into a new whole? Support your answer with evidence from the essay.

3. De Zengotita begins his essay by contrasting *American Idol*'s ratings with those for the Grammy Awards. How does beginning with this compari-son foreshadow the conclusions he draws about the implications of the "virtual revolution" in popular culture?

4. **Other Methods** In addition to division, de Zengotita uses cause-and-effect analysis (Chapter 12) to show how *American Idol*'s individual elements ex-plain its popularity. What does this cause-and-effect analysis add to the analysis of *American Idol*? What would be lost without it?

Language

1. As is the case with most of de Zengotita's writing, this essay combines loose, informal language — "What's going on here?" (paragraph 1) and "that's so 19th century" (paragraph 2) — with scholarly vocabulary to

explore a complex idea. What do you suppose is the author's purpose in employing these different levels of diction? What is the effect on you as a reader? (If necessary, see *diction* in the Glossary.)

2. Notice that throughout his essay, de Zengotita shifts back and forth between first person (*we, us, our*), second person (*you*), and third person (*they/them*). Can you find an underlying purpose for the different uses? Do the shifts in point of view add or detract from the overall effect of the essay? Why?

Writing Topics

1. **Journal to Essay**   In your journal entry (p. 160) you reflected on your favorite television show. Now write a more formal essay in which you describe that TV show and explain what makes it so enjoyable for you. Just as de Zengotita took *American Idol* apart to understand its popularity, explain what elements contribute to the appeal of the show you selected. Does its appeal rest mostly on the actors involved, the places depicted, the story line, or other features? Does it make you think about who you are as a person or change your view of the world? If it is merely good "entertainment," describe what makes it so.

2. The concept of *mediation* runs throughout "*American Idol* Worship" and nearly everything else that Thomas de Zengotita has written. Although the idea may seem complicated, it boils down to a relatively simple concept: de Zengotita believes that popular culture influences the way we perceive the world and ourselves. What do you think of this notion? Do the media control how you think, or can you pick and choose among its offerings without being affected in any meaningful way? Write an essay that uses the concept of mediation to explore your relationship with an aspect of popular culture of your choosing (for example, you might examine how a fashion or "lifestyle" magazine has changed the way you look at yourself, or describe how a song changed your attitude toward a problem you were facing). Or, if you don't accept the concept of mediation, write an essay that uses examples from your own experience to explain why you disagree with de Zengotita. If time allows, consider doing additional research on de Zengotita's theories to inform your analysis.

3. **Cultural Considerations**   American television programs are watched all over the world: *Baywatch*, for example, is one of the most popular shows in Germany, and *Desperate Housewives* is popular in China. Global viewers not only enjoy the programming; many say they watch to improve their English language skills or to learn about American culture. But what are they learning? Write an essay that focuses on a particular type of programming—network news, for example, or medical dramas—and explores how a non-American viewer might interpret it. Does the pro-

gramming provide an accurate depiction of life in the United States, or does it distort American realities?

4. **Connections** De Zengotita and Dave Barry, in "Humvee Satisfies a Man's Lust for Winches" (p. 149), both refer to popular culture's power to make us feel better about ourselves. At the same time, both writers suggest that such good feelings are superficial at best, maybe even harmful on a deeper level. Write an essay in which you analyze the effects of popular culture on self-esteem, drawing on both essays and your own understanding of this issue.

Division or Analysis

Choose one of the following topics, or any other topic they suggest, for an essay developed by analysis. The topic you decide on should be something you care about so that analysis is a means of communicating an idea, not an end in itself.

PEOPLE, ANIMALS, AND OBJECTS

1. The personality of a friend or relative
2. The personality of a typical politician, teacher, or other professional
3. An animal such as a cat, dog, horse, cow, spider, or bat
4. A machine or appliance such as a car engine, harvesting combine, laptop computer, hair dryer, toaster, or sewing machine
5. A nonmotorized vehicle such as a skateboard, in-line skate, bicycle, or snowboard
6. A building such as a hospital, theater, or sports arena

IDEAS

7. The perfect city
8. The perfect crime
9. A theory or concept in a field such as psychology, sociology, economics, biology, physics, engineering, or astronomy
10. The evidence in a political argument (written, spoken, or reported in the news)
11. A liberal arts education

ASPECTS OF CULTURE

12. A style of dress or "look," such as that associated with the typical businessperson, bodybuilder, rap musician, or outdoors enthusiast
13. A typical hero or villain in science fiction, romance novels, war movies, or movies or novels about adolescents
14. A television or film comedy
15. A literary work: short story, novel, poem, essay
16. A visual work: painting, sculpture, building
17. A musical work: song, concerto, symphony, opera
18. A performance: sports, acting, dance, music, speech
19. The slang of a particular group or occupation

WRITING ABOUT THE THEME
Looking at Popular Culture

1. The essays by Dave Barry (p. 149), Shafeeq Sadiq (p. 155), and Thomas de Zengotita (p. 160) all include the theme that what you see—whether in consumer products, advertising, or entertainment—is not all you get. Think of something you have used, seen, or otherwise experienced that made you suspect a hidden message or agenda. Consider, for example, a childhood toy, a popular breakfast cereal, a political speech, a magazine, a textbook, a video game, a movie, or a visit to a theme park such as Disney World. Using the essays in this chapter as models, write an analysis of your subject, making sure to divide it into distinct elements, and conclude by reassembling these elements into a new whole.

2. Luci Tapahonso (p. 142) and Shafeeq Sadiq both analyze television advertising. Sadiq calls for a "public awakening" to racist and sexist advertising. Tapahonso, in contrast, thinks that Native Americans found cause for celebration in a positive commercial that "showed Indians as we live today." What do you think of television advertising? Is Sadiq's concern justified, or are the ads he singles out unusual? How common are ads like the one Tapahonso analyzes? Consider ads you've seen, or pay close attention to the ads as you're watching television over a week or so. Then write an essay addressing whether advertisers seem to treat the differences among people fairly or to exploit those differences. Are there notable exceptions in either case?

3. Thomas de Zengotita argues that popular culture is moving in a new direction that shifts power to the audience. Ours, he says, is a "mediated world," where "it's spectators against celebrities, with spectators demanding a share of the last scarce resource in the overdeveloped world—attention." How do de Zengotita's observations affect your reading of the other examples of popular culture described in this chapter? For instance, does Jon Pareles (p. 142) present Keith Richards as an "everyday hero" or a "performer hero"? Did Native American viewers appreciate the advertisement described by Luci Tapahonso because it made them the center of attention? Are some men drawn to Humvees because it makes them feel powerful? Write an essay using de Zengotita's concept of mediation to explain the appeal (or lack of appeal) of one or several of the popular culture examples discussed in this chapter. Quote de Zengotita's analysis and passages from other writers as necessary, being sure to use proper citation format to acknowledge your sources.

Chapter 8

CLASSIFICATION

Sorting Group Identities

We **classify** when we sort things into groups: kinds of cars, styles of writing, types of customers. Because it creates order, classification helps us make sense of our experiences and our surroundings. With it, we see the correspondences among like things and distinguish them from unlike things, similarities and distinctions that can be especially helpful when making a decision or encouraging others to see things from a new perspective. You use classification when you prioritize your bills, sort your laundry, or organize your music collection; you might also draw on the method to choose among types of cell phone plans, to propose new pay scales at your place of work, or argue at a town meeting that some types of community projects are more valuable than others. Because classification helps us name things, remember them, and discuss them with others, it is also a useful method for developing and sharing ideas in writing.

READING CLASSIFICATION

Writers classify primarily to explain a pattern in a subject that might not have been noticed before: a sportswriter, for instance, might observe that basketball players tend to fall into one of three groups based on the aggressiveness of their play. Sometimes, writers also classify to persuade readers that one group is superior: a sportswriter might argue that one style of basketball play is more effective than the other two.

Writers who classify follow a three-step process:

1. Separate things into their elements, using the method of division or analysis (previous chapter).
2. Isolate the similarities among the elements.
3. Group or classify the things based on those similarities, matching like with like.

The following diagram illustrates a classification essay that appears later in this chapter, "The People Next Door" by Jonathan R. Gould Jr. (p. 176). Gould's subject is neighbors, and he sees four distinct kinds:

All the members of Gould's overall group share at least one characteristic: they have been Gould's neighbors. The members of each subgroup also share at least one characteristic: they are too friendly, for instance, or unsociable. The people in each subgroup are independent of each other, and none of them is essential to the existence of the subgroup: the kind of neighbor would continue to exist even if at the moment Gould didn't live next door to such a person.

The number of groups in a classification scheme depends entirely on the basis for establishing the classes in the first place. There are two systems:

- In a **complex classification** like that used for neighbors, each individual fits firmly into one class because of at least one distinguishing feature shared with all members of that class but not with any members of any other classes. All the too-friendly neighbors are overly friendly, but none of the unsociable, irritable, or just-right neighbors is.

- In a **binary or two-part classification**, two classes are in opposition to each other, such as constructive and destructive neighbors. Often, one group has a certain characteristic that the other group lacks. For instance, neighbors could be classified into those who respect your privacy and those who don't. A binary scheme is useful to emphasize the possession of a particular characteristic, but it is limited if it specifies nothing about the members of the "other" class except that they lack the trait. (An old joke claims that there are two kinds of people in the world—those who classify and all others.)

Sorting items demands a **principle of classification** that determines the groups by distinguishing them. For instance, Gould's principle in identifying four groups of neighbors is their behavior toward him and his family. Principles for sorting a year's movies might be genre (action-adventure, comedy, drama); place of origin (domestic, foreign); or cost of production (low-budget, medium-priced, high-budget). The choice of a principle depends on the writer's main interest in the subject.

Although a writer may emphasize one class over the others, the classification itself must be complete and consistent. A classification of movies by genre would be incomplete if it omitted comedies. It would be inconsistent if it included action-adventures, comedies, dramas, low-budget films, and foreign films: such a system mixes *three* principles (genre, cost, origin); it omits whole classes (what of high-budget domestic dramas?); and it overlaps other classes (a low-budget foreign action-adventure would fit in three different groups).

ANALYZING CLASSIFICATION IN PARAGRAPHS

Max Eastman (1883–1969) was a political organizer and tract writer and also a poet and scholar of Russian. This paragraph comes from his book *Enjoyment of Poetry* (1913).

A simple experiment will distinguish two types of human nature. Gather a throng of people and pour them into a ferryboat. By the time the boat has swung into the river you will find that a certain proportion have taken the trouble to climb upstairs in order to be out on deck and see what is to be seen as they cross over. The rest have settled indoors to think what they will do upon reaching the other side, or perhaps lose themselves in apathy or tobacco smoke. But leaving out those apathetic, or addicted to a single enjoyment, we may divide all the alert passengers on the boat into two classes: those who are interested in crossing the

Principle of classification (topic sentences underlined toward end): attitude toward experience and goals

1. Poetic people: focused on experience

2. Practical people: focused on goals

river, and those who are merely interested in getting
across. And we may divide all the people on the earth, or
all the moods of people, in the same way. Some of them
are chiefly occupied with attaining ends, and some with
receiving experiences. The distinction of the two will be
more marked when we name the first kind practical, and
the second poetic, for common knowledge recognizes that
a person poetic or in a poetic mood is impractical, and a
practical person is intolerant of poetry.

E. B. White (1899–1985) is well loved for his essays, verse, and fiction, including the children's stories *Charlotte's Web* and *Stuart Little* and the classic writing guide *The Elements of Style* (written with his college professor William Strunk Jr.). The following paragraph is from White's long essay *Here Is New York* (1949), first published in *Holiday* magazine and later reprinted in book form.

There are roughly three New Yorks. There is, first, the New York of the man or woman who was born here, who takes the city for granted and accepts its size and its turbulence as natural and inevitable. Second, there is the New York of the commuter—the city that is devoured by locust each day and spat out each night. Third, there is the New York of the person who was born somewhere else and came to New York in quest of something. Of these three trembling cities the greatest is the last—the city that accounts for New York's high-strung disposition, its poetical deportment, its dedication to the arts, and its incomparable achievements. Commuters give the city its tidal restlessness; natives give it solidity and continuity; but the settlers give it passion. And whether it is a farmer arriving from Italy to set up a small grocery store in a slum, or a young girl arriving from a small town in Mississippi to escape the indignity of being observed by her neighbors, of a boy arriving from the Corn Belt with a manuscript in his suitcase and a pain in his heart, it makes no difference; each embraces New York with the intense excitement of first love, each absorbs New York with the fresh eyes of an adventurer, each generates heat and light to dwarf the Consolidated Edison Company.

Principle of classification: origins of people who live in New York City

Topic sentence and identification of groups (underlined): (1) natives, (2) commuters, (3) settlers

Expanded discussion of group 3, explaining its significance

DEVELOPING AN ESSAY BY CLASSIFICATION
Getting Started

Classification essays are often assigned in college: you might be asked to identify the major schools of therapy for a psychology class, for instance, or to categorize difficult personality types for a business communication course. When you need to develop your own subject for a classification essay, think of one large class of things whose members you've noticed fall into subclasses, such as study habits, midnight grocery shoppers, or political fund-raising appeals. Be sure that your general subject forms a class in its own right—that all its members share at least one important quality. Then look for your principle of classification, the quality or qualities that distinguish some members from others, providing poles for the members to group themselves around. One such principle for political fund-raising appeals might be the different methods of delivery, such as direct marketing, media advertising, meetings, or the Internet.

While generating ideas for your classification, keep track of them in a list, diagram, or outline to ensure that your principle is applied thoroughly (all classes) and consistently (each class relating to the principle). Fill in the list, diagram, or outline with the distinguishing features of each class and with examples that will clarify your scheme.

Forming a Thesis

You will want to state your principle of classification in a thesis sentence so that you know where you're going and your readers know where you're taking them. Be sure the sentence also conveys a *reason* for the classification so that the essay does not become a dull list of categories. The following tentative thesis sentence is mechanical; the revision is more interesting.

> TENTATIVE THESIS SENTENCE   Political fund-raising appeals are delivered in many ways.
>
> REVISED THESIS SENTENCE   Of the many ways to deliver political fund-raising appeals, the three that rely on personal contact are generally the most effective.

(Note that the revised thesis sentence implies a further classification based on whether the appeals involve personal contact or not.)

Organizing

The introduction to a classification essay should make clear why the classification is worthwhile: What situation prompted the essay? What do readers already know about the subject? What use might they make of the information you will provide? Unless your principle of classification is self-evident, you may want to explain it briefly—though save extensive explanation for the body of the essay.

In the body of the essay the classes may be arranged in order of decreasing familiarity or increasing importance or size—whatever pattern provides the emphasis you want and clarifies your scheme for readers. You should at least mention each class, but some classes may demand considerable space and detail.

A classification essay often ends with a conclusion that restores the wholeness of the subject. Among other uses, the conclusion might summarize the classes, comment on the significance of one particular class in relation to the whole, or point out a new understanding of the whole subject gained from the classification.

Drafting

For the first draft of your classification, your main goal will be to establish your scheme: spelling out the purpose and principle of classification and defining the groups so that they are complete and consistent, covering the subject without mixing principles or overlapping. The more you've been able to plan your scheme, the less difficult the draft will be. If you can also fill in the examples and other details needed to develop the groups, do so.

Be sure to consider your readers' needs as you draft. For a subject familiar to readers, such as study habits, you probably wouldn't need to justify your principle of classification, but you would need to enliven the classes themselves with vivid examples. For an unfamiliar subject, in contrast, you might need to take considerable care in explaining the principle of classification as well as in detailing the classes.

Revising and Editing

The following questions and the information in the box can help you revise and edit your classification.

- *Will readers see the purpose of your classification?* Let readers know early why you are troubling to classify your subject, and keep this purpose evident throughout the essay.
- *Is your classification complete?* Your principle of classification should create categories that encompass every representative of the general subject. If some representatives will not fit the scheme, you

---

FOCUS ON PARAGRAPH DEVELOPMENT

A crucial aim of revising a classification is to make sure each group is clear: what's counted in, what's counted out, and why. You'll provide the examples and other details that make the groups clear as you develop the paragraph(s) devoted to each group.

The following paragraph gives just the outline of one group in a four-part classification of ex-smokers into zealots, evangelists, the elect, and the serene:

> The second group, evangelists, does not condemn smokers but encourages them to quit. Evangelists think quitting is easy, and they preach this message, often earning the resentment of potential converts.

Contrast this bare-bones adaptation with the actual paragraphs written by Franklin E. Zimring in his essay "Confessions of a Former Smoker":

> By contrast, the antismoking evangelist does not condemn smokers. Unlike the zealot, he regards smoking as an easily curable condition, as a social disease, and not a sin. The evangelist spends an enormous amount of time seeking and preaching to the unconverted. He argues that kicking the habit is not *that* difficult. After all, *he* did it; moreover, as he describes it, the benefits of quitting are beyond measure and the disadvantages are nil.
>
> The hallmark of the evangelist is his insistence that he never misses tobacco. Though he is less hostile to smokers than the zealot, he is resented more. Friends and loved ones who have been the targets of his preachments frequently greet the resumption of smoking by the evangelist as an occasion for unmitigated glee.

In the second sentence of both paragraphs, Zimring explicitly contrasts evangelists with zealots, the group he previously defined. And he does more as well: he provides specific examples of the evangelist's message (first paragraph) and of others' reactions to him (second paragraph). These details pin down the group, making it distinct from other groups and clear in itself.

For more on paragraph development through specifics, see page 38.

may have to create a new category or revise the existing categories to include them.

- *Is your classification consistent?* Consistency is essential to save readers from confusion or irritation. Make sure all the classes reflect the same principle and that they do not overlap. Remedy flaws by adjusting the classes or creating new ones.

A NOTE ON THEMATIC CONNECTIONS

Writers classify people more than any other subject, perhaps because the method gives order and even humor to our relationships with each other. The authors in this chapter explore the group identities that give people a sense of where they fit in various kinds of communities. In a paragraph, Max Eastman identifies two types of people, the practical and the poets (p. 170). Also in a paragraph, E. B. White sorts New Yorkers by their places of origin (p. 171). Jonathan Gould's essay finds four kinds of next-door neighbors (p. 176). Marion Winik's essay categorizes her friends into nine groups (p. 180). And Walter Mosley's essay proposes a new system for determining one's place in the American class structure (p. 186).

We make our friends; we make our enemies; but God makes our next-door neighbor.   —G. K. Chesterton

Good fences make good neighbors.   —Proverb

For what do we live, but to make sport for our neighbours, and laugh at them in our turn?   —Jane Austen

Journal Response   Jot down a list of neighbors you have now and have had in the past. Then write a short journal entry about the different kinds of neighbors you have encountered.

———————— Jonathan R. Gould Jr. ————————

Jonathan R. Gould Jr. was born in 1968 in Little Falls, New York, and grew up on a dairy farm in nearby Fort Plain. Graduating from Little Falls Baptist Academy, he was valedictorian of his class. He served three years in the US Army, specializing in administration and computer programming. At the State University of New York (SUNY) at Oneonta, he was an honors student, received the Provost Award for academic distinction, and obtained a BS in mathematics education.

THE PEOPLE NEXT DOOR
(STUDENT ESSAY)

From his experiences in many different settings, Gould identifies four types of neighbors, only one of which could be considered truly neighborly. Gould wrote this essay in 1994 for a writing course at SUNY.

I have moved more often than I care to remember. However, one thing   1
always stays the same no matter where I have been. There is always a
house next door, and that house contains neighbors. Over time, I have
begun putting my neighbors into one of four categories: too friendly,
unsociable, irritable, and just right.

Neighbors who are too friendly can be seen just about anywhere.   2
I mean that both ways. They exist in every neighborhood I have ever
lived in and seem to appear everywhere I go. For some strange reason
these people become extremely attached to my family and stop in as

many as eight to ten times a day. No matter how tired I appear to be, nothing short of opening the door and suggesting they leave will make them go home at night. (I once told an unusually friendly neighbor that his house was on fire, in an attempt to make him leave, and he still took ten minutes to say goodbye.) What is truly interesting about these people is their strong desire to cook for us even though they have developed no culinary skill whatsoever. (This has always proved particularly disconcerting since they stay to watch us eat every bite as they continually ask if the food "tastes good.")

The unsociable neighbor is a different story altogether. For reasons 3 of his own, he has decided to pretend that we do not exist. I have always found that one or two neighbors of this type are in my neighborhood. It is not easy to identify these people, because they seldom leave the shelter of their own house. To be honest, the only way I know that someone lives in their building is the presence of a name on the mailbox and the lights shining through the windows at night. My wife often tries to befriend these unique people, and I have to admire her courage. However, even her serenity is shaken when she offers our neighbors a fresh-baked apple pie only to have them look at her as if she intended to poison them.

Probably the most difficult neighbor to deal with is the irritable 4 neighbor. This individual probably has several problems, but he has reduced all those problems down to one cause — the proximity of my family to his residence. Fortunately, I have only encountered this type of neighbor in a handful of settings. (He is usually too busy with one group of "troublemakers" to pick up a new set.) The times that I have encountered this rascal, however, have proved more than enough for my tastes. He is more than willing to talk to me. Unfortunately, all he wants to tell me is how miserable my family is making him. Ignoring this individual has not worked for me yet. (He just adds my "snobbishness" to his list of faults that my family displays.) Interestingly, this fellow will eat anything my wife (bless her soul) might make in an attempt to be sociable. Even though he never has anything good to say about the food, not a crumb will be left on the plate when he is finished (which leads me to wonder just how starved and impoverished he must be).

At the risk of sounding like Goldilocks, there is also a neighbor 5 who is "just right." One of the most wonderful things about this neighbor is that there has always been at least one everywhere I have gone. We meet often (though not too often), and our greetings are always sincere. Occasionally, our families will go out to eat or to shop, or just sit and talk. We tend to spend as much time at their house as they do at ours (two to three times a month), and everyone knows just when it is time to say goodnight. For some reason, this neighbor knows how to cook, and we frequently exchange baked goods as well as pleasantries. For obvious reasons, this type of neighbor is my favorite.

As I mentioned before, each type of neighbor I have encountered is   6 a common sight in any neighborhood. I have always felt it was important to identify the type of neighbors that were around me. Then I am better able to maintain a clear perspective on our relationship and understand their needs. After all, people do not really change; we just learn how to live with both the good and the bad aspects of their behavior.

Meaning

1. Where does Gould state his thesis?
2. What is the difference between unsociable and irritable neighbors in Gould's classification?
3. From their context in Gould's essay, try to guess the meanings of any of the following words that are unfamiliar to you. Check your definitions against a dictionary's, and then write a sentence or two using each new word.

culinary (2)   proximity (4)   pleasantries (5)
disconcerting (2)   impoverished (4)

Purpose and Audience

1. Why do you suppose Gould wrote this essay? Where does he give the clearest indication?
2. Does Gould make any assumptions about his audience? Does he seem to be writing for a certain type of reader?

Method and Structure

1. Why do you think Gould chose the method of classification to write about the subject of neighbors? How does the method help him achieve his purpose?
2. What is Gould's principle of classification? Do you think his classification is complete and consistent? How else might he have sorted neighbors?
3. Why do you think Gould stresses the fact that he has encountered most of these types of neighbors everywhere he has lived?
4. What does Gould accomplish in his conclusion?
5. **Other Methods**   Gould's categories lend themselves to comparison and contrast (Chapter 10). Based on his descriptions, what are the differences between the too-friendly neighbor and the just-right neighbor?

Language

1. What is Gould's tone? How seriously does he take the problem of difficult neighbors?
2. Point out several instances of hyperbole or overstatement in the essay. What effect do these have?

Writing Topics

1. **Journal to Essay**　In your journal entry (p. 176) you began a process of classification by focusing on neighbors you have had. Now think of a group to which you belong—a religious organization, your family, a club or committee, even a writing class. Write a classification essay in which you sort the group's members into categories according to a clear principle of classification. Be sure to label and define each type for your readers, to provide examples, and to position yourself in one of the categories. What does your classification reveal about the group as a whole?
2. Most of us have had at least one colorful or bothersome neighbor at some time or another—a busybody, a recluse, a Peeping Tom. Write a descriptive essay (with some narration) about an interesting neighbor you have known or a narrative essay (with some description) about a memorable run-in with a neighbor.
3. Television has provided us with a large array of eccentric neighbors— from the Nortons in *The Honeymooners* to Rhoda Morgenstern in *The Mary Tyler Moore Show* to Cosmo Kramer in *Seinfeld*. Write an essay in which you classify the kinds of neighbors depicted on TV. You may borrow Gould's principle of classification if it fits, or come up with an alternative one of your own.
4. **Cultural Considerations**　"Good fences make good neighbors," says a character in Robert Frost's poem "Mending Wall," and many people in our live-and-let-live society would seem to agree. Is the best neighbor an invisible one? Or do we lose something when we ignore those who are literally closest to us? Write an essay giving a definition of what it means to be a good neighbor. Or, if you prefer, write an essay in which you compare and contrast neighboring habits in different types of communities you have lived in or know of.
5. **Connections**　Both Gould and Marion Winik, in "What Are Friends For?" (p. 180), classify common relationships: Gould distinguishes four categories of neighbors, while Winik pinpoints nine types of friends. Write an essay in which you compare the two essays. How persuasive do you find each writer's groups? Which comes closest to your own experiences with neighbors or friends? Why?

I get by with a little help from my friends.

—John Lennon and Paul McCartney

If a man does not make new acquaintances as he advances through life, he will soon find himself alone.

—Samuel Johnson

We need new friends. Some of us are cannibals who have eaten their old friends up; others must have ever-renewed audiences before whom to reenact an ideal version of their lives.

—Logan Pearsall Smith

Journal Response   Draw up a list of your friends. Include people you see on a regular basis and others you haven't seen for a while. Can you sort them into categories—for instance, by the places you see them, the things you discuss with them, the ways they make you feel, or their importance to you?

Marion Winik

Marion Winik was born in New York City in 1958. She received her BA from Brown University and her MFA from Brooklyn College. Perhaps best known as a commentator for National Public Radio's All Things Considered, *Winik is a contributing editor for American Airlines' in-flight magazine and regularly publishes pieces in well-known print periodicals such as* Parenting, Cosmopolitan, Reader's Digest, *and the* Utne Reader. *Her books include* Telling: Confessions, Concessions, and Other Flashes of Light *(1995) and* First Comes Love *(1997), a memoir about life with her gay, AIDS-infected husband. She's also the author of* The Lunch Box Chronicles *(1999), which deals with single parenthood in the nineties.*

WHAT ARE FRIENDS FOR?

In "What Are Friends For?" Winik locates various kinds of friends, from "Faraway" to "Hero" to "Friends You Love to Hate." The essay appears in Winik's collection Telling: Confessions, Concessions, and Other Flashes of Light.

I was thinking about how everybody can't be everything to each other, but some people can be something to each other, thank God, from the ones whose shoulder you cry on to the ones whose half-slips you borrow to the nameless ones you chat with in the grocery line.   1

Buddies, for example, are the workhorses of the friendship world, 2
the people out there on the front lines, defending you from loneliness
and boredom. They call you up, they listen to your complaints, they celebrate your successes and curse your misfortunes, and you do the same
for them in return. They hold out through innumerable crises before
concluding that the person you're dating is no good, and even then understand if you ignore their good counsel. They accompany you to a
movie with subtitles or to see the diving pig at Aquarena Springs. They
feed your cat when you are out of town and pick you up from the airport when you get back. They come over to help you decide what to
wear on a date. Even if it is with that creep.

What about family members? Most of them are people you just got 3
stuck with, and though you love them, you may not have very much in
common. But there is that rare exception, the Relative Friend. It is your
cousin, your brother, maybe even your aunt. The two of you share the
same views of the other family members. Meg never should have divorced Martin. He was the best thing that ever happened to her. You
can confirm each other's memories of things that happened a long time
ago. Don't you remember when Uncle Hank and Daddy had that awful
fight in the middle of Thanksgiving dinner? Grandma always hated
Grandpa's stamp collection; she probably left the windows open during the hurricane on purpose.

While so many family relationships are tinged with guilt and obli- 4
gation, a relationship with a Relative Friend is relatively worry free.
You don't even have to hide your vices from this delightful person. When
you slip out Aunt Joan's back door for a cigarette, she is already there.

Then there is that special guy at work. Like all the other people at 5
the job site, at first he's just part of the scenery. But gradually he starts
to stand out from the crowd. Your friendship is cemented by jokes about
coworkers and thoughtful favors around the office. Did you see Ryan's
hair? Want half my bagel? Soon you know the names of his turtles, what
he did last Friday night, exactly which model CD player he wants for
his birthday. His handwriting is as familiar to you as your own.

Though you invite each other to parties, you somehow don't quite 6
fit into each other's outside lives. For this reason, the friendship may
not survive a job change. Company gossip, once an infallible source
of entertainment, soon awkwardly accentuates the distance between
you. But wait. Like School Friends, Work Friends share certain memories which acquire a nostalgic glow after about a decade.

A Faraway Friend is someone you grew up with or went to school 7
with or lived in the same town as until one of you moved away. Without

a Faraway Friend, you would never get any mail addressed in handwriting. A Faraway Friend calls late at night, invites you to her wedding, always says she is coming to visit but rarely shows up. An actual visit from a Faraway Friend is a cause for celebration and binges of all kinds. Cigarettes, Chips Ahoy, bottles of tequila.

Faraway Friends go through phases of intense communication, then may be out of touch for many months. Either way, the connection is always there. A conversation with your Faraway Friend always helps to put your life in perspective: when you feel you've hit a dead end, come to a confusing fork in the road, or gotten lost in some crackerbox subdivision of your life, the advice of the Faraway Friend—who has the big picture, who is so well acquainted with the route that brought you to this place—is indispensable. 8

Another useful function of the Faraway Friend is to help you remember things from a long time ago, like the name of your seventh-grade history teacher, what was in that really good stir-fry, or exactly what happened that night on the boat with the guys from Florida. 9

Ah, the Former Friend. A sad thing. At best a wistful memory, at worst a dangerous enemy who is in possession of many of your deepest secrets. But what was it that drove you apart? A misunderstanding, a betrayed confidence, an unpaid loan, an ill-conceived flirtation. A poor choice of spouse can do in a friendship just like that. Going into business together can be a serious mistake. Time, money, distance, cult religions: all noted friendship killers. You quit doing drugs, you're not such good friends with your dealer anymore. 10

And lest we forget, there are the Friends You Love to Hate. They call at inopportune times. They say stupid things. They butt in, they boss you around, they embarrass you in public. They invite themselves over. They take advantage. You've done the best you can, but they need professional help. On top of all this, they love you to death and are convinced they're your best friend on the planet. 11

So why do you continue to be involved with these people? Why do you tolerate them? On the contrary, the real question is, What would you do without them? Without Friends You Love to Hate, there would be nothing to talk about with your other friends. Their problems and their irritating stunts provide a reliable source of conversation for everyone they know. What's more, Friends You Love to Hate make you feel good about yourself, since you are obviously in so much better shape than they are. No matter what these people do, you will never get rid of them. As much as they need you, you need them too. 12

At the other end of the spectrum are Hero Friends. These people   *13*
are better than the rest of us, that's all there is to it. Their career is something you wanted to be when you grew up—painter, forest ranger, tireless doer of good. They have beautiful homes filled with special handmade things presented to them by villagers in the remote areas they
have visited in their extensive travels. Yet they are modest. They never
gossip. They are always helping others, especially those who have suffered a death in the family or an illness. You would think people like
this would just make you sick, but somehow they don't.

A New Friend is a tonic unlike any other. Say you meet her at a   *14*
party. In your bowling league. At a Japanese conversation class, perhaps.
Wherever, whenever, there's that spark of recognition. The first time you
talk, you can't believe how much you have in common. Suddenly, your
life story is interesting again, your insights fresh, your opinion valued.
Your various shortcomings are as yet completely invisible.

It's almost like falling in love.   *15*

Meaning

1. What is Winik's thesis? How does it relate to the question she poses in the title?
2. What label does Winik assign to each category of friend that she establishes? What functions does each group fulfill?
3. Winik concludes her essay by describing the experience of meeting a New
Friend (paragraph 14). How is a New Friend different from other types of
friends, and why does Winik compare this experience with falling in love?
4. Try to guess the meanings of the following words from their context in
Winik's essay. Look up the words in a dictionary to check your guesses.
Then use each word in a sentence or two of your own.

counsel (2)	binges (7)	inopportune (11)
tinged (4)	crackerbox (8)	butt in (11)
cemented (5)	wistful (10)	tonic (14)
infallible (6)	ill-conceived (10)	
nostalgic (6)	lest (11)	

Purpose and Audience

1. Winik begins her essay by saying, "I was thinking about . . . " (paragraph 1). What does this introductory sentence reveal about her purpose?

2. Is the essay addressed to both male and female readers? In your opinion, is it accessible to both sexes? Why, or why not? According to the information presented in this essay, does Winik believe that friends can be of either sex?

Method and Structure

1. Some people would not think of classifying relationships as intimate as friendships into such clear-cut categories. Does Winik's choice of method surprise you? Do you find it effective? What does this method enable her to do?

2. What is Winik's principle of classification? Does she group her friends based on differences among them independent of her or on differences in their relationships with her? Why do you think she just mentions but doesn't explain School Friends (paragraph 6)? Do you understand what she means by this category? Is it a flaw in the essay that Winik does not explain the category?

3. In paragraph 3, Winik asks "What about family members?" as a transition to the category of Relative Friends. Study how she moves from one category to another in the rest of the essay. Are her transitions appropriate and effective? Why, or why not?

4. **Other Methods**   How does Winik use definition (Chapter 11) to differentiate her categories of friends? Where in the essay does she seem to take the most care with definition? Why do you think she gives more attention to some categories than to others?

Language

1. Winik sometimes uses actual lines from conversation but without quotation marks. For example, in paragraph 3 she writes, "The two of you share the same views of the other family members. Meg should never have divorced Martin. He was the best thing that ever happened to her." Locate two other passages where dialogue blends into the text. What is the effect of this use of dialogue?

2. Winik sometimes omits words (such as *If* at the beginning of "You quit doing drugs, you're not such good friends with your dealer anymore," paragraph 10) or uses sentence fragments (such as "Even if it is with that creep," 2). Why do you think she chooses to break some rules of writing?

3. Winik uses several metaphors in the essay—for example, "Buddies . . . are the workhorses of the friendship world" (paragraph 2). Find other examples of metaphor. What do they contribute to the essay? (If necessary, review *metaphor* in the Glossary.)

Writing Topics

1. **Journal to Essay** Write an essay about one of the categories of friends that you described in your journal entry (p. 180) — for example, friends you study with, childhood friends, or friends you confide in. Using the method of classification, examine the *functions* this category of friends performs. What activities do you do with them that you don't do with others? What do you talk about? How relaxed or tense, happy or irritated, do they make you feel? Why are they significant to you? For each function, provide plenty of examples for readers.

2. Winik uses classification to explore friendship. Use the same method to develop your own essay about people with whom you do *not* get along. What categories do they fall into — for example, are some gossipy, others arrogant, still others unreliable? (Detail the categories with plenty of examples.) What does your dislike of these types of people ultimately reveal about yourself and your values?

3. **Cultural Considerations** Americans have a reputation for being very friendly, so that a stranger might smile, wish you a nice day, or even suggest having coffee together. What, in your view, is the appropriate way to interact (or not interact) with a stranger? In answering, ignore situations that might be risky, such as deserted nighttime streets or strangers who look clearly threatening. Think instead of a safe situation, such as a long line at the grocery store or coffee shop or the waiting room of a doctor's office. What are your "rules" for initiating conversation and for responding to a stranger's overtures? What informs your rules: experience? personality? upbringing? To what extent do you think your rules are invented by you or bred into you?

4. **Connections** Kaela Hobby-Reichstein's essay "Learning Race" (p. 102), like Winik's essay, touches on the importance of friendship. Hobby-Reichstein, however, writes about a category that is missing from Winik's classification: the best friend. Use Hobby-Reichstein's experience (or your own) to write a paragraph that adds the best friend to Winik's classification. As you draft, consider both what makes a person a best friend and why that kind of relationship is important to a person.

It's easy to have principles when you're rich. The important thing is to have principles when you're poor.
— Ray Kroc

Though I am grateful for the blessings of wealth, it hasn't changed who I am. My feet are still on the ground. I'm just wearing better shoes.
— Oprah Winfrey

There's nothing surer/the rich get rich and the poor get children.
— Gus Kahn and Raymond B. Egan

Journal Response   Write a short journal entry about your attitude toward money. How much is enough? Do you consider yourself wealthy? middle-class? working-class? poor? Why? How do you view people who are better-off than you are? How do you view those who are struggling to make ends meet?

Walter Mosley

A former computer programmer turned writer, Walter Mosley (born 1952) is best known for his critically acclaimed Easy Rawlins detective novels, which explore the moral ambiguities of crime in the African American neighborhoods of Los Angeles. Mosley grew up in the Watts section of Los Angeles, attended Goddard College, and received a BA in political science from Johnson State College. He worked for Mobil Oil for several years before pursuing a master's degree in writing from the City College of the City University of New York, where he later founded a publishing degree program for young urban students. In addition to the Easy Rawlins series, Mosley has published a number of mystery and science-fiction novels notable for examining issues of race and class—among them Blue Light *(1998),* Fearless Jones *(2001), and* The Wave *(2006)—as well as several collections of short stories, such as* Futureland: Nine Stories of an Imminent Future *(2001). An outspoken social critic and political activist, Mosley also writes provocative nonfiction, including regular essay contributions for the* New Yorker *and the* Nation. *He wrote the Grammy-winning liner notes for* Richard Pryor ... And It's Deep Too!: The Complete Warner Bros. Recordings (1968–1992) *(2000) and the book* Workin' on the Chain Gang: Shaking Off the Dead Hand of History *(2000), an analysis of capitalism's failings. He lives in New York.*

SHOW ME THE MONEY

In this essay Mosley draws on his research for Workin' on the Chain Gang *to propose a new system for understanding class structure in the United States. A longer version first appeared in the* Nation *on December 18, 2006, as part of a cycle of essays Mosley wrote to start a dialogue about American cultural issues that have, as he put it, "weakened our spirits to the point of collapse."*

"The rich get richer . . ." This truism is irrefutable. ". . . and the poor get poorer." We look away from ourselves, and our loved ones, when the latter phrase is used to complete the saying.

Often only the first part of this age-old axiom is quoted. It's as if we are silently saying, "There's no reason to talk about the poor, about poverty. Let's just accept the notion that money migrates toward money and leave it at that."

But where does this money, which moves so unerringly into rich folks' pockets, come from? This is one of the most important questions in everyday working people's lives. Because the money that makes the rich richer comes out of the sweat, the sacrifice, and ultimately the blood of working men and women. . . .

Most people I know consider themselves middle-class workers. They're making good money, they say, and have good credit at the bank. Their children will go to good colleges and get better jobs. They will retire in comfort and travel to Europe (or Africa) to see the genesis of their culture.

These self-proclaimed middle-class citizens feel a certain private smugness about their proven ability to make it in this world while those in the working and lower classes — because of upbringing, lack of intelligence or will, or bad luck — are merely the fuel for the wealth of the nation.

But how do you know where you fit in the class system? Is it a level of income? Is it defined by education or the kind of job you possess? Is class a function of your relationship to your labor? For instance, are you in the middle class because you own your own business? Or are we defined by our rung on the ladder? As long as we are not at the bottom (or the top), then we can say we are in the middle.

It's a difficult question because the economic state of every one's life in this world is in perpetual flux. Depression, inflation, recession — all these and many other economic events continually change our finances and redefine our position in society. Our money grows in the bank, but at the same time it loses value. Our property increases in value, but taxes and expenses also rise. We say that we own the mortgage on our home, but more often than not the mortgage controls us. To buy a $10,000 home we pay $40,000 over thirty years. Where did that extra $30,000 go?

It seems to me that we need a rule-of-thumb definition of class. We can't use the pristine forms of geometry to prove where we are and what we're worth. Mathematical sums don't define wealth; the ability to control your time and quality of life does.   8

I'd like to put forward a system of class definition that is grounded in what I believe to be a common-sense approach to the issue.   9

Poverty is defined, in my system, by people not being able to cover the basic necessities in their lives. Indispensable medical care, nutrition, a place to live: all these essentials, for poor people, are often and chronically beyond reach. If a poor person needs $10 a day to make ends meet, often he or she only makes eight and a half.   10

Wealth, in my definition, is when money is no longer an issue or a question. Wealthy people don't know how much money they have or how much they make. Their worth is gauged in property, natural resources and power, in doors they can go through and the way the law works. Wealth moves like a shark over the rockbound crustaceans of the poor and working classes.   11

The middle classes, which logic would tell us occupy the space between poverty and wealth, are made up of two very different subspecies. One is the working class; the other is the class of limited privilege.   12

It is my proposition that the great majority of us fall into the former group. The privileged middle class are people who have to work for a living but who can buy almost anything they desire: a summer cottage, a prestige car, berths at the finer schools for their children. These people are lawyers, real estate developers, the owners of small and successful businesses. If someone in the class of privilege were to lose his job or experience reversals in his business, he would have time (between nine and twelve months) to consider his options before any part of his lifestyle would necessitate change. His children could stay in private schools, he could still go to fine restaurants and the opera on Friday nights, and even donate to the same charities.   13

But if a person from the working class loses her job, she would have to find an equivalent one within the month or it'll be fast food and junior college for everyone in the family.   14

Working-class people are (excuse the Marxism) wage-slaves. Those in the working class live on the edge of poverty, saying to themselves that they are doing all right. They drink and watch far too much TV.   15

They buy Lotto tickets and live moderate lives that are far beyond their means. The profit they generate flows to the rich, and they borrow to fill out the coffers.

Most Americans are working-class wage-slaves, arguing that they're   16
better off. This fantasy, more than any other confusion, hobbles us. Because we fear to see how delicate our economic state is, we cannot motivate ourselves to demand change.

Capitalism, the accrual of wealth from labor, is the religion of   17
America; poverty our cardinal sin. To recognize our position in relation to wealth would be perceived as a confession of wrongdoing, and so we stoically bear up, pretending we are doing all right. And because we don't see ourselves clearly, we have poor healthcare, no adequate insurance for old age, poisons in our water and our food and the continual nagging fear that things may at any moment fall apart.

Where is the money? It's not in our bank accounts or serving our   18
people. It's not in affordable housing, quality education or the development of sciences that would better the species and the planet. It's not being used for the purpose of global peace.

America is the wealthiest nation in the world, by far, but we the   19
American people are not wealthy. We, most of us, live on the border of poverty. In the distance are towering silvery skyscrapers housing our corporations and our billionaires. But do not be fooled. This skyline does not belong to us. We are not partners in the corporation of America....

This knowledge, as depressing and oppressing as it is, is also a har-   20
binger of hope. Poverty is not our fault or our destiny. We, the poor and working class, have built this nation and it, along with all its fabulous wealth, belongs to us. From the Atlantic to the Pacific we, the workers, are the ones who hold sway. And every vault, every clinic, every drop of sweat fallen upon American soil is our democratic birthright....

A man can be rich, but only a nation can be wealthy. And if any   21
person of any age suffers from poverty, then our whole country bears the shame.

Meaning

1. What is the author's thesis? What reasons does he give for classifying?
2. In which category does Mosley place himself, and what does he say about this group in relation to the others?
3. In paragraph 3, Mosley writes, "The money that makes the rich richer comes out of the sweat, the sacrifice and ultimately the blood of working men and women." What does he mean?

4. Try to guess the meanings of any of the following words that are unfamiliar to you. Test your guesses in a dictionary, and then come up with a sentence or two using each new word.

truism (1)	pristine (8)	coffers (15)
irrefutable (1)	indispensable (10)	accrual (17)
axiom (2)	chronically (10)	cardinal (17)
genesis (4)	gauged (11)	stoically (17)
flux (7)	crustaceans (11)	harbinger (20)

Purpose and Audience

1. What do you think Mosley's purpose is? Do you think his classification is really motivated by a desire to offer a "harbinger of hope" (paragraph 20)?
2. Who is Mosley's intended audience? What in the text supports your answer?
3. What do you think of Mosley's categories? Are they complete? convincing? If you know people in these categories, do they match Mosley's description?

Method and Structure

1. How does or doesn't the method of classification lend itself to Mosley's purpose?
2. Summarize each of the groups Mosley identifies (even those he does not discuss in detail). What is Mosley's principle of classification? Why does he categorize the groups the way he does?
3. What do you notice about Mosley's organization and the space he devotes to each category? Why do you think he varies the amount of space he gives to the categories? Do some of the categories get shortchanged?
4. **Other Methods**   In addition to classification, Mosley relies heavily on definition (Chapter 11) to advance his argument. Why do you think he defines each class so painstakingly? What would the essay lose if Mosley didn't define his terms?

Language

1. Examine Mosley's tone. How would you characterize his attitude toward his subject? Is he angry, resigned, hopeful, something else? Does his overall tone strengthen his argument or weaken it? Why? (If necessary, see pp. 38–39 and 334–35 on tone.)

2. Mosley uses a lot of "five-dollar words," many of which appear in the vocabulary list. He also injects the first person (*I, me, we,* and *our*) throughout his essay. How do his diction and point of view relate to his purpose and to his audience?

3. Mosley asks his readers to "excuse the Marxism" when he introduces the phrase "wage-slaves" in paragraph 15. Look up the term *Marxism* in a dictionary or encyclopedia and identify other economic terms in Mosley's essay that hold Marxist connotations. (If necessary, see pp. 48–49 on connotation.) What does his use of such politically charged language reveal about Mosley's relationship to his subject?

Writing Topics

1. **Journal to Essay**   Building on your journal entry about your attitude toward money (p. 186), write a response to Mosley's essay. Does it anger you? irritate you? reassure you? inspire you? make you feel something else? Did it lead you to rethink your own class status? Do you find Mosley's categories, definitions, and conclusions to be fair? Why or why not? Support your response with details from Mosley's essay and examples from your own experience.

2. Using Mosley's essay as a model, write an essay that proposes a new classification of a group of people (teachers, bosses, or salesclerks, for example) for the purpose of advancing an argument about a larger issue. Sort your subject into classes according to a consistent principle, and provide plenty of details to clarify the classes you decide on. In your essay, be sure to explain to your readers why the classification should persuade them to accept your argument.

3. **Cultural Considerations**   Mosley's classification questions the foundations of the American dream, which holds that a person from even the most humble circumstances can achieve prosperity through determination and hard work. How realistic, or not, do you think the American dream is today? Write an essay answering this question. As evidence for your argument, you may want to discuss how, if at all, the American dream applies to you, given your social and economic background.

4. **Connections**   In his paragraph on page 171, E. B. White alludes to the financial struggles of newly arrived New Yorkers but prefers to celebrate their contributions to the city. Write a brief essay in which you compare and contrast White's and Mosley's attitudes toward economic hardship in America, as well as their assumptions about how it can be overcome. Be sure to support your analysis by citing details from each selection.

Classification

Choose one of the following topics, or any other topic they suggest, for an essay developed by classification. The topic you decide on should be something you care about so that classification is a means of communicating an idea, not an end in itself.

PEOPLE

1. People you like (or dislike)
2. Boring people
3. Laundromat users
4. Teachers or students
5. Friends or coworkers
6. Computer users
7. Parents

PSYCHOLOGY AND BEHAVIOR

8. Friendships
9. Ways of disciplining children
10. Ways of practicing religion
11. Obsessions
12. Diets
13. Dreams

THINGS

14. Buildings on campus
15. Junk foods
16. Computer games
17. Trucks

SPORTS AND PERFORMANCE

18. Styles of baseball pitching, tennis serving, football tackling, or another sports skill
19. Runners
20. Styles of dance, guitar playing, acting, or another performance art

COMMUNICATIONS MEDIA

21. Young male or female movie stars
22. Talk-show hosts
23. Electronic discussion groups
24. Sports announcers
25. Television programs
26. Radio stations
27. Magazines or newspapers

Sorting Group Identities

1. Max Eastman (p. 170) claims that there are two types of human beings: those who are poetic and those who are practical. Write a brief essay in which you apply Eastman's classification to E. B. White's categories of New Yorkers (p. 171). Be sure to define each type for your readers and explain why you assign White's groups the way you do. Remember to use evidence from White's paragraph to support your idea.

2. Jonathan Gould (p. 176) and Marion Winik (p. 180) classify and label people with some intention to amuse readers. However, not all labels used to classify people are harmless. Consider, for example, labels based on gender or race or sexual orientation. Write an essay in which you discuss both the benefits and the costs of assigning labels to people—for those using the labels, for those being labeled, and for society as a whole. Give plenty of specific examples.

3. Max Eastman, E. B. White, and Walter Mosley (p. 186) find that communities exist even among people who don't know one another. Write an essay in which you offer your definition of *community*. Consider not only what constitutes a group identity but also why people might seek (or reject) a connection with strangers. Are abstract communities like the ones described by Eastman, White, and Mosley real or imagined? beneficial or harmful? Why do you think so?

Chapter 9

PROCESS ANALYSIS

Examining the Human Body

Game rules, repair manuals, cookbooks, science textbooks—these and many other familiar works are essentially process analyses. They explain how to do something (play Monopoly, patch a hole in the wall), how to make something (an omelet), or how something happens (how our hormones affect our behavior, how a computer stores and retrieves data). That is, they explain a sequence of actions with a specified result (the **process**) by dividing it into its component steps (the **analysis**). You might use process analysis to explain how a hybrid engine saves gas, or how a student organization can influence cafeteria menus. You also use process analysis when you want to teach someone how to do something, such as create a Web page or follow a new office procedure.

Process analysis overlaps several other writing methods discussed in this book. The analysis component is the method examined in Chapter 7—dividing a thing or concept into its elements. And we analyze a process much as we analyze causes and effects (Chapter 12), except that cause-and-effect analysis asks mainly *why* something happens or *why* it has certain results, whereas process analysis asks *how*. Process analysis also overlaps narration (Chapter 5), for the steps involved are almost always presented in chronological sequence. But narration recounts a unique sequence of events with a unique result, whereas process analysis explains a series of steps with the same predictable result. You might narrate a particularly exciting baseball game, for instance, but you would analyze the process—the rules—of any baseball game.

READING PROCESS ANALYSIS

Almost always, the purpose of process analysis is to explain, but sometimes a parallel purpose is to prove something about a process or to evaluate it: a writer may want to show how easy it is to change a tire, for instance, or urge dieters to follow a weight-loss plan on the grounds of its safety and effectiveness.

Processes occur in several varieties, including mechanical (a car engine), natural (cell division), psychological (acquisition of sex roles), and political (the electoral process). Process analyses generally fall into one of two types:

- A **directive** process analysis tells how to do or make something: bake a cake, tune a guitar, negotiate a deal, write a process analysis. It outlines the steps in the process completely so that the reader who follows them can achieve the specified result. Generally, a directive process analysis addresses the reader directly, using the second-person *you* ("You should think of negotiation as collaboration rather than competition") or the imperative (commanding) mood of verbs ("Add one egg yolk and stir vigorously"). (See also p. 201.)

- An **explanatory** process analysis provides the information necessary for readers to understand the process, but more to satisfy their curiosity than to teach them how to perform it. It may address the reader directly, but the third-person *he, she, it,* and *they* are more common.

Whether directive or explanatory, process analyses usually follow a chronological sequence. Most processes can be divided into phases or stages, and these in turn can be divided into steps. The stages of changing a tire, for instance, may be jacking up the car, removing the flat, putting on the spare, and lowering the car. The steps within, say, jacking up the car may be setting the emergency brake, blocking the other wheels, loosening the lug nuts, positioning the jack, and raising the car. Following a chronological order, a writer covers the stages in sequence and, within each stage, covers the steps in sequence.

To ensure that the reader can duplicate the process or understand how it unfolds, a process analysis must fully detail each step and specify the reasons for it. In addition, the writer must ensure that the reader grasps the sequence of steps, their duration, and where they occur. To this end, transitional expressions that signal time and place—such as *after five minutes, meanwhile, to the left,* and *below*—can be invaluable.

Though a chronological sequence is usual for process analysis, the sequence may be interrupted or modified to suit the material. A writer may need to pause in a sequence to provide definitions of specialized terms or to explain why a step is necessary or how it relates to the preceding and following steps. Instructions on how to change a tire, for instance, might stop briefly to explain that the lug nuts should be loosened slightly *before* the car is jacked up in order to prevent the wheel from spinning afterward.

ANALYZING PROCESSES IN PARAGRAPHS

Jane E. Brody (born 1941) is a nutritionist with degrees in biochemistry and science writing. Her weekly *New York Times* column, "Personal Health," has been syndicated in more than one hundred newspapers for three decades. This paragraph is from her best-selling guide to sensible eating, *Jane Brody's Nutrition Book* (1981).

When you think about it, it's impossible to lose—as many … diets suggest—10 pounds of *fat* in ten days, even on a total fast. A pound of body fat represents 3,500 calories. To lose 1 pound of fat, you must expend 3,500 more calories than you consume. Let's say you weigh 170 pounds and, as a moderately active person, you burn 2,500 calories a day. If your diet contains only 1,500 calories, you'd have an energy deficit of 1,000 calories a day. In a week's time that would add up to a 7,000-calorie deficit, or 2 pounds of real fat. In ten days, the accumulated deficit would represent nearly 3 pounds of lost body fat. Even if you ate nothing at all for ten days and maintained your usual level of activity, your caloric deficit would add up to 25,000 calories (2,500 calories a day times 10). At 3,500 calories per pound of fat, that's still only 7 pounds of lost fat. So if you want to lose fat, which is all you should want to lose, the loss must be gradual—at most a pound or two a week.

Explanatory process analysis: tells how weight loss happens

Process divided into steps

Transitions (underlined) signal sequence

Goal of process

Janet Jones is a licensed social worker and a member of the Boston Women's Health Book Collective, a nonprofit organization best known for the popular feminist guide to women's health *Our Bodies, Ourselves*. This paragraph is from "Women in Motion," the fitness chapter of *The New Our Bodies, Ourselves* (1992).

Occasionally you will stretch the ligaments of a joint too far, maybe even tear them (a sprain) or pull a muscle or a tendon in much the same way (a strain). Unless the injury is severe, you can treat it yourself. . . . For a sprain, elevate and rest the injured part, applying cold immediately and for the next twenty-four to seventy-two hours. This minimizes pain and swelling. At the end of this period you can switch to moist heat. Begin gentle movement as soon as possible; when you are ready to start full-scale exercising again, bind it evenly (not too tight) for support and go easy. If in the meantime you are climbing the walls, be physical with the rest of your body; swimming might be a possibility, for example.

Directive process analysis: tells how to treat a sprain

Process divided into five steps, each signaled with a transition (underlined)

Chronological sequence altered to offer additional advice

DEVELOPING AN ESSAY BY PROCESS ANALYSIS
Getting Started

You'll find yourself writing process analyses for your courses in school (for instance, explaining how a drug affects brain chemistry), in memos at work (recommending a new procedure for approving cost estimates), or in life outside work (giving written directions to your home). To find a subject when an assignment doesn't make one obvious, examine your interests or hobbies or think of something whose workings you'd like to research in order to understand them better. Explore the subject by listing chronologically all the necessary stages and steps.

Remember your readers while you are generating ideas. Consider how much background information they need, where specialized terms must be defined, and where examples must be given. Especially if you are providing instructions, consider what special equipment readers will need, what hitches they may encounter, and what the interim results should be. To build a table, for instance, what tools would readers need? What should they do if the table wobbles even after the corners are braced? What should the table feel like after the first sanding or the first varnishing?

Forming a Thesis

While you are exploring your subject, decide on the point of your analysis and express it in a thesis sentence that will guide your writing and tell your readers what to expect. The simplest thesis states what the process is and outlines its basic stages. For instance:

> Building a table is a three-stage process of cutting, assembling, and finishing.

But you can increase your readers' interest in the process by also conveying your reason for writing about it. You might assert that a seemingly difficult process is actually quite simple, or vice versa:

> Changing a tire does not require a mechanic's skill or strength; on the contrary, a ten-year-old child can do it.

> Windsurfing may look easy, but it demands the knowledge of an experienced sailor and the balance of an acrobat.

You might show how the process demonstrates a more general principle:

> The process of getting a bill through Congress illustrates majority rule at work.

Or you might assert that a process is inefficient or unfair:

> The state's outdated registration procedure forces new car buyers to waste hours standing in line.

Regardless of how you structure your thesis sentence, try to make it clear that your process analysis has a point. Usually you will want to include a direct statement of your thesis in your introduction so that readers know what you're writing about and why the process should matter to them.

Organizing

Many successful process analyses begin with an overview of the process to which readers can relate each step. In such an introduction you can lead up to your thesis sentence by specifying when or where the process occurs, why it is useful or interesting or controversial, what its result is, and the like. Especially if you are providing instructions, you can also use the introduction (perhaps a separate paragraph) to provide essential background information, such as the materials readers will need.

After the introduction, you should present the stages distinctly, perhaps one or two paragraphs for each, and usually in chronological order. Within each stage, also chronologically, you then cover the necessary steps. This chronological sequence helps readers see how a process unfolds or how to perform it themselves. Try not to deviate from it unless you have good reason to—perhaps because your process requires you to group simultaneous steps or your readers need definitions of terms, reasons for steps, connections between separated steps, and other explanations.

A process essay may end simply with the result. But you might conclude with a summary of the major stages, with a comment on the significance or usefulness of the process, or with a recommendation for changing a process you have criticized. For a directive process essay, you might state the standards by which readers can measure their success or give an idea of how much practice may be necessary to master the process.

Drafting

While drafting your process analysis, concentrate on getting in as many details as you can: every step, how each relates to the one before and after, how each contributes to the result. In revising you can always delete unnecessary details and connective tissue if they seem cumbersome, but in the first draft it's better to overexplain than underexplain.

Drafting a process analysis is a good occasion to practice a straightforward, concise writing style, for clarity is more important than originality of expression. Stick to plain language and uncomplicated sentences. If you want to dress up your style a bit, you can always do so after you have made yourself clear.

Revising and Editing

When you've finished your draft, ask a friend to read it. If you have explained a process, he or she should be able to understand it. If you have given directions, he or she should be able to follow them, or imagine following them. Then examine the draft yourself against the following questions and the information in the box.

- *Have you adhered to a chronological sequence?* Unless there is a compelling and clear reason to use some other arrangement, the stages and steps of your analysis should proceed in chronological order. If you had to depart from that order—to define or explain or to sort out simultaneous steps—the reasons should be clear to your readers.

- *Have you included all necessary steps and omitted any unnecessary digressions?* The explanation should be as complete as possible but not cluttered with information, however interesting, that contributes nothing to the readers' understanding of the process.
- *Have you accurately gauged your readers' need for information?* You don't want to bore readers with explanations and details they don't need. But erring in the other direction is even worse, for your essay will achieve little if readers cannot understand it.
- *Have you shown readers how each step fits into the whole process and relates to the other steps?* If your analysis seems to break down into a multitude of isolated steps, you may need to organize them more clearly into stages.
- *Have you used plenty of informative transitions?* Transitions such as *at the same time* and *on the other side of the machine* indicate when steps start and stop, how long they last, and where they occur. (A list of such expressions appears in the Glossary under *transitions.*) The expressions should be as informative as possible; signals such as *first . . . second . . . third . . . fourteenth* and *next . . . next* do not help indicate movement in space or lapses in time, and they quickly grow tiresome.

FOCUS ON CONSISTENCY

While drafting a directive process analysis, telling readers how to do something, you may start off with subjects or verbs in one form and then shift to another form because the original choice felt awkward. These shifts occur most often with the subjects *a person* or *one*:

> INCONSISTENT   To keep the car from rolling while changing the tire, *one* should first set the car's emergency brake. Then *one* should block the other three tires with objects like rocks or chunks of wood. Before raising the car, *you* should loosen the lug nuts of the wheel.

To repair the inconsistency here, you could stick with *one* for the subject (*one should loosen*), but that usually sounds stiff. It's better to revise the earlier subjects to be *you*:

> CONSISTENT   To keep the car from rolling while changing the tire, *you* should set the car's emergency brake. Then *you* should block the other three tires with objects like rocks or chunks of wood. Before raising the car, *you* should loosen the lug nuts of the wheel.

Sometimes, writers try to avoid *one* or *a person* or even *you* with passive verbs that don't require actors:

> INCONSISTENT   To keep the car from rolling while changing the tire, you should first set the car's emergency brake. Then the other three tires *should be blocked* with objects like rocks or chunks of wood.

But the passive is wordy and potentially confusing, especially when directions should be making it clear who does what. (See p. 45 for more on passive verbs.)

One solution to the problem of inconsistent subjects and passive verbs is to use the imperative, or commanding, form of verbs, in which *you* is understood as the subject:

> CONSISTENT   To keep the car from rolling while changing the tire, first *set* the car's emergency brake. Then *block* the other three tires with objects like rocks or chunks of wood.

A NOTE ON THEMATIC CONNECTIONS

The authors represented in this chapter set out to examine the steps involved in maintaining or manipulating the human body, and for that purpose process analysis is the natural choice of method. In a paragraph, Jane Brody explains to dieters how calories translate into pounds (p. 197). In another paragraph, Janet Jones tells how to treat a muscle sprain (p. 198). Rachel Hannon's essay recommends a way to help sick and injured strangers (p. 203). Atul Gawande's essay examines how doctors learn by practicing on unsuspecting patients (p. 209). And in an excerpt from a classic book that still has the power to shock, Jessica Mitford analyzes the technique of embalming a corpse, which turns out to be gruesomely funny (p. 216).

A life isn't significant except for its impact on other lives. —Jackie Robinson

Some people give time, some money, some their skills and connections, some literally give their life's blood. But everyone has something to give.
—Barbara Bush

What is nobody's business is my business. —Clara Barton

Journal Response Have you ever donated blood? Have you had your bone marrow typed for potential matches? Does your driver's license identify you as an organ donor? Would you give a kidney to a loved one? In a paragraph, consider why you are—or are not—willing to give parts of your body to help others in need.

Rachel Hannon

Born in 1984, Rachel Hannon grew up in Norwood, Massachusetts. After graduating from the Fontbonne Academy, an all-girls Catholic high school, Hannon went on to the College of the Holy Cross, where she majored in English and theology. A dedicated volunteer, she has traveled to West Virginia, Kenya, and India on service trips for Habitat for Humanity and plans to pursue a career with a nonprofit organization.

HOW TO DONATE PLASMA AND SAVE MORE LIVES
(STUDENT ESSAY)

In the following how-to essay, Hannon explains her special twist on a form of volunteering that many students are familiar with—giving blood. Hannon wrote this piece especially for The Compact Reader *in her senior year of college. Notice that the essay, particularly the second paragraph, includes researched information. In accordance with MLA style, Hannon names her source in the text and lists it at the end. She does not include parenthetical citations because her source—a Web site—does not have page or paragraph numbers. (See the Appendix for information on using and citing sources.)*

Anybody who has participated in a blood drive knows how good it feels   1
to make a difference in a stranger's life. Hospitals rely on donations to

replace blood lost in accidents or surgery and to treat chronic diseases such as anemia and leukemia. That's why I have been making blood donations for the past four years. But did you know that you can also donate something called plasma? I didn't. Just a few months ago, I was on the American National Red Cross Web site looking for a phone number when I stumbled across an appeal for plasma donors. Intrigued, I immediately called the local center for more information. Plasma donations, I learned, enable the Red Cross to help people who have undergone transplant or cardiovascular surgery, chemotherapy, or severe burns. Instead of donating blood that month, I donated plasma, and I'm glad I did. Although giving plasma is more complicated and time-consuming than giving blood, every healthy person should set aside a day to do it.

You might wonder, as I did, what plasma is and why patients   2
would need it instead of whole blood. The Red Cross explains that human blood is made up of four components: red blood cells, white blood cells, platelets, and plasma. Blood plasma is a yellowish water-based protein that helps to stabilize blood pressure, improve immune responses, and control bleeding, making it an invaluable resource for treating newborn babies, cancer patients, burn victims, and hemophiliacs. The lifesaving fluid is obtained by a procedure called *apheresis*, in which blood is drawn and circulated through a machine that separates the blood components from one another, removing the plasma and returning the rest of the blood to the donor's body. Because the process extracts only the components that patients need, nothing is wasted: a single donation can help twice as many people. At the same time, concentrated transfusions from a single donor are less likely to be rejected by a recipient's immune system, making plasma safer than blood for people whose health is already compromised. Blood is always needed, of course, but giving blood does not and should not hinder you from donating plasma, too.

To donate plasma, the first thing you'll need to do is call your near-   3
est Red Cross center (check the phone book or *http://www.redcross.org* for locations). Schedule your appointment for a day when you know you do not have class or much homework, because the process can take up to two hours. Do not consume any products containing aspirin for at least forty-eight hours before your appointment, since aspirin can thin blood. The Red Cross recommends that you consume a lot of water before you arrive, because dehydrated donors have been known to experience extreme exhaustion. For added nourishment, eat something substantial the day of your appointment as well: a bagel or pasta should do the trick.

There will be a number of preparatory procedures to follow when   4
you arrive at the donation center. First, you will be asked to fill out
some paperwork regarding your medical history: be prepared to answer questions about any allergies you have, medications you're taking, immunizations you've received, and diseases in your family history.
The Red Cross asks that you be at least 17 years old, weigh at least
110 pounds, and not have given blood for 56 days prior to donating
plasma. (Even people with some chronic conditions, including diabetes
and hypertension, are eligible to donate as long as their symptoms are
under control.) After you complete the paperwork, you will be asked
to take an AIDS test to be sure your plasma isn't infected with HIV;
this takes only a few minutes. A nurse will take you to a station and
prick your finger for a small sample of blood.

Once the nurse has confirmed that you're healthy enough to do-   5
nate plasma, she or he will lead you to the room where the donation
takes place. Depending on the layout of your local Red Cross center,
you may have a hospital-like room all to yourself, or you may share a
ward with several people. You will be provided with a bed and a television, but bring a magazine or a book to occupy yourself just in case:
you wouldn't want to be stuck watching a boring show! Although the
bed is comfortable and typically equipped with a blanket, you will be
in it for two hours and unable to move your arm, so get as comfortable
as possible before the nurse leaves. Take a trip to the restroom and ask
for an extra pillow or anything else that might help you feel comfortable: you don't want to get a stiff neck or develop an urge to move your
arm.

Once you're situated, the nurse will hook you up to the apheresis   6
machine with an intravenous (IV) tube. If you have a queasy stomach,
like me, do not look at the tube. Although the procedure is painless (unless you move your arm and feel the needle pinch), it can be disconcerting to see your own blood flowing down the tube, disappearing into
the machine, and recirculating back into your body. Waiting for the
donation to be over is the hard part: concentrate on whatever entertainment you have, and remember how much help your plasma will be
to those who are suffering from cancer, blood disease, or cardiovascular disease.

When the time is up, the nurse will unhook you from the IV tube   7
and bring you to another room, where you will have a few minutes to
recuperate. At this point, your blood sugar will be low and you may
feel dizzy. Drink some water or nibble on one of the sugary snacks provided by the Red Cross center to give your body some nourishment.
When you feel rested—the timing varies from person to person—you

can leave. While you should feel relatively well, you will most likely be extremely tired. Plan on taking public transportation if it's available, or ask a friend or family member to accompany you home in case you feel too weak to drive. When you get home, take a good long nap. Do not plan to attend any parties or perform any extraneous activities for at least twenty-four hours, because you will most likely still be feeling exhausted up to a day after your donation.

After you've completed the entire process of donating your plasma—   8
from scheduling your appointment to recovering completely—consider donating again. The Red Cross allows you to donate up to twelve times a year. Just as I made donating blood a regular practice in my life, I now make regular plasma donations, too.

Work Cited

American National Red Cross. "Plasma Apheresis." *RedCross.org*. 2007. 31 Mar. 2007 <http://www.redcross.org/services/ biomed/0,1082,0_20_,00.html>.

Meaning

1. In the first draft of her essay, Hannon expressed her main point as follows: "The process for donating plasma is a little different from donating blood." Locate her final thesis statement, and explain how it improves on the earlier version.
2. How is plasma different from blood? Why is the distinction important?
3. If you are not familiar with any of the following words, try to guess their meanings based on their context in Hannon's essay. Check your guesses in a dictionary, and then use each new word in a sentence or two.

hemophiliacs (2)	hinder (2)	disconcerting (6)
concentrated (2)	hypertension (4)	cardiovascular (6)
compromised (2)	intravenous (6)	extraneous (7)

Purpose and Audience

1. Why do you think Hannon chose this topic for her essay? Does she have a reason for writing beyond explaining what it's like to donate plasma?
2. Is Hannon's purpose weakened by the unpleasant sensations she sometimes describes as side effects of plasma donation, such as dehydration (paragraph 3), immobility (5), nausea (6), and exhaustion (7)? Why, or why not?

3. While a student, Hannon composed this essay especially for the readers of *The Compact Reader*. What statements and references show that she is trying to appeal to other students? What assumptions does she make about her audience?

Method and Structure

1. Why is process analysis a particularly useful method for achieving Hannon's purpose?
2. At several points in her essay, Hannon draws on research to provide explanations and advice about her subject. How does the information from the American National Red Cross Web site strengthen her process analysis?
3. Point out transitional words and phrases that Hannon uses as guideposts in her process analysis.
4. **Other Methods**   Where and how does Hannon use definition (Chapter 11) to establish the significance of her subject?

Language

1. Hannon's title alludes to the old Red Cross slogan "Donate blood — save a life." What is the effect of this reference? (For a definition of *allusion*, see the Glossary.)
2. Although the essay is based on her own experience, Hannon uses the second person (*you*) and the future tense to explain the process of donating plasma. Why do you think she does this? How would the essay have been different if she had written in the first person (*I*) and the past tense?
3. How would you characterize the tone of the essay? How can you tell that the author is personally invested in the process she is explaining? How does her tone affect you as a reader?

Writing Topics

1. **Journal to Essay**   In your journal entry (p. 203), you wrote about your attitudes toward fluid, tissue, and organ donation. Now write an essay that explains your position on donating (or receiving) body parts for medical purposes. Why do you (or don't you) think a person should give of their bodies to help people they may not know?
2. Using Hannon's essay as a model, write a directive process analysis explaining how to do something that is important to you but that others may not know about. For instance, you might tell readers how to protect their homes from intruders, how to thwart identity thieves, how to reduce their

carbon footprints, or how to become foster parents. Be sure to explain why your subject is important and to identify all the steps involved.

3. **Cultural Considerations**   Look again at the quotations preceding Hannon's essay. Does our culture encourage volunteerism, or does it reward selfishness? What do communities do for people, and what do people owe their communities in return? How much can one person do? In an essay, examine the relationship between the community and the individual in American society, drawing a conclusion about the importance, relevance, or practicality of volunteering one's time, money, or talents.

4. **Connections**   In "Show Me the Money" (p. 186), Walter Mosley argues that the rich owe their prosperity to "the sweat, the sacrifice and ultimately the blood of working men and women" (paragraph 3). Although his focus is economic rather than physical, Mosley does, like Hannon, seem to believe that people have an obligation to help the less fortunate. In an essay, compare and contrast Mosley's and Hannon's attitudes toward charity. Consider not only what each writer says about the social benefits and personal responsibilities of giving, but also his or her tone and assumptions about how readers might respond to his or her position. Which author is more successful at persuading readers to make sacrifices for the greater good, and why?

The greatest mistake you can make in life is to be continually fearing you will make one. —Elbert Hubbard

A mistake is simply another way of doing things. —Katharine Graham

Mistakes are a part of being human. Appreciate your mistakes for what they are: precious life lessons that can only be learned the hard way. Unless it's a fatal mistake, which, at least, others can learn from. —Al Franken

Journal Response   At one time or another, everybody makes mistakes, whether in the process of learning something new or doing something relatively familiar. In a paragraph, describe one such error in your life—a time when you did something wrong because you didn't know what you were doing or weren't being careful. What happened? Did you learn anything from the experience?

——————————— Atul Gawande ———————————

A general surgeon at Brigham and Women's Hospital, an assistant professor at Harvard Medical School and the Harvard School of Public Health, and a staff writer for the New Yorker, *Atul Gawande has been praised for his uncanny ability to "find the right balance between intimacy and respectfulness" in his practice and his prose. Gawande was born in 1965 in Brooklyn, New York, and raised in Athens, Ohio, where his physician parents, both from India, still see patients. He did his undergraduate work at Stanford University; won a Rhodes scholarship to study at Oxford; and took his medical training at Harvard, where he also completed a master's degree in public health. Although Gawande never planned to be a writer (his first freshman composition essay earned a C), he has developed a solid reputation as a man of letters. In addition to regular contributions to the* New Yorker *and the online magazine* Slate, *Gawande has published several articles in the* New England Journal of Medicine *and served as editor for* The Best American Science Writing 2006. *He is the author of two books:* Complications: A Surgeon's Notes on an Imperfect Science *(2002), a National Book Award finalist, and* Better: A Surgeon's Notes on Performance *(2007), completed with the support of a MacArthur "genius" grant. Gawande lives in Newton, Massachusetts.*

THE CENTRAL LINE

Gawande's Complications *is a thought-provoking exploration of the ethical and moral tensions between doctors' need for training and patients' desire for the best possible care. "The uncomfortable truth about teaching" surgery, he says, is that "we want perfection without practice." And, of course, that's not possible. In this excerpt from the book's first chapter, Gawande explains how one of the first procedures he performed as a new resident went wrong.*

The patient needed a central line. "Here's your chance," S., the chief   1
resident, said. I had never done one before. "Get set up and then page
me when you're ready to start.". . .

This will be good, I tried to tell myself: my first real procedure. My   2
patient—fiftyish, stout, taciturn—was recovering from abdominal
surgery he'd had about a week before. His bowel function hadn't yet
returned, leaving him unable to eat. I explained to him that he needed
intravenous nutrition and that this required a "special line" that would
go into his chest. I said that I would put the line in him while he was
in his bed, and that it would involve my laying him out flat, numbing
up a spot on his chest with local anesthetic, and then threading the line
in. I did not say that the line was eight inches long and would go into
his vena cava, the main blood vessel to his heart. Nor did I say how
tricky the procedure would be. There were "slight risks" involved, I
said, such as bleeding or lung collapse; in experienced hands, problems
of this sort occur in fewer than one case in a hundred.

But, of course, mine were not experienced hands. And the disasters   3
I knew about weighed on my mind: the woman who had died from
massive bleeding when a resident lacerated her vena cava; the man who
had had to have his chest opened because a resident lost hold of the
wire inside the line which then floated down to the patient's heart; the
man who had had a cardiac arrest when the procedure put him into
ventricular fibrillation. But I said nothing of such things when I asked
my patient's permission to do his line. And he said, "OK," I could go
ahead.

I had seen S. do two central lines; one was the day before, and I'd   4
attended to every step. I watched how she set out her instruments and
laid down her patient and put a rolled towel between his shoulder
blades to make his chest arch out. I watched how she swabbed his chest
with antiseptic, injected lidocaine, which is a local anesthetic, and then,
in full sterile garb, punctured his chest near his clavicle with a fat three-

inch needle on a syringe. The patient didn't even flinch. S. told me how to avoid hitting the lung with the needle ("Go in at a steep angle; stay *right* under the clavicle"), and how to find the subclavian vein, a branch to the vena cava lying atop the lung near its apex ("Go in at a steep angle; stay *right* under the clavicle"). She pushed the needle in almost all the way. She drew back on the syringe. And she was in. You knew because the syringe filled with maroon blood. ("If it's bright red, you've hit an artery," she said. "That's not good.")

Once you have the tip of this needle poking in the vein, you have to widen the hole in the vein wall, fit the catheter in, and thread it in the right direction—down to the heart rather than up to the brain—all without tearing through vessels, lung, or anything else. To do this, S. explained, you start by getting a guidewire in place. She pulled the syringe off, leaving the needle in place. Blood flowed out. She picked up a two-foot-long twenty-gauge wire that looked like the steel D string of an electric guitar, and passed nearly its full length through the needle's bore, into the vein, and onward toward the vena cava. "Never force it in," she warned, "and never ever let go of it." A string of rapid heartbeats fired off on the cardiac monitor, and she quickly pulled the wire back an inch. It had poked into the heart, causing momentary fibrillation. "Guess we're in the right place," she said to me quietly. Then to the patient: "You're doing great. Only a couple minutes now." She pulled the needle out over the wire and replaced it with a bullet of thick, stiff plastic, which she pushed in tight to widen the vein opening. She then removed this dilator and threaded the central line—a spaghetti-thick, yellow, flexible plastic tube—over the wire until it was all the way in. Now she could remove the wire. She flushed the line with a heparin solution and sutured it to his chest. And that was it.

I had seen the procedure done. Now it was my turn to try. I set about gathering the supplies—a central-line kit, gloves, gown, cap, mask, lidocaine—and that alone took me forever. When I finally had the stuff together, I stopped outside my patient's door and just stood there staring, silently trying to recall the steps. They remained frustratingly hazy. But I couldn't put it off any longer. . . . I took a deep breath, put on my best don't-worry-I-know-what-I'm-doing look, and went in to do the line.

I placed the supplies on a bedside table, untied the patient's gown behind his neck, and laid him down flat on the mattress, with his chest bare and his arms at his sides. I flipped on a fluorescent overhead light and raised his bed to my height. I paged S. to come. I put on my gown and gloves and, on a sterile tray, laid out the central line, guidewire, and other materials from the kit the way I remembered S. doing it. I drew up five cc's of lidocaine in a syringe, soaked two sponge-sticks in the yellow-brown Betadine antiseptic solution, and opened up the suture packaging. I was good to go.

S. arrived. "What's his platelet count?"   8

My stomach knotted. I hadn't checked. That was bad: too low and   9 he could have a serious bleed from the procedure. She went to check a computer. The count was acceptable.

Chastened, I started swabbing his chest with the sponge-sticks.   10 "Got the shoulder roll underneath him?" S. asked. Well, no. I had forgotten this, too. The patient gave me a look. S., saying nothing, got a towel, rolled it up, and slipped it under his back for me. I finished applying the antiseptic and then draped him so only his right upper chest was exposed. He squirmed a bit beneath the drapes. S. now inspected my tray. I girded myself.

"Where's the extra syringe for flushing the line when it's in?"   11 Damn. She went out and got it.

I felt for landmarks on the patient's chest. *Here?* I asked with my   12 eyes, not wanting to undermine my patient's confidence any further. She nodded. I numbed the spot with lidocaine. ("You'll feel a stick and a burn now, sir.") Next, I took the three-inch needle in hand and poked it through the skin. I advanced it slowly and uncertainly, a few millimeters at a time, afraid to plunge it into something bad. This is a big . . . needle, I kept thinking. I couldn't believe I was sticking it into someone's chest. I concentrated on maintaining a steep angle of entry, but kept spearing his clavicle instead of slipping beneath it.

"Ow!" he shouted.   13

"Sorry," I said. S. signaled with a kind of surfing hand gesture to   14 go underneath the clavicle. This time it did. I drew back on the syringe. Nothing. She pointed deeper. I went in deeper. Nothing. I took the needle out, flushed out some bits of tissue clogging it, and tried again.

"*Ow!*"   15

Too superficial again. I found my way underneath the clavicle once   16 more. I drew the syringe back. Still nothing. He's too obese, I thought to myself. S. slipped on gloves and a gown. "How about I have a look," she said. I handed her the needle and stepped aside. She plunged the needle in, drew back on the syringe, and, just like that, she was in. "We'll be done shortly," she told the patient. I felt utterly inept.

She let me continue with the next steps, which I bumbled through.   17 I didn't realize how long and floppy the guidewire was until I pulled the coil out of its plastic sleeve, and, putting one end of it into the patient, I very nearly let the other touch his unsterile bedsheet. I forgot about the dilating step until she reminded me. Then, when I put in the dilator, I didn't push quite hard enough, and it was really S. who pushed it all the way in. Finally we got the line in, flushed it, and sutured it in place.

Outside the room, S. said that I could be less tentative the next   *18* time, but that I shouldn't worry too much about how things had gone. "You'll get it," she said. "It just takes practice." I wasn't so sure. . . .

There is a saying about surgeons, meant as a reproof: "Sometimes   *19* wrong; never in doubt." But this seemed to me their strength. Every day, surgeons are faced with uncertainties. Information is inadequate; the science is ambiguous; one's knowledge and abilities are never perfect. Even with the simplest operation, it cannot be taken for granted that a patient will come through better off—or even alive. Standing at the table my first time, I wondered how the surgeon knew that he would do this patient good, that all the steps would go as planned, that bleeding would be controlled and infection would not take hold and organs would not be injured. He didn't, of course. But still he cut. . . .

In surgery, as in anything else, skill and confidence are learned   *20* through experience—haltingly and humiliatingly. Like the tennis player and the oboist and the guy who fixes hard drives, we need practice to get good at what we do. There is one difference in medicine, though: it is people we practice upon.

Meaning

1. What exactly is a central line? How does the essay explain it?
2. What does Gawande mean when he says, "But, of course, mine were not experienced hands" (paragraph 3)? What is he implying about his conversation with his patient?
3. Do you think that Gawande really believes, as he says in paragraph 19, that surgeons can never be sure a patient will survive a procedure? If that's true, why do they operate?
4. What is Gawande's point? Which sentences best convey his main idea?
5. Some of the following words may be new to you. Before looking them up in a dictionary, try to guess their meanings from their context in Gawande's piece. Then use each new word in a sentence or two.

taciturn (2)	draped (10)	bumbled (17)
lacerated (3)	girded (10)	tentative (18)
apex (4)	superficial (16)	reproof (19)
chastened (10)	inept (16)	ambiguous (19)

Purpose and Audience

1. What is Gawande's purpose? To teach inexperienced doctors how to insert a central line? To relate his own difficulties with surgery? Something else? How do you know?
2. Whom does Gawande seem to imagine as his audience? Is he writing for patients who have undergone or will soon require surgery? for medical students? for hospital administrators? for general readers? What evidence in the essay supports your answer?
3. From what perspective does Gawande write this process analysis: that of a novice hospital resident? an experienced surgeon? both? someone else? Support your answer with examples from the text.

Method and Structure

1. What process (or processes) is the subject of Gawande's analysis, and what steps does he include? How does process analysis help him achieve his purpose?
2. Process analysis can be explanatory or directive (see p. 196), and Gawande's piece has examples of both types. In which paragraphs does Gawande use each type or combine them? Does he intend for his readers to attempt the procedures he describes? If not, what do the examples of directive process analysis contribute to his essay?
3. What transitions does Gawande use to guide the reader through the steps of his process analysis? Is his use of transitions effective?
4. **Other Methods**   In addition to process analysis, Gawande uses narration (Chapter 5) to describe his first attempt at putting in a central line. How does he differentiate his personal experience from the general process?

Language

1. Gawande mixes specialized medical terminology with colloquial language throughout his process analysis. What is the effect of this combination? How, if at all, does he ensure that people without a medical background can understand what he means?
2. This selection has many grimace-inducing images, such as "a fat three-inch needle on a syringe" plunging into a patient's chest (paragraph 4) and a catheter "tearing through vessels" (5). List some images that made a particular impression on you, and explain their effect.
3. Gawande uses several figures of speech in his process analysis. For instance, he says that a guide wire "looked like the steel D string of an electric guitar" (paragraph 5)—a simile. And the central line itself is "spaghetti-thick"

(5) — a metaphor. What other figures of speech do you notice? What do they contribute to Gawande's essay?

4. Describe the author's tone: Is it basically personal and informal? professional? defensive? thoughtful? Is the tone appropriate, given Gawande's purpose?

Writing Topics

1. **Journal to Essay**   In your journal entry (p. 209), you wrote about a time when you made a mistake. Now write an essay about that event, telling the story in concrete, specific detail, providing insight into your thoughts as well as your response to the error, making the incident come alive. (You may use humor, too, if it comes naturally.) What conclusions can you draw about your experience?

2. Write a process analysis explaining how to do a task that you have struggled with in the past but have now mastered, such as organizing your computer files, painting or wallpapering a room, or cooking a meal. Explain the process step by step so that a reader can follow it, and be sure to cover solutions to problems along the way. For instance, in organizing computer files, how should one label folders and documents? What should one do when a downloaded document gets lost on the computer? How should one manage multiple drafts of a writing assignment?

3. **Cultural Considerations**   We are usually taught to respect doctors and other authority figures, but as Gawande makes clear, they don't always know what they're doing. Are there times when we can — even should — question authority? Write an essay about a time when you felt you had no choice but to disregard the advice of someone you would normally listen to — or, in contrast, when you heeded advice even though it seemed wrong or ignored advice and eventually regretted doing so. How difficult was your action? How did the situation turn out? Looking back, do you believe you did the right thing?

4. **Connections**   Like Gawande, Perri Klass, in "She's Your Basic L.O.L. in N.A.D." (p. 130), writes about her first few months as a hospital resident. Both writers express some ambivalence about their experiences as new doctors, pointing to the negative as well as the positive aspects of what they learned. How might Klass's or Gawande's patients respond to what these doctors have to say? Drawing on their essays for examples, write an essay of your own that explores the role of disillusionment in medical education. Why is it necessary to recognize the bad with the good? Who benefits when doctors discover their own weaknesses, and how?

The last the poor will let go, however miserable their lot in life, is the hope of a decent burial.   —Jacob Riis

The Bustle in a House / The Morning after Death / Is solemnest of industries / Enacted upon Earth   —Emily Dickinson

As is always the case with the dead, his face was handsomer and above all more dignified than when he was alive.   —Leo Tolstoy

Journal Response   Think of a modern custom or practice that you find point-less, barbaric, tedious, or otherwise objectionable. Write down all the steps of that process in a detailed list.

————— Jessica Mitford —————

Tough-minded, commonsensical, and witty, Jessica Mitford was described by Time *as the "Queen of Muckrakers." She was born in England in 1917, the sixth of Lord and Lady Redesdale's seven children, and was educated entirely at home. Her highly eccentric family is the subject of novels by her sister Nancy Mitford and of her own autobiographical* Daughters and Rebels *(1960). In 1939, a few years after she left home, Mitford took up permanent residence in the United States, becoming a naturalized American citizen in 1944. Shortly afterward, moved by her long-standing antifascism and the promise of equal-ity in a socialist society, she joined the American Communist Party; her years as a "Red Menace" are recounted in* A Fine Old Conflict *(1977). In the late 1950s she turned to investigative journalism, researching and exposing nu-merous instances of deception, greed, and foolishness in American society. Her articles appeared in the* Nation, Esquire, *the* Atlantic, *and other magazines, and many of them are collected in* Poison Penmanship: The Gentle Art of Muck-raking *(1979). Her book-length exposés include* The Trial of Dr. Spock *(1969),* Kind and Usual Punishment: The Prison Business *(1973), and* The American Way of Birth *(1992). Mitford died in 1996.*

EMBALMING MR. JONES

In 1963 Mitford published The American Way of Death, *a daring and influ-ential look at the standard practices of the American funeral industry. (*The American Way of Death Revisited, *nearly complete at Mitford's death, was published in 1998.) Mitford pegs the modern American funeral as "the most* *irrational and weirdest" custom of our affluent society, in which "the trappings of Gracious Living are transformed, as in a nightmare, into the trappings of Gracious Dying." This excerpt from the book, an analysis of the process of embalming a corpse and restoring it for viewing, demonstrates Mitford's sharp eye for detail, commanding style, and caustic wit.*

The drama begins to unfold with the arrival of the corpse at the mortuary.   *1*

Alas, poor Yorick![1] How surprised he would be to see how his   *2*
counterpart of today is whisked off to a funeral parlor and is in short
order, sprayed, sliced, pierced, pickled, trussed, trimmed, creamed,
waxed, painted, rouged, and neatly dressed—transformed from a common corpse into a Beautiful Memory Picture. This process is known
in the trade as embalming and restorative art, and is so universally employed in the United States and Canada that the funeral director does
it routinely, without consulting corpse or kin. He regards as eccentric
those few who are hardy enough to suggest that it might be dispensed
with. Yet no law requires embalming, no religious doctrine commends
it, nor is it dictated by considerations of health, sanitation, or even of
personal daintiness. In no part of the world but in Northern America
is it widely used. The purpose of embalming is to make the corpse presentable for viewing in a suitably costly container; and here too the funeral director routinely, without first consulting the family, prepares
the body for public display.

Is all this legal? The processes to which a dead body may be subjected are after all to some extent circumscribed by law. In most states,   *3*
for instance, the signature of next of kin must be obtained before an
autopsy may be performed, before the deceased may be cremated, before the body may be turned over to a medical school for research purposes; or such provision must be made in the decedent's will. In the case
of embalming, no such permission is required nor is it ever sought.[2] A

---

[1] A line from Shakespeare's *Hamlet*, spoken by Hamlet in a graveyard as he contemplates the skull of the former jester in his father's court. [Editor's note.]

[2] In 1982, nineteen years after this was written, the Federal Trade Commission issued comprehensive regulations on the funeral industry, including the requirement that funeral providers prepare an itemized price list for their goods and services. The list must include a notice that embalming is not required by law, along with an indication of the charge for embalming and an explanation of the alternatives. Consumers must give permission for embalming before they may be charged for it. Shortly before her death, however, Mitford wrote that thirteen years after the ruling, the FTC had "watered down" the regulations and "routinely ignored" consumer complaints against the funeral industry, enforcing the regulations only forty-two times. [Editor's note.]

textbook, *The Principles and Practices of Embalming*, comments on this: "There is some question regarding the legality of much that is done within the preparation room." The author points out that it would be most unusual for a responsible member of a bereaved family to instruct the mortician, in so many words, to "*embalm*" the body of a deceased relative. The very term *embalming* is so seldom used that the mortician must rely upon custom in the matter. The author concludes that unless the family specifies otherwise, the act of entrusting the body to the care of a funeral establishment carries with it an implied permission to go ahead and embalm.

Embalming is indeed a most extraordinary procedure, and one   4
must wonder at the docility of Americans who each year pay hundreds of millions of dollars for its perpetuation, blissfully ignorant of what it is all about, what is done, how it is done. Not one in ten thousand has any idea of what actually takes place. Books on the subject are extremely hard to come by. They are not to be found in most libraries or bookshops.

In an era when huge television audiences watch surgical operations   5
in the comfort of their living rooms, when, thanks to the animated cartoon, the geography of the digestive system has become familiar territory even to the nursery school set, in a land where the satisfaction of curiosity about all matters is a national pastime, the secrecy surrounding embalming can, surely, hardly be attributed to the inherent gruesomeness of the subject. Custom in this regard has within this century suffered a complete reversal. In the early days of American embalming, when it was performed in the home of the deceased, it was almost mandatory for some relative to stay by the embalmer's side and witness the procedure. Today, family members who might wish to be in attendance would certainly be dissuaded by the funeral director. All others, except apprentices, are excluded by law from the preparation room.

A close look at what does actually take place may explain in large   6
measure the undertaker's intractable reticence concerning a procedure that has become his major *raison d'être*.[3] Is it possible he fears that public information about embalming might lead patrons to wonder if they really want this service? If the funeral men are loath to discuss the subject outside the trade, the reader may, understandably, be equally loath to go on reading at this point. For those who have the stomach for it, let us part the formaldehyde curtain. . . .

[3] French, meaning "reason for being." [Editor's note.]

The body is first laid out in the undertaker's morgue — or rather, 7
Mr. Jones is reposing in the preparation room — to be readied to bid
the world farewell.

The preparation room in any of the better funeral establishments 8
has the tiled and sterile look of a surgery, and indeed the embalmer–
restorative artist who does his chores there is beginning to adopt the
term "dermasurgeon" (appropriately corrupted by some mortician-
writers as "demisurgeon") to describe his calling. His equipment, consisting of scalpels, scissors, augers, forceps, clamps, needles, pumps,
tubes, bowls and basins, is crudely imitative of the surgeon's, as is his
technique, acquired in a nine- or twelve-month post–high school course
in an embalming school. He is supplied by an advanced chemical industry with a bewildering array of fluids, sprays, pastes, oils, powders,
creams, to fix or soften tissue, shrink or distend it as needed, dry it here,
restore the moisture there. There are cosmetics, waxes, and paints to
fill and cover features, even plaster of Paris to replace entire limbs.
There are ingenious aids to prop and stabilize the cadaver: a Vari-Pose
Head Rest, the Edwards Arm and Hand Positioner, the Repose Block
(to support the shoulders during the embalming), and the Throop Foot
Positioner, which resembles an old-fashioned stocks.

Mr. John H. Eckels, president of the Eckels College of Mortuary 9
Science, thus describes the first part of the embalming procedure: "In
the hands of a skilled practitioner, this work may be done in a comparatively short time and without mutilating the body other than by
slight incision — so slight that it scarcely would cause serious inconve-
nience if made upon a living person. It is necessary to remove the blood,
and doing this not only helps in the disinfecting, but removes the principal cause of disfigurements due to discoloration."

Another textbook discusses the all-important time element: "The 10
earlier this is done, the better, for every hour that elapses between death
and embalming will add to the problems and complications encountered. . . ." Just how soon should one get going on the embalming? The
author tells us, "On the basis of such scanty information made available to this profession through its rudimentary and haphazard system
of technical research, we must conclude that the best results are to be
obtained if the subject is embalmed before life is completely extinct —
that is, before cellular death has occurred. In the average case, this
would mean within an hour after somatic death." For those who feel
that there is something a little rudimentary, not to say haphazard,
about this advice, a comforting thought is offered by another writer.
Speaking of fears entertained in early days of premature burial, he

points out, "One of the effects of embalming by chemical injection, however, has been to dispel fears of live burial." How true; once the blood is removed, chances of live burial are indeed remote.

To return to Mr. Jones, the blood is drained out through the veins   11
and replaced by embalming fluid pumped in through the arteries. As noted in *The Principles and Practices of Embalming,* "every operator has a favorite injection and drainage point—a fact which becomes a handicap only if he fails or refuses to forsake his favorites when conditions demand it." Typical favorites are the carotid artery, femoral artery, jugular vein, subclavian vein. There are various choices of embalming fluid. If Flextone is used, it will produce a "mild, flexible rigidity. The skin retains a velvety softness, the tissues are rubbery and pliable. Ideal for women and children." It may be blended with B. and G. Products Company's Lyf-Lyk tint, which is guaranteed to reproduce "nature's own skin texture . . . the velvety appearance of living tissue." Suntone comes in three separate tints: Suntan; Special Cosmetic Tint, a pink shade "especially indicated for young female subjects"; and Regular Cosmetic Tint, moderately pink.

About three to six gallons of a dyed and perfumed solution of   12
formaldehyde, glycerin, borax, phenol, alcohol, and water is soon circulating through Mr. Jones, whose mouth has been sewn together with a "needle directed upward between the upper lip and gum and brought out through the left nostril," with the corners raised slightly "for a more pleasant expression." If he should be bucktoothed, his teeth are cleaned with Bon Ami and coated with colorless nail polish. His eyes, meanwhile, are closed with flesh-tinted eye caps and eye cement.

The next step is to have at Mr. Jones with a thing called a trocar.   13
This is a long, hollow needle attached to a tube. It is jabbed into the abdomen, poked around the entrails and chest cavity, the contents of which are pumped out and replaced with "cavity fluid." This done, and the hole in the abdomen sewn up, Mr. Jones's face is heavily creamed (to protect the skin from burns which may be caused by leakage of the chemicals), and he is covered with a sheet and left unmolested for a while. But not for long—there is more, much more, in store for him. He has been embalmed, but not yet restored, and the best time to start the restorative work is eight to ten hours after embalming, when the tissues have become firm and dry.

The object of all this attention to the corpse, it must be remembered,   14
is to make it presentable for viewing in an attitude of healthy repose. "Our customs require the presentation of our dead in the semblance of normality . . . unmarred by the ravages of illness, disease or mutilation,"

says Mr. J. Sheridan Mayer in his *Restorative Art*. This is a rather large order since few people die in the full bloom of health, unravaged by illness and unmarked by some disfigurement. The funeral industry is equal to the challenge: "In some cases the gruesome appearance of a mutilated or disease-ridden subject may be quite discouraging. The task of restoration may seem impossible and shake the confidence of the embalmer. This is the time for intestinal fortitude and determination. Once the formative work is begun and affected tissues are cleaned or removed, all doubts of success vanish. It is surprising and gratifying to discover the results which may be obtained."

The embalmer, having allowed an appropriate interval to elapse, 15 returns to the attack, but now he brings into play the skill and equipment of sculptor and cosmetician. Is a hand missing? Casting one in plaster of Paris is a simple matter. "For replacement purposes, only a cast of the back of the hand is necessary; this is within the ability of the average operator and is quite adequate." If a lip or two, a nose or an ear should be missing, the embalmer has at hand a variety of restorative waxes with which to model replacements. Pores and skin texture are simulated by stippling with a little brush, and over this cosmetics are laid on. Head off? Decapitation cases are rather routinely handled. Ragged edges are trimmed, and head joined to torso with a series of splints, wires and sutures. It is a good idea to have a little something at the neck — a scarf or high collar — when time for viewing comes. Swollen mouth? Cut out tissue as needed from inside the lips. If too much is removed, the surface contour can easily be restored by padding with cotton. Swollen necks and cheeks are reduced by removing tissue through vertical incisions made down each side of the neck. "When the deceased is casketed, the pillow will hide the suture incisions . . . as an extra precaution against leakage, the suture may be painted with liquid sealer."

The opposite condition is more likely to present itself — that of 16 emaciation. His hypodermic syringe now loaded with massage cream, the embalmer seeks out and fills the hollowed and sunken areas by injection. In this procedure the backs of the hands and fingers and the under-chin area should not be neglected.

Positioning the lips is a problem that recurrently challenges the 17 ingenuity of the embalmer. Closed too tightly they tend to give a stern, even disapproving expression. Ideally, embalmers feel, the lips should give the impression of being ever so slightly parted, the upper lip protruding slightly for a more youthful appearance. This takes some engineering, however, as the lips tend to drift apart. Lip drift can sometimes be remedied by pushing one or two straight pins through the inner margin of the lower lip and then inserting them between the two upper front teeth. If Mr. Jones happens to have no teeth, the pins can just as easily be anchored in his Armstrong Face Former and Denture Replacer. Another method to maintain lip closure is to dislocate the lower jaw, which is then held in its new position by a wire run through holes which have been drilled through the upper and lower jaws at the midline. As the French are fond of saying, *il faut souffrir pour être belle.*[4]

If Mr. Jones has died of jaundice, the embalming fluid will very likely turn him green. Does this deter the embalmer? Not if he has intestinal fortitude. Masking pastes and cosmetics are heavily laid on, burial garments and casket interiors are color-correlated with particular care, and Jones is displayed beneath rose-colored lights. Friends will say, "How *well* he looks." Death by carbon monoxide, on the other hand, can be rather a good thing from the embalmer's viewpoint: "One advantage is the fact that this type of discoloration is an exaggerated form of a natural pink coloration." This is nice because the healthy glow is already present and needs but little attention.   18

The patching and filling completed, Mr. Jones is now shaved,   19
washed, and dressed. Cream-based cosmetic, available in pink, flesh, suntan, brunette, and blond, is applied to his hands and face, his hair is shampooed and combed (and, in the case of Mrs. Jones, set), his hands manicured. For the horny-handed son of toil special care must be taken; cream should be applied to remove ingrained grime, and the nails cleaned. "If he were not in the habit of having them manicured in life, trimming and shaping is advised for better appearance — never questioned by kin."

Jones is now ready for casketing (this is the present participle of   20
the verb "to casket"). In this operation his right shoulder should be depressed slightly "to turn the body a bit to the right and soften the appearance of lying flat on the back." Positioning the hands is a matter of importance, and special rubber positioning blocks may be used. The hands should be cupped slightly for a more lifelike, relaxed appearance. Proper placement of the body requires a delicate sense of balance. It should lie as high as possible in the casket, yet not so high that the lid, when lowered, will hit the nose. On the other hand, we are cautioned,

---

[4] French, meaning "It is necessary to suffer in order to be beautiful." [Editor's note.]

placing the body too low "creates the impression that the body is in a box."

Jones is next wheeled into the appointed slumber room where a   *21*
few last touches may be added — his favorite pipe placed in his hand or, if he was a great reader, a book propped into position. (In the case of little Master Jones a Teddy bear may be clutched.) Here he will hold open house for a few days, visiting hours 10 a.m. to 9 p.m.

Meaning

1. According to Mitford, what is the purpose of embalming and restoration (see paragraphs 2 and 14)? If they are not required by law or religion or "considerations of health, sanitation, or even of personal daintiness (2)," why are they routinely performed?
2. Why do Americans know so little about embalming (paragraphs 3–6)? Does Mitford blame Americans themselves, the funeral industry, or both?
3. Some of the following words may be new to you. Before looking them up in a dictionary, try to guess their meanings from their context in Mitford's essay. Then use each new word in a sentence or more.

mortuary (1)	mandatory (5)	cadaver (8)
counterpart (2)	apprentices (5)	rudimentary (10)
circumscribed (3)	intractable (6)	somatic (10)
decedent (3)	reticence (6)	haphazard (10)
bereaved (3)	loath (6)	pliable (11)
docility (4)	formaldehyde (6)	semblance (14)
perpetuation (4)	augers (8)	jaundice (18)
inherent (5)	distend (8)	

Purpose and Audience

1. What does Mitford reveal about her purpose when she questions whether the undertaker "fears that public information about embalming might lead patrons to wonder if they really want this service" (paragraph 6)? To discover how different the essay would be if Mitford had wanted only to explain the process, reread the essay from the point of view of an undertaker. What comments and details would the undertaker object to or find embarrassing?
2. Mitford's chief assumption about her readers is evident in paragraph 4. What is it?

3. Most readers find Mitford's essay humorous. Assuming you did, too, which details or comments struck you as especially amusing? How does Mitford use humor to achieve her purpose?

Method and Structure

1. Why do you think Mitford chose the method of process analysis to explore this particular social custom? What does the method allow her to convey about the custom? How does this information help her achieve her purpose?
2. Despite the fact that her purpose goes beyond mere explanation, does Mitford explain the process of embalming and restoration clearly enough for you to understand how it's done and what the reasons for each step are? Starting at paragraph 7, what are the main steps in the process?
3. Mitford interrupts the sequence of steps in the process several times. What information does she provide in paragraphs 8, 10, and 14 to make the interruptions worthwhile?
4. **Other Methods**   Mitford occasionally uses other methods to develop her process analysis — for instance, in paragraph 8 she combines description (Chapter 4) and classification (Chapter 8) to present the embalmer's preparation room and tools; and in paragraph 5 she uses contrast (Chapter 10) to note changes in the family's knowledge of embalming. What does this contrast suggest about our current attitudes toward death and the dead?

Language

1. How would you characterize Mitford's tone? Support your answer with specific details, sentence structures, and words in the essay. (See pp. 38–39 and 334–35 for more on *tone*.)
2. Mitford is more than a little ironic — that is, she often says one thing when she means another or deliberately understates her meaning. Here are two examples from paragraph 10: "the all-important time element" in the embalming of a corpse; "How true; once the blood is removed, chances of live burial are indeed remote." What additional examples do you find? What does this persistent irony contribute to Mitford's tone? (For a fuller explanation of *irony*, consult the Glossary.)
3. Mitford's style in this essay is often informal, even conversational, as in "The next step is to have at Mr. Jones with a thing called a trocar" (paragraph 13). But equally often she seems to imitate the technical, impersonal style of the embalming textbooks she quotes so extensively, as in "Another method to maintain lip closure is to dislocate the lower jaw" (17). What other examples of each style do you find? What does each style contribute

to Mitford's purpose? Is the contrast effective, or would a consistent style, one way or the other, be more effective? Why?

Writing Topics

1. **Journal to Essay**   For your journal entry (p. 216), you listed the steps of a process you find objectionable. Expand that list into a formal essay that analyzes the process by which your chosen custom or practice unfolds. Following Mitford's model, explain the process clearly while also conveying your attitude toward it.

2. Elsewhere in her book *The American Way of Death*, Mitford notes that the open casket at funerals, which creates the need for embalming and restoration, is "a custom unknown in other parts of the world. Foreigners are astonished by it." Write an essay in which you explore the possible reasons for the custom in the United States. Or, if you have strong feelings about closed or open caskets at funerals—derived from religious beliefs, family tradition, or some other source—write an essay agreeing or disagreeing with Mitford's treatment of embalming and restoration.

3. **Cultural Considerations**   Read about funeral customs in another country. (The library's catalog or a periodical database such as the *Social Sciences Index* can direct you to appropriate books or articles.) Write an essay in which you analyze the process covered in your sources, and use it as the basis for agreeing or disagreeing with Mitford's opinion of embalming and restoration.

4. **Connections**   In "The Squeeze" (p. 301), Charles Fishman argues that a large commercial industry (in his case, Wal-Mart) has the power to create artificial demand for products that people wouldn't otherwise want or need. Write an essay analyzing embalming and restoration—which Mitford notes are widely practiced only in North America—as a consumer product. How do funeral industry expectations and assumptions influence these practices? What is the customer really buying?

Process Analysis

Choose one of the following topics, or any other topic they suggest, for an essay developed by process analysis. The topic you decide on should be something you care about so that process analysis is a means of communicating an idea, not an end in itself.

TECHNOLOGY AND THE ENVIRONMENT

1. How an engine or other machine works
2. How the Internet works
3. Winterizing a car
4. Setting up a recycling program in a home or an office
5. How solar energy can be converted into electricity

EDUCATION AND CAREER

6. How children learn to dress themselves, play with others, read, or write
7. Reading a newspaper
8. Interviewing for a job
9. Succeeding in biology, history, computer science, or another course
10. Learning a foreign language
11. Coping with a bad boss

ENTERTAINMENT AND HOBBIES

12. Keeping a car in good shape
13. Making a model car, airplane, or ship
14. Performing a magic trick
15. Playing a board or card game, or performing one maneuver in that game
16. Throwing a really *bad* party
17. Playing a sport or a musical instrument
18. Making great chili or some other dish

HEALTH AND APPEARANCE

19. Getting physically fit
20. Climbing a mountain
21. Dieting
22. Cutting or dyeing one's own hair

FAMILY AND FRIENDS

23. Offering constructive criticism to a friend
24. Driving your parents, brother, sister, friend, or roommate crazy
25. Minimizing sibling rivalry
26. Making new friends in a new place

Examining the Human Body

1. Health means different things to different people, as the selections in this chapter show. Jane Brody (p. 197) is concerned with nutrition. Janet Jones (p. 198) focuses on muscle injuries. Atul Gawande (p. 209) emphasizes surgical intervention. Rachel Hannon (p. 203) believes that the healthy have an obligation to help the sick. Write an essay explaining one of your health priorities, such as eating well, exercising, building muscle, losing weight, quitting smoking, battling depression, or managing stress. What steps should you or someone else take to improve an aspect of health that you think is important?

2. The writers in this chapter reveal mixed feelings about the professionals whose work involves the human body. Jane Brody implies that many diet gurus lie, Atul Gawande confesses that doctors make mistakes, and Jessica Mitford (p. 216) argues that mortuary surgeons routinely violate corpses for no real purpose. Rachel Hannon, in contrast, exhibits a great deal of faith in nurses and the Red Cross. How do you feel about the health industry? Do you trust doctors, nurses, and others who practice medicine or offer health advice, or are you wary of them? What do you think accounts for your attitude? Drawing on the readings in this chapter and your own experience, write an essay that explains why you do, or don't, have faith in Western medicine.

3. Is biology destiny? That is, to what extent are our lives determined by the bodies we are born with? Write an essay that addresses this question. You could write a narrative about someone you know who worked through a physical disability to achieve a life goal, for instance, or someone whose life was forever changed by a devastating injury. You could compare and contrast social attitudes toward the obese and the very thin. You could examine the cause-and-effect relationship between skin color and career opportunities. You could define traditional gender roles or consider ways that men and women reject them. You could argue for or against a particular form of elective surgery, such as breast enhancement or facial reconstruction. Just be sure that your essay has a clear, limited thesis and plenty of details to support it.

Chapter 10

COMPARISON AND CONTRAST

Evaluating Stereotypes

An insomniac watching late-night television faces a choice between two World War II movies broadcasting at the same time. To make up his mind, he uses the dual method of comparison and contrast.

- **Comparison** shows the similarities between two or more subjects: the similar broadcast times and topics of the two movies force the insomniac to choose between them.
- **Contrast** shows the differences between subjects: the different actors, locations, and reputations of the two movies make it possible for the insomniac to choose one.

As in the example, comparison and contrast usually work together, because any subjects that warrant side-by-side examination usually resemble each other in some respects and differ in others. (Since comparison and contrast are so closely related, the terms *comparison* and *compare* will be used from now on to designate both.) You use the method instinctively whenever you need to choose among options—for instance, two political candidates, four tiers of company health benefits, or several pairs of running shoes. You might also use comparison to make sense of competing proposals for calming traffic in a congested neighborhood, to explain how nursing has changed in the past ten years, or to understand why some environmentalists warn of global warming while others are concerned about global cooling. Writers, too, often draw on the method, especially when a comparison can explain something that may be unfamiliar to their readers.

READING COMPARISON AND CONTRAST

Writers generally use comparison for one of two purposes:

- To **explain** the similarities and differences between subjects so as to make either or both of them clear.
- To **evaluate** subjects so as to establish their advantages and disadvantages, strengths and weaknesses.

The explanatory comparison does not take a position on the relative merits of the subjects; the evaluative comparison does, and it usually concludes with a preference or a suggested course of action. An explanatory comparison in a health magazine, for example, might show the similarities and differences between two popular diet plans; an evaluative comparison on the same subject might argue that one plan is better than the other.

Whether explanatory or evaluative, comparisons treat two or more subjects in the same general class or group: tax laws, religions, attitudes toward marriage, diseases, advertising strategies, diets, contact sports, friends. A writer may define the class to suit his or her interest — for instance, a television critic might focus on medical dramas, on cable news programs, or on classic situation comedies. The class likeness ensures that the subjects share enough features to make comparison worthwhile. With subjects from different classes, such as an insect and a tree, the similarities are so few and differences so numerous — and both are so obvious — that explaining them would be pointless.

In putting together a comparison, a writer selects subjects from the same class and then, using division or analysis, identifies the features shared by the subjects. These **points of comparison** are the attributes of the class and thus of the subjects within the class. For instance, the points of comparison for diets may be forbidden foods, allowed foods, speed of weight loss, and nutritional quality; for air pollutants they may be sources and dangers to plants, animals, and humans. These points help to arrange similarities and differences between subjects, and, more important, they ensure direct comparison rather than a random listing of unrelated characteristics.

In an effective comparison, a thesis or controlling idea governs the choice of class, points of comparison, and specific similarities and differences, while also making the comparison worthwhile for the reader.

With two or more subjects, several points of comparison, many similarities and differences, and a particular emphasis, comparison clearly requires a firm organizational hand. Writers have two options for arranging a comparison:

- **Subject-by-subject**, in which the points of comparison are grouped under each subject so that the *subjects* are covered one at a time.
- **Point-by-point**, in which the subjects are grouped under each point of comparison so that the *points* are covered one at a time.

The following brief outlines illustrate the different arrangements as they might be applied to diets:

Subject-by-subject

Harris's diet
  Speed of weight loss
  Required self-discipline
  Nutritional risk
Marconi's diet
  Speed of weight loss
  Required self-discipline
  Nutritional risk

Point-by-point

Speed of weight loss
  Harris's diet
  Marconi's diet
Required self-discipline
  Harris's diet
  Marconi's diet
Nutritional risk
  Harris's diet
  Marconi's diet

Since the subject-by-subject arrangement presents each subject as a coherent unit, it is particularly useful for comparing impressions of subjects: the dissimilar characters of two friends, for instance. However, covering the subjects one at a time can break an essay into discrete pieces and strain readers' memories, so this arrangement is usually confined to essays that are short or that compare several subjects briefly. For longer comparisons requiring precise treatment of the individual points—say, an evaluation of two proposals for a new student-aid policy—the point-by-point arrangement is more useful. Its chief disadvantage is that the reader can get lost in the details and fail to see any subject as a whole. Because each arrangement has its strengths and weaknesses, writers sometimes combine the two in a single work, using the divided arrangement to introduce or summarize overall impressions of the subjects and using the alternating arrangement to deal specifically with the points of comparison.

ANALYZING COMPARISON AND CONTRAST IN PARAGRAPHS

Michael Dorris (1945–97) was a fiction and nonfiction writer who, as a member of the Modoc tribe, explored Native American issues and experiences. The following paragraph comes from "Noble Savages? We'll Drink to That," first published in the *New York Times* in April 1992.

For centuries, flesh and blood Indians have been assigned the role of a popular-culture metaphor. Today, their evocation instantly connotes fuzzy images of Nature, the Past, Plight, or Summer Camp. War-bonneted apparitions pasted to football helmets or baseball caps act as opaque, impermeable curtains, solid walls of white noise that for many citizens block or distort all vision of the nearly two million Native Americans today. And why not? Such honoring relegates Indians to the long ago and thus makes them magically disappear from public consciousness and conscience. What do the 300 federally recognized tribes, and their various complicated treaties governing land rights and protections, their crippling teenage suicide rates, their manifold health problems have in common with jolly (or menacing) cartoon caricatures, wistful braves, or raven-tressed Mazola girls?

Subject-by-subject organization

1. The image in popular culture

Comparison clarified by transitions (underlined once) and repetition and restatement (underlined twice) (see pp. 147–48)

2. The reality of Native American life

Julia Álvarez (born 1950) is a novelist, poet, essayist, and teacher. Born in New York and raised in the Dominican Republic until the age of ten (political upheaval forced her family to flee the country at that time), she often writes about the complexities of immigration and bicultural identity. In this paragraph from her essay "A White Woman of Color," she examines class tensions within her immediate family.

It was Mami's family who were *really* white. They were white in terms of race, and white also in terms of class. From them came the fine features, the pale skin, the lank hair. Her brothers and uncles went to schools abroad and had important businesses in the country.... Not that Papi's family weren't smart and enterprising, all twenty-five brothers and sisters. (The size of the family

Point-by-point organization

1. Education

in and of itself was considered very country by some members of <u>Mami's family</u>.) Many of <u>Papi's brothers</u> had gone to the university and become professionals. But <u>their</u> education was totally island—no fancy degrees from Andover and Cornell and Yale, no summer camps or school songs in another language. <u>Papi's family</u> still lived in the interior versus the capital, in old-fashioned houses without air conditioning, decorated in ways my <u>mother's family</u> would have considered, well, tasteless.... <u>They</u> were *criollos*—creoles—<u>rather than</u> cosmopolitans, expansive, proud, colorful.... <u>Their</u> features were less aquiline than <u>Mother's family's</u>, the skin darker, the hair coarse and curly. <u>Their</u> money still had the smell of the earth on it and was kept in a wad in their back pockets, <u>whereas</u> my <u>mother's family</u> had money in the Chase Manhattan Bank, most of it with George Washington's picture on it, not Juan Pablo Duarte's.

> Comparison clarified by transitions (underlined once) and repetition and restatement (underlined twice) (see pp. 147–48)
>
> 2. Housing
>
> 3. Appearance
>
> 4. Money

DEVELOPING AN ESSAY BY COMPARISON AND CONTRAST
Getting Started

Whenever you observe similarities or differences between two or more members of the same general class—activities, people, ideas, things, places—you have a possible subject for comparison and contrast. Just be sure that the subjects are worth comparing and that you can do the job in the space and time allowed. For instance, if you have a week to complete a three-page paper, don't try to show all the similarities and differences between country-and-western music and rhythm and blues. The effort can only frustrate you and irritate your readers. Instead, limit the subjects to a manageable size—for instance, the lyrics of a representative song in each type of music—so that you can develop the comparisons completely and specifically.

To generate ideas for a comparison, explore each subject separately to pick out its characteristics, and then explore the subjects together to see what characteristics one suggests for the other. Look for points of comparison. Early on, you can use division or analysis (Chapter 7) to identify points of comparison by breaking the subjects' general class into its elements. A song lyric, for instance, could be divided into story line or plot, basic emotion, and special language such as dialect or slang. After you have explored your subjects fully, you can use classification (Chapter 8) to group your characteristics under the points of comparison. For instance, you might classify characteristics of two proposals for a new student-aid policy into qualifications for aid, minimum and maximum amounts to be made available, and repayment terms.

As you gain increasing control over your material, consider also the needs of your readers:

- Do they know your subjects well, or will you need to take special care to explain one or both of them?
- Will your readers be equally interested in similarities and differences, or will they find one more enlightening than the other?

Forming a Thesis

While you are shaping your ideas, you should also begin formulating your controlling idea, your thesis. The first thing you should do is look over your points of comparison and determine whether they suggest an explanatory or evaluative approach.

The thesis of an evaluative comparison will generally emerge naturally because it coincides with your purpose of supporting a preference for one subject over another:

THESIS SENTENCE (EVALUATION)   The two diets result in similarly rapid weight loss, but Harris's requires much more self-discipline and is nutritionally much riskier than Marconi's.

In an explanatory comparison, however, your thesis will need to do more than merely reflect your general purpose in explaining. It should go beyond the obvious and begin to identify the points of comparison. For example:

TENTATIVE THESIS SENTENCE (EXPLANATION)   Rugby and American football are the same in some respects and different in others.

REVISED THESIS SENTENCE (EXPLANATION)   Though rugby requires less strength and more stamina than American football, the two games are very much alike in their rules and strategies.

These examples suggest other decisions you must make when formulating a thesis:

- Will you emphasize both subjects equally or stress one over the other?
- Will you emphasize differences, similarities, or both?

Keeping your readers in mind as you make these decisions will make it easier to use your thesis to shape the body of your essay. For instance, if you decide to write an evaluative comparison and your readers are likely to be biased against your preference or recommendation, you will need to support your case with plenty of specific reasons. If the subjects are equally familiar or important to your readers (as the diets are in the previous example), you'll want to give them equal emphasis, but if one subject is unfamiliar (as rugby is in this country), you will probably need to stress it over the other.

Knowing your audience will also help you decide whether to focus on similarities, differences, or both. Generally, you'll stress the differences between subjects your readers consider similar (such as diets) and the similarities between subjects they are likely to consider different (such as rugby and American football).

Organizing

Your readers' needs and expectations can also help you plan your essay's organization. An effective introduction to a comparison essay often provides some context for readers—the situation that prompts the comparison, for instance, or the need for the comparison. Placing your thesis sentence in the introduction also informs readers of your purpose and point, and it may help keep you focused while you write.

For the body of the essay, choose the arrangement that will present your material most clearly and effectively. Remember that the subject-by-subject arrangement suits brief essays comparing dominant impressions of the subjects, whereas the point-by-point arrangement suits longer essays requiring emphasis on the individual points of comparison. If you are torn between the two—wanting both to sum up each subject and to show the two side by side—then a combined arrangement may be your wisest choice.

A rough outline like the models on page 231 can help you plan the basic arrangement of your essay and also the order of the subjects and points of comparison. If your subjects are equally familiar to your readers and equally important to you, then it may not matter which subject you treat first, even in a subject-by-subject arrangement. But if one subject is less familiar or if you favor one, then that one should probably come second. You can also arrange the points themselves to reflect their importance and your readers' knowledge: from least to most significant or complex, from most to least familiar. Be sure to use the same order for both subjects.

Most readers know intuitively how comparison and contrast works, so they will expect you to balance your comparison feature for feature as well. In other words, all the features mentioned for the first subject should be mentioned as well for the second, and any features not mentioned for the first subject should not suddenly materialize for the second.

The conclusion to a comparison essay can help readers see the whole picture: the chief similarities and differences between two subjects compared in a divided arrangement, or the chief characteristics of subjects compared in an alternating arrangement. In addition, you may want to comment on the significance of your comparison, advise readers on how they can use the information you have provided, or recommend a specific course of action for them to follow. As with all other methods of development, the choice of conclusion should reflect the impression you want to leave with readers.

Drafting

Drafting your essay gives you the chance to spell out your comparison so that it supports your thesis or, if your thesis is still tentative, to find your idea by writing into it. You can use paragraphs to help manage the comparison as it unfolds:

- In a subject-by-subject arrangement, if you devote two paragraphs to the first subject, try to do the same for the second subject. For both subjects, try to cover the points of comparison in the same order and group the same ones in paragraphs.
- In a point-by-point arrangement, balance the paragraphs as you move back and forth between subjects. If you treat several points of comparison for the first subject in one paragraph, do the same for the second subject. If you apply a single point of comparison to both subjects in one paragraph, do the same for the next point of comparison.

This way of drafting will help you achieve balance in your comparison and see where you may need more information to flesh out your subjects and your points. If the finished draft seems to march too rigidly in its pattern, you can always loosen things up when revising.

Revising and Editing

When you are revising and editing your draft, use the following questions and the information in the box to be certain that your essay meets the principal requirements of the comparative method.

- *Are your subjects drawn from the same class?* The subjects must have notable differences *and* notable similarities to make comparison worthwhile — though, of course, you may stress one group over the other.

- *Does your essay have a clear purpose and say something significant about the subject?* Your purpose of explaining or evaluating *and* the point you are making should be evident in your thesis *and* throughout the essay. A vague, pointless comparison will quickly bore readers.

- *Do you apply all points of comparison to both subjects?* Even if you emphasize one subject, the two subjects must match feature for feature. An unmatched comparison may leave readers with unanswered questions or weaken their confidence in your authority.

- *Does the pattern of comparison suit readers' needs and the complexity of the material?* Although readers will appreciate a clear organization and roughly equal treatment of your subjects and points of comparison, they will also appreciate some variety in the way you move back and forth. You needn't devote a sentence to each point, first for one subject and then for the other, or alternate subjects sentence by sentence through several paragraphs. Instead, you might write a single sentence on one point or subject but four sentences on the other — if that's what your information requires.

FOCUS ON PARALLELISM

With several points of comparison and alternating subjects, a comparison will be easier for your readers to follow if you emphasize the relative importance of the subjects in each of the points you are discussing. To help readers keep your comparison straight, take advantage of the technique of parallelism discussed on page 47. Parallelism — the use of similar grammatical structures for elements of similar importance — balances a comparison and clarifies the relationship between elements. At the same time, lack of parallelism can distract or confuse readers.

To make the elements of a comparison parallel, repeat the forms of related words, phrases, and sentences:

NONPARALLEL   Harris expects dieters to give up bread, dairy, and eating meat.

PARALLEL   Harris expects dieters to give up bread, dairy, and meat.

NONPARALLEL   Harris emphasizes self-denial, but with Marconi's plan you can eat whatever you want in moderation.

PARALLEL   Harris emphasizes self-denial, but Marconi emphasizes moderation.

NONPARALLEL   If you want to lose weight quickly, try the Harris diet. You'll have more success keeping the weight off if you follow Marconi's plan.

PARALLEL   If you want to lose weight quickly, choose the Harris diet. If you want to keep weight off, choose Marconi.

For more on parallelism, see page 47.

A NOTE ON THEMATIC CONNECTIONS

Each writer represented in this chapter uses comparison and contrast to understand or challenge stereotypes that have been applied to a minority group. A paragraph by Michael Dorris contrasts media images of Native Americans with the group's reality (p. 232). Another paragraph, by Julia Álvarez, evaluates the differences between the "cosmopolitan" and "creole" sides of a Dominican family (p. 232). Leanita McClain distinguishes her experience as a middle-class African American from the misperceptions of both blacks and whites (p. 239), while Cheryl Peck describes how hostility toward overweight people has affected her (p. 245). And Alaina Wong explains how playing with dolls helped a young girl come to terms with her Chinese features (p. 251).

*What is repugnant to every human being is to be reckoned always as a
member of a class and not as an individual person.* —Dorothy L. Sayers

*It is utterly exhausting being Black in America—physically, mentally, and
emotionally. While many minority groups and women feel similar stress,
there is no respite or escape from your badge of color.*

—Marian Wright Edelman

Prejudices are the chains forged by ignorance to keep men apart.

—Countess of Blessington

Journal Response Prejudice is so pervasive in our society that it is hard to avoid
it. Think of a time when somebody made an assumption about you because of
your membership in a group (as an ethnic, religious, or sexual minority; as a club
member; as a woman or man; as a "jock," "nerd," "homeboy," and so on).
Write a journal entry about the incident and how it made you feel.

Leanita McClain

*An African American journalist, Leanita McClain earned a reputation for hon-
est, if sometimes bitter, reporting on racism in America. She was born in 1952
on Chicago's South Side and grew up in a housing project there. She attended
Chicago State University and the Medill School of Journalism at Northwestern
University. Immediately after graduate school she began working as a reporter
for the* Chicago Tribune, *and over the next decade she advanced to writing a
twice-weekly column and serving as the first African American member of the
paper's editorial board. In 1983 she published an essay in the* Washington Post,
*"How Chicago Taught Me to Hate Whites," that expressed her anguish over a
racially divisive election in Chicago. The essay caused a furious controversy that
probably undermined McClain's already fragile psychological state. Long suffering from severe depression, she committed suicide in 1984, at the age of
thirty-two. In the words of her husband, Clarence Page, she could no longer
"distinguish between the world's problems and her own."*

THE MIDDLE-CLASS BLACK'S BURDEN

McClain wrote this essay for the "My Turn" column in Newsweek *magazine
in October 1980, and it was reprinted in a collection of her essays,* A Foot in

Each World (1986). As her comparison makes disturbingly clear, McClain's position as an economically successful African American subjected her to mistaken judgments by both blacks and whites.

I am a member of the black middle class who has had it with being pat-   1
ted on the head by white hands and slapped in the face by black hands
for my success.

   Here's a discovery that too many people still find startling: when   2
given equal opportunities at white-collar pencil pushing, blacks want
the same things from life that everyone else wants. These include the
proverbial dream house, two cars, an above-average school, and a vacation for the kids at Disneyland. We may, in fact, want these things
more than other Americans because most of us have been denied them
so long.

   Meanwhile, a considerable number of the folks we left behind in   3
the "old country," commonly called the ghetto, and the militants we
left behind in their antiquated ideology can't berate middle-class blacks
enough for "forgetting where we came from." We have forsaken the
revolution, we are told, we have sold out. We are Oreos, they say, black
on the outside, white within.

   The truth is, we have not forgotten; we would not dare. We are   4
simply fighting on different fronts and are no less war weary, and possibly more heartbroken, for we know the black and white worlds can
meld, that there can be a better world.

   It is impossible for me to forget where I came from as long as I   5
am prey to the jive hustler who does not hesitate to exploit my childhood friendship. I am reminded, too, when I go back to the old neighborhood in fear—and have my purse snatched—and when I sit down
to a business lunch and have an old classmate wait on my table. I recall the girl I played dolls with who now rears five children on welfare, the boy from church who is in prison for murder, the pal found
dead of a drug overdose in the alley where we once played tag.

   My life abounds in incongruities. Fresh from a vacation in Paris, I   6
may, a week later, be on the milk-run Trailways bus in Deep South
backcountry attending the funeral of an ancient uncle whose world
stretched only fifty miles and who never learned to read. Sometimes
when I wait at the bus stop with my attaché case, I meet my aunt getting off the bus with other cleaning ladies on their way to do my neighbors' floors.

   But I am not ashamed. Black progress has surpassed our greatest   7
expectations; we never even saw much hope for it, and the achievement
has taken us by surprise.

In my heart, however, there is no safe distance from the wretched 8
past of my ancestors or the purposeless present of some of my contemporaries; I fear such a fate can reclaim me. I am not comfortably
middle class; I am uncomfortably middle class.

I have made it, but where? Racism still dogs my people. There are 9
still communities in which crosses are burned on the lawns of black
families who have the money and grit to move in.

What a hollow victory we have won when my sister, dressed in her 10
designer everything, is driven to the rear door of the luxury high rise in
which she lives because the cab driver, noting only her skin color, assumes she is the maid, or the nanny, or the cook, but certainly not the
lady of any house at this address.

I have heard the immigrants' bootstrap tales, the simplistic re- 11
proach of "why can't you people be like us." I have fulfilled the entry
requirements of the American middle class, yet I am left, at times, feeling unwelcome and stereotyped. I have overcome the problems of food,
clothing and shelter, but I have not overcome my old nemesis, prejudice. Life is easier, being black is not.

I am burdened daily with showing whites that blacks are people. I 12
am, in the old vernacular, a credit to my race. I am my brothers' keeper,
and my sisters', though many of them have abandoned me because they
think that I have abandoned them.

I run a gauntlet between two worlds, and I am cursed and blessed 13
by both. I travel, observe, and take part in both; I can also be used by
both. I am a rope in a tug of war. If I am a token in my downtown office, so am I at my cousin's church tea. I assuage white guilt. I disprove
black inadequacy and prove to my parents' generation that their patience was indeed a virtue.

I have a foot in each world, but I cannot fool myself about either. I 14
can see the transparent deceptions of some whites and the bitter hopelessness of some blacks. I know how tenuous my grip on one way of life
is, and how strangling the grip of the other way of life can be.

Many whites have lulled themselves into thinking that race rela- 15
tions are just grand because they were the first on their block to discuss
crab grass with the new black family. Yet too few blacks and whites
in this country send their children to school together, entertain each
other, or call each other friend. Blacks and whites dining out together
draw stares. Many of my coworkers see no black faces from the time
the train pulls out Friday evening until they meet me at the coffee machine Monday morning. I remain a novelty.

Some of my "liberal" white acquaintances pat me on the head, 16
hinting that I am a freak, that my success is less a matter of talent than

of luck and affirmative action. I may live among them, but it is difficult to live with them. How can they be sincere about respecting me, yet hold my fellows in contempt? And if I am silent when they attempt to sever me from my own, how can I live with myself?

Whites won't believe I remain culturally different; blacks won't believe I remain culturally the same.   17

I need only look in a mirror to know my true allegiance, and I am painfully aware that, even with my off-white trappings, I am prejudged by my color.   18

As for the envy of my own people, am I to give up my career, my standard of living, to pacify them and set my conscience at ease? No. I have worked for these amenities and deserve them, though I can never enjoy them without feeling guilty.   19

These comforts do not make me less black, nor oblivious to the woe in which many of my people are drowning. As long as we are denigrated as a group, no one of us has made it. Inasmuch as we all suffer for every one left behind, we all gain for every one who conquers the hurdle.   20

Meaning

1. McClain states, "My life abounds in incongruities" (paragraph 6). What does the word *incongruities* mean? How does it apply to McClain's life?
2. What is the "middle-class black's burden" to which the title refers? What is McClain's main idea?
3. McClain writes that "there is no safe distance from the wretched past of my ancestors or the purposeless present of some of my contemporaries" (paragraph 8). What do you think she means by this statement?
4. If any of the following words are new to you, try to guess their meanings from their context in McClain's essay. Check your guesses against a dictionary's definitions, and then try to use each word in a sentence or two of your own.

proverbial (2)	nemesis (11)	tenuous (14)
antiquated (3)	vernacular (12)	amenities (19)
ideology (3)	gauntlet (13)	oblivious (20)
berate (3)	assuage (13)	denigrated (20)
reproach (11)		

Purpose and Audience

1. What seems to be McClain's primary purpose in this piece? Does she simply want to express her frustration at whites and blacks, or is she trying to do something else here?

2. Is McClain writing primarily to whites or to blacks or to both? What feelings do you think she might evoke in white readers? in black readers? What is *your* reaction to this essay?
3. McClain's essay poses several questions, including "I have made it, but where?" (paragraph 9) and "How can they be sincere about respecting me, yet hold my fellows in contempt?" (16). What is the purpose of such questions?

Method and Structure

1. What exactly is McClain comparing here? What are her main points of comparison?
2. Paragraph 6 on "incongruities" represents a turning point in McClain's essay. What does she discuss before this paragraph? What does she discuss after?
3. McClain uses many expressions to make her comparison clear, such as "Meanwhile" (paragraph 3) and "different fronts" (4). Locate three more such expressions, and explain what relationship each one establishes.
4. **Other Methods**   McClain relies on many other methods to develop her comparison. Locate one instance each of description (Chapter 4), narration (Chapter 5), example (Chapter 6), and cause-and-effect analysis (Chapter 12). What does each contribute to the essay?

Language

1. McClain sets the tone for this essay in the very first sentence. How would you describe this tone? Is it appropriate, do you think?
2. In her opening sentence, does McClain use the words *patted* and *slapped* literally? How would you explain her use of these words in the context of her essay?
3. Notice McClain's use of parallelism in paragraph 8: "I am not comfortably middle class; I am uncomfortably middle class." Locate two or three other uses of parallelism. How does this technique serve McClain's comparison? (For more on parallelism, see p. 46 and *parallelism* in the Glossary.)
4. In paragraph 16, McClain uses quotation marks around the term *liberal* in reference to her white acquaintances. Why do you think she uses the quotation marks here? What effect does this achieve?

Writing Topics

1. **Journal to Essay**   McClain writes about prejudices that plague her, and in your journal entry (p. 239) you recorded a personal experience of being prejudged because of your membership in a group. Now write a narrative in which you recount this experience in more detail. How were you

perceived, and by whom? What about this perception was accurate? What was unfair? How did the experience affect you? Write for a reader who is not a member of the group in question, being sure to include enough detail to bring the experience to life.

2. McClain's essay reports in part her experience of conflict resulting from her growth beyond the boundaries of her childhood and community. Think of a time when you outgrew a particular group or community. What conflicts and satisfactions did you experience? Write an essay comparing your experience with McClain's.

3. **Cultural Considerations**   Are there any ways in which you feel, like McClain, that you have "a foot in each world" (paragraph 14)? These worlds might be related to race and affluence, as McClain's worlds are, or they might be aligned by gender, social class, religion, or some other characteristic. Write an essay describing your own experience in balancing these two worlds. Are there ways in which you appreciate having a dual membership, or is it only a burden? What have you learned from your experience?

4. **Connections**   Like McClain, Kaela Hobby-Reichstein, in "Learning Race" (p. 102), writes poignantly about the burdens of being classified by skin color. The two women address similar issues, but their perspectives on racial discrimination are quite different. In an essay of your own, compare the tones and viewpoints of these two authors.

Thou seest I have more flesh than another man, and therefore more frailty.
— William Shakespeare

Except for smoking, obesity is now the number one preventable cause of death in this country. Three hundred thousand people die of obesity every year. — Dr. C. Everett Koop

Fat people may not be chortling all day long, but they're a hell of a lot nicer than the wizened and shriveled. — Suzanne Britt

Journal Response If you're like most people, you've probably been dissatis-fied with your size at one point or another, whether you wanted to be taller or shorter, lose a few pounds, build some muscle, or simply avoid weight gain. Write a journal entry in which you describe your attitude toward your body. What, if anything, would you change about it? Why?

Cheryl Peck

Cheryl Peck (born 1951) has always lived in Michigan—first with her par-ents and four younger siblings on a nonworking farm bordering a gravel pit; now in a small town with her "Beloved," Nancy, and her cat, Babycakes. She attended the University of Michigan, holds a full-time job in a welfare office, and has been trying—unsuccessfully—to write the great American novel since she was thirteen years old. After friends encouraged her to write down the per-sonal stories she was always amusing them with, Peck reluctantly started sub-mitting humorous and poignant articles to a Kalamazoo lesbian newsletter and giving readings at a community church. Another friend, who owns a combined printing and composting business, convinced Peck to self-publish a collection of her essays, on the theory that "she could always use unsold copies for worm bedding." Fat Girls and Lawn Chairs (2004) caught the attention of an editor at Warner Books, who brought the essays to a wider audience and cult-favorite status. Peck followed it a year later with Revenge of the Paste Eaters: Memoirs of a Misfit (2005) and is currently "contemplating writing a book about some-thing more interesting than my own life."

FATSO

In most of her writing, Peck uses her ample size— "three hundred pounds (plus change)"—to fuel her self-deprecating brand of humor. This essay from Re-venge of the Paste Eaters, however, takes a decidedly different approach to the weight issues that have plagued the author all her life.

My friend Annie and I were having lunch and we fell into a discussion   *1*
of people of size. She told me she had gone to the fair with a friend of
hers who is a young man of substance, and while he was standing in
the midway, thinking about his elephant ear,[1] someone walked past
him, said, "You don't need to eat that," and kept on walking away.
Gone before he could register what had been said, much less formulate
a stunning retort.

And that person was probably right: he did not need to eat that ele-   *2*
phant ear. Given what they are made of, the question then becomes:
Who *does* need to eat an elephant ear? And to what benefit? Are elephant ears inherently better for thin people than for fat ones? Do we
suppose that that one particular elephant ear will somehow alter the
course of this man's life in some way that all of the elephant ears before it, or all of the elephant ears to follow, might not? And last but not
least, what qualifies any of us for the mission of telling other people
what they should or should not eat?

I have probably spent most of my life listening to other people tell   *3*
me that as a middle-class white person, I have no idea what it is like to
be discriminated against. I have never experienced the look that tells me
I am not welcome, I have never been treated rudely on a bus, I have
never been reminded to keep my place, I have never been laughed at,
ridiculed, threatened, snubbed, not waited on, or received well-meaning
service I would just as soon have done without. I have never had to
choose which streets I will walk down and which streets I will avoid. I
have never been told that my needs cannot be met in this store. I have
never experienced that lack of social status that can debilitate the soul.

My feelings were not hurt when I was twelve years old and the shoe   *4*
salesman measured my feet and said he had no women's shoes large
enough for me, but perhaps I could wear the boxes.

I have never been called crude names, like "fatso" or "lard-   *5*
bucket." . . . My nickname on the school bus was never "Bismarck,"
as in the famous battleship. No one ever assumed I was totally inept
in all sports except those that involved hitting things because — and
everyone knows — the more weight you can put behind it, the farther
you can kick or bat or just bully the ball.

I have never picked up a magazine with the photograph of a naked   *6*
woman of substance on the cover, to read, in the following issue, thirty
letters to the editor addressing sizism, including the one that said, "She

---

[1] Fried dough. [Editor's note.]

should be ashamed of herself. She should go on a diet immediately and demonstrate some self-control. She is going to develop diabetes, arthritis, hypertension, and stroke, she will die an ugly death at an early age and she will take down the entire American health system with her." And that would, of course, be the only letter I remember. I would not need some other calm voice to say, "You don't know that—and you don't know that the same fate would not befall a thin woman."

No one has ever assumed I am lazy, undisciplined, prone to self- 7 pity, and emotionally unstable purely based on my size. No one has ever told me all I need is a little self-discipline and I too could be thin, pretty—a knockout, probably, because I have a "pretty face"—probably very popular because I have a "good personality." My mother never told me boys would never pay any attention to me because I'm fat.

I have never assumed an admirer would never pay any attention to 8 me because I'm fat. I have never mishandled a sexual situation because I have been trained to think of myself as asexual. Unattractive. Repugnant.

Total strangers have never walked up to me in the street and started 9 to tell me about weight loss programs their second cousin in Tulsa tried with incredible results, nor would they ever do so with the manner and demeanor of someone doing me a nearly unparalleled favor. I have never walked across a parking lot to have a herd of young men break into song about loving women with big butts. When I walk down the street or ride my bicycle, no one has ever hung out the car window to yell crude insults. When I walk into the houses of friends I have never been directed to the "safe" chairs as if I just woke up this morning this size and am incapable of gauging for myself what will or will not hold me.

I have never internalized any of this nonexistent presumption of 10 who I am or what I feel. I would never discriminate against another woman of substance. I would never look at a heavy person and think, "self-pitying, undisciplined tub of lard." I would never admit that while I admire beautiful bodies, I rarely give the inhabitants the same attention and respect I would a soul mate because I do not expect they would ever become a soul mate. I would never tell you that I was probably thirty years old before I realized you really *can* be too small or too thin, or that the condition causes real emotional pain.

I have never skipped a high school reunion until I "lose a few 11 pounds." I have never hesitated to reconnect with an old friend. I will appear anywhere in a bathing suit. If my pants split, I assume—and I assume everyone assumes—it was caused by poor materials.

I have always understood why attractive women are offended when 12 men whistle at them.

I have never felt self-conscious standing next to my male friend   *13*
who is five foot ten and weighs 145 pounds.

I am not angry about any of this.   *14*

Meaning

1. Throughout her essay Peck repeats that she has never experienced, done, or felt any of the things she describes. Is she telling the truth? How do you know? (Hint: look up *irony* in the Glossary.)
2. How does Peck feel about the discrimination she faces as an overweight woman? Why does she feel this way?
3. Several times in her essay, Peck refers to people "of substance" (paragraphs 1, 6, and 10). How might this phrase have a double meaning?
4. If any of the following words are new to you, try to guess their meanings from their context in Peck's essay. Check your guesses against a dictionary's definitions, and then try to use each word in a sentence or two of your own.

register (1)	crude (5)	demeanor (9)
retort (1)	prone (7)	gauging (9)
debilitate (3)	asexual (8)	presumption (10)

Purpose and Audience

1. For whom is Peck writing? Fat people? Thin people? Herself? What clues in the essay bring you to your conclusion?
2. What lesson might readers take from Peck's essay?

Method and Structure

1. What, precisely, is Peck comparing and contrasting in this essay? Identify a few of the points of comparison she uses to develop her main idea. Which of these points seem most important to her?
2. Where does Peck's comparison begin? How does she use a subtle shift in point of view to indicate that she does, indeed, know "what it is like to be discriminated against" (paragraph 3)? (If necessary, see *point of view* in the Glossary.)
3. **Other Methods**   Peck's comparison relies heavily on example (Chapter 6), focusing on a series of hurtful incidents from her own life. Choose two examples, and consider what each contributes to Peck's point.

Language

1. Peck is cautious in the words she to uses to refer to overweight people, preferring terms such as "woman of substance" (paragraphs 6 and 10) and "heavy person" (10) over the judgmental terms that some people have used to describe her (and that she has caught herself thinking about others). Why, then, does she use the obviously insulting "Fatso" as the title of her essay?

2. Peck uses the phrase "I have never" repeatedly (seventeen times, to be exact), as well as variations such as "I would never" and "I have not." What is the effect of this repetition?

3. How would you characterize the tone of this essay? How does it affect you as a reader?

Writing Topics

1. **Journal to Essay**   In your journal entry (p. 245), you described your attitude toward your body. Where do you think that attitude came from? Was it influenced in any way by your family, your friends, or the media? Write an essay in which you examine how other people's opinions affect a person's self-image. In your essay, describe your own thoughts about the ideal body, and explain the origins of those thoughts as best you can.

2. Peck's essay is in some respects an imagined response to the person who insulted her friend's friend. Think of a time when a stranger made an inappropriate or insensitive comment directed at you or someone close to you (or of a time when you overheard such a remark intended for someone else). Write an essay that responds to the person in question, explaining why his or her comment was offensive.

3. Write an essay expressing your opinion of Peck's essay. For instance, how would you respond to her complaint that people treat overweight individuals unfairly? Does she overlook important considerations about health? Do you think she exaggerates any of her points? Agree or disagree with Peck, supporting your opinion with your own examples.

4. **Cultural Considerations**   American society is famously obsessed with people's size. Media outlets have focused recently on what has been described as an "obesity epidemic," and weight loss is a multibillion-dollar industry in this country. But in many cultures (Samoan and Polynesian, for example), large bodies are prized over small ones. Identify one such culture, and find two or three brief sources that explain that culture's attitudes toward body shape (a librarian can help you). Write an essay that compares that culture's standards of physical beauty with America's. Which culture's ideals seem more reasonable to you? Express your preference in a clear thesis statement and support your evaluation with details. Be sure to document your sources, referring to pages 383–95 of the Appendix as necessary.

4. **Connections**   Peck suggests that discrimination against people of size is comparable, if not equivalent, to discrimination against people of color. In "The Middle-Class Black's Burden" (p. 239), Leanita McClain describes her own experiences with racial discrimination, and like Peck, she is angry. How do you think McClain would respond to Peck's characterization of race? Write an imaginary conversation between these two authors, inventing dialogue that mimics each writer's language and reflects the point of view she takes in her essay.

If Barbie is so popular, why do you have to buy her friends? —Steven Wright

I think they should have a Barbie with a buzz cut. —Ellen DeGeneres

Barbie is just a doll. —Mary Schmich

Journal Response   Think of a toy you wanted desperately when you were a child. Write a brief journal entry that explains why you wanted it. What was so special about it? If you did receive the toy, did it live up to your expectations? If you didn't get it, how did you react to your disappointment?

Alaina Wong

Alaina Wong was born in 1981 and grew up in New Jersey. As an English major at the University of Pennsylvania, she served as managing editor of Mosaic, a magazine for Asian American students. Wong graduated in 2002 and worked for several years in the marketing department at the publishing company Simon & Schuster. She is currently a marketing manager in the children's division at Penguin Books.

CHINA DOLL

(STUDENT ESSAY)

Wong wrote "China Doll" when she was a college junior as a submission for the teen anthology YELL-Oh Girls! Emerging Voices Explore Culture, Identity, and Growing Up Asian American *(2001). The essay, Wong explains, "provides a whimsical glimpse into the mind of a child, detailing the ways girls may come to terms with their Asian features, which so often contrast with the media-defined ideal of beauty."*

I wanted Princess Barbie, with long blond hair that you could brush   *1* and a beautiful shiny gown. She even came with a shimmery white tiara, which, in my eight-year-old mind, crowned her at the top of her Barbie world. My parents looked at me expectantly as I tore through the wrapping paper in childlike excitement. As the pile of shredded paper around me grew larger, so did my anticipation.

251

But instead of a beautiful princess with golden tresses, what I found   2
was an unfamiliar black-haired "friend" of Barbie, who wore a floral
wrap skirt over a pink bathing suit.

Disappointment passed over my eyes as I examined the doll more   3
closely. With her dark hair and slanted eyes, she was a dull comparison to her blond friend. My other dolls were all alike and beautiful with
their clouds of blond (or light-brown) hair, broad, toothy smiles, and
wide-open eyes. Even Ken had a perfectly painted-on coif of blond hair
and flashed a winning grin. I didn't think this new doll would go rid-
ing in Barbie's convertible with Ken. Why would he pick her when he
already had so many blond friends to choose from? Besides, instead
of a wide movie-star grin, her lips were curved into a more secretive,
sly smile. I wondered what secrets she was hiding. Maybe she had
crooked teeth.

I announced that I loved my new doll. I didn't want my mom and   4
dad to feel bad. Maybe the store didn't have any more Princess Barbie
dolls, so they had to buy me the leftovers, or the ones that no one wanted.
I looked at the name of this new black-haired addition to my perfect Barbie family. Kira. Kira didn't even have shoes, though her feet were still
arched up, as if they were waiting expectantly for their missing shoes. She
seemed incomplete. She was probably missing lots of things besides her
shoes. My other Barbies all had colorful plastic high heels to complement
their fashionable dresses. Their outfits were perfect.

"Alaina," my mom said, "get your things ready so I can drive you   5
over to Sarah's house!" I threw the dark-haired doll into my backpack
with the other Barbies I was bringing; Sarah and I always shared the latest additions to our Barbie collections. Everyone always said that Sarah
would grow up to look like Goldie Hawn, some famous movie star. I
didn't think I would grow up to look like anybody important, not unless I was like Cinderella, and a fairy godmother went Zap! so I could
be transformed, like magic. Sarah's hair fell in soft waves down her
back, while my own black hair was slippery and straight, like uncooked
spaghetti. I bet Sarah had gotten the Princess Barbie for Christmas.

I liked going over to Sarah's house. Her mom didn't care if we ate   6
raspberries from the backyard without washing them. The last time I
went there, I saw my best friend pluck a juicy purple berry right off the
bush and into her mouth. I was amazed that she didn't care about dirt.
Sarah's mom let us taste cookie dough from the batter when she baked
cookies. I guess only Chinese people cared about germs. My mother
never baked cookies anyway. Baking cookies is what white mothers do
all the time—they like to make things from "scratch" that turn out soft

and chewy, while Chinese mothers buy cookies from the supermarket that are dry and go crunch, unless you dip them in milk. Sarah's mother made the best macaroni and cheese too. Obviously she made it from "scratch." I hoped I was eating lunch there today.

After we pulled into Sarah's driveway, I jumped out of the car and said good-bye to my mom. Inside, Sarah and I ran up the stairs so I could look at her new dollhouse. On the way, we passed piles of laundry warm from the dryer, toys spread out on the floor in front of the TV, and newspapers scattered on the kitchen table. I was jealous. Sarah's mother probably didn't make them clean up every time someone came over. 7

Upstairs, I dumped my Barbies out of my backpack so we could compare our collections. Before I could even look at her dolls, Sarah turned to me. 8

"Look what I got!" she said proudly. 9

I knew it. Sarah had gotten the Princess Barbie. 10

And what did I have to show her? A plain Barbie friend with a funny name, Kira, in an ordinary bathing suit and a skirt that was just a piece of cloth that needed to be tied; it didn't even slip on like real clothes. My doll had straight black hair, no shoes, and worst of all, she didn't even know how to smile right. 11

"Well ... she has pretty flowers on her skirt," Sarah said helpfully. "And she looks kind of like you!" 12

She did? But I didn't want to look like this strange new "friend" of Barbie. Everyone knew that the Barbies with the blond hair were the best. They were the original ones. And they always got to wear the prettiest dresses. I noticed something, but I didn't want to say it out loud. The best dolls, the most glamorous ones, were always the ones that seemed to look like Sarah. 13

"Sarah, honey," her mom called. "Why don't you help me bring up some cookies for you and Alaina?" 14

My best friend turned to me. "I'll be right back!" she chirped. "If you want to, your dolls can try on Princess Barbie's clothes," she offered generously. 15

Sarah skipped out of the room, her blond pigtails swinging around her head. I turned to my Kira doll, regarding her simple outfit. I highly doubted that Princess Barbie's costume would look right on her. Whoever heard of a black-haired doll with slanted eyes wearing a crown? Maybe it wouldn't even fit right. Hesitatingly, I picked up Sarah's Princess Barbie. She really was beautiful. Slowly, I slipped off her gown and dressed her in one of the extra doll outfits, a shiny purple top and 16 silver pants. Princess Barbie continued smiling blankly at me. I was glad she didn't mind that I had changed her clothes.

Carefully, I buttoned my Kira doll into the glittery princess gown. *17*
No Velcro closures here; this dress was glamorous, like what a princess would wear in real life. The sunlight through Sarah's bedroom window made the dress sparkle, as if my plain dark-haired Kira doll was actually a princess. The doll's secretive smile began to comfort me, as if we shared a secret together. We both knew this wasn't her real gown, but maybe she could be princess for a day. Just maybe. I stared at her. Finally I placed Barbie's iridescent tiara on top of Kira's jet-black hair. And what do you know? It fit perfectly.

Meaning

1. In her opening paragraphs Wong compares her new Kira doll with the other Barbie dolls in her collection. How were they different?
2. In paragraph 4, an eight-year-old Wong wonders why her parents didn't get her the doll she wanted, contemplating that "maybe the store didn't have any more Princess Barbie dolls, so they had to buy me the leftovers, or the ones that no one wanted." By the end of the essay, however, Wong seems to realize that her parents may have had a different reason. Why do you think they chose the Kira doll for their daughter?
3. Wong's essay compares both her Kira doll with Princess Barbie and herself with her best friend, Sarah. In what ways do the dolls function as symbols for the girls? (If necessary, see *symbol* in the Glossary.)
4. Based on their context in Wong's essay, try to guess the meanings of any of the following words that you don't already know. Test your guesses in a dictionary, and then use each new word in a sentence or two of your own.

tresses (2)	complement (4)	chirped (15)
coif (3)	scratch (6)	regarding (16)
sly (3)	glamorous (13)	iridescent (17)

Purpose and Audience

1. What do you think might have prompted Wong to write about a doll she received as a child? What evidence from the text can you use to support your opinion?
2. Although this essay speaks from the perspective of an eight-year-old Chinese American girl and was written specifically for a collection aimed at young Asian girls, to what extent can other readers — adults, males, or Caucasians, for example — sympathize with Wong's experience? How

does she try to make sure that they can do so? Find examples from the essay that show she is addressing people who might not share her experience, as well as girls who may have had similar feelings growing up.

Method and Structure

1. Why is comparison and contrast particularly well suited to Wong's subject and purpose?
2. Where in the essay does Wong focus on similarities between herself and her best friend? Where does she focus on differences? Why do you think she might have chosen to organize her essay as she does?
3. **Other Methods**   Description (Chapter 4) features prominently in Wong's essay. She also uses narration (Chapter 5) to explain her experience. What dimensions do these other methods add to the piece?

Language

1. What is the overall tone of the essay?
2. Throughout "China Doll" Wong uses metaphors and similes to make her comparisons vivid and immediate. Find two or three examples and comment on their effectiveness.

Writing Topics

1. **Journal to Essay**   In your journal entry (p. 251), you wrote about a toy that you wanted as a child. Now think about that toy more critically. Did it carry meanings besides pure entertainment? Make a list of messages that the makers of the toy might intentionally or unintentionally have been sending to children. Using Wong's essay as a model, write an analysis of what the toy represented to you. Your essay may be serious or humorous, but it should include plenty of description so that readers unfamiliar with the toy can picture it in their minds.
2. Although Wong's essay is written with greater skill and range of vocabulary than an eight-year-old would be capable of, it reveals the many facets of a young girl's emotional life. Write an essay in which you analyze the girlish concerns evident in "China Doll," demonstrating how Wong's writing captures a girl's frame of mind. Consider, for example, the way she compares Chinese and white people's attitudes toward food (paragraph 6), or her certainty that "Sarah had gotten the Princess Barbie for Christmas" (paragraph 5). How does the author use diction and point of view to evoke the childhood naïveté she no longer has?

3. In her essay Wong explores the complex reasons behind her initial dislike for a doll with Asian features, commenting that "the best dolls, the most glamorous ones, were always the ones that seemed to look like Sarah" (paragraph 13). In other words, the most popular dolls were unmistakably white. Write an essay in which you consider the implications of Wong's observation. To what extent do contemporary fashion dolls (or some other aspect of popular entertainment) reflect, reinforce, or reject racial stereotypes? How might their popularity affect girls' self-esteem? You may draw on Wong's essay or your own experience for examples, or, if none come to mind, consider doing some research on the topic. (See the Appendix for tips on writing from sources.)

4. **Cultural Considerations**   The inspiration for Barbie was a racy adult doll made in Germany after World War II. In the 1950s, the U.S. toy manufacturer Mattel transformed the original doll into a toy for American girls. What characteristics of Barbie strike you as especially American? How might the doll have been different if it had been designed for girls in other cultures? Why do you think toy manufacturers might feel a need to create alternative versions like Wong's Kira doll or the recently popular Bratz line? Write an essay analyzing Barbie in which you answer these questions. The characteristics you identify may come from Wong's comparisons or your own experience, but be sure to explain why you think they are distinctly American.

5. **Connections**   Like Wong, Kaela Hobby-Reichstein, in "Learning Race" (p. 102), explores the first time she became aware of race. Though the two authors undoubtedly made parallel discoveries as children, the positions they write from are nearly opposite. Write a comparison of the two essays in which you explore the authors' tones and purposes.

Comparison and Contrast

Choose one of the following topics, or any other topic they suggest, for an essay developed by comparison and contrast. The topic you decide on should be something you care about so that the comparison and contrast is a means of communicating an idea, not an end in itself.

EXPERIENCE

1. Two jobs you have held
2. Two experiences with discrimination
3. Your own version of an event you witnessed or participated in and someone else's view of the same event (perhaps a friend's or a newspaper reporter's)
4. A good and a bad job interview

PEOPLE

5. Your relationships with two friends
6. Someone before and after marriage or the birth of a child
7. Two or more candidates for public office
8. Two relatives

PLACES AND THINGS

9. A place as it is now and as it was years ago
10. Two cars
11. Contact lenses and glasses
12. Two towns or cities
13. Nature in the city and in the country

ART AND ENTERTAINMENT

14. The work of two artists or writers, or two works by the same artist or writer
15. Two or more forms of jazz, classical music, or pop music
16. Movies or television today and when you were a child
17. A novel and a movie or television show on which it's based
18. A high school or college football, baseball, or basketball game and a professional game in the same sport
19. The advertisements during two very different television programs, or in two very different magazines

EDUCATION AND IDEAS

20. Talent and skill
21. Learning and teaching
22. Two styles of teaching
23. Two religions
24. Humanities courses and science or mathematics courses
25. A passive student and an active student

Evaluating Stereotypes

1. The writers in this chapter wrestle with questions of identity, debating issues as diverse as the emotional impact of negative stereotypes (Michael Dorris, p. 232; Leanita McClain, p. 239; Cheryl Peck, p. 245; and Alaina Wong, p. 251), the role of peers and family in the development of an individual's sense of self (Julia Álvarez, p. 232, McClain, Peck, and Wong), and the relationship between body image and self-esteem (Peck and Wong). All five authors rely on comparison and contrast, but otherwise they go about their tasks very differently. Most notably, perhaps, their tones vary widely, from irony to vulnerability to anger. Choose the two works that seem most different in this respect, and analyze how the tone of each helps the author achieve his or her purpose. Give specific examples to support your ideas. Does your analysis lead you to conclude that one tone is likely to be more effective than another in comparing stereotypes with reality? (For more on tone, see pp. 38–39 and 334–35.)

2. Michael Dorris, Leanita McClain, and Cheryl Peck refer to misperceptions of a minority group on the part of the dominant society. Think of a minority group to which you belong. It could be based on race, ethnicity, language, sexual orientation, religion, physical disability, or any other characteristic. How is your minority perceived in the dominant culture, and how does this perception resemble or differ from the reality as you know it? Write an essay comparing the perception of and the reality of your group.

3. All of the authors in this chapter suggest that stereotypes play a significant part in our perceptions of others and ourselves. Dorris refers to the "white noise" of Indian images in the media, Álvarez to her parents' negative assessments of each other's extended families, McClain to a distorted image of African Americans, Peck to perceptions about overweight individuals, and Wong to her misguided preference for blond Barbie dolls. To what extent, if at all, are these misconceptions the result of media hype or distortion, whether in advertising, news stories, television programming, movies, or elsewhere? What else might contribute to the misconceptions in each case? Write an essay explaining how such notions arise in the first place. You could use the misconceptions identified by the authors in this chapter for your examples, or you could supply examples of your own.

Chapter 11

DEFINITION

Clarifying Family Relationships

Definition sets the boundaries of a thing, a concept, an emotion, or a value. In answering "What is it?" and also "What is it *not*?" definition specifies the main qualities of a subject and its essential nature. Since words are only symbols, pinning down their precise meanings is essential for us to understand ourselves and one another. Thus we use definition constantly, whether we are explaining a new word like *muggle* to someone who has never heard it, specifying what we're after when we tell a friend we want to do something *fun,* or asking a physician to clarify what she means when she diagnoses a child as *hyperactive.*

We use definition often in sentences or paragraphs to explain their meaning—stopping to define *success,* for instance, in a business or research proposal, or giving the sense of a technical term in an engineering study. But we may also need to define words at length, especially when they are abstract, complicated, or controversial. Drawing on other methods of development, such as example, analysis, or comparison and contrast, entire essays might be devoted to debated phrases (such as *family values*), to the current uses of a word (*monopoly* in business), or to the meanings of a term in a particular context (like *personality* in psychological theory). Definition is, in other words, essential whenever we want to be certain that we are understood.

READING DEFINITION

There are several kinds of definition, each with different uses. One is the **formal definition**, usually a statement of the general class of things to which the word belongs, followed by the distinction(s) between it and other members of the class. For example:

	General class	*Distinction(s)*
A submarine is	a seagoing vessel	that operates underwater.
A parable is	a brief, simple story	that illustrates a moral or religious principle.
Pressure is	the force	applied to a given surface.
Insanity is	a mental condition	in which a defendant does not know right from wrong.

A formal definition usually gives a standard dictionary meaning of the word (as in the first two examples) or a specialized meaning agreed to by the members of a profession or discipline (as in the last two examples, from physics and criminal law, respectively). Writers use formal definition to explain the basic meaning of a term so that readers can understand the rest of a discussion. Occasionally, a formal definition can serve as a springboard to a more elaborate, detailed exploration of a word. For instance, an essay might define *pride* simply as "a sense of self-respect" before probing the varied meanings of the word as people actually understand it and then settling on a fuller and more precise meaning of the author's own devising.

This more detailed definition of *pride* could fall into one of two other types of definition: stipulative and extended. A **stipulative definition** clarifies the particular way a writer is using a word: it stipulates, or specifies, a meaning to suit a larger purpose; the definition is part of a larger whole. For example, to show how pride can destroy personal relationships, a writer might first stipulate a meaning of *pride* that ties in with that purpose. Though a stipulative definition may sometimes take the form of a brief formal definition, most require several sentences or even paragraphs. In a physics textbook, for instance, the physicist's definition of *pressure* quoted above probably would not suffice to give readers a good sense of the term and eliminate all the other possible meanings they may have in mind.

Whereas a writer may use a formal or stipulative definition for some larger purpose, he or she would use an **extended definition** for the sake of defining—that is, for the purpose of exploring a thing, quality, or idea in its full complexity and drawing boundaries around it until its meaning is complete and precise. Extended definitions usually treat subjects so complex, vague, or laden with emotions or values that people misunderstand or disagree over their meanings. The subject may be an abstract concept like *patriotism*, a controversial phrase like *beginnings of life*, a colloquial or slang expression like *hype*, a thing like *nanobot*, a scientific idea like *natural selection*, even an everyday expression like *nagging*. Besides defining, the purpose may be to persuade readers to accept a definition (for instance, that life begins at conception, or at birth), to explain (what is natural selection?), or to amuse (nagging as exemplified by great nags).

As the variety of possible subjects and purposes may suggest, an extended definition may draw on whatever methods will best accomplish the goal of specifying what the subject encompasses and distinguishing it from similar things, qualities, or concepts. Several strategies are unique to definition:

- **Synonyms,** or words of similar meaning, can convey the range of the word's meanings. For example, a writer could equate *misery* with *wretchedness* and *distress.*
- **Negation,** or saying what a word does not mean, can limit the meaning, particularly when a writer wants to focus on only one sense of an abstract term, such as *pride*, that is open to diverse interpretations.
- The **etymology** of a word—its history—may illuminate its meaning, perhaps by showing the direction and extent of its change (*pride*, for instance, comes from a Latin word meaning "to be beneficial or useful") or by uncovering buried origins that remain implicit in the modern meaning (*patriotism* comes from the Greek word for "father"; *happy* comes from the Old Norse word for "good luck").

These strategies of definition may be used alone or together, and they may occupy whole paragraphs in an essay-length definition; but they rarely provide enough range to surround the subject completely. That's why most definition essays draw on at least some of the other methods discussed in this book. One or two methods may predominate: an essay on nagging, for instance, might be developed with brief narratives. Or several methods may be combined: a definition of *patriotism* might compare it with *nationalism*, analyze its effects (such as the actions people take on its behalf), and give examples of patriotic individuals. The goal is not to employ every method in a sort of catalog of methods but to use those which best illuminate the subject. By drawing on the appropriate methods, a writer defines and clarifies a specific perspective on the subject so that the reader understands the meaning exactly.

ANALYZING DEFINITION IN PARAGRAPHS

David Popenoe (born 1932), a professor of sociology at Rutgers University, has written numerous books and articles about family life and marriage in modern societies. This paragraph comes from his book *Life without Father: Compelling New Evidence That Fatherhood and Marriage Are Indispensable for the Good of Children and Society* (1996).

What do fathers do? Partly, of course, it is simply being a second adult in the home. Bringing up children is demanding, stressful, and often exhausting. Two adults can support and spell each other; they can also offset each other's deficiencies and build on each other's strengths. Beyond that, fathers — men — bring an array of unique and irreplaceable qualities that women do not ordinarily bring. Some of these are familiar, if sometimes overlooked or taken for granted. The father as protector, for example, has by no means outlived his usefulness. And he is important as a role model. Teenage boys without fathers are notoriously prone to trouble. The pathway to adulthood for daughters is somewhat easier, but they still must learn from their fathers, as they cannot from their mothers, how to relate to men. They learn from their fathers about heterosexual trust, intimacy, and difference. They learn to appreciate their own femininity from the one male who is most special in their lives (assuming that they love and respect their fathers). Most important, through loving and being loved by their fathers, they learn that they are worthy of love.

> Question — topic sentence — introduces role to be defined. Roles and qualities of fathers:
> Second adult in home
>
> Protector
> Role model
>   For sons
>   For daughters

Firoozeh Dumas (born 1966), a California-based writer who emigrated from Iran with her family at the age of seven, hopes to dispel American fears of Iranian people by revealing their "shared humanity." The following paragraph is from her best-selling book *Funny in Farsi: A Memoir of Growing Up Iranian in America* (2003).

When we lived in Abadan, we lived near my father's oldest sister, Sedigeh. She is my *ameh*, my father's sister. Her four sons are my *pessar ameh*,

> Early sentence introduces role to be defined

"sons of father's sister." Our families spent every free moment together and I always thought of my aunt Sedigeh and uncle Abdullah as a second set of parents. Since my aunt Sedigeh never had a daughter, she regarded me as her own. Always warm and affectionate, she showered me with compliments that stayed with me long after our visits had ended. She often told me that I was smart and patient and that she wished that I were her daughter. She never criticized me, but loved me as only a father's sister could. To me, the word *ameh* still conjures up feelings of being enveloped with love.

Roles and qualities of an *ameh*:

Parent figure

Warm and affectionate

Uncritical and loving

Concluding topic sentence: summarizes meaning of word for author

DEVELOPING AN ESSAY BY DEFINITION
Getting Started

You'll sometimes be asked to write definition essays, as when a psychology exam asks for a discussion of *schizophrenia* or a political science assignment calls for an explanation of the term *totalitarianism*. To come up with a subject on your own, consider words that have complex meanings and are either unfamiliar to readers or open to varied interpretations. The subject should be something you know and care enough about to explore in great detail and surround completely. An idea for a subject may come from an overheard conversation (for instance, a reference to someone as "too patriotic"), a personal experience (a broken marriage you think attributable to one spouse's pride), or something you've seen or read (another writer's definition of *jazz*).

Begin exploring your subject by examining and listing its conventional meanings (consulting an unabridged dictionary may help here, and the dictionary will also give you synonyms and etymology). Also examine the differences of opinion about the word's meanings — the different ways, wrong or right, that you have heard or seen it used. Run through the other methods to see what fresh approaches to the subject they open up:

- How can the subject be described?
- What are some examples?
- Can the subject be divided into qualities or characteristics?
- Can its functions help define it?
- Will comparing and contrasting it with something else help sharpen its meaning?
- Do its causes or effects help clarify its sense?

Some of the questions may turn up nothing, but others may open your eyes to meanings you had not seen.

Forming a Thesis

When you have generated a good list of ideas about your subject, settle on the purpose of your definition. Do you mostly want to explain a word that is unfamiliar to readers? Do you want to express your own view so that readers see a familiar subject from a new angle? Do you want to argue in favor of a particular definition or perhaps persuade readers to look more critically at themselves or their surroundings? Try to work your purpose into a thesis sentence that summarizes your definition and — just as important — asserts something about the subject. For example:

> TENTATIVE THESIS STATEMENT   The prevailing concept of *patriotism* is dangerously wrong.

> REVISED THESIS STATEMENT   Though generally considered entirely positive in meaning, *patriotism* in fact reflects selfish, childish emotions that have no place in a global society.

(Note that the revised thesis statement not only summarizes the writer's definition and makes an assertion about the subject, but it also identifies the prevailing definition she intends to counter in her essay.)

With a thesis sentence formulated, reevaluate your ideas in light of it and pause to consider the needs of your readers:

- What do readers already know about your subject, and what do they need to be told in order to understand it as you do?
- Are your readers likely to be biased for or against your subject? If you were defining *patriotism*, for example, you might assume that your readers see the word as representing a constructive, even essential value that contributes to the strength of the country. If your purpose were to contest this view, as implied by the revised thesis statement, you would have to build your case carefully to win readers to your side.

Organizing

The introduction to a definition essay should provide a base from which to expand and at the same time explain to readers why the forthcoming definition is useful, significant, or necessary. You may want to report the incident that prompted you to define, say, why the subject itself is important, or specify the common understandings, or misunderstandings, about its meaning. Several devices can serve as effective beginnings: the etymology of the word; a quotation from another writer supporting or contradicting your definition; or an explanation of what the word does *not* mean (negation). (Try to avoid the overused opening that cites a dictionary: "According to *The American Heritage Dictionary*, _____ means...." Your readers have probably seen this opening many times before.) If it is not implied in the rest of your introduction, you may want to state your thesis so that readers know precisely what your purpose and point are.

The body of the essay should then proceed, paragraph by paragraph, to refine the characteristics or qualities of the subject, using the arrangement and methods that will distinguish it from anything similar and provide your perspective. For instance:

- You might draw increasingly tight boundaries around the subject, moving from broader, more familiar meanings to the one you have in mind.
- You might arrange your points in order of increasing drama.
- You might begin with your own experience of the subject and then show how you see it operating in your surroundings.

The conclusion to a definition essay is equally a matter of choice. You might summarize your definition, indicate its superiority to other definitions of the same subject, quote another writer whose view supports your own, or recommend that readers make some use of the information you have provided. The choice depends—as it does in any kind of essay—on your purpose and the impression you want to leave with readers.

Drafting

While drafting your extended definition, keep your subject vividly in mind. Say too much rather than too little about it to ensure that you capture its essence; you can always cut when you revise. And be sure to provide plenty of details and examples to support your view. Such evidence is particularly important when, as in the earlier example of patriotism, you wish to change readers' perceptions of your subject.

In definition the words you use are especially important. Abstractions and generalities cannot draw precise boundaries around a subject, so your words must be as concrete and specific as you can make them. You'll have chances during revising and editing to work on your words, but try during drafting to pin down your meanings. Use words and phrases that appeal directly to the senses and experiences of readers. When appropriate, use figures of speech to make meaning inescapably clear; instead of "Patriotism is childish," for example, write "The blindly patriotic person is like a small child who sees his or her parents as gods, all-knowing, always right." The connotations of words—the associations called up in readers' minds by words like *home, ambitious,* and *generous*—can contribute to your definition as well. But be sure that connotative words trigger associations suited to your purpose. And when you are trying to explain something precisely, rely most heavily on words with generally neutral meanings. (See pp. 49–50 for more on concrete and specific language and figures of speech. See pp. 48–49 for more on connotation.)

Revising and Editing

When you are satisfied that your draft is complete, revise and edit it against the following questions and the information in the box.

- *Have you surrounded your subject completely and tightly?* Your definition should not leave gaps, nor should the boundaries be so broadly drawn that the subject overlaps something else. For instance, a definition of *hype* that focused on exaggerated and deliberately misleading claims should include all such claims (some political speeches, say, as well as some advertisements), and it should exclude appeals that do not fit the basic definition (some public-service advertising, for instance).

- *Does your definition reflect the conventional meanings of the word?* Even if you are providing a fresh slant on your subject, you can't change its meaning entirely, or you will confuse your readers and perhaps undermine your own credibility. *Patriotism,* for example, could not be defined from the first as "hatred of foreigners," for that definition strays into an entirely different realm. The conventional meaning of "love of country" would have to serve as the starting point, though your essay might interpret the meaning in an original way.

FOCUS ON PARAGRAPH AND ESSAY UNITY

When drafting a definition, you may find yourself being pulled away from your subject by the descriptions, examples, comparisons, and other methods you use to specify meaning. Let yourself explore byways of your subject — doing so will help you discover what you think. But in revising you'll need to direct all paragraphs to your thesis, and within paragraphs you'll need to direct all sentences to the paragraph topic. In other words, you'll need to ensure that your essay and its paragraphs are unified.

One way to achieve unity is to focus each paragraph on some part of your definition and then to focus each sentence within the paragraph on that part. Judy Brady's "I Want a Wife" (p. 277) proceeds in just such a pattern, as the following outline shows. The sentences from paragraphs 3–9 specify the paragraph topics. A look at Brady's essay will show you that each of the paragraphs elaborates on its topic.

THESIS (PARAGRAPH 2)   I ... would like to have a wife.

PARAGRAPH 3   I want a wife who will work and send me to school. And ... I want a wife to take care of my children.

PARAGRAPH 4   I want a wife who will take care of *my* physical needs.

PARAGRAPH 5   I want a wife who will not bother me with rambling complaints.... But I want a wife who will listen to me.

PARAGRAPH 6   I want a wife who will take care of the details of my social life.

PARAGRAPH 7   I want a wife who is sensitive to my sexual needs.

PARAGRAPH 8   I want the liberty to replace my present wife with another one.

PARAGRAPH 9   When I am through with school and have a job, I want my wife to quit working and remain at home.

If some part of your definition requires more than a single paragraph, by all means expand it. But keep the group of paragraphs focused on a single idea.

For more on unity in essays and paragraphs, see pages 33–35.

A NOTE ON THEMATIC CONNECTIONS

Family is the core topic of this chapter. The authors represented here are all seeking to define, or redefine, a complex set of relationships that many of us take for granted. David Popenoe, in a paragraph, considers the ever-important role a father plays in the lives of his children (p. 263), while Firoozeh Dumas, in another paragraph, explains the special place held by the paternal aunt in an Iranian family (p. 263). Reena Nadler, an identical twin, writes about her need to carve out an identity separate from that of her sister (p. 270). In defining a wife, Judy Brady questions male and female roles in traditional families (p. 277). And Andrew Sullivan, a single gay man with conservative values, examines the very personal meanings of marriage as a public institution (p. 282).

Resolve to be thyself. —Matthew Arnold

It is easier to live through someone else than to become complete yourself.
—Betty Friedan

Man's main task in life is to give birth to himself. —Eric Fromm

Journal Response Achieving our individuality—one of life's greatest challenges—often involves differentiating ourselves from others. In a short journal entry, compare yourself with a sibling or another family member. How are you similar to this person? How are you different?

Reena Nadler

Reena Nadler was born in 1984 and grew up in New York City. As a student at Swarthmore College, she pursued diverse interests: she was a member of the rugby and track-and-field teams, a senior editor and columnist for her school's student-run magazine, and a peer leader committed to mentoring fellow classmates. Nadler also organized school programs that encouraged students to appreciate cultural diversity, and she participated in a national student diversity leadership conference. She graduated in 2006.

CHROMOSOMES IN COMMON
(STUDENT ESSAY)

"Do you like being a twin?" is a question that Nadler frequently hears. In this essay, written for an English class on autobiography, she responds to this question by discussing how it feels always to be defined as part of a pair.

"Hey, Reena, do you like being a twin?" 1

"Is that your sister, Reena? You guys look exactly alike, that's so 2
cute."

"Do you guys ever switch classes or take tests for the other one?" 3

"Hold on, stand together so I can compare you. Your nose is 4
rounder, I think, Reena, and Susannah, your face is a little wider."

"Hey, stay next to each other, I want a picture of the two of you 5
together."

"Yeah, let's get a picture of the twins." 6

Susannah and I sighed, moved next to each other and grinned for the 7
flash. We were in Disneyland, surrounded by a group of goggling friends,
half of whom had been on Susannah's summer trip and had never met
me and the other half of whom had been on my summer trip and had
never met her. The flood of questions washed over my armor—armor
built up after sixteen years of the same thing. I didn't say that the comments and comparisons always make me feel as if I have no identity. I
didn't say that they always make me feel as if I'm on display, like all the
cartoon characters that day at Disneyland. I didn't say that they always
make me feel as if I am not myself, but simply a comparison to Susannah. I didn't say that they always put a layer of bitterness over one of the
most precious things I have—my relationship with my sister. After all, I
told myself, these were my friends. They meant well, and they couldn't
help it if they couldn't understand. I have never met anyone who could
know both me and my sister and not compare us, and that will last all
my life.

The picture came out so well that one of my friends sent it to 8
me—the cute twins right next to each other in the foreground and
some Disneyland trees in the background. It is a close-up down to our
shoulders; Susannah and I are next to each other in similar shirts, hair
pulled back, each with one arm raised, presenting our identities as twins
to the flock of picture takers. We're both wearing that extra wide picture smile one gets when too many pictures in a row have been taken
and the smile muscles are getting tired. Our faces reflect the wry sense
of humor—the essence of armor—that we have developed because the
alternative is animosity. The picture is in black and white; singularly
appropriate because it presents only one dimension of its subjects. Our
attention is not focused on each other but on the camera, both enjoying and despising the attention. Though we stand next to each other
in space, the picture does not record our connection. Instead it is about
the connection of each to the role she plays for the world.

So what is that other dimension, that intimate bond? There is an- 9
other picture of us, back from when we were two. We are sitting in a
big plush golden brown armchair which served as the center and meeting place of the room we shared. The chair is wide enough to hold the
two of us side by side, and long enough for our purple-pajamaed feet
to barely reach the edge. We each have one of those large children's
books in our laps, easily bigger than we are, and we look as though we

are settling in for an evening of companionable reading. Two tufts of light brown hair wisp gently over two concentrated foreheads as each examines her book. Our shoulders lean up against each other and our books overlap; our hands are touching as we hold down the pages. Each is interested in her own endeavor, but a quick glance could reveal what interesting activity the other one is up to, and a word or two could enlist the other's help and attention in our own. Our comfortable companionship whispers that we are long accustomed to sharing space, sharing discoveries, living with the spheres of our lives intertwining, overlapping, fusing, and re-forming in response to each other.

Our favorite number is two. We can break a cookie perfectly down 10 the middle. When it is time to go to bed, we will not cry to stay up with the grown-ups because anything interesting that will be going on is probably going to be right there between the two of us. When we are together there is a relaxation of boundaries that is almost like one self being alone. We do not understand the concept of being truly alone.

I have found, however, that often in life the more meaningful some- 11 thing is to a person, the more difficulties it raises. The difficulties of being a twin are not restricted to other people's reactions but are also often about this connection we have shared since we were little. When I had just turned thirteen, I had the best summer of my life. That year Susannah, disappointed with her experiences at our old camp, decided to build new experiences for herself in a new camp. For herself, and by herself. I was contented to stay at the old camp and try my first solo flight in familiar surroundings. That summer I laughed and cried and talked with my friends at camp. My friends, not ours. I had a place that was mine alone, a place to make memories that no one else would ever have but me. That idea may sound ordinary to other people, but to me it was the first time ever that my sense of my life and my identity expanded into its own perfect sphere. It was the first time I knew it could. But Susannah's new camp experiment was a failure — the atmosphere and the people there did not complement her, but crushed her. I came home two months later with my arms flung wide to the world and to its possibilities. She came back curled up into a ball. The next summer everything I had created for myself was threatened: Susannah asked me if she could come back to the old camp and share it with me, and she wanted to be in my bunk. She needed somewhere safe where she could revive, and she needed me to be that safety. I needed desperately to keep my one separate plateau.

No one knows how to share the way a twin does. Twins share a 12 family, a face, a body, a life. They swim in the same sea before birth and develop hands, feet, eyes, ears, brains in conjunction. For up to ten days after conception, during the planning of nearly all patterns of personhood, they are even a single entity. How could I invite my sister to share the one space I had exuberantly and painstakingly carved around myself? How could I deny it to her? What could I do with our needs in such direct opposition?

It is a very powerful thing when you realize that you love someone 13 as much as you love yourself. Not just the concept dwelt on in various religious texts, which is treating other people as you wish to be treated, but knowing that in some deep and shrouded part of yourself another person's needs are as important to you as your own. It is a feeling of absolute selfishness and absolute generosity. I got my only glimpse of this part of myself when I was thirteen. I decided that my sister's needs were stronger than my own; she came to camp with me. It is a decision I still feel in conflict about today.

This was not an ultimate sacrifice, however. Searching for an iden- 14 tity and defining the boundaries and differences between oneself and other people is an exploration that everyone is faced with. Only with me, the search is much more complex and urgent. Far from being an isolated story, the camp incident merely illustrates one of many conflicts that have always been and will always be a part of my life; I deal with other people's comments and questions about being a twin and my reactions to them every day. Sometimes I don't want Susannah to read a book I have loved or to have a teacher I have had simply because I want something so desperately to be mine. Competition between us is both repressed and secretly flourishing.

Sometimes I look at her, so similar to me, and see all my insecurities 15 incarnated in a person who is with me all the time and whom people cannot distinguish from me. When I am uncomfortable with myself, therefore, it often translates into hating my sister. I remember my frustration once when I was very angry at my sister, and I caught a glimpse of my crying face in the mirror—looking exactly like hers does when she is upset. Ironically, the only person who truly understands these and many other conflicts is Susannah herself, and as in everything else, we help each other through the experience. On the track team, for example, we are especially protective and supportive of one another by an unspoken instinctive agreement, because the other option is to spoil the experience by hating the other one for being on the team too. She is my partner in the conflicts caused by her as she is my partner in everything else.

So back to the question that began this essay: "Hey, Reena, do you 16 like being a twin?" The answer, I have found, is often so complex that it can be encompassed only in the experience of a lifetime. On another level, however, the answer is quite simple. I am Me, my sister is She, and together there is another entity, a We. I wouldn't trade it in for anything.

Meaning

1. In her opening paragraphs Nadler describes the way that friends treat her and her twin sister. How does she react to their "comments and comparisons (paragraph 7)"? Why?
2. Nadler refers to an "intimate bond" with Susannah (paragraph 9). How does this bond manifest itself during her life, and what benefits does it provide?
3. In paragraph 11, Nadler claims that "often in life the more meaningful something is to a person, the more difficulties it raises." In addition to dealing with the "group of goggling friends" (7), what other conflicts is Nadler compelled to face as a result of being a twin? How does she attempt to resolve them? Is she successful?
4. Based on their context in Nadler's essay, try to guess the meanings of any of the following words that you don't already know. Test your guesses in a dictionary, and then use each new word in a sentence or two of your own.

goggling (7)	plateau (11)	shrouded (13)
wry (8)	exuberantly (12)	incarnated (15)
companionable (9)	painstakingly (12)	encompassed (16)
enlist (9)		

Purpose and Audience

1. What do you think might have prompted Nadler to write so personally about being a twin? What evidence from the text can you use to support your opinion?
2. Although this essay is certainly written from the particular perspective of an identical twin, to what extent can nontwins sympathize with Nadler's experience? How does she try to make sure that they can do so? Find examples from the essay that show she is addressing people who might not share her experience.

Method and Structure

1. Why is definition particularly well suited to Nadler's subject and purpose?
2. Analyze the organization Nadler uses for her definition of what it means to be a twin. Where in the essay does she focus on similarities between her-

self and her sister? Where does she focus on differences? Why do you think she might have chosen to structure her essay as she does?

3. **Other Methods**   Narration (Chapter 5) features prominently in Nadler's essay, and in paragraphs 8 and 9 she uses description (Chapter 4) of photographic images to complement her comparison. What dimensions do these other methods add to the piece?

Language

1. What is the overall tone of the essay?
2. In her first paragraphs, Nadler quotes comments made by her friends at Disneyland. How do these quotations set up the main idea of the essay?
3. Nadler frequently uses words in pairs, such as "exuberantly and painstakingly" (paragraph 12), "deep and shrouded" (13), and "complex and urgent" (14). Find other paired words in the essay. How does this device help to mirror Nadler's experience?

Writing Topics

1. **Journal to Essay**   As an identical twin, Nadler is in a special position to write an essay of definition about a family bond. Most of us cannot entirely understand the experience of being so intimately involved with another person, yet certainly we have all struggled to differentiate ourselves from siblings or peers. Expanding on your journal entry (p. 270), write an essay in which you explore one of these relationships, focusing on moments that involved distancing yourself from others. For example, did you ever have a wonderful experience that a parent could not understand, or did a rift ever form between you and a sibling?

2. Like Nadler, you may recall the first time you felt that your sense of your life and your identity "expanded into its own perfect sphere" (paragraph 11). Write an essay in which you describe an experience that made you feel you were on your own, independent and in charge of your own life. This could be, for example, the first time you drove a car alone, traveled abroad, or left home for college. How did it feel to be so independent? Was it intimidating or liberating?

3. Deeply loving another person can often bring both joys and difficulties. In fact, most people would probably agree with Nadler when she states, "It is a very powerful thing when you realize that you love someone as much as you love yourself" (paragraph 13). Write an essay about a similarly meaningful relationship you have had in your life. Describe the ups and downs of this relationship, from feelings of support and tenderness to moments of conflict and anger.

4. **Cultural Considerations**   Contemporary American society places great importance on the individual, encouraging people to "be themselves," to develop original insights and tastes, and to voice their own opinions. In contrast, many other cultures emphasize conformity for the greater good. Write an essay in which you explain how either the pressure to be yourself or the pressure to conform with others has affected you in a personal way. For example, how have these pressures affected your college experience in situations such as classroom participation or writing term papers? Do you often feel compelled to be different or to conform? How do you tend to react to these pressures?

5. **Connections**   Like Nadler, Julia Álvarez, in her paragraph from "A White Woman of Color" (p. 232), explores how her immediate family contributed to her sense of who she is. Though both authors undoubtedly struggled to forge independent identities, the experiences they describe demonstrate how family relationships play into people's definitions of themselves. In a brief essay, analyze how the writers convey their feelings about their relatives. Focus on their words and especially on their figures of speech.

A woman's place is in the home.   —Mid-nineteenth-century proverb

Motherhood and homemaking are honorable choices for any woman,
provided it is the woman who makes those decisions.   —Molly Yard

We haven't come a long way, we've come a short way. If we hadn't come a
short way, no one would be calling us "baby."   —Elizabeth Janeway

Journal Response   Write a journal entry about gender roles today. How
have they changed in the past few decades? How might they continue to
evolve?

Judy Brady

Judy Brady was born in 1937 in San Francisco. She attended the University of
Iowa and graduated with a bachelor's degree in painting in 1962. Married in
1960, she was raising two daughters by the mid-1960s. She began working in
the women's movement in 1969 and through it developed an ongoing concern
with political and social issues, especially women's rights. She believes that "as
long as women continue to tolerate a society which places profits above the needs
of people, we will continue to be exploited as workers and as wives." Besides
the essay reprinted here, Brady has written articles for various magazines and
edited 1 in 3: Women with Cancer Confront an Epidemic *(1991), motivated*
by her own struggle with the disease. She is also cofounder of the Toxic Links
Coalition and a volunteer at the Women's Cancer Resource Center in Berkeley,
California.

I WANT A WIFE

Writing after eleven years of marriage, and before divorcing her husband, Brady
here pins down the meaning of the word wife *from the perspective of one per-*
son who lives the role. This essay was published in the first issue of Ms. *maga-*
zine in December 1971, and it has since been reprinted widely. Is its harsh
portrayal still relevant today?

I belong to that classification of people known as wives. I am A Wife.   1
And, not altogether incidentally, I am a mother.

Not too long ago a male friend of mine appeared on the scene fresh   2
from a recent divorce. He had one child, who is, of course, with his

277

ex-wife. He is looking for another wife. As I thought about him while I was ironing one evening, it suddenly occurred to me that I, too, would like to have a wife. Why do I want a wife?

I would like to go back to school so that I can become economically   3 independent, support myself, and, if need be, support those dependent upon me. I want a wife who will work and send me to school. And while I am going to school I want a wife to take care of my children. I want a wife to keep track of the children's doctor and dentist appointments. And to keep track of mine, too. I want a wife to make sure my children eat properly and are kept clean. I want a wife who will wash the children's clothes and keep them mended. I want a wife who is a good nurturant attendant to my children, who arranges for their schooling, makes sure that they have an adequate social life with their peers, takes them to the park, the zoo, etc. I want a wife who takes care of the children when they are sick, a wife who arranges to be around when the children need special care, because, of course, I cannot miss classes at school. My wife must arrange to lose time at work and not lose the job. It may mean a small cut in my wife's income from time to time, but I guess I can tolerate that. Needless to say, my wife will arrange and pay for the care of the children while my wife is working.

I want a wife who will take care of *my* physical needs. I want a wife   4 who will keep my house clean. A wife who will pick up after my children, a wife who will pick up after me. I want a wife who will keep my clothes clean, ironed, mended, replaced when need be, and who will see to it that my personal things are kept in their proper place so that I can find what I need the minute I need it. I want a wife who cooks the meals, a wife who is a *good* cook. I want a wife who will plan the menus, do the necessary grocery shopping, prepare the meals, serve them pleasantly, and then do the cleaning up while I do my studying. I want a wife who will care for me when I am sick and sympathize with my pain and loss of time from school. I want a wife to go along when our family takes a vacation so that someone can continue to care for me and my children when I need a rest and change of scene.

I want a wife who will not bother me with rambling complaints   5 about a wife's duties. But I want a wife who will listen to me when I feel the need to explain a rather difficult point I have come across in my course of studies. And I want a wife who will type my papers for me when I have written them.

I want a wife who will take care of the details of my social life.   6 When my wife and I are invited out by friends, I want a wife who will take care of the babysitting arrangements. When I meet people at school that I like and want to entertain, I want a wife who will have the house clean, will prepare a special meal, serve it to me and my friends, and not interrupt when I talk about things that interest me and my friends. I want a wife who will have arranged that the children are fed and ready for bed before my guests arrive so that the children do not bother us. I want a wife who takes care of the needs of my guests so that they feel comfortable, who makes sure that they have an ashtray, that they are passed the hors d'oeuvres, that they are offered a second helping of the food, that their wine glasses are replenished when necessary, that their coffee is served to them as they like it. And I want a wife who knows that sometimes I need a night out by myself.

I want a wife who is sensitive to my sexual needs, a wife who   7
makes love passionately and eagerly when I feel like it, a wife who makes sure that I am satisfied. And, of course, I want a wife who will not demand sexual attention when I am not in the mood for it. I want a wife who assumes the complete responsibility for birth control, because I do not want more children. I want a wife who will remain sexually faithful to me so that I do not have to clutter up my intellectual life with jealousies. And I want a wife who understands that *my* sexual needs may entail more than strict adherence to monogamy. I must, after all, be able to relate to people as fully as possible.

If, by chance, I find another person more suitable as a wife than the   8
wife I already have, I want the liberty to replace my present wife with another one. Naturally, I will expect a fresh, new life; my wife will take the children and be solely responsible for them so that I am left free.

When I am through with school and have a job, I want my wife   9
to quit working and remain at home so that my wife can more fully and completely take care of a wife's duties.

My God, who *wouldn't* want a wife?   10

Meaning

1. In one or two sentences, summarize Brady's definition of a wife. Consider not only the functions she mentions but also the relationship she portrays.
2. Brady provides many instances of a double standard of behavior and responsibility for the wife and the wife's spouse. What are the wife's chief responsibilities and expected behaviors? What are the spouse's?
3. If any of the following words are unfamiliar, try to guess what they mean from the context of Brady's essay. Look the words up in a dictionary to check your guesses, and then use each one in a sentence or two of your own.

nurturant (3)	replenished (6)	monogamy (7)
hors d'oeuvres (6)	adherence (7)	

Purpose and Audience

1. Why do you think Brady wrote this essay? Was her purpose to explain a wife's duties, to complain about her own situation, to poke fun at men, to attack men, to attack society's attitudes toward women, or something else? Was she trying to provide a realistic and fair definition of *wife*? What passages in the essay support your answers?

2. What does Brady seem to assume about her readers' gender (male or female) and their attitudes toward women's roles in society, relations between the sexes, and work inside and outside the home? Does she seem to write from the perspective of a particular age-group or social and economic background? In answering these questions, cite specific passages from the essay.

3. Brady clearly intended to provoke a reaction from readers. What is *your* reaction to this essay: do you think it is realistic or exaggerated, fair or unfair to men, relevant or irrelevant to the present time? Why?

Method and Structure

1. Why would anybody need to write an essay defining a term like *wife*? Don't we know what a wife is already? How does Brady use definition in an original way to achieve her purpose?

2. Analyze Brady's essay as a piece of definition, considering its thoroughness, its specificity, and its effectiveness in distinguishing the subject from anything similar.

3. Analyze the introduction to Brady's essay. What function does paragraph 1 serve? In what way does paragraph 2 confirm Brady's definition? How does the question at the end of the introduction relate to the question at the end of the essay?

4. **Other Methods**   Brady develops her definition primarily by classification (Chapter 8). What does she classify, and what categories does she form? What determines her arrangement of these categories? What does the classification contribute to the essay?

Language

1. How would you characterize Brady's tone: whining, amused, angry, contemptuous, or something else? What phrases in the essay support your answer? (If necessary, see pp. 38–39 and pp. 334–35 on tone.)

2. Why does Brady repeat "I want a wife" in almost every sentence, often at the beginning of the sentence? What does this stylistic device convey about the person who wants a wife? How does it fit in with Brady's main idea and purpose?

3. Why does Brady never substitute the personal pronoun "she" for "my wife"? Does the effect gained by repeating "my wife" justify the occasionally awkward sentences, such as the last one in paragraph 3?
4. What effect does Brady achieve with the expressions "of course" (paragraphs 3 and 7), "Needless to say" (3), "after all" (7), and "Naturally" (8)?

Writing Topics

1. **Journal to Essay**   Using your journal entry (p. 277) and ideas generated by Brady's essay, analyze a role that is defined by gender, such as that of a wife or husband, mother or father, sister or brother, daughter or son. First write down the responsibilities, activities, and relationships that define that role, and then elaborate your ideas into an essay defining this role as you see it. You could, if appropriate, follow Brady's model by showing how the role is influenced by the expectations of another person or people.

2. Combine the methods of definition and comparison (Chapter 10) in an essay that compares a wife or a husband you know with Brady's definition of either role. Be sure that the point of your comparison is clear and that you use specific examples to illustrate the similarities or differences you see.

3. **Cultural Considerations**   Brady's essay was written in the specific cultural context of 1971. Undoubtedly, many cultural changes have taken place since then, particularly changes in gender roles. However, one could also argue that much remains the same. Write an essay in which you compare the stereotypical role of a wife now with the role Brady defines. In addition to your own observations and experiences, consider contemporary images of wives that the media present — for instance, in television advertising or sitcoms.

4. **Connections**   Both Brady and David Popenoe (p. 263) make reference to the demands of children in a family, mentioning their needs to be fed, kept clean, clothed, entertained, and guided, among others. Brady complains that most of these tasks fall on women's shoulders and wishes that her spouse would help more, but Popenoe, while acknowledging the need to have two people involved, distinguishes the unique role that fathers play in bringing up their children. Write an essay in which you examine and compare the roles that mothers and fathers play in their children's upbringing. Are there tasks for which one parent is particularly suited? Or is the gender of the parent less relevant than people sometimes think?

Happiness in marriage is entirely a matter of chance. — Jane Austen

Our nation must defend the sanctity of marriage. — George W. Bush

What is fascinating about marriage is why anyone wants to get married.
— Alain de Botton

Journal Response Contemporary society exerts great pressure on single adults to form lasting romantic partnerships. Many unattached people, however, insist that they are perfectly happy to be alone, and many couples are content to live together without a formal commitment. Is marriage a prerequisite for happiness, or is it overrated? Reflect for a moment on what marriage means to you, and write a journal entry that explains your feelings on the subject.

Andrew Sullivan

Andrew Sullivan was born in 1963 in southern England and raised Catholic in a working-class suburb of London. He studied modern history at Magdalen College of Oxford University and holds an MA in public administration and a PhD in political science from Harvard University. A senior editor of the Atlantic *and the author of countless articles dealing with issues of homosexuality, AIDS, and conservative politics, Sullivan is perhaps best known for his popular blog the* Daily Dish *(http://andrewsullivan.theatlantic.com) and for his book* Virtually Normal: An Argument about Homosexuality *(1995). Sullivan's other titles include* Same-Sex Marriage: Pro and Con: A Reader *(1997),* Love Undetectable: Notes on Friendship, Sex, and Survival *(1998), and* The Conservative Soul: How We Lost It, How to Get It Back *(2006). He lives in Washington, DC, and is a frequent guest on television and radio talk shows.*

THE "M-WORD": WHY IT MATTERS TO ME

In early 2004, the Massachusetts Supreme Court declared the state's ban on same-sex marriage to be unconstitutional, and the mayor of San Francisco permitted city officials to issue marriage licenses to same-sex couples. Both events added fuel to a national debate over gay marriage. "The 'M-Word': Why It Matters to Me" first appeared in an issue of Time *magazine devoted to the controversy. In the essay Sullivan offers a very personal definition of marriage to explain why he and many other gay Americans want it for themselves.*

What's in a name?   1

Perhaps the best answer is a memory.   2

As a child, I had no idea what homosexuality was. I grew up in a   3
traditional home—Catholic, conservative, middle class. Life was relatively simple: education, work, family. I was brought up to aim high
in life, even though my parents hadn't gone to college. But one thing
was instilled in me. What matters is not how far you go in life, how
much money you make, how big a name you make for yourself. What
really matters is family, and the love you have for one another. The
most important day of your life was not graduation from college or
your first day at work or a raise or even your first house. The most important day of your life was when you got married. It was on that day
that all your friends and all your family got together to celebrate the
most important thing in life: your happiness, your ability to make a
new home, to form a new but connected family, to find love that puts
everything else into perspective.

But as I grew older, I found that this was somehow not available   4
to me. I didn't feel the things for girls that my peers did. All the emotions and social rituals and bonding of teenage heterosexual life eluded
me. I didn't know why. No one explained it. My emotional bonds to
other boys were one-sided; each time I felt myself falling in love, they
sensed it, pushed it away. I didn't and couldn't blame them. I got along
fine with my buds in a nonemotional context; but something was awry,
something not right. I came to know almost instinctively that I would
never be a part of my family the way my siblings one day might be. The
love I had inside me was unmentionable, anathema—even, in the
words of the Church I attended every Sunday, evil. I remember writing
in my teenage journal one day: "I'm a professional human being. But
what do I do in my private life?"

So, like many gay men of my generation, I retreated. I never dis-   5
cussed my real life. I couldn't date girls and so immersed myself in
schoolwork, in the debate team, school plays, anything to give me an
excuse not to confront reality. When I looked toward the years ahead,
I couldn't see a future. There was just a void. Was I going to be alone
my whole life? Would I ever have a "most important day" in my life?
It seemed impossible, a negation, an undoing. To be a full part of my
family I had to somehow not be me. So like many gay teens, I withdrew, became neurotic, depressed, at times close to suicidal. I shut myself in my room with my books, night after night, while my peers
developed the skills needed to form real relationships, and loves. In

wounded pride, I even voiced a rejection of family and marriage. It was the only way I could explain my isolation.

It took years for me to realize that I was gay, years later to tell others, and more time yet to form any kind of stable emotional bond with another man. Because my sexuality had emerged in solitude—and without any link to the idea of an actual relationship—it was hard later to reconnect sex to love and self-esteem. It still is. But I persevered, each relationship slowly growing longer than the last, learning in my twenties and thirties what my straight friends found out in their teens. But even then, my parents and friends never asked the question they would have asked automatically if I were straight: So when are you going to get married? When is your relationship going to be public? When will we be able to celebrate it and affirm it and support it? In fact, no one—no one—has yet asked me that question.

When people talk about "gay marriage," they miss the point. This isn't about gay marriage. It's about marriage. It's about family. It's about love. It isn't about religion. It's about civil marriage licenses—available to atheists as well as believers. These family values are not options for a happy and stable life. They are necessities. Putting gay relationships in some other category—civil unions, domestic partnerships, civil partnerships, whatever—may alleviate real human needs, but, by their very euphemism, by their very separateness, they actually build a wall between gay people and their own families. They put back the barrier many of us have spent a lifetime trying to erase.

It's too late for me to undo my own past. But I want above everything else to remember a young kid out there who may even be reading this now. I want to let him know that he doesn't have to choose between himself and his family anymore. I want him to know that his love has dignity, that he does indeed have a future as a full and equal part of the human race. Only marriage will do that. Only marriage can bring him home.

Meaning

1. Where does Sullivan stand on the issue of gay marriage? Does he insist on full marriage rights for same-sex couples, or does he accept the alternative of civil unions? Where in the essay does he make his position clear?
2. Sullivan devotes the beginning of his essay to explaining his family's attitudes toward marriage. What was the significance of marriage in the Sullivan household? How did his family's expectations shape his own desires?

3. In paragraph 7, Sullivan writes, "This isn't about gay marriage. It's about marriage." What does he mean? What difference does he see in the concepts of "gay marriage" and "marriage"?

4. If any of the following words are unfamiliar, try to guess what they mean from the context of Sullivan's essay. Look up the words in a dictionary to check your guesses, and then use each one in a sentence or two of your own.

instilled (3)	anathema (4)	persevered (6)
eluded (4)	neurotic (5)	alleviate (7)
awry (4)	solitude (6)	euphemism (7)

Purpose and Audience

1. Why do you think Sullivan wrote this essay?

2. In his conclusion (paragraph 8), Sullivan mentions the "young kid out there who may even be reading this now" but doesn't speak to him directly. What does this suggest about Sullivan's vision of his readers?

3. How do you think Sullivan expects his audience to react to this essay? Does he seem to assume his audience's agreement, does he write defensively to forestall criticism, or does he assume some other response? What in the essay makes you think as you do?

Method and Structure

1. Why is definition an appropriate method for Sullivan to use in developing his ideas? What specific features of this method serve him?

2. In developing his definition, Sullivan relies heavily on personal anecdotes. What do the anecdotes contribute to his essay? Do they weaken his case in any way?

3. **Other Methods**   In what ways does Sullivan use narration (Chapter 5) and cause-and-effect analysis (Chapter 12) as part of his definition? Why are these methods important in developing his point?

Language

1. Why does Sullivan use "the 'M-Word'" instead of *marriage* in his title?

2. Sullivan's opening question — "What's in a name?" — is a line from Shakespeare's *Romeo and Juliet*. How does this reference establish the overall tone of Sullivan's argument? Is his tone appropriate to his subject? Why, or why not?

3. Point out some examples that show Sullivan's use of emotional appeal to argue his point. What is the effect of these examples?

Writing Topics

1. **Journal to Essay**   In your journal entry (p. 282), you explained what marriage means to you. Now expand your thoughts into an essay-length definition of marriage. Does your definition correspond to traditional assumptions about marriage, or is it unconventional? What characteristics does your definition *not* include?
2. Write a response to Sullivan's essay in which you establish your own position on the debate over gay marriage. Do you agree with Sullivan that marriage between same-sex partners is not only acceptable but necessary, or do you take the view that marriage should be limited to heterosexual couples? Or does your opinion fall somewhere between the two extremes? Draw on the definition of marriage you constructed for your answer to question 1 as necessary or appropriate, and as much as possible, use examples from your own experience (or from the experiences of those close to you) to support your argument.
3. **Cultural Considerations**   As Sullivan's experience suggests, our adult relationships are often shaped by the examples set by older members of our families — though not always in the ways they might have expected. In an essay explore how your parents or other relatives have influenced your own attitudes toward romance and commitment.
4. **Connections**   In this essay Sullivan argues that marriage is the primary source of an adult's happiness. Judy Brady, in "I Want a Wife" (p. 277), could hardly disagree more. Write an essay in which you compare and contrast the opinions and tones of these two writers.

Definition

Choose one of the following topics, or any other topic they suggest, for an essay developed by definition. The topic you decide on should be something you care about so that definition is a means of communicating an idea, not an end in itself.

PERSONAL QUALITIES

1. Ignorance
2. Sophistication
3. Spirituality or worldliness
4. Selflessness or selfishness
5. Loyalty or disloyalty
6. Responsibility
7. A good sport
8. Hypocrisy

EXPERIENCES AND FEELINGS

9. A nightmare
10. A good teacher, coach, parent, or friend
11. A good joke or a tasteless joke
12. Religious faith

ASPIRATIONS

13. The good life
14. Success or failure
15. A good job

SOCIAL CONCERNS

16. Poverty
17. Education
18. Domestic violence
19. Substance abuse
20. Prejudice
21. An American ethnic group such as Italians, WASPs, Japanese, Norwegians, or Chinese

ART AND ENTERTAINMENT

22. Jazz or some other kind of music
23. A good novel, movie, or television program
24. Impressionist painting or some other school of art

IDEAS

25. Freedom
26. Nostalgia
27. Feminism
28. A key concept in a course you're taking

WRITING ABOUT THE THEME
Clarifying Family Relationships

1. David Popenoe (p. 263), Reena Nadler (p. 270), and Andrew Sullivan (p. 282) all write of the impact that family members have on a child's development into adulthood. How important is family (immediate or extended) in shaping young people's sense of who they are and what they want out of life? To what extent does the larger community—friends, teachers, neighbors—also play a significant role in forming a person's identity? Answer in a brief essay, citing as examples the selections in this chapter and observations of your own.

2. Several of the authors in this section deal with gender roles. David Popenoe focuses on the role of the man as father, Judy Brady (p. 277) is concerned with unreasonable demands on married women, and Andrew Sullivan argues that gender should not factor into a couple's ability to marry. In your experience, are traditional gender roles helpful or harmful to individuals in a relationship? to society in general? Write an essay that supports your opinion with examples drawn from your own experience.

3. Firoozeh Dumas (p. 263), Judy Brady, and Andrew Sullivan each question at least one traditional notion of the nuclear family as it is understood in the United States. What, in your mind, constitutes a family? How—if at all—has the typical American family changed since your parents or grandparents were your age? Do you think that these relationships will continue to evolve? What predictions can you make about how families might be structured in the future?

Chapter 12

CAUSE-AND-EFFECT
ANALYSIS

Understanding Markets
and Consumers

Why did free agency become so important in professional baseball, and how has it affected the sport? What caused the recent warming of the Pacific Ocean, and how did the warming affect the earth's weather? We answer questions like these with **cause-and-effect analysis**, the method of dividing occurrences into their elements to find relationships among them. Cause-and-effect analysis is a specific kind of analysis, the method discussed in Chapter 7.

When we analyze **causes**, we try to discover which of the events preceding a specified outcome actually made it happen:

> What caused Adolf Hitler's rise in Germany?
>
> Why have herbal medicines become so popular?

When we analyze **effects,** we try to discover which of the events following a specified occurrence actually resulted from it:

> What do we do for (or to) drug addicts when we imprison them?
>
> What happens to our foreign policy when the president's advisers disagree over its conduct?

These are existing effects of past or current situations, but effects are often predicted for the future:

> How would a cure for cancer affect the average life expectancy of men and women?

> How might your decision to take family leave affect your future job prospects?

Causes and effects can also be analyzed together, as the questions opening this chapter illustrate.

Like everyone else, you probably consider causes and effects many times a day: Why is the traffic so heavy? What will happen if I major in art rather than business? In writing you'll also draw often on cause-and-effect analysis, perhaps explaining why the school's basketball team has been so successful this year, what made a bridge collapse, or how a new stoplight has worsened rush-hour traffic. You'll use the method for persuasion, too, as in arguing that the family, not the mass media, bears responsibility for children's violence (focusing on causes) or that adult illiteracy threatens American democracy (focusing on possible effects). Because cause-and-effect analysis attempts to answer *why* and *what if*—two of the most basic questions of human experience—you'll find the method often in your reading as well.

READING CAUSE-AND-EFFECT ANALYSIS

Cause-and-effect analysis is found in just about every discipline and occupation, including history, social science, natural science, engineering, medicine, law, business, and sports. In any of these fields, as well as in writing done for college courses, the purpose in analyzing may be to explain or to persuade. In explaining why something happened or what its outcome was or will be, writers try to order experience and pin down the connections in it. In arguing with cause-and-effect analysis, they try to demonstrate why one explanation of causes is more accurate than another or how a proposed action will produce desirable or undesirable consequences.

The possibility of arguing about causes and effects points to the main challenge of this method. Related events sometimes overlap, sometimes follow one another immediately, and sometimes connect over gaps in time. They vary in their duration and complexity. They vary in their importance. Analyzing causes and effects thus requires not only identifying them but also discerning their relationships accurately and weighing their significance fairly.

Causes and effects often do occur in a sequence, each contributing to the next in what is called a **causal chain**. For instance, an unlucky man named Jones ends up in prison, and the causal chain leading to his imprisonment can be outlined as follows: Jones's neighbor, Smith, dumped trash on Jones's lawn. In reprisal, Jones set a small brush fire in Smith's yard. A spark from the fire accidentally ignited Smith's house. Jones was prosecuted for the fire and sent to jail. In this chain each event is the cause of an effect, which in turn is the cause of another effect, and so on to the unhappy conclusion.

Identifying a causal chain partly involves sorting out events in time:

- **Immediate** causes or effects occur nearest an event. For instance, the immediate cause of a town's high unemployment rate may be the closing of a large manufacturing plant where many townspeople work.
- **Remote** causes or effects occur further away in time. The remote cause of the town's unemployment rate may be a drastic decline in the company's sales or (more remote) a weak regional or national economy.

Analyzing causes also requires distinguishing their relative importance in the sequence:

- **Major** causes are directly and primarily responsible for the outcome. For instance, if a weak economy is responsible for low sales, it is a major cause of the manufacturing plant's closing.
- **Minor** causes (also called **contributory** causes) merely contribute to the outcome. The manufacturing plant may have closed for the additional reason that the owners could not afford to make repairs to its machines.

As these examples illustrate, time and significance can overlap in cause-and-effect analysis: a weak economy, for instance, is both a remote and a major cause; the lack of funds for repairs is both an immediate and a minor cause.

Since most cause-and-effect relationships are complex, several pitfalls can weaken an analysis or its presentation. One is a confusion of coincidence and cause—that is, an assumption that because one event preceded another, it must have caused the other. This error is nicknamed **post hoc**, from the Latin *post hoc, ergo propter hoc*, meaning "after this, therefore because of this." Superstitions often illustrate post hoc: a basketball player believes that a charm once ended her shooting slump, so she now wears the charm whenever she plays. But post hoc also occurs in more serious matters. For instance, the office of a school administrator is vandalized, and he blames the incident on a recent speech by the student-government president criticizing the administration. But the administrator has no grounds for his accusation unless he can prove that the speech incited the vandals. In the absence of proof, the administrator commits the error of post hoc by asserting that the speech caused the vandalism simply because the speech preceded the vandalism.

Another potential problem in cause-and-effect writing is **oversimplification**. An effective analysis must consider not just the causes and effects that seem obvious or important but all the possibilities: remote as well as immediate, minor as well as major. One form of oversimplification confuses a necessary cause with a sufficient cause:

- A **necessary** cause, as the term implies, is one that must happen in order for an effect to come about; an effect can have more than one necessary cause. For example, if emissions from a factory cause a high rate of illness in a neighborhood, the emissions are a necessary cause.

- A **sufficient** cause, in contrast, is one that brings about the effect *by itself*. The emissions are not a sufficient cause of the illness rate unless all other possible causes—such as water pollution or infection—can be eliminated.

Oversimplification can also occur if opinions or emotions are allowed to cloud the interpretation of evidence. Suppose that a writer is examining the reasons a gun-control bill she opposed was passed by the state legislature. Some of the evidence strongly suggests that a member of the legislature, a vocal supporter of the bill, was unduly influenced by lobbyists. But if the writer attributed the passage of the bill solely to this legislator, she would be exaggerating the significance of a single legislator and ignoring the opinions of the many others who also voted for the bill. To achieve a balanced analysis, she would have to put aside her personal feelings and consider all possible causes for the bill's passage.

ANALYZING CAUSES AND EFFECTS IN PARAGRAPHS

David Foster Wallace (born 1962) is a popular and controversial novelist, the author of *Infinite Jest* (1996), *A Supposedly Fun Thing I'll Never Do Again* (1997), and *Oblivion* (2004). He also writes short stories, history, and general nonfiction. The following paragraph is from

"Consider the Lobster," an article written for *Gourmet* magazine and selected for *The Best American Essays 2005*.

[Lobsters] are themselves good eating. Or so we think now. Up until sometime in the 1800s, though, lobster was literally low-class food, eaten only by the poor and institutionalized. Even in the harsh penal environment of early America, some colonies had laws against feeding lobsters to inmates more than once a week because it was thought to be cruel and unusual, like making people eat rats. One reason for their low status was how plentiful lobsters were in old New England. "Unbelievable abundance" is how one source describes the situation, including accounts of Plymouth pilgrims wading out and capturing all they wanted by hand, and of early Boston's seashore being littered with lobsters after hard storms — these latter were treated as a smelly nuisance and ground up for fertilizer. There is also the fact that premodern lobster was cooked dead and then preserved, usually packed in salt or crude hermetic containers. Maine's earliest lobster industry was based around a dozen such seaside canneries in the 1840s, from which lobster was shipped as far away as California, in demand only because it was cheap and high in protein, basically chewable fuel.

Effect (topic sentence underlined): lobster's low-class status

Causes:
Plentiful supply

Preparation

Distribution

Barbara Ehrenreich (born 1941) is an essayist, historian, and investigative journalist. A contributing writer for a wide range of periodicals, she is probably best known for her books about contemporary class struggles in the United States: *Fear of Falling: The Inner Life of the Middle Class* (1989), *Nickel and Dimed: On (Not) Getting By in America* (2001), and *Bait and Switch: The (Futile) Pursuit of the American Dream* (2005). The following paragraph is from *Nickel and Dimed*.

The problem of rents is easy for a noneconomist, even a sparsely educated low-wage worker, to grasp. . . . When the rich and the poor compete for housing on the open market, the poor don't stand a chance. The rich can always outbid them, buy up their tenements or trailer parks, and replace them with condos, McMansions, golf courses, or whatever they like. Since the rich have become more numerous, thanks largely to rising

Cause (topic sentence underlined): competition for housing between rich and poor

Effects:

Rich can purchase inexpensive properties for themselves

stock prices and executive salaries, the poor have necessarily been forced into housing that is more expensive, more dilapidated, or more distant from their
places of work.... Insofar as the poor have to work
near the dwellings of the rich — as in the case of so
many service and retail jobs — they are stuck with
lengthy commutes or dauntingly expensive housing.

> Poor are forced to
> pay more, accept
> less, or move

DEVELOPING AN ESSAY BY
CAUSE-AND-EFFECT ANALYSIS
Getting Started

Assignments in almost any course or line of work ask for cause-and-effect
analysis: What caused the Vietnam War? In the theory of sociobiology,
what are the effects of altruism on the survival of the group? Why did costs
exceed the budget last month? You can find your own subject for cause-
and-effect analysis from your experiences, from observation of others,
from your course work, or from your reading outside school. Anytime
you find yourself wondering what happened or why or what if, you may
be onto an appropriate subject.

Remember that your treatment of causes or effects or both must be
thorough; thus your subject must be manageable within the constraints
of time and space imposed on you. Broad subjects like those in the following examples must be narrowed to something whose complexities
you can cover adequately.

BROAD SUBJECT   Causes of the increase in American industrial productivity

NARROWER SUBJECT   Causes of increasing productivity on one assembly
line

BROAD SUBJECT   Effects of cigarette smoke

NARROWER SUBJECT   Effects of parents' secondhand smoke on small children

Whether your subject suggests a focus on causes or effects or both,
list as many of them as you can from memory or from further reading. If the subject does not suggest a focus, then ask yourself questions
to begin exploring it:

- Why did it happen?
- What contributed to it?
- What were or are its results?
- What might its consequences be?

One or more of these questions should lead you to a focus and, as you explore further, to a more complete list of ideas.

But you cannot stop with a simple list, for you must arrange the causes or effects in sequence and weigh their relative importance: Do the events break down into a causal chain? Besides the immediate causes and effects, are there also less obvious, more remote ones? Besides the major causes or effects, are there also minor ones? At this stage, you may find that diagraming relationships helps you see them more clearly. The following diagram illustrates the earlier example of the plant closing (see p. 292):

Though uncomplicated, the diagram does sort out the causes and effects and show their relationships and sequence.

While you are developing a clear picture of your subject, you should also be anticipating the expectations and needs of your readers. As with the other methods of essay development, consider especially what your readers already know about your subject and what they need to be told:

- Do readers require background information?
- Are they likely to be familiar with some of the causes or effects you are analyzing, or should you explain every one completely?
- Which causes or effects might readers already accept?
- Which ones might they disagree with? If, for instance, the plant closing affected many of your readers—putting them or their relatives out of work—they might blame the company's owners rather than economic forces beyond the owners' control. You would have to address these preconceptions and provide plenty of evidence for your own interpretation.

Forming a Thesis

To help manage your ideas and information, try to develop a working thesis sentence that states your subject, your perspective on it, and your purpose. For instance:

> EXPLANATORY THESIS SENTENCE   Being caught in the middle of a family quarrel has affected not only my feelings about my family but also my relations with friends.

> PERSUASIVE THESIS SENTENCE   Contrary to local opinion, the many people put out of work by the closing of Windsor Manufacturing were victims not of the owners' incompetence but of the nation's weak economy.

Notice that these thesis sentences reflect clear judgments about the relative significance of possible causes or effects. Such judgments can be difficult to reach and may not be apparent when you start writing. Often you will need to complete a draft of your analysis before you are confident about the relationship between cause and effect. And even if you start with an idea of how cause and effect are connected, you may change your mind after you've mapped out the relationship in a draft. That's fine: just remember to revise your thesis sentence accordingly.

Organizing

The introduction to a cause-and-effect essay can pull readers in by describing the situation whose causes or effects you plan to analyze, such as the passage of a bill in the legislature or a town's high unemployment rate. The introduction may also provide background, such as a brief narrative of a family quarrel; or it may summarize the analysis of causes or effects that the essay disputes, such as townspeople blaming owners for a plant's closing. If your thesis is not already apparent in the introduction, stating it explicitly can tell readers exactly what your purpose is and which causes or effects or both you plan to highlight. But if you anticipate that readers will oppose your thesis, you may want to delay stating it until the end of the essay, after you have provided the evidence to support it.

The arrangement of the body of the essay depends primarily on your material and your emphasis. If events unfold in a causal chain with each effect becoming the cause of another effect, and if stressing these links coincides with your purpose, then a simple chronological sequence will probably be clearest. But if events overlap and vary in significance, their organization will require more planning. Probably the most effective way to arrange either causes or effects is in order of increasing importance. Such an arrangement helps readers see which causes or effects you consider minor and which major, while it also reserves your most significant (and probably most detailed) point for last. The groups of minor or major events may then fit into a chronological framework.

To avoid being preoccupied with organization while you are drafting your essay, prepare some sort of outline before you start writing. The outline need not be detailed so long as you have written the details elsewhere or can retrieve them easily from your mind. But it should show all the causes or effects you want to discuss and the order in which you will cover them.

To conclude your essay, you may want to restate your thesis — or state it, if you deliberately withheld it for the end — so that readers are left with the point of your analysis. If your analysis is complex, readers may also benefit from a summary of the relationships you have identified. And depending on your purpose, you may want to specify why your analysis is significant, what use your readers can make of it, or what action you hope they will take.

Drafting

While drafting your essay, strive primarily for clarity — sharp details, strong examples, concrete explanations. To make readers see not only *what* you see but also *why* you see it, you can draw on just about any method of writing discussed in this book. For instance, you might narrate the effect of a situation on one person, analyze a process, or compare and contrast two interpretations of cause. Particularly if your thesis is debatable (like the earlier example asserting the owners' blamelessness for the plant's closing), you will need accurate, representative facts to back up your interpretation, and you may also need quotations from experts such as witnesses and scholars. If you do not support your assertions specifically, your readers will have no reason to believe them. (For more on evidence in persuasive writing, see pp. 321–22 and 329–30. For more on finding and documenting sources, see the Appendix.)

Revising and Editing

While revising and editing your draft, consider the following questions and the box to be sure your analysis is sound and clear.

- *Have you explained causes or effects clearly and specifically?* Readers will need to see the pattern of causes or effects—their sequence and relative importance. And readers will need facts, examples, and other evidence to understand and accept your analysis.
- *Have you demonstrated that causes are not merely coincidences?* Avoid the error of post hoc, of assuming that one event caused another just because it preceded the other. To be convincing, a claim that one event caused another must be supported with ample evidence.
- *Have you considered all the possible causes or effects?* Your analysis should go beyond what is most immediate or obvious so that you do not oversimplify the cause-and-effect relationships. Your readers will expect you to present the relationships in all their complexity.
- *Have you represented the cause-and-effect relationships honestly?* Don't deliberately ignore or exaggerate causes or effects in a misguided effort to strengthen your essay. If a cause fails to support your thesis but still does not invalidate it, mention the cause and explain why you believe it to be unimportant. If a change you are proposing will have bad effects as well as good, mention the bad effects and explain how they are outweighed by the good. As long as your reasoning and evidence are sound, such admissions will not weaken your essay; on the contrary, readers will appreciate your fairness.
- *Have you used transitions to signal the sequence and relative importance of events?* Transitions between sentences can help you pinpoint causes or effects (*for this reason, as a result*), show the steps in a sequence (*first, second, third*), link events in time (*in the same month*), specify duration (*a year later*), and indicate the weights you assign events (*equally important, even more crucial*). (See also *transitions* in the Glossary.)

FOCUS ON CLARITY AND CONCISENESS

While drafting a cause-and-effect analysis, you may need to grope a bit to discover just what you think about the sequence and relative importance of reasons and consequences. As a result, your sentences may grope a bit, too, reflecting your initial confusion or your need to circle around your ideas in order to find them. The following draft passage reveals such difficulties:

WORDY AND UNCLEAR   Employees often worry about suggestive comments from others. The employee may not only worry but feel the need to discuss the situation with coworkers. One thing that is an effect of sexual harassment, even verbal harassment, in the workplace is that productivity is lost. Plans also need to be made to figure out how to deal with future comments. Engaging in these activities is sure to take time and concentration from work.

Drafting this passage, the writer seems to have built up to the idea about lost productivity (third sentence) after providing support for it in the first two sentences. The fourth sentence then adds more support. And sentences 2–4 all show a writer working out his ideas: sentence subjects and verbs do not focus on the main actors and actions of the sentences, words repeat unnecessarily, and word groups run longer than needed for clarity.

These problems disappear from the edited version below, which moves the main ideas up front, uses subjects and verbs to state what the sentences are about, and cuts unneeded words.

CONCISE AND CLEAR   Even verbal sexual harassment in the workplace causes a loss of productivity. Worrying about suggestive comments from others, discussing those comments with coworkers, planning how to deal with future comments—all these activities take time and concentration that a harassed employee could spend on work.

For more on editing for conciseness and clarity, see pages 44–45.

A NOTE ON THEMATIC CONNECTIONS

Analyzing the marketplace often prompts writers to ask what leads to success or failure or what may result from a business decision. The authors in this chapter all attempt to pinpoint a cause-and-effect relationship between business practices and consumer behaviors. In a paragraph (p. 293), David Foster Wallace explains why lobster was once highly unpopular. In another paragraph (p. 294), Barbara Ehrenreich considers how the real estate market makes housing less affordable. In essays, journalist Charles Fishman (opposite) and student writers Stephanie Alaimo and Mark Koester (p. 307) discuss the consequences of our shopping choices, while *New York Times* guest columnist Gerald Early tries to understand why more African Americans don't attend professional baseball games (p. 312).

For millions of people, Wal-Mart is a lifesaver that provides what they want at prices they can afford.
— Jeremy J. Siegel

Every time you see the Wal-Mart smiley face, whistling and knocking down the prices, somewhere there's a factory worker being kicked in the stomach.
— Sherrie Ford

There is only one boss: the customer. And he can fire everybody in the company, from the chairman on down, simply by spending his money somewhere else.
— Sam Walton (Wal-Mart's founder)

Journal Response Nearly every American family (93 percent of us, in fact) shops at Wal-Mart at least once a year; the chain is also one of the country's largest employers. How do you feel about the retail giant? Are you a fan of the store, do you shop there reluctantly, or do you go out of your way to avoid the place? Have you, or has somebody you know, ever worked there? In your journal, write a few paragraphs about your experiences with Wal-Mart, whether good or bad.

Charles Fishman

Business journalist Charles Fishman (born 1961) grew up in Miami, Florida, and earned his BA from Harvard University. He reported for the Harvard Independent, *the* Washington Post, *the* Orlando Sentinel's Sunday magazine, *and the* Raleigh News & Observer *before taking his current post as senior editor for the business magazine* Fast Company. *Fishman's prizewinning 2004 cover story for* Fast Company, *"The Wal-Mart You Don't Know," generated such an overwhelming response that he extended his research to write his first book* — The Wal-Mart Effect: How the World's Most Powerful Company Really Works — *and How It's Transforming the American Economy (2006), a* New York Times *best seller and the* Economist's *choice for best book of 2006. Known for his ability to access tightly guarded work environments, including a Tupperware factory and a bomb manufacturing plant, Fishman won the Gerald Loeb Award for distinguished business journalism in 2005 and 2007. He lives in Philadelphia with his wife and family.*

THE SQUEEZE

The Wal-Mart Effect has been praised for offering a balanced look at Wal-Mart's impact on the global economy. In this excerpt from the book, Fishman relates a story about a gallon of pickles to show how the world's largest retailer is able to "defy the laws of supply, demand, and competition."

A gallon-sized jar of whole pickles is something to behold. The jar it-   1
self is the size of a small aquarium. The fat green pickles, floating in
swampy juice, look reptilian, their shapes exaggerated by the glass of
the jar. The jar weighs twelve pounds, too big to carry with one hand.

The gallon jar of pickles is a display of abundance and excess. It   2
is entrancing, and also vaguely unsettling. Wal-Mart fell in love with
Vlasic's gallon jar of pickles.

Wal-Mart priced it at $2.97 — a year's supply of pickles for less   3
than $3! "They were using it as a 'statement' item," says Pat Hunn,
who calls himself the mad scientist of the gallon jar of pickles at Vlasic. "Wal-Mart was putting it before consumers, saying this represents
what Wal-Mart's about: *You can buy a stinkin' gallon of pickles for
$2.97*. And it's the nation's number-one brand."

Because of Wal-Mart's scale, the Wal-Mart effect isn't just about   4
delivering "always low prices." It's also about how Wal-Mart gets
those low prices, and what impact the low prices have far beyond Wal-
Mart's shelves, and beyond our own wallets: the cost of low prices to
the companies that supply Wal-Mart, and to the people who work for
those companies. That story can be found floating in Vlasic's gallon jar
of pickles, the tale of how that gallon jar came to be sold at Wal-Mart.

Back in the late 1990s, Vlasic wasn't looking to build its brand on   5
a gallon of whole pickles. Pickle companies make money on "the cut,"
slicing cucumbers into specialty items like spears and hamburger chips.
"Cucumbers in the jar, you don't make a whole lot of money there,"
says Steve Young, who was then vice president of marketing for pickles at Vlasic, but has since left the company. But a Wal-Mart buyer saw
the gallon jar at some point in the late 1990s, and started talking to Pat
Hunn about it. Hunn, who has also since left Vlasic, was then head of
Vlasic's Wal-Mart sales team, based in Dallas.

The gallon intrigued the buyer. For Vlasic, it was a niche product   6
aimed at small businesses and people having large events. Still, in sales
tests in Wal-Mart stores, priced somewhere over $3, "the gallon sold
like crazy," says Hunn, "surprising us all." The Wal-Mart pickle buyer
had a brainstorm: What would happen to the gallon if they offered it

nationwide, and got it below $3? Hunn was skeptical, but his job was to look for ways to sell pickles at Wal-Mart. Why not?

And so in 1998, Vlasic's gallon jar of pickles went into every Wal-Mart, 2,500 stores, at $2.97, a price so low that Vlasic and Wal-Mart were only making a penny or two on a jar, if that. The gallon was showcased on a big, freestanding pallet display near the front of stores. It was an abundance of abundance.   *7*

"They went through the roof," says Hunn.   *8*

Says Young, "It was selling eighty jars a week, on average, in every store." Doesn't sound like much until you do the math: That's 200,000 gallons of pickles, just in gallon jars, just at Wal-Mart, every week. Whole fields of cucumbers were heading out the door.   *9*

The gallon jar of pickles became what you might call a "devastating success" for Vlasic. "Quickly, it started cannibalizing our non-Wal-Mart business," says Young. "We saw consumers who used to buy the spears and the chips in supermarkets"—where a small quart jar of Vlasic pickles cost $2.49—"buying the Wal-Mart gallons. They'd eat a quarter of a jar and throw the thing away when they got moldy. A family can't eat them fast enough."   *10*

The gallon jar reshaped Vlasic's pickle business: It chewed up the profit margin of the business with Wal-Mart, and of pickles generally; procurement had to scramble to find enough pickles to fill the gallons. The volume also gave Vlasic strong sales numbers, strong growth numbers, and a powerful place in the world of pickles at Wal-Mart.   *11*

The gallon was hoisting Vlasic and hurting it at the same time. Indeed, Steve Young, Vlasic's marketing guy, and Pat Hunn, Vlasic's Wal-Mart sales guy, agree on the details of the gallon, but years later they disagree over whether it was good or bad for Vlasic.   *12*

Hunn remembers cutting a deal with Wal-Mart whereby the retailer could only increase its sales of gallons if it increased its sales of the more profitable spears and chips in lockstep. The gallon was good.   *13*

Young remembers begging Wal-Mart for relief. "They said, 'No way,'" says Young. "We said we'll increase the price"—even $3.49 would have helped tremendously—"and they said, 'If you do that, all the other products of yours we buy, we'll stop buying.' It was a clear threat."   *14*

Hunn remembers the conversations differently. Things were more complicated, more subtle. "They did not put a gun to our head and say, 'It's $2.97 or you're out of here,'" says Hunn. "They said, 'We want the $2.97 gallon of pickles. If you don't do it, we'll see if someone else might.' I knew our competitors were saying to Wal-Mart, 'We'll do the $2.97 gallons if you give us your other business.'   *15*

"We're all big boys," Hunn says. "We all make decisions."   *16*

Wal-Mart's business was so indispensable to Vlasic, and the gal- *17*
lon so central to the Wal-Mart relationship, that decisions about the
future of the gallon were made at the CEO level. "One option was to
call their bluff," says Young. But Vlasic was struggling as an independent spin-off of Campbell Soup Company, and couldn't afford to risk
the Wal-Mart business. The pain didn't continue for weeks or months
—the $2.97 gallon of Vlasic dills was on the shelves at Wal-Mart for
two and a half years.

Finally, Wal-Mart let Vlasic up for air. "The Wal-Mart guy's re- *18*
sponse was classic," says Young. "He said, 'Well, we've done to pickles what we did to orange juice. We've killed it. We can back off.'"

Vlasic got to take the product down to half a gallon of pickles, for *19*
$2.49. By that point, Young says, profits in pickles had been cut by
50 percent—millions of dollars in lost profit, even as the business itself grew. Devastating success, indeed.

The meaning of the Vlasic story is complicated, but it cuts to the *20*
heart of how Wal-Mart does business. It shows the impact of Wal-Mart's
scale and power in what we all think is a market economy. Wal-Mart's
focus on pricing, and its ability to hold a supplier's business hostage to
its own agenda, distorts markets in ways that consumers don't see, and
ways the suppliers can't effectively counter. Wal-Mart is so large that it
can often defy the laws of supply, demand, and competition.

That's the scary part of the Vlasic story: The market didn't cre- *21*
ate the $2.97 gallon of pickles, nor did waning consumer demand or
a wild abundance of cucumbers. Wal-Mart created the $2.97 gallon
jar of pickles. The price—a number that is a critical piece of information to buyers, sellers, and competitors about the state of the pickle
market—the price was a lie. It was unrelated to either the supply of
cucumbers or the demand for pickles. The price was a fiction imposed
on the pickle market in Bentonville. Consumers saw a bargain; Vlasic saw no way out. Both were responding not to real market forces,
but to a pickle price gimmick imposed by Wal-Mart as a way of making a statement.

Meaning

1. Why, according to Fishman, did Wal-Mart want to sell a gallon jar of
   pickles for under three dollars? What was the store trying to accomplish
   by offering such a low price, and what was the actual result?
2. What is a "devastating success" (paragraphs 10 and 19)? How does the
   Vlasic story illustrate this concept?

3. What does Fishman mean when he says that "the price was a lie" (paragraph 21)? Is he accusing Wal-Mart of being unethical, or is he saying something else? Put the idea in your own words.
4. If any of the following words are new to you, try to guess their meanings from their context in Fishman's essay. Look up the words in a dictionary to check your guesses, and then use each word in a sentence or two of your own.

behold (1)	niche (6)	hoisting (12)
reptilian (1)	pallet (7)	lockstep (13)
entrancing (2)	cannibalizing (10)	indispensable (17)
scale (4)	procurement (11)	waning (21)

Purpose and Audience

1. What seems to be Fishman's primary purpose in this piece? Does he want to express his opinion about Wal-Mart's business practices? persuade shoppers to boycott the store? educate his readers? How can you tell?
2. To whom does Fishman seem to be writing here? Why do you think so?

Method and Structure

1. How well does cause-and-effect analysis suit Fishman's subject? In what way does this method provide an effective means of achieving his purpose?
2. Summarize the causal chain Fishman identifies in paragraphs 5–11.
3. Do you think Fishman oversimplifies the cause-and-effect relationship between Wal-Mart's pricing and Vlasic's profit losses? Why, or why not?
4. Fishman's evidence consists largely of quotations from interviews with former Wal-Mart executives and suppliers. How convincing do you find this evidence? Do you think the analysis would have been weaker or stronger if Fishman had talked to current employees? Why?
5. **Other Methods** Aside from cause-and-effect analysis, what other method does Fishman use extensively to show how Wal-Mart affects its suppliers? Why does he use it?

Language

1. Fishman introduces his essay by using a metaphor to describe a gallon jar of pickles. What is the metaphor, and how effective is it? Why do you think the author chose to start this way? (If necessary, review *metaphor* in the Glossary.)

2. Fishman uses the word *abundance* several times in this essay. How does repetition of this key word emphasize the author's point? In what ways does context affect the word's meaning?

3. How would you characterize Fishman's tone? Is it appropriate, given his purpose and his audience?

Writing Topics

1. **Journal to Essay**   In your journal entry (p. 301), you wrote about some of your experiences with Wal-Mart. Look again at the quotations that precede the journal assignment, then use your journal entry as the starting point for an essay that takes a position on the ongoing debate over the chain's impact on America. Is Wal-Mart good or bad for the economy? In what ways might the store's overwhelming success affect our way of life? Why do you think so? (If you wish, you may research and quote expert opinion to support your argument, as Fishman does in his consideration of the subject. See the Appendix for advice on finding sources and integrating them in an essay.)

2. Although Fishman is interested primarily in Wal-Mart's and Vlasic's business choices, his essay can also be read as an illustration of the Latin phrase *caveat emptor*, or "buyer beware." Most of the pickles in a gallon jar, after all, end up in the trash. Look back on your own experience and think of another example of a consumer product or service that isn't as good as it seems. (For example, you might consider a digital music service whose files won't transfer between players, an "as-seen-on-TV" gadget that didn't deliver on its promises, or low-fat convenience foods that are loaded with high-fructose corn syrup.) Write an essay that explains to readers why they shouldn't buy the item or use the service, providing plenty of details to clarify your reasons.

3. **Cultural Considerations**   As Fishman's pickle example suggests, Americans are notorious for snapping up products they don't need in quantities that border on the absurd. Many cultures, however, actively discourage this kind of behavior, prizing thrift and generosity over personal acquisition. Write an essay that defends or argues against consumption for its own sake, making a point of explaining what, in your mind, constitutes a necessity and what is a luxury. Do we have a right—even an obligation—to spend money on things we don't truly need? Why, or why not?

4. **Connections**   In "The Squeeze," Charles Fishman shows how a large company can take advantage of a smaller one for its own benefit. Similarly, Walter Mosley, in "Show Me the Money" (p. 186), asserts that wealthy Americans have gained their position at the expense of less powerful workers. Write an essay that compares the two authors' beliefs about competition and fairness in a capitalist economy. What assumptions, if any, do both writers share? Where do their perspectives diverge? How do their attitudes reinforce or conflict with your own views?

There is no reason that the universe should be designed for our convenience.
— John D. Barrow

All of the biggest technological inventions created by man — the airplane, the automobile, the computer — says little about his intelligence, but speaks volumes about his laziness.
— Mark Kennedy

Besides black art [such as voodoo and witchcraft], there is only automation and mechanization.
— Federico García Lorca

Journal Response Write a short journal entry about a modern convenience that you dislike. (Examples might include online banking, multifunction mobile phones, vending machines, cruise control, or automated call centers.) Why don't you care for it? In what ways is this technology harmful, or just more trouble than it's worth?

— Stephanie Alaimo and Mark Koester —

Stephanie Alaimo (born 1984) and Mark Koester (born 1983) studied at DePaul University of Chicago. Alaimo, a Spanish major, volunteered as a tutor in English as a Second Language and as an intern with the Interfaith Committee for Worker Justice. Koester, a native of Omaha, Nebraska, majored in philosophy. Both are currently pursuing advanced degrees and teaching English in Strasbourg, France.

THE BACKDRAFT OF TECHNOLOGY

(STUDENT ESSAY)

How important is it to save a few minutes in the supermarket? Would you stand in line to save someone else's job? Alaimo and Koester think you should — and they explain why by analyzing the causes and effects of self-service checkout machines. They collaborated on this op-ed piece for the DePaulia, *a student newspaper, in 2006.*

You have picked up the bread and the milk and the day's miscellaneous 1
foodstuffs at your local grocery store. The lines at the traditional, human-operated checkouts are a shocking two customers deep. Who wants to wait? Who would wait when we have society's newest upgrade in not having to wait: the- self-checkout?

Welcome to the automated grocery store. "Please scan your next   2
item," a repetitively chilling, mechanical voice orders you.

If you have yet to see it at your nearest grocer, a new technological   3
advance has been reached. Instead of waiting for some minimally waged,
minimally educated, and, most likely, immigrant cashier to scan and bag
your groceries for you, you can now do it yourself. In a consumer-driven,
hyperactive, "I want" world, an increase in speed is easily accepted
thoughtlessly. We're too busy. But, in gaining efficiency and ease, a number of jobs have been lost, particularly at the entry level, and a moment
of personal, human engagement with actual people has vanished.

It seems easy enough to forget about the consequences when you   4
are rushed and your belly is grumbling. The previously utilized checkout lanes at local grocery stores and super, mega, we-have-everything
stores are now routinely left unattended during the peak hours. In these
moments, your options are using the self-checkout or waiting for a real
human being. Often in a hurried moment we choose the easiest, fastest,
and least mentally involved option without much consideration.

We forget to consider that with the aid of the self-checkout at least   5
two jobs have been lost. As a result, a human cashier and grocery
bagger are now waiting in the unemployment line. Furthermore, self-
checkout machines are probably not manufactured in the United States,
thus shipping more jobs overseas. And sadly, the job openings are now
shrinking by putting consumers to work. The wages from these jobs
are stockpiled by those least in need—corporations and those who own
them.

The mechanization of the service industry has been occurring   6
throughout our lifetimes. Gas stations were once full-service. Human
bank tellers handled simple cash withdrawals, instead of ATMs. Even
video stores are being marginalized from people ordering online from
companies like Netflix. And did you know that you can now order a
pizza for delivery online without even talking to a person?

Sure, these new robots and computers reduce work, which could   7
potentially be a really good thing. But these mechanizations have only
increased profit margins for large corporations and have reduced the
need to hire employees. Jobs are lost along with means of providing for
one's self and family.

For those who find the loss of grocery store labor to be meaning-   8
less and, quite frankly, beyond impacting their future lives as accoun-
tants or lawyers, it does not seem to be entirely implausible that almost
any job or task could become entirely technologically mechanized and
your elitist job market nuked.

We are a society trapped in a precarious fork in the road. We can   9
either eliminate the time and toil of the human workload and still allow
people to have jobs and maintain the same standard of living, though
working less, or, in a darker scenario, we can eliminate human work
in terms of actual human jobs and make the situation of the lower
classes more tenuous. Is it our goal to reduce the overall time that individuals spend laboring? Or is it our goal to increase corporate profits at the loss of many livelihoods?

At present, corporations and their executives put consumers to   10
work, cut the cost of labor through the use of technology such as self-
checkouts and ATMs, and profit tremendously. But a host of workers are now scrambling to find a way to subsist. To choose the self-
checkout simply as a convenience cannot be morally justified unless
these jobs remain.

The choices we make on a daily basis affect the whole of our soci-   11
ety. Choosing convenience often translates to eliminating actual jobs
that provide livelihoods and opportunities to many. Think before you
simply follow the next technological innovation. Maybe it could be you
in their soon-to-be-jobless shoes. Say "No!" to self-checkout.

Meaning

1. What do you make of the title of this essay? What is a backdraft, and what
   does it have to do with technology?
2. In paragraph 4, Alaimo and Koester write, "Often in a hurried moment
   we choose the easiest, fastest, and least mentally involved option without
   much consideration." Do they condemn this tendency?
3. Try to guess the meanings of the following words, based on their context
   in Alaimo and Koester's essay. Test your guesses in a dictionary, and then
   try to use each word in a sentence or two of your own.

   stockpiled (5)   implausible (8)   tenuous (9)
   marginalized (6)   precarious (9)   subsist (10)

Purpose and Audience

1. Do you believe that Alaimo and Koester are writing mainly to express their
   viewpoint or to persuade readers to do something? Make specific references to the text to support your opinion.
2. Who is the "you" being addressed in the two opening paragraphs? What
   do these paragraphs and the rest of the essay tell you about the authors'
   conception of their audience?

Method and Structure

1. Why do you think Alaimo and Koester rely on cause-and-effect analysis to develop their ideas? What are some causes of long checkout lines, in their opinion? What is the effect of the option to serve ourselves rather than wait for a cashier?
2. The authors open and close their essay by having their readers imagine waiting in line at the supermarket. What is the effect of this scenario?
3. In your opinion, is the cause-and-effect analysis in this essay sufficiently thorough and convincing? Why, or why not?
4. **Other Methods** In addition to cause-and-effect analysis, Alaimo and Koester rely on example (Chapter 6) and argument and persuasion (Chapter 13). What does each of these other methods contribute to their essay?

Language

1. How would you describe the authors' tone? Are they angry? optimistic? passionate? earnest? hesitant? friendly?
2. Alaimo and Koester begin paragraph 7 with the interjection "Sure." They also use phrases such as "miscellaneous foodstuffs" (1), "super, mega, we-have-everything stores" (4), "nuked" (8), and "fork in the road" (9). How would you characterize this language? What does it add to (or take away from) the essay?

Writing Topics

1. **Journal to Essay** On the basis of your journal entry and your reaction to the quotations at the beginning of this essay (p. 307), expand your ideas about the drawbacks of a modern convenience. Do you agree with Alaimo and Koester that "the choices we make on a daily basis affect the whole of our society" (paragraph 11)? When do technological conveniences help us? At what point does convenience for ourselves become harmful and destructive for others? Write to persuade your readers to change their behavior, as Alaimo and Koester do, or from a narrower personal perspective. If you choose the latter course, however, be sure to make your experience meaningful to others with plenty of details and examples.
2. Alaimo and Koester challenge their readers to reject self-service opportunities because they believe mechanization deprives unskilled workers of desperately needed jobs. But are such menial, low-paying jobs really worth saving? Write an essay that offers an alternative solution to the employment issue Alaimo and Koester describe. Define the problem as you interpret it, and explain its causes. In your proposal, outline the changes you would like to see take place, identify who would have to make them, and predict how they would improve things.

3. **Cultural Considerations**   In paragraph 3, Alaimo and Koester say that many cashiers are immigrants; later they express concern that American jobs are being shipped to other countries (5). What is your response to these remarks? Write an essay that considers the impact of foreign labor on the US job market. What are some sources of friction? What are some advantages? To what extent should the United States encourage immigration and globalization, and to what extent should the country restrict them? Why? Use examples from your own experience, observations, and reading.

4. **Connections**   Like Alaimo and Koester, Dave Barry, in "Humvee Satisfies a Man's Lust for Winches" (p. 149), questions the need for a modern technology while understanding why people use it anyway. But whereas Alaimo and Koester take their subject quite seriously, Barry draws on humor to make his point. Compare and contrast these writers' strategies in an effort to determine when humor is appropriate and when it detracts from a writer's purpose. How, for example, would "The Backdraft of Technology" have worked if the authors had taken a more lighthearted approach? What would be lost in Barry's essay if he hadn't tried to make his readers laugh?

Baseball is an allegorical play about America, a poetic, complex, and subtle play of courage, fear, good luck, mistakes, patience about fate, and sober self-esteem. — Saul Steinberg

Baseball is a game, yes. It is also a business. But what it most truly is, is disguised combat. For all its gentility, its almost leisurely pace, baseball is violence under wraps. — Willie Mays

Baseball is reassuring. It makes me feel as if the world is not going to blow up. — Sharon Olds

Journal Response What is your favorite pastime? Perhaps you like to watch baseball, play a musical instrument, tinker in a workshop, or go mountain biking. Whatever you do for fun, have you been puzzled by your own behavior, wondered why more people don't enjoy the pastime, or noticed anything odd about other people who do enjoy it? Write a journal entry describing one such curiosity.

Gerald Early

Gerald Early was born in 1952 in Philadelphia. He graduated from the University of Pennsylvania, received a PhD from Cornell University, and teaches English and African American studies at Washington University in St. Louis. His essays, reviews, and poetry have appeared in a range of publications, including the New York Times Book Review, *the* Kenyon Review, Harper's Magazine, *the* New Republic, *and* Obsidian II. *Early's scholarly and popular books include* Culture of Bruising: Essays on Prizefighting, Literature, and Modern American Culture *(1994), which won the National Book Critics Circle Award for criticism;* Daughters: On Family and Fatherhood *(1994);* One Nation under a Groove: Motown and American Culture *(1995); and* This Is Where I Came In: Black America in the 1960s *(2003). An avid fan of sports and music, Early is also a National Public Radio commentator and a sought-after script consultant. He has lent his expertise to the television series* The Mississippi *(1983) as well as to Ken Burns's popular PBS documentaries* Baseball *(1994),* Jazz *(2001),* Unforgivable Blackness: The Rise and Fall of Jack Johnson *(2004), and* The War *(2007). He is currently working on a novel for young readers.*

BLACK BALL

Early wrote several short pieces on popular culture and politics for the New York Times *as a guest columnist in the spring of 2006. "Black Ball," a post from a blog he kept during that time, presents a complex answer to a simple question.*

I am a passionate baseball fan. I have been a Cardinals season ticket holder for many years. I resell a lot of the tickets, and some I just give away, but I still go to 25 to 30 games a season. Whenever I look around the stands, I see very few black people, often fewer than 50.

In the entire St. Louis region (both city and suburbs), blacks make up about 19 percent of the population (50 percent of the population of the city itself). The Cardinals almost always draw 35,000 fans a game, and often more than 40,000. Yet I never see anything approaching 7,000 to 8,000 blacks at the park. The Cardinals are a very successful franchise with a strong fan base. Plus, the team has been particularly successful the last two years, winning more regular season games than any other major league team.[1]

Why don't black people go to baseball games? Some blacks I know suggest that the game is too slow. But why would only blacks find that objectionable and not any other group? Besides, wouldn't that mostly affect the young, who have shorter attention spans and the need for MTV-like editing? Don't middle-aged blacks like baseball?

Some have suggested that not enough African Americans play the game anymore. Less than 10 percent of major league players are African American. Most "colored" players today come from Latin America and the Caribbean and consider themselves Hispanic or Latino. Black Americans do not necessarily identify with them, nor do they necessarily identify with black Americans. But the problem with this theory is that it supposes that blacks are only attracted to sports where they have a dominant or pronounced presence, like professional football or basketball. The opposite is clearly not true for whites. After all, most of the people who attend professional sporting events in America — including football and basketball — are white.

If this theory is true about blacks, what does it say about them? Do they have a need for a certain level of representation because they are

[1] The St. Louis Cardinals won the 2006 World Series, seven months after Early wrote this piece. [Editor's note.]

a minority? Sports are supposed to encourage a larger sort of identification, beyond the merely racial. Athletes are supposed to possess a larger sense of representation. If not, Michael Jordan, Tiger Woods, and the Williams sisters would not have amounted to so much in our culture.

Others say blacks don't go to baseball games because they are too 6 expensive. But blacks make up a somewhat larger portion of the attendance at football and basketball games, and tickets to those events are even more expensive. Within reason, expense does not stop the average person from consuming something. Some have argued that blacks don't feel welcome at baseball games because too many whites are there. This is the price one pays for being a minority. There are too many of the majority everywhere. It doesn't stop blacks from shopping at suburban malls.

Or maybe black people have never really liked baseball that much, 7 even back in the days of segregation, when they briefly had racial leagues. For some or maybe all of these reasons, black people and baseball have become a form of nostalgia in America. We indulged in a bit of that as a culture this week when 17 people from the Negro Leagues[2] and the era preceding them were elected to the Baseball Hall of Fame. We might look back now on the era of segregation as a time when black people loved baseball and supported it. We might also look back at it as a time when blacks owned and operated the business of baseball. This aspect of the game's history was also commemorated with these elections and rightly so.

But as is usually the case with dealing with blacks in America, the 8 celebratory (which is the only way we seem able to speak about black history now) imperils intelligibility. Indeed, the need to celebrate becomes almost patronizing—as if the fact that blacks accomplished anything is now worth giving them a pat on the head. (The victims organized and did something!) Celebration can even imperil the primary importance of an achievement, by turning it into a simplistic story about the triumph over adversity. The Negro Leagues now exist in the American Valhalla of sports mythmaking as the triumph over racism and segregation.

---

[2] African American players were excluded from the National League and the American League through the first half of the twentieth century. The segregated Negro National League and Negro American League, along with several regional organizations, were created in the 1920s. The color line was not broken until 1947, when Jackie Robinson joined the Brooklyn Dodgers. [Editor's note.]

I suggest that view is blatantly dishonest. The Negro Leagues were   9
the result of racism and segregation, not the triumph over them. The
Negro Leagues were a sign of black people's weakness and inability
to function fully in American society. The Negro Leagues were a sign,
not of black people's pathology, but of America's pathology.

Effa Manley was largely the focus of the news stories about the spe-   10
cial election because she became the first woman inducted into the Hall
of Fame (our society loves firsts). The fact that she was a white woman
passing for black makes her all the more intriguing. What the newspapers gave us was an image of Effa Manley, the famed co-owner of
the Newark Eagles, as a fiery, independent woman who fought for
black baseball and tried to protect her players. But the Negro Leagues,
with the exception of the years during World War II when black income exploded, were never solvent, always undercapitalized, didn't
control their venues, and were, in most cases, hardly a league at all, except on paper....

Manley, like most whites and blacks who ran businesses that were   11
made possible solely by segregation, never wanted integration in the
way that it came. She wanted the Negro Leagues to become a minor
league for professional baseball, to be the special place to create the
black ballplayer. In essence, she wanted a sort of institutionalized segregation so that a black business could maintain itself. But racialized
businesses confine both the black entrepreneur and the black consumer.
I point this out not to disparage Manley but to point out the dilemma
of black institutions in the United States, of which Negro League baseball was one.

Because of the conditions under which black churches, black col-   12
leges and universities, and black businesses were established, it is impossible not to see them in a stigmatized way. They were established
not to make black people independent nor even to help them establish
a culture but to remind them every day that they were inferior to
whites. Because of this, I think most blacks have wound up secretly hating both segregation and integration. Disappointed by institutions of
their own making, they ended up desiring alien institutions with a history of saying they weren't good enough to be there.

The story of blacks and baseball is not a nostalgia story but a story   13
about the group memory of institutionalized racism. It is a complex
story about ambivalence and adaptation, precariousness, limitation
and pride. It is not a story of triumph or tragedy. It is the story of a
conflicted people trying, with some success, to make the most of their
conflicts.

Meaning

1. This essay is built around a central question: "Why don't black people go to baseball games?" (paragraph 3). What is the author's answer?

2. Early's subject does not become clear until paragraphs 8 and 9, and he withholds his thesis until paragraph 13. Is he writing solely about baseball? What, exactly, is his point?

3. What does Early mean by "institutionalized racism" (paragraph 13)? What associations does this phrase have? To what extent does it capture the main idea of this essay?

4. If any of the following words are new to you, try to guess their meanings from their context in Early's essay. Check your guesses in a dictionary, and then use each word in a sentence or two of your own.

commemorated (7)	pathology (9)	stigmatized (12)
imperils (8)	solvent (10)	alien (12)
intelligibility (8)	undercapitalized (10)	ambivalence (13)
Valhalla (8)	disparage (11)	precariousness (13)

Purpose and Audience

1. What seems to have inspired Early to write this essay? How is "Black Ball" a reaction to a particular cultural moment?

2. Is Early writing primarily for black baseball fans who, like himself, wonder why they don't see more African Americans in the stands? Or is he writing for a broader audience? How can you tell?

3. What assumptions does Early seem to make about his readers' familiarity with baseball in general, and with the history of the Negro Leagues in particular? What details help clarify the context of his analysis for those who don't already know it?

Method and Structure

1. What are the two main cause-and-effect relationships that Early explores in this essay? How are these central to his purpose for writing?

2. Why does Early open his essay by identifying himself as a "passionate baseball fan" (paragraph 1)? How does this personal information affect the implications of his conclusion?

3. In paragraphs 3–6, Early considers—and rejects—several possible causes that might explain why African Americans don't go to baseball games. Why does he devote nearly a third of his essay to these ideas? What does he accomplish by including them?

4. **Other Methods**   In paragraphs 7–11, Early brings in comparison and contrast (Chapter 10). What is he comparing? What point does the comparison and contrast help him make?

Language

1. Early's title has a double meaning. What is it? How does it reinforce the point of his essay?
2. How would you describe Early's tone in this essay? Is it consistent throughout?

Writing Topics

1. **Journal to Essay**   In your journal entry (p. 312), you described something about your favorite pastime that made you curious. Express that curiosity in the form of a question. Then, following Early's essay as a model, use cause-and-effect analysis to try to answer it.
2. Write an essay critiquing Early's essay. For instance, how persuasive do you find his explanation for low African American attendance at ball games? Is his cause-and-effect analysis thorough? What do you think of his examples? Does he overstate his point? Are you intrigued by his argument? Agree or disagree with Early, supporting your opinion with your own examples.
3. **Cultural Considerations**   Toward the end of his essay, Early refers to historically "black churches, black colleges and universities, and black businesses," asserting that "it is impossible not to see them in a stigmatized way" (paragraph 12). Many African American leaders, however, have argued the opposite: that such institutions help to build up disadvantaged communities, develop pride, and offer social and economic opportunities not available in the wider culture. Write an essay in which you explore your thoughts on this issue. Is there a difference between segregation chosen by a minority group and segregation forced by the majority? What are the benefits, if any, of self-imposed segregation? What are the drawbacks? If you're not sure, you may want to conduct a little research on the topic to learn more about the arguments on both sides of the debate. (See the Appendix for advice on finding and documenting sources.)
4. **Connections**   Thomas de Zengotita, in "*American Idol* Worship" (p. 160), considers what draws fans to a particular form of entertainment and offers an unusual perspective on the power of heroes and representation in popular culture. In an essay consider how de Zengotita's ideas may (or may not) complicate Early's assessment of why African Americans don't attend baseball games.

Cause-and-Effect Analysis

Choose one of the following questions, or any other question they suggest, and answer it in an essay developed by analyzing causes or effects. The question you decide on should concern a topic you care about so that your analysis of causes or effects is a means of communicating an idea, not an end in itself.

PEOPLE AND THEIR BEHAVIOR

1. Why is a past or present politician, athlete, police officer, or firefighter considered a hero?
2. Why did one couple you know marry or divorce?
3. What does a sound body contribute to a sound mind?
4. Why is a particular friend or relative always getting into trouble?
5. Why do people root for the underdog?
6. How does a person's alcohol or drug dependency affect others in his or her family?

WORK

7. At what age should a person start working for pay, and why?
8. What effects do you expect your education to have on your choice of career and your performance in it?
9. Why would a man or woman enter a field that has traditionally been filled by the opposite sex, such as nursing or engineering?
10. What effect has the job market had on you and your friends?

ART AND ENTERTAINMENT

11. Why do teenagers like hip-hop music?
12. Why have art museums become so popular?
13. What makes a professional sports team succeed in a new city?
14. Why is (or was) a particular television show or movie so popular?

CONTEMPORARY ISSUES

15. Why does the United States spend so much money on defense?
16. What are the possible effects of rising college tuitions?
17. How can a long period of involuntary unemployment affect a person?
18. Why is a college education important?
19. Why do marriages between teenagers fail more often than marriages between people in other age-groups?
20. Why might someone resort to a public act of violence, such as bombing a building?

--- WRITING ABOUT THE THEME ---
Understanding Markets and Consumers

1. Most of the writers in this chapter examine the unintended consequences of actions taken by companies and consumers. Charles Fishman's story about Wal-Mart's low prices (p. 301) and Stephanie Alaimo and Mark Koester's warning against self-service checkout (p. 307) are most notable in this respect, but even Barbara Ehrenreich's analysis of high rents (p. 294) suggests how difficult it is to predict the social effects of a personal purchase, and Gerald Early's look at the long-term effects of the Negro Leagues (p. 312) shows how a bad decision can haunt a business for decades. Think of a contemporary product or service that you believe holds the potential to do unexpected harm — or that could bring unanticipated benefits — and write an essay predicting its consequences. (Be sure to review the cause-and-effect guidelines on pp. 295–99 before beginning your analysis.)

2. David Foster Wallace (p. 293), Gerald Early, and Stephanie Alaimo and Mark Koester all consider the stigma attached to a particular consumer option: Wallace looks at why most Americans rejected lobster until the middle of the nineteenth century, Early explains how segregation turned African Americans away from professional baseball, and Alaimo and Koester attempt to persuade readers that self-checkout machines are morally wrong. Write an essay in which you consider the power of negative publicity. Can regular people influence the behavior of large corporations by boycotting what they have to offer? To what extent does big business control the marketplace regardless of how customers might object? You may, if you wish, center your discussion on the current debate over Wal-Mart (see Fishman), or you may focus on any business that concerns you. Perhaps you'd like to propose a boycott of your own. Just be sure that your essay has a clear, limited thesis and plenty of details to support it.

3. Although the writers represented in this chapter focus on a common subject, their tones vary widely, from objective to moralistic to resigned. Choose the two authors who seem most different in tone, and analyze how their tones help clarify their points. Is one author's tone more effective than the other's? If so, why? (For more on tone, see pp. 38–39 and 334–35.)

Chapter 13

ARGUMENT AND PERSUASION

Debating Law and Order

Since we argue all the time — with relatives, with friends, with the auto mechanic or the shop clerk — a chapter devoted to argument and persuasion may at first seem unnecessary. But arguing with an auto mechanic over the cost of repairs is quite a different process from arguing with readers over a complex issue. In both cases we are trying to find common ground with our audience, perhaps to change its views or even to compel it to act as we wish. But the mechanic is in front of us; we can shift our tactics in response to his or her gestures, expressions, and words. The reader, in contrast, is "out there"; we have to anticipate those gestures, expressions, and words in the way we structure the argument, the kinds of evidence we use to support it, even the way we conceive of the subject.

A great many assertions that are worth making are debatable at some level — whether over the facts on which the assertions are based or over the values they imply. Two witnesses to an accident cannot agree on what they saw; two scientists cannot agree on what an experiment shows; two economists cannot agree on what measures will reduce unemployment; two doctors cannot agree on what constitutes life or death. We see such disagreements play out in writing all the time, whether we're reading an accident report, a magazine article claiming the benefits of unemployment rates, or an editorial responding to a Supreme Court decision.

READING ARGUMENT AND PERSUASION

Technically, argument and persuasion are two different processes:

- **Argument** appeals mainly to an audience's sense of reason in order to negotiate a common understanding or to win agreement with a claim. It is the method of a columnist who defends a president's foreign policy on the grounds of economics and defense strategy.
- **Persuasion** appeals mainly to an audience's feelings and values in order to compel some action, or at least to win support for an action. It is the method of a mayoral candidate who urges voters to support her because she is sensitive to the poor.

But argument and persuasion so often mingle that we will use the one term *argument* to mean a deliberate appeal to an audience's reason and emotions in order to create compromise, win agreement, or compel action. Making an effective case for an opinion requires upholding certain responsibilities and attending to several established techniques of argumentation, most of them dating back to ancient Greece.

The Elements of Argument

All arguments share certain elements.

- The core of any argument is an **assertion** or **proposition**, a debatable claim about the subject. Generally, this assertion is expressed as a thesis statement. It may defend or attack a position, suggest a solution to a problem, recommend a change in policy, or challenge a value or belief. Here are a few examples:

  > The college should give first priority for on-campus jobs to students who need financial aid.

  > School prayer has been rightly declared unconstitutional and should not be reinstituted in any form.

  > Smokers who wish to poison themselves should be allowed to do so, but not in any place where their smoke will poison others.

- The central assertion is broken down into subclaims, each one supported by evidence.

- Significant opposing arguments are raised and dispensed with, again with the support of evidence.
- The parts of the argument are organized into a clear, logical structure that pushes steadily toward the conclusion.

A writer may draw on classification, comparison, or any other rhetorical method to develop the entire argument or to introduce evidence or strengthen the conclusion. For instance, in a proposal arguing for raising a college's standards of admission, a dean might contrast the existing standards with the proposed standards, analyze a process for raising the standards over a period of years, and predict the effects of the new standards on future students' preparedness for college work.

Appeals to Readers

Effective arguments appeal to readers: they ask others to listen to what someone has to say, judge the words fairly, and, as much as possible, agree with the writer. Most arguments combine three kinds of appeals to readers: ethical, emotional, and rational.

Ethical Appeal

The **ethical appeal** is often not explicit in an argument, yet it pervades the whole. It is the sense a writer conveys of his or her expertise and character, projected by the reasonableness of the argument, by the use of evidence, and by tone. A rational argument shows readers that the writer is thinking logically and fairly (see pp. 324–26). Strong evidence establishes credibility (see pp. 324–25 and 329–31). And a sincere, reasonable tone demonstrates balance and goodwill (see pp. 334–35).

Emotional Appeal

The **emotional appeal** in an argument aims directly for the readers' hearts — for the complex of beliefs, values, and feelings deeply embedded in all of us. We are just as often motivated by these ingrained ideas and emotions as by our intellects. Even scientists, who stress the rational interpretation of facts above all else, are sometimes influenced in their interpretations by emotions deriving from, say, competition with other scientists. And the willingness of a nation's citizens to go to war may result more from their fear and pride than from their reasoned considerations of risks and gains. An emotional appeal in an argument attempts to tap such feelings for any of several reasons:

- To heighten the responsiveness of readers
- To inspire readers to new beliefs
- To compel readers to act
- To assure readers that their values remain unchallenged

An emotional appeal may be explicit, as when an argument against capital punishment appeals to readers' religious values by citing the Bible's Sixth Commandment, "Thou shalt not kill." But an emotional appeal may also be less obvious, because individual words may have connotations that elicit emotional responses from readers. For instance, one writer may characterize an environmental group as "a well-organized team representing diverse interests," while another may call the same group "a hodgepodge of nature lovers and irresponsible businesspeople." The first appeals to readers' preference for order and balance, the second to readers' fear of extremism and disdain for unsound business practices. (See pp. 48–49 and 335 for more on connotation.)

The use of emotional appeals requires care:

- The appeal must be directed at the audience's actual beliefs and feelings.
- The appeal must be presented dispassionately enough so that readers have no reason to doubt the fairness in the rest of the argument.
- The appeal must be appropriate to the subject and to the argument. For instance, in arguing against a pay raise for city councilors, a legislator might be tempted to appeal to voters' resentment and distrust of wealthy people by pointing out that two of the councilors are rich enough to work for nothing. But such an appeal would divert attention from the issue of whether the pay raise is justified for all councilors on the basis of the work they do and the city's ability to pay the extra cost.

Carefully used, emotional appeals have great force, particularly when they contribute to an argument based largely on sound reasoning and evidence. The appropriate mix of emotion and reason in a given essay is entirely dependent on the subject, the writer's purpose, and the audience. Emotional appeals are out of place in most arguments in the natural and social sciences, where rational interpretations of factual evidence are all that will convince readers of the truth of an assertion. But emotional appeals may be essential to persuade an audience to support or take an action, for emotion is a stronger motivator than reason.

Rational Appeal

A **rational appeal** is one that, as the name implies, addresses the rational faculties of readers—their capacity to reason logically about a problem. It establishes the truth of a proposition or claim by moving through a series of related subclaims, each supported by evidence. In doing so, rational appeals follow processes of reasoning that are natural to all of us. These processes are induction and deduction.

Inductive reasoning moves from the particular to the general, from evidence to a generalization or conclusion about the evidence. It is a process we begin learning in infancy and use daily throughout our lives: a child burns herself the three times she touches a stove, so she concludes that stoves burn; a moviegoer has liked four movies directed by Clint Eastwood, so he forms the generalization that Clint Eastwood makes good movies. Inductive reasoning is also very common in argument: a nurse administrator might offer facts showing that chronic patients in the state's mental hospitals receive only drugs as treatment, and then conclude that the state's hospitals rely exclusively on drugs to treat chronic patients.

The movement from particular to general is called an **inductive leap** because we must make something of a jump to conclude that what is true of some instances (the chronic patients whose records were available) is also true of all other instances in the class (the rest of the chronic patients). In an ideal world we could perhaps avoid the inductive leap by pinning down every conceivable instance, but in the real world such thoroughness is usually impractical and often impossible. Instead, we gather enough evidence to make our generalizations probable. The evidence for induction may be of several kinds:

- Facts: statistics or other hard data that are verifiable or, failing that, attested to by reliable sources (for instance, the number of drug doses per chronic patient, derived from hospital records).
- The opinions of recognized experts on the subject, opinions that are themselves conclusions based on research and observation (for instance, the testimony of an experienced hospital doctor).
- Examples illustrating the evidence (for instance, the treatment history of one patient).

A sound inductive generalization can form the basis for the second reasoning process, **deductive reasoning**. Working from the general to the particular, we start with such a generalization and apply it to a new situation in order to draw a conclusion about that situation. Like induction, deduction is a process we use constantly to order our experience. The child who learns from three experiences that all stoves burn then sees a new stove and concludes that this stove also will burn. The child's thought process can be written in the form of a **syllogism**, a three-step outline of deductive reasoning:

> All stoves burn me.
> This is a stove.
> Therefore, this stove will burn me.

The first statement, the generalization derived from induction, is called the **major premise**. The second statement, a more specific assertion about some element of the major premise, is called the **minor premise**. And the third statement, an assertion of the logical connection between the premises, is called the **conclusion**. The following syllogism takes the earlier example about mental hospitals one step further:

> MAJOR PREMISE   The state hospitals' treatment of chronic patients relies exclusively on drugs.
>
> MINOR PREMISE   Drugs do not cure chronic patients.
>
> CONCLUSION   Therefore, the state hospitals' treatment of chronic patients will not cure them.

Unlike an inductive conclusion, which requires a leap, the deductive conclusion derives necessarily from the premises: as long as the reasoning process is valid and the premises are accepted as true, then the conclusion must also be true. To be valid, the reasoning must conform to the process outlined earlier. The following syllogism is *not* valid, even though the premises are true:

> All radicals want to change the system.
> Georgia Allport wants to change the system.
> Therefore, Georgia Allport is a radical.

The flaw in this syllogism is that not *only* radicals want to change the system, so Allport does not *necessarily* fall within the class of radicals just because she wants to change the system. The conclusion, then, is invalid.

A syllogism can be valid without being true if either of the premises is untrue. For example:

> All people who want political change are radicals.
> Georgia Allport wants political change.
> Therefore, Georgia Allport is a radical.

The conclusion here is valid because Allport falls within the class of people who want political change. But the conclusion is untrue because the major premise is untrue. As commonly defined, a radical seeks extreme change, often by revolutionary means. But other forms and means of change are also possible; Allport, for instance, may be interested in improving the delivery of services to the poor and in achieving passage of tougher environmental-protection laws — both political changes, to be sure, but neither radical.

In arguments, syllogisms are rarely spelled out as neatly as in these examples. Sometimes the order of the statements is reversed, as in this sentence paraphrasing a Supreme Court decision:

> The state may not imprison a man just because he is too poor to pay a fine; the only justification for imprisonment is a certain danger to society, and poverty does not constitute certain danger.

The buried syllogism can be stated thus:

> MAJOR PREMISE   The state may imprison only those who are a certain danger to society.
>
> MINOR PREMISE   A man who is too poor to pay a fine is not a certain danger to society.
>
> CONCLUSION   Therefore, the state cannot imprison a man just because he is too poor to pay a fine.

Often, one of a syllogism's premises or even its conclusion is implied but not expressed. Each of the following sentences omits one part of the same syllogism:

> All five students cheated, so they should be expelled. [Implied major premise: cheaters should be expelled.]
>
> Cheaters should be punished by expulsion, so all five students should be expelled. [Implied minor premise: all five students cheated.]
>
> Cheaters should be punished by expulsion, and all five students cheated. [Implied conclusion: all five students should be expelled.]

Fallacies

Inappropriate emotional appeals and flaws in reasoning — called **fallacies** — can trap writers as they construct arguments. Writers must watch out for the following:

- **Hasty generalization:** an inductive conclusion that leaps to include *all* instances when at best only *some* instances provide any evidence. Hasty generalizations form some of our worst stereotypes:

Physically challenged people are mentally challenged, too.

African Americans are good athletes.

Italian Americans are volatile.

- **Oversimplification:** an inductive conclusion that ignores complexities in the evidence that, if heeded, would weaken the conclusion or suggest an entirely different one. For example:

    The newspaper folded because it couldn't compete with television.

Although television may have taken some business from the paper, hundreds of other papers continue to thrive; thus television could not be the only cause of the paper's failure.

- **Begging the question:** assuming a conclusion in the statement of a premise, and thus begging readers to accept the conclusion—the question—before it is proved. For example:

    We can trust the president not to neglect the needy, because he is a compassionate man.

This sentence asserts in a circular fashion that the president is not uncompassionate because he is compassionate. He may indeed be compassionate, but this is the question that needs addressing.

- **Ignoring the question:** introducing an issue or consideration that shifts the argument away from the real issue. Offering an emotional appeal as a premise in a logical argument is a form of ignoring the question. The following sentence, for instance, appeals to pity, not to logic:

    The mayor was badly used by people he loved and trusted, so we should not blame him for the corruption in his administration.

- **Ad hominem** (Latin for "to the man"): a form of ignoring the question by attacking the opponents instead of the opponents' arguments. For example:

    O'Brien is married to a convict, so her proposals for prison reform should not be taken seriously.

- **Either-or:** requiring that readers choose between two interpretations or actions when in fact the choices are more numerous.

    Either we imprison all drug users, or we will become their prisoners.

The factors contributing to drug addiction, and the choices for dealing with it, are obviously more complex than this statement suggests. Not all either-or arguments are invalid, for sometimes the alternatives encompass all the possibilities. But when they do not, the argument is false.

- **Non sequitur** (Latin for "it does not follow"): a conclusion derived illogically or erroneously from stated or implied premises. For instance:

  > Young children are too immature to engage in sex, so they should not be taught about it.

  This sentence implies one of two meanings, both of them questionable: only the sexually active can learn anything about sex, or teaching young children about sex will cause them to engage in it.

- **Post hoc** (from the Latin *post hoc, ergo propter hoc*, "after this, therefore because of this"): assuming that because one thing preceded another, it must have caused the other. For example:

  > After the town banned smoking in closed public places, the incidence of vandalism went up.

  Many things may have caused the rise in vandalism, including improved weather and a climbing unemployment rate. It does not follow that the ban on smoking, and that alone, caused the rise.

ANALYZING ARGUMENT AND PERSUASION IN PARAGRAPHS

David Lindorff (born 1949) is a freelance journalist who has written extensively about the death penalty. The following paragraph is adapted from "The Death Penalty's Other Victims," an article Lindorff wrote for the online magazine *Salon* in 2001. The paragraph offers an inductive argument.

A major and controversial element of the death-penalty system is being largely ignored: the right of prosecutors and judges to eliminate, "for cause," any potential jurors who say they might not be willing or able to vote for death during the penalty phase of a murder trial. Whatever one might think about the death penalty itself, the trouble with screening out death-penalty skeptics—a process known as "death-qualifying"

the jury — is that it does a lot more than simply eliminate jurors opposed to capital punishment. It makes for
juries that tend to be white, male, and significantly
more likely to convict the person accused of the crime
in the first place. In a 1968 landmark study, Hans
Zeisel found that death-qualifying juries led to an 80
percent increase in the conviction rate. In a 1994 study
Craig Haney, Aida Hurtado, and Luis Vega reported
that while minorities accounted for 18.5% of the people in California jury pools they examined, they represented 26.3 percent of those excluded from jury panels
through the death-qualifying process. And a North
Carolina jury study conducted in 1982 found an even
greater disparity, with 55.2 percent of black potential
jurors being excluded during the death-penalty quali-
fying process, in contrast to 20.7 percent of whites.
Studies also indicate that women tend to be excluded,
since they are also more likely to oppose the death
penalty.

The generalization: death-qualifying creates juries that are more white, male, and likely to convict

Evidence: Increase in convictions

Exclusion of minorities

Exclusion of women

Martin Luther King Jr. (1929–1968) was a revered and powerful leader
of the civil rights movement during the 1950s and 1960s. When leading sit-ins, boycotts, and marches, he always insisted on nonviolent resistance. In this paragraph from "Letter from Birmingham Jail" (1963),
King uses deduction to argue in favor of civil disobedience.

You express a great deal of anxiety over our willingness to break laws. This is certainly a legitimate concern. Since we so diligently urge people to obey the
Supreme Court's decision of 1954 outlawing segregation in the public schools, at first glance it may seem
rather paradoxical for us consciously to break laws.
One may well ask: "How can you advocate breaking
some laws and obeying others?" The answer lies in the
fact that there are two types of laws: just and unjust. I
would be the first to advocate obeying just laws. One
has not only a legal but a moral responsibility to obey
just laws. Conversely, one has a moral responsibility to
disobey unjust laws. I would agree with St. Augustine
that "an unjust law is no law at all."

Major premise: laws should be obeyed

Minor premise: some laws are unjust and therefore are not laws

Conclusion: unjust laws should not be obeyed

DEVELOPING AN ARGUMENTATIVE
AND PERSUASIVE ESSAY
Getting Started

You will have many chances to write arguments, from defending or opposing a policy such as progressive taxation in an economics course to justifying a new procedure at work to persuading a company to refund your money for a bad product. To choose a subject for an argumentative essay, consider a behavior or policy that irks you, an opinion you want to defend, a change you would like to see implemented, or a way to solve a problem. The subject you pick should meet certain criteria:

- It should be something you have some knowledge of from your own experience or observations, from class discussions, or from reading, although you may need to do further research as well.
- It should be limited to a topic you can treat thoroughly in the space and time available to you — for instance, the quality of computer instruction at your school rather than in the whole nation.
- It should be something that you feel strongly about so that you can make a convincing case. (However, it's best to avoid subjects that you cannot view with some objectivity, seeing the opposite side as well as your own; otherwise, you may not be open to flaws in your argument, and you may not be able to represent the opposition fairly.)

Once you have selected a subject, do some preliminary research to make sure that you will have enough evidence to support your opinion. This step is especially important with an issue like welfare cheating or tax advantages for the wealthy that we all tend to have opinions about whether we know the facts or not. Where to seek evidence depends on the nature of your argument.

- For an argument derived from your own experiences and observations, such as a recommendation that all students work part-time for the education if not for the money, gathering evidence will be primarily a matter of searching your own thoughts and also uncovering opposing views, perhaps by consulting others.
- Some arguments derived from personal experience can be strengthened by the judicious use of facts and opinions from other sources. An essay arguing in favor of vegetarianism, for instance, could mix the benefits you have felt with those demonstrated by scientific data.

- Nonpersonal and controversial subjects require the evidence of other sources. Though you might strongly favor or oppose a massive federal investment in solar-energy research, your opinions would count little if they were not supported with facts and the opinions of experts.

For advice on conducting research and using the evidence you find, see the Appendix.

In addition to evidence, knowledge of readers' needs and expectations is absolutely crucial in planning an argument. In explanatory writing, detail and clarity alone may accomplish your purpose; but you cannot hope to move readers in a certain direction unless you have some idea of where they stand. You need a sense of their background in your subject, of course. But even more, you need a good idea of their values and beliefs, their attitudes toward your subject — in short, their willingness to be convinced. In a composition class, your readers will probably be your instructor and your classmates, a small but diverse group. A good target when you are addressing a diverse audience is the reader who is neutral or mildly biased one way or the other toward your subject. This person you can hope to influence as long as your argument is reasonable, your evidence is thorough and convincing, your treatment of opposing views is fair, and your appeals to readers' emotions are appropriate to your purpose, your subject, and especially your readers' values and feelings.

Forming a Thesis

With your subject and some evidence in hand, you should develop a tentative thesis. But don't feel you have to prove your thesis at this early stage; fixing it too firmly may make you unwilling to reshape it if further evidence, your audience, or the structure of your argument so demands.

Stating your thesis in a preliminary thesis sentence can help you form your idea. Make this sentence as clear and specific as possible. Don't resort to a vague generality or a nondebatable statement of fact. Instead, state the precise opinion you want readers to accept or the precise action you want them to take or support. For instance:

VAGUE   Computer instruction is important.

NONDEBATABLE   The school's investment in computer instruction is less than the average investment of the nation's colleges and universities.

PRECISE   Money designated for new dormitories and athletic facilities should be diverted to constructing computer facilities and hiring first-rate computer faculty.

VAGUE   Cloning research is promising.

NONDEBATABLE   Scientists have been experimenting with cloning procedures for many years.

PRECISE   Those who oppose cloning research should consider the potentially valuable applications of the research for human health and development.

Since the thesis is essentially a conclusion from evidence, you will probably need to do some additional reading to ensure that you have a broad range of facts and opinions supporting not only your view of the subject but also any opposing views. Though it may be tempting to ignore your opposition in the hope that readers know nothing of it, it is dishonest and probably futile to do so. Acknowledging and, whenever possible, refuting significant opposing views will enhance your credibility with readers. If you find that some counterarguments damage your own argument too greatly, then you will have to rethink your thesis.

Organizing

Once you have formulated your thesis and evaluated your reasons and evidence against the needs and expectations of your audience, begin planning how you will arrange your argument.

The introduction to your essay should draw readers into your framework, making them see how the subject affects them and predisposing them to consider your argument. Sometimes, a forthright approach works best, but an eye-opening anecdote or quotation can also be effective. Your thesis sentence may end your introduction. But if you think readers will not even entertain your thesis until they have seen some or all of your evidence, then withhold your thesis for later.

The main part of the essay consists of your reasons and your evidence for them. The evidence you generated or collected should suggest the reasons that will support the claim of your thesis — essentially the minor arguments that bolster the main argument. In an essay favoring federal investment in solar-energy research, for instance, the minor arguments might include the need for solar power, the feasibility of its widespread use, and its cost and safety compared with the cost and safety of other energy sources. It is in developing these minor arguments that you are most likely to use induction and deduction consciously — generalizing from specifics or applying generalizations to new information. Thus the minor arguments provide the entry points for your evidence, and together they should encompass all the relevant evidence.

Unless the minor arguments form a chain, with each growing out of the one before, their order should be determined by their potential effects on readers. In general, it is most effective to arrange the reasons in order of increasing importance or strength so as to finish powerfully. But to engage readers in the argument from the start, try to begin with a reason that they will find compelling or that they already know and accept; that way, the weaker reasons will be sandwiched between a strong beginning and an even stronger ending.

The views opposing yours can be raised and dispensed with wherever it seems most appropriate to do so. If a counterargument pertains to just one of your minor arguments, then dispose of it at that point. But if the counterarguments are more basic, pertaining to your whole thesis, you should dispose of them either after the introduction or shortly before the conclusion. Use the former strategy if the opposition is particularly strong and you fear that readers will be disinclined to listen unless you address their concerns first. Use the latter strategy when the counterarguments are generally weak or easily dispensed with once you've presented your case.

In the conclusion to your essay, you may summarize the main point of your argument and state your thesis for the first time, if you have saved it for the end, or restate it from your introduction. An effective quotation, an appropriate emotional appeal, or a call for support or action can often provide a strong finish to an argument.

Drafting

While you are drafting the essay, work to make your reasoning clear by showing how each bit of evidence relates to the reason or minor argument being discussed, and how each minor argument relates to the main argument contained in the thesis. In working through the reasons and evidence, you may find it helpful to state each reason as the first sentence in a paragraph and then support it in the following sentences. If this scheme seems too rigid or creates overlong paragraphs, you can always make changes after you have written your draft. Draw on a range of methods to clarify your points. For instance, define specialized terms or those you use in a special sense, compare and contrast one policy or piece of evidence with another, or carefully analyze causes or effects.

Revising and Editing

When your draft is complete, use the following questions and the box to guide your revision and editing.

- *Is your thesis debatable, precise, and clear?* Readers must know what you are trying to convince them of, at least by the end of the essay if not up front.
- *Is your argument unified?* Does each minor claim support the thesis? Do all opinions, facts, and examples provide evidence for a minor claim? On behalf of your readers, question every sentence you have written to be sure it contributes to the point you are making and to the argument as a whole.
- *Is the structure of your argument clear and compelling?* Readers should be able to follow easily, seeing when and why you move from one idea to the next.
- *Is the evidence specific, representative, and adequate?* Facts, examples, and expert opinions should be well detailed, should fairly represent the available information, and should be sufficient to support your claim.
- *Have you slipped into any logical fallacies?* Detecting fallacies in your own work can be difficult, but your readers will find them if you don't. Look for the following fallacies discussed earlier (pp. 326–28): hasty generalization, oversimplification, begging the question, ignoring the question, ad hominem, either-or, non sequitur, and post hoc. (All of these are also listed in the Glossary under *fallacies*.)

FOCUS ON TONE

Readers are most likely to be persuaded by an argument when they sense a writer who is reasonable, trustworthy, and sincere. A rational appeal, strong evidence, and acknowledgment of opposing views do much to convey these attributes, but so does tone, the attitude implied by choice of words and sentence structures.

Generally, you should try for a tone of moderation in your view of your subject and a tone of respectfulness and goodwill toward readers and opponents.

- State opinions and facts calmly:

  OVEREXCITED   One clueless administrator was quoted in the newspaper as saying she thought many students who claim learning disabilities are faking their difficulties to obtain special treatment! Has she never heard of dyslexia, attention deficit disorder, and other well-established disabilities?

CALM   Particularly worrisome was one administrator's statement, quoted in the newspaper, that many students who claim learning disabilities may be "faking" their difficulties to obtain special treatment.

• Replace arrogance with deference and sarcasm with plain speaking:

ARROGANT   I happen to know that many students would rather party or just bury their heads in the sand than get involved in a serious, worthy campaign against the school's unjust learning-disabled policies.

DEFERENTIAL   Time pressures and lack of information about the issues may be what prevents students from joining the campaign against the school's unjust learning-disabled policies.

SARCASTIC   Of course, the administration knows even without meeting students what is best for every one of them.

PLAIN SPEAKING   The administration should agree to meet with each learning-disabled student to learn about his or her needs.

• Choose words whose connotations convey reasonableness rather than anger, hostility, or another negative emotion:

HOSTILE   The administration *coerced* some students into dropping their lawsuits. [*Coerced* implies the use of threats or even violence.]

REASONABLE   The administration *convinced* some students to drop their lawsuits. [*Convinced* implies the use of reason.]

See pages 38–39 for more on tone and pages 48–49 for more on connotation.

A NOTE ON THEMATIC CONNECTIONS

Argument and persuasion is the ideal method for presenting an opinion or a proposal on a controversial issue, making it a natural choice for the writers in this chapter, all of whom wanted to make a case about criminal justice. In a paragraph (p. 328), David Lindorff takes a stand against screening out certain jurors in death-penalty cases. In another paragraph (p. 329), Martin Luther King Jr. urges readers to condone civil disobedience. Jeremy Steben's essay (p. 336) takes an unusual tack to criticize police activity in his town. Anna Quindlen (p. 343) asserts that changing our attitude toward mental illness may help to prevent school shootings. In an essay drawing on his own experience as an inmate, Wilbert Rideau (p. 349) argues for prison reform. And in the final two essays, Ira Glasser (p. 355) and James R. McDonough (p. 361) take opposing positions on the war on drugs.

The end must justify the means. — Matthew Prior

The right of the people to be secure in their persons, houses, papers, and effects, against unreasonable searches and seizures, shall not be violated, and no warrants shall issue but upon probable cause.

— Fourth Amendment to the US Constitution

Every society gets the kind of criminal it deserves. What is equally true is that every community gets the kind of law enforcement it insists on.

— Robert Kennedy

Journal Response Write about a recent time when you were aware of law enforcement in your community—perhaps a noteworthy arrest, a controversy involving police methods, a report of rising or falling crime, even a personal experience. What did you read, hear, or experience, and what did you think about it?

Jeremy Steben

Jeremy Steben was born in 1981 and grew up in Avon, Connecticut. He studied for two years at Boston College before taking time off from school to marshal in aircraft at Nantucket Memorial Airport and to teach Alpine skiing. Steben transferred to Vermont's Marlboro College in 2002. His interests include reading, collecting comic books, sailing, and skiing.

SMALL TOWN, QUIET TOWN, SAFE TOWN

(STUDENT ESSAY)

Steben wrote the following essay for his freshman writing course at Boston College. The police in his suburban hometown had been sued in 2000 for pulling over drivers not because of wrongdoing but just because of the driver's or the car's appearance. The question is whether such police behavior unacceptably violates civil liberties or constitutes a reasonable price for public safety. To get Steben's answer, pay careful attention to his tone.

The streets of my town can be dangerous places. I know; I drive them 1 all the time. On the surface my town is a quiet, upscale little suburb in

Connecticut, with the occasional cow pasture and golf course lending a sense of serenity and simplicity. But underneath the sugarcoated topping lies a not-so-sweet reality. Criminal elements travel our streets at night, while good citizens sleep, or boldly prowl our avenues in the glare of daylight. Thankfully, our streets are patrolled by a valiant police force that takes up the thankless task of stamping out crime with a vigor and enthusiasm that are to be commended. These dauntless men and women are the only bastion of defense against the darkness that constantly threatens to boil over and consume our fair community. These unsung heroes should be extolled and held up as an example to police forces all over the nation. One might presume that most officers patrol the streets regularly, setting speed traps and staying alert for any sign of traffic infractions or other criminal activity. However, my town's officers are far more proactive in their duties. They dislike waiting until they actually observe a crime being committed. Our officers have learned to be on the lookout for various indications ("clues," if you will) that action may be required. Occasionally these leads may prove false, but only diligent pursuit of them guarantees that order is maintained, and the innocent parties involved are only mildly inconvenienced.

For instance, our officers are quite aware of the problem of teenagers. It's common knowledge that teenagers have a tendency to be up to no good. Now, I happen to be a member of this group, and by no means do I suggest that we all engage in such things, but enough of us do that teenagers warrant special attention by the police. Especially on weekend nights, or when there are more than one of us in a car, we can count on a watchful eye being turned on us. Police pull us over regularly to ensure that there is nothing illegal going on. Officers rely on their instincts and observation when determining which cars to pull over. Should some smart aleck demand a specific reason for being stopped, our officers placate him by saying that he was driving "erratically." This could mean that a tire touched the median or the white strip or that the driver jerked the wheel a little too sharply on the last turn, but it lets the officer get on with the investigation unimpeded.

But knowing which cars to target is only half of proper law enforcement; a thorough officer doesn't stop there. Once the cars have been stopped, the officer must determine whether he has discovered a crime. Unfortunately this can be a difficult task. Our constitutional protection from unwarranted search and seizure is, sadly, often abused by criminals, and the laws regulating when and how an officer can conduct a search are numerous and cloying. Thankfully, over years of experience, our police have developed a system by which they can easily search any car that they feel is suspicious, and rarely do they concern themselves over such bothersome things as constitutional rights.

The first thing that a young or minority driver will notice upon   4
being stopped by an officer is the demeanor of the officer. The brisk and abrasive bearing, which seems to say, "I know you're guilty of *something*, and I'm going to find out *exactly* what," is of course intended to scare criminals, make them nervous, and make it easier for the officer to do his job. I appreciate this because it establishes the proper relationship between the officer and me right off the bat. The appropriate pressure is applied at once as the officer attempts to ascertain whether any illegal substances have been consumed. "So, you boys been doing some drinking tonight?" This question is then repeated several times throughout the ensuing conversation in slightly varied forms, such as "So, what, you guys have a few beers tonight?" or "So, you been partying, having a little fun?" This is just in case the driver forgot that he *had* in fact been drinking and accidentally answered "no" the first time. After five minutes of this the driver begins to think maybe he *did* have a few beers that night, even if he didn't. This interrogation gives the officer time to shine his flashlight all through the interior of the car in a visual examination.

What happens next depends on what the officer sees and, to some   5
extent, on the driver's reaction. For instance, if the driver turns around in his seat for any reason, perhaps to speak to somebody in the back seat, the following exchange is likely to occur:

> "Hey! What did you just throw back there?" the officer might say.
> "What? Nothing, I was just saying . . ." would be the stammered reply.
> "Step out of the vehicle. We're going to search it."

Suspicious clues like air fresheners hanging from the rearview mirror can also provide a reason to search, as they may be intended to cover up the scent of alcohol or marijuana. Even a twig can help officers do their job:

> "What's that on your floor? It looks like a stem."
> "It's just a twig."
> "I think it's a stem. Please exit the vehicle."

If all else fails, the officer can always claim the car smells like alcohol or marijuana or simply that the driver appears high or slightly drunk. In this way officers can feel free to pursue their suspicions and ensure that no crime is being committed.

Teenagers and minorities are not the only "problem" groups that 6
are habitually targeted. Drivers of vehicles that do not look expensive,
are not well kept, or are particularly old must be investigated. In a town
full of Grand Cherokees and Mercedes, such cars tend to be a bit out of
place. The police are consistent about checking these vehicles, as my
friend Ellie can personally attest. When she received her license she was
given a car that looked, to put it kindly, like a piece of junk. Driving a
car that was dented in many places, rusting in spots, and with several
panels caved in, it was no wonder that within a few months she had
been pulled over no less than fifteen times. The only reason this impres-
sive number stopped growing was that eventually Ellie had been pulled
over at least once by every patrolman on the force and it was established that she did indeed belong in town. She expressed a slight
annoyance at all the trouble, but I assured her that it was absolutely
necessary to our town's continued safety, and besides, she got to know
several officers much better than she might have.

Diligent, dogged, and thorough, our officers are doing the best they 7
can. It is truly a pity that not everyone sees their efforts for the blessings they are. The recent lawsuits against our maligned department
have brought our town to the attention of the entire state of Connecticut. The fact that we have been portrayed with infamy rather than
respect in the papers is truly a wrong. I don't see what all the fuss is
about. The plaintiffs claim that the police stop cars based on the looks
of the car and the driver and that cars traveling out of or into Hartford
are flagged for inspection. But as I stated above, certain seemingly superficial clues do indeed indicate suspicious persons and motives, and
paying attention to such details is an important part of law enforcement. Strangely, the lawsuits don't mention police victimizing minors,
although the police pay just as much special attention to the age of the
driver as they do to these other factors. Whenever some indignant
teenager complains about his treatment by the police, adults just shrug,
especially if he is particularly scruffy looking. "What do you expect?"
is the common reply. Indeed, what can you expect if you're a member
of a group commonly associated with criminal activity? And what's
more, if you further differentiate yourself from proper citizens by being
unkempt, you can't help but draw suspicion.

If police treated everybody the same they would be hampered in 8
their ability to fight crime. I accept my position and realize that to safe-
guard the greater good I must occasionally give up a few constitutional
rights, a sacrifice that I make gladly. In fact, I think it rather petty that
some individuals seek to shirk this shared civic responsibility. I can only

hope that these lawsuits have a fleeting impact on the methods of our police. In the future our officers must feel free to enforce the law as they see fit, and if their methods circumvent a few of our civil liberties, well, that's the price that we must pay for living in a quiet, safe town.

Meaning

1. What is the main point of Steben's essay? How far along were you when you realized the irony of his approach? (See *irony* in the Glossary if you need a definition.) What clues in the first paragraph hint at this approach?
2. What, exactly, does Steben believe the police do wrong? Whom do they victimize, and how?
3. How does Steben explain police officers' justification for their actions? Does he believe their methods are at all justified?
4. If you are unsure of the meanings of any of the following words, try to guess them from their context in Steben's essay. Look up the words in a dictionary to check your guesses, and then practice using each word in a sentence or two of your own.

upscale (1)	unimpeded (2)	plaintiffs (7)
bastion (1)	cloying (3)	hampered (8)
extolled (1)	demeanor (4)	petty (8)
proactive (1)	dogged (7)	shirk (8)
diligent (1)	infamy (7)	circumvent (8)
placate (2)		

Purpose and Audience

1. Why do you believe Steben wrote this essay? To make fun of the police? To express his indignation? To argue for or against something? (If so, what?) For some other purpose?
2. Whom do you believe Steben imagines as his primary readers? Teenagers, minorities, and the poor—the groups he says are habitually targeted by the police? The "good citizens" (paragraph 1) whom the police are protecting? The police, of whom he is so critical? Support your answer with specific examples from the text.

Method and Structure

1. Steben's irony requires that he say the opposite of what he means, and in doing so he sometimes turns the principles of argument on end. For instance, can you find examples of some of the fallacies listed on pages 326–28? How do they support Steben's purpose?

2. How effective do you find Steben's choice to present his argument indirectly, cloaked in a counterargument? Your answer may depend on many factors, such as how confusing, amusing, offensive, or powerful you find the essay.

3. **Other Methods** In paragraphs 2–5 Steben uses process analysis (Chapter 9) to detail police methods. What does this lengthy passage contribute to the essay?

Language

1. Steben's language is quite formal, with phrases such as "One might presume" (paragraph 1) and "by no means do I suggest" (2). Some of the language mimics oldsters speaking of youngsters, such as teenagers who are "up to no good" and the "smart aleck" teen (2). Some of the language even mimics a speech by a city mayor who is handing out awards to police officers—phrases such as "These dauntless men and women" (1). Why do you think Steben chose this formal style? How effective is it?

2. Why does Steben quote dialogue in paragraphs 4 and 5? What function or functions do these exchanges play?

Writing Topics

1. **Journal to Essay** Starting from your journal entry (p. 336), write an essay about the state of law enforcement in your community, as you see it. You could focus on a particular incident involving the police or on more general patterns of action illustrated with examples. Do the police do their jobs effectively and fairly? Do they contribute to easing or to increasing tensions among groups of people? Do some groups support the police while others don't?

2. Choose a social or other kind of problem you care about—it could be the difficulty of obtaining health insurance, overcrowding in public schools, violence in the media, child neglect, or anything else. Describe the problem as you understand it, particularly how it affects people. Then discuss your solution to the problem or some part of it. Be sure at least to acknowledge opposing views. You may choose to write ironically, as Steben does, or straightforwardly.

3. **Cultural Considerations** Steben refers to the "constitutional protection from unwarranted search and seizure" (paragraph 3)—a reference to the Fourth Amendment to the US Constitution, quoted before the essay (p. 336). The United States is noteworthy among nations for the protections it affords citizens and others who might be suspected or accused of a crime. In some other countries, for instance, law-enforcement officers may use almost any means deemed necessary to obtain evidence against

a suspected wrongdoer, whereas in the United States not only the Constitution but also federal, state, and local laws tightly restrict when and how evidence may be gathered. Still, many in the United States are concerned that individual rights are not protected enough or that the protections are not equally enforced. Do you think the US system achieves an appropriate balance between fairness to individuals and effectiveness in deterring or stopping crime, or does it lean one way or the other? Write an essay stating your opinion and supporting it with examples from your experience, observations, and reading. If you are familiar with individual rights and law-enforcement procedures in another country, you may want to use comparison and contrast (Chapter 10) to help make your point.

4. **Connections**   Steben writes about the experience of being falsely accused just because he is young. In contrast, Annie Dillard, in "The Chase" (p. 90), narrates an incident in which she was rightly accused of playing a childish prank. Although the incidents described by these authors differ greatly, both Steben and Dillard are subject to adults' negative attitudes about young people. Write an essay in which you outline adult society's attitudes toward young people, both just and unjust, using evidence from Steben's and Dillard's essays and from your own experience and observations.

ON SCHOOL SHOOTINGS

*I am not insane. I am angry.... I killed because people like me are
mistreated every day.*
— Luke Woodham

He just seemed strange.... He didn't seem dangerous in any way.
— Karan Grewal

The reality is that schools are very safe environments for our kids.
— Jim Mercy

Journal Response   School shootings seem to have become an epidemic in the
United States. Most notoriously, in 1999 two students at Columbine High
School killed thirteen people, and in 2007 a student at Virginia Tech killed
thirty-three people. Every time a new tragedy makes the news, we hear demands for tighter security and closer attention to warning signs. Many high-
school (and even grade-school) students now pass through metal detectors on
their way to class, and several school districts have initiated "zero tolerance"
policies that call for the removal of children who show any potential to do
harm. How do you feel about all of this? In a journal entry, comment on the
problem of student violence. How extensive is it? What causes it? What should
be done about it?

---------------------- Anna Quindlen ----------------------

*Winner of the Pulitzer Prize for commentary in 1992, Anna Quindlen writes
sharp, candid columns on subjects ranging from family life to social issues to
international politics. She was born in 1953 in Philadelphia, where she grew
up, as she puts it, "an antsy kid with a fresh mouth." After graduating from
Barnard College, Quindlen began writing for the* New York Post *and two years
later joined the staff of the* New York Times, *where she quickly worked her
way up from a city hall reporter to a regular columnist. Quindlen left the* Times
*in 1995 to focus on writing novels, and since 1999 she has written a biweekly
column for* Newsweek *magazine. Her columns have been collected in* Living
Out Loud *(1988),* Thinking Out Loud *(1993), and* Loud and Clear *(2004).
Quindlen is also the author of* A Short Guide to a Happy Life *(2000) and the
novels* Object Lessons *(1991),* One True Thing *(1994),* Black and Blue *(1998),*
Blessings *(2002), and* Rise and Shine *(2006).*

THE C WORD IN THE HALLWAYS

Quindlen wrote this selection from Loud and Clear *in November 1999, a few months after the massacre at Columbine High School and several years before the carnage at Virginia Tech in 2007. Read in the wake of this later tragedy, her message seems more urgent than ever.*

The saddest phrase I've read in a long time is this one: psychological   1
autopsy. That's what the doctors call it when a kid kills himself, and
they go back over the plowed ground of his short life, and discover all
the hidden markers that led to the rope, the blade, the gun.

There's a plague on all our houses, and since it doesn't announce   2
itself with lumps or spots or protest marches, it has gone unremarked
in the quiet suburbs and busy cities where it has been laying waste. The
number of suicides and homicides committed by teenagers, most often
young men, has exploded in the last three decades, until it has become
routine to have black-bordered photographs in yearbooks and murder suspects with acne problems. And everyone searches for reasons,
and scapegoats, and solutions, most often punitive. Yet one solution
continues to elude us, and that is ending the ignorance about mental
health, and moving it from the margins of care and into the mainstream
where it belongs. As surely as any vaccine, this would save lives.

So many have already been lost. This month Kip Kinkel was sen-   3
tenced to life in prison in Oregon for the murders of his parents and a
shooting rampage at his high school that killed two students. A psychiatrist who specializes in the care of adolescents testified that Kinkel,
now seventeen, had been hearing voices since he was twelve. Sam
Manzie is also seventeen. He is serving a seventy-year sentence for luring an eleven-year-old boy named Eddie Werner into his New Jersey
home and strangling him with the cord to an alarm clock because his
Sega Genesis was out of reach. Manzie had his first psychological evaluation in the first grade.

Excuses, excuses. That's what so many think of the underlying   4
pathology in such hideous crimes. In the 1956 movie *The Bad Seed*, little Patty McCormack played what was then called a "homicidal maniac" and the film censors demanded a ludicrous mock curtain call in
which the child actress was taken over the knee of her screen father and
spanked. There are still some representatives of the "good spanking"
school out there, although today the spanking may wind up being life

in prison. And there's still plenty of that useless adult "what in the world does a sixteen-year-old have to be depressed about" mind-set to keep depressed sixteen-year-olds from getting help.

It's true that both the Kinkel and the Manzie boys had already been introduced to the mental health system before their crimes. Concerned by her son's fascination with weapons, Faith Kinkel took him for nine sessions with a psychologist in the year before the shootings. Because of his rages and his continuing relationship with a pedophile, Sam's parents had tried to have him admitted to a residential facility just days before their son invited Eddie in.

But they were threading their way through a mental health system that is marginalized by shame, ignorance, custom, the courts, even by business practice. Kip Kinkel's father made no secret of his disapproval of therapy. During its course he bought his son the Glock that Kip would later use on his killing spree, which speaks sad volumes about our peculiar standards of masculinity. Sam's father, on the other hand, spent days trying to figure out how much of the cost of a home for troubled kids his insurance would cover. In the meantime, a psychiatrist who examined his son for less time than it takes to eat a Happy Meal concluded that he was no danger to himself or others, and a judge lectured Sam from the bench: "You know the difference between right and wrong, don't you?"

The federal Center for Mental Health Services estimates that at least six million children in this country have some serious emotional disturbance and, for some of them, right and wrong take second seat to the voices in their heads. Fifty years ago their parents might have surrendered them to life in an institution, or a doctor flying blind with an ice pick might have performed a lobotomy, leaving them to loll away their days. Now lots of them wind up in jail. Warm fuzzies aside, consider this from a utilitarian point of view: Psychological intervention is cheaper than incarceration.

The most optimistic estimate is that two thirds of these emotionally disturbed children are not getting any treatment. Imagine how we would respond if two thirds of America's babies were not being immunized. Many health insurance plans do not provide coverage for necessary treatment, or financially penalize those who need a psychiatrist instead of an oncologist. Teachers are not trained to recognize mental illness, and some dismiss it, "Bad Seed" fashion, as bad behavior. Parents are afraid, and ashamed, creating a home environment, and national atmosphere, too, that tells teenagers their demons are a disgrace.

And then there are the teenagers themselves, slouching toward adulthood in a world that loves conformity. Add to the horror of creeping depression or delusions that of peer derision, the sound of the C word in the hallways: crazy, man, he's crazy, haven't you seen him, didn't you hear? Boys, especially, still suspect that talk therapy, or even heartfelt talk, is somehow sissified, weak. Sometimes even their own fathers think so, at least until they have to identify the body.

Another sad little phrase is "If only," and there are always plenty   10
of them littering the valleys of tragedy. If only there had been long-term intervention and medication, Kip Kinkel might be out of jail, off the taxpayers' tab, and perhaps leading a productive life. If only Sam Manzie had been treated aggressively earlier, new psychotropic drugs might have slowed or stilled his downward slide. And if only those things had happened, Faith Kinkel, William Kinkel, Mikael Nickolauson, Ben Walker, and Eddie Werner might all be alive today. Mental health care is health care, too, and mental illness is an illness, not a character flaw. Insurance providers should act like it. Hospitals and schools should act like it. Above all, we parents should act like it. Then maybe the kids will believe it.

Meaning

1. What is Quindlen's main idea, and where do you find it in the essay?
2. What examples of teen violence does Quindlen give? What reason does she provide to explain these students' behavior?
3. Why is Quindlen so alarmed about our attitudes toward mental illness? Whom does she blame for the problems experienced by troubled teenagers?
4. In paragraph 6, Quindlen writes that William Kinkel's purchase of a gun for his son "speaks sad volumes about our peculiar standards of masculinity." What does she mean?
5. If you are unsure of any of the following words used by Quindlen, try to determine their meanings from their context in the essay. Check their meanings in a dictionary to test your guesses. Then use each word in a sentence or two of your own.

scapegoats (2)	loll (7)	derision (9)
pathology (4)	utilitarian (7)	psychotropic (10)
ludicrous (4)	incarceration (7)	
marginalized (6)	oncologist (8)	

Purpose and Audience

1. What seems to be Quindlen's purpose in writing this essay? Is she writing mainly to express a concern, offer a solution to a problem, influence gov-

ernment decisions, change individuals' attitudes, or do something else? What evidence from the text supports your answer?

2. Who do you think is the author's target audience? How does Quindlen engage these readers' support?

3. Although this essay was written only a few months after the tragedy at Columbine (which at the time was the deadliest school shooting in American history), Quindlen makes no mention of the shooters there, Eric Harris and Dylan Klebold. Why do you suppose she leaves them out of her discussion?

Method and Structure

1. Is Quindlen's appeal mostly emotional or mostly rational? Explain your answer with examples from the essay.

2. Where in the essay does Quindlen address opposing viewpoints? How fair is her depiction of people with conflicting opinions?

3. Quindlen makes two literary references in this essay: "a plague on all our houses" (paragraph 2) is an allusion to Shakespeare's play *Romeo and Juliet*, and "slouching toward adulthood" (9) is an allusion to William Butler Yeats's poem "The Second Coming." What is the effect of these references?

4. **Other Methods**   Quindlen supports her argument with other methods, such as example (Chapter 6), comparison and contrast (Chapter 10), and cause-and-effect analysis (Chapter 12). Locate one instance of each method. What does each contribute to the essay?

Language

1. What is the "*C* Word" to which Quindlen refers in her title? Why do you suppose she waits until the end of the essay to use the word itself?

2. How does Quindlen use parallel sentence structure in her conclusion to drive home her point?

3. How would you describe Quindlen's tone? Is it consistent throughout? Is it appropriate for her subject?

Writing Topics

1. **Journal to Essay**   Take off from the comments you made in your journal entry (p. 343) to write an essay that agrees or disagrees with Quindlen. Has the incidence of teenage suicide and homicide really "exploded" (paragraph 2) to the degree that Quindlen describes? Are teenage killers victims of inadequate mental health care? Is better psychological treatment the answer to the problem? Are there other solutions we should consider?

Your essay may be, but need not be, an argument: that is, you could explain your answer to any of these questions or argue a specific point. Either way, use examples and details to support your ideas.

2. Although Quindlen's essay demonstrates a large degree of compassion for troubled teenagers, some scholars and psychologists would caution that the cause-and-effect relationship she draws between mental illness and violence is misinformed. Using the library or the Internet, research articles or studies concerning media stigmatization of the mentally ill. In an essay, discuss whether you think Quindlen's analysis of teen violence reflects negative stereotypes. If you find that it does, consider whether such stereotypes affect the persuasiveness of her argument. (For advice on finding and using research sources, see the Appendix.)

3. **Cultural Considerations**   At several points in her essay, Quindlen suggests that American codes of masculinity are at least partly to blame for teenage boys' tendency toward violence. Write an essay that explores what our culture expects of boys and men, and how those expectations might translate into inappropriate behavior. How does American culture define manhood? Do we, in fact, pressure boys to keep silent about their emotions? To what extent is masculine aggression encouraged or rewarded? How does society respond to boys—and men—who don't conform to expectations? And to what extent are individuals responsible for their own behavior? In formulating your analysis, consider also how a person from another culture might respond—a resident of, say, Mexico or Japan or France.

4. **Connections**   Both Quindlen and Andrew Sullivan, in "The 'M-Word': Why It Matters to Me" (p. 282), write with strong emotion about a social issue—mental illness in Quindlen's case, gay marriage in Sullivan's—and both writers use a similar titling strategy. In an essay, explore how the concept of personal shame, or social taboo, informs each writer's approach. Why do these writers hesitate to name their subjects in their titles, and what does this hesitation say about how they imagine their readers will respond to their arguments? How effective is each writer's strategy of tackling a controversial issue from an emotional perspective? What would these essays have lost (or gained) if they had been written from a more psychologically distant point of view?

Prison continues, on those who are entrusted to it, a work begun elsewhere, which the whole of society pursues on each individual through innumerable mechanisms of discipline.
                                                                    —Michel Foucault

Man is not made better by being degraded; he is seldom restrained from crime by harsh measures, except the principle of fear predominates in his character; and then he is never made radically better for its influence.
                                                                    —Dorothea Dix

Of the three official objects of our prison system—vengeance, deterrence, and reformation of the criminal—only one is achieved; and that is the one which is nakedly abominable.
                                                                    —George Bernard Shaw

Journal Response What is the purpose of prison in a civilized society? Do we jail people to punish them, to rehabilitate them, or to protect others from them? Are there other ways to respond to crime? In your journal, write a few paragraphs exploring your thoughts on these questions.

Wilbert Rideau

Born in 1942 in Lawtell, Louisiana, Wilbert Rideau had a troubled youth. When he was just nineteen, an all-white jury convicted the African American teenager of murder for his role in the death of a bank teller during a robbery. After several appeals the conviction was overturned on the grounds of bias, and his sentence was switched to life imprisonment. In a 2005 retrial the verdict was reduced to manslaughter, and since Rideau had already served the maximum sentence for that crime, he was released. During his time on death row, the eighth-grade dropout educated himself through extensive reading and sought a position on the Angolite, *Louisiana State Penitentiary's newsletter. Turned down because of his race, he started his own publication,* Lifer, *and began writing a syndicated weekly column for black newspapers in Louisiana and Mississippi. After being named editor of the* Angolite *in 1975, he succeeded in transforming it into an award-winning national magazine. The coauthor of* The Wall Is Strong *(1991), a college reader, and* Life Sentences *(1992), a collection of prison writing, Rideau is now a recognized authority on criminal justice. He has also collaborated on several radio and film productions, most notably* The Farm *(1998), an Oscar nominee and the Sundance Film Festival's winner for best documentary.*

WHY PRISONS DON'T WORK

Not surprisingly, Rideau is an outspoken advocate for prison reform. Although crime prevention is important, he says, we're going at it the wrong way. He wrote this essay, commissioned by Time *magazine in 1994, while he was still serving a sentence of life in prison.*

I was among thirty-one murderers sent to the Louisiana State Penitentiary in 1962 to be executed or imprisoned for life. We weren't much different from those we found here, or those who had preceded us. We were unskilled, impulsive, and uneducated misfits, mostly black, who had done dumb, impulsive things — failures, rejects from the larger society. Now a generation has come of age and gone since I've been here, and everything is much the same as I found it. The faces of prisoners are different, but behind them are the same impulsive, uneducated, unskilled minds that made dumb, impulsive choices that got them into more trouble than they ever thought existed. The vast majority of us are consigned to suffer and die here so politicians can sell the illusion that permanently exiling people to prison will make society safe.

Getting tough has always been a "silver bullet," a quick fix for the crime and violence that society fears. Each year in Louisiana — where excess is a way of life — lawmakers have tried to outdo each other in legislating harsher mandatory penalties and in reducing avenues of release. The only thing to do with criminals, they say, is get tougher. They have. In the process, the purpose of prison began to change. The state boasts one of the highest lockup rates in the country, imposes the most severe penalties in the nation, and vies to execute more criminals per capita than anywhere else. This state is so tough that last year, when prison authorities here wanted to punish an inmate in solitary confinement for an infraction, the most they could inflict on him was to deprive him of his underwear. It was all he had left.

If getting tough resulted in public safety, Louisiana citizens would be the safest in the nation. They're not. Louisiana has the highest murder rate among states. Prison, like the police and the courts, has a minimal impact on crime because it is a response after the fact, a mop-up operation. It doesn't work. The idea of punishing the few to deter the many is counterfeit because potential criminals either think they're not going to get caught or they're so emotionally desperate or psychologically distressed that they don't care about the consequences of their actions. The threatened punishment, regardless of its severity, is never a factor in the equation. But society, like the incorrigible criminal it abhors, is unable to learn from its mistakes.

Prison has a role in public safety, but it is not a cure-all. Its value 4 is limited, and its use should also be limited to what it does best: isolating young criminals long enough to give them a chance to grow up and get a grip on their impulses. It is a traumatic experience, certainly, but it should only be a temporary one, not a way of life. Prisoners kept too long tend to embrace the criminal culture, its distorted values and beliefs; they have little choice—prison is their life. There are some prisoners who cannot be returned to society—serial killers, serial rapists, professional hit men, and the like—but the monsters who need to die in prison are rare exceptions in the criminal landscape.

Crime is a young man's game. Most of the nation's random vio- 5 lence is committed by young urban terrorists. But because of long, mandatory sentences, most prisoners here are much older, having spent fifteen, twenty, thirty, or more years behind bars, long past necessity. Rather than pay for new prisons, society would be well served by releasing some of its older prisoners who pose no threat and using the money to catch young street thugs. Warden John Whitely agrees that many older prisoners here could be freed tomorrow with little or no danger to society. Release, however, is governed by law or by politicians, not by penal professionals. Even murderers, those most feared by society, pose little risk. Historically, for example, the domestic staff at Louisiana's Governor's mansion has been made up of murderers, hand-picked to work among the chief-of-state and his family. Penologists have long known that murder is almost always a once-in-a-lifetime act. The most dangerous criminal is the one who has not yet killed but has a history of escalating offenses. He's the one to watch.

Rehabilitation can work. Everyone changes in time. The trick is 6 to influence the direction that change takes. The problem with prisons is that they don't do more to rehabilitate those confined in them. The convict who enters prison illiterate will probably leave the same way. Most convicts want to be better than they are, but education is not a priority. This prison houses 4,600 men and offers academic training to 240, vocational training to a like number. Perhaps it doesn't matter. About 90 percent of the men here may never leave this prison alive.

The only effective way to curb crime is for society to work to pre- 7 vent the criminal act in the first place, to come between the perpetrator and crime. Our youngsters must be taught to respect the humanity of others and to handle disputes without violence. It is essential to educate and equip them with the skills to pursue their life ambitions in a meaningful way. As a community, we must address the adverse life circumstances that spawn criminality. These things are not quick, and they're not easy, but they're effective. Politicians think that's too hard a sell. They want to be on record for doing something now, something they can point to at reelection time. So the drumbeat goes on for more police, more prisons, more of the same failed policies.

Ever see a dog chase its tail?   8

Meaning

1. According to Rideau, what is the purpose of sending people to prison? Where in the text does he state the central assumption that grounds his argument?
2. Why don't prisons work? Locate the author's thesis statement or summarize his main idea in your own words.
3. How, according to Rideau, can we better protect society from violent criminals?
4. Some of the following words may be new to you. Try to guess their meanings from the context of Rideau's essay. Test your guesses in a dictionary, and then use each new word in a sentence or two of your own.

consigned (1)	infraction (2)	curb (7)
legislating (2)	incorrigible (3)	perpetrator (7)
vies (2)	abhors (3)	
per capita (2)	escalating (5)	

Purpose and Audience

1. In light of the fact that *Time* magazine asked Rideau to write this essay, what do you suppose his purpose is? Can an essay like this one, published in a magazine with a circulation in the millions, have an effect on legislation? What would the intermediary steps have to be?
2. Who would Rideau's ideal readers be? Politicians? Prisoners? Average citizens? Why do you think so?

Method and Structure

1. Explain how Rideau uses deductive and inductive reasoning to form his argument. How might his main idea be phrased as a syllogism (see pp. 325–26)?
2. How would you rate Rideau's ethical appeal? What strategies does he use to overcome readers' potential doubts about his objectivity?

3. How does Rideau handle opposing viewpoints? What is the effect of acknowledging some of the benefits of prisons in paragraphs 4 and 6?
4. **Other Methods**   In paragraphs 2 and 3, Rideau uses cause-and-effect analysis (Chapter 12) to examine the results of one instance of "getting tough" on crime. What were the consequences of Louisiana's strong stance on punishment? How does this cause-and-effect analysis further Rideau's argument for reform?

Language

1. How would you describe Rideau's attitude toward his subject? What is the overall tone of his argument?
2. Why does Rideau take such pains to describe himself and his fellow inmates as "unskilled, impulsive, and uneducated misfits" (paragraph 1)? How does he use repetition of key words to preview his solution to crime?
3. What is the purpose of the question with which Rideau ends his essay?

Writing Topics

1. **Journal to Essay**   The United States imprisons more of its citizens than almost any other country. Why is this the case? Reread the quotations and the journal entry you wrote before reading Rideau's essay (p. 349). Develop your ideas into an essay that explains and supports your thoughts on the uses of imprisonment in America. Do we, as Rideau argues, jail people in an effort to protect society from dangerous criminals, or do other motives come into play? Are such motives reasonable? Is imprisonment effective at accomplishing the purposes assigned to it? Is the institution abused or misused in any way? Whatever your position, be sure to support it with plenty of details and examples and to consider how others might disagree with you.
2. Prison is a perennially popular subject in fiction. Find a novel or film that takes prison, or something related to prison (such as involuntary commitment to a mental hospital), as its subject. (For novels, you might consider Charles Dickens's *Little Dorrit*, Malcolm Braly's *On the Yard*, or Kurt Vonnegut's *Hocus Pocus*. Films touching on this subject include *Cool Hand Luke*, *Escape from Alcatraz*, *Bad Boys*, *The Green Mile*, and *The Shawshank Redemption*, the last two based on stories by Stephen King.) Write an essay comparing and contrasting the novel's or film's attitudes toward prison with Rideau's views. Are the criticisms the same? Where do they differ?
3. **Cultural Considerations**   As the quotation from Michel Foucault (p. 349) suggests, laws reflect and reinforce basic social values: What behaviors are

acceptable? What transgressions are punishable? How far should we go to enforce social norms? Although incarceration practices might seem reasonable in a contemporary cultural context, viewed from an outsider's perspective they can often be quite surprising. For much of American history, for instance, whole families — including dependent infants — were routinely placed in debtors' prisons for a father's failure to provide for them. And in the early twentieth century, unmarried women could be jailed for pregnancy. Think of a past or current law that strikes you as absurd or extreme and look for the underlying social value that it's meant to enforce. Then write an essay that explains the law to somebody from another culture, or another time, who might have trouble understanding it. You may be ironic or satiric, if you wish, or you may prefer a more straightforward informative approach.

4. **Connections**   Rideau and Anna Quindlen, in "The C Word in the Hallways" (p. 343), both impart a sense of urgency about crime prevention, but their approaches are as different as their last lines: Rideau's "Ever see a dog chase its tail?" (paragraph 8) versus Quindlen's "Then maybe the kids will believe it" (10). What do these lines and others like them reveal about these authors' attitudes toward their subjects and their readers? Are both approaches equally effective? Why, or why not?

Just say no.
—Nancy Reagan

There seems to be no stopping drug frenzy once it takes hold of a nation. What starts with an innocuous HUGS, NOT DRUGS bumper sticker soon leads to wild talk of shooting dealers and making urine tests a condition for employment—anywhere.
—Barbara Ehrenreich

The entire war on drugs disproportionately targets poor people and people of color.
—Ethan Nadelmann

Journal Response   Is there any illegal drug that you think should be legalized? Is there any legal drug that you think should not be legal? What would be the effects, both positive and negative, of changing the legislation on this drug? Consider, for example, whether a change in status would increase or decrease use of the drug, whether it would hurt or harm users, and what the social and economic repercussions might be.

Ira Glasser

Ira Glasser was born in Brooklyn, New York, in 1938. After obtaining degrees from Queens College of the City College of New York (BS, 1959) and Ohio State University (MA, 1960), he taught college mathematics and edited the public affairs magazine Current *for several years before finding his life's work with the American Civil Liberties Union (ACLU). First as associate director of the organization's New York branch and then as national director from 1978 to 2001, Glasser developed a reputation for protecting the dispossessed from government abuses of power and for taking on unpopular causes in the name of First Amendment rights. (Most notoriously, he defended a neo-Nazi group's right to march through Skokie, Illinois.) He is generally credited with transforming the ACLU from a small legal service to an influential—if often controversial—national presence. Glasser has published essays in periodicals ranging from* USA Today *to* Christianity and Crisis *to* Harper's Magazine, *as well as two books,* Doing Good: The Limits of Benevolence *(coauthored with Willard Gaylin and others, 1978) and* Visions of Liberty *(1991). Now retired from the ACLU, he is president of the board of the Drug Policy Alliance, a lobbying group dedicated to ending the war on drugs.*

DRUG BUSTS = JIM CROW

From the 1870s through the first half of the twentieth century, a system of state and federal laws denied African Americans the right to use the same public facilities (such as restrooms and water fountains) and institutions (such as schools and housing developments) available to the white majority. This widespread and officially sanctioned segregation, called "Jim Crow" after the title of a popular nineteenth-century song, stayed in place until the civil rights movement successfully forced the creation of new laws against racial discrimination in the 1960s. But is legal segregation truly history? In this essay, first published in the Nation *in 2006, Glasser suggests that it is not.*

I was born in 1938, grew up on the working-class, immigrant streets 1
of East Flatbush in Brooklyn during World War II, and came to political consciousness during the postwar years. As children, we were told that World War II was a war fought against racism, against the idea that a whole class of people could be separated, subjugated and even murdered because of their race or religion. But back home in the United States, racial separation and subjugation remained entrenched by law in the Deep South and by custom nearly everywhere else.

This moral contradiction between what America said it stood for and 2
the way it was actually organized was largely unrecognized by the American public as World War II drew to a close. The first major postwar event that challenged this contradiction and made it unavoidable was the coming of Jackie Robinson to the Brooklyn Dodgers in 1947. It engaged people, including children, in a drama of racial integration, and it created what may have been the first racially integrated public accommodation—at Ebbets Field, where the Dodgers played. The following year President Harry Truman issued an executive order desegregating the armed forces. In 1950 *Brown v. Board of Education* was filed, signaling the start of the modern civil rights era. Four years later a surprisingly unanimous Supreme Court struck down legally enforced racial separation in public schools, and seventeen months after that, Rosa Parks refused to give her seat to a white man on a Montgomery, Alabama, bus. Nine years later, after countless protests, marches, sit-ins and freedom rides, as well as murders and beatings of civil rights workers, the Civil Rights Act of 1964 was passed, outlawing racial discrimination in public accommodations, employment and education. A year later the Voting Rights Act of 1965 outlawed racial discrimination in voting, and three years after that, the Fair Housing Act of 1968 outlawed racial dis-

crimination in the purchase and rental of homes. By 1968 the legal infrastructure of Jim Crow subjugation had been destroyed and a new legal infrastructure of federal civil rights enforcement was erected in its place. America had, for the first time, abolished legalized racial discrimination and replaced it with a system of formal legal equality.

As it turned out, actual equality of opportunity did not follow automatically, easily or quickly from legal equality. But over the succeeding decades it has been assumed that at the very least, no legalized racial discrimination remains, and certainly no new forms of legalized skin-color subjugation have arisen. This is true, with one substantial exception: the system of drug prohibition and its enforcement, which is the major, and still insufficiently recognized, civil rights issue of our day. 3

In the late 1960s, at the peak of the civil rights movement, there were fewer than 200,000 people in state and federal prisons for all criminal offenses; by 2004 there were over 1.4 million. Another 700,000-plus in local jails brought the total to 2.2 million. This explosion of incarceration has been heavily due to nonviolent drug offenses—mostly possession and petty sales, not involving guns or violence—resulting from the exponential escalation of the "war on drugs," beginning in 1968 and accelerating again after 1980. 4

Since 1980 drug arrests have tripled, to 1.6 million annually—nearly half for marijuana, 88 percent of those for possession, not sale or manufacture. Since 1980 the proportion of all state prisoners who are in for drug offenses increased from 6 percent to 21 percent. Since 1980 the proportion of all federal prisoners who are in for drug offenses increased from 25 percent to 57 percent. 5

At the same time, the racial disparity of arrests, convictions and imprisonment for these offenses has become pronounced. According to federal statistics gathered by the Sentencing Project, only 13 percent of monthly drug users of all illegal drugs—defined as those who use a drug at least once a month on a regular basis—are black, about their proportion of the population. But 37 percent of drug-offense arrests are black; 53 percent of convictions are black; and 67 percent of all people imprisoned for drug offenses are black. Adding in Latinos, about 22 percent of all monthly drug users are black or Latino, but 80 percent of people in prison for drug offenses are black or Latino. Even in presumptively liberal New York State, 92 percent of all inmates who are there for drug offenses are black or Latino. 6

The fact that so many people arrested, convicted and imprisoned for drug offenses are black or Latino is not because they are mostly the ones 7 doing the crime; it is because they are mostly the ones being targeted. This is not a phenomenon of the Deep South. It is nationwide. And it is not accidental. As the racial profiling scandals a few years ago showed, blacks are disproportionately targeted while driving cars on the highway; for example, in a lawsuit challenging this practice, it was revealed that although only 17 percent of drivers on a stretch of I-95 in Maryland were black, 73 percent of all the cars stopped and searched for drugs were driven by blacks. Nor was this an isolated example. In Florida blacks were seventy-five times more likely than whites to be stopped and searched for drugs while driving. And it turned out that these racially targeted stops were the explicit result of a Drug Enforcement Administration program begun in 1986, called Operation Pipeline, that "trained" 27,000 state troopers in forty-eight states to spot cars that might contain drugs. Most of the cars spotted were driven by blacks. And this happened even though three-quarters of monthly drug users are white! . . .

Despite these patterns of racial targeting, it has not been fashionable 8 among liberals to see drug prohibition as a massive civil rights problem of racial discrimination. Perhaps it would be easier if we examined the way racially targeted drug-war incarceration has damaged the right to vote, a right quintessentially part of the rights we thought we had won in the 1960s with the demise of Jim Crow laws.

Until recently (there have been some changes in the past few years in 9 some states), every state but two barred felons from voting—some permanently, some in a way that allowed, theoretically but often not as a practical matter, for the restoration of voting rights. Because of the explosion of incarceration driven by drug prohibition, more than 5 million people are now barred from voting. The United States is the only industrial democracy that does this. And the origin of most of these laws—no surprise—is the post-Reconstruction period after slavery was abolished. Felony disenfranchisement laws, like poll taxes and literacy tests, were historically part of the system that arose after slavery to bar blacks from exercising equal rights and, in particular, equal voting rights. Felony disenfranchisement laws were, to a large extent, part of a replacement system for subjugating blacks after slavery was abolished. . . .

The fact is, just as Jim Crow laws were a successor system to slav- 10 ery, so drug prohibition has been a successor to Jim Crow laws in targeting blacks, removing them from civil society and then denying them the right to vote. . . . Drug prohibition is now the last significant instance of legalized racial discrimination in America.

That many liberals have been at best timid in opposing the drug 11 war and at worst accomplices to its continued escalation is, in light of the racial politics of drug prohibition, a special outrage.... Liberals especially, therefore, need to consider attacking the premises upon which this edifice of racial subjugation is based. If they do not, who will?

Meaning

1. Where does Glasser identify the issue he is going to address? Where does he state his thesis?
2. What disparity does Glasser see in drug arrest statistics? Why are the numbers problematic?
3. Some of the following words may be new to you. Try to guess their meanings from the context of Glasser's essay. Test your guesses in a dictionary, and then use each new word in a sentence or two of your own.

subjugated (1)	pronounced (6)	demise (8)
infrastructure (2)	presumptively (6)	disenfranchisement (9)
exponential (4)	disproportionately (7)	successor (10)
escalation (4)	quintessentially (8)	edifice (11)

Purpose and Audience

1. For whom is Glasser writing? People who already favor drug law reform? People who think the laws are beneficial? Someone else? What does the author seem to assume about his readers?
2. Why do you think Glasser wrote this essay? What does he hope to accomplish by making his argument?

Method and Structure

1. Which part of the essay is more explanatory than argumentative? Is this part entirely objective? What does it contribute to Glasser's argument?
2. What kinds of evidence does the author provide? Where does it come from, and is it reliable and convincing? Why, or why not? (See pp. 376–77 for information on evaluating sources.)
3. Can you find any reference to opposing viewpoints in Glasser's essay? How, if at all, does his treatment of alternative perspectives on the issue affect the persuasiveness of his argument?
4. **Other Methods** In paragraphs 8–10, Glasser uses cause-and-effect analysis (Chapter 12) to explain how imprisonment can take away convicts' voting rights. What, then, are the political consequences of targeting racial minorities for drug arrests? How does this analysis further Glasser's argument against current law-enforcement practices?

Language

1. How does Glasser's tone help convey the "special outrage" (paragraph 11) he feels about liberals' failure to oppose drug laws more aggressively? Point out three or four examples of language that establishes that mood.
2. Glasser uses several difficult words, many of which appear in the vocabulary list. He also avoids use of the first-person *I* beyond his introductory paragraphs. How do his diction and point of view relate to his purpose and audience?
3. What is the effect of the question that closes the essay?

Writing Topics

1. **Journal to Essay**   Starting from your journal notes (p. 355), write an argument in favor of changing the existing laws on the drug you have chosen. Make sure to present both sides of the argument and demonstrate why your side makes more sense.
2. Using the library or the Internet, research a political lobbying organization that is concerned with the war on drugs, such as the Drug Policy Alliance, the Sentencing Project, or DARE. In an essay summarize the global vision the organization outlines in its mission statement, which may include goals met to date as well as plans for the future. Then discuss whether you agree with the organization's assessment of current drug issues, its proposed solutions, and its methods for achieving those solutions. (You may need to narrow this discussion to a particular issue.)
3. **Cultural Considerations**   Glasser writes that with the exception of drug-enforcement practices that target minorities, "no legalized racial discrimination remains, and certainly no new forms of legalized skin-color subjugation have arisen" in the United States (paragraph 3). What do you think of this statement? Do you agree with Glasser, or can you think of other forms of racial discrimination that are built into current government policies? And to what extent does it matter whether discrimination is legal or not? Write an essay in which you examine the state of racial discrimination in contemporary American politics or culture. You may wish to think broadly about this issue, but bring your essay down to earth by focusing on a specific form of discrimination—perhaps one that you've experienced or witnessed in your own life.
4. **Connections**   Unlike Glasser, James R. McDonough, the author of the next essay ("Critics Scapegoat the Antidrug Laws") is strongly in favor of the war on drugs. On what major points do the authors agree and disagree? How do the tones of the two essays compare? Does either writer seem more convinced of being in the right? Which essay do you find more convincing, and why?

*I oppose intrusions of the state into the private realm—as in abortion,
sodomy, prostitution, pornography, drug use, or suicide, all of which I
would strongly defend as matters of free choice in a representative
democracy.*
　　　　　　　　　　　　　　　　　　　　　　　　　—Camille Paglia

*To punish drug takers is like a drunk striking the bleary face it sees in the
mirror. Drugs will not be brought under control until society itself changes.*
　　　　　　　　　　　　　　　　　　　　　　　　　—Brian Inglis

*Let us not forget who we are. Drug abuse is a repudiation of everything
America is.*
　　　　　　　　　　　　　　　　　　　　　　　　　—Ronald Reagan

Journal Response　In a journal entry, comment on one example of an addictive substance, such as cocaine, heroin, tobacco, alcohol, or caffeine. Who uses this substance, and why? How does it affect the user? What effects, if any, does it have on those who do not use it? Does society condone its use or forbid it? Why?

———————— **James R. McDonough** ————————

*Born in 1946 in New York City, retired Lieutenant Colonel James R.
McDonough attended Brooklyn Polytechnic Institute and the US Military Academy at West Point, earned a Purple Heart along with several other medals as a
troop leader in the Vietnam War, and went on to receive a master's degree in
political science at the Massachusetts Institute of Technology. During a full career as an officer in the US Army, McDonough served in Europe, Africa, Korea,
and Bosnia; taught at West Point; and advised the Defense Nuclear Agency and
the US State Department. The author of several publications for the military,
including* National Compulsory Service *and* Text on International Relations
(both 1977), McDonough has also published the memoir Platoon Leader *(1985)
and two novels,* The Defense of Hill 781 *(1988) and* The Limits of Glory *(1991).
As director of strategy for the Office of National Drug Control Policy from
1996 to 1999, McDonough influenced many laws that make up the country's
ongoing war on drugs. He served as director of Florida's Office of Drug Control from 1999 to 2006 and is currently secretary of the Florida Department of
Corrections.*

CRITICS SCAPEGOAT THE ANTIDRUG LAWS

A former drug-enforcement official himself, McDonough strongly supports the war on drugs. As he sees it, drug abuse is not a personal issue but a major social problem that needs to be resolved. In this essay, first published in 2003 in the conservative current events magazine Insight, *McDonough explains why drug laws are not only reasonable but necessary.*

An oft-repeated mantra of both the liberal left and the far right is that   1 antidrug laws do greater harm to society than illicit drugs. To defend this claim, they cite high rates of incarceration in the United States compared with more drug-tolerant societies. In this bumper-sticker vernacular, the drug war in the United States has created an "incarceration nation."

But is it true? Certainly rates of incarceration in the United States   2 are up (and crime is down). Do harsh antidrug laws drive up the numbers? Are the laws causing more harm than the drugs themselves? These are questions worth exploring, especially if their presumptive outcome is to change policy by, say, decriminalizing drug use....

In essence, the advocates of decriminalization of illegal drug use   3 assert that incarceration rates are increasing because of bad drug laws resulting from an inane drug war, most of whose victims otherwise are well-behaved citizens who happen to use illegal drugs. But that infraction alone, they say, has led directly to their arrest, prosecution and imprisonment, thereby attacking the public purse by fostering growth of the prison population.

Almost constant repetition of such assertions, unanswered by   4 voices challenging their validity, has resulted in the decriminalizers gaining many converts. This in turn has begotten yet stronger assertions: the drug war is racist (because the prison population is overrepresentative of minorities); major illegal drugs are benign (ecstasy is "therapeutic," "medical" marijuana is a "wonder" drug, etc.); policies are polarized as "either-or" options ("treatment not criminalization") instead of a search for balance between demand reduction and other law-enforcement programs; harm reduction (read: needle distribution, heroin-shooting "clinics," "safe drug-use" brochures, etc.) becomes the only "responsible" public policy on drugs.

But the central assertion, that drug laws are driving high prison 5
populations, begins to break down upon closer scrutiny. Consider these
numbers from the U.S. Bureau of Justice Statistics compilation, *Felony
Sentences in State Courts, 2000.* Across the United States, state courts
convicted about 924,700 adults of a felony in 2000. About one-third
of these (34.6 percent) were drug offenders. Of the total number of convicted felons for all charges, about one-third (32 percent) went straight
to probation. Some of these were rearrested for subsequent violations,
as were other probationers from past years. In the end 1,195,714 offenders entered state correctional facilities in 2000 for all categories
of felonies. Of that number, 21 percent were drug offenders. Seventy-
nine percent were imprisoned for other crimes.

Therefore, about one-fifth of those entering state prisons in 2000 6
were there for drug offenses. But drug offenses comprise a category
consisting of several different charges, of which possession is but one.
Also included are trafficking, delivery and manufacturing. Of those incarcerated for drug offenses only about one-fourth (27 percent) were
convicted of possession. One-fourth of one-fifth is 5 percent. Of that
small amount, 13 percent were incarcerated for marijuana possession,
meaning that in the end less than 1 percent (0.73 percent to be exact)
of all those incarcerated in state-level facilities were there for marijuana
possession. The data are similar in state after state. At the high end, the
rates stay under 2 percent. Alabama's rate, for example, was 1.72 percent. At the low end, it falls under one-tenth of 1 percent. Maryland's
rate, for example, was 0.08 percent. The rate among federal prisoners
is 0.27 percent.

If we consider cocaine possession, the rates of incarceration also 7
remain low — 2.75 percent for state inmates, 0.34 percent for federal.
The data, in short, present a far different picture from the one projected
by drug critics such as [Ethan] Nadelmann,[1] who decries the wanton
imprisonment of people whose offense is only the "sin of drug use."

But what of those who are behind bars for possession? Are they 8
not otherwise productive and contributing citizens whose only offense
was smoking a joint? If Florida's data are reflective of the other states
— and there is no reason why they should not be — the answer is no.
In early 2003, Florida had a total of 88 inmates in state prison for possession of marijuana out of an overall population of 75,236 (0.12 per-

[1] Ethan Nadelmann is the founder and executive director of the Drug Policy Alliance,
a lobbying group opposed to current drug laws. [Editor's note.]

cent). And of those 88, 40 (45 percent) had been in prison before. Of the remaining 48 who were in prison for the first time, 43 (90 percent) had prior probation sentences and the probation of all but four of them had been revoked at least once. Similar profiles appear for those in Florida prisons for cocaine possession (3.2 percent of the prison population in early 2003). They typically have extensive arrest histories for offenses ranging from burglary and prostitution to violent crimes such as armed robbery, sexual battery and aggravated assault. The overwhelming majority (70.2 percent) had been in prison before. Of those who had not been imprisoned previously, 90 percent had prior probation sentences and the supervision of 96 percent had been revoked at least once.

The notion that harsh drug laws are to blame for filling prisons to   9
the bursting point, therefore, appears to be dubious. Simultaneously, the proposition that drug laws do more harm than illegal drugs themselves falls into disarray even if we restrict our examination to the realm of drugs and crime, overlooking the extensive damage drug use causes to public health, family cohesion, the workplace and the community.

Law-enforcement officers routinely report that the majority (i.e.,   10
between 60 and 80 percent) of crime stems from a relationship to substance abuse, a view that the bulk of crimes are committed by people who are high, seeking ways to obtain money to get high or both. These observations are supported by the data. The national Arrests and Drug Abuse Monitoring (ADAM) program reports on drugs present in arrestees at the time of their arrest in various urban areas around the country. In 2000, more than 70 percent of people arrested in Atlanta had drugs in their system; 80 percent in New York City; 75 percent in Chicago; and so on. For all cities measured, the median was 64.2 percent. The results are equally disturbing for cocaine use alone, according to Department of Justice statistics for 2000. In Atlanta, 49 percent of those arrested tested positive for cocaine; in New York City, 49 percent; in Chicago, 37 percent. Moreover, more than one-fifth of all arrestees reviewed in 35 cities around the nation had more than one drug in their bodies at the time of their arrest, according to the National Household Survey on Drug Abuse.

If the correlation between drug use and criminality is high for adults,   11
the correlation between drug use and misbehavior among youth is equally high. For children ages 12 to 17, delinquency and marijuana use show a proportional relationship. The greater the frequency of marijuana use, the greater the incidents of cutting class, stealing, physically attack-

ing others and destroying other people's property. A youth who smoked marijuana six times in the last year was twice as likely physically to attack someone else than one who didn't smoke marijuana at all. A child who smoked marijuana six times a month in the last year was five times as likely to assault another than a child who did not smoke marijuana. Both delinquent and aggressive antisocial behavior were linked to marijuana use—the more marijuana, the worse the behavior.

Even more tragic is the suffering caused children by substance 12 abuse within their families. A survey of state child-welfare agencies by the National Committee to Prevent Child Abuse found substance abuse to be one of the top two problems exhibited by 81 percent of families reported for child maltreatment. Additional research found that chemical dependence is present in one-half of the families involved in the child-welfare system. In a report entitled *No Safe Haven: Children of Substance-Abusing Parents*, the National Center on Addiction and Substance Abuse at Columbia University estimates that substance abuse causes or contributes to seven of 10 cases of child maltreatment and puts the federal, state and local bill for dealing with it at $10 billion.

Are the drug laws, therefore, the root of a burgeoning prison pop- 13 ulation? And are the drug laws themselves a greater evil than the drugs themselves? The answer to the first question is a clear no. When we restricted our review to incarcerated felons, we found only about one-fifth of them were in prison for crimes related to drug laws. And even the minuscule proportion that were behind bars for possession seemed to have serious criminal records that indicate criminal behavior well beyond the possession charge for which they may have plea-bargained, and it is noteworthy that 95 percent of all convicted felons in state courts in 2000 pleaded guilty, according to the Bureau of Justice Statistics.

The answer to the second question also is no. Looking only at 14 crime and drugs, it is apparent that drugs drive crime. While it is true that no traffickers, dealers or manufacturers of drugs would be arrested if all drugs were legal, the same could be said of drunk drivers if drunken driving were legalized. Indeed, we could bring [the] prison population down to zero if there were no laws at all. But we do have laws, and for good reason. When we look beyond the crime driven by drugs and factor in the lost human potential, the family tragedies, massive health costs, business losses and neighborhood blights instigated by drug use, it is clear that the greater harm is in the drugs themselves, not in the laws that curtail their use.

Meaning

1. What two questions does McDonough seek to answer in this essay? Where does he state his thesis?
2. According to McDonough, what is the relationship between drug use and other crimes? Why is the relationship important?
3. Some of the following words may be new to you. Try to guess their meanings from the context of McDonough's essay. Test your guesses in a dictionary, and then use each new word in a sentence or two of your own.

mantra (1)	benign (4)	correlation (11)
vernacular (1)	decries (7)	burgeoning (13)
presumptive (2)	wanton (7)	blights (14)
fostering (3)	median (10)	instigated (14)

Purpose and Audience

1. For whom is McDonough writing? People who already favor drug law reform? People who think the laws are beneficial? Someone else? What does the author seem to assume about his readers?
2. Against whom is McDonough arguing? Why does he say it is necessary to debate them?
3. Why do you think McDonough wrote this essay? What does he hope to accomplish by making his argument?

Method and Structure

1. What kinds of evidence does the author provide? Where does it come from, and is it reliable and convincing? Why, or why not? (See pp. 376–77 for information on evaluating sources.)
2. McDonough suggests that some of his opponents' arguments are based on faulty reasoning. What logical fallacies does he implicitly or explicitly identify? Does McDonough lapse into any logical fallacies himself? If so, where?
3. Analyze the organization of McDonough's argument. Which of his opponents' major points does he call into question? Where does he introduce new points? How does he use his introduction and conclusion to frame the debate?
4. **Other Methods** McDonough's argument draws on several methods of development, including division or analysis (Chapter 7), classification (Chapter 8), and cause-and-effect analysis (Chapter 12). Locate one instance of each of these methods. How does using them help the author to support his points?

Language

1. How would you describe McDonough's attitude toward his subject? What is the tone of the last paragraph in particular?
2. McDonough puts quotation marks around many of the words he uses to describe his opponents' position on illegal drugs (see, for instance, paragraph 4). What is the purpose of these quotation marks? What is their effect?
3. What is the difference between the decriminalization (paragraphs 2, 3, and 4) and the legalization (14) of drugs? Does McDonough distinguish between the two?

Writing Topics

1. **Journal to Essay** Take off from the comments you made in your journal entry (p. 361) to write an essay about drug abuse. Do you regard drug use or addiction as a critical problem? Do you believe that the government is taking adequate steps to protect society from users and dealers? Do you believe that individuals have the right to indulge in whatever mind-altering substances they choose? Why are some addictive substances socially acceptable while others are forbidden by law? Who, if anybody, is harmed by drugs? Your essay may be, but need not be, an argument: that is, you could explain your answer to any of these questions or argue a specific point. Either way, use examples and details to support your ideas.
2. McDonough asserts in paragraph 11 that youths who smoke marijuana tend to be more violent than those who do not. At your library or video store, try to find *Reefer Madness*, a film made in 1936 that shows middle-class teenagers descending from uncontrollable laughter to murder after smoking marijuana. What tactics does the film use to persuade viewers of the dangers of marijuana? What assumptions does it make? Write an essay analyzing the film as a component of a decades-long campaign against drugs. Do you see any parallels between the movie's approach and McDonough's? Can either work be classified as propaganda? Why, or why not?
3. **Cultural Considerations** Think of a drug that is or was illegal in the United States but is legal in another country. An example is hashish, which is legal in the Netherlands but not in this country, or absinthe, a hallucinogenic liqueur that is available in France but banned here. Do some research on the drug and the debates surrounding it. Can the differences in acceptance be accounted for by different cultural contexts in the two countries? Did scientific studies in the two countries yield different results? Is there a historical explanation? Write an essay in which you compare and contrast attitudes toward the drug in the two countries, and try to explain why the authorities in those countries came to different conclusions about its legality.

4. **Connections**   Both McDonough and Ira Glasser, in "Drug Busts = Jim Crow" (p. 355), use statistics from published sources to support their arguments. But there seems to be discrepancy in their data. Both writers state that 21 percent of state prisoners are drug offenders (see paragraph 5 in both essays); but while McDonough asserts that only 13 percent of jailed drug offenders were convicted for possession of marijuana (6), Glasser claims that possession of marijuana accounts for nearly half of all drug arrests (5). What might explain the apparent contradiction in these numbers? Take a close look at the use of statistics in both essays, considering the sources from which they were obtained, the authors' reasons for citing them, and the way each author frames the information. Is either author guilty of misrepresentation, or are there subtle differences in how they define their terms? What does the difference in their numbers tell you about the objectivity of statistics? Are all numerical data automatically authoritative, or can writers manipulate numbers to serve their purposes? Explain your answer in an essay, citing examples from both writers' arguments. If time allows, you might want to look up the sources they cite to check their figures yourself.

WRITING WITH THE METHOD
Argument and Persuasion

Choose one of the following statements, or any other statement they suggest, and support *or* refute it in an argumentative essay. The statement you decide on should concern a topic you care about so that argument is a means of convincing readers to accept an idea, not an end in itself.

MEDIA

1. Pornographic magazines and films should be banned.
2. Violence and sex should be banned from television.
3. Advertisements for consumer products (or political candidates) should be recognized as serving useful purposes.
4. Recordings of popular music should be specially labeled if their lyrics contain violent or sexual references.

SPORTS

5. Professional athletes should not be allowed to compete in the Olympics.
6. Professional athletes are overpaid for their work.
7. The school's costly athletic programs should be eliminated in favor of improving the academic curriculum.

HEALTH AND TECHNOLOGY

8. People should have the right to choose when to die without interference from the government or the medical community.
9. Private automobiles should be restricted in cities.
10. Laboratory experiments on dogs, cats, and primates should be banned.
11. Smoking should be banned in all public places, including outdoors in congested places.

EDUCATION

12. Students caught in any form of academic cheating should be expelled.
13. Students should not be granted high-school diplomas until they can demonstrate reasonable competence in writing and mathematics.
14. Like high-school textbooks, college textbooks should be purchased by the school and loaned to students for the duration of a course.

SOCIAL AND POLITICAL ISSUES

15. The elderly are entitled to unlimited free medical care.
16. Private institutions should have the right to make rules that would be unconstitutional outside those institutions.
17. Children should be able to sue their parents for negligence or abuse.
18. A citizen should be able to buy and keep a handgun for protection without having to register it.
19. When adopted children turn eighteen, they should have free access to information about their birth parents.

WRITING ABOUT THE THEME
Debating Law and Order

1. Several of the essays in this chapter discuss crimes committed by young adults, yet the authors write from very different perspectives with widely varied purposes. Jeremy Steben (p. 336), for instance, takes a sarcastic tone in complaining that authority figures abuse their power over high-school students, while Anna Quindlen (p. 343) takes an earnest tone in urging authority figures to do more to protect teenagers. Similarly, Wilbert Rideau (p. 349) argues that people shouldn't have to spend their lives paying for the "dumb, impulsive choices" (paragraph 1) of their youth, while James R. McDonough (p. 361) suggests that young drug offenders aren't punished harshly enough. Think of an illegal or dangerous behavior typical of teenagers or young adults and write an essay that argues your position on how legal authorities should respond to it. For instance, you might write about underage drinking, reckless driving, or downloading music without paying for it. How harshly should such behavior be punished, if at all? In your essay, be sure to consider the potential consequences of both the behavior and the response, and to support your opinion with plenty of examples and details to explain your reasons.

2. Many of the authors in this chapter disagree on the success and failure of prison in American society. Wilbert Rideau, for instance, argues that long prison terms for one-time offenders are both ineffective and counterproductive, and Ira Glasser (p. 355) claims that prison sentences for drug arrests have reinstituted legalized racial segregation. Martin Luther King Jr. (p. 329), advocating civil disobedience from his prison cell, and David Lindorff, examining the jury selection process (p. 328), both suggest that incarceration is often unjust. James R. McDonough, in contrast, believes that jail time is the best way to prevent drug-related crimes. Write an essay in which you defend or propose a reform to the American penal system. In your essay, explain what about prison does or doesn't work, what should change, how that change should be effected, and what the outcome might be if your reform was put into effect. (If you don't see a need for reform, write an essay explaining why reform advocates such as Rideau and Glasser are wrong to seek a change.)

3. Most of the topics chosen by the writers in this chapter—miscarriage of justice, jury selection, police profiling, mental illness, prison sentencing, and drug laws—are concerned to some extent with crime prevention and public safety. Select the topic that you think is the most important for society to focus on. (You may pick a topic discussed in this chapter or identify one of your own choosing.) Predict the outcome, twenty or thirty years from now, if steps are not taken to adequately address this issue. Describe the best way to deal with the controversy surrounding the problem you have chosen.

Appendix

WORKING WITH SOURCES

Writing is a means of communicating, a conversation between writers and readers—and between writers and other writers. Finding out what others have said about a subject, or looking for information to support and develop your thesis, is a natural part of the composing process.

A **source** is any work that you draw on for ideas or evidence in the course of writing your essay. If you are analyzing or responding to a work—such as an essay in this book or an advertisement—you may need to summarize, paraphrase, and quote passages from the work to give your readers a clear understanding of both your subject and your interpretation of it. In many instances, you will also want to do some research to bolster your evidence or add support to your interpretation of a subject. In either case, the guidelines in this appendix will help you to use the work of others effectively in your own writing.

WRITING ABOUT READINGS

Many of the writing assignments that follow the readings in this book ask you to respond directly to an essay or to write about it in relation to one or more other essays—to analyze two writers' approaches, to compare several writers' ideas about a subject, or to use the ideas in one reading to investigate the meanings of another. The same will be true of much writing you do throughout college, whether you are examining literary works, psychological theories, business case studies, historical documents, or lesson plans.

In some academic writing, you'll be able to use an idea in a selection as a springboard for an essay about your own opinions or experiences, as Grace Patterson does in her response to Barbara Lazear Ascher's writing in Chapter 3 (p. 41). However, much academic writing requires you to write *about* one or more readings: you analyze the material (see Chapter 7), and you synthesize, or recombine, the elements of that analysis to support an original idea of your own (see pp. 377–81). Your goal is not to report what other writers have said, but to think critically about what they have said and how they have said it (see Chapter 1) in a quest to draw your own conclusions about the subject.

When writing about reading, always assume that readers do not have the work in front of them, even when it's been assigned or discussed in class. Refer to the writer's ideas directly, and draw on evidence from the reading to support your conclusions. Use summary, paraphrase, and quotation (see pp. 378–80) to give readers a sense of the work, a clear picture of the elements that you are responding to, and a measured understanding of how those elements contribute to your thesis.

USING RESEARCH TO SUPPORT A THESIS

Often, when you draft an essay, you'll discover that you need more information to clarify part of your subject or to develop a few of your points more fully. This was the case for student writer Rachel Hannon, whose essay "How to Donate Plasma and Save More Lives" appears in Chapter 9 (p. 203). Upon reviewing an early draft of her essay, Hannon realized that her readers might not understand what blood plasma is. Unsure herself, she checked the American National Red Cross Web site, found exactly what she needed, and added a short explanatory paragraph to her draft. The entire research project took all of fifteen minutes.

Other times, you'll want to conduct more extensive research—for instance, when you need several examples to develop your draft, when you are troubled by conflicting assertions in essays you're comparing, or when you want to include a few expert opinions to support your argument. Shafeeq Sadiq, whose student essay appears in Chapter 7

(p. 155), chose to research current ads to build his argument that advertisers use racist and sexist tactics to sell their products. Tae Andrews, whose essay appears later in this Appendix (p. 396), sought out the work of experts to add credibility to his critique of entertainment media. Because even a little outside material can contribute compelling and informative support for an essay, many of the writing assignments in this book ask you to conduct a similar level of research to find supporting information. This section explains the basics of researching sources and using what you find responsibly and correctly.

Finding Sources

You have two basic options for locating research sources: the library and the Internet. Although both can be good sources of information, in general you should prefer printed sources or information located through your library's electronic research portals (such as subject directories and databases) over material you might pull up with a popular Web search engine such as Google. The material you reach through your library is more likely to have gone through an editorial review process designed to ensure that the information is accurate, reliable, and accepted by experts in the field. Material on the open Internet, in contrast, could have been written and posted by just about anybody, leaving plenty of room for doubt. The exception is printed material that has been uploaded to the Web, such as magazine and newspaper content, although you should check that the entity responsible for posting the material is trustworthy (see the next section, "Evaluating Sources").

When you're looking for sources, never be shy about asking librarians for help. These information professionals are eager to show you how to use the library's resources and to help you track down whatever you need. Make a point of familiarizing yourself with the most useful basic research tools.

- *Subject directories* organize material on the Web into categories. As noted above, the open Internet is riskier than the library for research, but a good directory can be a helpful starting point because it can show the broad dimensions of a subject and help you narrow your topic. The best directories are those that have been compiled by librarians, particularly the Librarians' Internet Index (*http://www.lii.org*) and directories created for individual colleges (check your library's home page).

- *Library catalogs* offer a comprehensive listing of the printed materials (books, magazines, newspapers, reference works, and the like) housed in a library. Most college library catalogs are computerized, which means you can plug in a search term — subject keyword, author, or title, for instance — and pull up a list of what the library has. Most colleges also belong to consortiums that let you search the holdings of related libraries and arrange for interlibrary loan (allow plenty of time to arrange for transfers).
- *Periodical indexes* provide listings of the articles in thousands of magazines, scholarly journals, and newspapers. Some indexes are available as electronic subscription services, such as EBSCO and ProQuest, that can be accessed from the library or a remote location (such as a home computer with an Internet connection). Often a database will provide full-text copies of at least some of the articles located in a search; in other cases you will need to use the information listed in the citation to track down the relevant issue on the library shelves.

Evaluating Sources

When you read a written work for an assignment, you read it critically, digging beneath the surface of the words to tease out the author's intentions and analyze the author's use of evidence (see Chapter 1). The same is true when you use outside sources to support your own ideas. You don't want to weaken your essay by drawing on unreliable information or repeating overly biased opinions.

Luckily, you need not read everything you find as closely as you would a reading assignment. Instead, you can scan potential sources to see how well they satisfy the following criteria:

- *Is the source relevant?* Obviously, you should focus on sources that are directly related to your subject, but pay attention as well to the format of documents you find. A summary or abstract that you locate in a database search is not a relevant source, nor is an excerpt from an article or book posted on a Web site. To use information you find in incomplete sources such as these, you'll need to use the publication information to find a copy of the full document in its original form.
- *How current is the information?* In most cases, the more recently your source was published or updated, the better.
- *Are you looking at a primary or a secondary source?* A primary source is an original document written by a creator or an eyewit-

ness: for instance, a short story, a lab report, or a letter describing an event. A secondary source is a writer's interpretation of a primary source or sources: a literary analysis, a summary of recent scientific discoveries, or a historian's explanation of an event. While secondary sources can be very helpful in providing factual data and general overviews of a subject, primary sources usually provide more valuable, detailed information.

- *What is the author's purpose, and who is the intended audience?* Consider, for instance, whether a source is meant to provide information, argue a point, or sell a product. Material written for general readers will usually be easier to understand but less detailed than something written for an audience of specialists. When you're looking at a Web site, the URL can give you a sense of the purpose of the source: sites ending in *.com* (commercial) are generally created to sell, market, or entertain; sites ending in *.gov* (government), *.net* (network), or *.org* (nonprofit organization) more often exist to provide information.

- *Is the author reliable?* Determine not only who wrote the material but also the author's qualifications for writing on the subject. Learning about the author is relatively easy with most printed sources, which generally provide biographical notes on authors. But you may have to do some detective work to figure out who created or posted an online source. Detective work may be needed as well to discover any bias that might weaken the credibility of a print or online author.

- *How does the author use evidence?* Unreliable writers make assertions without supporting evidence. Reliable writers provide detailed evidence for their ideas, distinguish between facts and opinions, acknowledge opposing viewpoints, and cite their sources. Keep in mind that evidence can be faulty or misused. If something gives you pause, check one or two related sources to see if you can verify the information. If you find that similar evidence used by other writers conflicts with the information in your source, you may have good reason to doubt that writer's credibility.

Once you've determined that a source is worth using, the checklist for critical reading on page 6 can help you to examine it more closely.

SYNTHESIZING SOURCE MATERIAL

When you bring information and ideas from outside sources into your writing, your goal is to develop and support your own thesis, not to create a patchwork of facts and quotations from other writers. It can be tempting to string together materials from your sources and to think that they speak for themselves — or for you — but the practice always leads to weak essays. Aim instead for **synthesis**, weaving the elements into a new whole: gather related information and ideas from your sources, then recombine them to support an idea of your own making. To synthesize, you'll usually do better to complete a first draft without relying on your research, then turn to your sources for a handful of summaries, paraphrases, and quotations that support your points. Always strive to maintain your own voice when you're writing.

Summarizing

A **summary** is a condensed statement, *in your own words*, of the main meaning of a longer work. Summaries omit supporting details and examples to focus on the original author's thesis. You can find short summaries of essays throughout this book in the sections "A Note on Thematic Connections," which appear in Chapters 4–13. For example:

> Langston Hughes pinpoints the moment during a church revival when he lost his faith (97–99).

> Perri Klass's essay grapples with why doctors use peculiar and often cruel jargon and how it affects them (130–33).

Notice that each summary names the author of the work being summarized and provides page numbers; it also refrains from using any of the original author's language.

Summarizing is one of the most effective ways to bring the ideas of others into your writing without losing your voice or bogging down your essay with unnecessary details. Depending on the length of the original work and your reasons for using it, your summary might be a single sentence or paragraph; keep it as short as possible — generally no longer than 10 percent of the original. If you're responding to a short essay, for example, a handful of sentences will usually be enough to distill its meaning.

Paraphrasing

A **paraphrase** is a restatement, again *in your own words*, of a short passage from another writer's work. While summarizing makes it possible to explain someone else's main idea without repeating specifics, paraphrasing lets you incorporate important details that support your own main idea.

A paraphrase is about the same length as the original, but it does not use any of the other writer's unique words, phrasings, or sentence structures. Simply replacing a few words with synonyms won't suffice; in fact, that shortcut counts as plagiarism (see pp. 382–83). If you cannot avoid using some of the writer's language, put it in quotation marks. For example:

ORIGINAL PASSAGE   "Poverty is defined, in my system, by people not being able to cover the basic necessities in their lives. Indispensable medical care, nutrition, a place to live: all these essentials, for poor people, are often and chronically beyond reach. If a poor person needs $10 a day to make ends meet, often he or she only makes eight and a half." (Walter Mosley, "Show Me the Money," p. 188)

PARAPHRASE   As Walter Mosley sees it, poverty is a matter of inadequate resources. The poor have difficulty obtaining adequate health care, food, and shelter—things most of us take for granted—not because they have no income at all, but because the money they earn is not enough to cover these basic expenses (188).

ORIGINAL PASSAGE   "Wealth, in my definition, is when money is no longer an issue or a question. Wealthy people don't know how much money they have or how much they make. Their worth is gauged in property, natural resources and power, in doors they can go through and the way the law works." (Walter Mosley, "Show Me the Money," p. 188)

PARAPHRASE   Wealth, in contrast, is defined by Mosley as freedom. The rich don't have to worry about finances; indeed, their "property, natural resources and power" confer social and legal privileges far more significant than freely available cash (188).

Notice here, too, that a paraphrase identifies the original source and provides a page number. Even if the words are your own, the ideas are someone else's, and so they must be credited.

Quoting

Sometimes a writer's or speaker's exact words will be so well phrased or important to your own meaning that you will want to quote them. When you are responding to or analyzing passages in a written work, such as an essay or a novel, direct **quotations** will be essential evidence as you develop your points. Even when you are borrowing ideas from other writers, however, quoting can be useful if the author's original wording makes a strong impression that you want to share with your readers.

Be sparing in your use of quotations. Limit yourself to those lines of primary sources to which you're responding directly, and perhaps a handful of choice passages from secondary sources that would lose their punch or meaning if you paraphrased them. Quoting others too often will make you vanish as a writer, leaving your readers to wonder what *you* have to say and why they should care.

When you do use a quotation, be careful to copy the original words and punctuation exactly, and to identify clearly the boundaries and source of the quotation:

- Put *quotation marks* around all quoted material shorter than four typed lines.
- Use *block quotations* for quoted passages longer than four typed lines. Start the quotation on a new line and indent the whole passage ten spaces. Don't use quotation marks; the indenting shows that the material is quoted.
- Include a *parenthetical citation* that provides a page number for your source (see pp. 384–86). For short quotations, place the citation after the final quotation mark and before the period. For block quotations, place the citation after the final period.

You can make changes in quotations so that they fit the flow of your own sentences — say, by deleting a word or sentence that is not relevant to your purpose, or by inserting a word or punctuation mark to clarify meaning. However, such changes must be obvious:

- Use an *ellipsis*, or three spaced periods (. . .), to show a deletion.

    Stewart and Elizabeth Ewen have suggested that "for hard-working, ill-housed immigrants, . . . clothing offered one of the few avenues by which people could assume a sense of belonging" (156).

- Use *brackets* ([ ]) around any change or addition you make.

    Most fashion historians echo Thorstein Veblen's assertion that "members of each [social] stratum accept as their ideal of decency the scheme of life in vogue in the next higher stratum" (84).

For examples of the use and formatting of quotations, see the sample documented essay by Tae Andrews (p. 396).

Integrating

When you do incorporate material from outside sources, make a point to introduce every summary, paraphrase, or quotation and to specify why it's relevant to your thesis. You may know perfectly well what a particular piece of information or a quotation contributes to your essay, but your readers shouldn't have to guess why it's there or how it supports your point. At the same time, your readers shouldn't have to decipher where your thoughts end and someone else's thoughts begin. Three techniques are especially helpful in giving your readers the necessary guidance.

- *Use signal phrases to introduce summaries, paraphrases, and quotations.* A signal phrase names the author of the borrowed material and thus provides a transition between your idea and someone else's. If the information is relevant, you might also explain why the author is an authoritative source or name the article or book you're referring to. Here are some examples of signal phrases:

    As financial planner Zora Klyberg points out in the pamphlet *Start Saving for Retirement NOW* ...

    U.S. Census Bureau data reveal ...

    Not everyone agrees. Wilbert Rideau, for example, believes that ...

    Be careful to craft each signal phrase to reflect your reasons for including a source. Using the same signal phrase over and over (such as "According to so-and-so") does nothing to frame your sources and will frustrate your readers.

- *Mark the end of borrowed material with a parenthetical note identifying at least the page number of your source* (see pp. 384–86). The citation is required, and it makes clear that you've finished with the source and are returning to your own argument.

- *Follow up with a brief explanation of how the material supports your point.* To show that the borrowed material backs up your ideas, comment afterward on what it contributes to your essay. You might, for example, comment on the meaning of the borrowed material, dispute it, or summarize it in the context of a new idea. Such follow-ups are especially necessary after block quotations, which can distract readers from your thesis.

For examples of effective integration of source materials, see any of the documented student essays in this book: Grace Patterson's "A Rock and a Hard Place" (p. 53), Shafeeq Sadiq's "Racism and Sexism in Advertising" (p. 155), Rachel Hannon's "How to Donate Plasma and Save More Lives" (p. 203), and Tae Andrews's "Urban Neanderthals: The Damaging Effects of Media Stereotypes on Young African American Males" (p. 396).

AVOIDING PLAGIARISM

Claiming credit for writing that you didn't compose yourself is **pla-giarism**, a form of academic dishonesty that can carry serious con-sequences. Purchasing or copying whole essays—from the Internet or a friend, for instance—is the most obvious and dishonest form of plagiarism. But plagiarism is often unintentional, caused not by de-liberate cheating but by misunderstanding or sloppiness. It's impor-tant to be aware of the rules and responsibilities that come with using the work of others in your writing and to follow them as carefully as you can.

- *Take careful notes.* No matter what your system for researching—formal note cards, dedicated notebooks, photocopies, computer files—keep thorough and accurate records. It's all too easy to for-get, when you return to your notes, which words are your own and which ones are borrowed. If you copy down the exact words of a source, enclose them in quotation marks. If you paraphrase or sum-marize, make a note to remind yourself that the language is your own, and double-check that you haven't inadvertently picked up any of the original phrasing. (It's a good idea to keep a photocopy of the original for this purpose.) Always record full source infor-mation for any material you find, using the models on pages 387–95. Few things are more frustrating than having to redo your research at the last minute to fill in missing information.

- *Use electronic sources with care.* Just because something appears on the Internet doesn't mean you're free to use it however you wish. Any language or idea you find, regardless of where you find it, must be credited to its source. At the same time, resist the urge to cut and paste snippets from online sources directly into your working draft. Doing so may seem like a time-saver, but later on you won't be able to distinguish the borrowed text from your own words. Print electronic documents for your records, or at least save them as clearly labeled individual files.

- *Know the definition of* common knowledge. *Common knowledge* is general information that is so widely known or broadly accepted that it can't be traced to a particular writer. Verifiable facts that you can find in multiple sources—the date of a historic event, the weight of a chemical element, the population of a major city—are considered common knowledge and do not need to be credited. In contrast, original material that has been distributed widely—the lyrics to a popular song, a magazine article posted on the Web, a video uploaded to YouTube—remains the intellectual property of its creator and must be cited. Note, too, that even if a piece of information is common knowledge, the wording of that information is not; always put factual material into your own words.

- *Never include someone else's ideas in your writing without identifying the borrowed material and acknowledging its source.* Whether you quote directly or rephrase information in your own words, you must make it clear to readers when words and ideas are not your own. If you use another writer's exact words, enclose them in quotation marks and identify the source. If you summarize or paraphrase, clearly distinguish your ideas from the source author's with a signal phrase and a source citation. Then, at the end of your paper, list all your sources in a works-cited list (see the next section, "Documenting Sources").

When in doubt, err on the side of caution. Ask an instructor or librarian for help, or simply cite your sources for everything that you're not sure of. It's better to have too much documentation in your essay than not enough.

DOCUMENTING SOURCES (MLA STYLE)

The purpose of citing your sources is twofold: you acknowledge the sources that helped you, and you enable curious readers to verify and explore your information by looking it up themselves.

In your English and language classes, and in some other humanities as well, you will be expected to document your sources with the system outlined by the Modern Language Association in *MLA Handbook for Writers of Research Papers*, 6th ed., by Joseph Gibaldi (2003). MLA style provides a brief parenthetical citation for each use of a source within the body of the essay. Then at the end of the essay, a comprehensive list of works cited provides complete publication information for every source.

PARENTHETICAL TEXT CITATION

```
In the essay "The Box Man" Barbara Lazear Ascher says that
a homeless man who has chosen solitude can show the rest
of us how to "find ... a friend in our own voice" (11).
```

WORKS-CITED ENTRY

Ascher, Barbara Lazear. "The Box Man." The Compact
        Reader: Short Essays by Method and Theme. Ed. Jane
        E. Aaron. 8th ed. Boston: Bedford, 2008. 7-11.

Parenthetical Text Citations

Citations within the body of your essay include just enough information for readers to recognize the boundaries of borrowed material and
to locate the full citation in the works-cited list. Generally, they name
the author of a source and the page number on which you found the
information or idea cited.

To keep in-text citations unobtrusive, strive to make them as brief
as possible without sacrificing necessary information. The best way to
do this is to name the author of the source in a signal phrase, limiting
the parenthetical information to the page number. If you don't name
the author in a signal phrase, include the author's name in the parenthetical citation.

AUTHOR NAMED IN THE TEXT

Historian Thomas French notes that Mount Auburn Cemetery quickly became a popular leisure destination for
city residents and tourists (37).

AUTHOR NOT NAMED IN THE TEXT

Mount Auburn Cemetery quickly became a popular leisure
destination for city residents and tourists (French 37).

A work by multiple authors

If a source has two or three authors, list all of their names.

Some of the most successful organized tours in New York
bring visitors on guided walks or bus rides to locations that are featured in popular television shows
(Espinosa and Herbst 228).

In the case of four or more authors, you may list all of the names or
shorten the reference by naming the first author and following with "et
al." (Latin abbreviation for "and others"). Whichever option you
choose, use the same format for your works cited list (see p. 388).

As early as 1988, leading scholars cautioned against educators' dependence on computers, warning that technology is "accompanied by rapid change, instability, and general feelings of insecurity and isolation" (Ferrante, Hayman, Carlson, and Phillips 1).

As early as 1988, leading scholars cautioned against educators' dependence on computers, warning that technology is "accompanied by rapid change, instability, and general feelings of insecurity and isolation" (Ferrante et al. 1).

A work by a corporate or government author

For works written in the name of an organization, company, or government that doesn't list individual authors, treat the name of the group as the author.

The National Multiple Sclerosis Society reports that progressive neurological disorders damage the body in repeated but unpredictable intervals, forcing patients to adapt to new losses several times over (2).

Two or more works by the same author(s)

If your essay cites more than one work by the same author(s), include the title of the specific source within each citation. In the following examples, both works are by Fredey, who is named in the text.

Maura Fredey notes that most of the nurses at the Boston Home have been on staff for more than five years, and at least seven boast a quarter century or more of service ("21st Century Home" 26).

The home's high level of care includes not only medical, dental, and vision treatment as needed, says Fredey, but also round-the-clock nursing attention and extensive social and rehabilitative services ("Bridges" 13).

If the title is long, you may shorten it. (The complete titles for the articles cited above are "The 21st Century Home: How Technology Is Helping to Improve the Lives of Patients at the Boston Home" and "Bridges to Care: The Boston Home Reaches Out.")

An anonymous work

If the author of a work is unnamed (as is often the case in newspaper editorials and Web sites, for instance), include the title within the parentheses. You may shorten the title if it is long.

```
The population of Pass Christian, Mississippi, is less
than a third of what it was before Hurricane Katrina
("New Town Crier" 22).
```

An indirect source

To cite a direct quotation that you find in another writer's work, use the abbreviation "qtd. in" (for "quoted in") to indicate that you're not using the original source.

```
Elizabeth Cady Stanton was delighted that "all sorts of
new ideas [were] seething" among the transcendental
community's female residents (qtd. in Griffith 45).
```

An electronic source

Treat most electronic sources as you would any other source—cite the author's name if it is available, or cite the title if a work is anonymous. For electronic sources that number paragraphs instead of pages, insert a comma between the author's name and the abbreviation "par." (for "paragraph"). If no numbering is available, include the author's name only, either in a signal phrase or in parentheses.

```
One former teacher who successfully brought computers
into his classroom argues that to use new technologies
effectively, teachers need to become "side-by-side
learners" with their students (Rogers, par. 10).
```

```
Outback Steakhouse does not provide nutritional infor-
mation on its Web site, but the company does offer menu
suggestions for customers with dietary restrictions.
```

List of Works Cited

The works-cited list provides complete publication information for every source you refer to within your essay. Format the list as follows:

- Start the list on a new page following the conclusion of your essay.
- Center the title "Works Cited" (without quotation marks) at the top of the page.
- Double-space everything in the list.
- Alphabetize the entries by the authors' last names. If a work doesn't have a listed author, alphabetize it by the title, ignoring the initial words *a*, *an*, and *the*.
- For each entry, align the first line with the left margin and indent subsequent lines five spaces or one-half inch.

The elements of individual entries will vary somewhat, as shown in the models in this section. However, the basic content and formatting rules can be summarized in a few general guidelines:

- Start with the author's last name, followed by a comma and the author's first name. (For more than one author, list the names as they appear in the work, reversing the first author's name only.)
- Provide the full title of the work, with all major words capitalized. Underline the titles of books, periodicals, whole Web sites, and longer creative works such as plays or television series; put quotation marks around the titles of book chapters, periodical articles, pages on Web sites, and short creative works such as stories, poems, and song titles.
- Include complete publication information. At a minimum this includes city of publication, publisher, and date (for books); volume number, date, and inclusive page numbers (for periodicals); and access date and URL (for Web sites).
- Separate the elements of an entry (author, title, publication information) with periods.

BOOKS

A book by one author

Ehrenreich, Barbara. <u>Bait and Switch: The (Futile) Pursuit of the American Dream</u>. New York: Metropolitan, 2005.

A book by multiple authors

List all of the authors; if there are more than three authors, you may provide the first author's name followed by "et al." (Latin abbreviaton for "and others"). Whichever option you choose, use the same format for your in-text citations (see p. 384).

```
Cooper, Martha, and Joseph Sciorra. R.I.P.: Memorial
    Wall Art. London: Thames, 1994.
Ferrante, Reynolds, John Hayman, Mary Susan Carlson,
    and Harry Phillips. Planning for Microcomputers in
    Higher Education: Strategies for the Next Genera-
    tion. Washington, DC: Assn. for Study of Higher
    Educ., 1988.
Ferrante, Reynolds, et al. Planning for Microcomputers
    in Higher Education: Strategies for the Next Gener-
    ation. Washington, DC: Assn. for Study of Higher
    Educ., 1988.
```

A book by a corporate or government author

For books written in the name of an organization, company, or government that doesn't list individual authors, treat the name of the group as the author.

```
National Commission on Terrorist Attacks. The 9/11
    Commission Report: Final Report of the National
    Commission on Terrorist Attacks upon the United
    States. New York: Norton, 2004.
```

More than one work by the same author(s)

```
Pollan, Michael. The Omnivore's Dilemma: A Natural His-
    tory of Four Meals. New York: Penguin, 2006.
---. Second Nature: A Gardener's Education. New York:
    Grove, 1991.
```

Edition other than the first

```
Favazza, Armando R. Bodies under Siege: Self-Mutilation
    and Body Modification in Culture and Psychiatry.
    2nd ed. Baltimore: Johns Hopkins UP, 1996.
```

A book with an editor

Wheeler, Marjorie Spruill, ed. Votes for Women! The
    Woman Suffrage Movement in Tennessee, the South,
    and the Nation. Knoxville: U of Tennessee P, 1995.

A book with an author and an editor

Bellamy, Edward. Looking Backward: 2000-1887. Ed.
    Daniel H. Borus. Boston: Bedford, 1995.

An anthology

James, Rosemary, ed. My New Orleans: Ballads to the Big
    Easy by Her Sons, Daughters, and Lovers. New York:
    Touchstone, 2006.

Cite the whole anthology only when you are referring to the editor's
material or cross-referencing multiple selections that appear within it
(as shown below).

A selection from an anthology

List the work under the selection author's name. Include the page numbers for the entire selection at the end of the citation.

Early, Gerald. "Black Ball." The Compact Reader: Short
    Essays by Method and Theme. Ed. Jane E. Aaron.
    8th ed. Boston: Bedford, 2008. 312-15.

If you are citing two or more selections from the same anthology, you
can avoid unnecessary repetition by listing the anthology in its own
entry and cross-referencing it in the selection entries. Alphabetize each
entry separately.

Aaron, Jane E., ed. The Compact Reader: Short Essays
    by Method and Theme. 8th ed. Boston: Bedford,
    2008.

Hobby-Reichstein, Kaela. "Learning Race." Aaron 102-5.

Wong, Alaina. "China Doll." Aaron 251-54.

A section of a book

When referring to only part of a book (such as an introduction, fore-
word, or specific chapter), name the author and indicate the part of the
book you are citing, with page numbers.

> Ephron, Nora. "Parenting in Three Stages." I Feel Bad
>   about My Neck: And Other Thoughts on Being a Woman.
>   New York: Knopf, 2006. 54-64.
> Lipsitz, George. Foreword. Race Rebels: Culture, Poli-
>   tics, and the Black Working Class. By Robin D. G.
>   Kelley. New York: Free Press, 1996. xi-xiii.

A reference work

> "Social Security." The Encyclopedia Americana. 2006 ed.

PERIODICALS: JOURNALS, MAGAZINES, AND NEWSPAPERS

An article in a journal with continuous pagination

For many scholarly journals, all of the issues in a year are considered
a single volume: page numbers start at 1 in the first issue, with subsequent issues numbered consecutively, so that the first page of a Sep-
tember issue might be numbered 555. When citing an article from this
kind of journal, follow the journal title with the volume number, the
volume year in parentheses, a colon, and the page numbers for the
whole article.

> Douglas, Susan J. "The Turn Within: The Irony of Tech-
>   nology in a Globalized World." American Quarterly
>   58 (2006): 619-38.

An article in a journal that pages issues separately

When citing an article from a journal that starts each issue with page 1,
follow the volume number with a period and the issue number.

> Armstrong, Alan. "Arthur's Fall." Shakespeare Bulletin
>   24.1 (2006): 1-10.

An article in a monthly or bimonthly magazine

```
Rosin, Hanna. "Striking a Pose." Atlantic Dec. 2006:
    114-19.
```

An article in a weekly magazine

```
Ordoñez, Jennifer. "Baby Needs a New Pair of Shoes."
    Newsweek 14 May 2007: 50-54.
```

An article in a newspaper

Many newspapers appear in more than one edition, so you need to specify which edition you used ("New England ed." in the model below). Give the section label as part of the page number when the newspaper does the same ("A1" in the model). Otherwise, give the section after the edition (for example, "natl. ed., sec. 3: 7"). Cite an article that runs on nonconsecutive pages with the starting page number followed by a plus sign ("+").

```
Kanter, James, and Andrew C. Revkin. "Scientists Detail
    Climate Changes, Poles to Tropics." New York Times
    7 Apr. 2007, New England ed.: A1+.
```

A letter to the editor

```
Skinner, Briahnna. Letter. Boston Sunday Globe 8 Apr.
    2007: E8.
```

An unsigned article or editorial

```
"War Stories Told on a T-Shirt." Reader's Digest Feb.
    2007: 26.
"Time to Go Back to Government 101." Editorial. Salem
    Observer 12 Apr. 2007: A6.
```

ONLINE SOURCES

Cite sources you locate through an online database or on the Internet in much the same way as print materials, with the author (if any) and publication information. But online sources need additional information as well, usually the electronic address, or URL, and the date you accessed the source. This information enables readers to find the source. If the source has changed or disappeared, as can happen with online sources, the information at least tells readers what version you used. Place the access date and then the URL at the end of the entry, and enclose the URL in angle brackets. If you must break a long URL to fit, break it only after a slash and do not add a hyphen.

A work from a library subscription service

Start with the standard publication details, followed by the database name, the service name, the library name and location, the access date, and the URL of the database provider.

> al-Khalifa, Raya. "Cover-up: The New Black." The New
>   Statesman 23 Oct. 2006: 17. Academic Search
>   Premier. EBSCO. U of Massachusetts, Boston, Healey
>   Lib. 2 Dec. 2006 <http://www.epnet.com>.

An entire Web site

Start with the title of the site, followed by the name(s) of any editor(s), the date of publication or most recent update, the name of the sponsoring organization, the date you visited the site, and the URL. If any of this information is unavailable, include as much as you can find.

> The Martin Luther King, Jr., Papers Project. Ed. Clay-
>   borne Carson. Dec. 2006. The Martin Luther King,
>   Jr., Research and Education Institute, Stanford U.
>   8 Dec. 2006 <http://www.stanford.edu/group/King>.
> Urban Legends Reference Pages. Ed. Barbara Mikkelson
>   and David P. Mikkelson. 1995-2007. 14 Sept. 2007
>   <http://www.snopes.com>.

A short work from a Web site

> "Lets Talk Facts about College Students and Alcohol
>   Abuse." Healthyminds.org. 2006. American Psychi-
>   atric Assoc. 6 July 2007 <http://
>   www.healthyminds.org/factsheets/LTF-CollSAA.pdf>.

An online book

Include the standard details about the original publication (see pp. 387–90), followed by as much information about the Web version as you can locate (site title, editor, date of online publication, sponsor name), the date of access, and the URL.

> Lovecraft, H. P. The Dunwich Horror. 1928. Arkham, MA:
> Miskatonic UP, 2002. YankeeClassic.com. 2 Dec. 2006
> <http://www.yankeeclassic.com/miskatonic/library/
> stacks/literature/lovecraft/novellas/dunwich.htm>.

An article in an online scholarly journal

Start with the basic entry for an article in a print journal (see pp. 390–91), followed by the date of access and the URL. Provide whatever numbering the online version uses — pages, paragraphs, or sections. Omit numbers if the source doesn't use them.

> Cooper, Melinda. "The Unborn Born Again: Neo-Imperialism,
> the Evangelical Right, and the Culture of Life."
> Postmodern Culture 17.1 (2006): 42 pars. 2 Feb.
> 2007 <http://www3.iath.virginia.edu/pmc/
> current.issue/17.1cooper.html>.

An article in an online newspaper

> Hernandez, Daniel. "Year One of the Immigrant Rights
> Movement: Washington Drags Its Feet While the Rest
> of Society Adapts to Reality." Los Angeles Times
> 25 Mar. 2007. 28 Mar. 2007 <http://
> pqasb.pqarchiver.com/latimes/search.html>.

An article in an online magazine

> Dickinson, Debra J. "Not in My Backyard, Either." Salon
> 18 Dec. 2006. 7 Jan. 2007 <http://www.salon.com/
> opinion/feature/2006/12/18/Katrina/index.html>.

E-mail

Start with the name of the person who wrote the e-mail, use the subject line as the title, and follow with "E-mail to" and the name of the recipient (if you are the recipient, use "author" instead of your name). End with the date the e-mail was sent.

```
Rawls, Florence P. "Possible Perkins Connection."
    E-mail to author. 9 May 2006.
Stone, Martha. "Your Query re Cordelia Harmon." E-mail
    to Stephen Gallant. 12 July 2006.
```

OTHER SOURCES

An interview

```
Angelou, Maya. Interview with Lucinda Moore. Smithsonian
    34.1 (2003): 96-99.
Conti, Regina. Personal interview. 3 Nov. 2007.
```

A television or radio program

Include as much of the following as available: episode or segment title, program title, series title, network, local station, broadcast date. Include the name of the director ("Dir."), performers ("Perf."), narrator ("Narr."), or host ("Host") if such information is significant.

```
"Pole to Pole." Planet Earth. Discovery Channel. 25 Mar.
    2007.
"Tijuana's Drug Boom Reflects Mexico's New Problem."
    Narr. Lourdes Garcia-Navarro. All Things Consid-
    ered. Natl. Public Radio. WEVH, Plymouth, NH.
    16 Oct. 2006.
```

A sound recording

```
James, Etta. "Sugar on the Floor." Live from San Fran-
    cisco. On the Spot-Private, 1994.
Pink Martini. Hey Eugene! Heinz Records, 2007.
```

A film, video, or DVD

Donnie Darko. Dir. Richard Kelly. Perf. Jake Gyllen-
haal, Jena Malone, Drew Barrymore, Noah Wyle,
Patrick Swayze, and Mary McDonnell. 2001. DVD. 20th
Century Fox, 2004.

A musical composition or work of art

Tchaikovsky, Peter Ilyich. The Nutcracker Suite, op. 71A.
Magritte, René. The Human Condition II. 1935. Collection Madame E. Happé-Lorge, Brussels. Surrealists
and Surrealism. By Gaëtan Picon. New York: Rizzoli,
1983. 145.

An advertisement

Eco-Drive by Citizen. Advertisement. Entertainment
Weekly 4 May 2007: 19.
Mastercard. Advertisement. NBC. WNKY, Bowling Green,
Ky. 16 Sept. 2007.
N95 by Nokia. Advertisement. 7 Apr. 2007 <http://
www.greatpockets.com>.

SAMPLE DOCUMENTED ESSAY

The sample essay included here was written by Tae Andrews, a student at the University of Notre Dame. Born in San Antonio, Texas,
in 1986, Andrews grew up in Long Island, Connecticut, and upstate
New York. He is majoring in American studies and was recently chosen to be a features editor for the *Observer*, Notre Dame's student
newspaper.

Andrews wrote "Urban Neanderthals" for his first-year composition course and revised it for *The Compact Reader*. He chose the topic,
he explains, because as both an aspiring journalist and "a multiracial
person … attending a heavily white campus," he was bothered by
stereotypes of young African American men in the media and felt that
"the issues at hand were (and are) pressing."

As you read his essay, notice how Andrews integrates primary and
secondary sources to develop and support his original ideas without relying on them to speak for him.

Urban Neanderthals:

The Damaging Effects of Media Stereotypes

on Young African American Males

"Bust a n*gga head, smack a ho, shoot the club
up." These lyrics from "You Don't Want No Drama,"
a popular rap song by Eightball and MJG, neatly
capture both cause and consequence of stereotyping young black men as violent, women-hating
thugs. By falsely portraying what it is to be an
African American man, lyrics such as these are
fueling a downward spiral for black male youth.
At the same time, they contribute to prejudice
and discrimination by reinforcing the idea that
black men are unintelligent, aggressive brutes.
This one-two punch is an extremely damaging
combination--both to African Americans and to
race relations in America. It is time for the
media to start paying more attention to how they
portray black men in fields that permeate youth
culture, especially in two areas where young
African American males are highly visible and
successful: hip-hop music and professional
sports. The misrepresentations are too prevalent,
and too dangerous, to ignore.

Let's look first at music. The songs and
videos created by artists such as 50 Cent, Dr. Dre,
and Snoop Dogg have built a youth culture centered
in violence and disrespect. These negative ideals
are perfectly represented in what I will term
"the Urban Neanderthal," the image of a "man"
projected by hip-hop culture. The Urban Neanderthal wears his pants low, turns his baseball cap
backward, and usually has diamond-encrusted
jewelry hanging from his neck. His value as a man
is determined by his ability to intimidate and
physically impose his will on others and to treat

Shocking quotation grabs readers' attention and sets up main idea; source identified in following sentence

Thesis statement

First major point: music

Andrews's own idea

women badly. The Urban Neanderthal uses his fists
to do his talking.

The danger posed by the Urban Neanderthal
lies not in teenagers' copying 50 Cent's look
but in their absorbing the social norms presented
in his lyrics. Those norms are not real but
invented: rappers, after all, don't use the names
on their birth certificates; they create stage
names and characters that they play onstage and
in their albums. However, as developmental psychologist L. Monique Ward has warned, this invented culture creates codes of conduct for young
black males and influences their self-image (284-
85). By presenting the edgy Urban Neanderthal as
the personification of black masculinity, the
media send out two messages with devastating
consequences. First, impressionable black adolescents, many of whom are surrounded by the brutal-
ity and abuse glorified by the Urban Neanderthal,
begin to fashion the idea that behaving violently
is what it means to be a man. Second, the white
community, observing this self-representation of
black manhood, develops the idea that all young
blacks are criminals and feels justified in its
prejudiced opinions of the black community.

Recording companies champion Urban Neanderthals like 50 Cent because controversy sells
records. Although an essential component of hip-
hop as a genre is its emphasis on social justice
through social commentary, the positive messages
have been lost in the mix. Take, for example, the
rapper Tupac Shakur. He will forever be remembered more for his bullet-ridden death than for
his songs about improving the ghettos and raising
the African American community out of poverty. In
his single "Changes," Shakur delivers a soapbox

Signal phrase names
author and provides
credentials

Citation for summary
identifies all pages
summarized

Andrews applies
idea from source to
his own idea

Andrews's own idea

sermon on the need for collective action from the
black community to end drug abuse and crime. In
an interlude during the song, he stops rapping
and speaks directly to his audience:

> We gotta make a change. It's time for
> us as a people to start makin' some
> changes. Let's change the way we eat,
> let's change the way we live, and let's
> change the way we treat each other. You
> see the old way wasn't working so it's
> on us to do what we gotta do, to survive.

Block format for long quotation

No citation needed because author and title are named in text and song lyrics don't have page numbers

Songs of social commentary from the street such
as Shakur's, however, are usually passed over by
record company marketers when they identify singles
for airwave play. In the effort to sell records
and boost ratings, labels and disc jockeys ignore
positive tracks in favor of harder, more provocative songs based on the image of the Urban Neanderthal. As a result, instead of hearing quality
songs of social uplift from artists such as the
Roots, John Legend, and Common, we hear 50 Cent
rapping about shooting people.

Follow-up comments explain significance of direct quotation

With hip-hop culture promoting the stereotype of the Urban Neanderthal so vigorously, perhaps it should be expected that sports journalists
would adopt the stereotype in their portrayals of
African Americans. Black quarterbacks in the
National Football League, for instance, are regularly portrayed as being somehow less intelligent
than their white counterparts, even when they're
being praised. Media scholar Toni Bruce points
out that Caucasian play-callers such as Peyton
Manning and Tom Brady are celebrated for their
leadership, sound decision making, and "knowledge
of the game"--skills generally attributed to
intelligence and hard work--while African Ameri-

Second major point: sports

Source provides a supporting point

Paraphrase integrates direct quotations

can quarterbacks such as Daunte Culpepper and
Steve McNair are highly touted for their "natural
athleticism" (861). This seeming compliment is
actually a subtle insult: by implying that black
quarterbacks' success is a result of natural
physical prowess, the media pointedly ignore the
hours of hard work and dedication black athletes
put into their training, reinforcing the long-
standing stereotype of the African American male
as a stupid brute blessed with tremendous
physical capability but little mental facility.

    An even more telling example of the Urban
Neanderthal in sports can be found in media coverage of professional basketball. More than any other
sport, professional basketball is composed mainly
of young African American athletes. Basketball is
also the professional sport most closely associated
with hip-hop culture. Many crossover promotions
feature rap artists--such as rapper Jay-Z--selling
basketball shoes, and players--such as Shaquille
O'Neal, Allen Iverson, and Ron Artest--releasing
rap albums. Not surprisingly, the National
Basketball Association (NBA) is portrayed by many
sportswriters as a league filled with lazy, overpaid
thugs--a league, that is, of Urban Neanderthals.

    One of the most common criticisms leveled at
the NBA is that pro athletes don't play "real"
basketball. This criticism reflects the same bias
directed at African American quarterbacks--
namely, that the black athletes of the NBA are
tremendously gifted physical specimens but lack
the intelligence to play a fundamentally sound
game. Consider the words of New York Times Magazine writer Michael Sokolove, who writes that the
NBA's "players are the best athletes in all of
pro sports--oversize, swift and agile--but

Margin notes:

Citation includes page number only because author is named in text

Follow-up comments elaborate on mean-ing of paraphrase

Andrews's own ob-servations and ideas

Andrews's own ob-servations and ideas

Signal phrase names author and provides credentials

weirdly they are also the first to have devolved
to a point where they can no longer play their
own game" (44). Sokolove goes on to criticize the
NBA for its emphasis on individual ability as
opposed to a team-first concept of basketball:
"The concept of being part of a team," he says,
"is one that seems to elude a great many [NBA]
players" (46). All of the players he praises for
breaking this mold and playing unselfish, technically skilled (in other words, intelligent)
basketball are either white or foreign-born. At
the same time, Sokolove makes no mention of the
predominantly African American Detroit Pistons,
who won the league championship in 2004 with a
commitment to team play. Again, we see a pointed
accusation through omission that black NBA players are selfish, unintelligent players who don't
work together and get by on pure athleticism
alone. Omissions such as this are as sharp a
slight as a direct criticism would be, perhaps
even more damaging for their subtlety.

        In both sports and hip-hop, African American
males have experienced success not seen in other
industries. Unfortunately, this success goes hand
in hand with unbalanced and biased depictions.
Media culture has embraced a stereotype of black
men--even successful black men--as violent,
aggressive, and ignorant brutes who regularly
engage in harmful behaviors and threaten society
at large. To undo the damage caused by this
stereotype, the media should focus more on positive examples of black manhood both in hip-hop
and in sports, such as music artist Kanye West or
Philadelphia Eagles quarterback Donovan McNabb.
There are plenty of better role models out there
than Urban Neanderthals.

Marginal notes:

Direct quotations used because exact words illustrate Andrews's point

Brackets indicate material inserted for clarity

Follow-up comments analyze quotations

Conclusion summarizes major points, restates thesis, and offers a solution

Works Cited

Bruce, Toni. "Marking the Boundaries of the
     'Normal' in Televised Sports: The Play-by-
     Play of Race." Media, Culture & Society 26
     (2004): 861-79. Academic Search Premier.
     EBSCO. Notre Dame U Lib. 4 Feb. 2005
     <http://www.epnet.com>.

Eightball and MJG. "You Don't Want No Drama."
     Living Legends. Bad Boy Entertainment, 2004.

Shakur, Tupac. "Changes." Greatest Hits. Inter-
     scope, 1998.

Sokolove, Michael. "Clang!" New York Times Maga-
     zine 13 Feb. 2005: 42-47.

Ward, L. Monique. "Wading through the Stereo-
     types: Positive and Negative Associations
     between Media Use and Black Adolescents'
     Conceptions of Self." Developmental Psychol-
     ogy 40 (2004): 284-94.

List of works cited starts on a new page

Journal article from a library subscription service

Sound recording

Sound recording

Article from a weekly print magazine

Article from a journal that paginates issues continuously

GLOSSARY

abstract and concrete words   An **abstract** word refers to an idea, quality, attitude, or state that we cannot perceive with our senses: *democracy, generosity, love, grief.* It conveys a general concept or impression. A **concrete** word, in contrast, refers to an object, person, place, or state that we can perceive with our senses: *lawn mower, teacher, Chicago, moaning.* Concrete words make writing specific and vivid. See also pp. 49–50, 61, and *general and specific words.*

allusion   A brief reference to a real or fictitious person, place, object, or event. An allusion can convey considerable meaning with few words, as when a writer describes a movie as "potentially this decade's *Star Wars*" to imply both that the movie is a space adventure and that it may be a blockbuster. But to be effective, the allusion must refer to something readers know well.

analysis (also called **division**)   The method of development in which a subject is separated into its elements or parts and then reassembled into a new whole. See Chapter 7 on division or analysis, p. 140.

anecdote   A brief narrative that recounts an episode from a person's experience. See, for instance, Peck, paragraph 1, p. 246. See also Chapter 5 on narration, p. 81.

argument   The form of writing that appeals to readers' reason and emotions in order to win agreement with a claim or to compel some action. This definition encompasses both argument in a narrower sense — the appeal to reason to win agreement — and persuasion — the appeal to emotion to compel action. See Chapter 13 on argument and persuasion, p. 320.

assertion   A debatable claim about a subject; the central idea of an argument.

audience   A writer's audience is the group of readers for whom a particular work is intended. To communicate effectively, the writer should estimate readers' knowledge of the subject, their interest in it, and their biases toward it and should then consider these needs and expectations in choosing what to say and how to say it. For further discussion of audience, see pp. 2, 12–13, and 18–19.

body   The part of an essay that develops the main idea. See also p. 26.

cause-and-effect analysis   The method of development in which occurrences are divided into their elements to find what made an event happen (its causes) and what the consequences were (its effects). See Chapter 12 on cause-and-effect analysis, p. 290.

chronological order   A pattern of organization in which events are arranged as they occurred over time, earliest to latest. Narratives usually follow a chronological order; see Chapter 5 on narration, p. 81.

classification   The method of development in which the members of a group are sorted into classes or subgroups according to shared characteristics. See Chapter 8 on classification, p. 168.

cliché An expression that has become tired from overuse and that therefore deadens rather than enlivens writing. Examples: *in over their heads, turn over a new leaf, march to a different drummer, as heavy as lead, as clear as a bell.* See also p. 51.

climactic order A pattern of organization in which elements — words, sentences, examples, ideas — are arranged in order of increasing importance or drama. See also p. 37.

coherence The quality of effective writing that comes from clear, logical connections among all the parts, so that the reader can follow the writer's thought process without difficulty. See also pp. 35–37 and 147–48.

colloquial language The language of conversation, including contractions *(don't, can't)* and informal words and expressions *(hot* for new or popular, *boss* for employer, *ad* for advertisement, *get away with it, flunk the exam).* Most dictionaries label such words and expressions *colloquial* or *informal.* Colloquial language is inappropriate when the writing situation demands precision and formality, as a college term paper or a business report usually does. But in other situations it can be used selectively to relax a piece of writing and reduce the distance between writer and reader. (See, for instance, Hughes, p. 97.) See also *diction.*

comparison and contrast The method of development in which the similarities and differences between subjects are examined. Comparison examines similarities and contrast examines differences, but the two are generally used together. See Chapter 10 on comparison and contrast, p. 229.

conclusions The endings of written works — the sentences that bring the writing to a close. A conclusion provides readers with a sense of completion, with a sense that the writer has finished. Sometimes the final point in the body of an essay may accomplish this purpose, especially if it is very important or dramatic (for instance, see Winik, p. 180). But usually a separate conclusion is needed to achieve completion. It may be a single sentence or several paragraphs, depending on the length and complexity of the piece of writing. And it may include one of the following, or a combination, depending on your subject and purpose:

- A summary of the main points of the essay (see McDonough, p. 365)
- A statement of the main idea of the essay, if it has not been stated before (see Klass, p. 133), or a restatement of the main idea incorporating information from the body of the essay (see Nadler, p. 273)
- A comment on the significance or implications of the subject (see Gilb, p. 69; Dillard, p. 94; Hobby-Reichstein, p. 105; and Fishman, p. 304)
- A call for reflection, support, or action (see Sadiq, p. 157; Mosley, p. 189; Alaimo and Koester, p. 309; and Glasser, p. 358)
- A prediction for the future (see Sullivan, p. 284 and Quindlen, p. 346)
- An example, anecdote, question, or quotation that reinforces the point of the essay (see Barry, p. 152; Brady, p. 279; and Rideau, p. 352)

Excluded from this list are several endings that should be avoided because they tend to weaken the overall effect of an essay: (1) an example, fact, or quotation that pertains to only part of the essay; (2) an apology for your ideas, for the quality of the writing, or for omissions; (3) an attempt to enhance the significance of the essay by overgeneralizing from its ideas and evidence; (4) a new idea that requires the support of an entirely different essay.

concrete words   See *abstract and concrete words.*

connotation and denotation   A word's **denotation** is its literal meaning: *famous* denotes the quality of being well known. A word's **connotations** are the associations or suggestions that go beyond its literal meaning: *notorious* denotes fame but also connotes sensational, even unfavorable, recognition. See also pp. 48–49.

contrast   See *comparison and contrast.*

critical reading   Reading that looks beneath the surface of a work, seeking to uncover both its substance and the writer's interpretation of the substance. See Chapter 1 on reading, especially pp. 3–6.

deductive reasoning   The method of reasoning that moves from the general to the specific. See Chapter 13 on argument and persuasion, especially pp. 324–26.

definition   An explanation of the meaning of a word. An extended definition may serve as the primary method of developing an essay. See Chapter 11 on definition, p. 260.

denotation   See *connotation and denotation.*

description   The form of writing that conveys the perceptions of the senses — sight, hearing, smell, taste, touch — to make a person, place, object, or state of mind vivid and concrete. See Chapter 4 on description, p. 55.

diction   The choice of words you make to achieve a purpose and make meaning clear. Effective diction conveys your meaning exactly, emphatically, and concisely, and it is appropriate to your intentions and audience. **Standard English**, the written language of educated native speakers, is expected in all writing for college, business and the professions, and publication. The vocabulary of standard English is large and varied, encompassing, for instance, both *comestibles* and *food* for edible things, both *paroxysm* and *fit* for a sudden seizure. In some writing situations, standard English may also include words and expressions typical of conversation (see *colloquial language*). But it excludes other levels of diction that only certain groups understand or find acceptable. Most dictionaries label expressions at these levels as follows:

- **Nonstandard**: words spoken among particular social groups, such as *ain't, them guys, hisself,* and *nowheres.*
- **Slang**: words that are usually short-lived and that may not be understood by all readers, such as *tanked* for drunk, *bread* for money, and *honcho* for one in charge.
- **Regional** or **dialect**: words spoken in a particular region but not in the country as a whole, such as *poke* for a sack or bag, *holler* for a hollow or small valley.
- **Obsolete**: words that have passed out of use, such as *cleam* for smear.

See also *connotation and denotation* and *style.*

division or analysis   See *analysis.*

documentation   A system of identifying your sources so that readers know which ideas are borrowed and can locate the original material themselves. Papers written for English and other humanities courses typically follow the MLA (Modern Language Association) documentation system, which requires brief parenthetical citations within the body of the essay and a comprehensive list of works cited at the end. See the Appendix, especially pp. 383–95.

dominant impression   The central idea or feeling conveyed by a description of a person, place, object, or state of mind. See Chapter 4 on description, especially p. 56.

effect   See *cause-and-effect analysis.*

emotional appeal   In argumentative and persuasive writing, the appeal to readers' values, beliefs, or feelings in order to win agreement or compel action. See pp. 322–23.

essay   A prose composition on a single nonfictional topic or idea. An essay usually reflects the personal experiences and opinions of the writer.

ethical appeal   In argumentative and persuasive writing, the sense of the writer's expertise and character projected by the reasonableness of the argument, the use and quality of evidence, and the tone. See p. 322.

evidence   The details, examples, facts, statistics, or expert opinions that support any general statement or claim. See pp. 324 and 329–31 on the use of evidence in argumentative writing, pp. 374–76 on finding evidence in sources, and pp. 383–95 on documenting researched evidence.

example   An instance or representative of a general group or an abstract concept or quality. One or more examples may serve as the primary method of developing an essay. See Chapter 6 on example, p. 111.

exposition   The form of writing that explains or informs. Most of the essays in this book are primarily expository, and some essays whose primary purpose is self-expression or persuasion employ exposition to clarify ideas.

fallacies   Flaws in reasoning that weaken or invalidate an argument. Some of the most common fallacies follow (the page numbers refer to further discussion in the text).

- **Hasty generalization,** leaping to a conclusion on the basis of inadequate or unrepresentative evidence: *Every one of the twelve students polled supports the change in the grading system, so the administration should implement it* (pp. 326–27).
- **Oversimplification,** overlooking or ignoring inconsistencies or complexities in evidence: *If the United States banned immigration, our unemployment problems would be solved* (pp. 293, 327).
- **Begging the question,** assuming the truth of a conclusion that has not been proved: *Acid rain does not do serious damage, so it is not a serious problem* (p. 327).
- **Ignoring the question,** shifting the argument away from the real issue: *A fine, churchgoing man like Charles Harold would make an excellent mayor* (p. 327).
- **Ad hominem** ("to the man") **argument,** attacking an opponent instead of the opponent's argument: *She is just a student, so we need not listen to her criticisms of foreign policy* (p. 327).
- **Either-or,** presenting only two alternatives when the choices are more numerous: *If you want to do well in college, you have to cheat a little* (p. 327).
- **Non sequitur** ("It does not follow"), deriving a wrong or illogical conclusion from stated premises: *Because students are actually in school, they should be the ones to determine our educational policies* (p. 328).
- **Post hoc** (from *post hoc, ergo propter hoc,* "after this, therefore because of this"), assuming that one thing caused another simply because it preceded the

other: *Two students left school in the week after the new policies were announced, proving that the policies will eventually cause a reduction in enrollments* (pp. 292–93, 328).

figures of speech   Expressions that imply meanings beyond or different from their literal meanings in order to achieve vividness or force. See p. 50 for discussion and examples of specific figures.

formal style   See *style.*

freewriting   A technique for discovering ideas for writing: writing for a fixed amount of time without stopping to reread or edit. See pp. 20–21.

general and specific words   A **general** word refers to a group or class: *car, mood, book.* A **specific** word refers to a particular member of a group or class: *Toyota, irritation, dictionary.* Usually, the more specific a word is, the more interesting and informative it will be for readers. See also pp. 49–50, p. 61, and *abstract and concrete words.*

generalization   A statement about a group or a class derived from knowledge of some or all of its members: for instance, *Dolphins can be trained to count* or *Television news rarely penetrates beneath the headlines.* The more instances the generalization is based on, the more accurate it is likely to be. A generalization is the result of inductive reasoning; see pp. 324–25.

hasty generalization   See *fallacies.*

hyperbole   Deliberate overstatement or exaggeration: *The desk provided an acre of work surface.* See also p. 50. (The opposite of hyperbole is understatement, discussed under *irony.*)

image   A verbal representation of sensory experience — that is, of something seen, heard, felt, tasted, or smelled. Images may be literal: *Snow stuck to her eyelashes; The red car sped past us.* Or they may be figures of speech: *Her eyelashes were snowy feathers; The car rocketed past us like a red missile.* (See pp. 49–50.) Through images, a writer touches the readers' experiences, thus sharpening meaning and adding immediacy. See also *abstract and concrete words.*

inductive reasoning   The method of reasoning that moves from the particular to the general. See Chapter 13 on argument and persuasion, especially pp. 324–25.

informal style   See *style.*

introductions   The openings of written works, the sentences that set the stage for what follows. An introduction to an essay identifies and restricts the subject while establishing the writer's attitude toward it. Accomplishing these purposes may require anything from a single sentence to several paragraphs, depending on the writer's purpose and how much readers need to know before they can begin to grasp the ideas in the essay. The introduction often includes a thesis sentence stating the main idea of the essay (see pp. 24–25). To set up the thesis sentence, or as a substitute for it, any of the following openings, or a combination, may be effective:

- Background on the subject that establishes a time or place or that provides essential information (see Gilb, p. 72; Gould, p. 176; Hannon, p. 203; McClain, p. 238; and Glasser, p. 355)
- An anecdote or other reference to the writer's experience that forecasts or illustrates the main idea or that explains what prompted the essay (see Dillard, p. 90; Peck, p. 245; and Brady, p. 277)

- An explanation of the significance of the subject (see Mosley, p. 186; Alaimo and Koester, p. 307; and Quindlen, p. 343)
- An outline of the situation or problem that the essay will address, perhaps using interesting facts or statistics (see Sadiq, p. 155; de Zengotita, p. 160; and Early, p. 312)
- A statement or quotation of an opinion that the writer will modify or disagree with (see Johnson, p. 124; Steben, p. 336; and McDonough, p. 361)
- An example, quotation, or question that reinforces the main idea (see Kessler, p. 119, and Klass, p. 130)

A good introduction does not mislead readers by exaggerating the significance of the subject or the essay, and it does not bore readers by saying more than is necessary. In addition, a good introduction avoids three openings that are always clumsy: (1) beginning with *The purpose of this essay is . . .* or something similar; (2) referring to the title of the essay in the first sentence, as in *This is not as hard as it looks* or *This is a serious problem*; and (3) starting too broadly or vaguely, as in *Ever since humans walked upright . . .* or *In today's world. . . .*

irony   In writing, irony is the use of words to suggest a meaning different from their literal meaning. Steben's "Small Town, Quiet Town, Safe Town" (p. 336) presents an ironic statement relying on reversal: he says the opposite of what he really means. But irony can also derive from understatement (saying less than is meant) or hyperbole (exaggeration). Irony can be witty, teasing, biting, or cruel. At its most humorless and heavily contemptuous, it becomes **sarcasm**: *Thanks a lot for telling Dad we stayed out all night; that was really bright of you.*

metaphor   A figure of speech that compares two unlike things by saying that one is the other: *Bright circles of ebony, her eyes smiled back at me.* See also p. 50.

narration   The form of writing that tells a story, relating a sequence of events. See Chapter 5 on narration, p. 81.

nonstandard English   See *diction*.

oversimplification   See *fallacies*.

paragraph   A group of related sentences, set off by an initial indentation, that develops an idea. By breaking continuous text into units, paragraphing helps the writer manage ideas and helps the reader follow those ideas. Each paragraph makes a distinct contribution to the main idea governing the entire piece of writing. The idea of the paragraph itself is often stated in a topic sentence (see pp. 33–34), and it is supported with sentences containing specific details, examples, and reasons. Like the larger piece of writing to which it contributes, the paragraph should be unified, coherent, and well developed. For examples of successful paragraphs, see the paragraph analyses in the introduction to each method of development (Chapters 4–13). See also pp. 33–34 and 268 (unity), pp. 26 and 147–48 (coherence), and pp. 38 and 174–75 (development).

parallelism   The use of similar grammatical forms for ideas of equal importance. Parallelism occurs within sentences: *The doctor recommends swimming, bicycling, or walking.* It also occurs among sentences: *Strumming her guitar, she made listeners feel her anger. Singing lines, she made listeners believe her pain.* See also p. 47.

paraphrase   A restatement — in your own words — of another writer's ideas. A paraphrase is about the same length as the original passage, but it does not repeat words, phrases, or sentence patterns. See also pp. 378–79.

personification   A figure of speech that gives human qualities to things or abstractions: *The bright day smirked at my bad mood.* See also p. 50.

persuasion   See *argument.*

plagiarism   The failure to identify and acknowledge the sources of words, information, or ideas that are not your own. Whether intentional or accidental, plagiarism is a serious offense and should always be avoided. See pp. 382–83.

point of view   The position of the writer in relation to the subject. In description, point of view depends on the writer's physical and psychological relation to the subject (see pp. 56–57). In narration, point of view depends on the writer's place in the story and on his or her relation to it in time (see p. 83). More broadly, point of view can also mean the writer's particular mental stance or attitude. For instance, an employee and an employer might have different points of view toward the employee's absenteeism or the employer's sick-leave policies.

premise   The generalization or assumption on which an argument is based. See *syllogism.*

process analysis   The method of development in which a sequence of actions with a specified result is divided into its component steps. See Chapter 9 on process analysis, p. 195.

pronoun   A word that refers to a noun or other pronoun: *Six days after King picked up his Nobel Peace Prize in Norway, he was jailed in Alabama.* The personal pronouns (the most common) are *I, you, he, she, it, we,* and *they.* See also pp. 35–36 (pronouns and coherence), pp. 57 and 83 (pronouns and point of view), and pp. 201–2 (consistency in pronouns).

proposition   A debatable claim about a subject; the central idea of an argument.

purpose   The reason for writing, the goal the writer wants to achieve. The purpose may be primarily to explain the subject so that readers understand it or see it in a new light; to convince readers to accept or reject an opinion or to take a certain action; to entertain readers with a humorous or exciting story; or to express the thoughts and emotions triggered by a revealing or instructive experience. The writer's purpose overlaps the main idea—the particular point being made about the subject. In effective writing, the two together direct and control every choice the writer makes. See also pp. 12–13 and 18–19, *thesis,* and *unity.*

quotation   The exact words of another writer or speaker, copied word for word and clearly identified. Short quotations are enclosed in quotation marks; longer quotations are set off from the text by indenting. See p. 380.

rational appeal   In argumentative and persuasive writing, the appeal to readers' rational faculties—to their ability to reason logically—in order to win agreement or compel action. See pp. 324–26.

repetition and restatement   The careful use of the same words or close parallels to clarify meaning and tie sentences together. See also pp. 35–36 and 147–48.

revision   The stage of the writing process devoted to "re-seeing" a draft, divided into fundamental changes in content and structure (revision) and more superficial changes in grammar, word choice, and the like (editing). See Chapter 3 on writing, p. 31.

rhetoric   The art of using words effectively to communicate with an audience, or the study of that art. To the ancient Greeks, rhetoric was the art of the *rhetor*—orator, or public speaker—and included the art of persuasion. Later the word shifted to mean elegant language, and a version of that meaning persists in today's occasional use of *rhetoric* to mean pretentious or hollow language, as in *Their argument was mere rhetoric.*

sarcasm　See *irony.*

satire　The combination of wit and criticism to mock or condemn human foolishness or evil. The intent of satire is to arouse readers to contempt or action, and thus it differs from comedy, which seeks simply to amuse. Much satire relies on irony—saying one thing but meaning another (see *irony*).

simile　A figure of speech that equates two unlike things using *like* or *as: The crowd was restless, like bees in a hive.* See also p. 50.

slang　See *diction.*

source　Any outside or researched material that helps to develop a writer's ideas. A source may be the subject of an essay, such as when you are writing about a reading in this book, or it may provide evidence to support a particular point. However a source is used, it must always be documented. See the Appendix on working with sources, p. 373.

spatial organization　A pattern of organization that views an object, scene, or person by paralleling the way we normally scan things—for instance, top to bottom or near to far. See also pp. 37 and 59.

specific words　See *general and specific words.*

Standard English　See *diction.*

style　The *way* something is said, as opposed to *what* is said. Style results primarily from a writer's characteristic word choices and sentence structures. A person's writing style, like his or her voice or manner of speaking, is distinctive. Style can also be viewed more broadly as ranging from formal to informal. A very formal style adheres strictly to the conventions of Standard English (see *diction*); tends toward long sentences with sophisticated structures; and relies on learned words, such as *malodorous* and *psychopathic.* A very informal style, in contrast, is more conversational (see *colloquial language*); tends toward short, uncomplicated sentences; and relies on words typical of casual speech, such as *smelly* or *crazy.* Among the writers represented in this book, Glasser (p. 355) writes quite formally, Hughes (p. 97) quite informally. The formality of style may often be modified to suit a particular audience or occasion: a college term paper, for instance, demands a more formal style than an essay narrating a personal experience. See also *tone.*

summary　A condensed version—in your own words—of the main idea of a longer work. A summary is much shorter than the original and leaves out most of the supporting details. See also p. 378.

syllogism　The basic form of deductive reasoning, in which a conclusion derives necessarily from proven or accepted premises. For example: *The roof always leaks when it rains* (the major premise). *It is raining* (the minor premise). *Therefore, the roof will leak* (the conclusion). See Chapter 13 on argument and persuasion, especially pp. 260–63.

symbol　A person, place, or thing that represents an abstract quality or concept. A red heart symbolizes love; the Golden Gate Bridge symbolizes San Francisco's dramatic beauty; a cross symbolizes Christianity.

synthesis　The practice of combining elements into a new whole. In writing, synthesis usually involves connecting related ideas from multiple sources to form an original idea of your own. See pp. 377–81.

thesis   The main idea of a piece of writing, to which all other ideas and details relate. The main idea is often stated in a **thesis sentence** (or sentences), which asserts something about the subject and conveys the writer's purpose. The thesis sentence is often included near the beginning of an essay. Even when the writer does not state the main idea and purpose, however, they govern all the ideas and details in the essay. See also pp. 11–12, pp. 22–24, and *unity*.

tone   The attitude toward the subject, and sometimes toward the audience and the writer's own self, expressed in choice of words and sentence structures as well as in what is said. Tone in writing is similar to tone of voice in speaking, from warm to serious, amused to angry, joyful to sorrowful, sympathetic to contemptuous. For examples of strong tone in writing, see Barry (p. 149), McClain (p. 238), Brady (p. 277), Peck (p. 245), and Steben (p. 336). See also pp. 38–39 and 334–35.

topic sentence   See *paragraph*.

transitions   Links between sentences and paragraphs that relate ideas and thus contribute to clarity and smoothness. Transitions may be sentences beginning paragraphs or brief paragraphs that shift the focus or introduce new ideas. They may also be words and phrases that signal and specify relationships. Some of these words and phrases—but by no means all—are listed here:

- **Space**: above, below, beyond, farther away, here, nearby, opposite, there, to the right
- **Time**: afterward, at last, earlier, later, meanwhile, simultaneously, soon, then
- **Illustration**: for example, for instance, specifically, that is
- **Comparison**: also, in the same way, likewise, similarly
- **Contrast**: but, even so, however, in contrast, on the contrary, still, yet
- **Addition or repetition**: again, also, finally, furthermore, in addition, moreover, next, that is
- **Cause or effect**: as a result, consequently, equally important, hence, then, therefore, thus
- **Summary or conclusion**: all in all, in brief, in conclusion, in short, in summary, therefore, thus
- **Intensification**: indeed, in fact, of course, truly

understatement   See *irony*.

unity   The quality of effective writing that occurs when all the parts relate to the main idea and contribute to the writer's purpose. See also pp. 33–35 and 268.

Acknowledgments (continued from page ii)

Joan Didion. "The Santa Ana." Excerpt from "Los Angeles Notebook" in *Slouching Towards Bethlehem* by Joan Didion. Copyright © 1966, 1968 and renewed 1996 by Joan Didion. Reprinted by permission of Farrar, Straus & Giroux, LLC.

Annie Dillard. Pages 44–49 from *An American Childhood* by Annie Dillard. Copyright © 1987 by Annie Dillard. Reprinted by permission of HarperCollins Publishers, Inc.

Gerald Early. "Black Ball." From *The New York Times*, March 1, 2006. Copyright © 2006 by The New York Times Company. Reprinted by permission.

Barbara Ehrenreich. Excerpt from "Evaluation" in *Nickel and Dimed: On (Not) Getting By in America* by Barbara Ehrenreich. Copyright © 2001 by Barbara Ehrenreich. Reprinted by permission of Henry Holt and Company, LLC.

Charles Fishman. "The Squeeze." From *The Wal-Mart Effect* by Charles Fishman. Copyright © 2006 by Charles Fishman. Used by permission of The Penguin Press, a division of Penguin Group (USA) Inc.

Atul Gawande. "The Central Line." From *Complications: A Surgeon's Notes on an Imperfect Science.* Copyright © 2002 by Atul Gawande. Reprinted by permission of Henry Holt and Company, LLC.

Dagoberto Gilb. "My Landlady's Yard." From *Gritos: Essays* by Dagoberto Gilb. Copyright © 2003 by Dagoberto Gilb. Reprinted by permission of the author.

Ira Glasser. "Drug Busts = Jim Crow." Reprinted with permission from the July 10, 2006, issue of *The Nation*. For subscription information, call 1-800-333-8536. Portions of each week's *Nation* magazine can be accessed at http://www.thenation.com.

Langston Hughes. "Salvation." From *The Big Sea* by Langston Hughes. Copyright © 1940 by Langston Hughes. Copyright renewed ©1968 by Arna Bontemps and George Houston Bass. Reprinted by permission of Hill and Wang, a division of Farrar, Straus and Giroux, LLC.

Kirk Johnson. "Today's Kids Are, Like, Killing the English Language." From *The New York Times*, August 9, 1998. Copyright © 1998 by The New York Times Company. Reprinted by permission.

Janet Jones. Excerpt from "Women in Motion" in *The New Our Bodies, Ourselves: A Book by and for Women* by the Boston Women's Health Book Collective. Copyright © 1992. Published by Touchstone, an imprint of Simon & Schuster, Inc. Reprinted by permission of Janet Jones.

Perri Klass. "She's Your Basic L.O.L. in N.A.D." From *A Not Entirely Benign Procedure* by Perri Klass. Copyright © 1987 by Perri Klass. Used by permission of G.P. Putnam's Sons, a division of Penguin Group (USA) Inc.

Leanita McClain. "The Middle-Class Black's Burden." From *A Foot in Each World: Essays and Articles* by Leanita McClain. Copyright © 1986 by Leanita McClain. Reprinted by permission of Northwestern University Press.

James R. McDonough. "Critics Scapegoat the Antidrug Laws." From *Insight on the News.* Copyright © November 11–24, 2003. Reprinted by permission of the author.

Jessica Mitford. "Embalming Mr. Jones." From *The American Way of Death* by Jessica Mitford. Copyright © 1963, 1978 by Jessica Mitford. Reprinted by permission of the Estate of Jessica Mitford. All rights reserved.

Walter Mosley. "Show Me the Money. " Reprinted with permission from the December 18, 2006, issue of *The Nation*. For subscription information, call 1-800-333-8536. Portions of each week's *Nation* magazine can be accessed at http://www.thenation.com.

Cheryl Peck. "Fatso." From *Revenge of the Paste Eaters* by Cheryl Peck. Copyright © 2005 by Cheryl Peck. By permission of Grand Central Publishing.

Anna Quindlen. "The C Word in the Hallways." From *Loud and Clear* by Anna Quindlen. Copyright © 2004 by Anna Quindlen. Used by permission of International Creative Management, Inc.

Wilbert Rideau. "Why Prisons Don't Work." From *Time*, March 21, 1994. Copyright © 1994 by Wilbert Rideau. Reprinted with the permission of the author, c/o The Permissions Company. www.permissionscompany.com.

Shafeeq Sadiq. "Racism and Sexism in Advertising." First published in *Delta Winds*, a collection of student writing from San Joaquin Delta College (1997). Reprinted by permission of the author.

Andrew Sullivan. "The 'M-Word': Why It Matters to Me." From *Time* Magazine, February 16, 2004. Copyright © 2004, Time Inc. All rights reserved. Reprinted by permission.

Marion Winik. "What Are Friends For?" From *Telling: Confessions, Concessions and Other Flashes of Light* by Marion Winik. Copyright © 1994 by Marion Winik. Used by permission of Random House, Inc.

Alaina Wong. "China Doll." Pages 117–121 from *YELL-OH GIRLS!* by Vickie Nam. Copyright © 2001 by Vickie Nam. Reprinted by permission of HarperCollins Publishers.

INDEX OF AUTHORS
AND TITLES

Guide to the Elements of Writing

The Compact Reader offers advice on writing from the general, such as organizing and revising, to the particular, such as tightening sentences and choosing words. Consult the page numbers here for answers to questions you may have about the elements of writing. To find the meaning of a particular term or concept, consult the Glossary on pages 402–10.

Resources for Teaching

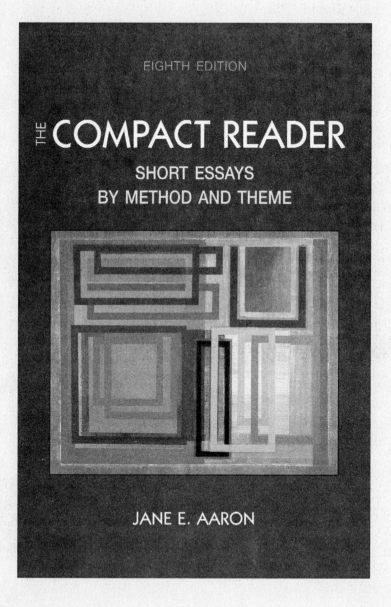

EIGHTH EDITION

THE COMPACT READER

SHORT ESSAYS
BY METHOD AND THEME

JANE E. AARON

1 0 9 8 7
f e d c b a

For information, write: Bedford/St. Martin's, 75 Arlington Street, Boston, MA 02116   (617-399-4000)

ISBN-10: 0-312-43431-6
ISBN-13: 978-0-312-43431-1

PREFACE

This manual has three parts, all intended to help you take maximum advantage of *The Compact Reader* as a classroom text. Part I discusses the content and possible classroom uses of the three introductory chapters, each element of the editorial apparatus in the rhetorical chapters, and the research appendix. Part II discusses the kinds of course materials with which *The Compact Reader* may be combined. And Part III offers teaching suggestions, a content quiz, and a vocabulary quiz for each essay in the book, as well as possible answers to the reading questions following each essay. Further, the manual offers annotations for one essay from each of the book's chapters. These annotations highlight the thesis and show how the author draws on diverse methods to develop the essay.

CONTENTS

I
USING *THE COMPACT READER*

The Compact Reader's structure is uncomplicated: three introductory chapters coach students on reading and writing, ten chapters explain and illustrate ten rhetorical methods of development, an appendix offers guidelines for using and documenting sources in writing, and a glossary defines key writing terms.

THREE INTRODUCTORY CHAPTERS
ON READING AND WRITING

You may wish to discuss these chapters explicitly in class, adapting all or parts of them to your syllabus, or you may find the chapters self-explanatory enough simply to ask students to read them on their own. Either way, these chapters lay useful groundwork for a reading and writing course. They explain and illustrate how critical reading is linked to good writing, how to read a text critically, how to work productively through the initial stages of writing, and how to revise and edit one's own drafts.

Reading (Chapter 1)

The introduction to critical reading is organized as follows:

Reading Attentively, p. 2

Reading Critically, p. 3

> Preparing, p. 4
> Reading Actively, p. 4
> Using a Reading Checklist, p. 5
> CHECKLIST FOR CRITICAL READING, p. 6

Analyzing a Sample Essay, p. 6

> Barbara Lazear Ascher, "The Box Man," p. 7
> Meaning, p. 11
> Purpose and Audience, p. 12
> Method and Structure, p. 13
> Language, p. 14

A highlight of the chapter is the discussion of Barbara Lazear Ascher's essay "The Box Man," showing how a critical reader might approach an essay and what conclusions might result. This discussion is organized around generalized versions of the questions that appear after each essay in Chapters 4–13. These questions — divided into the four categories of meaning, purpose and audience, method and structure, and language — invite students to consider the elements an author calls upon in constructing an essay. By observing how a critical reader might answer these questions for Ascher's essay, students have an opportunity to see what kinds of answers they might provide to the questions following the other essays in the book — and, more significant, to begin honing their own skills as critical readers.

Ascher's essay combines many of the methods of development (definition, example, description, etc.), thus providing an overview of the methods treated separately in the subsequent chapters. At the same time, the discussion of Ascher's essay introduces a point assumed throughout *The Compact Reader*: writers rarely use a single method alone, but rather gain shape, texture, and clarity for their writing by applying whatever method is best suited to a particular point or purpose.

To engage students actively in writing during the first or second class period, you might ask them to do some prewriting as preparation for reading the Ascher essay. Possible questions: What's the difference between solitude and loneliness? What kind of people would you describe as lonely? solitary? Or, to move in another direction: What is your impression of the homeless? Do you think some people choose to be homeless? Can one find dignity in such a situation? After reading Ascher's essay, students could compare their responses with hers and with one another's. They may see Ascher's as more complete and insightful than their own, and they will probably note that she presents her characters quite vividly, perhaps even prompting some students to recall similar characters in their own experiences. This comparison would provide a useful springboard to a discussion of the writer's task — and to Chapters 2 and 3.

Writing: Getting Started through Drafting (Chapter 2)

This chapter and the next provide an overview and illustrations of the writing process, detailing the basic concepts, terms, and stages that are used in the introductions to the rhetorical methods. Chapter 2 is divided into the following sections:

Getting Started, p. 17

> Considering Your Subject and Purpose, p. 17
> Considering Your Audience, p. 18
> Discovering Ideas, p. 19

>> Journal Writing, p. 19
>> Freewriting, p. 20
>> Brainstorming, p. 21
>> Using the Methods of Development, p. 22

Forming a Thesis, p. 22

> Identifying Your Main Point, p. 23
> Drafting and Revising a Thesis Sentence, p. 24

The two-chapter introduction to the writing process focuses on the work in progress of a student, Grace Patterson, as she develops a response to Ascher's "The Box Man." Chapter 2 includes Patterson's journal writing (p. 20) and freewriting (p. 21), along with her complete first draft (p. 28). If your class does peer editing, you might ask students to comment on the draft as a beginning exercise. In discussing their own and their classmates' comments, they will come to see what kinds of responses are appropriate and how best to phrase them.

Writing: Revising and Editing
(Chapter 3)

Continuing the two-chapter introduction to the writing process, this chapter covers the crucial stages of revising and editing.

These sections aim to help students with questions they may have while revising and editing. In Chapter 3, concise text and specific examples explain each element of writing, and two boxed checklists guide students through rethinking and correcting their own work. Then, in the introduction to each rhetorical method, a more specific revision and editing checklist appears with a "Focus" box that treats an element of writing especially relevant to the method — for instance, verbs in narration, transitions in process analysis, and tone in argument. All discussions of the elements — both in Chapters 2 and 3 and in the method introductions — are indexed inside the book's back cover, so that students know just where to go for help.

TEN CHAPTERS ON THE METHODS OF DEVELOPMENT
Chapter Introductions

The introductions to Chapters 4–13 all proceed in the same way. The opening section, "Reading _____," discusses the purposes for which the method is suited and provides essential concepts and definitions while showing students what elements to look for when reading paragraphs and essays that use the method. The next section, "Analyzing _____ in Paragraphs," annotates two paragraphs that illustrate the method. As noted above, a "Focus" box in each chapter emphasizes a particular element that students should be aware of when revising or editing, whether it is concrete and specific language in description or parallelism in comparison and contrast. Finally, "A Note on Thematic Connections" highlights the common topic of the chapter's paragraphs and essays.

The two paragraphs in each introduction allow students to study the method in brief, uncomplicated examples before moving on to complete essays. If you discuss the methods of development in class, the annotated paragraphs can serve as concrete illustrations of each method's special concerns. In addition, the paragraphs can serve as models for students to follow in writing paragraphs of their own (perhaps drawing on the list of topics at the end of each chapter) before they move on to more complex, essay-length applications of the method.

Chapter 13, "Argument and Persuasion/Debating Law and Order," is slightly different from the chapters before it. Because argumentation is so central to academic writing, this chapter introduction is more extensive than the others, with detailed discussions of the elements of argument; ethical, emotional, and rational appeals; and common logical fallacies. The chapter also offers two extra essays that argue opposing viewpoints on a single issue (drug laws).

The Essays

The Compact Reader's thirty-five essays satisfy several criteria. Most important, they are interesting, and they plainly illustrate the rhetorical methods. The essays are also short, averaging two to four pages, so students will find them imitable; yet they are substantial enough for sharpening reading skills and encouraging lively discussion. A few longer essays provide transition to more challenging academic work. Significantly, more than a third of the readings in *The Compact Reader* were written by students, demonstrating what is possible while reassuring other students that they, too, can write essays that others will want to read.

Though mainly a rhetorical reader, *The Compact Reader* offers an alternative, thematic approach because the paragraphs and essays in each chapter relate in subject as well as form. Thus, for example, Chapter 5's narrative selections all deal with the subject of recalling childhood, and Chapter 11's definition essays all address family relationships. You might have students read two or three of a chapter's essays and then discuss in class their theme as an entry to a discussion of the rhetorical approach. Or you could focus discussion on just the theme. As noted on the following page, a "Connections" writing topic for each essay and a set of thematic topics for each chapter help students perceive and write about the thematic links both within and among chapters.

Prereading Activities

Provocative quotations from a wide variety of sources — pop culture to literature to cultural theory — precede each essay and focus on the essay's core theme. Journal prompts after these quotations emphasize writing *before* reading to encourage students to read more actively and critically.

Biographical and Essay Headnotes

The preface to each essay establishes a context for the essay, offering background on the writer's interests and expertise in his or her subject and providing information about his or her intended audience. Students are often inclined to skip such sections, so it may be worthwhile to point out how helpful the headnotes can be for analyzing the essays along with the discussion questions.

Critical Reading Questions

The questions following each essay help students analyze and evaluate the essay, either on their own or in class discussions. The questions are organized in four groups — meaning, purpose and audience, method and structure, and language — that lead students to examine the essay with an increasingly sharp focus. As mentioned earlier, the four groups of questions correspond to those following Ascher's essay in the chapter on reading (Chapter 1). Possible answers to the questions are provided in this manual.

Writing Topics

At least four writing topics follow each essay. Some relate to the essay's content; some suggest a subject compatible with the method introduced in the chapter; several ask students to do research on a subject raised by the essay. A topic for each essay, "Journal to Essay," offers guidance on developing each student's prereading journal entry into a work for readers. A topic labeled "Cultural Considerations" leads students to examine the differences and likenesses between cultures and subcultures. And a final topic, labeled "Connections," encourages students to tease out thematic or rhetorical links between the essay and either a sample paragraph or another essay in the book.

In addition to the topics following each essay, every chapter ends with two sets of supplementary writing suggestions. The first set, "Writing with the Method," includes many possibilities for applying the chapter's method of development. The second set, "Writing about the Theme," includes three detailed ideas for drawing on the chapter's resources to explore its topic.

APPENDIX ON WORKING WITH SOURCES

New to the eighth edition, a brief overview of research and documentation gives students guidance on incorporating material from their reading into essays of their own. The appendix covers the most important elements of source-based writing.

The overarching assumption of this new appendix is that students will be drawing on the readings in this book and ideas gathered from minor research to support their own ideas in short essays, rather than developing formal research or term papers. Accordingly, the emphasis is on synthesizing outside materials to develop an original idea, with a focus on summarizing, paraphrasing, quoting, integrating sources, and avoiding plagiarism. The appendix also offers a few pointers on finding and evaluating sources in the library and on the Web, along with several MLA documentation models — fourteen parenthetical and forty-eight works cited — for the types of sources students are most likely to use.

The appendix culminates in an annotated sample student essay that both demonstrates how a handful of sources can be used in the service of a student's own ideas and illustrates the most important mechanical aspects of documented writing. It is a brief essay, drawing on only five sources (two of them lyrics of popular hip-hop songs), but it effectively shows how sources can add to a thesis without overwhelming a student's voice.

Taking advantage of the addition of this new coverage, *The Compact Reader* now includes writing topics throughout the book that ask students to conduct some research on a subject as they respond to readings and develop their ideas. See, for instance, the writing prompts on pages 249, 256, 348, and 360.

GLOSSARY

This section provides definitions of terms used in the text. Because most entries include page references to longer text discussions, the glossary can serve as an index as well as a freestanding quick reference. In some cases, the glossary offers specific aids — such as options for essay introductions and conclusions, with cross-references to the book's essays — that could serve as the basis of class discussion.

II
COMBINING *THE COMPACT READER* WITH OTHER MATERIALS

Because of its brevity, *The Compact Reader* can easily be combined with other classroom materials and approaches. Teachers using previous editions report that they have successfully integrated the reader with other textbooks, library research, current newspaper and magazine articles, and the writing of their own students.

OTHER TEXTBOOKS

Though brief, *The Compact Reader* anticipates many student questions about the use of the methods of development; hence you can ask students to read the chapter introductions independently, reserving class time to discuss the chapter's theme or the application of the writing principles.

Given its coverage of the writing process, *The Compact Reader* can complement a handbook or a sentence-combining textbook. The reader can inspire writing assignments and guide students through the stages of drafting, revising, and editing. For more detailed discussion of their specific problems — such as paragraph coherence, clear sentences, or word choice — and for help with grammar and punctuation, students can consult the other textbook. A class that meets three days a week could spend one day discussing an essay from the reader, one day discussing and planning the students' own essays, and one day covering sentence-level issues.

Or you may want to pair *The Compact Reader* with a literature anthology, using the chapter introductions and the essay models to guide students as they construct their own essays in response to literature. The discussions of description (Chapter 4) and narration (Chapter 5) may help students analyze the descriptive and narrative passages they encounter in short stories or novels; and you may want to discuss the similarities and differences between fictional and nonfictional description and narration. Using these methods, students could experiment with either fiction or nonfiction (or both, contrasting in a class discussion the problems they encountered with each). You can also emphasize that much writing about literature relies heavily on example (Chapter 6), comparison and contrast (Chapter 10), cause-and-effect analysis (Chapter 12), and argument and persuasion (Chapter 13); and you can tailor assignments in which students use these methods to explain, analyze, or evaluate the readings in the literature anthology.

RESEARCH TOOLS

You may wish to help prepare students for academic writing by asking them to use outside sources in at least some of their writing. Many of the essays and themes in *The Compact Reader* invite further investigation — for example, Sadiq (p. 155), McClain (p. 238), Early (p. 312), and the issues in Chapter 13. Frequent suggestions for research writing ask students to consult a dictionary, an encyclopedia, *The New York Times Index*, or a book or article found through the library catalog, *The Readers' Guide*, or the Internet. The assignments are specific and limited so that students can quickly find and read the other sources, using most of their time to construct their essays.

If you incorporate research into the course, you may wish to spend a class period or two introducing students to the library and its basic reference tools. You may also teach formats for documentation of sources, such as the MLA system discussed in the Appendix or almost any handbook on writing.

READING FROM CURRENT SOURCES

One advantage of a brief collection like *The Compact Reader* is that you can supplement the paragraphs and essays with topical articles on the book's themes or examples of the methods of development, or both. Op-ed pieces, essays in *Time* and *Newsweek*, articles in the school paper or the local paper, letters to the editor — all of these are good sources. Students are often surprised to see how the "textbook" methods abound in current periodicals, and at the same time they often respond well to the immediacy of last week's or yesterday's news items. In small groups or in the class as a whole, students can analyze the structure of these samples using questions like those first presented in Chapter 1 on reading. Outside readings can also serve as the basis for in-class writing topics. For instance, Thomas de Zengotita's "*American Idol* Worship" might be compared with another article on the virtues or defects of reality TV shows.

You can also encourage students to look for thematic connections or applications of the methods and bring them to class. For instance, students may watch for ways they use the methods in their own lives: comparing and contrasting in order to buy a new car; analyzing causes and effects in order to uncover the reasons for an unexpectedly high or low grade. Or students may examine television programs, films, magazines, and other sources for ideas to support the readings' or the class's approach to a chapter topic such as using language or defining gender roles. And, of course, students can watch for the methods in the readings, lectures, and exams of their other courses: the descriptive lab report in chemistry, the cause-and-effect analysis in history, and so on.

STUDENT WRITING

Like many instructors, you may rely on students' own writing to provide the substance of some class discussion. Given drafts of student papers to read, students may work in small groups or in pairs, using the method of careful reading and analysis recommended in Chapter 1. Then, using as a model the comments on Grace Patterson's drafts in Chapters 2 and 3, students can evaluate their peers' writing, making specific recommendations for improving each draft. When the paper employs a particular method of development, students may tailor their recommendations by referring to the chapter introduction to that method. To instruct students in this kind of peer-editing procedure — or instead of the small-group work — you may want to go over a sample student essay with the whole class.

In addition to responding to the essays in the reader, students may respond, in writing, to one another's essays. Especially for topics in argument and persuasion (Chapter 13), you can circulate one or two provocative student essays and ask the class to write arguments countering (or reinforcing) the arguments in those essays. Or students can exchange their own argumentative essays blindly, then write an essay in response to the one they receive. Knowing that someone will be responding to their essays invites students to formulate their arguments specifically and persuasively — perhaps more so than if they were writing just for you.

---------------- CHAPTER 4 ----------------

DESCRIPTION
Sensing the Natural World

---------------- Marta K. Taylor ----------------
DESERT DANCE (p. 62)

Taylor's piece provides an excellent example of description and, as a student essay, is most inspiring. Her images are strong and fresh, relying on figures of speech throughout, so you might focus discussion on how Taylor's use of figures contributes to the emotion of her description. (See question 4 under "Language.") As noted in question 2 under "Method and Structure," the essay builds to a climax and effectively juxtaposes the two components of her piece: safety and violence.

Taylor's essay may remind students of significant places from their childhood, and the prereading journal prompt and "Journal to Essay" writing topic have them explore their memories in a subjective description. You might have students do some freewriting to help them recall as much detail as possible from their memories, exploring each of their senses in relation to the place.

Content Quiz

1. Why does Taylor's family drive through the night?
    [The hotels are filled because of the rodeo.]

2. Where did Taylor grow up?
    [Los Angeles.]

3. What phenomenon was seldom seen in Taylor's childhood?
    [Rain.]

4. What looks like old men to Taylor?
   [The twisted forms of the Joshua trees.]

5. What tells Taylor that she is not dreaming?
   [The cramp in her neck and the pain in her elbow.]

Vocabulary Quiz

1. *Paragon* (paragraph 3) is closest in meaning to
   a. tower   b. model   c. protection
   [b. model]

2. *Silhouette* (5) is closest in meaning to
   a. figure   b. outline   c. frame
   [b. outline]

3. *Gnarled* (6) is closest in meaning to
   a. contorted   b. mangled   c. extended
   [a. contorted]

4. *Frolicked* (6) is closest in meaning to
   a. played   b. zigzagged   c. lit
   [a. played]

5. *Gaudy* (7) is closest in meaning to
   a. magnificent   b. costly   c. showy
   [c. showy]

ANSWERS

Meaning

1. "State of grace" (paragraph 7) does seem to capture Taylor's dominant impression. For her, this state consists of feeling safe (e.g., "motionless, soundless, protective paragon" [3]) while witnessing a violent, God-created lightning storm (5, 6). Taylor's trip through the desert resembles a religious experience: besides "state of grace," she refers to "sacred silence" (2), draws an image of her father's haloed head (3), notes the timelessness of the experience (4), and alludes to God (6).

Purpose and Audience

1. Taylor's opening sentence explains why she and her family are traveling at night and at the same time pulls the reader quickly into the story. By using the pronoun *we* without any initial explanation of who "we" is, she captures her reader's interest.

2. Students' answers will vary, perhaps depending on whether they're familiar with the desert. Some especially vivid images: the Joshua trees like old men, God taking a photograph, the flashing fireworks of the lightning (all paragraph 6).

Method and Structure

1. Taylor is trying to convey a contrast between the interior peace of the car and the exterior chaos of the storm. The "violent, gaudy display" (paragraph 7) going on outside makes her feel even safer and more cocooned in the car, where her father, the "protective paragon of security and strength" (3) is in control, there is no noise, her sleeping brother's chest rises and falls, and the "gentle heat of the engine" (5) keeps her warm.

2. The structure builds to a climax and evenly juxtaposes safety and violence, the components of Taylor's "state of grace" (paragraph 7).

3. Taylor's emotions appear, for example, in "wicked" and "cleverly" (paragraph 1), "sacred silence" (2), "protective paragon" (3), "violent sucking rush of air" (4), "gentle heat of the engine" (5), the "empty and lonely" road (6).

4. Since the narrative framework builds to a climax at Taylor's "state of grace" (paragraph 7), it rivets attention on that impression.

Language

1. Taylor's language creates an atmosphere of peace, stillness, and protection: "sacred silence" (paragraph 2); "protective paragon of security and strength" (3); "gentle heat of the engine" (3); "still in silence, still in darkness" (6).

2. The title refers to the "dance" of the lightning, and several phrases in paragraphs 6 and 7 support the notion of movement: the "natural strobe" of the lightning, the "hobble" of the trees, the fireworks that "frolicked," the "movements of a marionette," the "gaudy display."

3. The Joshua trees are "twisted" and look like "old men" with a "feeble hobble" (paragraph 6). This is a vivid if economical description of the trees, which are thought to have been named after Joshua, the biblical leader of Israel, because their limbs angle upward like arms. In the desert, they stand taller than their surroundings and do resemble gnarled humans.

4. Similes: hair playing with light "like tinsel" (paragraph 3), the lightning "like a rapidly growing twig" (5), a flash "as if God were taking a photograph" (6), the road that "shone like a dagger" (6), the trees that "looked like old men" (6).

5. The final long sentence intensifies the sense that Taylor is coming out of the spell of the storm. The rush of words parallels the rush of feeling in her neck and elbow.

13

————————— Dagoberto Gilb —————————

MY LANDLADY'S YARD (p. 66)

Gilb's essay is perhaps the most challenging of the readings in this chapter, subtly using a description of a barren desert lawn to explore issues of immigration and assimilation without ever explicitly naming either as his subject. But even if students miss Gilb's deeper point, "My Landlady's Yard" offers a promising subject for writing: those immediate surroundings that we all too often take for granted. Gilb's relationship with the landscape is unusually intimate: he finds meaning in details that most other observers would overlook, from the general dustiness of El Paso down to the brand names of discarded wrappers scattered around his yard. Gilb's perceptions are highly personal, and his descriptions more impressionistic than precise, yet he succeeds in creating a pervasive sense of melancholy and hope that his readers can easily appreciate.

You might want to ask students to try applying Gilb's strategy to a description of their own homes, relying on mood rather than precision to create a dominant impression. Alternatively, if you think your students are up to it, you could explore with the class how the author uses description of a mundane subject to make a point about something else altogether.

Content Quiz

1. Where is Gilb's rental house located?
   [El Paso, Texas.]

2. What kinds of plants grow well in the desert?
   [Gilb names four: creosote, mesquite, ocotillo, and yucca.]

3. What kind of plants did the landlady plant in the yard?
   ["Yankee plants and . . . imported grass" better suited to nondesert climates.]

4. What cultural institution is located in the author's backyard?
   [The local high school.]

5. Who makes up the majority of El Paso's population?
   [Mexican immigrants and their descendants, or, as the local media refer to them, "Hispanics."]

Vocabulary Quiz

1. *Lush* (paragraph 1) is closest in meaning to
   a. drunk   b. colorful   c. plentiful
   [c. plentiful]

2. *Digits* (3) is closest in meaning to
   a. numbers   b. fingers   c. scars
   [b. fingers]

3. *Misconception* (5) is closest in meaning to
   a. knowledge   b. mistake   c. creation
   [b. mistake]

4. *Aspiration* (6) is closest in meaning to
   a. goal   b. sweat   c. breath
   [a. goal]

5. *Husks* (6) is closest in meaning to
   a. dogs   b. seeds   c. shells
   [c. shells]

ANSWERS
Meaning

1. On the surface, Gilb waters the lawn because his landlady expects him to, and he doesn't want to give her a reason to evict him. On a deeper level, he tends the grass because he, too, would like a green suburban lawn. (On an even deeper level, Gilb is using the grass as a symbol for himself: he does the work because he wants to survive. See question 1 under "Purpose and Audience.")

2. By the end of the essay (paragraph 7), close readers will have caught on to Gilb's use of symbolism. If Gilb is writing about his own cultural ambivalence as a Mexican American, the sentence captures his main point perfectly: he may be trying to assimilate, but the process is incomplete (or "patchy at best"), and he's not sure that he should be making the effort. Ultimately, his "Mexican" self ("the brown dirt") still dominates over his "American" self ("the green").

Purpose and Audience

1. Gilb uses grass to symbolize Mexican immigrants and their descendants in the Southwest, particularly El Paso. The first clue appears in the introduction: both the plants and the people are "imported" (paragraph 1). Once students see this connection, the essay will take on levels of meaning that many may have missed. Gilb describes the grass in an effort to discuss assimilation without diving into the contentiousness of the current debate over immigration. Students may notice several parallels between the grass and the Mexican community in Texas: both have trouble thriving in the American desert; both seem out of place; both require an extraordinary amount of care to survive. Yet Gilb — a Mexican American himself — embraces the ideals of the dominant culture (symbolized by his landlady) and is determined to thrive in the harsh environment, even if he's not convinced that he should.

2. Gilb's shift in possessive pronouns is part of his assimilation argument. He is saying (again, very subtly) that the work he does to maintain and improve the house and yard will eventually make the property his own (as

15

he already considers it by the end of the essay). In many ways, that property is a metaphor for the United States as a whole: Gilb is pressing readers to accept Mexican Americans as full participants in American culture.

3. Gilb can assume that his readers are intimately familiar with the desert landscape he describes, so he doesn't need to describe the general landscape in much detail. (Notice, for example, that he rattles off the names of desert plants without bothering to explain what they are.) Instead, he focuses on the details that his readers may not know: the specific kinds of trash he finds in the yard, for instance. Because the *Texas Observer* devotes many pages to politics and tends to take a liberal stance, Gilb can also assume that his readers will be well versed in the cultural and political tensions surrounding immigration issues. He doesn't feel a need to make his argument explicit because he can count on his readers to pick up his subtler meanings without much effort. For readers unfamiliar with Texas and its politics, of course, this assumption could pose problems.

Method and Structure

1. The yard Gilb describes is dusty, neglected, and strewn with litter, but it also shows signs of effort and hope.

2. Gilb takes a psychological point of view but builds his description around the physical process of tending to the grass in front of and back of his house.

3. The label is important to Gilb because it gets at the crux of his argument. The culturally dominant "Anglo" population sees the numerically dominant Mexican American population solely in terms of "otherness" — focusing on language but ignoring a shared history and culture that is only superficially divided by a political border. The label allows the Anglo community to define members of the majority community as minorities.

Language

1. Although readers may reasonably object to Gilb's casual way with his sentences and argue that the grammar flaws weaken his credibility as a writer, he is using fragments and run-ons to approximate a spoken voice. The author is trying to establish a connection with his readers by assuming a conversational style, encouraging readers to imagine that he is talking with them, perhaps over the fence, in a neighborly way. This point of view helps to temper the controversial argument he is making under the surface of his words. At the same time, the chatty tone may cause less discerning readers to miss the larger point of his essay entirely.

2. Just a few examples of Gilb's abundant figures of speech include personifications such as "shrubs and evergreens that snuggle the walls of the house" and "suburbs [that] moved on to east and west many years ago" (paragraph 1); metaphors such as "*gold*, colorless and liquid, is pouring out onto this desert" (2) and "concrete river" (5); similes such as "an offering as unquenchable and ruthless as to any Aztec deity" (2); and hyperbole such

as the "non-Indian hunter eating one meal, then leaving behind the car-cass" (6).

3. Gilb appeals to four of the five senses: sight ("trash blowing by, snared by limbs and curbs and fences" [paragraph 6]); touch ("with my thumb over the brass fittings and squeezed against the water" [3]); taste ("the slimy remains of what goes for cheese on nachos" [3]); and sound ("police cars squealed" [5]). Although he doesn't directly invoke smell, some sensitive readers may even get a sense of it in his descriptions of the area's unyielding dryness.

ANNOTATED ESSAY

Cause and effect

Description

Comparison

It's been a very dry season here. Not enough rain. And the sun's beginning to feel closer. Which, of course, explains why this is called the desert. Why the kinds of plants that do well enough in the region — creosote, mesquite, ocotillo, yucca — aren't what you'd consider lush, tropical blooms. All that's obvious, right? To you, I'm sure, it's obvious, and to me it is, too, but not to my landlady. My landlady doesn't think of this rock house I rent in central El Paso as being in the desert. To her, it's the big city. She's from the country, from a ranch proba-bly just like the one she now calls home, a few miles up the paved highway in Chaparral, New Mexico, where the roads are graded dirt. She must still see the house as she did when she lived here as a young wife and mother, as part of the city's peaceful suburbs, which it certainly was thirty years ago. She probably planted the shrubs and evergreens that snuggle the walls of the house now, probably seeded the back- and front-yard grass herself. And she wants those Yankee plants and that imported grass to continue to thrive as they would in all other American, nondesert neighborhoods, even if these West Texas suburbs moved on the east and west many years ago, even if the population has quadrupled and water is more scarce, and expensive, than back then.

Comparison

So I go ahead and drag around a green hose despite my per-ception that *gold*, colorless and liquid, is pouring out onto this desert, an offering as unquenchable and ruthless as to any Aztec deity (don't water a couple of days and watch how fast it dries away). Superstitions, if you don't mind my calling them that, die hard, and property values are dependent on shared impres-sions. I'm not ready to rent and load another U-Haul truck.

Example

With my thumb over the brass fitting and squeezed against the water, I use the digits on my other hand to pluck up loose garbage. You've heard, maybe, of West Texas wind. That explains why so much of it lands here on my front yard, but also a high school is my backyard: the school's rear exit is only a dirt alley and fence away from my garage, and teenagers pass by in the morning, during lunch, and when school lets out. I find the lat-est Salsa Rio branch of Doritos, Big Gulp Grande cups, paper

1

2

3

(or plastic or both) bowls with the slimy remains of what goes for cheese on nachos from the smiley-faced Good Time Store two blocks away, used napkins, orange burger pouches, the new glossy-clean plastic soda containers, waxy candy wrappers from Mounds and Mars and Milky Way. Also beer cans and bottles, grocery-store bags both plastic and paper, and fragments from everything else (believe me) possible.

I'm betting you think I'm not too happy about accumulating such evidence. You're right. But I'm not mentioning it to complain. I want the image of all the trash, as well as the one of me spraying precious water onto this dusty alkaline soil, to get your attention. Because both stand for the odd way we live and think out here, a few hundred miles (at least) from everyplace else in the United States.

My green grass in the desert, for instance. My landlady wants thick, luxuriant grass because that's the way of this side of the border, and this side is undeniably better, whatever misconception of place and history and natural resources the desire for that image depends on. It's not just her, and it's not just lawns. Take another example: a year ago about this time, police cars squealed onto the asphalt handball and basketball courts on the other side of the school fence to regain control of a hundred or so students lumped around a fight, most of them watching, some swinging baseball bats. What happened? According to the local newspaper, the fight broke out between a group of black students, all of them dependents of Fort Bliss military personnel (as their jargon has it), and a group of Hispanic students. "Hispanic" is the current media term for those of descent from South of the Border. Even around here. Which is the point: that even in this town — the other side of the concrete river considered the official land of Spanish-language history and culture — the latest minority-language terminology is used to describe its historic, multigenerational majority population. With the exception of one high school on the more affluent west side of town, Anglos are the overwhelming minority; at the high school behind my backyard the ratio must be ten to one. Though Mexico has been the mother of this region, and remains so, it's the language and understanding of The North that labels the account of the school incident: "Hispanic" students, black dependents of GIs.

If green grass is the aspiration, the realization of an American fantasy, then the trash is from the past, the husks of a frontier mentality that it took to be here, and stay, in the first place. Trash blowing by, snared by limbs and curbs and fences, is a display of what was the attitude of the West. The endlessness of its range. The ultimate principle of every man, woman, animal, and thing for itself. The meanness required to survive. The wild joy that could abandon rules. The immediacy of life. Or the stupidity of the non-Indian hunter eating one meal, then leaving behind the carcass. Except that vultures and coyotes and finally

Margin annotations:
4 — Description
5 — Cause and effect
Narration
Description
Definition
6 — Description
Comparison

ants used to clean that mess up. The remains of the modernized hunt don't balance well in nature or its hybrid shrubs, do not biodegrade. And there are a lot more hunters than before.

Trash contradicts the well-tended lawn. And in my neighborhood, not all is Saint Augustine or Bermuda. Hardy weeds sprout and grow tall everywhere, gray-green century plants shoot stalks beside many homes. El Paso is still crossing cultures and times, the wind blows often, particularly this time of year, the sun will be getting bigger, but the pretty nights cool things off here on the desert. Let me admit this: I'd like it if grass grew well in my backyard. What I've got is patchy at best, and neglected, the brown dirt is a stronger color than the green. So the other day, I soaked that hard soil, drug it up, threw seed grown and packaged in Missouri, covered it with peat humus from Menard, Texas, and I'm waiting.

7

Description

DOMINANT
IMPRESSION
(THESIS)

Narration

Joan Didion

THE SANTA ANA (p. 72)

Joan Didion's piece is an excellent example of descriptive writing. Her colorful yet unsettling images appeal to the senses — sight, sound, taste, and touch. Didion's precision permits the reader to share her sensual impressions of and experiences with the "persistent [and] malevolent" (paragraph 3) Santa Ana wind. Perhaps the most interesting question to begin discussion with your students is whether Didion admires the destructive force she writes about. (See the fourth writing topic.) Because it may remind them of one, Didion's essay could start a discussion about a "phenomenon" that drives students crazy where they live, leading into the first and second writing topics.

Content Quiz

1. Where does the Santa Ana come from?
   [From the northeast, down mountains and through canyons.]

2. Has Didion lived in Los Angeles all her life?
   [No: "when I first moved to Los Angeles."]

3. What color is the sky right before the Santa Ana comes?
   [Yellow.]

4. What are the two extremes of weather in Southern California?
   [The rainy season and the dry season of the Santa Ana.]

5. How long does the Santa Ana usually last?
   [Three or four days.]

Vocabulary Quiz

1. *Mechanistic* (paragraph 1) is closest in meaning to
   a. conniving   b. determined   c. complex
   [b. determined]

2. *Malevolent* (3) is closest in meaning to
   a. evil   b. powerful   c. dangerous
   [a. evil]

3. *Mitigating* (3) is closest in meaning to
   a. aggravating   b. circumstantial   c. excusing
   [c. excusing]

4. *Incendiary* (4) is closest in meaning to
   a. inflammatory   b. insensitive   c. windy
   [a. inflammatory]

5. *Apocalypse* (6) is closest in meaning to
   a. drought   b. end of the world   c. winter
   [b. end of the world]

ANSWERS

Meaning

1. Didion's statement of thesis is found in paragraph 6: "[T]he violence and the unpredictability of the Santa Ana affect the entire quality of life in Los Angeles, accentuate its impermanence, its unreliability. The wind shows us how close to the edge we are."

2. The wind leaves the city dry, hot, and still. It makes people a little crazy, "drying the hills and the nerves to the flash point" (paragraph 1). "The baby frets. The maid sulks" (1). It makes Didion testy and argumentative, causing her to "rekindle a waning argument with the telephone company" (1). Indians used to throw themselves into the sea when the Santa Ana came. Didion's neighbor holes up inside, and the neighbor's husband runs around with a machete. People go to their doctors complaining of "headaches and nausea and allergies, about 'nervousness,' about 'depression'" (3). Schoolchildren become unmanageable. People have even committed murder.

3. A mechanistic view holds that human behavior is entirely controlled by outside forces (in this case, a force of nature). The opposite view would be that humans act of their own accord, that they have free will.

4. The last sentence could be read both literally (Los Angeles is on the edge of the continent) and figuratively (life in Los Angeles pushes residents to the edge of sanity).

Purpose and Audience

1. The essay uses the Santa Ana to make a larger point about the craziness of life in Los Angeles. Didion seems to be responding to the problem she states in paragraph 6: "It is hard for people who have not lived in Los Angeles to realize how radically the Santa Ana figures in the local imagination." At the same time, there is a self-expressive element to the essay: such a potent force begs to be written about and affords Didion the opportunity to explore its dramatic effects on herself and her surroundings.

2. Didion is writing for the outsider as well: "It is hard for people who have not lived in Los Angeles to realize how radically the Santa Ana figures in the local imagination" (paragraph 6). We know she is from the city because the essay is written from a personal, insider's point of view and she uses the first person: "when I first moved to Los Angeles" (2); "just as we had always known it would be in the end" (6).

Method and Structure

1. Because the wind itself is nearly intangible, Didion is limited to describing its physical and psychological effects: on nature (the Pacific, peacocks, the sky [paragraph 2]), on property (the fires and property damage described in paragraph 4), and on people (see question 2 under "Meaning"). By describing these effects so vividly and thoroughly, she brings to life a phenomenon that people who have not lived in Los Angeles would otherwise have trouble understanding.

2. Paragraphs 1 and 2 are mostly subjective: Didion describes the first signs of a Santa Ana coming on as she is writing, then goes on to describe its effects on herself and on her neighbors. Paragraphs 3–5 are mostly objective, based on literary and journalistic sources: Didion situates the Santa Ana in the context of other malevolent winds throughout the world, attempts a scientific explanation for its effects, discusses the two violent seasons in Los Angeles, and recounts a particularly devastating Santa Ana in 1957. Paragraph 6 returns to a subjective point of view: Didion suggests that the Santa Ana is emblematic of life in southern California.

3. The quotation helps move the essay from examples based on Didion's personal experience to examples she has heard or read about.

4. Didion's description relies on concrete examples because what she's trying to describe is essentially intangible. Her examples are colorful and memorable and paint a vivid portrait for the outsider of what it's like to live with such a malign phenomenon.

Language

1. The first person makes the description more personal and intimate, helping us feel the effects of the Santa Ana as though we were there. The present

21

tense gives a sense of immediacy to the essay, creating the impression that Didion is spontaneously recording her thoughts.

2. The colorful images (the glossy ocean, screaming peacocks in trees, the yellow sky) bring the effects of the Santa Ana to life and make them memorable. The imagery is surreal because it's jarring, otherworldly.

CHAPTER 5

NARRATION
Recalling Childhood

Annie Dillard
THE CHASE (p. 90)

Students should enjoy Dillard's dramatic rendering of a childhood thrill, which is likely to inspire them to write their own tales of glories past. Dillard is at her narrative and descriptive best here, capturing the feeling of childhood and the rhythm of the chase. Vivid, convincing detail is, of course, the key to making a story compelling, and only through careful word choice will students be able to re-create their excitement as effectively as Dillard does hers. The narrative provides rich opportunity to discuss how such description operates: see question 4 under "Method and Structure" and question 3 under "Language."

Content Quiz

1. How old was Dillard when the snowball event took place?
   [Seven years old.]

2. What kind of car did Dillard and her friends throw snowballs at?
   [A black Buick.]

3. Who got chased by the driver?
   [Dillard and Mike Fahey.]

4. What did the driver say when he finally caught them?
   ["You stupid kids."]

5. How would Dillard have reacted if the driver "cut off [their] heads"?
   [She would have "died happy."]

Vocabulary Quiz

1. *Translucent* (paragraph 6) is closest in meaning to
   a. clear   b. frozen   c. solid
   [a. clear]

2. *Impelled* (14) is closest in meaning to
   a. chased   b. drove   c. knocked
   [b. drove]

3. *Compelled* (14) is closest in meaning to
   a. forced   b. teased   c. chased
   [a. forced]

4. *Obscure* (16) is closest in meaning to
   a. mountainous   b. hidden   c. empty
   [b. hidden]

5. *Exalting* (20) is closest in meaning to
   a. furious   b. close   c. glorious
   [c. glorious]

ANSWERS

Meaning

1. "[T]hat you have to fling yourself at what you're doing, you have to point yourself, forget yourself, aim, dive" (paragraph 13); that the unbridled, unfettered enthusiasm of childhood comes from wholehearted concentration on whatever you're doing; that the courage to do it is simultaneously the catalyst for and reward of childhood enthusiasms, enthusiasms most adults (though not the driver of the Buick) abandon.

2. Getting in trouble is not per se a means to happiness — total concentration and courage and commitment, to the point of forgetting yourself, is. Being open to this kind of abandon may well get you into trouble, but it's the *abandon* rather than the trouble that leads to happiness.

Purpose and Audience

1. To recapture the glories of childhood, to re-create its adrenaline rush, and possibly to remind adults what they are missing — getting the most out of life.

2. Dillard's shift to *you* moves the spotlight from herself, the narrator, to the reader. The reader becomes an active participant in the football plays described, thus increasing the immediacy and intensity of the scene Dillard is trying to create.

Method and Structure

1. Dillard could have chosen to illustrate the enthusiasm of youth and its loss in adulthood through example, which would have brought concreteness to a general observation (much as the narration, a kind of extended example, does here), or comparison and contrast, which would have placed the change at the center of the essay. But the vivid narration brings with it an immediacy and a memorableness that might be hard to achieve through these other methods.

2. The elaborate detail in paragraph 12 — including specific homes, a woodpile, and an intersection — gives a feel for the intricacy and length of the chase. But to go on in this way, mentioning every feature of the landscape,

would probably try readers' patience. Thus, in succeeding paragraphs, Dillard summarizes: the chase runs "block after block" (13, 14).

3. This sentence entices readers to read on and also lets readers know that whatever "trouble" Dillard got into was not serious. Hence, readers can relax, become fully engaged in the story, and vicariously enjoy the chase.

4. Description contributes specific concrete details that bring the scene to life. Some are "up to our boot tops in snow" (paragraph 3), "tire chains come clanking from afar" (7), "a smashed star with a hump in the middle" (8), "every breath tore my throat" (14), "there was a prow of snow beneath [the man's cuffs] on his shoes and socks" (16).

Language

1. Dillard seamlessly interweaves the straightforward, declarative language and limited experience of a child ("Some boys taught me to play football" [paragraph 1]; "we all popped it one" [5]; "this time, the only time in all of life" [9]) with the greater powers of observation and more sophisticated perspective of an adult ("complex trail of beige chunks like crenellated castle walls" [5]; "we reverted to the natural solitude of children" [5]).

2. Dillard feels admiration and approval because the man throws himself into the chase with the same verve she and her friends do. Some evidence: "a man got out of it [the car], running. He didn't even close the car door" (paragraph 9); "incredibly, he was still after us" (10); "Any normal adult would have quit. . . . He was a thin man, all action. All of a sudden, we were running for our lives" (10); all of paragraph 13; "He impelled us forward" (14); "he would never give up, this man" (14); "The point was that he had chased us passionately without giving up, and so he had caught us" (19).

3. Both images suggest presents, gifts, magic, enchantment, a childhood fantasy world.

———— Langston Hughes ————

SALVATION (p. 97)

Students usually understand and identify with Hughes's childhood emotions, for nearly everyone can recall an early experience of disappointed expectations. That point of connection can provide a starting place for discussion of the essay.

Though Hughes does provide informative details on the revival, students who are unfamiliar with the ideas of sin, salvation, and the like may participate in discussion more actively if they are given some brief background information. In contrast, students whose own religious experiences parallel those of Hughes's aunt, rather than of Hughes himself, may bring to the essay their own strong convictions and may therefore have difficulty understanding (and accepting, even as a different opinion) Hughes's point.

Content Quiz

1. What is Hughes "not really" saved from?
   [Sin.]

2. Where is "Salvation" mainly set?
   [In Hughes's Auntie Reed's church.]

3. What is the "mourner's bench"?
   [The place in church for those who had not yet been "saved."]

4. Who is Westley?
   [The last boy to be saved besides Hughes.]

5. What did Hughes do the night of the day he was saved?
   [Cried in bed.]

Vocabulary Quiz

1. *Dire* (paragraph 3) is closest in meaning to
   a. dreadful   b. angry   c. sacrilegious
   [a. dreadful]

2. *Fold* (3) is closest in meaning to
   a. class   b. bevy   c. flock
   [c. flock]

3. *Rounder* (6) is closest in meaning to
   a. minister   b. watchman   c. mortician
   [b. watchman]

4. *Deacons* (6) is closest in meaning to
   a. fathers   b. minister's assistants   c. singers
   [b. minister's assistants]

5. *Rejoicing* (13) is closest in meaning to
   a. singing   b. praying   c. expressing joy
   [c. expressing joy]

ANSWERS

Meaning

1. Hughes's point seems to be that his faith was shattered because he was not saved and because his lie passed for salvation. Whereas at first he is naively faithful, in the end he feels shameful and betrayed.

2. Hughes decides to get up because of the pressure he feels and because Westley has lied without suffering for it. Afterward, however, he feels betrayed that Jesus did not save him from the pressure or from lying.

3. Hughes plays on the word *salvation*. In saying that he "was saved from sin. . . . But not really saved" (first two sentences), he means that he performed the ritual convincingly yet felt no spiritual change. He pretended to be saved and in doing so lost his faith. For Hughes, at least, salvation seems a sham. (It is also possible that the adult Hughes felt that he *had* in a sense been saved — from hypocrisy.)

Purpose and Audience

1. Clearly, the experience was a significant one for Hughes (paragraph 15), and that fact alone could explain his including the essay in his autobiography. He does not seem critical of his aunt and the other adults in the congregation; as an adult he seems to understand that they would "see" Jesus in other than the literal way he expected to "see" (15). But this play on *see* itself may point out another purpose of the essay: to underscore the literal-mindedness of children, their inability to comprehend the abstractions by which adults live. Hughes may also have wanted to illustrate the point at which a child learns to rely on himself or herself, not on others, for truth.

2. Hughes does not assume that his readers are familiar with the kind of service he describes. Particularly in paragraphs 1, 3, 4, 11, 13, and 14, he provides details that clarify the procedure, such as the purpose and activity of a revival (1), the appeals made to the children (3, 4), and the blessing of the children (14).

3. The dialogue, lines from hymns, and descriptions of the noise level in the church (e.g., paragraphs 3, 7) re-create the pressure Hughes felt in a way that simple assertions such as "Everyone was after me to get up" could not possibly do. Besides sound, the details contributing to the sense of pressure include heat (6), loneliness (6, 11), time (6, 11), the aunt's presence (7), and Westley's proud grin (11).

Method and Structure

1. The autobiographical narrative form makes this more personal, and probably more memorable, than an argumentative essay would be. A title of an argumentative essay on the same subject might be "Hypocrisy in Organized Religion." Such an essay would probably also be more objective, presenting both sides of the subject, and possibly more objectionable to those who disagreed with the author's opinion.

2. Examples of explanation in Hughes's narrative: what he expects salvation to be like (paragraph 2); who Westley is (6). Examples of compression of time: several weeks of the revival retold in just a few sentences (1); the procession of children to the altar (6). Example of omitted events: the gap between the end of the meeting (14) and Hughes in bed that night (15). Example of expanded time: the moments before Hughes decides to be saved (7–12).

   By condensing or omitting some events, Hughes keeps the narrative moving and emphasizes the crucial moments of pressure leading to his decision. These moments are drawn out in a way that makes us sympathize with Hughes's predicament, understand his reason for lying, and share his sense of shame and betrayal.

3. Examples of transitions: "then" (paragraph 3); "still" (5); "finally," "now" (6); "then," "while" (7); "now" (11); "suddenly" (13); "when," "then" (14); "that night," "now," "anymore" (15).

4. The process analysis is important because many readers will not have been to a revival meeting or will not understand how one works. It also puts us inside the process, allowing us to see it through Hughes's eyes.

Language

1. Hughes as an adult seems both amused and sorrowful. His use of "young sinners" (paragraph 1) is ironic, and a similar wryness runs through his descriptions of Westley (6, 11) and even of his own predicament (7, 11). But there is no amusement in the last paragraph, where Hughes conveys his pain and a sense of loss. Here the juxtaposition of Hughes's wish not to cry (because it is childish and he does not want his aunt to hear) with his inability to keep from crying (some form of *cry* appears four times) intensifies the sense of sorrow.

2. Hughes achieves the breathless pattern of a child reporting an overwhelming experience, thus leading us to see the experience from a child's point of view rather than an adult's.

3. The young Hughes seems to expect a literal physical experience (paragraphs 5, 7, 15); he will "see" something that "comes to" him from the outside. Hughes's aunt, in contrast, believes that one can "see" Jesus in one's soul (2); the seeing is not literal but spiritual. Hughes's understanding of *see* makes his disappointment and sense of betrayal inevitable.

ANNOTATED ESSAY

I was saved from sin when I was going on thirteen. But not really saved. It happened like this. There was a big revival at my Auntie Reed's church. Every night for weeks there had been much preaching, singing, praying, and shouting, and some very hardened sinners had been brought to Christ, and the membership of the church had grown by leaps and bounds. Then just before the revival ended, they held a special meeting for children, "to bring the young lambs to the fold." My aunt spoke of it for days ahead. That night, I was escorted to the front row and placed on the mourner's bench with all other young sinners, who had not yet been brought to Jesus. | 1

Narration

My aunt told me that when you were saved you saw a light, and something happened to you inside! And Jesus came into your life! And God was with you from then on! She said you could see and hear and feel Jesus in your soul. I believed her. I have heard a great many old people say the same thing and it seemed to me they ought to know. So I sat there calmly in the hot, crowded church, waiting for Jesus to come to me. | 2

The preacher preached a wonderful rhythmical sermon, all moans and shouts and lonely cries and dire pictures of hell, and then he sang a song about the ninety and nine safe in the fold, but one little lamb was left out in the cold. Then he said: "Won't you come? Won't you come to Jesus? Young lambs, won't you come?" And he held out his arms to all us young sinners, there on the mourner's bench. And the little girls cried. And some of them jumped up and went to Jesus right away. But most of us just sat there.

3 ⎤
Description

Narration and process analysis

A great many old people came and knelt around us and prayed, old women with jet-black faces and braided hair, old men with work-gnarled hands. And the church sang a song about the lower lights are burning, some poor sinners to be saved. And the whole building rocked with prayer and song.

4
Description

Still I kept waiting to *see* Jesus.

5

Finally all the young people had gone to the altar and were saved, but one boy and me. He was a rounder's son named Westley. Westley and I were surrounded by sisters and deacons praying. It was very hot in the church, and getting late now. Finally Westley said to me in a whisper: "God damn! I'm tired o' sitting here. Let's get up and be saved." So he got up and was saved.

6

Then I was left all alone on the mourner's bench. My aunt came and knelt at my knees and cried, while prayers and songs swirled all around me in the little church. The whole congregation prayed for me alone, in a mighty wail of moans and voices. And I kept waiting serenely for Jesus, waiting, waiting — but he didn't come. I wanted to see him, but nothing happened to me. Nothing! I wanted something to happen to me, but nothing happened.

7
Narration and process analysis

Description

I heard the songs and the minister saying: "Why don't you come? My dear child, why don't you come to Jesus? Jesus is waiting for you. He wants you. Why don't you come? Sister Reed, what is this child's name?"

8

"Langston," my aunt sobbed.

9

"Langston, why don't you come and be saved? Oh, Lamb of God! Why don't you come?"

10

Now it was really getting late. I began to be ashamed of myself, holding everything up so long. I began to wonder what God thought about Westley, who certainly hadn't seen Jesus either, but who was now sitting proudly on the platform, swinging his knickerbockered legs and grinning down at me, surrounded by deacons and old women on their knees praying. God had not struck Westley dead for taking his name in vain or for lying in the temple. So I decided that maybe to save further trouble, I'd better lie, too, and say that Jesus had come, and get up and be saved.

11

Description

So I got up.

12

Suddenly the whole room broke into a sea of shouting, as 13
they saw me rise. Waves of rejoicing swept the place. Women
leaped in the air. My aunt threw her arms around me. The min-   Description
ister took me by the hand and led me to the platform.

When things quieted down, in a hushed silence, punctuated 14
by a few ecstatic "Amens," all the new young lambs were blessed
in the name of God. Then joyous singing filled the room.

That night, for the last time in my life but one — for I was a 15
big boy twelve years old — I cried. I cried, in bed alone, and
couldn't stop. I buried my head under the quilts, but my aunt
heard me. She woke up and told my uncle I was crying because   Narration
the Holy Ghost had come into my life, and because I had seen
Jesus. But I was really crying because I couldn't bear to tell her
that I had lied, that I had deceived everybody in the church, that   THESIS
I hadn't seen Jesus, and that now I didn't believe there was a
Jesus anymore, since he didn't come to help me.

Kaela Hobby-Reichstein

LEARNING RACE (p. 102)

In this frank account of a difficult lesson learned in her childhood, Hobby-
Reichstein tackles a controversial issue with grace and equanimity. Her disarm-
ing and forthright tone may encourage students to explore a challenging discovery in their own childhoods — one they can now view with perspective.

Hobby-Reichstein's student essay is an excellent example of a first-person
narrative with a strong thesis. She relates her story not merely for the sake of
telling it but also to make a point about how racism is taught to children — and
to urge her readers to reject the stereotypes they may have been taught (or may
inadvertently be teaching). Her details are clear and engaging, her figures of
speech are strong and fresh, and her manipulation of narrative time is deliberate
and logical. Hobby-Reichstein also effectively incorporates dialogue to emphasize
her points. You might want to spend some time with your students analyzing the
way she weaves together her own experience with the words of others not only
to give her story immediacy and to highlight different perceptions of race but
also to persuade readers that the childish perceptions are more reasonable.

Content Quiz

1. How long have the author and her best friend known each other?
   [Since Hobby-Reichstein was two years old.]

2. What item did Hobby-Reichstein always include in her kindergarten artwork?
   [A rainbow.]

3. What paint colors did Hobby-Reichstein use for her family members' skin?
   [She used peach for herself and her mother; brown for her father and half
   brother.]

4. Why did the kindergarten teacher say Hobby-Reichstein's painting was wrong?
[Because she knew that Hobby-Reichstein's father and half brother were white.]

5. What kind of neighborhood did Ryan's grandmother live in?
[Fort Richmond was an Italian working-class neighborhood.]

Vocabulary Quiz

1. *Swimming* (paragraph 2) is closest in meaning to
   a. dancing   b. gesturing   c. too small for
   [c. too small for]

2. *Grits* (8) is closest in meaning to
   a. hot cereal   b. bacon   c. bugs
   [a. hot cereal]

3. *Degraded* (8) is closest in meaning to
   a. represented   b. improved   c. insulted
   [c. insulted]

4. *Attributes* (8) is closest in meaning to
   a. characteristics   b. credits   c. histories
   [a. characteristics]

5. *Bigotry* (9) is closest in meaning to
   a. having more than one spouse   b. prejudice   c. poverty
   [b. prejudice]

ANSWERS

Meaning

1. Hobby-Reichstein does not explicitly define the meaning of race in her essay, but in her conclusion she suggests that race is a system of "ignorance and hatred" (paragraph 15) that is taught to children just as it was taught to her. She didn't recognize racial difference between herself and her best friend as a child. As an adult, she rejects the idea that black and white people are inherently different and is angered by the bigotry that she has witnessed. She hopes to use her personal experiences to teach others not to hate.

2. The author's belief stemmed from the relative skin tones of the male and female members of both families: Ryan was the daughter of a black mother and an Italian American father, and Hobby-Reichstein's father and half brother were darker than she and her mother were (yet still Caucasian), so it seemed logical to conclude that gender, rather than race, determined color within any given family. Her misunderstanding suggests that although she recognized that people could be different, she didn't comprehend the cultural implications of race.

Purpose and Audience

1. Hobby-Reichstein's reasons for writing are revealed in her conclusion: she wants to draw on strength gained from her painful experiences "to speak [her] mind and possibly end some ignorance and hatred in the process" (paragraph 15).

2. Although the use of racial slurs is fraught with danger, Hobby-Reichstein's intent is not to offend but to put her readers in the same uncomfortable position she was in when the words were used in her presence. She takes great care to follow the offensive dialogue with an expression of her own anger and hurt to clarify that she does not condone the language. All the same, some students may reasonably question the wisdom of her choice.

Method and Structure

1. Narration is all about telling a story, and that's what Hobby-Reichstein sets out to do here. She makes full use of summary, descriptive details, dialogue, and narrative time to share her experience.

2. The long passage of time between episodes helps to dramatize and reinforce the author's introductory explanation that it took several years before she understood the meaning of race. The three major periods touched on in the essay coincide with the three stages of her learning process: first, she found out in kindergarten that skin color correlates with race; then she discovered around fourth grade that race difference fuels hatred; finally, as an adult she learned that she could use her knowledge of bigotry to reeducate others.

3. The differences Hobby-Reichstein saw between herself and Ryan as a young girl were cultural: their families ate different foods, used different levels of formality in their language, and listened to different kinds of music (Hobby-Reichstein implies that she preferred Ryan's family's style). At the same time, both girls lived in the same building, hated having their hair done, and "picked up a number of each other's cultural attributes" (paragraph 8). Hobby-Reichstein didn't give much thought to their skin colors until the difference was pointed out to her. She doesn't dwell on them in her comparison — or elsewhere in her narrative — because she wants her readers to understand that she refuses to judge others by their race.

Language

1. Hobby-Reichstein demonstrates considerable skill in crafting and using original figures of speech. In particular, the notion that "shards of childlike innocence caught in [her] throat" (paragraph 14) effectively invokes a major idea of her essay: that the experiences she describes not only shattered her innocence but left her unable to articulate her anguish for many years.

2. The simple structure of Hobby-Reichstein's sentences reflects the simplicity of her childhood perspective.

CHAPTER 6

EXAMPLE
Using Language

Kim Kessler

BLAH BLAH BLAH (p. 119)

Kessler wrote this essay as a student to comment on a seemingly meaningless phrase common among her peers. Using examples, she shows that the phrase "blah blah blah" does have meaning — "generic rhetoric" (paragraph 2), "an intimacy that transcends . . . language" (4), and finally a "cover-up" (5). For this last meaning, Kessler provides a narrative example whose concrete, specific details are particularly effective.

One way to initiate class discussion may be to ask students who Kessler's audience is. Building on this question, have students discuss the various audiences they write to when they create compositions. Their instructors? Their friends? The free world? How do their examples change according to their audience?

Content Quiz

1. What are two other versions of "blah blah blah" used by Kessler's friends? ["yadda yadda" and "etc., etc."]

2. What are some of the "good reasons" that people use "blah blah blah"? [What one is about to say is so trite that it's not worth repeating; one wants to cut to the chase; the speakers are intimates who understand each other without words.]

3. Whom does Kessler bump into while walking across campus? [An acquaintance.]

4. What caused Kessler to have a mini-breakdown? [She was caught in the rain, lonely, wet, and carrying a heavy trombone.]

5. What solution does Kessler offer to "this 'blah blah' thing"? ["Put on your Walkman and avoid it all."]

Vocabulary Quiz

1. *Articulate* (paragraph 2) is closest in meaning to
   a. intelligent   b. well-spoken   c. interesting
   [b. well-spoken]

2. *Transcends* (4) is closest in meaning to
   a. rises above   b. eliminates   c. climbs
   [a. rises above]

3. *Accosted* (6) is closest in meaning to
   a. molested   b. priced   c. approached
   [c. approached]

4. *Gratuitous* (6) is closest in meaning to
   a. pointless   b. typical   c. tedious
   [a. pointless]

5. *Repercussions* (9) is closest in meaning to
   a. reasons   b. consequences   c. drumbeats
   [b. consequences]

ANSWERS

Meaning

1. Kessler feels that she's being deceptive by using the phrase to avoid a subject she doesn't want to talk about. She uses it "in place of the atypical" rather than to "impl[y] the typical" (paragraph 7).

2. The "symbol of generic rhetoric" (paragraph 2) is "blah blah blah." The phrase is symbolic in that it takes the place of something else — it has no meaning of its own. It's generic because it can mean anything. This captures Kessler's main idea: that the phrase is deceptive because it is open to almost any interpretation the listener chooses to assign to it. The speaker can use this ambiguity to avoid speaking the truth without actually lying.

Purpose and Audience

1. Both: although Kessler says she is on the fence about "blah blah blah," most of her examples imply criticism of the phrase. She disparagingly refers to her "oh-so-articulate friends" (paragraph 2) who use it, and she feels dismissed and rejected when its use implies that "it is not worth their time or their energy to actually recount a story for my sake" (4). Equally, she feels guilty when she finds herself using the phrase to cover up something she doesn't want to talk about. Kessler may also be trying to amuse, as is indicated by her ironic tone: "oh-so-articulate friends" (2), "yeah, it's a verb" (4), "It's not very often that I share like that" (6).

2. Kessler is writing for an audience of her fellow college students. The subject is current slang among young adults, her peers; the evidence consists

of anecdotes from campus life; and the tone is ironic and informal (see question 1 under "Language").

Method and Structure

1. It's hard to talk about language in the abstract; it's a subject that calls for examples. The long example in paragraph 6 shows us exactly how Kessler uses "blah blah blah" to avoid subjects she doesn't want to talk about. Without it we'd have no idea what she means.

2. In paragraph 4, the examples illustrate the "couple of good reasons" for the prevalence of the phrase: many conversations are trite, and intimates do not always require language. The extended example in paragraph 6 shows that for the author the expression is "a refuge, a wall of meaningless words with which to protect myself" (7).

3. The introduction consists of paragraphs 1–3: these provide the background of the phenomenon and Kessler's main idea. In the body of the essay (4–8), Kessler gives examples that illustrate her main idea, showing how the phrase is used and misused. Paragraph 9 serves as the conclusion, offering a "solution" to the problem.

4. Kessler not only shows how "blah blah blah" is used but also explains what it may mean in these uses. "Blah blah blah" can be a shortcut for something trite or obvious; it can suggest that the person speaking doesn't want to waste his or her time; it can indicate intimacy between the speakers; and it can mean that the speaker doesn't wish to tell the whole truth. This use of definition helps Kessler demonstrate her thesis from paragraph 2.

Language

1. Kessler's tone is partly serious, partly ironic. Her style is at times very informal, almost like spoken language: "The thing about it is" (paragraph 2); "Well, maybe 'lie' isn't the best word" (5); "But, hey" (9); and all of her parenthetical remarks. This informality is appropriate for an audience of college peers: she writes as if she were talking to a group of friends. At other times she takes on a mock-serious tone, imitating an earnest academic analysis: "It has come to my attention," "symbol of generic rhetoric" (2); "recently noticed phenomenon" (3); much of paragraph 4. Kessler means everything she says (until the last paragraph), but she seems to realize that there are more important problems than this one.

2. "[O]h-so-articulate friends" (paragraph 2); "I hope you can all handle that open display of vulnerability. It's not very often that I share like that" (6); the "reasonable solution" at the end of paragraph 9.

3. Kessler gives the piece an informal, chatty feel and makes it clear that she is writing for her peers.

Kirk Johnson

TODAY'S KIDS ARE, LIKE, KILLING
THE ENGLISH LANGUAGE (p. 124)

Students might be surprised to find Johnson, a writer and father, proclaim with thinly veiled humor that "*Duh* has elegance. *Duh* has shades of meaning, even sophistication" (paragraph 2). These unorthodox views are bound to inspire debate about the way young people express themselves and the impact their slang has on older generations.

An interesting class discussion might revolve around the compilation of a "master list" of slang expressions that students commonly use and an objective, academic study of the function of these terms. Johnson's essay asks us to think about the role of language in conveying identity and in communicating with others.

Content Quiz

1. When was the author born?
   [The 1950s.]

2. Which two cities do *duh* and *yeah, right* represent?
   [New York and Los Angeles.]

3. Who is Marcel Danesi?
   [Professor of linguistics and semiotics, who coined the term "pubilect."]

4. In the sentence "He was, *like, duh!*" what is the function of the word *like*?
   [It is a "crucial helping verb . . . , a verbal springboard."]

5. Why does the computer represent the paradox of the age?
   [It is built around a binary code of black and white, but the information it transmits represents the gray scale of modern life.]

Vocabulary Quiz

1. *Hyperbole* (paragraph 3) is closest in meaning to
   a. understatement   b. exaggeration   c. sarcasm
   [b. exaggeration]

2. *Incisive* (7) is closest in meaning to
   a. complaining   b. sharp   c. indirect
   [b. sharp]

3. *Overwrought* (11) is closest in meaning to
   a. overstressed   b. unintended   c. fascinating
   [a. overstressed]

4. *Unpalatable* (16) is closest in meaning to
   a. uninteresting   b. unpleasant   c. unavailable
   [b. unpleasant]

5. *Steeped* (21) is closest in meaning to
   a. saturated   b. devoid   c. related
   [a. saturated]

ANSWERS
Meaning

1. Johnson's main point is that slang terms, although commonly decried as a deterioration in language use, in fact reflect the times and convey a wide array of meanings. He states that terms such as *duh* and *yeah, right* are "the ideal terms to usher in the millennium and the information age, and to highlight the differences from the stolid old twentieth century" (paragraph 2).

2. Johnson focuses first on the paired terms *duh* and *yeah, right*. They reflect opposite attitudes and replace the black-and-white, right-and-wrong approach of past generations. He also gives special attention to *like*, while admitting that its uses are more difficult to pinpoint. The variety of the first two expressions and the ambivalence of the third powerfully represent the complexity of the modern world.

3. Although *duh* and *yeah, right* spring from a desire to think more flexibly, they also reflect a world governed by yes-or-no, binary-based computers.

Purpose and Audience

1. The author appears to write for a variety of reasons. On the one hand, opening with "they are all quite wrong" (paragraph 1) and "hear me out" (3) and his detailed analyses of meaning indicate an explanatory and persuasive purpose. On the other hand, his examples and many of his statements are clearly intended to amuse — for instance, "almost any politician's speech cries out for heaping helpings of both [*duh* and *yeah, right*] at various moments" (paragraph 10).

2. Johnson addresses readers who, like the *New York Times* audience, are adults and probably parents: he is bringing them news of young people's language and analyzing it at a level of detail that would be unnecessary for the young people who use it (and would not be tolerated by them, as Johnson asserts of his own sons). The audience is a general one, not a group of linguistic specialists, or Johnson would surely present his argument in a more academic manner by, for instance, citing more than a single scholar.

3. The author evidently expects disagreement from the "educators, linguistic Brahmins and purists" (paragraph 1) with whom he disagrees, and he expects dismissal from his own sons. He responds by asking readers to hear him out and then by presenting a reasoned, well-supported case for

his view. Students' own responses will vary. The most interesting may come from those who use the terms that Johnson analyzes.

Method and Structure

1. The examples are so interesting that more would be welcome, but there seem to be enough to get Johnson's points across. We see the difference between *duh* and *yeah, right* in the paragraphs of contrast (8–10). And *like* comes through clearly in the three very different examples in paragraphs 13 and 16.

2. Johnson may have saved *like* for a climax: *duh* and *yeah, right* assert complementary meanings, but *like* is actually "altering the structure of the English language" (paragraph 12). At the same time, all three expressions "convey the sense of reflected reality that is part of the age we live in" (17). Some students may fault Johnson for not pulling all his ideas together at the beginning of the essay, while others might find that the essay takes an interesting new turn in paragraph 12.

3. Johnson's experiences with his sons both prompted the essay and support it. They also add immediacy and humor. But Johnson also strengthens his opinions with more objective evidence, such as historical references (paragraph 3), serious analysis of his examples (for instance, paragraph 14), and perhaps most impressively, the opinion of an expert (12). Students may find the mixture of personal and objective evidence more convincing than either alone.

4. In Johnson's definitions, *duh* "undercut[s] mindless understatement or insulting repetition," and *yeah, right* responds coolly to overstatement (paragraph 9); the more complex *like* softens statements, serves as quotation marks around often ironic quotations, serves as a helping verb, and distinguishes what seems to be from what is. Summarizing, Johnson says, "[L]*ike* reflects modern life, and *duh* and *yeah, right* are the tools with which such a life can be negotiated and mastered" (18).

Language

1. Of the given adjectives, *reassuring, humorous*, and *serious* seem to be the most appropriate to describe Johnson's tone. At times the author sounds academic, quoting "a professor of linguistics and semiotics . . . who has studied the language of youth" (paragraph 12). At other times Johnson imitates the speech he is describing, as in "*Like* is, like, dangerous" (11). Overall, he reassures readers that *duh* and the other words are valid, sophisticated, even creative — for instance, "drenched with content" (6), "matchless tools of savvy" (7), "ideal terms" (2). For *New York Times* readers — a general audience consisting mostly of educated adults, many of them parents — this mix seems quite appropriate.

2. Other contrasting word pairs include "black and white" in paragraph 4, "understatement or overstatement" and others in paragraph 6, and "for

better or worse" in paragraph 17. Johnson continually reinforces his point that *duh*; *yeah, right*; and *like* allow discourse on a "gray scale" between extremes.

3. The quoted examples and colloquial language (for example, "Good old *yes* and *no*" [paragraph 4] and "throw in a whole basket" [8]) keep the essay easygoing and accessible. The more precise, formal language (for example, "exquisitely differentiated universe" [6] and *"Yeah, right* is . . . the antithesis to *duh's* empathetic thesis" [9]) conveys a serious purpose and also helps to pin down meaning more exactly. Students who have difficulty with the more formal vocabulary may be engaged enough by the examples and colloquialisms (and the subject itself) to explore and master the passages they didn't initially understand.

——— Perri Klass ———

SHE'S YOUR BASIC L.O.L. IN N.A.D. (p. 130)

Klass's subject is inherently interesting to students: even if they don't hope or plan to go to medical school, they are at least intrigued by doctors. This essay addresses the issue of how language establishes the boundaries of groups. As such, it could initiate a discussion of special languages — in particular, technical terminology, jargon, and slang. Before or after reading the essay, students could discuss (in class or in writing) the purposes and effects of special language — is it alienating? mysterious? authoritative? Other sources of jargon worth examining include a sports broadcast, a conversation between computer specialists, or the writing class itself (for example, what effects do expressions such as *comma splice* and *relative clause* have on students?). The goal of any of these discussions is to arrive at an understanding of when jargon is useful, necessary, and effective, and when it is superfluous, distracting, or downright harmful.

Klass's essay beautifully surmounts a central difficulty in essays developed by example: how to weave together many examples without sounding monotonous. She avoids tedium through sentence variety (see the box on p. 117 in the text) and also by varying the way she presents her examples: she explains some medical terms in parenthetical comments, others by anecdote; she treats some briefly, lingers over others; she groups those having to do with baseball into a separate class. Students often overlook the importance of variety — or, if they are aware that their writing lacks it, don't quite know how to remedy the problem. Klass's essay provides a useful model. (Question 2 under "Method and Structure" focuses their attention on this point.)

Content Quiz

1. What does the abbreviation "N.A.D." stand for in this essay?
   [No apparent distress.]

2. In medical jargon, what is a "no-hitter"?
   [A night without any new admissions.]

3. In medical jargon what is the accepted abbreviation for "nasogastric"?
   [NG.]

4. What nickname did the interns give the medical student who liked to cite syndromes named after researchers?
   [Mr. Eponym.]

5. In neurological research, what is a "brainstem preparation"?
   ["An animal whose higher brain functions have been destroyed."]

Vocabulary Quiz

1. *Primeval* (paragraph 2) is closest in meaning to
   a. mean   b. blissful   c. earliest
   [c. earliest]

2. *Terminal* (6) is closest in meaning to
   a. dead   b. final   c. calloused
   [b. final]

3. *Pompous* (15) is closest in meaning to
   a. pretentious   b. important   c. principled
   [a. pretentious]

4. *Locutions* (15) is closest in meaning to
   a. phrases   b. exclamations   c. jokes
   [a. phrases]

5. *Jurisdiction* (17) is closest in meaning to
   a. government   b. authority   c. guidance
   [b. authority]

ANSWERS
Meaning

1. Klass's point: learning medical jargon marks a rite of passage into doctor-hood, a passage mitigated by her realization that the "new alien assumptions" (paragraph 18) of the language are not wholly positive or for the better. She reveals her full point in the final paragraph.

2. To Klass, medical jargon serves two useful purposes: the language builds "closeness and professional spirit" (paragraph 8), and it creates distance between doctors and patients (17). Given Klass's evident distaste for the disrespectful and even inhumane jargon illustrated in paragraphs 10–16, those particular expressions seem unlikely to build her professional spirit. They certainly do create distance between doctor and patient.

Purpose and Audience

1. Klass implies that she lost something by becoming a doctor; that there was something idyllic about the lack of knowledge she had before and something corrupted about her now complex life. The phrase suggests that she wants to explain a process that medical students must go through and also *why* they must go through it — in part, why the corrupted state is necessary for doctors.

2. Klass is halfway between a nondoctor and a doctor; she's looking ahead, gaining knowledge, but still clearly remembers that state of "primeval innocence" (paragraph 2). She expects her readers not to know about the doctor side, which she is at pains to explain to them in paragraphs 1, 2, 4, and many others, but she expects readers to identify with the nondoctor side: see, for example, "endless jargon and abbreviations" (2), terms that go "a little too far" (10), "I had resolved not to be shy" (11), jargon that makes "the beginning medical student nervous about the effects of medical training" (15).

3. Answers will vary. Klass does not define every term (for example, "nasogastric" [paragraph 3]; "cardiac enzymes" [4]; "sickle-cell" [15]). But in most if not all cases, her meaning is clear without definitions: we don't need to know exactly what's wrong with the patient to see the point being made about jargon.

Method and Structure

1. Klass begins with an example for the sake of interest — and to create a sense of mystery: What are these terms? Will they be defined? She immediately makes her audience feel befuddled, thus putting them in the position she was in when she started working in the hospital — and in the position of a patient. The opening example in effect gives readers a capsule version of Klass's experience, which is what she wants to explain.

2. Other examples: "This sort of construction probably reflects . . . profound irritation" (paragraph 4); "Baseball metaphor is pervasive" (6); "Some people seem to become enamored of the jargon for its own sake" (8); "Then there are the more pompous locutions" (15).

3. Effects: camaraderie (paragraph 8), excitement (8, 18), arrogance and pomposity (8–15), discomfort (15, 18), distance (17).

Language

1. Klass is deeply concerned about the desensitizing effects that medical jargon has had on her and her colleagues. This seriousness toward her subject is most evident in the last paragraph: the tone becomes graver as Klass makes her concerns explicit. The essay's black humor is cautionary, serving to expose a troubling phenomenon.

2. Answers will vary. The shifts between *we/us* and *they/them* may be seen as emphasizing that Klass's own role is shifting: she doesn't identify fully with the doctors. The shifts between *I* and *you* are more difficult to justify thematically, though Klass evidently uses *you* — especially in paragraph 18 — to extend her conclusions beyond herself.

3. Positive: "thrills," "communicate effectively," "professional speech," "closer and closer to being a doctor." Negative: "uncomfortably," "peculiarities and even atrocities," "avoid," "strange," "afraid," "alien."

ANNOTATED ESSAY

"Mrs. Tolstoy is your basic L.O.L. in N.A.D., admitted for a soft rule-out M.I.," the intern announces. I scribble that on my patient list. In other words Mrs. Tolstoy is a Little Old Lady in No Apparent Distress who is in the hospital to make sure she hasn't had a heart attack (rule out a myocardial infarction). And we think it's unlikely that she has had a heart attack (a *soft* rule-out). `1` *Definition*

If I learned nothing else during my first three months of working in the hospital as a medical student, I learned endless jargon and abbreviations. I started out in a state of primeval innocence, in which I didn't even know that "s̄ C.P., S.O.B., N/V" meant "without chest pain, shortness of breath, or nausea and vomiting." By the end I took the abbreviations so for granted that I would complain to my mother the English professor, "And can you believe I had to put down *three* NG tubes last night?" `2` *Example and definition*

"You'll have to tell me what an NG tube is if you want me to sympathize properly," my mother said. NG, nasogastric — isn't it obvious? `3`

I picked up not only the specific expressions but also the patterns of speech and the grammatical conventions; for example, you never say that a patient's blood pressure fell or that his cardiac enzymes rose. Instead, the patient is always the subject of the verb: "He dropped his pressure." "He bumped his enzymes." This sort of construction probably reflects that profound irritation of the intern when the nurses come in the middle of the night to say that Mr. Dickinson has disturbingly low blood pressure. "Oh, he's gonna hurt me bad tonight," the intern may say, inevitably angry at Mr. Dickinson for dropping his pressure and creating a problem. `4` *Division or analysis*

When chemotherapy fails to cure Mrs. Bacon's cancer, what we say is, "Mrs. Bacon failed chemotherapy." `5`

"Well, we've already had one hit today, and we're up next, but at least we've got mostly stable players on our team." This means that our team (group of doctors and medical students) has already gotten one new admission today, and it is our turn again, so we'll get whoever is next admitted in emergency, but at least most of the patients we already have are fairly stable, `6` *Example and definition* that is, unlikely to drop their pressures or in any other way get suddenly sicker and hurt us bad. Baseball metaphor is pervasive: a no-hitter is a night without any new admissions. A player is always a patient — a nitrate player is a patient on nitrates, a unit player is a patient in the intensive-care unit and so on, until you reach the terminal player.

It is interesting to consider what it means to be winning, or doing well, in this perennial baseball game. When the intern hangs up the phone and announces, "I got a hit," that is not cause for congratulations. The team is not scoring points; rather, it is getting hit, being bombarded with new patients. The object of the game from the point of view of the doctors, considering the players for whom they are already responsible, is to get as few new hits as possible.

These special languages contribute to a sense of closeness and professional spirit among people who are under a great deal of stress. As a medical student, it was exciting for me to discover that I'd finally cracked the code, that I could understand what doctors said and wrote and could use the same formulations myself. Some people seem to become enamored of the jargon for its own sake, perhaps because they are so deeply thrilled with the idea of medicine, with the idea of themselves as doctors.

I knew a medical student who was referred to by the interns on the team as Mr. Eponym because he was so infatuated with eponymous terminology, the more obscure the better. He never said "capillary pulsation" if he could say "Quincke's pulses." He would lovingly tell over the multinamed syndromes — Wolff-Parkinson-White, Lown-Ganong-Levine, Henoch-Schonlein — until the temptation to suggest Schleswig-Holstein or Stevenson-Kefauver or Baskin-Robbins became irresistible to his less reverent colleagues.

And there is the jargon that you don't ever want to hear yourself using. You know that your training is changing you, but there are certain changes you think would be going a little too far.

The resident was describing a man with devastating terminal pancreatic cancer. "Basically he's C.T.D.," the resident concluded. I reminded myself that I had resolved not to be shy about asking when I didn't understand things. "C.T.D.?"I asked timidly.

The resident smirked at me. "Circling The Drain."

The images are vivid and terrible. "What happened to Mrs. Melville?"

"Oh, she boxed last night." To box is to die, of course.

Then there are the more pompous locutions that can make the beginning medical student nervous about the effects of medical training. A friend of mine was told by his resident, "A pregnant woman with sickle-cell represents a failure of genetic counseling."

Division or analysis

7

Division or analysis

8

Cause and effect

9

Classification

Example

10

11

Example and definition

12

13

14

15

Classification

Mr. Eponym, who tried hard to talk like the doctors, once
explained to me, "An infant is basically a brainstem preparation." A brainstem preparation, as used in eurological research,
is an animal whose higher brain functions have been destroyed
so that only the most primitive reflexes remain, like the sucking
reflex, the startle reflex, and the rooting reflex. 16

The more extreme forms aside, one most important function
of medical jargon is to help doctors maintain some distance
from their patients. By reformulating a patient's pain and problems into a language that the patient doesn't even speak, I suppose we are in some sense taking those pains and problems
under our jurisdiction and also reducing their emotional impact.
This linguistic separation between doctors and patients allows
conversations to go on at the bedside that are unintelligible to
the patient. "Naturally, we're worried about adeno-C.A.," the
intern can say to the medical student, and lung cancer need never
be mentioned. 17

> Cause and effect

> Example

I learned a new language this past summer. At times it
thrills me to hear myself using it. It enables me to understand
my colleagues, to communicate effectively in the hospital. Yet I
am uncomfortably aware that I will never again notice the peculiarities and even atrocities of medical language as keenly as I
did this summer. There may be specific expressions I manage to
avoid, but even as I remark them, promising myself I will never
use them, I find that this language is becoming my professional
speech. It no longer sounds strange in my ears — or coming
from my mouth. And I am afraid that as with any new language, to use it properly you must absorb not only the vocabulary but also the structure, the logic, the attitudes. At first you
may notice these new alien assumptions every time you put
together a sentence, but with time and increased fluency you
stop being aware of them at all. And as you lose that awareness,
for better or for worse, you move closer and closer to being a
doctor instead of just talking like one. 18

> THESIS

CHAPTER 7

DIVISION OR ANALYSIS
Looking at Popular Culture

Dave Barry
HUMVEE SATISFIES A MAN'S LUST
FOR WINCHES (p. 149)

This laugh-out-loud-funny analysis of Humvees criticizes consumer excess by making fun of it. Although Barry's purpose is obviously to get a chuckle from his readers, some of your students may have strong feelings about over-size, fuel-guzzling vehicles. Barry's references to the Humvee's military origins and to the first American invasion of Iraq may also raise difficult political issues. Whether or not you encourage discussion on these points will, of course, depend on your reasons for teaching the essay and what kinds of responses will be most productive to that end. If you wish to focus on style and method, for instance, you might want to steer conversation away from latent environmental and political controversies. If, however, you are more inter-ested in getting your students fully engaged in a subject, allowing them to digress into these issues may prove fruitful.

What is perhaps most interesting about Barry's essay is the way he plays with a standard written genre: the automotive review. You might remind your students that readers unconsciously expect an essay to follow the conventions of its genre. Although veering from those expectations will usually frustrate readers, if it is done with purposeful intent (as is the case with Barry), the result can be insightful or very entertaining — a point that is suggested in question 2 under "Method and Structure." For an interesting class exercise, consider bringing, or asking your students to bring, a sample of a traditional auto review and comparing it with Barry's. Students will quickly notice that although Barry follows the standard format, he subverts it just enough to high-light the inherent absurdity of his subject — and, of course, to get a laugh.

Content Quiz

1. When did Americans first notice the Humvee?
   [Most learned of its existence during the Persian Gulf War of 1991.]

2. According to Barry, what do the letters in *Humvee* stand for?
   ["Hugely Masculine VEEhickle."]

3. What color was the Humvee that Barry test-drove?
    [Bright yellow.]

4. Name at least one feature of the Humvee that Barry highlights.
    [The tires can be inflated while driving; it has an enormous winch; it has an engine; the ride is uncomfortable.]

5. What use does Barry suggest for a winch?
    [He suggests using it to pull down the house of a person who runs you off the road.]

Vocabulary Quiz

1. *Protuberances* (paragraph 5) is closest in meaning to
    a. decorations   b. bulges   c. tools
    [b. bulges]

2. *Wanton* (8) is closest in meaning to
    a. excessive   b. restrained   c. Chinese
    [a. excessive]

3. *Carnality* (8) is closest in meaning to
    a. playfulness   b. meat   c. sex
    [c. sex]

4. *Winch* (title, 12) is closest in meaning to
    a. hood ornament   b. crank   c. grill
    [b. crank]

5. *Foolhardy* (15) is closest in meaning to
    a. stupid   b. careless   c. silly
    [b. careless]

ANSWERS

Meaning

1. This sentence provides a good tongue-in-cheek summary of Barry's main point: that the Humvee is hypermasculine to the point of absurdity, yet it doesn't succeed in conferring manhood on its driver (after all, it can't grow hair).

2. The title plays on the similarity in pronunciation of *winches* and *wenches*: the former is a crank used for pulling heavy items, and the latter is a derogatory and somewhat antiquated term for women, especially prostitutes. The pun hints very strongly that Barry believes not only that the Humvee appeals to men's sexual identity but also that it falls short in fulfilling their desires.

Purpose and Audience

1. Barry's purpose is to entertain, as evidenced by his humor throughout.

2. Just a few examples of his hyperbolic statements: "This led to some mishaps, most notably when Arnold Schwarzenegger, attempting to open his garage door, accidentally launched a missile" (paragraph 3); the Humvee was "covered with puddles of drool deposited by passing guys" (5); the winch "can pull down a house" (12); "a truly masculine, big-winched man does not need comfort" (14); "I was competing for the one available space with roughly 20,000 other motorists" (16). Barry uses irony to eke out some laughs, to underscore just how ridiculous the Humvee is in civilian life, and to point out the violent aspects of the car's appeal.

Method and Structure

1. Barry examines those features of the Humvee that appeal specifically to men, or, more specifically, "guys." He divides the vehicle into five elements: military function (2, 3), appearance (5), gadgets (6–12, 16), engine (13), and comfort (14).

2. Barry injects humor into his analysis by subverting readers' expectations. Although he follows the general format of an automotive review, he uses the method to highlight the more ridiculous elements of the Humvee. In the process, he is able to undermine the very features that appeal to a stereotypical male driver.

3. Barry means to show that the sexual appeal of the Humvee fails to make its drivers any more successful as men. Contrasting men's admiration of particular features to women's perplexed response effectively demonstrates that the car does not make its drivers more attractive to women; in fact, it does quite the opposite.

Language

1. Barry's tone is decidedly sarcastic. It would be difficult to argue that he takes his subject seriously.

2. Barry counts himself among the men foolish enough to be seduced by the Humvee's promise of masculinity. By peppering the essay with slang and colloquialisms, he establishes himself as the object of his own joke. Doing this enables him to forge a bond both with the men he mocks and with those readers (male and female) who would laugh at Humvee owners.

Shafeeq Sadiq

RACISM AND SEXISM IN ADVERTISING (p. 155)

This student essay provides a thought-provoking critique of advertising tactics and a good example of division or analysis. With the thesis that "minorities

47

and women are constantly being exploited in everyday advertisements" (paragraph 1), the analysis may surprise students who do not view television commercials critically. Sadiq demonstrates the elements of advertisements that make them exploitative and then reassembles these elements to draw his conclusion that "[t]here needs to be a public awakening, for racism and sexism should not be used in any situation" (6).

Sadiq's piece could open up a class discussion about how minorities and women are exploited in the media. As an assignment, have students bring in magazine and newspaper articles or descriptions of television shows or commercials in order to analyze the stereotypes used. Students should feel free to explore other areas of American society where stereotypes may appear, such as the fashion industry or the music industry.

Content Quiz

1. What two products are frequently associated with sexist advertising?
   [Beer and cars.]

2. Who is the target audience for the GoDaddy.com ad?
   [Men.]

3. How does the ad for Boost Mobile perpetuate stereotypes of African American men?
   [It implies that African American men prefer white women and that sex is their ultimate goal in life.]

4. What is the implication of the ad for Citibank?
   [That immigrants are all buffoons.]

5. Which advertisers does Sadiq suggest may be the most guilty of using stereotypes?
   [Beer companies.]

Vocabulary Quiz

1. *Gimmicks* (paragraph 1) is closest in meaning to
   a. strategies   b. images   c. stereotypes
   [a. strategies]

2. *Notorious* (3) is closest in meaning to
   a. guilty   b. irresponsible   c. infamous
   [c. infamous]

3. *Materialize* (3) is closest in meaning to
   a. dance   b. appear   c. drink
   [b. appear]

4. *Unabashedly* (4) is closest in meaning to
   a. shamelessly   b. excessively   c. enduringly
   [a. shamelessly]

5. *Perpetrator* (5) is closest in meaning to
    a. criminal   b. sinner   c. guilty party
    [c. guilty party]

ANSWERS
Meaning

1. "Television, print media, and billboards no longer show products, but rather show gimmicks in order to sell the products. Often, these gimmicks reinforce racial stereotypes and portray women in a negative light" (paragraph 1).

2. Advertisers attempt to associate their products with sexual success: they are selling the notion that buying their products will make their male customers more attractive to women. In doing so, they exploit women, reducing them to objects to stimulate male fantasies.

3. Sadiq thinks the depiction plays into stereotypes of African Americans as being hypersexual and more interested in seducing white women than in pursuing loftier goals.

Purpose and Audience

1. Sadiq wants to convince readers that sexism and racism are alive and well in advertising today, despite the "political correctness" (paragraph 1) of society today. But, as he indicates in the last paragraph, he also wants to encourage a grassroots movement to boycott companies that use racism and sexism to sell their products.

2. Sadiq is writing for a multiracial audience made up of both men and women. He seems to assume that his readers will be receptive to his message. He spends no time justifying why exploitation of women and minorities is undesirable or why advertisers should not engage in exploitation. At the same time, he seems to assume that his readers are not aware of the "gimmicks" (paragraph 1) that advertisers use to exploit women and minorities. His purpose is to bring them to light.

Method and Structure

1. Because the questionable aspects of ads may not be immediately apparent, Sadiq's analysis of the ads — revealing their elements — is necessary for him to show readers the offensive components.

2. The principle of analysis (the second topic sentence) is the elements of the ad that cause it to exploit stereotypes of African Americans. These elements are the hot tub, the multiple women, and the caption and tagline that suggest sex is the ultimate goal.

3. Sadiq's first paragraph is a formal introduction that sets up the subject in a no-nonsense, right-to-the-point way. His last paragraph is a formal conclusion calling for action that grows out of his thesis.

4. Sadiq probably doesn't think racism is a more serious problem. But he sees only one group of people — women — as exploited by sexism, whereas any number of racial or ethnic groups suffer from racism, each in a distinct way.

5. The description is necessary to translate a message from a visual medium into a written one. Viewers might not notice that the actors are attractive, that the women appear so quickly after the man opens the beer (paragraph 3), that the African American man is in a hot tub (4), or that the immigrants speak with an accent (5).

Language

1. Sadiq takes his subject very seriously; one might even accuse him of humorlessness. But this tone is in keeping with his high-minded purpose.

2. Answers will vary. Some students may find the irony inconsistent with Sadiq's otherwise serious tone. Others may appreciate the occasional lightness.

ANNOTATED ESSAY

Political correctness is an inherent part of society today. Whether it involves minorities or women, racist and sexist comments are rightfully no longer tolerated in places such as the schoolyard and the workplace. Why is it, then, that minorities and women are constantly being exploited in everyday advertisements? Television, print media, and billboards no longer show products, but rather show gimmicks in order to sell the products. Often, these gimmicks reinforce racial stereotypes and portray women in a negative light.

1

THESIS

2

Example

Description and division or analysis

On every television channel, commercials sell products with the use of beautiful women. These commercials range from alcoholic beverages to Internet domain registrations. Who can forget the GoDaddy.com ad campaign, with scantily clad Candice Michelle selling the Web site with a series of commercials that had nothing to do with the webpage itself? These commercials, still available for viewing on the Go Daddy Web site, featured "window cleaner" Michelle rubbing her breasts against an office window, "car washer" Michelle doing the same at a car wash, and spokesperson Michelle having a "wardrobe malfunction" during a congressional hearing on censorship. The product is mentioned only in passing. Advertisements like the Go Daddy campaign exploit women en route to their actual target: men. The series of commercials would routinely air during sporting events such as the NFL playoffs and Super Bowl, when the majority of the viewers are male. They tied in quite nicely with similar commercials that are designed to sell beer.

Beer companies have been notorious for exploiting women in their everyday promotions. Watching a sporting event, you can usually find an attractive young lady being swept off her feet by a less than attractive man after he opens the beer of his choice. Or,

3

if you are lucky, you can witness several young women materialize on a desert island with the male drinker after, of course, he opens his can of beer. These advertisements present women as a goal, a trophy if you will, that can only be attained with the proper beverage. The women seldom have anything to say besides "Yes," solidifying their portrayal as unintelligent sex objects.

Description and division or analysis

Example

Unfortunately, the exploitation does not stop with women. It touches minority groups as well, especially the African American community. In a recent issue of *Cosmopolitan* magazine, for example, an ad for Boost Mobile features a young, African American male sitting in a hot tub and staring into the sky. He is joined by three attractive women — two white, one under each arm, and one African American, watching the action farther to his left. The caption, "Pick up on a plan that pays off," is followed by the company's tag line: "Where You At?" In promoting the product in a women's magazine, Boost unabashedly reinforces long-standing stereotypes of African American male sexuality. Is that *really* where we are at? Are white women *really* the big "payoff" plan for today's young, African American male? Boost Mobile would like us to think so.

4

Description and division or analysis

Example

African Americans are not the only minority group exploited in advertising. Immigrants are regularly subjected to abuse as well. The most recent perpetrator, Citibank, promoted its credit card rewards program in 2006 and 2007 with commercials featuring two cartoonish immigrant characters: Roman, a man with a thick European accent, mustache, and polyester suit, and his sidekick, Victor. According to Citibank's ad agency, the campaign was supposed to have "unique humor and charm" (qtd. in Petracca). Viewers disagreed. More than half the consumers polled for *USA Today*'s weekly Ad Track survey said they disliked the ads (Petracca). In the commercial, Roman states in his accented English that Citibank's cards are rewarding. "Very, very, very rewarding." The poll shows that most of us found the ads to be annoying. Very, very, very annoying.

5

Description and comparison

Example

Racism and sexism in advertising is a problem that often goes unnoticed by the consumer today. Nevertheless, it must be dealt with. The only winners in these types of ad campaigns are the advertisers themselves, who make money when we purchase their products. There needs to be a public awakening, for racism and sexism should not be used in any situation, especially not to sell products. Advertisers need to take responsibility for their own actions and end this type of exploitation. But if they do not do so willingly, we the consumers can always force them. After all, we have the dollars and the sense.

6

Cause and effect

——————————————— Thomas de Zengotita ———————————————

AMERICAN IDOL WORSHIP (p. 160)

De Zengotita's essay focuses on a popular culture phenomenon that many students enjoy but probably have not thought about critically: the reality show *American Idol*. His assumption that most fans never stop to think about why the show is so popular resembles the underlying assumption of Shafecq Sadiq (p. 155) — that readers haven't really analyzed advertisements. Students may wonder, Why *not* take *American Idol* for granted? After all, it's just a TV show, right? De Zengotita suggests some reasons in his second and third paragraphs: the "virtual revolution" epitomized by *American Idol* affects our perceptions not only of the world around us but of ourselves as well. Questions 1 and 3 under "Meaning" and question 1 under "Purpose and Audience" are intended to help students begin to think about this question, as are the second and fourth writing topics.

The concept of "mediation" may prove challenging to some of your students, but most of them, having grown up thoroughly immersed in popular culture and implicitly trained to question its messages, will probably grasp the idea intuitively right away. Try not to let them get caught up in the jargon of de Zengotita's scholarly theorizing: the complexities of mediational theory are not essential to understanding his analysis of *American Idol*. If students are interested, however, the author's book *Mediated: How the Media Shapes Your World and the Way You Live in It* (2005) is a relatively accessible and consistently fascinating read. The introductory chapter, in particular, does a good job of explaining the basics of the author's conceptual framework.

Content Quiz

1. How many people watch *American Idol*?
   [The show has nearly 35 million viewers every week.]

2. What is the "virtual revolution"?
   [It's the recent phenomenon in which regular people produce and distribute their own forms of entertainment, such as blogs, podcasts, chat room posts, YouTube videos, and the like.]

3. Whom do most people identify as their heroes?
   [According to de Zengotita, most people would name somebody from their own lives or a performer/entertainer from popular culture.]

4. Why do musicians wield so much influence in contemporary culture?
   [De Zengotita offers two reasons: (1) they "create an experience of belonging that their fans would otherwise never know" by making "us the focus of attention," and (2) music is a profoundly personal and very powerful medium.]

5. What makes the humiliation of *American Idol* contestants unique?
   [Unlike contestants on other reality shows, *American Idol* hopefuls are per-

forming music, which, because it is so personal, leaves the performer psychically exposed and tremendously vulnerable.]

Vocabulary Quiz

1. *Nexus* (paragraph 2) is closest in meaning to
   a. vanity   b. combination   c. height
   [b. combination]

2. *Ruckus* (3) is closest in meaning to
   a. commotion   b. fistfight   c. explanation
   [a. commotion]

3. *Aura* (3) is closest in meaning to
   a. light   b. quality   c. crown
   [b. quality]

4. *Unironic* (7) is closest in meaning to
   a. predictable   b. sincere   c. self-conscious
   [b. sincere]

5. *Articulated* (7) is closest in meaning to
   a. literal   b. implied   c. spoken
   [c. spoken]

ANSWERS

Meaning

1. De Zengotita's thesis can be found in the first and last lines of paragraph 2. The reasons behind *American Idol*'s popularity, he asserts, lie in "a nexus of factors shaping the 'virtual revolution' unfolding all around us. . . . The *American Idol* format combines essential elements of this revolution." He repeats his thesis in the last two one-sentence paragraphs: "*American Idol* gives you so many ways to feel good about yourself. No wonder it's a hit."

2. For de Zengotita, the "virtual revolution" is marked by the audience's unwillingness to be "mere spectators" (paragraph 2) of the media. Recent technologies — notably, Internet file-sharing venues and the easy accessibility of digital photography and recording — make it easy for regular people to create and distribute their own media productions. *American Idol* takes the democratic impulses of the virtual revolution and repackages it for audience members, who in turn get to feel as if they had a hand in creating not only the show but also the individual "idols" themselves.

3. Students may struggle with this concept at first, but it's actually pretty simple. The central conceit of *American Idol* is that it turns everyday people — the fans — into musical heroes. The people watching the show are encouraged to imagine themselves as contestants, and they are given the voting power to decide which contestants will win, so they form a double identity in which they have the ability to transform themselves into superstars.

Stardom is the ultimate fantasy for people immersed in a popular culture that repeatedly tells them they're the center of the media universe, hence the "magic" of the show.

Purpose and Audience

1. De Zengotita sets out to explain why *American Idol* is popular. His primary purpose is, therefore, explanatory. But in encouraging his readers to examine the show closely, he's also trying to persuade them to develop a critical understanding of their own relationships with the "mediated world," as he describes it. By breaking a popular reality show down into its component parts, he forces us to look more closely at why it appeals to us. And by taking a critical rather than a personal stance toward his subject (he never explicitly identifies himself as a fan), the author attempts to exempt himself from the mediating influences he analyzes. How successful he is in that effort is open to debate.

2. De Zengotita assumes that he is addressing people who have seen *American Idol* and enjoyed it (the show draws "close to 35 million viewers" every week, as he acknowledges in the first paragraph, and it's nearly impossible to avoid being exposed to it by way of other media venues) but who have not thought fully about the show's implications. At the same time, the author is careful to describe individual elements of the show in enough detail so that the rare reader who has not seen it would probably have no trouble following his analysis.

   The question of being well versed in de Zengotita's *mediation* theory is a little trickier. Certainly, if readers are well versed in the concept of *mediation* as he defines it, it will help them follow his analysis of *American Idol*. All the same, perceptive readers should be able to grasp the basic idea — that popular culture influences how we perceive ourselves — from the context of the essay. Even if *mediation* means nothing to readers, however, de Zengotita's analysis of *American Idol* is developed thoroughly enough to make sense on its own merit and to open a few eyes to a new way of looking at the show.

Method and Structure

1. In de Zengotita's assessment, the unprecedented popularity of *American Idol* epitomizes the implications of the "virtual revolution" for consumers and producers of media products. Any of the examples the author cites in paragraph 2 — chat rooms, live journals, etc. — could serve to illustrate his point that new technologies and platforms are profoundly transforming the ways we interact with the media. But *American Idol* is so popular, and its influence is so wide-reaching, that it's an ideal subject for his analysis of this phenomenon.

2. De Zengotita is interested in the elements of *American Idol* that draw on the "'virtual revolution' unfolding all around us" (paragraph 2). Those elements, as he sees them, are the show's appeal to the "everyday hero" (3), its creation of "performer heroes" (4), the "power of music" in general (7), and the program's infamous exploitation of the contestants' "voluntary

personal humiliation" (8). All of these elements combine to make "you . . . feel good about yourself" (9).

3. De Zengotita finds it striking that "a show that features amateurs" (paragraph 1) is more popular than one that features professional musicians, but younger readers in particular won't be surprised by the discrepancy. And that is the essence of the author's point: just as the Grammy Awards and *American Idol* compete for viewership, the current media landscape as a whole pits "spectators against celebrities" (2) in a bid for attention. The spectators are winning, de Zengotita argues, because the deck is stacked in their favor. If the major function of popular culture is to make the spectator feel good, as the author believes, any program that directly involves the spectator in the spectacle is going to win.

4. The cause-and-effect component allows de Zengotita to anticipate and answer the question so often raised by division or analysis: so what? The author could have analyzed the elements of the show without examining the reasons for (and the implications of) its popularity, but the exercise would have seemed empty to most readers. Certainly, it wouldn't have satisfied de Zengotita, whose long-abiding interest in the media's effect on individual consciousness was his reason for examining the show in the first place.

Language

1. Your students may be relieved to know that several reviewers of *Mediated* complained about de Zengotita's predilection for mixing colloquial and scholarly language. He attempts to make complex ideas more accessible and "hip" by speaking the language of his high school students — hoping both to draw in readers who would normally avoid academic or philosophical subjects and to present himself as a savvy participant in media culture (rather than as an objective or disconnected academic observer). The effect depends on each reader's attitude. Some readers find it jarring and distracting to the point of invalidating de Zengotita's authority as a writer; others find it a reassuring source of the kind of performer-audience fusion that de Zengotita writes about.

2. The different points of view are part of de Zengotita's effort to form a common bond with his readers. Astute readers might suggest that the author uses first person when he wants to count himself among the audience of a particular form of entertainment, third person when he's trying to appear objective, and second person only at the end. Unfortunately, however, there appears to be no discernible pattern of his usage, probably a consequence of his original writing situation. (The essay originated as a newspaper column, so presumably it was written quickly.) As an exercise, you might try asking your students to revise the essay (or parts of it) to use a consistent point of view. Then ask them how the changes affect the piece's readability.

CHAPTER 8

CLASSIFICATION
Sorting Group Identities

—————————— Jonathan R. Gould Jr. ——————————
THE PEOPLE NEXT DOOR (p. 176)

Writing for a composition course, Gould puts classification to good use in rendering his experiences with neighbors. Students may be inspired to write their own classifications of the types of neighbors they've encountered. Gould's style is sometimes simple, sometimes humorous, but always direct and engaging — as reflected in his classification system. You might ask students what kind of neighbor Gould himself seems to be, based on his narratives, portrayals of his wife, and references to his family: too friendly, unsociable, irritable, or just right? You may then want to ask students what kind of neighbors they are: what category would their neighbors place them in?

Another way to prompt discussion is suggested by the first writing topic. Ask students to classify the members of a group they belong to, such as one centering on family background, ethnic group, musical interest, or political belief. Gould's distinct classes and clear examples can provide a model for such a discussion.

Content Quiz

1. How often has Gould moved?
   [More often than he "care[s] to remember."]

2. How does Gould get rid of neighbors who are too friendly?
   [He opens the door and suggests they leave, or tells them their house is on fire.]

3. What is the rarest type of neighbor?
   [The irritable neighbor. ("Fortunately, I have only encountered this type of neighbor in a handful of settings.")]

4. Which neighbors like to cook?
   [Too-friendly neighbors and just-right neighbors. But too-friendly neighbors cook poorly.]

5. Can a neighbor change from one type to another?
   [Not according to Gould: "people do not really change."]

Vocabulary Quiz

1. *Culinary* (paragraph 2) is closest in meaning to
   a. social   b. tasteful   c. cooking related
   [c. cooking related]

2. *Disconcerting* (2) is closest in meaning to
   a. deceitful   b. ironic   c. disturbing
   [c. disturbing]

3. *Proximity* (4) is closest in meaning to
   a. approximateness   b. nearness   c. togetherness
   [b. nearness]

4. *Impoverished* (4) is closest in meaning to
   a. hungry   b. poor   c. dirty
   [b. poor]

5. *Pleasantries* (5) is closest in meaning to
   a. small talk   b. advice   c. niceties
   [a. small talk]

ANSWERS
Meaning

1. "Over time, I have begun putting my neighbors into one of four categories: too friendly, unsociable, irritable, and just right" (paragraph 1).

2. Unsociable neighbors try to pretend that Gould and his family don't exist, while irritable neighbors blame the Goulds for everything wrong in their lives.

Purpose and Audience

1. Gould's conclusion makes his purpose clear: identifying neighbors by type, he (and by extension his readers) will be better able to understand and deal with them. Gould wants to share his system so that others might use it, and at the same time, it seems, he wants to entertain readers with types they'll recognize.

2. Not really; his essay could register with anyone who has ever had a neighbor.

Method and Structure

1. Classification helps Gould arrange neighbors — an otherwise unmanageably diverse group — into recognizable and amusing categories.

2. His classification is based on levels of friendliness or hostility toward his family. The classification seems complete and consistent on its own terms. He could have chosen to classify neighbors by how well they kept up appearances, their level of activity, their wealth, or any number of other criteria.

3. Gould wants to show that his categories are universal, not just based on his own limited or unrepresentative experience.

4. He restores the wholeness of the subject and suggests one reason for writing the essay: the ability to recognize the four types of neighbors makes for better relations with them.

5. The too-friendly neighbor doesn't seem to recognize boundaries (actual or psychological) between himself and Gould. The just-right neighbor has good instincts about Gould's need for privacy and sociability.

Language

1. Gould's tone is deadpan: "For some strange reason these people become extremely attached to my family" (paragraph 2); "the only way I know that someone lives in their building is the presence of a name on the mailbox and the lights shining through the windows at night" (3); "Interestingly, this fellow will eat anything my wife (bless her soul) might make in an attempt to be sociable" (4). In the final paragraph, he shows that his true attitude toward bad neighbors is one of good-humored resignation: he sees them as unavoidable nuisances to be taken in stride.

2. "[S]top in as many as eight to ten times a day" (paragraph 2); Gould's pretending his neighbor's house is on fire (2); "no culinary skill whatsoever" (2); "the only way I know that someone lives in their building is the presence of a name on the mailbox and the lights shining through the windows at night" (3); "I have to admire her courage" (3); "have them look at her as if she intended to poison them" (3); "will eat anything" (4); "not a crumb" (4); "starved and impoverished" (4). Students may make a case for other examples. The effect is to create humor by exaggerating the faults of bad neighbors.

——————————— **Marion Winik** ———————————

WHAT ARE FRIENDS FOR? (p. 180)

Winik's essay deals with the topic of friendship, a concept that arouses an immediate and profound emotional response. She uses the method of classification to help her account for the complexity of experiences that we share with all those whom we regard as our "friends." Class discussion could begin by eliciting information about students' friends and proceed to differentiate the varying relationships and activities that develop among individuals and groups.

Winik also relies on definition as a way to name the groups she is classifying. This technique can be quite useful to students in their own writing, and classroom discussion might revolve around how to combine classification and definition effectively.

Content Quiz

1. Who are the "workhorses of the friendship world"?
   ["Buddies."]

2. What does Winik think about a relative who is also a friend?
   [She describes this person as "the rare exception" but says that a relationship with a "Relative Friend" is comparatively worry-free.]

3. With what kind of friend might you share big celebrations and binges?
   [A "Faraway Friend."]

4. Is it good or bad to have a "Former Friend"?
   [It could be both. Winik describes this friend as "[a]t best a wistful memory, at worst a dangerous enemy."]

5. Which kind of friend is on the other end of the spectrum from the "Friends You Love to Hate"?
   [The "Hero Friend."]

Vocabulary Quiz

1. *Counsel* (paragraph 2) is closest in meaning to
   a. advice   b. stories   c. conversation
   [a. advice]

2. *Infallible* (6) is closest in meaning to
   a. undependable   b. reliable   c. unflinching
   [b. reliable]

3. *Wistful* (10) is closest in meaning to
   a. unrelenting   b. nostalgic   c. profound
   [b. nostalgic]

4. *Lest* (11) is closest in meaning to
   a. indeed   b. in fact   c. in case
   [c. in case]

5. *Inopportune* (11) is closest in meaning to
   a. optimal   b. suitable   c. inconvenient
   [c. inconvenient]

ANSWERS
Meaning

1. Winik's thesis is that different people fulfill different functions for each other. In her first sentence, she states clearly, "[E]verybody can't be everything to each other, but some people can be something to each other." In showing what people can be to each other, the rest of the essay answers the title question, "What Are Friends For?"

2. There are nine categories of friends, according to Winik, and they all fulfill different functions. Buddies, described as the "workhorses of the friendship world" (paragraph 2), perform myriad important and insignificant tasks. Relative Friends offer insights into family affairs. Work Friends are vital at work but do not function outside the workplace. They resemble School Friends in eventually providing nostalgic memories. Faraway Friends offer a map of your past. Former Friends are either sad memories or dangerous enemies. Friends You Love to Hate are people you can gossip about. Hero Friends somehow do not annoy you because they really are perfect. New Friends are a pleasure, a "tonic unlike any other" (14).

3. New Friends are different from other kinds of friends in that they do not know you well enough to judge you: Winik remarks, "Your various shortcomings are as yet completely invisible" (paragraph 14). Finding a New Friend is like falling in love because it has the same freshness and unspoiled romantic glow.

Purpose and Audience

1. The opening sentence implies that Winik intends the essay not to be taken as gospel: she's just thinking, reminiscing about her own friendships, sharing ideas, not especially trying to win readers over to her opinion. "I was thinking" (paragraph 1) is typical of conversation and establishes the conversational tone of the essay.

2. While this essay is written from a decidedly female viewpoint (for instance, the first paragraph mentions the friends "whose half-slips you borrow"), Winik's examples make clear that at least two categories — Relative Friends (paragraph 3) and Work Friends (5) — can be of either sex. Perhaps the others can, too. This openness may make the essay more accessible to both male and female readers, although some students may not agree that the two sexes can be more than casual friends.

Method and Structure

1. Winik's thesis at the beginning of the essay — that different people play different roles in our lives — begs for the classification method and entices the audience to learn just what those differences are.

2. Winik establishes these groups based not on inherent differences between her friends but on the role that each type of friend plays for her. For example, the Work Friend is important to her because together they can make jokes about coworkers (paragraphs 5, 6). In contrast, the Faraway Friend is invaluable in retracing the author's past (7–9). As for why Winik gives short shrift to School Friends (simply comparing them to Work Friends), perhaps she thinks the category is one all readers will have experience with and thus understand. Some students may question the lack of development of the category, even in an informal classification like Winik's.

3. Winik makes few explicit transitions between categories besides those in paragraphs 3, 5, 11, and 13. Some of her moves are rather abrupt, such

as those in paragraphs 7, 10, and 14. Some students may prefer a more guided approach. Others may find Winik's approach appropriate for her casual, informal tone.

4. Winik takes the most care to define Buddies (paragraph 2), Relative Friends (3, 4), Work Friends (5, 6), Faraway Friends (7–9), Friends You Love to Hate (11, 12), and possibly Hero Friends (13). These, presumably, are the categories she finds most important or most problematic (needing the most explanation). Winik elaborates on the titles she assigns to the groups by giving specific definitions. For example, we might initially confuse Faraway Friends with Former Friends. However, the definitions of these friends (7, 10) clearly differentiate between the two categories.

Language

1. The other instances appear later in paragraph 3 and in this passage from paragraph 5: "Your friendship is cemented by jokes about coworkers and thoughtful favors around the office. Did you see Ryan's hair? Want half my bagel?" These unmarked lines of dialogue intensify the informal, conversational tone of the piece.

2. Omitted words, incomplete sentences, and other rule bending all add to the impression that Winik is engaging in a conversation with the reader, since they are more typical of oral rather than written style.

3. Other metaphors include the description of the Work Friend as initially "just part of the scenery" (paragraph 5) and eventually sharing memories with "a nostalgic glow" (6). In an extended metaphor on Faraway Friends, Winik likens them to guides when "you've hit a dead end, come to a confusing fork in the road, or gotten lost in some crackerbox subdivision of your life" — guides who have "the big picture," who know "the route that brought you to this place" (8). In addition, "[a] New Friend is a tonic" (14). These and other metaphors convey meaning vividly and economically by calling on readers' associations.

ANNOTATED ESSAY

I was thinking about how everybody can't be everything to each other, but some people can be something to each other, thank God, from the ones whose shoulder you cry on to the ones whose half-slips you borrow to the nameless ones you chat with in the grocery line.

Buddies, for example, are the workhorses of the friendship world, the people out there on the front lines, defending you from loneliness and boredom. They call you up, they listen to your complaints, they celebrate your successes and curse your misfortunes, and you do the same for them in return. They hold out through innumerable crises before concluding that the person you're dating is no good, and even then understand if you ignore their good counsel. They accompany you to a movie

1   THESIS

2

Definition
and
example

Classification

with subtitles or to see the diving pig at Aquarena Springs. They feed your cat when you are out of town and pick you up from the airport when you get back. They come over to help you decide what to wear on a date. Even if it is with that creep.

What about family members? Most of them are people you just got stuck with, and though you love them, you may not have very much in common. But there is that rare exception, the Relative Friend. It is your cousin, your brother, maybe even your aunt. The two of you share the same views of the other family members. Meg never should have divorced Martin. He was the best thing that ever happened to her. You can confirm each other's memories of things that happened a long time ago. Don't you remember when Uncle Hank and Daddy had that awful fight in the middle of Thanksgiving dinner? Grandma always hated Grandpa's stamp collection; she probably left the windows open during the hurricane on purpose.

While so many family relationships are tinged with guilt and obligation, a relationship with a Relative Friend is relatively worry free. You don't even have to hide your vices from this delightful person. When you slip out Aunt Joan's back door for a cigarette, she is already there.

Then there is that special guy at work. Like all the other people at the job site, at first he's just part of the scenery. But gradually he starts to stand out from the crowd. Your friendship is cemented by jokes about coworkers and thoughtful favors around the office. Did you see Ryan's hair? Want half my bagel? Soon you know the names of his turtles, what he did last Friday night, exactly which model CD player he wants for his birthday. His handwriting is as familiar to you as your own.

Though you invite each other to parties, you somehow don't quite fit into each other's outside lives. For this reason, the friendship may not survive a job change. Company gossip, once an infallible source of entertainment, soon awkwardly accentuates the distance between you. But wait. Like School Friends, Work Friends share certain memories which acquire a nostalgic glow after about a decade.

A Faraway Friend is someone you grew up with or went to school with or lived in the same town as until one of you moved away. Without a Faraway Friend, you would never get any mail addressed in handwriting. A Faraway Friend calls late at night, invites you to her wedding, always says she is coming to visit but rarely shows up. An actual visit from a Faraway Friend is a cause for celebration and binges of all kinds. Cigarettes, Chips Ahoy, bottles of tequila.

Faraway Friends go through phases of intense communication, then may be out of touch for many months. Either way, the connection is always there. A conversation with your Faraway Friend always helps to put your life in perspective: when you feel you've hit a dead end, come to a confusing fork in the road, or gotten lost in some crackerbox subdivision of your life, the

3

Definition
and example

Classification

4

5

Definition

Example

6

Cause and
effect

7

Definition
and example

Example

Definition

8

Process
analysis

advice of the Faraway Friend — who has the big picture, who is so well acquainted with the route that brought you to this place — is indispensable.

Another useful function of the Faraway Friend is to help you remember things from a long time ago, like the name of your seventh-grade history teacher, what was in that really good stir-fry, or exactly what happened that night on the boat with the guys from Florida.

Ah, the Former Friend. A sad thing. At best a wistful memory, at worst a dangerous enemy who is in possession of many of your deepest secrets. But what was it that drove you apart? A misunderstanding, a betrayed confidence, an unrepaid loan, an ill-conceived flirtation. A poor choice of spouse can do in a friendship just like that. Going into business together can be a serious mistake. Time, money, distance, cult religions: all noted friendship killers. You quit doing drugs, you're not such good friends with your dealer anymore.

And lest we forget, there are the Friends You Love to Hate. They call at inopportune times. They say stupid things. They butt in, they boss you around, they embarrass you in public. They invite themselves over. They take advantage. You've done the best you can, but they need professional help. On top of all this, they love you to death and are convinced they're your best friend on the planet.

So why do you continue to be involved with these people? Why do you tolerate them? On the contrary, the real question is, What would you do without them? Without Friends You Love to Hate, there would be nothing to talk about with your other friends. Their problems and their irritating stunts provide a reliable source of conversation for everyone they know. What's more, Friends You Love to Hate make you feel good about yourself, since you are obviously in so much better shape than they are. No matter what these people do, you will never get rid of them. As much as they need you, you need them too.

At the other end of the spectrum are Hero Friends. These people are better than the rest of us, that's all there is to it. Their career is something you wanted to be when you grew up — painter, forest ranger, tireless doer of good. They have beautiful homes filled with special handmade things presented to them by villagers in the remote areas they have visited in their extensive travels. Yet they are modest. They never gossip. They are always helping others, especially those who have suffered a death in the family or an illness. You would think people like this would just make you sick, but somehow they don't.

A New Friend is a tonic unlike any other. Say you meet her at a party. In your bowling league. At a Japanese conversation class, perhaps. Wherever, whenever, there's that spark of recognition. The first time you talk, you can't believe how much you have in common. Suddenly, your life story is interesting again,

9   Example

10   Classification

Definition and cause and effect

11   Example

Definition

12

Comparison

13

Definition, example, and comparison

Classification

14

Definition, and cause and effect

your insights fresh, your opinion valued. Your various short-comings are as yet completely invisible.

It's almost like falling in love.

15
Comparison

Walter Mosley

SHOW ME THE MONEY (p. 186)

Mosley's essay is both more serious and more challenging than the other essays in the chapter, but it should capture students' interest because it touches on a subject that affects everyone: money. Whether students approach his classification from the belief that America is a classless society or from a conviction that class is endemic, Mosley's categorizations of wealth are likely to come as a surprise — especially to those who define themselves as middle-class.

Some students will surely be put off by Mosley's strong language, while others may embrace the writer's socialist perspective. Such political divisions could lead to compelling (if contentious) classroom debate, provided you set some ground rules for mutual respect and thoughtful deliberation. Alternatively, you might focus on how Mosley structures his argument, noting how a third of the essay sets up his reasons for categorizing Americans by class (paragraphs 1–9) and another third explains the implications of his system (17–21). Mosley uses classification, which comprises the middle of the essay (10–16), to advance a serious (and controversial) argument, not as an end in itself.

Content Quiz

1. What economic class do most Americans consider themselves to be?
   [Most think of themselves as "middle-class workers."]

2. How is poverty defined?
   [By the inability to meet basic needs, such as food, medicine, and shelter.]

3. How is wealth defined?
   [By not having to think about money.]

4. What are the two subcategories of the middle class?
   [The "working class" and "the class of limited privilege."]

5. What is a "wage-slave"?
   [A working-class person whose labor generates money for someone else.]

Vocabulary Quiz

1. *Irrefutable* (paragraph 1) is closest in meaning to
   a. garbage   b. undeniable   c. incorrect
   [b. undeniable]

2. *Genesis* (4) is closest in meaning to
   a. origin   b. perfection   c. opposite
   [a. origin]

3. *Flux* (7) is closest in meaning to
   a. trouble   b. growth   c. change
   [c. change]

4. *Gauged* (11) is closest in meaning to
   a. measured   b. earned   c. spent
   [a. measured]

5. *Harbinger* (20) is closest in meaning to
   a. destroyer   b. sign   c. result
   [b. sign]

ANSWERS

Meaning

1. Mosley's thesis, which he uses as a transition between his classification system and his assessment of its implications, appears in the middle of his essay. "Most Americans," he says, "are working-class wage-slaves, arguing that they're better off. This fantasy, more than any other confusion, hobbles us. Because we fear to see how delicate our economic state is, we cannot motivate ourselves to demand change" (paragraph 16).

2. Even though he's a successful writer with a large list of best-selling novels to his credit, Mosley counts himself among the majority: he considers himself working-class. This group, he says, is by far the predominant class in America, even if most people think of themselves as middle-class.

3. The statement is an effective summary of the Marxist critique of capitalism. Mosley's point is that the rich don't earn their wealth. Rather, he argues, the money enjoyed by the upper classes is derived from the hard work of the working class. In other words, the rich exploit the labors of the poor for their own benefit.

Purpose and Audience

1. Mosley's essay is a call to arms intended to inspire readers to fight the system. He may indeed mean to offer some consolation to those of us who are struggling under the financial structure of American society, but more than that, he wants to "motivate [readers] to demand change" (paragraph 16).

2. Mosley wrote this for the *Nation,* a progressive magazine with a strong political focus and a well-educated, high-income subscriber base. According to the magazine's own demographic profiles, more than three-quarters of its readers hold a college degree, more than half hold a graduate degree, nearly half earn $75,000 or more a year, and the vast majority are employed in a professional or managerial position. Mosley knows this

about his readers, but despite their relative affluence, he tries to shake them out of their belief that they are middle-class or better, at least partly by his continual use of the first person plural (*we, us*) to refer to the working class.

3. Mosley's categories are surprising if nothing else. He strengthens his unconventional classification by offering his own definitions of terms. In Mosley's system, most of us are working-class not because we hold blue-collar jobs or struggle financially, but because he defines the working class as those who depend on a regular paycheck to stay afloat — regardless of the size of the paycheck.

Method and Structure

1. Classification is the perfect method for Mosley's purpose, which is to change his readers' conception of how the American class system is structured and where they fit into that system. Re-sorting the classes according to his own principle of analysis is a very effective way to get his readers to rethink their positions. Classification lets him redraw the lines around poor, middle-class, and rich and to position his readers in a class to which they would never have assigned themselves.

2. Mosley groups Americans into three major classes: rich, poor, and middle class, the last of which he further subdivides into the "working class" and "the class of limited privilege" (paragraph 12). His principle of classification is outlined in paragraphs 10 and 11: he defines class not by the conventional markers of bank balance or job description, but by people's "ability to cover the basic necessities in their lives" and the options they have available to them. He makes these distinctions because although most of his readers think of themselves as middle-class and comfortable, he wants to show that they're closer to the working class than they are to the wealthy. By changing his readers' perceptions of their own financial status, he hopes to realign their political allegiances and redirect their goals.

3. The heart of Mosley's classification appears in paragraphs 10–16, and it shouldn't be surprising that he devotes most of that space to explaining what he means by the "working class." He needs to briefly explain what he means by "poverty" (10) and "wealth" (11), but to truly convince his readers that they are actually working-class, he needs to define that category with the most detail.

4. Definition is essential to Mosley's purpose because he is proposing new understandings of terms that most people interpret far differently than he wants them to. If he didn't clarify his use of the terms "poverty," "wealth," "middle class," "working class," and "class of limited privilege," readers would assume these terms' traditional meanings, which would cause them to misunderstand Mosley's classification entirely.

Language

1. Mosley's tone is ponderous and highly polemical. He is quite serious, verging on angry and certainly determined. Whether that strengthens or weak-

ens the effectiveness of his argument depends on each reader's preference. Many readers will be put off by his tone; others will find that it aligns with their own views.

2. Mosley's diction suggests that his audience is educated (as the readers of the *Nation* tend to be), which further implies that they also earn above-average salaries (also true of *Nation* readers). By using the first person to address this audience, he emphasizes their (and his own) position among the working class, which is the primary subject of his essay.

3. Mosley's position is undoubtedly that of a Marxist, as his explicit reference to Marxism makes clear. Additional examples of overtly Marxist language include "the sweat, the sacrifice and ultimately the blood of working men and women" (paragraph 3); "citizens" (5); "relationship to your labor" (6); "capitalism, the accrual of wealth from labor" (17); and "we are not partners in the corporation of America" (19).

CHAPTER 9

PROCESS ANALYSIS
Examining the Human Body

Rachel Hannon

HOW TO DONATE PLASMA AND
SAVE MORE LIVES (p. 203)

One of the most accessible pieces in *The Compact Reader*, "How to Donate Plasma and Save More Lives" is a clear and uncomplicated example of directive process analysis that should certainly persuade students that they are capable of writing a similar essay themselves. Hannon's purpose is simple, her language is engaging, and her approach is straightforward.

Hannon was commissioned to write this essay, but the topic was entirely her idea. An enthusiastic volunteer who plans to dedicate her life to nonprofit work, she feels strongly about the benefits of helping others and wanted to encourage other students to give of themselves. To help your students prepare for the second writing topic, you might ask them about their own passions. What do they do in their spare time? What do they think is most important in life? How can they draw on their own experiences to encourage others to try something new?

Content Quiz

1. Who is helped by plasma donations?
   [Beneficiaries include recipients of transplant and cardiovascular surgery, chemotherapy patients, burn victims, hemophiliacs, and newborns.]

2. What are the four components of whole blood?
   [Red blood cells, white blood cells, platelets, and plasma.]

3. How does apheresis work?
   [Blood is pumped through an intravenous tube into a machine that extracts the plasma and returns the rest of the blood to the donor's body.]

4. How is a plasma donor likely to feel when the procedure is over?
   [Extremely tired.]

5. How often can a person donate plasma?
   [Twelve times a year.]

Vocabulary Quiz

1. *Concentrated* (paragraph 2) is closest in meaning to
   a. thoughtful   b. undiluted   c. imprisoned
   [b. undiluted]

2. *Hinder* (2) is closest in meaning to
   a. prevent   b. qualify   c. enable
   [a. prevent]

3. *Compromised* (2) is closest in meaning to
   a. acceptable   b. different   c. weakened
   [c. weakened]

4. *Disconcerting* (6) is closest in meaning to
   a. upsetting   b. loud   c. confusing
   [a. upsetting]

5. *Extraneous* (7) is closest in meaning to
   a. strenuous   b. unnecessary   c. educational
   [b. unnecessary]

ANSWERS

Meaning

1. The first draft of Hannon's thesis statement merely expressed a fact; it was also unnecessarily vague. Her revised thesis statement is much stronger because it expresses her purpose for writing and makes an assertion about her subject, challenging her readers to try the process she describes.

2. Plasma is one of four components of whole blood. The distinction is important because the Red Cross uses plasma for specific purposes that don't call for the other components. By extracting only the plasma, the Red Cross can be more efficient and prevent waste.

Purpose and Audience

1. Hannon's purpose is implied in her thesis statement and expressed directly in her conclusion: she hopes to persuade readers to donate plasma and to do so regularly.

2. The side effects that Hannon describes may discourage some readers from donating plasma, but her forthrightness in describing negative as well as positive aspects of the process establishes her credibility and will help to persuade readers that the discomforts involved are minor.

3. Several examples in Hannon's essay demonstrate that she is writing for students: she instructs her readers to choose "a day when you know you do not have class or much homework" (paragraph 3), jokes about being "stuck watching a boring show" (5), and warns them not to "attend any parties or extraneous activities" (7) for at least a day after the donation. A student

herself, Hannon seems to assume that her readers are as volunteer-minded as she is. (This may be true of many college students, but in taking for granted that most of her readers have "participated in a blood drive" and know "how good it feels to make a difference in a stranger's life" (1), Hannon risks alienating readers who are not already blood donors.)

Method and Structure

1. Many readers might be reluctant to volunteer for something they perceive as complicated or painful. By outlining the procedures and explaining what potential donors can expect at each stage, Hannon demystifies the process and tries to dispel readers' fears, persuading them that what she is asking of them is not only worthwhile but also relatively easy and painless.

2. Hannon's research was minimal (just a few basic facts from an informative Web site), but she provides all the information readers need to understand, as Hannon puts it, "what plasma is and why patients would need it instead of whole blood" (paragraph 2). She also offers authoritative advice from the Red Cross about who may donate and how donors should prepare for an appointment (4), adding important objective details to a process analysis that draws on a subjective experience.

3. Transitions, which Hannon varies to hold readers' interest, clarify the sequence of actions: "the first thing" (paragraph 3), "for at least 48 hours" (3), "when you arrive" (4), "after you complete" (4), "once the nurse has confirmed" (5), "when the time is up" (7), "at this point" (7).

4. Hannon uses definition in paragraph 2 to explain what plasma is and to clarify how it is different from whole blood. This is important, because many readers will not otherwise understand the point of donating plasma.

Language

1. Most readers will have heard the Red Cross slogan before. By building on a concept that readers already know and most likely accept as true, Hannon is able to suggest that plasma donation is beneficial without having to justify her suggestion. If readers already believe in the value of saving one life, the author can reasonably assume that they will be intrigued by the prospect of saving more.

2. If Hannon's essay had been written in the past tense from a first-person point of view, it would have been a personal narrative rather than a directive process analysis, weakening its ability to persuade readers that they can (and should) donate plasma themselves.

3. Hannon's tone might best be described as eager, lighthearted, and idealistic. She attempts to create a sense of camaraderie with her readers. Some may find her enthusiasm infectious, but others may feel that it is presumptuous.

ANNOTATED ESSAY

Anybody who has participated in a blood drive knows how   1
good it feels to make a difference in a stranger's life. Hospitals
rely on donations to replace blood lost in accidents or surgery
and to treat chronic diseases such as anemia and leukemia.
That's why I have been making blood donations for the past
four years. But did you know that you can also donate something called plasma? I didn't. Just a few months ago, I was on
the American National Red Cross Web site looking for a phone
number when I stumbled across an appeal for plasma donors.
Intrigued, I immediately called the local center for more information. Plasma donations, I learned, enable the Red Cross to help
people who have undergone transplant or cardiovascular surgery, chemotherapy, or severe burns. Instead of donating blood
that month, I donated plasma, and I'm glad I did. Although giving plasma is more complicated and time-consuming than giv-   THESIS
ing blood, every healthy person should set aside a day to do it.

You might wonder, as I did, what plasma is and why   2
patients would need it instead of whole blood. The Red Cross
explains that human blood is made up of four components: red
blood cells, white blood cells, platelets, and plasma. Blood plasma is a yellowish water-based protein that helps to stabilize
blood pressure, improve immune responses, and control bleed-   Definition
ing, making it an invaluable resource for treating newborn
babies, cancer patients, burn victims, and hemophiliacs. The
lifesaving fluid is obtained by a procedure called *apheresis*, in
which blood is drawn and circulated through a machine that   Process
separates the blood components from one another, removing   analysis
the plasma and returning the rest of the blood to the donor's
body. Because the process extracts only the components that
patients need, nothing is wasted: a single donation can help
twice as many people. At the same time, concentrated transfu-   Cause
sions from a single donor are less likely to be rejected by a re-   and
cipient's immune system, making plasma safer than blood for   effect
people whose health is already compromised. Blood is always
needed, of course, but giving blood does not and should not
hinder you from donating plasma, too.

To donate plasma, the first thing you'll need to do is call   3
your nearest Red Cross center (check the phone book or
http://www.redcross.org for locations). Schedule your appointment for a day when you know you do not have class or much
homework, because the process can take up to two hours. Do
not consume any products containing aspirin for at least forty-   Process
eight hours before your appointment, since aspirin can thin   analysis
blood. The Red Cross recommends that you consume a lot of
water before you arrive, because dehydrated donors have been
known to experience extreme exhaustion. For added nourishment, eat something substantial the day of your appointment as
well: a bagel or pasta should do the trick.

There will be a number of preparatory procedures to follow 4
when you arrive at the donation center. First, you will be asked
to fill out some paperwork regarding your medical history: Be
prepared to answer questions about any allergies you have,
medications you're taking, immunizations you've received, and
diseases in your family history. The Red Cross asks that you be   Process
at least 17 years old, weigh at least 110 pounds, and not have   analysis
given blood for 56 days prior to donating plasma. (Even people
with some chronic conditions, including diabetes and hypertension, are eligible to donate as long as their symptoms are under
control.) After you complete the paperwork, you will be asked
to take an AIDS test to be sure your plasma isn't infected with
HIV; this takes only a few minutes. A nurse will take you to a
station and prick your finger for a small sample of blood.

Once the nurse has confirmed that you're healthy enough to 5
donate plasma, she or he will lead you to the room where the
donation takes place. Depending on the layout of your local
Red Cross center, you may have a hospital-like room all to your-   Description
self, or you may share a ward with several people. You will be
provided with a bed and a television, but bring a magazine or a
book to occupy yourself just in case: you wouldn't want to be
stuck watching a boring show! Although the bed is comfortable
and typically equipped with a blanket, you will be in it for two
hours and unable to move your arm, so get as comfortable as
possible before the nurse leaves. Take a trip to the restroom and
ask for an extra pillow or anything else that might help you feel
comfortable: you don't want to get a stiff neck or develop an
urge to move your arm.

Once you're situated, the nurse will hook you up to the 6
apheresis machine with an intravenous (IV) tube. If you have a
queasy stomach, like me, do not look at the tube. Although the
procedure is painless (unless you move your arm and feel the
needle pinch), it can be disconcerting to see your own blood
flowing down the tube, disappearing into the machine, and
recirculating back into your body. Waiting for the donation to
be over is the hard part: concentrate on whatever entertainment
you have, and remember how much help your plasma will be
to those who are suffering from cancer, blood disease, or cardiovascular disease.

When the time is up, the nurse will unhook you from the IV 7
tube and bring you to another room, where you will have a few
minutes to recuperate. At this point, your blood sugar will be
low and you may feel dizzy. Drink some water or nibble on one   Cause
of the sugary snacks provided by the Red Cross center to give   and
your body some nourishment. When you feel rested — the tim-   effect
ing varies from person to person — you can leave. While you
should feel relatively well, you will most likely be extremely
tired. Plan on taking public transportation if it's available, or
ask a friend or family member to accompany you home in case
you feel too weak to drive. When you get home, take a good

long nap! Do not plan to attend any parties or perform any extraneous activities for at least twenty-four hours, because you will most likely still be feeling exhausted up to a day after your donation.

After you've completed the entire process of donating your plasma — from scheduling your appointment to recovering completely — consider donating again. The Red Cross allows you to donate up to twelve times a year. Just as I made donating blood a regular practice in my life, I now make regular plasma donations, too.

8

Atul Gawande

THE CENTRAL LINE (p. 209)

Given the enduring popularity of hospital dramas on television and the resulting debates over medical issues, students are sure to respond to Gawande's firsthand account of one of the most troublesome paradoxes of modern medicine — the unavoidable necessity of practicing new techniques on people who would rather have more skilled surgeons doing the work. Students might have a strong reaction to the grisly details in the piece, in the form of either morbid fascination or indignant revulsion.

A good way to initiate discussion of Gawande's central dilemma (doctors can't learn without practicing, but patients deserve the highest quality of care) might be to ask your students to share some of their own hospital experiences. Did it ever occur to them that the doctors they trust with their lives might not know what they're doing? How do they feel about being essentially human guinea pigs? Having read Gawande's essay, are they more or less likely to demand an experienced surgeon or to refuse to let a student doctor touch them? Can there be any solution to the problem Gawande assumes is unsolvable?

Content Quiz

1. Why did Gawande's patient need a central line?
   [The man was recuperating from abdominal surgery and couldn't eat. He needed a central line to deliver nutrients to his body.]

2. What is the vena cava?
   [The major artery that delivers blood to the heart.]

3. What are some of the risks associated with a central line?
   [Bleeding, laceration, collapsed lung, loose foreign objects in the body, cardiac arrest, ventricular fibrillation.]

4. What does the guidewire used for a central line look like?
   [It's two feet long and quite thick. Gawande compares it to "the steel D string of an electric guitar."]

5. What is the purpose of putting a rolled towel under the patient's back? [It makes the chest arch out.]

Vocabulary Quiz

1. *Taciturn* (paragraph 2) is closest in meaning to
   a. obese   b. mean   c. quiet
   [c. quiet]

2. *Apex* (4) is closest in meaning to
   a. bottom   b. middle   c. top
   [c. top]

3. *Chastened* (10) is closest in meaning to
   a. pure   b. embarrassed   c. stubborn
   [b. embarrassed]

4. *Girded* (10) is closest in meaning to
   a. prepared   b. scolded   c. humiliated
   [a. prepared]

5. *Reproof* (19) is closest in meaning to
   a. evidence   b. criticism   c. praise
   [b. criticism]

ANSWERS

Meaning

1. As the author explains in paragraph 2, "central line" is the term for both a catheter and the relatively simple medical procedure in which that catheter is threaded into a patient's body and sewn into place. In the case Gawande describes, the line would be used to deliver nutrients into a major artery of a patient who couldn't eat, and the procedure proved to be not nearly as simple as one might expect.

2. Gawande told the patient that the procedure rarely involves complications when it is performed by "experienced hands," but he neglected to mention that he had never done it before. The implication is that the young resident lied (through omission) to get the patient's permission for him to practice.

3. He does believe it. His own experience with the central line (not to mention examples of complications in the rest of the book) demonstrates that even routine procedures can go wrong, and surgery doesn't always have the desired effect. As Gawande says in paragraph 19, surgeons learn to be confident despite uncertainty.

4. Gawande's thesis statement, provided as a clue in the headnote on page 210, appears later in his chapter: "The uncomfortable truth about teaching" surgery is that "we want perfection without practice." He goes on to say, "[Y]et everyone is harmed if no one is trained for the future. So learning is

hidden, behind drapes and anesthesia and the elisions of language." The excerpt reprinted in *The Compact Reader* comes closest to expressing this point — implied in the telling of the central line story at all — when Gawande writes, "[I]t is people we practice upon" (paragraph 20).

Purpose and Audience

1. Gawande exposes his fumbling with the procedure to make a point about the ethics of medical training and to persuade readers that although mistakes are inevitable, novice doctors must be allowed to learn by doing. He wants readers to cringe at the story but also to recognize that learning medicine is a process and that mistakes are inevitable. Some students may recognize that the author is responding to an ongoing cultural debate about teaching hospitals, which train doctors by letting them work on patients who may or may not realize that they're not getting the best possible care.

2. He is writing for a general audience of intelligent, curious readers with an interest in medicine and ethics. Clues to his audience can be found in his effort to make his subject feel immediate and not a little scary, in his confessional tone, and in his mixture of professional jargon and colloquial language.

3. The bulk of the process is described from the point of view of an experienced doctor remembering what it was like to be an inexperienced resident frightened by a particular task. His novice perspective is evident in the immediacy of comments such as "this will be good . . . my first real procedure" (paragraph 2), "I couldn't put it off any longer" (6), "that was bad" (9), "damn" (11), and "this is a big . . . needle" (12). At the same time, he keeps some distance from his earlier fumbling by intermingling present and past tense, as well as by framing the narrative with explanations of how the procedure should go and ruminations on what he has learned since then: "once you have the tip of the needle poking in the vein, you have to widen the hole in the vein wall" (5) and "every day, surgeons are faced with uncertainties" (19).

Method and Structure

1. Gawande is describing two processes: (1) how a central line is inserted and (2) how doctors learn. He summarizes the steps of the first process in paragraph 2: "[I]t would involve my laying him out flat, numbing up a spot on his chest with local anesthetic, and then threading the line in." Paragraphs 4–17 explain these steps in excruciating detail. The steps of the second process are less explicit and might be summarized as "[Y]ou have to keep trying, and making mistakes, until you get the hang of it."

2. Most of the essay uses explanatory process, but in paragraph 5, Gawande speaks directly to readers in the second person, as though he were teaching them how to insert a central line. Obviously, he doesn't intend for readers to attempt the procedure; his strategy is to show how it feels to be in the uncomfortable position of trying to understand the instructions.

3. Transitions clarify the sequence of actions and thoughts: "I did not say" (paragraph 2), "Nor did I say" (2), "But, of course" (3), "once you have the tip of the needle poking in the vein" (5), "To do this" (5), "She then removed" (5), "Now it was my turn" (6), "When I finally had the stuff together" (6), "Next" (12), "This time" (14), "Finally" (18).

4. Although the essay is a personal narrative about his first central line, Gawande makes a point throughout of explaining the process that applies anytime a doctor performs the procedure, especially in paragraphs 4 and 5, where he reports how the chief resident did it, and then again in paragraphs 6–17, where he relates his step-by-step attempt (and failure) to replicate what he saw her do.

Language

1. The sometimes jarring combination of medical terminology — "ventricular fibrillation" (paragraph 3), "subclavian vein" (4), "dilator" (5), "cc's" (7), "platelet count" (8) — with unmistakably informal words and phrases — "flinch" (4), "you knew because" (4), "took me forever" (6), and "stuff" (6) — nicely re-creates a medical resident's ambivalent sense of knowing something about medicine while really knowing nothing. Gawande follows many of his medical terms with a brief definition for general readers; the ones he doesn't define create for his readers the same sense of confusion that he felt as a resident.

2. Gawande can be very explicit in his descriptions; students should have no trouble identifying vivid imagery that makes them cringe. The author includes them to stress the risks of surgery and highlight doctors' fears. Readers can't miss his point that even routine surgery is dangerous.

3. Other examples: "a string of rapid heartbeats fired off on the cardiac monitor" (paragraph 5), "a bullet of thick, stiff plastic" (5), "spearing his clavicle" (12), "surfing hand gesture" (14). By comparing obscure medical equipment and procedures to familiar objects, Gawande suggests how new they were to him while simultaneously making them vivid for readers who aren't familiar with surgery either.

4. Gawande's tone is thoughtful, confessional, and deliberately naive. Some readers might find him disingenuous, but the tone seems appropriate for a personal introduction to the "complications" of hospital training.

Jessica Mitford

EMBALMING MR. JONES (p. 216)

Mitford's essay shows students that process analysis need not be a dull series of directions and demonstrates how the method can be used to explain and support a strongly held belief. But her sardonic view of funeral customs may shock some students. Discussing the underlying seriousness of the essay and Mitford's probable reasons for choosing such an approach helps answer those concerns. As an alternative, you may want to elicit defenses of funeral directors, their profession, and American funeral customs.

Content Quiz

1. In what part of the world is embalming most widely used?
   [North America.]

2. Is embalming required by law?
   [No.]

3. What is a dermasurgeon?
   [An embalmer.]

4. What is the first step in the embalming process?
   [Removing the blood from the body.]

5. When is the best time to begin the embalming process?
   ["Before life is completely extinct — that is, before cellular death has occurred."]

Vocabulary Quiz

1. *Mortuary* (paragraph 1) is closest in meaning to
   a. graveyard   b. funeral home   c. morgue
   [b. funeral home]

2. *Decedent* (3) is closest in meaning to
   a. deceased   b. relative   c. mortician
   [a. deceased]

3. *Intractable* (6) is closest in meaning to
   a. stubborn   b. unclear   c. consistent
   [a. stubborn]

4. *Rudimentary* (10) is closest in meaning to
   a. refined   b. undeveloped   c. secondary
   [b. undeveloped]

5. *Somatic* (10) is closest in meaning to
   a. bodily   b. brain   c. technical
   [a. bodily]

ANSWERS

Meaning

1. Embalming and restoration make the corpse suitable for viewing by using costly measures to erase all traces of the cause of death. They are performed, Mitford seems to believe, because people are ignorant of the procedures (paragraphs 4, 5).

2. Americans know as little as they do because no effort is made to erase their ignorance. Mitford aims most of her attack at the funeral industry, which, she says, perpetuates the practices without any clearly defined legal rights and seems deliberately to keep relatives and the general public in the dark.

Purpose and Audience

1. Mitford analyzes the processes of embalming and restoration in the hope and expectation that readers will then question the practices themselves. An undertaker would be offended by nearly every sentence in the piece, including the quotations from embalming textbooks.

2. Mitford assumes that her audience is completely ignorant about the process of embalming — what is done, how it is done, why it is done, even what it costs.

3. Students will find their own examples of humor. Mitford uses humor to show how ludicrous funeral customs are when they are examined objectively, rather than under the emotional stress of bereavement. Humor also mitigates some of the gruesomeness of the process.

Method and Structure

1. Process analysis helps Mitford expose the custom of embalming for the morbid and absurd practice she sees it to be, allowing her to present the process in all its unsettling detail. She hopes to convince readers to reexamine their tacit approval of the practice by exposing the ugly secrets that lie behind a beautified corpse. The unusual process analysis allows her simultaneously to shock and to amuse her audience.

2. Mitford explains the process quite clearly. The main steps are removing the blood and replacing it with embalming fluid (paragraphs 9–11); removing the entrails and replacing them with cavity fluid (13); replacing missing parts and repairing defects (15, 16); "lip closure" (17); applying cosmetics, washing hair, manicuring, and so on (18, 19); and "casketing" (20).

3. In paragraph 8, Mitford describes the undertaker's tools. In paragraph 10, she explains the "time element" in the process (while also illustrating the rudimentary quality of information on embalming). And in paragraph 14, she explains the objective of the process of restoration.

4. The contrast suggests that we, unlike our ancestors, are fearful and shy about death and the dead and thus acquiesce in the funeral industry's wish to keep us ignorant of its practices.

Language

1. Mitford's tone is bitingly sarcastic, overlaid with a good dollop of black humor. Some examples: the brand names of the "aids" she mentions, such as "Throop Foot Positioner" (paragraph 8); sentences such as "Head off?" (15); terms such as "jabbed" (13) and "routinely handled" (15).

2. Mitford's irony contributes substantially to her sarcastic tone and to the humor of the piece. Other examples of irony: "Beautiful Memory Picture" (paragraph 2), when the trussing, trimming, and slicing earlier in the sentence would produce quite the opposite effect; "For those who feel that there is something a little rudimentary, not to say haphazard, about this advice, a comforting thought is offered" (10); "The funeral industry is equal to the challenge" (14).

3. The contrast of informal style and formal textbook style underlines the discrepancy Mitford sees between the outward dignity and solemnity of funeral practices and their actual grotesqueness and humorousness. Other examples of informal style: "Just how soon should one get going on embalming?" (paragraph 10); "jabbed into the abdomen, poked around the entrails" (13). Other examples of textbook style: "any of the better funeral establishments" (8); "the embalmer has at hand a variety of restorative waxes" (15).

CHAPTER 10

COMPARISON AND CONTRAST
Evaluating Stereotypes

Leanita McClain

THE MIDDLE-CLASS BLACK'S BURDEN (p. 239)

McClain's essay addresses the significant issues of race and class relations both thoughtfully and uncompromisingly. Positioning herself among middle-class African Americans, McClain directly confronts the mistaken assumptions she faces among both other African Americans and middle-class white Americans. Throughout her essay, she poses some rather difficult rhetorical questions, as indicated in question 3 under "Purpose and Audience." You might direct students' attention to these questions: what does McClain hope to gain with them?

Content Quiz

1. What has McClain "had it" with?
   ["Being patted on the head by white hands and slapped in the face by black hands for [her] success."]

2. What do other African Americans call middle-class African Americans like McClain?
   ["Oreos . . . black on the outside, white within."]

3. What has happened to some of McClain's childhood friends?
   [Old classmate waits on her table, girl she played with has five children and is on welfare, boy from church is imprisoned for murder, pal died of drug overdose.]

4. What is McClain's relationship to the middle class?
   [She is "uncomfortably" in it.]

5. What is it that blacks and whites will not believe about McClain?
   ["Whites won't believe I remain culturally different; blacks won't believe I remain culturally the same."]

Vocabulary Quiz

1. *Proverbial* (paragraph 2) is closest in meaning to
   a. desired   b. commonly expressed   c. everywhere evident
   [b. commonly expressed]

2. *Berate* (3) is closest in meaning to
   a. scold   b. punish   c. frown at
   [a. scold]

3. *Nemesis* (11) is closest in meaning to
   a. friend   b. rival   c. source of harm
   [c. source of harm]

4. *Vernacular* (12) is closest in meaning to
   a. idiom   b. rule   c. advice
   [a. idiom]

5. *Assuage* (13) is closest in meaning to
   a. inflame   b. erase   c. calm
   [c. calm]

ANSWERS
Meaning

1. "Incongruities" (paragraph 6) are inconsistencies (Latin *in-*, "not," and *congruere*, "to agree"). As a middle-class African American, McClain feels that she fits well in neither the predominantly white middle class nor the angry and fear-ridden African American community. Her examples include being called an "Oreo" (3), a trip to Paris back-to-back with a backcountry funeral (6), and an aunt who cleans for one of her neighbors (6). See also paragraphs 10, 13, and 14.

2. Paragraph 1 sums up the "middle-class black's burden" and states McClain's main idea — that she's "had it with being patted on the head by white hands and slapped in the face by black hands for my success." (See also "Language," question 2.)

3. McClain's "ancestors" are, of course, slaves and the oppressed African Americans who descended from them. "The purposeless present" of her contemporaries presumably refers to the endemic poverty and social problems of many present-day African Americans (paragraph 8).

Purpose and Audience

1. McClain is trying to communicate the burden she feels and ultimately to promote change: "We [middle-class blacks] know the black and white worlds can meld, that there can be a better world" (paragraph 4); "Racism still dogs my people" (9); "Inasmuch as we all suffer for every one left behind, we all gain for every one who conquers the hurdle" (20).

2. McClain addresses both whites and blacks, trying to educate members of both worlds about the prejudice she experiences and convince both to change their attitudes and behavior.

3. McClain's questions are rhetorical: they do not have easy answers, if they have answers at all. She includes them because they are the questions she confronts every day; writing the essay is a way of posing them to those who may not have thought of them.

Method and Structure

1. McClain is comparing her feelings among and misjudgment by African Americans and whites. Her points of comparison include life goals (paragraph 2), respect for roots (3, 4, 19, 20), congruence (5, 6), racism (9–12, 15, 16, 18), and tokenism (13).

2. In paragraph 6, McClain shifts from her life among other African Americans to her life among whites. The paragraph merges the two worlds.

3. Other clarifying expressions: "too" (paragraph 5), "however" (8), "still" (9), "yet" (11), "two worlds" (13), "each world" (14), "but" (16), "As for" (19), "nor" (20).

4. Description, narration, and example all appear in paragraphs 5 and 6. The entire essay analyzes the causes and effects of McClain's "burden" as a middle-class African American; specific instances appear in paragraphs 5 and 20.

Language

1. McClain's tone is angry, her language strong and uncompromising: "who has had it" (paragraph 1), "pencil pushing" (2), "antiquated ideology" (3), "wretched past . . . purposeless present" (8), "hollow victory" (10), "simplistic reproach" (11), "transparent deceptions . . . bitter hopelessness" (14), "lulled themselves" (15), "freak" (16), "No" (19), "drowning" (20). Some students will find her moral outrage appropriate given the gravity of her subject and what is at stake: the state of race relations in America. Others may wish she had tempered her anger.

2. McClain does not use "patted" and "slapped" (paragraph 1) literally, of course; they are metaphors for her experiences. Whites pat her on the head by applauding her for succeeding when they might not have expected her to; blacks slap her by berating her for her success and insisting that she has forsaken her people.

3. Parallelism reinforces McClain's comparisons because similar grammatical structures encompass contrasting ideas. Other examples: "patted on the head . . . and slapped in the face" (paragraph 1); "I have overcome . . . , but I have not overcome" (11); "Life is easier, being black is not" (11); "I know how tenuous my grip on one way of life is, and how strangling the grip of the other way of life can be" (14).

4. The use of quotation marks around "liberal" (paragraph 16) emphasizes the term and also questions its sincerity, given the context. We are meant to distrust McClain's white acquaintances and their avowed respect for her.

ANNOTATED ESSAY

I am a member of the black middle class who has had it with being patted on the head by white hands and slapped in the face by black hands for my success.

1
THESIS

Here's a discovery that too many people find startling: when given equal opportunities at white-collar pencil pushing, blacks want the same things from life that everyone else wants. These include the proverbial dream house, two cars, an above-average school, and a vacation for the kids at Disneyland. We may, in fact, want these things more than other Americans because most of us have been denied them so long.

2
Comparison

Example

Meanwhile, a considerable number of the folks we left behind in the "old country," commonly called the ghetto, and the militants we left behind in their antiquated ideology can't berate middle-class blacks enough for "forgetting where we came from." We have forsaken the revolution, we are told, we have sold out. We are Oreos, they say, black on the outside, white within.

3

Definition

The truth is, we have not forgotten; we would not dare. We are simply fighting on different fronts and are no less war weary, and possibly more heartbroken, for we know the black and white worlds can meld, that there can be a better world.

4

It is impossible for me to forget where I came from as long as I am prey to the jive hustler who does not hesitate to exploit childhood friendship. I am reminded, too, when I go back to the old neighborhood in fear — and have my purse snatched — and when I sit down to a business lunch and have an old classmate wait on my table. I recall the girl I played dolls with who now rears five children on welfare, the boy from church who is in prison for murder, the pal found dead of a drug overdose in the alley where we once played tag.

5

Example and cause and effect

My life abounds in incongruities. Fresh from a vacation in Paris, I may, a week later, be on the milk-run Trailways bus in Deep South backcountry attending the funeral of an ancient uncle whose world stretched only fifty miles and who never learned to read. Sometimes when I wait at the bus stop with my attaché case, I meet my aunt getting off the bus with other cleaning ladies on their way to do my neighbors' floors.

6
Example and narration

But I am not ashamed. Black progress has surpassed our greatest expectations; we never even saw much hope for it, and the achievement has taken us by surprise.

7

Comparison

In my heart, however, there is no safe distance from the wretched past of my ancestors or the purposeless present of some of my contemporaries; I fear such a fate can reclaim me. I am not comfortably middle class; I am uncomfortably middle class.

8

I have made it, but where? Racism still dogs my people. There are still communities in which crosses are burned on the lawns of black families who have the money and grit to move in.

9
Example

What a hollow victory we have won when my sister, dressed in her designer everything, is driven to the rear door of the luxury high rise in which she lives because the cab driver, noting only her skin color, assumes she is the maid, or the nanny, or the cook, but certainly not the lady of any house at this address.

10

Example and narration

I have heard the immigrants' bootstrap tales, the simplistic reproach of "why can't you people be like us." I have fulfilled the entry requirements of the American middle class, yet I am left, at times, feeling unwelcome and stereotyped. I have overcome the problems of food, clothing, and shelter, but I have not overcome my old nemesis, prejudice. Life is easier, being black is not.

11

Cause and effect

I am burdened daily with showing whites that blacks are people. I am, in the old vernacular, a credit to my race. I am my brothers' keeper, and my sisters', though many of them have abandoned me because they think that I have abandoned them.

12

I run a gauntlet between two worlds, and I am cursed and blessed by both. I travel, observe, and take part in both; I can also be used by both. I am a rope in a tug of war. If I am a token in my downtown office, so am I at my cousin's church tea. I assuage white guilt. I disprove black inadequacy and prove to my parents' generation that their patience was indeed a virtue.

13

I have a foot in each world, but I cannot fool myself about either. I can see the transparent deceptions of some whites and the bitter hopelessness of some blacks. I know how tenuous my grip on one way of life is, and how strangling the grip of the other way of life can be.

14

Many whites have lulled themselves into thinking that race relations are just grand because they were the first on their block to discuss crab grass with the new black family. Yet too few blacks and whites in this country send their children to school together, entertain each other, or call each other friend. Blacks and whites dining out together draw stares. Many of my coworkers see no black faces from the time the train pulls out Friday evening until they meet me at the coffee machine Monday morning. I remain a novelty.

15

Example

Some of my "liberal" white acquaintances pat me on the head, hinting that I am a freak, that my success is less a matter of talent than of luck and affirmative action. I may live among them, but it is difficult to live with them. How can they be sincere about respecting me, yet hold my fellows in contempt? And if I am silent when they attempt to sever me from my own, how can I live with myself?

16

Cause and effect

Whites won't believe I remain culturally different; blacks won't believe I remain culturally the same.

17

Comparison

I need only look in a mirror to know my true allegiance, and I am painfully aware that, even with my off-white trappings, I am prejudged by my color.

18

As for the envy of my own people, am I to give up my   19
career, my standard of living, to pacify them and set my conscience at ease? No. I have worked for these amenities and
deserve them, though I can never enjoy them without feeling
guilty.

These comforts do not make me less black, nor oblivious to   20
the woe in which many of my people are drowning. As long as
we are denigrated as a group, no one of us has made it. Inasmuch   Cause and
as we all suffer for every one left behind, we all gain for every   effect
one who conquers the hurdle.

Cheryl Peck

FATSO (p. 245)

Peck's essay, both ironic and angry, addresses a heated topic: obesity. Though
not specifically about the public health and political issues that comprise the
current obesity debate, the essay does succeed in raising many issues and attitudes involved in it. As a large woman herself, Peck identifies several types of
hostility and discrimination that overweight people face every day. She directly
compares others' perceptions of her with her own perception of herself, finding disturbing similarities in the negative attitudes about "people of substance"
on both sides. At the same time, she obliquely compares sizism with racism, a
connection that some readers will appreciate and others will undoubtedly
reject outright. Currently or formerly overweight students are sure to see themselves in some of her examples, but so might those who are "normal" weight
or underweight; most readers will find her essay quite moving regardless of
where they fit on the spectrum.

Students who connect with Peck's writing will undoubtedly enjoy her
essay collections *Fat Girls and Lawn Chairs* (2004) and *Revenge of the Paste Eaters*
(2005). Both books are filled with personal reflections and very funny stories
that resonate with readers regardless of their backgrounds. It's worth reminding students that although Peck has published two books, she is not a professional writer. She works full-time in a welfare office and writes primarily for
her own satisfaction. Yet she has developed both a strong style and a wide
audience, a source of inspiration for other aspiring writers.

Content Quiz

1. What hurtful comment did a stranger make to a large man who was eating
   an elephant ear at a fair?
   ["You don't need to eat that."]

2. Why have people told Peck that she doesn't have any experience with discrimination?
   [Because she is white and middle-class.]

3. What did a salesperson suggest that Peck could wear on her large feet?
   [Shoe boxes.]

4. What were some of Peck's nicknames in school?
   [She was called "fatso," "lardbucket," and "Bismarck."]

5. What unsolicited information did a stranger give Peck in the street?
   [She told Peck about a weight-loss program that worked for her "second cousin in Tulsa."]

Vocabulary Quiz

1. *Register* (paragraph 1) is closest in meaning to
   a. understand   b. repeat   c. weigh
   [a. understand]

2. *Debilitate* (3) is closest in meaning to
   a. energize   b. repair   c. cripple
   [c. cripple]

3. *Crude* (5, 9) is closest in meaning to
   a. raw   b. tactless   c. simple
   [b. tactless]

4. *Asexual* (8) is closest in meaning to
   a. gay   b. promiscuous   c. gender neutral
   [c. gender neutral]

5. *Demeanor* (9) is closest in meaning to
   a. attitude   b. cruelty   c. language
   [a. attitude]

ANSWERS

Meaning

1. Peck does not mean any of her "I have never" statements literally. Each example is drawn from her personal experience, as her references to specific incidents — such the shoe store clerk's rude joke (paragraph 5), the grade school nicknames (5), or the hurtful letter she read in a magazine (6) — make clear. She is being bitterly ironic to underscore the difference between what people assume about her and what is actually true.

2. She is angry — an emotion Peck (again, ironically) denies in her last paragraph — not only because others have treated her badly but also because she has internalized many of the negative stereotypes applied to obese people and often treats herself as poorly as others do.

3. Although "person of substance" is a politically correct euphemism for an overweight person, the connotations of the word *substance* also suggest that these people are important and that there is more to them than their size alone.

Purpose and Audience

1. Peck is writing primarily to judgmental thin people — specifically, she is responding to the person who made the hurtful comment to her friend at a fair and to the people who have told her that because she is a "middle-class white person" she has "no idea what it is like to be discriminated against" (paragraph 3). At the same time, however, because Peck is very forthright in counting herself among those who stereotype overweight people, we can also conclude that she is writing a cautionary tale for others who have internalized society's negative assessments of fat people.

2. Peck is trying to teach her readers not to discriminate against people of size by revealing the pain caused by snap judgments and insensitive comments. She underscores the importance of her message by implicitly comparing sizism to racism early in her essay (paragraph 3): both forms of discrimination, she insists, are equally hurtful. Peck acknowledges, however, that her lesson is a difficult one to learn. At three hundred pounds, she has caught herself making negative assumptions about other overweight people.

Method and Structure

1. This essay is based primarily on a point-by-point contrast between Peck's life as it is and her life as she imagines it would be if she were smaller. At the same time, she compares what others assume about her with how she sees herself. Her major points of comparison include interpersonal relationships (paragraphs 5, 9, 11), media representations (6), and self-esteem (7, 8, 10). Peck also suggests an implicit comparison between racism and sizism (3), but she uses that to bolster her main point, not as the focus of the essay itself.

2. The comparison begins in Peck's discussion of racial discrimination in the third paragraph, but she deliberately waits until the fourth paragraph to make it clear that she is writing a comparison and contrast essay. On the first reading of paragraph 3, most readers will assume that she is writing from a somewhat detached point of view, interpreting her "I have never" statements literally. When Peck shifts to an obviously personal example of discrimination in paragraph 4 ("My feelings were not hurt"), however, she makes it clear that the types of racial discrimination outlined in the previous paragraph are actually meant to serve as examples of the discrimination she has experienced as a large woman.

3. Although she is writing about sizism in general, Peck uses profoundly personal examples to make her point. Some of the more notable examples include her humiliation in the shoe store (paragraph 4), her sexual awkwardness (8), and her encounter with the woman who suggested a weight-loss program (9). Obesity is a charged topic in contemporary America. By exposing her vulnerabilities in such a raw manner, Peck makes the subject personal and tries to form a bond with her readers, which increases her chances of success in making readers sympathetic to the difficulties and social stigmas that overweight people face.

Language

1. The title serves a couple of functions. It has a shock value that draws readers in more effectively than, say, "Obesity" would. At the same time, it recalls the name-calling that Peck experienced as a child and predicts the self-loathing that is a major theme of her essay. It could also serve as a verbalization of the prejudice that she describes in her introduction and responds to in the body of her comparison.

2. Peck's repeated invocation of the phrase "I have never" (as well as its variations) gives the essay coherence as well as a rhythm that is difficult to resist. At the same time, the parallelism created by her usage emphasizes that each incident she describes is equally important and on a par with the racial discrimination she discusses in paragraph 3. Some readers may also find in the phrase an echo of the exclamation "Well, I never!" — often uttered to express exasperation at an insult.

3. Peck is unmistakably sarcastic, bitter, and angry. Her tone will likely put some readers on the defensive despite her efforts to form a bond with them (see question 3, under "Method and Structure"). Other readers, particularly those who have had experiences similar to the author's, may feel that the tone strengthens the essay and gives it a punch it might not otherwise have.

Alaina Wong

CHINA DOLL (p. 251)

Wong skillfully interweaves a number of complex comparisons into this account of learning to embrace her Chinese American identity when she was a girl. Students will be intrigued by the differences between Wong and her best friend, the girls' families, the Barbie and Kira dolls, and Wong's initial and revised views of herself.

Our families' and friends' influence on our self-perceptions are, of course, topics of enduring interest and could lead to a discussion of the question we are all asked at one point or another: who is your role model?

Content Quiz

1. What did Wong want for Christmas?
   [A Princess Barbie doll.]

2. What, to Wong's mind, made the Princess Barbie special?
   [Besides its general glamour and beauty, it came with a tiara.]

3. What did Sarah's hair look like?
   [She had long blond hair that "fell in soft waves down her back."]

4. What did Wong's hair look like?
   [Her "black hair was slippery and straight, like uncooked spaghetti."]

5. Why did Wong like to eat at her friend's house?
[Because Sarah's mother let them eat things (such as raspberries off the bush and raw cookie dough) that Wong's mother would have forbidden because of germs, she cooked from "scratch," and she "made the best macaroni and cheese."]

Vocabulary Quiz

1. *Tresses* (paragraph 2) is closest in meaning to
   a. clothing   b. hair   c. skin
   [b. hair]

2. *Sly* (3) is closest in meaning to
   a. evil   b. tight   c. mischievous
   [c. mischievous]

3. *Complement* (4) is closest in meaning to
   a. praise   b. wear   c. match
   [c. match]

4. *Glamorous* (13, 17) is closest in meaning to
   a. beautiful   b. famous   c. expensive
   [a. beautiful]

5. *Iridescent* (17) is closest in meaning to
   a. heavy   b. borrowed   c. shiny
   [c. shiny]

ANSWERS

Meaning

1. Wong's doll collection is populated by "real," brand-name Barbies. They are "all alike and beautiful with their clouds of blond (or light-brown) hair, broad toothy smiles, and wide-open eyes" (paragraph 3), and they all have "colorful plastic high heels to complement their fashionable dresses" and "perfect" outfits (4). The Kira doll, on the other hand, is not a Barbie but a "'friend' of Barbie" (2), features "dark hair and slanted eyes" (3), has "lips . . . curved into a more secretive, sly smile" (3), wears a "floral wrap skirt" (2) that is "just a piece of cloth that need[s] to be tied" (11), and came without shoes. As far as Wong is concerned, Kira is clearly inferior to Barbie.

2. We can't be sure, of course, but Wong's parents almost certainly selected the Kira doll for their daughter precisely because it has vaguely Asian features rather than Barbie's overtly Caucasian ones. Like many parents of ethnic girls, they probably wanted her to have a doll that she could identify with, and they probably meant for it to make young Alaina feel good about herself. Wong fails to appreciate that the doll "looks kind of like" (paragraph 12) her until her friend Sarah points it out to her, but she slowly comes to see herself in it and in the process to find promise in her own appearance.

3. The "dark-haired" Kira and the blond Princess Barbie stand for Wong's sense of herself and her friend Sarah. The parallels are rather obvious, although Wong does reinforce them by stressing that Kira is Barbie's "friend" (paragraph 2). What may not be so obvious to students is the way Wong projects her feelings about her own appearance onto the dolls. At first she rejects the Kira doll, who to her mind is neither as pretty nor as glamorous as the Barbies, and she wonders how Kira could possibly be attractive to men (in the form of Ken), who "already had so many blond friends to choose from" (3). She assumes that the Asian-looking doll has defects even beneath her unsatisfactory appearance — "crooked teeth," for example (3), and "probably missing lots of things" (4) — an assumption that suggests the state of Wong's own lack of self-esteem as a Chinese American girl growing up in a predominantly white community. When Wong dresses her doll in Princess Barbie's clothes with her friend Sarah's encouragement, she feels as if she's doing something slightly wrong, although she's not sure why she feels that way. The borrowed clothes symbolize, perhaps, Wong's ambivalence about assimilating into white culture — although her discovery that Barbie's tiara "fit perfectly" suggests the beginning of Wong's comfort with her own identity.

Purpose and Audience

1. In comments she wrote for the introduction to "China Doll" in *YELL-Oh Girls!* Wong explained that her "experiences growing up and slowly becoming race conscious inspired [her] to write this story." She continued, "I hope to evoke a sense of familiarity and understanding from people who may have also experienced these feelings."

2. Wong justifiably assumed that the young Asian girls for whom *YELL-Oh Girls!* was published would recognize themselves in at least some aspects of her story. At the same time, Wong was aware that her feelings might be unfamiliar to readers beyond the *YELL-Oh Girls!* audience, so she took care to emphasize whatever universal experiences she could find. For example, her disappointment with a gift (paragraphs 1–3) and the guilt that accompanied that feeling (4) are emotions that most readers felt at some point in their childhoods or have witnessed in their own or other children.

Method and Structure

1. The method works for Wong's story because she is trying to understand the source of her disappointment in the Kira doll. By comparing the doll she received with the one she wanted, she can explore the positive and negative aspects of each and determine whether one is indeed better than the other. And because the dolls symbolize the writer and her best friend, the method of comparison and contrast lets her recognize not only how they are different but also how they are alike.

2. In paragraphs 2–4, Wong emphasizes the differences between her Kira doll and her Barbie dolls (and, by extension, herself and Sarah); in paragraphs 5–7, she outlines her reasons for liking Sarah's family better than her own; and in paragraphs 8–15, she emphasizes (again with the dolls serving as

stand-ins) her perception of her friend's superiority. It is only in the last two paragraphs (16, 17) that Wong begins to see the possibility that they are more alike than they are different, and even then her assessment is tentative. This organization reflects her own emotional journey, from rejection to a hesitant acceptance of her Chinese American identity.

3. Because Wong's self-image in this essay is based on her appearance, the descriptions of the dolls' features are essential in conveying her meaning. Without them, the essay would be based on abstractions and would lack immediacy for readers, especially for those not acquainted with girls' fashion dolls. The narration, however, puts Wong's comparison in a familiar context that most readers will understand. It not only personalizes her experience but encourages readers to connect it with their own childhoods.

Language

1. Wong manages to write the essay with a voice that combines a girl's naïveté and insecurity with an adult's perspective of her youthful feelings. Her tone is innocent, measured, and imbued with a sense of childlike wonder.

2. Examples include Wong's assertion that Princess Barbie's tiara "crowned her at the top of her Barbie world" (paragraph 1), her description of her dolls' "clouds of blond (or light-brown) hair" (3), and her disparaging assessment of her own hair as being "like uncooked spaghetti" (5). Wong's metaphors and similes catch readers' attention without distracting them from her message, and they bring color and wit to her writing.

CHAPTER 11

DEFINITION
Clarifying Family Relationships

Reena Nadler
CHROMOSOMES IN COMMON (p. 270)

How many of us have wondered what it would be like to have an identical twin? In this introspective and moving essay, Nadler, a student writer, explains just how hard but also how wonderful it can be to grow up with someone who looks just like you.

Nadler is, of course, in a unique position to construct a definition essay on this chapter's theme of clarifying family relationships, since in attempting to define a twin, she is also trying to define herself. Yet this struggle to "become complete," "give birth" to ourselves, and "resolve to be" ourselves (the words of Friedan, Fromm, and Arnold in the prereading quotations) is in a sense part of the journey we all travel in quest of our own identities — a journey that involves distinguishing ourselves from family, peers, and colleagues. The simple question "Who are you?" would be a good starting point for a class discussion that could blossom into some excellent material for writing comparison and contrast essays.

Content Quiz

1. In the photo of the twins taken at Disneyland, what emotion do their faces show?
   [A "wry sense of humor."]

2. What activity were the two-year-old twins engaged in when the picture of them was taken?
   [Reading.]

3. Why didn't the young twins cry when they were sent to bed?
   [They were more interested in each other's company than in the grown-ups' conversation.]

4. How old were the twins when they were first separated?
   [Thirteen.]

5. In what situation are the twins especially protective and supportive of one another?
   [On the track team.]

Vocabulary Quiz

1. *Goggling* (paragraph 8) is closest in meaning to
    a. spying   b. staring   c. giggling
    [b. staring]

2. *Wry* (9) is closest in meaning to
    a. hysterical   b. strange   c. ironic
    [c. ironic]

3. *Enlist* (10) is closest in meaning to
    a. secure   b. ignore   c. reject
    [a. secure]

4. *Painstakingly* (13) is closest in meaning to
    a. methodically   b. effortlessly   c. enthusiastically
    [a. methodically]

5. *Encompassed* (17) is closest in meaning to
    a. directed   b. contained   c. carved
    [b. contained]

ANSWERS

Meaning

1. The comparisons that people always make between Nadler and her sister not only rob her of her identity but also make her feel as if she is constantly on display, even prompting inner feelings of bitterness. She suggests that the struggle to establish her own identity has been especially difficult for her because she is an identical twin.

2. The twins rely on each other a great deal for companionship (paragraph 4), entertainment (5), and support (10). Nadler describes the bond as providing her with comfort, security, and protection.

3. Despite the intimacy of her relationship with her sister, Nadler also feels the need to assert her own identity and shield herself from the perception that she is the mirror image of her sister (paragraph 2). Sometimes she has had to sacrifice her own desires: for example, when Susannah expressed a wish to attend camp with her, Nadler "decided that my sister's needs were stronger than my own" (14), even though she preferred to attend by herself (8). Although it is supremely difficult to resolve these questions, Nadler concludes that her relationship with her sister is a precious gift that is worth the sacrifice (14).

Purpose and Audience

1. Nadler appears to have various reasons for writing this essay. Certainly, she is partly responding to the question posed in paragraph 1, a question many readers may be curious about. She also realizes that all young people are struggling to define themselves and wants to make the point that for

twins this struggle is all the greater (15). Finally, she seems to be using the essay as an opportunity for self-reflection, an attempt to articulate the inner conflicts she feels and perhaps come to terms with them.

2. Nadler is aware that she is writing about experiences unfamiliar to most people, so she does what she can to relate these to experiences shared by others. For example, she makes the point that the quest for personal identity is a common one, an exploration "that everyone is faced with" (paragraph 15). She also acknowledges, though, that no one who is not a twin can fully understand her feelings (13).

Method and Structure

1. Identical twins fascinate people, as Nadler acknowledges. But most of us don't recognize that twins need to discover differences between themselves, which can be a source of great inner conflict. Definition allows Nadler to explain both what twins are and how that relationship defines her.

2. In paragraphs 9 and 10, Nadler describes photographs of herself and her sister that emphasize their similarities, a theme that she continues to develop in paragraph 11. Then, in paragraphs 12–15, she describes the summer they attended separate camps — when she discovered that she could be different from her sister, a liberating experience — followed by her agonizing decision to allow her sister, who had a very different solo experience, to return to camp with her the following year. Her point here is that she feels the need to be different from her sister, but this desire is constantly thwarted by the closeness of their relationship. Finally, in paragraphs 13 and 14, she returns to consider their inevitable similarities, reaching a sort of peace with her inner conflict. This organization suggests her own emotional journey, from childhood acceptance to adolescent rebellion to a gradually maturing outlook.

3. Nadler uses narration at the beginning of her essay to relate a typical incident for her and her sister — the uncomfortable experience of being compared by friends and acquaintances — which exemplifies the conflicts she will go on to discuss. She uses narration again beginning in paragraph 12, relating the sisters' solo camp experiences; this culminates in Nadler's central realization that her identity as a twin will always be a source of inner conflict. Her descriptions of the two photographs — one taken at age sixteen, the other at age two — suggest the emotional evolution of their relationship, though they have remained physically so similar.

Language

1. Nadler's tone is serious and deeply thoughtful: "Our faces reflect the wry sense of humor — the essence of armor — that we have developed because the alternative is animosity" (paragraph 9). Her tone is also passionate: "It is a very powerful thing when you realize that you love someone as much as you love yourself" (14). Her vocabulary is sophisticated and carefully chosen and her sentence structure appropriately complex to reflect her feelings.

2. The opening quotations represent exactly the kinds of responses to her and her identical twin that so trouble Nadler's sense of self-identity. "I have never met anyone who could know both me and my sister and not compare us," she writes at the end of paragraph 8, "and that will last all my life."

3. Other examples of paired words include "help and attention" (paragraph 10), "absolute selfishness and absolute generosity" (14), and "repressed" and "flourishing" (15). This skillful linguistic device subtly calls attention to the dualities — two sisters, two lives, and two identities — that are the focus of the essay.

Judy Brady

I WANT A WIFE (p. 277)

Brady's definition uses carefully selected examples to present an angry statement about a wife's place in the home and in society. Some students may initially misunderstand the essay and think that Brady really does want a slave of her own. Other students may see the essay as excessively hostile toward wives, husbands, and marriage. And still other students may find Brady's sense of oppression somewhat passé, not as much of an issue now as it was in the less liberated early 1970s. Class discussion may be guided by the questions under "Purpose and Audience" and by the second and third writing topics.

Content Quiz

1. With whom does the child of Brady's recently divorced male friend live?
   [The child's mother.]

2. Why does Brady want to go back to school?
   [So she can become economically independent and support herself and her family.]

3. Why should a wife go on family vacations?
   [To continue caring for her partner and for the children.]

4. According to Brady's definition, which partner in a marriage must remain sexually faithful to the other?
   [The wife.]

5. What should the first wife do if a new wife is taken?
   ["Take the children and be solely responsible for them."]

Vocabulary Quiz

1. *Nurturant* (paragraph 3) is closest in meaning to
   a. compassionate   b. gentle   c. nourishing
   [c. nourishing]

2. *Hors d'oeuvres* (6) is closest in meaning to
   a. appetizers   b. cocktails   c. napkins
   [a. appetizers]

3. *Replenished* (6) is closest in meaning to
   a. removed   b. refilled   c. rewashed
   [b. refilled]

4. *Adherence* (7) is closest in meaning to
   a. indifference   b. attachment   c. attention
   [b. attachment]

5. *Monogamy* (7) is closest in meaning to
   a. sexual faithfulness   b. equality in a marriage
   c. marriage to only one person
   [c. marriage to only one person]

ANSWERS
Meaning

1. A wife is a person whose entire function is the selfless serving of others, especially the husband.

2. The wife's chief responsibilities are to work when doing so is beneficial to the spouse, to care for the children, to care for the house and to cook, to meet the spouse's physical and emotional needs, and to arrange and run social events. The wife's behavior should be entirely selfless. The spouse's responsibilities are to attend school and study and eventually to support dependents "if need be" (paragraph 3) — but nothing is required or contributed at home. The spouse's behavior may be entirely selfish.

Purpose and Audience

1. Brady's purpose is to attack society's — and men's — attitudes toward the role of wife. She presents a deliberately one-sided definition, exaggerating to achieve this purpose.

2. Brady seems to assume that her readers are mostly women who will understand and appreciate her anger. Her perspective seems to be that of a middle-class woman in her twenties or early thirties: the wife works to put the spouse through school; the children are relatively young; the family lives in a house; and the couple has an active social life.

3. Answers will vary widely.

Method and Structure

1. Readers may take the role of a wife for granted — or may have in 1971 — but Brady sees a need to show how the wife is taken advantage of. By presenting a slanted definition, she encourages readers to see things her way.

2. The definition is highly specific and clearly distinguishes the role of a wife from, say, the role of a housekeeper or a lover. It is also thorough in that it covers a wide range of responsibilities and behaviors. But some readers may think that the omission of any positive elements in the relationship between wife and spouse — what keeps the wife at the job? love? security? — makes the definition less than complete.

3. Paragraph 1 suggests that the author is defined by society according to her role as a wife. Paragraph 2 presents a man who seems to view a wife's role just as Brady goes on to define it: he is divorced; he has left his child to his wife; and he wants "a wife" — as if anyone might do. The question at the end of the introduction leads into the definition; once the earlier question is answered, the final rhetorical question opens up the divorced man's wish and Brady's wish to everyone.

4. With classification, Brady makes the definition more manageable. She classifies the wife's responsibilities into financial support and child care (paragraph 3), housekeeping and cooking (4), emotional support (5), social organization (6), and sexual fulfillment (7). The categories are increasingly personal and intrusive, thus emphasizing the exploitation of women in marriage.

Language

1. Brady's tone is angry and contemptuous, and it is achieved largely through irony: "It may mean a small cut in my wife's income . . . , but I guess I can tolerate that" (paragraph 3); "I want a wife who will not bother me with rambling complaints about a wife's duties" but "will listen to me when I feel the need to explain a rather difficult point I have come across in my course of studies" (5).

2. The repetition portrays the spouse as childish, demanding, and selfish.

3. Use of the phrase "my wife" emphasizes the spouse's depersonalization and possession of the wife. At the same time, the phrase allows Brady to avoid expressing a wish for another woman, which might be more distracting than the occasionally awkward sentences now in the essay.

4. Such expressions underline the irony.

--------- Andrew Sullivan ---------

THE "M-WORD": WHY IT MATTERS TO ME (p. 282)

Sullivan's essay deftly addresses what is probably the most contentious topic among all of the selections in *The Compact Reader*: the ongoing debate over gay marriage. Writing from a calm yet earnest point of view shortly after the Massachusetts Supreme Court announced that the state would begin issuing marriage licenses to same-sex couples, the author provides a very personal perspective on what has quickly become a very public issue. In defining marriage as the pursuit of happiness (a subtle constitutional argument), Sullivan deftly sidesteps the more controversial elements of the debate by reframing its terms. As he puts it toward the end of his essay, the debate "isn't about gay marriage. It's about marriage" (paragraph 7). Some students will agree wholeheartedly, of course, while others will reject Sullivan's angle altogether.

A good place to begin a discussion of Sullivan's topic would be to focus on students' journal entries, exploring their assumptions about marriage in general before delving into what could easily become a heated argument about gay rights and the proposed boundaries for civil unions and legal marriage on both the federal and state levels. Regardless of where students stand on the issue, they should come to recognize that the debate itself is largely a struggle over agreeing on definitions.

Content Quiz

1. How does Sullivan characterize his upbringing?
   [He describes growing up in a "traditional home — Catholic, conservative, middle class" — and explains that "life was relatively simple: education, work, family."]

2. In Sullivan's family, what was "the most important day in your life"?
   [Your wedding day.]

3. What happened whenever the young Sullivan developed feelings for another boy?
   [The other boy "sensed it, pushed it away."]

4. What extracurricular activities did Sullivan pursue as a student?
   [Debate team and drama.]

5. What question have Sullivan's family and friends never asked him?
   [When he is going to get married.]

Vocabulary Quiz

1. *Eluded* (paragraph 4) is closest in meaning to
   a. confused   b. escaped   c. shaped
   [b. escaped]

2. *Awry* (4) is closest in meaning to
   a. wrong   b. terrible   c. amusing
   [a. wrong]

3. *Anathema* (4) is closest in meaning to
   a. numb   b. hateful   c. important
   [b. hateful]

4. *Solitude* (6) is closest in meaning to
   a. secret b. shame c. isolation
   [c. isolation]

5. *Alleviate* (7) is closest in meaning to
   a. intensify b. cheapen c. help
   [c. help]

ANSWERS

Meaning

1. Sullivan believes that marriage — not "civil unions, domestic partnerships, civil partnerships, whatever" (paragraph 7) — is the only acceptable option for same-sex partners who want to make a lifelong commitment to each other. In his opinion, marriage is essential because it's the only label that allows a person to fully participate in society. The alternatives that have been suggested, he argues, create unnecessary and harmful barriers. He makes his position clear in paragraph 7 and in the last three sentences of his essay.

2. For Sullivan's family, marriage is the most important part of a person's life. Not only does a wedding trump every other accomplishment, but it also establishes the basis for a person's relationship to the world at large. That expectation caused great pain for Sullivan as he was growing up, because he gradually came to realize that he was forbidden by society and law to take part in this life-defining event. His family's assumptions have led him to want marriage desperately, but as things stand right now (outside of Massachusetts), he cannot have it.

3. Sullivan's point here is that putting the adjective *gay* in front of the word *marriage* creates a distinction that is unnecessary and divisive, much the same as *male nurse* or *lady doctor* do. Marriage, in Sullivan's view, has nothing to do with gender; it is a commitment made by two people and sanctioned by law.

Purpose and Audience

1. Although Sullivan is quite open about his personal struggles in coming to terms with his sexuality, he is now secure in it, even as he accepts that "it's too late . . . to undo [his] own past" (paragraph 7) and aspire to marriage himself. Rather than trying to justify his marital status or his own desires, Sullivan is trying to persuade his readers to approve of legally sanctioned marriage for others — particularly for those still young enough to benefit from marriage as Sullivan characterizes it.

2. Certainly, the last paragraph suggests that Sullivan believes that at least some of his readers are young gay men who dream of marriage. But by not addressing that "young kid" directly, Sullivan emphasizes that his essay is directed at those who would deny a boy (or, presumably, a girl) that dream.

3. Although Sullivan seems to assume that his readers are willing to keep an open mind, he clearly expects them to resist his argument even if they don't reject it outright. To engage his readers' empathy, he devotes more than half of his essay to relating his painful personal experiences and withholds his statement of thesis until he can be reasonably sure that his audience is ready to hear it. He is also careful throughout to establish common ground with heterosexual readers who might be hostile to his point of view. Consider, for example, his acceptance of heterosexual preferences in his statement that "he didn't and couldn't blame" the boys who turned away from him (paragraph 4), his use of the second person "you" in paragraph 3 to explain the importance of marriage, and his wholehearted embrace of "family values" in paragraph 7.

Method and Structure

1. To get his readers to understand and even accept his controversial position on gay marriage, Sullivan first has to explain what *marriage* means to him. He defines it mainly through narration (paragraphs 3 and 4) and cause-and-effect analysis (5 and 6), showing depths of meaning that might not be apparent to readers whose sexuality allows them to take the word for granted.

2. Sullivan suggests in the opening of his essay that the best answer to the question of gay marriage "is a memory" (paragraph 2) — specifically, his memory. The anecdotes give him a particular authority on the subject and also make his points concrete. Moreover, revealing such deeply personal experiences seems itself to exemplify the personal nature of a very public debate. The anecdotes thus strengthen the essay. However, some readers might say that Sullivan's approach limits the definition or makes it unconvincing for anyone besides the author himself.

3. Sullivan uses narration in paragraphs 3 and 4 to establish pathos and to explain why marriage has always been important to him. He uses cause-and-effect analysis in paragraphs 5 and 6 to help readers understand how denying marriage on the basis of sex inflicts deep and lasting wounds on individuals and on society as a whole. These methods help the author personalize the debate before he explores its larger implications.

Language

1. Using "The 'M-Word'" instead of "Marriage" acknowledges the point that for many readers, the idea of marriage between same-sex partners is an unutterable horror. Sullivan uses it in the same way a child might nervously tell his parents that a sibling used "the f-word" — with a sense of simultaneous shame and titillation and the implicit intention of not becoming a transgressor himself.

2. On one level, Sullivan's reference to *Romeo and Juliet* signals to readers that he holds the same respect for Western traditions of love and romance as they do. Readers familiar with Shakespeare's story will recognize several parallels between the star-crossed lovers' forbidden passion and "the love

that dare not speak its name." Sullivan means to imply that refusing to allow gay men (and women) to marry is just as wrong-headed and tragic as was the feud between the Capulets and the Montagues. At the same time, the passage establishes the plaintive tone that Sullivan uses throughout. His essay is filled with emotion and pathos, rather than the militancy or aggressive politics that characterize many of the arguments on both sides of the ongoing debate. Whether this tone is appropriate or effective will depend on the reader, but it does get Sullivan's point across without turning angry.

3. Examples include Sullivan's unbridled enthusiasm for marriage as "the most important thing in your life" (paragraph 3); the descriptions of his awkward teenage years in paragraph 4; his painful realization that he "would never be a part of my family the way my siblings one day might be" (4); his reference to himself as "neurotic, depressed, at times close to suicidal" (5); and his resigned acceptance that "it's too late for me to undo my own past" (8). By exposing his own vulnerability and emotional trauma, Sullivan hopes to engage his readers' empathy for the plight of others like him.

ANNOTATED ESSAY

What's in a name?

Perhaps the best answer is a memory.

As a child, I had no idea what homosexuality was. I grew up in a traditional home — Catholic, conservative, middle class. Life was relatively simple: education, work, family. I was brought up to aim high in life, even though my parents hadn't gone to college. But one thing was instilled in me. What matters is not how far you go in life, how much money you make, how big a name you make for yourself. What really matters is family, and the love you have for one another. The most important day of your life was not graduation from college or your first day at work or a raise or even your first house. The most important day of your life was when you got married. It was on that day that all your friends and all your family got together to celebrate the most important thing in life: your happiness, your ability to make a new home, to form a new but connected family, to find love that puts everything else into perspective.

But as I grew older, I found that this was somehow not available to me. I didn't feel the things for girls that my peers did. All the emotions and social rituals and bonding of teenage heterosexual life eluded me. I didn't know why. No one explained it. My emotional bonds to other boys were one-sided; each time I felt myself falling in love, they sensed it, pushed it away. I didn't and couldn't blame them. I got along fine with my buds in a nonemotional context; but something was awry, something not right. I came to know almost instinctively that I would never be a part of my family the way my siblings one day might be. The love I had inside me was unmentionable,

1
2
3

Division or analysis

Definition

4

Narration

anathema — even, in the words of the Church I attended every Sunday, evil. I remember writing in my teenage journal one day: "I'm a professional human being. But what do I do in my private life?"

So, like many gay men of my generation, I retreated. I never discussed my real life. I couldn't date girls and so immersed myself in schoolwork, in the debate team, school plays, anything to give me an excuse not to confront reality. When I looked toward the years ahead, I couldn't see a future. There was just a void. Was I going to be alone my whole life? Would I ever have a "most important day" in my life? It seemed impossible, a negation, an undoing. To be a full part of my family I had to somehow not be me. So like many gay teens, I withdrew, became neurotic, depressed, at times close to suicidal. I shut myself in my room with my books, night after night, while my peers developed the skills needed to form real relationships, and loves. In wounded pride, I even voiced a rejection of family and marriage. It was the only way I could explain my isolation.

It took years for me to realize that I was gay, years later to tell others, and more time yet to form any kind of stable emotional bond with another man. Because my sexuality had emerged in solitude — and without any link to the idea of an actual relationship — it was hard later to reconnect sex to love and self-esteem. It still is. But I persevered, each relationship slowly growing longer than the last, learning in my twenties and thirties what my straight friends found out in their teens. But even then, my parents and friends never asked the question they would have asked automatically if I were straight: So when are you going to get married? When is your relationship going to be public? When will we be able to celebrate it and affirm it and support it? In fact, no one — no one — has yet asked me that question.

When people talk about "gay marriage," they miss the point. This isn't about gay marriage. It's about marriage. It's about family. It's about love. It isn't about religion. It's about civil marriage licenses — available to atheists as well as believers. These family values are not options for a happy and stable life. They are necessities. Putting gay relationships in some other category — civil unions, domestic partnerships, civil partnerships, whatever — may alleviate real human needs, but, by their very euphemism, by their very separateness, they actually build a wall between gay people and their own families. They put back the barrier many of us have spent a lifetime trying to erase.

It's too late for me to undo my own past. But I want above everything else to remember a young kid out there who may even be reading this now. I want to let him know that he doesn't have to choose between himself and his family any more. I want him to know that his love has dignity, that he does indeed have a future as a full and equal part of the human race. Only marriage will do that. Only marriage can bring him home.

5   Definition

Narration

6   Cause and effect

7   Comparison and contrast

8   Definition

Cause and effect

THESIS

CHAPTER 12

CAUSE-AND-EFFECT ANALYSIS

Understanding Markets and Consumers

Charles Fishman

THE SQUEEZE (p. 301)

Most of us love to hate Wal-Mart. Although many economists and social commentators repeatedly warn that the retail behemoth is destroying small retailers and exploiting workers, others point out that the store's trademark low prices have effectively improved the standard of living of working-class Americans by making necessities and luxuries alike more affordable. This excerpt from Fishman's book is especially interesting because it looks at an aspect of Wal-Mart that often escapes public notice: that the mega-business has the power to make — and destroy — other businesses. As Fishman warns, the "Wal-Mart effect" reaches farther than even the most vocal opponents recognize.

Students may be interested to know that the source of Barbara Ehrenreich's cause-and-effect paragraph on p. 294 of the text (*Nickel and Dimed*) includes a lengthy and critical chapter about her undercover stint as a Wal-Mart associate. Other recent entries in the Wal-Mart debate include *The Wal-Mart Revolution: How Big-Box Stores Benefit Consumers, Workers, and the Economy* (2007), by Richard Vedder and Wendell Cox; *Wal-Mart: The Face of Twenty-First-Century Capitalism* (2005), edited by Nelson Lichtenstein; *The United States of Wal-Mart* (2005), by John Dicker; *Wal-Mart: The High Cost of Low Price* (2005), by Greg Spotts; and *No One Makes You Shop at Wal-Mart: The Surprising Deceptions of Individual Choice* (2006), by Tom Slee.

Content Quiz

1. For what price did Wal-Mart insist on selling Vlasic's gallon-size jar of pickles?
   [Less than $3 — specifically, $2.97.]

2. How much profit did Wal-Mart and Vlasic make on each gallon?
   [A few pennies at most.]

3. How did Wal-Mart respond when Vlasic asked to raise the price of the gallon jar?
   [It refused and, depending on whom you believe, might have threatened to offer the business to a competitor.]

4. From what larger company is Vlasic a spin-off?
[Campbell Soup.]

5. For how long did Wal-Mart keep the price of a gallon of pickles artificially low?
[Two and a half years.]

Vocabulary Quiz

1. *Entrancing* (paragraph 2) is closest in meaning to
   a. magical   b. dangerous   c. expensive
   [a. magical]

2. *Niche* (6) is closest in meaning to
   a. specialty   b. general   c. new
   [a. specialty]

3. *Pallet* (7) is closest in meaning to
   a. color   b. platform   c. paddle
   [b. platform]

4. *Hoisting* (12) is closest in meaning to
   a. punching   b. insulting   c. lifting
   [c. lifting]

5. *Waning* (21) is closest in meaning to
   a. complaining   b. decreasing   c. rising
   [b. decreasing]

ANSWERS

Meaning

1. As one of Fishman's informants explains, Wal-Mart wanted to use the $2.97 gallon as a "'statement' item" (paragraph 3). The idea was to impress customers with an incredible value and demonstrate what Wal-Mart had to offer. Although executives knew that pickle profits would be minimal, their goal was to drive business and increase the volume of sales throughout the chain. The result was good for Wal-Mart: customers bought the pickles in droves. But for the supplier, Wal-Mart's success came at a steep cost, sharply reducing its profits even as sales increased. Worse, the gallon jars kept customers from buying Vlasic's more profitable products.

2. A "devastating success" is a deliberate oxymoron that might be summed up by the saying "Be careful what you wish for; you just might get it." The term describes a seemingly positive accomplishment that turns out to be damaging. In Vlasic's case, Wal-Mart helped the company to increase pickle sales dramatically, yet Vlasic's profits dropped precipitously, leaving them no better off than they had been before they made the arrangement with Wal-Mart — and possibly much worse off.

3. Fishman isn't really accusing Wal-Mart of deceptive business practices, although readers might certainly interpret his essay that way. He uses the word "lie" (paragraph 21) to emphasize that Wal-Mart's price was a gimmick rather than a true reflection of market conditions. His point is that the chain is so large and has such power over its suppliers that it has managed to exempt itself from the laws of supply and demand.

Purpose and Audience

1. Fishman's relatively objective reportorial approach to telling the Vlasic story suggests that he wants to educate readers rather than express his opinion or spark outrage. As he explains his purpose in paragraph 20, the story "shows the impact of Wal-Mart's scale and power in what we all think is a market economy." If anything, he hopes to convince readers that we need to rethink the old laws of supply and demand, because Wal-Mart has rendered them meaningless (a point implied in the subtitle of his book and stated explicitly in its concluding chapter).

2. Fishman wrote his book for an intelligent general audience, rather than for, say, economists or business leaders. (Remember that the book started as a cover story for *Fast Company*, a business magazine aimed at a popular readership.) His understanding of his audience can be seen in his storytelling approach, his preference for colloquial language, and his avoidance of economic and business jargon. He does seem to assume that his readers shop at Wal-Mart at least occasionally, and he takes for granted that they have at least a basic grasp of major economic principles, such as a "market economy" and the "laws of supply, demand, and competition."

Method and Structure

1. Given the author's purpose in explaining Wal-Mart's impact on the economy, cause-and-effect analysis is almost inevitable as the choice of method. The subject (Wal-Mart's effect) lends itself to the method perfectly.

2. A possible summary: A Wal-Mart buyer noticed the gallon jar of pickles and convinced Vlasic to experiment with selling it for a low price at a few stores. Both companies were shocked by the product's popularity and decided to try selling it even more cheaply on a national level. Sales were overwhelming, and Vlasic was forced to increase production, but profits fell as volume increased. Worse, customers started buying the gallon jars instead of (rather than in addition to) more profitable variations, putting Vlasic in a pickle.

3. Readers could easily argue that Fishman focuses too squarely on Wal-Mart's artificial price and ignores a host of possible mitigating factors. An academic economist, for example, would probably want to see a more nuanced consideration of both companies' business models, of market fluctuations, and of customers' buying habits. All the same, given Fishman's purpose and audience, the depth of his analysis seems sufficient.

4. Fishman's sources could be seen as both a strength and a weakness. Former employees can be more open, but they can also be more bitter. Current employees may be reluctant to speak ill of the company that pays their salaries. In either case, the quotations work well as expert testimony, even if they may not be perfectly objective. (Students may catch on that the author could not interview current employees of either Wal-Mart or its suppliers. Wal-Mart is notoriously unwilling to talk to reporters, and its suppliers are understandably reluctant to say anything publicly that might jeopardize their relationships with their most important distributor.)

5. As a reporter, Fishman naturally turns to narrative to make his point. (He also chooses to focus the analysis on a single example.) By presenting his analysis in the form of a story, he makes it more interesting and accessible to a general audience.

Language

1. Fishman compares pickles in a jar to reptiles in a dank aquarium. It's a wonderful metaphor invoking images of swamp creatures and sea monsters, and it grabs readers' attention by portraying a harmless consumer product as a lurking menace. Notice, too, that Fishman returns to the monster metaphor ever so subtly in other parts of the essay, describing the "story . . . floating in Vlasic's gallon jar" (paragraph 4), referring to "whole fields of cucumbers . . . heading out the door" as though they were an advancing army of mutants (9), commenting that the "cannibalizing" (10) pickles "chewed up" Vlasic's profits (11), and repeating Young's comment that Wal-Mart "killed" the pickles (18) as though it were the victor in an epic battle.

2. In many ways, "abundance" (paragraphs 2, 7, 21) captures the image Wal-Mart sought to create for itself. The word evokes a sense of plenty and of satisfaction. Each time Fishman repeats the word, however, his use becomes more ironic, ultimately implying that Wal-Mart's quantity comes closer to greed than to necessity.

3. Fishman's tone is simultaneously balanced and ironic — no small feat. He cultivates the sense of balance by relying on quotations from Wal-Mart insiders to tell the story, hovering in the background as an objective reporter. But at the same time, he weaves an understated story about the "devastating success" Wal-Mart inflicted on a supplier, leaving readers with what is ultimately a cautionary tale about the perils of victory.

ANNOTATED ESSAY

A gallon-sized jar of whole pickles is something to behold. The jar itself is the size of a small aquarium. The fat green pickles, floating in swampy juice, look reptilian, their shapes exaggerated by the glass of the jar. The jar weighs twelve pounds, too big to carry with one hand.

1

Description

Cause and effect

The gallon jar of pickles is a display of abundance and ex-   2
cess. It is entrancing, and also vaguely unsettling. Wal-Mart fell
in love with Vlasic's gallon jar of pickles.

Wal-Mart priced it at $2.97 — a year's supply of pickles for   3
less than $3! "They were using it as a 'statement' item," says Pat
Hunn, who calls himself the mad scientist of the gallon jar of pick-   Division or
les at Vlasic. "Wal-Mart was putting it before consumers, saying   analysis
this represents what Wal-Mart's about: *You can buy a stinkin' gallon
of pickles for $2.97.* And it's the nation's number-one brand."

Because of Wal-Mart's scale, the Wal-Mart effect isn't just   4
about delivering "always low prices." It's also about how Wal-
Mart gets those low prices, and what impact the low prices have
far beyond Wal-Mart's shelves, and beyond our own wallets:
the cost of low prices to the companies that supply Wal-Mart,
and to the people who work for those companies. That story can
be found floating in Vlasic's gallon jar of pickles, the tale of how
that gallon jar came to be sold at Wal-Mart.

Back in the late 1990s, Vlasic wasn't looking to build its   5
brand on a gallon of whole pickles. Pickle companies make
money on "the cut," slicing cucumbers into specialty items like
spears and hamburger chips. "Cucumbers in the jar, you don't
make a whole lot of money there," says Steve Young, who was   Cause
then vice president of marketing for pickles at Vlasic, but has   and
since left the company. But a Wal-Mart buyer saw the gallon jar   effect
at some point in the late 1990s, and started talking to Pat Hunn
about it. Hunn, who has also since left Vlasic, was then head of
Vlasic's Wal-Mart sales team, based in Dallas.   Narration

The gallon intrigued the buyer. For Vlasic, it was a niche   6
product aimed at small businesses and people having large
events. Still, in sales tests in Wal-Mart stores, priced somewhere
over $3, "the gallon sold like crazy," says Hunn, "surprising us
all." The Wal-Mart pickle buyer had a brainstorm: What would
happen to the gallon if they offered it nationwide, and got it
below $3? Hunn was skeptical, but his job was to look for ways
to sell pickles at Wal-Mart. Why not?

And so in 1998, Vlasic's gallon jar of pickles went into every   7
Wal-Mart, 2,500 stores, at $2.97, a price so low that Vlasic and
Wal-Mart were only making a penny or two on a jar, if that. The
gallon was showcased on a big, freestanding pallet display near
the front of stores. It was an abundance of abundance.

"They went through the roof," says Hunn.   8

Says Young, "It was selling eighty jars a week, on average,   9
in every store." Doesn't sound like much until you do the math:
That's 200,000 gallons of pickles, just in gallon jars, just at Wal-
Mart, every week. Whole fields of cucumbers were heading out
the door.

The gallon jar of pickles became what you might call a "dev-   10
astating success" for Vlasic. "Quickly, it started cannibalizing
our non-Wal-Mart business," says Young. "We saw consumers   Comparison
who used to buy the spears and the chips in supermarkets"—

where a small quart jar of Vlasic pickles cost $2.49 — "buying the Wal-Mart gallons. They'd eat a quarter of a jar and throw the thing away when they got moldy. A family can't eat them fast enough."

The gallon jar reshaped Vlasic's pickle business: It chewed   **11**
up the profit margin of the business with Wal-Mart, and of pickles generally; procurement had to scramble to find enough pickles to fill the gallons. The volume also gave Vlasic strong sales numbers, strong growth numbers, and a powerful place in the world of pickles at Wal-Mart.

Cause
and
effect

The gallon was hoisting Vlasic and hurting it at the same   **12**
time. Indeed, Steve Young, Vlasic's marketing guy, and Pat Hunn, Vlasic's Wal-Mart sales guy, agree on the details of the gallon, but years later they disagree over whether it was good or bad for Vlasic.

Hunn remembers cutting a deal with Wal-Mart whereby the   **13**
retailer could only increase its sales of gallons if it increased its sales of the more profitable spears and chips in lockstep. The Comparison
gallon was good.

Young remembers begging Wal-Mart for relief. "They said,   **14**
'No way,' " says Young. "We said we'll increase the price" — even $3.49 would have helped tremendously — "and they said, 'If you do that, all the other products of yours we buy, we'll stop buying.' It was a clear threat."

Narration

Hunn remembers the conversations differently. Things were   **15**
more complicated, more subtle. "They did not put a gun to our head and say, 'It's $2.97 or you're out of here,'" says Hunn. "They said, 'We want the $2.97 gallon of pickles. If you don't do it, we'll see if someone else might.' I knew our competitors were saying to Wal-Mart, 'We'll do the $2.97 gallons if you give us your other business.'

"We're all big boys," Hunn says. "We all make decisions."   **16**

Wal-Mart's business was so indispensable to Vlasic, and the   **17**
gallon so central to the Wal-Mart relationship, that decisions about the future of the gallon were made at the CEO level. "One option was to call their bluff," says Young. But Vlasic was struggling as an independent spin-off of Campbell Soup Company, and couldn't afford to risk the Wal-Mart business. The pain didn't continue for weeks or months — the $2.97 gallon of Vlasic dills was on the shelves at Wal-Mart for two and a half years.

Finally, Wal-Mart let Vlasic up for air. "The Wal-Mart guy's   **18**
response was classic," says Young. "He said, 'Well, we've done to pickles what we did to orange juice. We've killed it. We can back off.' "

Cause
and
effect

Vlasic got to take the product down to half a gallon of pick-   **19**
les, for $2.49. By that point, Young says, profits in pickles had been cut by 50 percent — millions of dollars in lost profit, even as the business itself grew. Devastating success, indeed.

The meaning of the Vlasic story is complicated, but it cuts to the heart of how Wal-Mart does business. It shows the impact of Wal-Mart's scale and power in what we all think is a market economy. Wal-Mart's focus on pricing, and its ability to hold a supplier's business hostage to its own agenda, distorts markets in ways that consumers don't see, and ways the suppliers can't effectively counter. Wal-Mart is so large that it can often defy the laws of supply, demand, and competition.

That's the scary part of the Vlasic story: The market didn't create the $2.97 gallon of pickles, nor did waning consumer demand or a wild abundance of cucumbers. Wal-Mart created the $2.97 gallon jar of pickles. The price — a number that is a critical piece of information to buyers, sellers, and competitors about the state of the pickle market — the price was a lie. It was unrelated to either the supply of cucumbers or the demand for pickles. The price was a fiction imposed on the pickle market in Bentonville. Consumers saw a bargain; Vlasic saw no way out. Both were responding not to real market forces, but to a pickle price gimmick imposed by Wal-Mart as a way of making a statement.

20

Division or analysis

21

THESIS

Cause and effect

Stephanie Alaimo and Mark Koester
THE BACKDRAFT OF TECHNOLOGY (p. 307)

Students sometimes complain that writing an essay for an English class is an empty exercise because nobody but the teacher will read it and the task has no purpose beyond earning a grade. This strong student op-ed piece suggests an effective way to counter objections that writing assignments are pointless. Most school newspapers, as well as many national publications (*Newsweek* comes to mind), encourage students to submit their essays for publication. You might consider framing at least one assignment as a newspaper or magazine submission, encouraging (or even requiring) students to send their essays to a local, regional, or national publication for consideration. Knowing that their writing will have a broad and clearly defined audience usually gives even the most reluctant student writers a real sense of purpose and seriousness that too often seems missing.

The Compact Reader is always looking for new student essays as well. We would be thrilled if your students sent their work to Bedford/St. Martin's for possible inclusion in the next edition. Simply ask them to include their name, address, and phone number on the first page of their essay and send their finished essay(s) to *Compact Reader* Editor, Bedford/St. Martin's, 75 Arlington Street, Boston, MA 02116.

Content Quiz

1. What do the authors describe as "society's newest upgrade in not having to wait"?
   [The self-service checkout machine.]

2. What do the authors believe are the hidden costs of self-service checkouts?
    [Jobs and human interaction.]

3. Where, according to the authors, are self-checkout machines manufactured?
    [Somewhere other than the United States.]

4. Give at least two examples of the mechanization of customer service identified in the essay.
    [Self-service gas pumps, ATM machines, video rental services such as Netflix, online pizza orders.]

5. Who do the authors say gains the most from mechanizing customer service?
    [Corporations.]

Vocabulary Quiz

1. *Stockpiled* (paragraph 5) is closest in meaning to
    a. saved   b. paid   c. cut
    [a. saved]

2. *Implausible* (8) is closest in meaning to
    a. possible   b. unlikely   c. believable
    [b. unlikely]

3. *Precarious* (9) is closest in meaning to
    a. split   b. dangerous   c. scenic
    [b. dangerous]

4. *Tenuous* (9) is closest in meaning to
    a. unstable   b. promising   c. angry
    [a. unstable]

5. *Subsist* (10) is closest in meaning to
    a. employ   b. argue   c. live
    [c. live]

ANSWERS

Meaning

1. *Backdraft* is a firefighters' term for a sudden explosion that occurs when a fire seems to be under control; it is caused by the introduction of fresh air to smoldering embers in a room that has been depleted of oxygen. (Students may have difficulty finding the word in a general or college dictionary, but explanations are easily found online. A few may recognize the concept from the 1991 Kurt Russell movie.) Using the word in the title allows Alaimo and Koester to imply something that is left unsaid in the essay itself yet informs at least part of their purpose. The idea is that even a seemingly innocuous technology has the potential to blow up in our faces.

2. Alaimo and Koester understand the tendency, as students may notice in the authors' use of "we" to implicate themselves in the behavior, as well as in their effort to acknowledge that their readers are reasonable people ("who wants to wait?" [paragraph 1]; "it seems easy enough to forget" [4]; "Sure, these new robots and computers reduce work" [7]). Ultimately, however, they condemn the unthinking preference for what's easy. They express their opinion unequivocally in paragraph 10: "To choose the self-checkout simply as a convenience cannot be morally justified unless these jobs remain."

Purpose and Audience

1. The purpose of this essay is unmistakably persuasive, as the last sentence makes clear. Alaimo and Koester urge their readers to "[s]ay 'No!' to self-checkout" (paragraph 11). In other words, they're calling for a boycott.

2. Presumably, they're addressing other students at DePaul University. You may need to point out to your students that DePaul is a large, urban Catholic university with a tradition of faith, community service, and social justice — although the authors' emphasis on morality in paragraph 10 might tip them off. Alaimo and Koester seem to believe that their readers are, like themselves, at least nominally religious and committed to social justice (which is why they don't feel a need to explain what they mean by "morally justified" [10]). They also assume that their fellow students are somewhat advantaged and have lofty aspirations for their own futures (as we can infer from their warning that "your elitist job market [could be] nuked" [8]).

Method and Structure

1. Cause-and-effect analysis enables Alaimo and Koester to explore how self-checkout came to be and explain how the convenience actually harms us. They explain that retailers like self-checkout because it lets them reduce payroll expenses. The authors further suggest that the existence of the self-checkout option is one of the reasons for long lines at registers that do have cashiers: stores are cutting back on staffing and forcing customers to serve themselves. And the more willing we are to do the work ourselves, the less need there will be for human cashiers, ironically making the staffed lines even longer. More important, Alaimo and Koester warn, our choice of convenience over human interaction is reducing the number of jobs available for unskilled workers.

2. The scenario encourages readers to consider how the issue affects them personally, making the authors' argument more immediate and compelling.

3. Opinions will vary. Students may notice that the authors fail to provide evidence for a few questionable assertions, such as their assumptions that "self-checkout machines are probably not manufactured in the United States" (paragraph 5) and that "any job or task could become entirely technologically mechanized" (8). Students might also reasonably accuse Alaimo and Koester of oversimplifying, because they rely almost exclusively on necessary causes, identifying no one (sufficient) cause for the popularity of

self-checkout or the loss of jobs (see pp. 308–9 of the text). At the same time, the authors do consider immediate, remote, major, and minor causes, lending their argument a respectable level of complexity given its length and the scope of their subject. Readers' own depth of knowledge and personal interests will affect how persuasive they deem the essay to be.

4. The examples of mechanization of customer service in paragraph 6 demonstrate that the problem is not limited to supermarket self-checkout lines, making the authors' subject more relevant for readers and suggesting the broader implications of their subject. The method of argument and persuasion, of course, pervades the essay as a whole and serves as the authors' primary reason for analyzing causes and effects in the first place.

Language

1. Although Alaimo and Koester obviously feel strongly about their message and are occasionally confrontational about it ("your elitist job market nuked" [paragraph 8]; "cannot be morally justified" [10]; "it could be you" [11]), their overall tone is probably best described as earnest. They seem honestly to believe that their essay may help people keep their jobs, if only readers will listen.

2. They seem to be attempting to create a friendly rapport with their readers by peppering an otherwise serious essay with slang and colloquialisms. Unfortunately, a few of the phrases are clichés, and one might go further to argue that "trapped in a precarious fork in the road" (paragraph 9) is a mixed metaphor disguised as a cliché. The casual language may cause some readers to conclude that the writing (and perhaps the thinking behind it) is unnecessarily sloppy.

——————————— Gerald Early ———————————

BLACK BALL (p. 312)

Early's blog entry offers an unusual perspective on the historical and psychological legacies of the Jim Crow era, examining how racial segregation continues to affect both public institutions, such as professional baseball, and African Americans as a group. His cause-and-effect analysis is compelling and surprising: not many people would argue that the segregation of fifty years ago explains the lack of African American baseball fans today. Early suggests this by raising (and rejecting) several other theories that have been put forth to explain the sport's overwhelmingly white spectator base. Many students will find Early's analysis eye-opening and provocative, while others might come away unsatisfied with his explanations. These potential differences in response offer a good lead-in to a class discussion: how convincing is Early's cause-and-effect analysis, and why?

Ira Glasser's argumentative essay in Chapter 13 of the text, "Drug Busts = Jim Crow" (p. 356), offers an interesting counterpoint to Early's musings. Glasser provides some informative background on the history of segregation (including Jackie Robinson's significance in the history of baseball and of segregation), which Early only alludes to. And if Early believes that the effects of segregation continue today, Glasser believes that legalized segregation itself is back in force. Taken together, these two essays demonstrate the complexity of race relations in contemporary society and offer a promising topic for discussion (suggested by the third writing topic that follows Early's essay): does segregation still exist, and if so, what are its effects?

Content Quiz

1. What is Early's favorite baseball team?
   [The St. Louis Cardinals.]

2. What percentage of professional baseball players are African American?
   [Less than 10 percent.]

3. What regions do most nonwhite baseball players in the United States come from?
   [Latin America and the Caribbean.]

4. In terms of attendance, to what sports does Early compare baseball?
   [Football and basketball.]

5. Who was Effa Manley?
   [The first woman inducted into the Baseball Hall of Fame. She was the co-owner of the Newark Eagles.]

Vocabulary Quiz

1. *Imperil* (paragraph 8) is closest in meaning to
   a. impale   b. threaten   c. celebrate
   [b. threaten]

2. *Pathology* (9) is closest in meaning to
   a. disease   b. mistake   c. opportunity
   [a. disease]

3. *Disparage* (11) is closest in meaning to
   a. praise   b. remove   c. belittle
   [c. belittle]

4. *Stigmatized* (12) is closest in meaning to
   a. funny   b. mistaken   c. disgraced
   [c. disgraced]

5. *Ambivalence* (13) is closest in meaning to
   a. uncertainty   b. balance   c. strength
   [a. uncertainty]

ANSWERS
Meaning

1. Early believes that African Americans shun professional baseball because of the history of the Negro Leagues, which he argues were created not to help black players (as many believe), but to keep them off of mainstream teams. The resulting stigma, as he sees it, is not necessarily conscious but hovers over collective memory, leaving "most blacks . . . secretly hating both segregation and integration" (paragraph 12), as well as the game that embodies both so solidly.

2. Early writes about baseball to make a point about the painful legacy of racial segregation in the United States, using the racism in baseball to illustrate the racism in the country at large. His thesis is stated in the last two sentences of the essay: "It is not a story of triumph or tragedy. It is the story of a conflicted people trying, with some success, to make the most of their conflicts." In other words, Early wants readers to accept his view that African Americans are engaged in a constant struggle to overcome the obstacles of racism and that although accomplishments are worth celebrating, we should not romanticize them or allow them to distort the memory of past injustices.

3. "Institutionalized racism" is a form of discrimination built into the very structure of society. The concept applies to whole organizations — sports leagues, businesses, schools, governments — rather than to individuals. Because it is endemic to a group's ways of thinking, institutionalized racism is both harder to recognize and more difficult to rout. In the case of professional baseball, racism is evident both in the formation of segregated leagues in the first place and in contemporary assumptions that segregation represented an accomplishment for black players, owners, and fans.

Purpose and Audience

1. As he suggests in paragraph 7, Early wrote "Black Ball" in response to the induction of Effa Manley and 17 Negro League players into the Baseball Hall of Fame in March 2006.

2. He is writing for a generalized audience of *New York Times* readers. His use of "blacks" and "them" rather than "us" is one clue that he is writing for a mixed audience; another clue can be found in his use of "we" when he speaks of American culture as a whole. Nowhere does he make any sort of appeal to sports fans or African American readers. Writing for a fairly broad audience, Early apparently assumes that readers are reasonably well educated (for example, some of his vocabulary is sophisticated) and that they will be open to new ideas.

3. Early assumes that his readers have at least some knowledge of baseball, the history of segregation in the United States, and the existence of the Negro Leagues. All the same, he is careful to explain references that may not be obvious to the uninitiated. For instance, he breaks down attendance at

Cardinals games and makes a point of explaining who Effa Manley was and why she was significant.

Method and Structure

1. Early considers the causes and effects surrounding the creation of the Negro Leagues as an explanation of the cause of low black attendance at baseball games today. It's worth noting that although the essay is presented as an answer to the question "Why don't black people go to baseball games?" (paragraph 3), he's analyzing causes and effects to explore the much larger issue of racial segregation in the United States.

2. The author's self-identification as a baseball fan creates a complexity in his argument that students may find difficult to grasp. After all, if African Americans reject baseball because of the historical stigmas attached to it, how can Early, a highly educated black man who is fully aware of that history, be a fan? The answer might be that he has ambivalent feelings about his passion for baseball. That ambivalence is evident throughout the essay and is summed up in his conclusion. Ultimately, Early neither celebrates nor condemns black baseball. Instead, he presents it as a chapter in the ongoing struggle of African American history.

3. He explores what might be considered opposing cause-and-effect relationships to emphasize that popular assumptions are inadequate to explain African Americans' lack of interest in baseball. In doing so, he underscores the complexity of his subject and prepares readers for the significance of his own theory.

4. Early is comparing and contrasting celebratory interpretations of the Negro Leagues' cultural significance with what he believes is the truth of their history and legacy. The comparison contributes to his point that African American history is too easily misinterpreted in a haze of nostalgia and that Americans must be more willing to examine their faults honestly.

Language

1. Early's title is really quite brilliant. "Black Ball" is a reference to African American baseball, of course, but the word *blackball* also means to vote against or to exclude from a group. The title perfectly captures the cause-and-effect relationship Early explores in the essay. As he sees it, the Negro Leagues represented the exclusion of African Americans from professional baseball, which then caused African American fans to reject the game as a whole.

2. His tone shifts from bemusement in the first half of the essay to a more formal and sternly worded analysis of the Negro Leagues' creation and legacy in terms of race relations in the United States. Ultimately, Early's overall tone might best be described as ambivalent. Although he loves baseball, he is pained by its cultural implications and fully understands why more African Americans don't join him at the ballpark.

CHAPTER 13

ARGUMENT AND PERSUASION
Debating Law and Order

Jeremy Steben
SMALL TOWN, QUIET TOWN, SAFE TOWN (p. 336)

Steben's idiosyncratic and carefully crafted comment on police profiling is sure to elicit a strong response from students. There is much to agree or disagree with in this essay, not only Stephen's viewpoint, but also his tone and his technique. The essay is exciting and ambitious because it is structured around a trick of irony: Steben disguises his real opinion by saying the exact opposite of what he means.

Class discussion could focus both on the issue of law enforcement and on Steben's ironic approach. The essay also invites further research into police profiling.

Content Quiz

1. Where does the author live?
   [In a quiet, upscale little suburb in Connecticut.]

2. According to the author, what is "common knowledge" about teenagers?
   [They have a tendency to be up to no good.]

3. What small mistakes often give rise to the police's opinion that a driver is driving "erratically"?
   [Having a tire touch the median or white strip, or jerking the wheel a little too sharply on a turn.]

4. What constitutes a "suspicious clue" in a teenager's car?
   [An air freshener hanging from the rearview mirror.]

5. What are some common makes of car in the author's town?
   [Grand Cherokee and Mercedes.]

Vocabulary Quiz

1. *Extolled* (paragraph 1) is closest in meaning to
   a. commended   b. disparaged   c. examined
   [a. commended]

2. *Placate* (2) is closest in meaning to
   a. alienate   b. appease   c. gratify
   [b. appease]

3. *Demeanor* (4) is closest in meaning to
   a. impression   b. conduct   c. distrust
   [b. conduct]

4. *Dogged* (7) is closest in meaning to
   a. complaint   b. irresolute   c. tenacious
   [c. tenacious]

5. *Shirk* (8) is closest in meaning to
   a. avoid   b. volunteer   c. pursue
   [a. avoid]

ANSWERS
Meaning

1. Steben's main idea is that the police violate some people's civil liberties by their aggressive, preemptive tactics. This thesis is not stated; in fact, statements to the contrary abound as the essay builds ironically around an exaggerated counterargument. An unknowing reader might take several paragraphs to see Steben's approach, but there are early clues in hyperbolic phrases such as the criminals who "boldly prowl our avenues in the glare of the daylight" or the "valiant," "dauntless" police, "the only bastion of defense against the darkness that constantly threatens to boil over and consume our fair community" (paragraph 1).

2. The police assume the worst of all members of certain groups — teenagers, minorities, drivers of less-than-stellars cars — that they associate with infractions or crimes. With little or no cause, the police harass members of these groups and violate their constitutional protections.

3. The police want to secure the safety of the community by being "proactive in their duties" (paragraph 1), uncovering hidden crimes or preferably stopping crimes before they occur. Steben does not appear to find any justification for methods that violate rights.

Purpose and Audience

1. Steben seems to have been targeted by the police himself, or can imagine being targeted ("we can count on a watchful eye being turned upon us" [paragraph 2]), and his satirical approach seems to be a way to vent frustration at such treatment. He's also clearly having a good time at the expense of the police. But the guiding purpose seems to be to raise an alarm about the subversion of civil rights in the supposed interest of law and order.

2. Since Steben wrote the essay for a college class, he doubtless envisions readers like himself — young, educated, affluent. Perhaps he expects these

readers to have experienced the same police harassment and to be amused by his satire. But just as likely he hopes the satire will focus their attention on a problem they haven't given much or any thought to. The "proper citizens" (paragraph 7), too, might have their eyes opened if they were to come across the essay. The police seem pretty definitely *not* to be Steben's target audience.

Method and Structure

1. The deliberate fallacies contribute to the satire by exaggerating the opposite of what the author believes. Examples: *Either/or*: "These dauntless men and women are the only bastion of defense against the darkness that constantly threatens to boil over and consume our fair community" (paragraph 1). *Ignoring the question*: "only diligent pursuit . . . guarantees that order is maintained, and the innocent parties involved are only mildly inconvenienced" (1). *Hasty generalization*: "It's common knowledge that teenagers have a tendency to be up to no good" (2). *Begging the question*: "if their methods circumvent a few of our civil liberties, well, that's the price that we must pay for living in a quiet, safe town" (8).

2. Satire like Steben's is risky because it can be misunderstood, hit a raw nerve, or simply fall flat. Students' responses will vary, of course.

3. The process analysis provides a very detailed example of the methods Steben says the police use, showing step-by-step how they harass and violate the rights of drivers and passengers just because they belong to a certain group.

Language

1. The formal language intensifies the irony. Steben, a teenager, writes like a fairly stuffy adult. Though seething at the injustice he sees, he writes loftily. Though disapproving of police conduct, he writes of it with exaggerated approval.

2. The dialogue brings the incident to life, giving it a specificity that mere summary would not. The dialogue also contributes to Steben's irony because it exaggerates the false chumminess (paragraph 4) and gruff suspicion (5) of the police, as well as the dopey innocence of the teenagers (5).

Anna Quindlen

THE C WORD IN THE HALLWAYS (p. 343)

The subject of student violence is a sensitive one, particularly for students who may have had a personal connection to Virginia Tech, as well as for those who worry about the possibility of a shooting incident on their own campus. All the same, Quindlen's essay offers an excellent opportunity to discuss the effectiveness of using emotional appeals in argument.

One way to initiate discussion might be to ask how much has changed since Quindlen wrote this essay. Teachers and administrators have indeed started paying more attention to students' mental health, but many would argue that the increased scrutiny has caused more problems than it has solved. Others might reply that mental illness is just as stigmatized — if not more so — than it was in 1999. Still others might point out that despite the media frenzies that accompany each new shooting, the problem (as devastating as it is) is neither as new nor as widespread as news reports imply.

If your students have trouble finding sources for the second writing topic (on media stigmatization of mental illness), you might suggest the following:

Fletcher, Carol. "Madness in Magazines: The Stigmatization of a Psychiatric Disability in American News Weeklies." AEJMC Conference Papers. 5 Nov. 2004.

Philo, G., et al. "The Impact of Mass Media on Public Images of Mental Illness: Media Content and Audience Belief." Health Education Journal 53 (1994): 271–81.

Smellie, Patrick. "Feeding Stereotypes." Quill 87.2 (1999): 25.

Smith Jr., Claude J. "Finding a Warm Place for Someone We Know: The Cultural Appeal of Recent Mental Patient and Asylum Films." Journal of Popular Film and Television 27.1 (Spring 1999): 40.

Wahl, Otto F. Media Madness: Public Images of Mental Illness. New Brunswick: Rutgers UP, 1997.

Content Quiz

1. What is a "psychological autopsy"?
   [It's the process by which doctors try to identify the reasons for a teenager's suicide or homicide.]

2. Who were Kip Kinkel and Sam Manzie?
   [Both were seventeen-year-olds who committed murders: Kinkel killed his parents and two classmates; Manzie killed an eleven-year-old boy.]

3. What ending did film censors insist be added to the 1956 movie *The Bad Seed*?
   [They forced the producers to add a scene in which the fictional father spanked the lead character as punishment for her killing spree.]

4. With what weapon did Kip Kinkel kill his father?
   [With the same gun (a Glock) that his father bought for him as an alternative to therapy.]

5. According to Quindlen, how many mentally ill children do not get psychological treatment?
   [Two-thirds of the total, which is estimated at six million.]

Vocabulary Quiz

1. *Ludicrous* (paragraph 4) is closest in meaning to
   a. laughable   b. cautious   c. thoughtful
   [a. laughable]

2. *Loll* (7) is closest in meaning to
   a. fight   b. droop   c. enjoy
   [b. droop]

3. *Utilitarian* (7) is closest in meaning to
   a. psychological   b. practical   c. financial
   [b. practical]

4. *Derision* (9) is closest in meaning to
   a. approval   b. support   c. ridicule
   [c. ridicule]

5. *Psychotropic* (10) is closest in meaning to
   a. mind-altering   b. recreational   c. legal
   [a. mind-altering]

ANSWERS

Meaning

1. The author's thesis is stated in the introduction: "Yet one solution contin-ues to elude us, and that is ending the ignorance about mental health, and moving it from the margins of care and into the mainstream where it belongs. As surely as any vaccine, this would save lives" (paragraph 2). In other words, Quindlen believes that if American culture destigmatized mental illness and became more willing to treat it like any other illness, fewer troubled teenagers would kill themselves or others.

2. Quindlen focuses her essay on relatively targeted teen killings, using as her primary examples Kip Kinkel (who killed his parents and two Oregon class-mates in November 1999) and Sam Manzie (who killed a young boy in his New Jersey home the same month), both of whom were sentenced to life in prison when they were seventeen years old. As she sees it, both boys were mentally ill. She further suggests that Kinkel's father aided and abetted his actions by buying him a gun and that Manzie was the victim of a pedophile.

3. Quindlen blames society for its actions, believing that these boys killed because their mental illnesses went untreated: in Kinkel's case because his father disapproved of therapy, and in Manzie's case because his parents couldn't afford the necessary care. Ultimately, she presents Kinkel and Manzie as victims.

4. She is implying that our culture encourages boys to use violence to solve their problems, a point she reinforces later when she remarks that "talk therapy, or even heartfelt talk, is somehow sissified, weak" (paragraph 9).

Purpose and Audience

1. Quindlen makes her purpose clear in her conclusion: she wants readers not only to recognize that "mental illness is an illness, and not a character flaw" (paragraph 10) but also to act on that understanding and ensure that troubled children get the treatment they need.

2. Her reference to "we parents" in paragraph 10 suggests that Quindlen is writing primarily to parents of teenagers, hoping to urge them to take their children's problems more seriously. By extension, her conclusion hints that she also imagines representatives of insurance providers, hospitals, and schools among her readers.

3. The omission will almost certainly trouble, or at least puzzle, some readers, but there are reasonable explanations for Quindlen's decision not to include the Columbine tragedy in her discussion. On the surface, her essay is a response to two very specific incidents that took place at around the same time. On a deeper level, however, it may be that the scale of Columbine is just too overwhelming to contemplate in a brief essay, that Quindlen doesn't put Harris and Klebold in the same category of untreated mental illness in which she places Kinkel and Manzie, or that she doesn't see fit to try to excuse their behavior — or to blame the massacre on society. (Such an attempt would probably have alienated readers.)

Method and Structure

1. Quindlen's argument is highly emotional. She sets the tone with her opening observation that the phrase "psychological autopsy" is "the saddest" one she's "read in a long time" (paragraph 1). Just a few examples of emotional appeal in her essay include her reference to "black-bordered photographs in yearbooks and murder suspects with acne problems" (2), her comment that "so many lives have already been lost" (3), her mention of Sam Manzie's relationship with a pedophile (5), her depiction of Manzie's father trying to navigate the insurance system (6), the sarcastic description of a "psychiatrist who examined his son for less time than it takes to eat a Happy Meal" (6), her chilling allusion to lobotomies (7), her acknowledgment that her argument has an element of the "warm fuzzies" to it (7), her question of "how we would respond if two thirds of America's babies were not being immunized" (8), and the "what if" scenario of her conclusion.

2. She tackles opposing viewpoints in paragraph 4, with her reference to the "ludicrous" solution to child homicides epitomized in the movie *The Bad Seed*, and in paragraphs 5 and 6, in which she acknowledges that Kinkel and Manzie did receive mental health care (but insists that it was inadequate). Although her discussion of the boys' treatment does seem balanced and reasonable, students may rightly object that in relying on a fifty-year-old movie to characterize those who disagree with her perspective, Quindlen is unfairly depicting her opponents as almost comically irrational.

3. Depending on readers' knowledge of Shakespeare's play and Yeats's poem, these quick allusions pack a lot of meaning. *Romeo and Juliet*, of course, is largely a story about teenagers who get caught up in circumstances that were not of their making. (It's no small coincidence that both of them die as an indirect result of their families' feuding.) "The Second Coming" describes the end of the world as the arrival of a terrible beast that destroys the innocent. Most college students (and many high school students) will have at least a passing familiarity with the play; you may want to bring a copy of the poem to class and share it with students.

4. Quindlen's examples of teenage killers (paragraph 3) and ineffective responses (4) establish the urgency of the problem and the need for a better solution. The paragraphs of comparison and contrast explaining the boys' treatment (5, 6) emphasize the inadequacy of contemporary mental health interventions. The essay as a whole could be read as a cause-and-effect analysis, but the dangerous relationship between current attitudes and teenage boys' violence is articulated most clearly in paragraphs 8 and 9.

Language

1. "The C Word" refers to *crazy*, a derisive word Quindlen doesn't utter until paragraph 9. The use of the euphemism in the title, along with the whispered quality of the word itself at the end of the essay, underscores the stigma that society attaches to mental illness.

2. After asserting that "mental illness is an illness, not a character flaw" (paragraph 10), Quindlen creates an emphatic rhythm by ending three of the last four sentences with the same phrase: insurance providers, hospitals and schools, and parents "should act like it." She then uses a variation of this phrase ("will believe it") to argue that her solution will work.

3. Quindlen's tone is consistently plaintive, begging readers to take seriously the problem of mental illness. Although some readers will consider it effective, others may find it cloying.

ANNOTATED ESSAY

The saddest phrase I've read in a long time is this one: psy-chological autopsy. That's what the doctors call it when a kid kills himself, and they go back over the plowed ground of his short life, and discover all the hidden markers that led to the rope, the blade, the gun. 1 | Definition

There's a plague on all our houses, and since it doesn't announce itself with lumps or spots or protest marches, it has gone unremarked in the quiet suburbs and busy cities where it has been laying waste. The number of suicides and homicides committed by teenagers, most often young men, has exploded in the last three decades, until it has become routine to have black-bordered photographs in yearbooks and murder suspects with acne problems. And everyone searches for reasons, and scapegoats, and solutions, most often punitive. Yet one solution 2 | Cause and effect continues to elude us, and that is ending the ignorance about mental health, and moving it from the margins of care and into the mainstream where it belongs. As surely as any vaccine, this would save lives.

So many have already been lost. This month Kip Kinkel was sentenced to life in prison in Oregon for the murders of his parents and a shooting rampage at his high school that killed two students. A psychiatrist who specializes in the care of adolescents testified that Kinkel, now seventeen, had been hearing voices since he was twelve. Sam Manzie is also seventeen. He is serving a seventy-year sentence for luring an eleven-year-old boy named Eddie Werner into his New Jersey home and strangling him with the cord to an alarm clock because his Sega Genesis was out of reach. Manzie had his first psychological evaluation in the first grade.

Excuses, excuses. That's what so many think of the underlying pathology in such hideous crimes. In the 1956 movie *The Bad Seed*, little Patty McCormack played what was then called a "homicidal maniac" and the film censors demanded a ludicrous mock curtain call in which the child actress was taken over the knee of her screen father and spanked. There are still some representatives of the "good spanking" school out there, although today the spanking may wind up being life in prison. And there's still plenty of that useless adult "what in the world does a sixteen-year-old have to be depressed about" mind-set to keep depressed sixteen-year-olds from getting help.

It's true that both the Kinkel and the Manzie boys had already been introduced to the mental health-system before their crimes. Concerned by her son's fascination with weapons, Faith Kinkel took him for nine sessions with a psychologist in the year before the shootings. Because of his rages and his continuing relationship with a pedophile, Sam's parents had tried to have him admitted to a residential facility just days before their son invited Eddie in.

But they were threading their way through a mental health system that is marginalized by shame, ignorance, custom, the courts, even by business practice. Kip Kinkel's father made no secret of his disapproval of therapy. During its course he bought his son the Glock that Kip would later use on his killing spree, which speaks sad volumes about our peculiar standards of masculinity. Sam's father, on the other hand, spent days trying to figure out how much of the cost of a home for troubled kids his insurance would cover. In the meantime, a psychiatrist who examined his son for less time than it takes to eat a Happy Meal concluded that he was no danger to himself or others, and a judge lectured Sam from the bench: "You know the difference between right and wrong, don't you?"

The federal Center for Mental Health Services estimates that at least six million children in this country have some serious emotional disturbance and, for some of them, right and wrong

Margin annotations: 3 Example · 4 Example · 5 Comparison · 6 · Cause and effect · 7 take second seat to the voices in their heads. Fifty years ago their parents might have surrendered them to life in an institution, or a doctor flying blind with an ice pick might have performed a lobotomy, leaving them to loll away their days. Now lots of them wind up in jail. Warm fuzzies aside, consider this from a utilitarian point of view: Psychological intervention is cheaper than incarceration.

Division or analysis and comparison

The most optimistic estimate is that two thirds of these emotionally disturbed children are not getting any treatment. Imagine how we would respond if two thirds of America's babies were not being immunized. Many health insurance plans do not provide coverage for necessary treatment, or financially penalize those who need a psychiatrist instead of an oncologist. Teachers are not trained to recognize mental illness, and some dismiss it, "Bad Seed" fashion, as bad behavior. Parents are afraid, and ashamed, creating a home environment, and a national atmosphere, too, that tells teenagers their demons are a disgrace.

8

Division and classification

And then there are the teenagers themselves, slouching toward adulthood in a world that loves conformity. Add to the horror of creeping depression or delusions that of peer derision, the sound of the *C* word in the hallways: crazy, man, he's crazy, haven't you seen him, didn't you hear? Boys, especially, still suspect that talk therapy, or even heartfelt talk, is somehow sissified, weak. Sometimes even their own fathers think so, at least until they have to identify the body.

9

Cause and effect

Another sad little phrase is "If only," and there are always plenty of them littering the valleys of tragedy. If only there had been long-term intervention and medication, Kip Kinkel might be out of jail, off the taxpayers' tab, and perhaps leading a productive life. If only Sam Manzie had been treated aggressively earlier, new psychotropic drugs might have slowed or stilled his downward slide. And if only those things had happened, Faith Kinkel, William Kinkel, Mikael Nickolauson, Ben Walker, and Eddie Werner might all be alive today. Mental health care is health care, too, and mental illness is an illness, not a character flaw. Insurance providers should act like it. Hospitals and schools should act like it. Above all, we parents should act like it. Then maybe the kids will believe it.

10

Example

THESIS

--------------------- Wilbert Rideau ---------------------

WHY PRISONS DON'T WORK (p. 349)

Rideau's essay is serious and his proposal controversial, but his argument is relatively easy to follow. Taking as his premise the idea that society is right to want to protect itself from crime, he skillfully establishes several reasons for his titular assertion that prisons don't work: tough sentencing hasn't reduced violent crime, the threat of jail has not stopped people from committing crimes, long prison terms harden criminals instead of reforming them, even the worst crime — murder — is usually an isolated mistake, and prisoners simply need more support to rise above their weaknesses. At each step of his argument, Rideau manages to knock down a common assumption without alienating his readers. If nothing else, he is a master at building common ground.

What is perhaps most instructive in Rideau's essay is that even a convicted killer arguing for prison reform can establish a strong ethical appeal. The author's personal history might offer a good opening for a class discussion (see question 2 under "Method and Structure"). How do Rideau's circumstances affect his credibility? How successfully does he overcome this potential problem? How can students apply the same strategies to their own arguments?

Content Quiz

1. Where was the author imprisoned, and for what?
   [He was at Louisiana State Penitentiary for murder.]

2. What did prison authorities in Louisiana take from an inmate in solitary confinement as punishment?
   [His underwear.]

3. What American state has the highest murder rate?
   [Louisiana.]

4. What category of prisoners work in the home of Louisiana's governor?
   [Murderers.]

5. Who, according to the author, is "the most dangerous criminal"?
   [The person "who has not yet killed but has a history of escalating offenses."]

Vocabulary Quiz

1. *Consigned* (paragraph 1) is closest in meaning to
   a. sold   b. committed   c. resigned
   [b. committed]

2. *Vies* (2) is closest in meaning to
   a. sins   b. competes   c. fails
   [b. competes]

3. *Incorrigible* (3) is closest in meaning to
   a. unreformable   b. violent   c. tricky
   [a. unreformable]

4. *Abhors* (3) is closest in meaning to
   a. hates   b. imprisons   c. releases
   [a. hates]

5. *Escalating* (5) is closest in meaning to
   a. driving b. petty c. increasing
   [c. increasing]

ANSWERS
Meaning

1. Rideau asserts his central assumption in paragraph 1. Prisons, he says, exist "so politicians can sell the illusion that permanently exiling people to prison will make society safe." In other words, the purpose of prison is to protect society. He refers again to this assumption in paragraphs 3 ("If getting tough resulted in public safety") and 4 ("Prison has a role in public safety"). Corollary to the goal of public safety are the intent of rehabilitating criminals (6) and the belief that the threat of jail is a deterrent to crime (7).

2. Put simply, prisons don't work because they don't accomplish what Rideau sees as their primary goal: they don't make society safe from crime. They don't deter people from committing crimes (paragraph 3), they hold people who no longer pose a threat to society (4, 5), and they don't do enough to rehabilitate those inmates who will ultimately be released (6, 7). Rideau's thesis might be summed up in a sentence from the middle of the essay: "Prison, like the police and the courts, has a minimal impact on crime because it is a response after the fact, a mop-up operation" (3).

3. The author believes that society should focus on prevention rather than punishment. He offers his proposal in his conclusion, where he insists that "our youngsters must be taught to respect the humanity of others and to handle disputes without violence. . . . As a community, we must address the adverse life circumstances that spawn criminality" (paragraph 7). Some readers may notice an implication here that social inequities (especially poverty) are the real cause of crime.

Purpose and Audience

1. It's a little difficult to gauge Rideau's purpose, but an astute reader might conclude that he wants to persuade politicians to change their "tough on crime" approach and refocus their efforts on measures that are more likely to prevent crime in the first place. It is conceivable that an opinion essay in a publication such as *Time* might play a small part in legislative change. Readers of such publications include policymakers, to be sure, but, more important, major news magazines influence public opinion, which in turn influences political opinion and action.

2. The ideal reader would probably be the governor of a state with a high rate of incarceration, such as Louisiana or Texas, since Rideau's purpose is to influence penal policy. Prisoners, of course, already have strong opinions on sentencing, and they probably don't need Rideau to persuade them that imprisonment doesn't help them. But average citizens are important to Rideau because a groundswell of prison reform sentiment could force politicians to act.

Method and Structure

1. Rideau's inductive reasoning is drawn from his experiences as a prisoner at Louisiana State Penitentiary. He provides examples of fellow prisoners' experiences and attitudes to generalize about inmates at other prisons. Similarly, he describes the failures of Louisiana's penal system to draw a conclusion about the effectiveness of prison in general. His deductive reasoning can be summarized in the following syllogism:

   MAJOR PREMISE: Prisons rely on deterrence, rehabilitation, and punishment to protect society.

   MINOR PREMISE: Most criminals do not think about the possibility of jail when they commit their crimes, prisons don't rehabilitate inmates, and punishment happens after the fact.

   CONCLUSION: Therefore, prisons don't protect society.

   Some students may notice that Rideau's entire argument rests on the assumption that prisons are meant to protect society — an assertion that is not universally agreed upon. If one assumes that prisons are meant solely to punish, for instance, Rideau's argument falls apart.

2. Most readers can be expected to doubt Rideau's objectivity. After all, how seriously can we take an admitted killer's claim that a life sentence is an ineffective way to protect society? Rideau's credibility is helped by his willingness to acknowledge his status as a lifer from the start. And in some ways, he turns his credibility problem to his advantage, most notably by sharing his firsthand knowledge of the prison population and of the effects that long sentences have on inmates, as well as by using his personal experience to bring in compelling examples (such as the prisoner whose underwear was taken away in paragraph 2). He wisely uses the expert testimony of a prison warden (5) to echo his claims, and he makes a point of introducing statistical and factual evidence to support individual points. Rideau also works to build common ground with his readers by acknowledging the validity of opposing viewpoints (see the next question).

3. Rideau anticipates that many readers will object to his argument, so he establishes common ground at every opportunity. Nearly every paragraph identifies an opposing viewpoint and attempts to discredit it. He begins paragraph 2, for instance, by describing the prevailing "tough on crime" ideology, then shows how one state (Louisiana) has taken that ideology too far. In the next paragraph (3), he accepts the need for public safety but argues that "getting tough" hasn't worked. In paragraphs 4–6, he acknowledges some valid uses of prisons, including temporary confinement and rehabilitation through education, but he insists that such uses should be limited or improved. And in his conclusion, he stresses that he shares with readers the desire to "curb crime," offering his own solution to the problem.

4. Louisiana has enacted some of the most stringent sentencing guidelines in the country, raising mandatory sentences and restricting parole, yet the state still "has the highest murder rate" (paragraph 3) in the country.

Rideau believes that the laws have failed because people don't think rationally when they're committing a crime. Rather, they're so caught up in desperate circumstances that any potential consequences are irrelevant at the time. He uses the example of Louisiana to emphasize his point that prison is not a deterrent to crime.

Language

1. Rideau accepts that crime is a problem, but he believes that prison is not the solution. Because he knows that his position will be controversial, he maintains a carefully measured tone that borders on conciliation.

2. His point is that most new inmates are stupid, immature kids rather than hardened, calculating criminals. By repeating the words "unskilled, impulsive, and uneducated misfits," as well as variations on them — "dumb," "failures," "rejects" — several times in his opening paragraph, he emphasizes the need to educate potential criminals and make them productive members of society *before* they get into trouble.

3. "Ever see a dog chase its tail?" (paragraph 8) is a rhetorical question. It summarizes Rideau's main point (that current prison laws are based on faulty circular logic) with a compelling visual image; it also highlights his frustration.

—————— Ira Glasser ——————

DRUG BUSTS = JIM CROW (p. 355)

Glasser's essay works with the piece by James R. McDonough (p. 361 in the text) to form an informal set of paired readings that take opposing positions on the same controversial issue: the nation's ongoing "war" on drugs. Although the writers don't speak to each other directly (McDonough's "response" was written a few years before Glasser's essay was published), their arguments do.

It should be no surprise that Glasser, the former head of the ACLU, opposes the war on drugs. What may surprise your students, however, are his grounds for opposing it. Glasser puts his own spin on fellow Drug Policy Alliance spokesperson Ethan Nadelmann's famous objection (summarized in his quotation on p. 355 in the text) that drug laws disproportionately target the poor and ethnic minorities. Not only do these laws put too many people of color in jail, Glasser says, but they also have effectively reinstituted legalized racial segregation.

You might want to start a discussion by asking students what they know about the Jim Crow era. Sadly, they may not be aware of the extent to which African Americans were denied the use of public facilities, institutions, and legal protections in the decades between Reconstruction and civil rights reform, so you may need to supplement Glasser's introductory historical overview with additional background information.

Content Quiz

1. What war was popularly believed to be a fight against racism?
   [World War II.]

2. What fabled moment in sports history does the author credit as "the first major postwar event that challenged" legal segregation in the popular imagination?
   [Jackie Robinson's joining the Brooklyn Dodgers in 1947.]

3. How did the size of the general prison population change between 1960 and 2004?
   [It grew enormously, from 200,000 federal and state prisoners in 1960 to 2.2 million in federal, state, and local jails in 2004.]

4. Statistically, who is more likely to be arrested on a drug charge — a white person or a black person?
   [A black person.]

5. What civic duty are many convicted felons barred from fulfilling?
   [Voting.]

Vocabulary Quiz

1. *Subjugate* (paragraphs 1, 3, 9, 11) is closest in meaning to
   a. discriminate   b. enslave   c. threaten
   [b. enslave]

2. *Infrastructure* (2) is closest in meaning to
   a. foundation   b. precedent   c. right
   [a. foundation]

3. *Presumptively* (6) is closest in meaning to
   a. arrogantly   b. supposedly   c. overwhelmingly
   [b. supposedly]

4. *Quintessentially* (8) is closest in meaning to
   a. fifth   b. theoretically   c. absolutely
   [c. absolutely]

5. *Demise* (8) is closest in meaning to
   a. death   b. half   c. beginning
   [a. death]

ANSWERS

Meaning

1. Glasser doesn't identify the subject of his essay until paragraph 3, where he states that "the system of drug prohibition and its enforcement . . . is the major, and still insufficiently recognized, civil rights issue of our day." His

thesis — "drug prohibition is now the last significant instance of legalized racial discrimination in America" (10) — appears in his conclusion.

2. Glasser asserts in paragraph 6 that although 13 percent of regular drug users are black, African Americans represent 37 percent of people arrested for drug use and 67 percent of those imprisoned for the crime. The racial disparity between drug use, arrests, and convictions is even wider when Latinos are taken into account (22 percent of the user population versus 80 percent of the prison population). His point is that minorities are disproportionately targeted by police and the courts, and that drug laws have created a convenient legal excuse for jailing (and, as he explains later, disenfranchising) people of color.

Purpose and Audience

1. As the headnote on page 356 of the text points out, Glasser's essay first appeared in the *Nation* — one of the most aggressively liberal publications in the country. The author states at several points in his argument that he is writing to fellow political liberals. He assumes that they already share his distrust of the legal system, that they're at least somewhat uneasy about the current state of drug enforcement, and that they share his desire to eliminate racial discrimination. It's quite clear that he imagines his readers to be highly educated: note, for instance, the high level of his vocabulary and the way he glosses over the history of Jim Crow. He also seems to assume that liberals have allowed themselves to be somewhat "timid in opposing the drug war" (paragraph 11) and that they can be shaken out of their complacency.

2. Glasser makes his purpose clear in the last paragraph: he wants his readers "to consider attacking the premises upon which this edifice of racial subjugation is based." In other words, his essay is a call to action aimed at liberals, whom he hopes will not only recognize the "racial politics of drug prohibition" but also do something to reverse current trends.

Method and Structure

1. The first two paragraphs, in which Glasser outlines the basic history of desegregation, are more explanatory than argumentative. They're not entirely objective: the author is making a somewhat emotional appeal to those who are (like himself) personally invested in the legacy of the civil rights movement and would be dismayed to think that legal equality is being undermined in any way. He establishes the background so that he can dismantle readers' assumption that legalized segregation has been abolished. At the same time, his description of the horrors of segregation suggests what may be the consequences of allowing legal discrimination to take hold once again.

2. His evidence includes personal observations of racial politics in the Jim Crow era and historical facts (paragraphs 1 and 2), but he relies most heavily on numbers (4–7) drawn from "federal statistics gathered by the Sentencing Project" (6). The Sentencing Project (*http://www.sentencingproject.org*) is a

prison-reform lobbying group with a strong agenda, so students may reasonably question the objectivity of data derived from it.

3. Glasser does not seem to address opposing viewpoints in this essay, unless one counts the introductory assertions that segregation is a thing of the past. The omission of conflicting arguments may present a problem for some readers, but the author's purpose is not so much to engage in a debate as to establish the existence of an unrecognized problem.

4. As Glasser explains, most states deny convicted felons the right to vote — not only during their prison terms but often permanently. The result has been that millions of people of color can no longer vote because they have been convicted of drug use. The author is arguing that, in effect, the U.S. government is systematically disenfranchising minorities — in spite of laws passed in the 1960s barring legal discrimination. The point expands his argument beyond drugs to civil rights in general, emphasizing the broader ramifications of denying convicted felons the right to vote.

Language

1. Because Glasser draws mostly on facts, his tone is relatively measured throughout the essay. On a first reading, then, some readers may be surprised by the word "outrage" in his conclusion (paragraph 11). However, several comments hint at his rising indignation. Examples include the phrase "moral contradiction" in paragraph 2, his assertion that the targeting of minorities "is not a phenomenon of the Deep South. . . . And it is not accidental" (7), and the exclamation that concludes paragraph 7: "And this happened even though three-quarters of monthly drug users are white!" Readers may also detect the sarcasm in Glasser's use of the word "fashionable" (8) to describe liberal attitudes, as well as the anger in his statement that "[t]he United States is the only industrial democracy that does this" (9).

2. Glasser takes the issue of racial discrimination very seriously and expects his readers to do so as well. The seriousness of his subject — and the urgency of his purpose — is reflected in the formality of his diction.

3. The last sentence in the piece — "If they do not, who will?" — is an appeal to liberal readers' sense of responsibility for those who are politically disadvantaged. Some students may rightly find it condescending toward minorities (who presumably are capable of political action themselves) and political conservatives (who presumably could be persuaded by a reasonable argument), but Glasser is trying to persuade liberals to take up the fight by implying that nobody else will do it.

———————————— James R. McDonough ————————————

CRITICS SCAPEGOAT THE ANTIDRUG LAWS (p. 361)

Written a few years before "Drug Busts = Jim Crow" (p. 355 in the text), this essay nonetheless seems to respond almost directly to Ira Glasser's piece. In the course of arguing against drug decriminalization, McDonough questions the validity of one of the major premises on which Glasser bases his own argument: that arrests for petty drug offenses have resulted in an explosive rise in the number of inmates in American prisons.

Just as students are unlikely to be surprised by Glasser's stance against the war on drugs, they might well expect that McDonough, in charge of drug enforcement in Florida and personally involved in the creation of American drug policies, supports the laws. As a law enforcement officer, McDonough has seen the personal and social damage inflicted by drug use, and he firmly believes that the majority of crimes committed in the United States can be traced back to drug use. Whether your students agree with him or not will be a matter of both personal experience and their evaluation of his argumentation techniques. For some readers, the essay will smack of antidrug propaganda; others will surely find it very persuasive.

You might want to start a discussion by asking students about their positions on the current drug laws. (The journal prompts that accompany Glasser's essay on p. 360 of the text ask them to write on this topic.) Do they favor decriminalization or legalization in any form, or do they think that most (if not all) illegal drugs should stay illegal? Why?

Content Quiz

1. According to McDonough, which is responsible for high rates of incarceration: drug law or drug use?
    [Drug use.]

2. Into what four categories does the author classify drug crimes?
    [Possession, trafficking, delivery, and manufacturing.]

3. Whose experience does the author cite to support his assertion that "the majority . . . of crime stems from a relationship to substance abuse"?
    [Law enforcement officers.]

4. Name at least two teenage behaviors that McDonough says can be blamed on smoking marijuana.
    [McDonough lists several examples of "delinquent and aggressive anti-social behavior" caused by marijuana: "cutting class, stealing, physically attacking others and destroying other people's property."]

5. What, according to the author, "causes or contributes to seven of 10 cases of child maltreatment"?
    [Substance abuse.]

2. McDonough is debating those on "the liberal left and the far right" (paragraph 1) who want to decriminalize illegal drugs on the basis that the antidrug laws cause more harm than the drugs do. It is important to question their arguments, he says in paragraph 3, because their unchallenged assertions have won several people over to their side and threaten to encourage further acceptance of dangerous drugs. Implied in his statements is the concern that drug use will become more common, thus causing more problems for society.

3. The author's goal is to persuade readers to reject arguments in favor of drug decriminalization and to support existing laws instead. He does not ask that they take action, only that they recognize what he sees as the truth.

Method and Structure

1. McDonough relies on several sources to advance his argument. He cites statistics from the Census Bureau publication *Felony Sentences in State Courts, 2000* (paragraphs 5–7) to undermine his opponents' argument that the prisons are overflowing with petty offenders, then draws on data from his own office in Florida to argue that those prisoners who were convicted of drug offenses are guilty of more serious crimes as well (8). He brings in additional information — anecdotal evidence, survey results, and statistics — from the National Arrests and Drug Monitoring (ADAM) Program (10), the U.S. Department of Justice (10 and 13), the National Household Survey on Drug Abuse (10), a survey conducted by the National Committee to Prevent Child Abuse (12), and a report by the National Center on Addiction and Substance Abuse titled *No Safe Haven: Children of Substance-Abusing Parents* (12). Some of these sources are more reliable than others (for instance, we can presume that the census data is more objective than *No Safe Haven*), but students may find the range and sheer quantity of evidence more convincing than any particular kind.

2. McDonough suggests from the beginning that people in favor of decriminalization are begging the question. They claim that drug laws are bad because drugs themselves don't do any real harm, but McDonough argues that the question of harm is itself the issue of the debate. He also accuses his opponents of oversimplification (for instance, in his effort in paragraphs 5–9 to explain the cause of higher rates of imprisonment). The one fallacy he cites explicitly is the tendency to present "policies . . . as 'either-or' options" (4). Calling attention to faulty reasoning helps McDonough to undermine opponents' premises while attempting to establish the superiority of his own reasoning.

    Some students may see an element of post hoc reasoning in McDonough's slippery slope claims in paragraph 4: that a willingness to decriminalize drugs has led to accusations that policies are racist as well as to encouraging illegal drug use. His question in paragraph 8 about whether people in jail for possession "are . . . not otherwise productive and contributing citizens whose only offense was smoking a joint," as well as his comment in paragraph 13 that "95 percent of all convicted felons . . . pleaded guilty," borders on an ad hominem attack as well. Finally, his concluding assertion

Vocabulary Quiz

1. *Mantra* (paragraph 1) is closest in meaning to
   a. lie   b. saying   c. joke
   [b. saying]

2. *Vernacular* (1) is closest in meaning to
   a. language   b. truth   c. glue
   [a. language]

3. *Benign* (4) is closest in meaning to
   a. pleasant   b. dangerous   c. harmless
   [c. harmless]

4. *Decries* (7) is closest in meaning to
   a. weeps   b. condemns   c. approves
   [b. condemns]

5. *Burgeoning* (13) is closest in meaning to
   a. growing   b. hitting   c. budgeting
   [a. growing]

ANSWERS
Meaning

1. McDonough asks his central questions in his introduction: "Do harsh antidrug laws drive up the [prison population] numbers? Are the laws causing more harm than the drugs themselves?" (paragraph 2). His thesis is framed as the answers to these questions in paragraphs 13 and 14 (in both cases, "no") and is summarized in his final sentence: "[T]he greater harm is in the drugs themselves, not in the laws that curtail their use."

2. McDonough asserts that drug use is the root cause of more serious crimes that "damage . . . public health, family cohesion, the workplace and the community" (paragraph 9). More than half of the crimes unrelated to drugs, he claims, "are committed by people who are high, seeking ways to get high or both" (10). He also argues that teenagers who smoke marijuana exhibit "delinquent and aggressive antisocial behavior" (11) and that substance users mistreat their children (12). The relationship between drug use and violence, he suggests, is the reason drugs are illegal in the first place.

Purpose and Audience

1. McDonough seems to be writing for people on the verge of being swayed by decriminalization arguments. His labored use of statistics and numerical logic suggests that he assumes that his readers are reasonable, intelligent people, but his use of scare tactics (particularly the threat that liberalizing attitudes toward drugs will raise the rate of violent crimes, increase the welfare rolls, and harm children [paragraphs 9–12]) also suggests that he believes they are afraid. It should be clear as well that McDonough assumes that his readers do not use drugs themselves.